How Machine Learning is
Innovating Today's World

Scrivener Publishing
100 Cummings Center, Suite 541J
Beverly, MA 01915-6106

Publishers at Scrivener
Martin Scrivener (martin@scrivenerpublishing.com)
Phillip Carmical (pcarmical@scrivenerpublishing.com)

How Machine Learning is Innovating Today's World

A Concise Technical Guide

Edited by

Arindam Dey
School of Computer Science, VIT-AP University, Andhra Pradesh, India

Sukanta Nayak
Dept. of Mathematics, VIT-AP University, Andhra Pradesh, India

Ranjan Kumar
Dept. of Mathematics, VIT-AP University, India

and

Sachi Nandan Mohanty
Dept. of Computer Science, VIT-AP University, Andhra Pradesh, India

Scrivener
Publishing

This edition first published 2024 by John Wiley & Sons, Inc., 111 River Street, Hoboken, NJ 07030, USA and Scrivener Publishing LLC, 100 Cummings Center, Suite 541J, Beverly, MA 01915, USA
© 2024 Scrivener Publishing LLC
For more information about Scrivener publications please visit www.scrivenerpublishing.com.

Wiley Global Headquarters
111 River Street, Hoboken, NJ 07030, USA

For details of our global editorial offices, customer services, and more information about Wiley products visit us at www. wiley.com.

Limit of Liability/Disclaimer of Warranty
While the publisher and authors have used their best efforts in preparing this work, they make no representations or warranties with respect to the accuracy or completeness of the contents of this work and specifically disclaim all warranties, including without limitation any implied warranties of merchant-ability or fitness for a particular purpose. No warranty may be created or extended by sales representatives, written sales materials, or promotional statements for this work. The fact that an organization, website, or product is referred to in this work as a citation and/or potential source of further information does not mean that the publisher and authors endorse the information or services the organization, website, or product may provide or recommendations it may make. This work is sold with the understanding that the publisher is not engaged in rendering professional services. The advice and strategies contained herein may not be suitable for your situation. You should consult with a specialist where appropriate. Neither the publisher nor authors shall be liable for any loss of profit or any other commercial damages, including but not limited to special, incidental, consequential, or other damages. Further, readers should be aware that websites listed in this work may have changed or disappeared between when this work was written and when it is read.

Library of Congress Cataloging-in-Publication Data

ISBN 978-1-394-21411-2

Cover image: Pixabay.Com
Cover design by Russell Richardson

Set in size of 11pt and Minion Pro by Manila Typesetting Company, Makati, Philippines

Printed in the USA

10 9 8 7 6 5 4 3 2 1

Contents

Preface

This timely book presents a diverse collection of chapters that delve into the remarkable ways that machine learning (ML) is transforming various fields and industries. It provides a comprehensive understanding of the latest advancements and practical applications of ML techniques.

Machine learning, a branch of artificial intelligence, has gained tremendous momentum in recent years, revolutionizing the way we analyze data, make predictions, and solve complex problems. As researchers and practitioners in the field, the editors of this book recognize the importance of disseminating knowledge and fostering collaboration to further advance this dynamic discipline.

The chapters herein cover a wide range of topics, each contributing a unique perspective to the broader landscape of machine learning. First is a comprehensive analysis of various tokenization techniques and the sequence-to-sequence model in natural language processing. Next, Chapter 2 explores the evaluation of English language readability using ML models, followed by a detailed study of text analysis for information retrieval through natural language processing in the subsequent chapter.

Chapter 4 investigates machine learning's role in maximizing cotton yield with a focus on fertilizer selection, and Chapter 5 delves into the application of reinforcement learning approaches to supply chain management. The following chapter examines the performance analysis of converting algorithms to source code using natural language processing in Java, and Chapter 7 presents an alternate approach to solving differential equations utilizing artificial neural networks with optimization techniques.

The exploration of the subject continues with a comparative study of different techniques of text-to-SQL query conversion in Chapter 8, and the next chapter examines ML approaches to catalysis. After that, Chapter 10 presents the systematic study of text generation and classification using tokenization in natural language processing, followed by the classification of livestock diseases using ML algorithms in Chapter 11.

Chapter 12 provides a closer look at the application of ML in image enhancement techniques, and the following chapter demonstrates the prediction of book genres using natural language processing. Additionally, Chapter 14 delves into efficient leader selection for inter-cluster flying ad-hoc networks, and the subsequent chapter provides a comprehensive survey of applications powered by GPT-3 and DALL-E.

Recommender systems' domain of application is discussed in Chapter 16, and the next chapter reviews mood detection, emoji generation, and classification using tokenization and CNN. Chapter 18 delves into a new variation of the exam scheduling problem using graph coloring, and Chapter 19 examines the intersection of software engineering and machine learning applications.

Moreover, Chapter 20 explores ML strategies for indeterminate information systems in complex bipolar neutrosophic environments, and the rise of AI-generated news videos is scrutinized in Chapter 21. The next section highlights ML applications in battery management systems, while the healthcare industry is covered in Chapter 23. The book's final chapter presents how to enhance resource management in precision farming through AI-based irrigation optimization.

This book will serve as a valuable resource for researchers, scholars, and enthusiasts seeking to understand the cutting-edge advancements in ML. The editors extend our gratitude to all the authors who have contributed their expertise, insights, and knowledge to make this book possible. Their commitment to advancing the frontiers of machine learning has greatly enriched the content and depth of this publication.

We also offer our sincere appreciation to Wiley and Scrivener Publishing for their support and guidance throughout the editorial process. Their commitment to publishing high-quality scientific literature has been instrumental in bringing this book to fruition.

We hope that readers find this book insightful, engaging, and thought-provoking. May it inspire you to explore new horizons in machine learning and contribute to the ongoing advancements that are reshaping our world.

The Editors
March 2024

Part 1
NATURAL LANGUAGE PROCESSING (NLP) APPLICATIONS

A Comprehensive Analysis of Various Tokenization Techniques and Sequence-to-Sequence Model in Natural Language Processing

Kuldeep Vayadande[1]*, Ashutosh M. Kulkarni[1], Gitanjali Bhimrao Yadav[1], R. Kumar[2] and Aparna R. Sawant[1]

[1]Vishwakarma Institute of Technology, Pune, India
[2]VIT-AP University, Inavolu, Beside AP Secretariat, Amaravati AP, India

Abstract

This research paper provides an in-depth examination of various tokenization techniques and Sequence-to-Sequence (Seq2Seq) models, with an emphasis on the LSTM, Transformer, and Attention-based LSTM models. The process of tokenization, which breaks down text into smaller units, plays a vital role in natural language processing (NLP). This study evaluates different tokenization methods, including word-based, character-based, and sub-word-based methods. It also explores the latest advancements in Seq2Seq models, such as the LSTM, Transformer, and Attention-based LSTM models, which have been successful in tasks like machine translation, text summarization, and dialog systems. The paper compares the performance of different tokenization techniques and Seq2Seq models on benchmark datasets. Additionally, it highlights the strengths and limitations of these models, which helps in understanding their suitability for various NLP applications. The aim of this study is to comprehensively understand the current advancements in tokenization and sequence-to-sequence modeling for NLP, particularly with regard to LSTM, Transformer, and Attention-based LSTM models.

Keywords: RNN, CRNN, LSTM, bidirectional-LSTM, text augmentation, tokenization, attention-based LSTM

1.1 Introduction

Tokenization is a fundamental step in natural language processing (NLP) that entails breaking down text into smaller units, such as words or characters. This process is critical for many NLP tasks, including text classification, machine translation, and text summarization. Different levels of granularity, such as word-level, character-level, and sub-word-level, can be used for tokenization.

In recent years, various tokenization techniques have been proposed, each with their unique advantages and disadvantages. The Multi-head Self-attention Mechanism in [1] is

*Corresponding author: kuldeep.vayadande1@vit.edu

Arindam Dey, Sukanta Nayak, Ranjan Kumar and Sachi Nandan Mohanty (eds.) *How Machine Learning is Innovating Today's World: A Concise Technical Guide*, (3–12) © 2024 Scrivener Publishing LLC

a type of attention mechanism that allows the model to concentrate on multiple parts of the input text simultaneously. Tokenization is the most straightforward approach, and it is widely used in many NLP tasks. However, it may not be as effective for languages with complex morphological structures, such as agglutinative languages. On the other hand, character-level tokenization can handle such languages better, but it may also introduce more noise into the data. Sub-word-level tokenization, such as byte-pair encoding (BPE) and unigram language modeling (ULM), has been proposed as a compromise between word-level and character-level tokenization.

The goal of this study is to provide a thorough understanding of the tokenization methods that have been introduced recently. The research will evaluate different tokenization methods, including word-based, character-based, and sub-word-based methods, and compare their performance on a set of benchmark datasets. Furthermore, the research will delve into the details of these techniques, their working principle, and their performance on various NLP tasks. Additionally, the research will also analyze the advantages and limitations of these techniques, which will assist in understanding their suitability for different types of NLP applications. The objective of this research is to gain a complete insight into the latest developments in tokenization for NLP. This research will be a valuable resource for researchers and practitioners in the field of NLP, supplying students with a thorough comprehension of the most advanced tokenization algorithms available at the time. The popularity of Sequence-to-Sequence (Seq2Seq) models in NLP has grown in recent times because of their capability to process input and output sequences of varying lengths. Seq2Seq models, also known as encoder–decoder models, have produced noteworthy outcomes in a number of NLP applications, including dialogue systems, machine translation, and text summarization. Different Seq2Seq models have been put forth through time, and each has merits and faults of its own. One such model is the Long Short-Term Memory (LSTM), a popular Seq2Seq model that has shown promise in a variety of NLP applications. Its limitation is that it is computationally expensive. An alternative to the LSTM model that has proven to be more effective is the Transformer model, which is built on the attention mechanism. Attention-based LSTM models are also proposed, which combine the advantages of LSTM and attention mechanisms. With an emphasis on the LSTM, Transformer, and Attention-based LSTM models, this survey seeks to provide a thorough understanding of the many Seq2Seq models that have been suggested in recent years. We will cover the details of these models, their working principle, and their performance on various NLP tasks. Furthermore, we also cover the advantages, limitations, and performance comparison of these models, which helps in understanding their suitability for different types of NLP applications.

Also, some non-tokenization technique as mentioned in [4] is focused on pre-training an efficient encoder that can operate without tokenization.

1.2 Literature Survey

The Multi-head Self-attention Mechanism [1] is a type of attention mechanism that enables the model to concentrate on multiple sections of the input text simultaneously. This is achieved by utilizing multiple "heads" to attend to different segments of the input. This can aid the model's understanding of the context and relationships between different parts of the input text, resulting in more accurate and coherent summaries.

The pointer network is a type of encoder–decoder [2] model that uses an attention mechanism to point to the part of the input text that should be included in the summary. It helps the model to generate the summary by copying relevant words from the input text, rather than generating them from scratch.

In summary, the research paper [3] focuses on improving the language generation performance by calibrating the likelihood of the generated sequences, while the research paper [4] focuses on Long Document Summarization and uses a combination of top-down and bottom-up inference to extract high-level concepts and specific details from the input text. Both papers provide different approaches to improve the performance of NLP tasks.

CANINE [4] is focused on pre-training an efficient encoder that can operate without tokenization, making the training process faster and more scalable. It uses a simple linear-layer-based architecture and employs a binary masking strategy to hide specific words during training, in order to predict them during inference.

FNet [5], on the other hand, introduces a new method of mixing tokens with Fourier transforms to capture long-range dependencies. This method can produce highly expressive representations and has the advantage of being computationally efficient. The paper shows that the approach outperforms traditional pre-training methods on various NLP tasks.

Charformer [6] focuses on the tokenization stage of pre-processing and proposes a novel method of sub-word tokenization that utilizes gradient information to identify the best sub-word splits. The authors show that their method is fast and results in improved performance on several NLP tasks.

The paper [7] proposes a new pre-training method for language models that leverages retrieval-based techniques. The authors show that this approach can effectively pre-train models on large-scale text corpora, leading to improved performance on a variety of NLP benchmarks.

The paper [8] focuses on enhancing the training efficiency of large-scale transformers, which are frequently employed in NLP applications like language modeling, text classification, and machine translation. The authors propose a new training method, "Random-LTD," which involves randomly dropping tokens and layers during the training process to speed up convergence and reduce memory requirements. The authors show that this method can effectively train large-scale transformers with improved efficiency.

Detecting Label Errors in Token Classification Data [9] focuses on a different challenge in NLP, which is detecting label errors in token classification data. The authors propose a method for detecting label errors in token classification datasets, which can negatively impact the performance of NLP models. The authors present experiments demonstrating the effectiveness of their method in detecting label errors in real-world datasets.

1.3   Sequence-to-Sequence Models

1.3.1   Convolutional Seq2Seq Models

Convolutional Seq2Seq (ConvSeq2Seq) models [10] are a variant of Seq2Seq models that incorporate (CNNs) into model architecture. ConvSeq2Seq models are particularly useful for processing sequences of data with a grid-like structure, such as image sequences or spectrograms.

Compared to traditional Seq2Seq models that use recurrent neural networks (RNNs), ConvSeq2Seq models have the advantage of being able to process sequences in parallel, which can lead to faster training and inference times. However, they may be less effective at capturing long-range dependencies in the data compared to RNN-based models.

1.3.2   Pointer Generator Model

Pointer Generator [11] models are a type of Seq2Seq model used for text summarization and other tasks where the output sequence is a subset of input sequence. The Seq2Seq model comprises of a decoder that generates the target sequence and an encoder that analyzes the input sequence and generates a fixed-length vector representation.

Pointer Generator models have been utilized for a wide range of tasks such as text summarization, headline generating, and question answering. Compared to traditional Seq2Seq models, attention-based models offer a more adaptable approach to handle the issue of Out-of-Vocabulary (OOV) words and can produce output sequences that are more reflective of the input data.

1.3.3   Attention-Based Model

Models that rely on attention [12, 13] are a category of Seq2Seq models that have recently become widespread for various NLP jobs such as machine translation, text summarization, and answering questions. The attention mechanism, which enables it to concentrate on various segments of the input sequence while producing the output sequence, is a key aspect of these models. The attention mechanism computes a score for each element in the input sequence that reflects its importance for the current task, and the decoder uses these scores to weight the contribution of each element when generating the output.

However, attention-based models can be computationally expensive and difficult to train, especially for large sequences, due to the need to compute attention scores for every element in the input sequence. Additionally, the attention mechanism can sometimes be unstable, leading to poor performance in some cases.

1.4   Comparison Table

Table 1.1 shows different Approach-based comparison [1–9]. Table 1.2 shows advantages and disadvantages of Tokenization and Seq2Seq Model [1–9]. Table 1.3 shows model performance [1–9].

Table 1.1 Approach-based comparison.

Paper	Approach used	Performance
[1]	Multi-head self-attention mechanism	Improved understanding of context and relationships in input text
[2]	Pointer network	Use of attention mechanism to point to relevant input text for summary generation

(Continued)

Table 1.1 Approach-based comparison. (*Continued*)

Paper	Approach used	Performance
[3]	Improved language generation performance by calibrating likelihood of generated sequences	[Performance not specified]
[4]	Long Document Summarization using top-down and bottom-up inference	[Performance not specified]
[5]	Pre-training an efficient encoder with binary masking strategy	Improved performance on NLP tasks
[6]	Novel sub-word tokenization method using gradient information	Improved performance on several NLP tasks
[7]	Retrieval-based pre-training method for language models	Improved performance on a variety of NLP benchmarks
[8]	Improving training efficiency of large-scale transformers	Improved efficiency in training large-scale transformers
[9]	Detecting label errors in token classification data	Effective method for detecting label errors in real-world datasets

Table 1.2 Advantages and disadvantages based on tokenization and Seq2Seq approach used.

Paper	Approach used	Performance
[1]	Multi-head self-attention mechanism	Improved understanding of context and relationships in input text
[2]	Pointer network	Use of attention mechanism to point to relevant input text for summary generation

(*Continued*)

Table 1.2 Advantages and disadvantages based on tokenization and Seq2Seq approach used. (*Continued*)

Paper	Approach used	Performance
[3]	Improved language generation performance by calibrating likelihood of generated sequences	[Performance not specified]
[4]	Long Document Summarization using top-down and bottom-up inference	[Performance not specified]
[5]	Pre-training an efficient encoder with binary masking strategy	Improved performance on NLP tasks
[6]	Novel sub-word tokenization method using gradient information	Improved performance on several NLP tasks
[7]	Retrieval-based pre-training method for language models	Improved performance on a variety of NLP benchmarks
[8]	Improving training efficiency of large-scale transformers	Improved efficiency in training large-scale transformers
[9]	Detecting label errors in token classification data	Effective method for detecting label errors in real-world datasets

Table 1.3 Model performance comparison w.r.t accuracy and RMSE.

Model	Accuracy
BERT model	94
Multi-head self-attention pointer model	96
Bidirectional LSTM model	97.5
Encoder–decoder model	97
Encoder–decoder model with attention layer	98

1.5   Comparison Graphs

This section contains comparison graphs of various techniques. Figure 1.1 shows accuracy comparison graph pf five different sequence-to-sequence models [1–9] and Figure 1.2 shows RMSE comparison graph of five different sequence-to-sequence models [1–9].

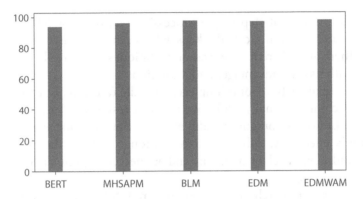

Figure 1.1 Accuracy comparison graph of five different sequence-to-sequence models [1–9].

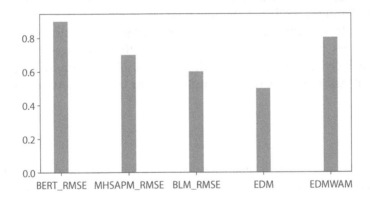

Figure 1.2 RMSE comparison graph of five different sequence-to-sequence models [1–9].

1.6   Research Gap Identified

The current available models lack multi-sentence summarization tasks, and the existing model does not work for large datasets and is limited to character-level data. Handling long sequences: Seq2Seq models tend to struggle with long sequences, especially when the sequence is much longer than the training data. This leads to a drop in performance, and a need to address this challenge. Despite the impressive results achieved by Seq2Seq models, it is often difficult to understand how the model makes its predictions. Improving the interpretability of these models is an important research area. Seq2Seq models are trained on large amounts of data, and any biases in the data are likely to be reflected in the model's predictions. Addressing data bias is an important research area in Seq2Seq models.

Overall, the research gap in Seq2Seq models is to continue to improve the models' accuracy, interpretability, scalability, robustness, and ability to handle diverse data types, while addressing data bias and other challenges.

1.7 Conclusion

Tokenization is an important step in pre-processing text data for NLP tasks. It involves dividing a text into smaller units, called tokens, which can be words, characters, sub-words, or even bytes. There are different tokenization techniques that have been proposed in the literature, each with its own advantages and limitations.

Character-level tokenization, for example, can handle rare and out-of-vocabulary words effectively, but is computationally expensive and can result in a large number of tokens. Word-level tokenization is computationally efficient, but may not handle rare or out-of-vocabulary words effectively. Sub-word tokenization combines the advantages of both character-level and word-level tokenization, and has become a popular choice in many NLP tasks.

In addition, recent research has proposed novel tokenization techniques such as gradient-based sub-word tokenization and token dropping to address the challenges of processing large amounts of text efficiently. These techniques show promise in improving the efficiency of NLP models while maintaining their accuracy.

In conclusion, tokenization is a critical step in NLP pre-processing, and different tokenization techniques have been proposed to address the challenges of processing large amounts of text effectively and efficiently. The choice of tokenization technique depends on the specific NLP task, the size of the text corpus, and the computational resources available.

References

1. Qiu, D. and Yang, B., Text summarization based on multi-head self-attention mechanism and pointer network. *Complex Intell. Syst.*, 8, 555–567, 2022, https://doi.org/10.1007/s40747-021-00527-2.
2. Li, Z., Peng, Z., Tang, S., Zhang, C., Ma, H., Text summarization method based on double attention pointer network. *IEEE Access*, 4, 1–1, 2016.
3. Zhao, Y., Khalman, M., Joshi, R., Narayan, S., Saleh, M., Liu, P.J., Calibrating sequence likelihood improves conditional language generation. *ArXiv*, 2022, https://doi.org/10.48550/arXiv.2210.00045.
4. Clark, J.H., Garrette, D., Turc, I., Wieting, J., CANINE: Pre-training an efficient tokenization-free encoder for language representation. 5, 11 March, 2021.
6. Lee-Thorp, J., Ainslie, J., Eckstein, I., Ontanon, S., FNet: Mixing tokens with fourier transforms, NAACL, in: *Proceedings of the 2022 Conference of the North American Chapter of the Association for Computational Linguistics: Human Language Technologies*, pp. 4296–4313, 2022.
7. Tay, Y., Tran, V.Q., Ruder, S., Gupta, J., Chung, H.W., Bahri, D., Qin, Z., Baumgartner, S., Yu, C., Metzler, D., Charformer: Fast character transformers via gradient-based subword tokenization, ICLR, 2022.
8. Borgeaud, S., Mensch, A., Hoffmann, J., Cai, T., Rutherford, E., Millican, K., van den Driessche, G., Lespiau, J.-B., Damoc, B., Clark, A., de Las Casas, D., Guy, A., Menick, J., Ring, R., Hennigan,

T., Huang, S., Maggiore, L., Jones, C., Cassirer, A., Brock, A., Paganini, M., Irving, G., Vinyals, O., Osindero, S., Simonyan, K., Rae, J.W., Elsen, E., SIfre, L., Improving language models by retrieving from trillions of tokens, Feb 2022.

9. Yao, Z., Wu, X., Li, C., Holmes, C., Zhang, M., Li, C., He, Y., Random-LTD: Random and layerwise token dropping brings efficient training for large-scale transformers, 17 Nov 2022.

10. Wang, W.-C. and Mueller, J., Detecting label errors in token classification data, 8 Oct 2022.

11. Gehring, J., Auli, M., Grangier, D., Yarats, D., Dauphin, Y.N., Convolutional sequence to sequence learning, 25 July, 2017.

12. See, A., Liu, P.J., Manning, C.D., The point: Summarization with pointer-generator networks, 25 April 2017.

13. Chorowski, J., Bahdanau, D., Serdyuk, D., Cho, K., Bengio, Y., Attention-based models for speech recognition, 24 June 2015.

A Review on Text Analysis Using NLP

Kuldeep Vayadande[1]*, Preeti A. Bailke[1], Lokesh Sheshrao Khedekar[1], R. Kumar[2] and Varsha R. Dange[1]

[1]Vishwakarma Institute of Technology, Pune, Maharashtra, India
[2]VIT-AP University, Inavolu, Beside AP Secretariat, Amaravati, AP, India

Abstract

The application of natural language processing (NLP) methods in text analysis for information retrieval is examined in this research. First, a summary of the importance and role of text analysis in information retrieval is presented. The study then looks at text pre-processing methods such as tokenization, stemming, and stop-word elimination. Additionally, other NLP techniques are investigated, including sentiment analysis, part-of-speech tagging, and named entity identification. The following section of the study looks at several text representation models, such as word embeddings, TF-IDF, and bag-of-words. Text analytics is the process of interpreting unorganized textual material and converting it into useful data for study in order to provide a measurable number that provides some crucial information. Text analysis is being used by businesses more and more. It helps with the research of unstructured information, such as customer feedback, as well as the identification of patterns and trend predictions. Solutions, databases, analysis, automated process programs, data gathering, and extraction-based tools are only a few examples of the technology solutions for text analysis that are available for converting text data into meaningful data for analysis. This research will cover the principles of textual data, several text mining methodologies, and the most popular text analysis tools. We examine text categorization methods including Support Machines, Deep Learning and Naive Bayes, Information retrieval systems, NLP tools and libraries, text summarization strategies, and case examples in diverse disciplines, which are covered in the conclusion. An overview of text analysis for information retrieval using NLP methods is the goal of this research. Information retrieval systems, NLP tools, text summarization, text representation models, text classification, text similarity measures, and text pre-processing are all covered in the study. The emphasis is on describing the various strategies and how they are used in information retrieval. The relevance of text analysis for information retrieval and its future possibilities are covered in the conclusion.

Keywords: Natural language processing (NLP), information recovery, text recovery

*Corresponding author: kuldeep.vayadande1@vit.edu

Arindam Dey, Sukanta Nayak, Ranjan Kumar and Sachi Nandan Mohanty (eds.) How Machine Learning is Innovating Today's World: A Concise Technical Guide, (13–24) © 2024 Scrivener Publishing LLC

2.1   Introduction

An introduction to text analysis for information retrieval using NLP methods is given in this study. It focuses on describing the various approaches and the ways in which they are used in information retrieval.

In numerous fields, including online search, legal document analysis, customer service, and more, information retrieval from large text corpora has gained importance. Text analysis requires the use of natural language processing (NLP), which offers methods for extracting, representing, and comprehending human language.

Unstructured text data are transformed into structured or useful information through the process of text analysis. Numerous information retrieval activities, including document retrieval, question answering, and summarization, can be supported by these data. Text analysis relies heavily on NLP approaches, which provide ways to pre-process text data, extract linguistic aspects, categorize text, and assess text similarity.

- Text pre-processing is the research of techniques for purifying and converting unprocessed text data into a format appropriate for subsequent analysis. Tokenization, stemming, stop-word removal, and other pre-processing procedures are included.
- Sentiment analysis, Text representation models: The examination of various text representation models, such as bag-of-words, TF-IDF, and word embeddings, and their effects on the effectiveness of information retrieval.
- Text categorization: The study of methods for dividing text into multiple groups, including sentiment analysis, subject categorization, and spam detection. Using machine learning (ML) methods like Naive Bayes, SVM, and Deep Learning falls under this.
- Text similarity measures: The investigation of methods for gauging textual document similarity, such as cosine similarity, Jaccard similarity, and Euclidean distance, and their effects on the effectiveness of information retrieval.
- The Information recovery systems: Investigation of different information recovery techniques, such as keyword-based, Boolean, and latent semantic indexing (LSI), and how well they function in diverse domains.
- NLP tools and libraries: The investigation of the benefits and drawbacks of well-known NLP tools and libraries, including NLTK, spaCy, and Gensim, as well as their effects on the effectiveness of information retrieval.
- Text summarizing is the study of methods for producing text summaries, such as abstractive and extractive methods, and how to use them in information retrieval.

These are only a few of the numerous subjects that may be examined in depth in a study of text analysis for NLP-based information retrieval. A complete understanding of this subject necessitates both theoretical understanding and hands-on proficiency using NLP tools and procedures. The goal of this research is to present a thorough and understandable overview of text analysis for NLP-based information retrieval.

2.2   Literature Review

In the paper by Martin Krallinger [1], he explains that the most typical medium for the official exchange of information in this contemporary civilization is text. Even if extracting relevant information from texts is not a simple operation, having a business intelligence tool that can do it quickly and inexpensively is essential in today's world. Text analytics is a new and intriguing track of study that tackles the problem and provides the intelligence tool. The methodologies, applications, and difficult problems in text mining have been provided in this work as an overview. Basic text mining techniques have been the focus of attention. The techniques include NLP and information extraction and application domains have been briefly reviewed.

In the paper by Paul Thompson [2], he explains that by automatically choosing instances of intriguing biological occurrences from big document collections, Information Extraction (IE), a text mining component, makes it easier to uncover new information. Understanding the semantic behavior and syntactic of these terms is vital since verbs and nominalized verbs are typically the focus of events. In the biomedical sector, the GREC is a singular resource since it offers not only the fundamental links between entities but also a wide range of additional crucial characteristics, such as their context, chronology, method, and environmental elements. It therefore strives to support the creation of information and technologies that are specifically related to biology.

In [3], Fei Wu explains that to extract semantic relations from natural language text, IE systems are constrained by the availability of training data, because the majority of these systems rely on supervised learning of relation-specific instances. Open IE solutions, such as Text Runner, aim to manage the web's infinite number of relationships. This study introduces WOE, a novel open IE method that combines a heuristic evaluation of Wikipedia info boxes and relevant material with self-supervised learning over unlexicalized features. The two operating modes for WOE are a pattern classifier trained on dependency path patterns and a CRF extractor trained on shallow features like POS tags.

In [5], Shaidah Jusoh explains that the most typical medium for the official exchange of information in this contemporary civilization is text. Even if extracting relevant information from texts is not a simple operation, having a business intelligence tool that can do it quickly and inexpensively is essential in today's world. Text analysis is a new and intriguing field of study that tackles the problem and provides an intelligence tool. The methodologies, applications, and difficult problems in text mining have been provided in this work as an overview. Basic text mining techniques have been the focus of attention. The techniques include information recovery and NLP. Application domains have been briefly reviewed.

In the paper by Laura Chiticariu [6], she explains the majority of contemporary academic research in this field works under the presumption that statistical ML is the most effective strategy for handling information extraction issues. While rule-based IE rules the business sphere, academics often reject it as being outdated. To the practitioners in the industry, we argued the value of rule-based methods. We suggested approaches for resolving the divide by drawing inspiration from SQL's and the database community's achievements. In particular, we demand the standardization of an IE rule language and lay forth a bold research agenda for NLP academics who want to work on issues that are highly valuable and of broad interest in the field.

In [7], Tanu Verma paper explains that the examination of data that are found in natural language text is known as text mining [11, 12]. In order to gather potentially useful business insights, a company may use text-based material, such as emails, word documents, and postings on social media streams. Data analysis, case-based reasoning, NLP, statistics, information recovery, and ML are a few of the well-known scientific disciplines whose methodologies are used in the study and applications of text mining, a burgeoning subject. This study investigates a technique for extracting structured databases using an information extraction system that is self-taught.

In [8], Dr. S. Vijayarani explains that finding or extracting meaningful information from text is a process called text mining. It is an interesting field of research since it seeks to understand unstructured texts. Data analysis (TDM) and the Knowledge recovery or Discovery in Textual Databases (KDT) are its official names. In modern applications like text comprehension, KDT is becoming more significant. Finding or extracting meaningful information from text is a process called text mining. It searches through big databases for intriguing patterns. Many pre-processing methods are used, including stemming and stop-word elimination. In-depth information on text mining pre-processing approaches is provided in this article.

In [9], Honey Gupta explains that in today's rapidly developing information era, text summary has developed into a key tool for assisting and comprehending textual material. Today's world is surrounded by an atmosphere of the internet, which includes a wealth of information in many formats. However, a person cannot read all of these data. A huge quantity of data, which keeps growing every day, needs to be condensed so that people can readily understand it and find it helpful and productive. Text summarization provides pertinent and exact information from the content to cut down on reading time. Implementing abstractive summaries of single and many papers has been suggested in this research. Tokenization, POS-tagging, chunking, and parsing are the first pre-processing steps for the document.

In [10], Ahsan Mahmood clarifies that text-based information makes up the vast bulk of data in the current information age, and these data are expanding incredibly rapidly as more and more internet users flock to social media, where they often share new text-based information. The main use of this project is to produce a data retrieval system using Sahih Bukhari's hadith data. We have used a number of techniques and procedures to accomplish this.

In [11], Yanshan Wang explains that gathering data and information from electronic health records (EHRs) is desired to assist automated systems at the point of treatment and to use them as secondary sources for clinical and translational research. EHRs have swiftly acquired popularity. They have carefully searched many databases for papers that were published in these databases between January 1, 2009, and September 6, 2016. Editorials, reviews, errata, letters, notes, and comments were not included; only papers that are in English language were included.

In [12], Li Shi explains that numerous studies on the use of big data in a variety of fields, including business, healthcare, security, education, and so on have been conducted since the discovery of the large data. The national large data strategy is beginning to place more emphasis on geoscience big data research. To undertake research in the large data, we must find more organized and unstructured geological reports, technical reports, and publications-related geoscience exploration data as we can. This paper suggests using CNN classification to obtain important prospecting data from text data in geoscience.

In [13], Kiran Adnan clarifies, by extracting relations, entities, events, objects, and many more categories, that the IE technique transforms unstructured data into valuable structured information. In order to prepare it for analysis, unstructured data are mined for information. As a result, the data analysis is enhanced by the precise and effective process of transformation of unstructured information in the IE process. Text, picture, audio, and video data formats have all given rise to a variety of methodologies. The systematic literature review's objective is to assess the most recent approaches for IE from unstructured big data sources, such as text, images, audio, and video.

In [14], Baban Gain explains that the judicial sphere has a significant influence and high demand for automated systems based on language technology. It will, for instance, lessen the issue of manually reviewing several old files to determine if they are relevant to a current case. This type of technology would be highly useful to attorneys and speed up the process of rendering a judgment in a particular case. Previously, it took a few months or even a year to reach a decision on a given instance. It has been noted that there are several instances where lawyers pull material from old court case records in an effort to make the information relevant to their present case. In everyday practice, they carry out the procedure by hand.

In [15], Jiayuan He states that our civilization is always in need of new medication discovery and development. Our healthcare systems need new pharmaceuticals that are used to treat medical needs nowadays, and pharmaceutical companies work to sell better treatments; this process of creating all new medications is expensive and time-consuming. They explained why we chose to host the lab, the tasks it offered, and the structure for its evaluation.

In [16], Guillaume Cabanac explains in this special issue that authors from various backgrounds provide essays and NLP, a new actor with growing relevance for all of the aforementioned domains. However, they all share the utilization of academic data that are well-known in scient metrics and the resolution of challenges that are typical of scient metric research. The research that is presented in their papers includes ideas from each of these domains. As is customary in SCIM, citations are modeled and mined together with metadata from bibliographic records (authorships, titles, and sporadically abstracts).

In [17], Aarti Chugh states that due to the changing usage patterns and cutting-edge features provided by popular social networking sites, social media has emerged. The future of social media is seen as a speed bump that improves learning and processing of enormous amounts of data. Deep RNN is used to analyze the sentiment to increase the accuracy of sentiment categorization drastically.

In [18], Phayung Meesad explains that internet users have significantly risen as a result of information and communication technology development. Both news presenters and newsreaders benefit from the change from the conventional to the digital method on how people consume information and news, which results in greater comfort and efficiency for everyone.

2.3   Comparison Table of Previous Techniques

Table 2.1 shows comparison of different techniques [1–20].

Table 2.1 Comparisons.

Authors	Year	Outcome
Martin Krallinger, Alfonso Valencia, and Lynette Hirschman [1]	2008	Future uses of text-mining techniques based on labor-intensive manual literature searches and curation pipelines could be feasible, but only if the conclusions drawn from automatically generated text-based outputs are reliable and pertinent.
John McNaught, Paul Thompson, Sophia Ananiadou, Syed A Iqbal, [2]	2009	The authors have created a special method that concentrates on both verbs and nominalized verbs for annotating sentence-bound gene regulatory events.
Fei Wu, Daniel S. Weld [3]	2010	They conducted their studies using three corpora: the WSJ from Penn Treebank, Wikipedia, and the whole Web. They chose 300 phrases at random from each dataset.
F. S. Gharehchopogh and Z. A. Khalifelu [4]	2011	The effectiveness of text and web mining techniques employing the resulting model is demonstrated. This finding also demonstrates that the unexpected outcomes may be included into an unstructured data model to reduce the quality of the information.
Shaidah Jusoh and Hejab M. Alfawareh [5]	2012	The fundamental methods of text mining have been the emphasis. Some of the approaches include information extraction and natural language processing. An immediate evaluation of application domains has been conducted.
Laura Chiticariu, Yunyao Li, Frederick R. Reiss [6]	2013	They have persuaded business professionals of the value of rule-based methods. They have recommended strategies for resolving the gap. They demand that an IE rule language be standardized.
Tanu Verma, Renu, Deepti Gaur [7]	2014	They have provided a method for extracting structured databases using an autonomously learned information extraction system.
Ms. Nithya, Ms. J. Ilamathi [8]	2015	From a big amount of data, relevant information may be extracted via data mining. Many research challenges are handled and solved using data mining approaches.

(Continued)

Table 2.1 Comparisons. (*Continued*)

Authors	Year	Outcome
Honey Gupta, Sheetal Chaudhari, Aveena Kottwani [9]	2016	Topical analysis, phrase frequency, and POS labeling are all included in the text summary. All of these are utilized to produce a thorough synopsis of the papers' content.
Ahsan Mahmood, Wahab Khan, Zahoor-ur-Rehman [10]	2017	Named Entity Recognition has been utilized by them (NER). Catboats and speech recognition are a few examples of NER's applications. They suggest a framework for knowledge extraction to extract Named entities.
Yanshan Wang, Sungrim Moon, Wang, Majid Rastegar-Mojarad [11]	2018	Clinical research that employs EHR data and studies that use clinical IE differ greatly from one another, despite the fact that clinical IE has been employed for a variety of purposes.
Li Shi, Chen Jianping, and Xiang Jie [12]	2018	In this research, a method is suggested for text mining important prospecting data from geoscience text data using CNN classification.
Kiran Adnan and Rehan Akbar [13]	2019	From unstructured or semi-structured data, usable information is extracted using the information extraction (IE) process. The findings and suggestions from the research will assist to enhance big data analytics by increasing its effectiveness.
Baban Gain, Dibyanayan Bandyopadhyay, Tanik Saikh [14]	2019	Different metrics were established by the task organizers to assess the participating systems. Precision, recall, and F-measure are used in tasks 1 and 2, respectively.
Jiayuan He, Christian Druckenbrodt, Saber A. Akhondi [15]	2020	They have examined how our evaluation's results are affected by how comparable the training and test sets are. Three distinct train–test commonalities were examined.
Guillaume Cabanac, Ingo Frommholz, Philipp Mayr [16]	2020	The research that is presented in their publications combines concepts from each of these fields, but they all share the use of academic data that are well-known in scient metrics and the resolution of issues that are typical of scient metric research.
Aarti Chugh, Vivek Kumar Sharma, Sandeep Kumar [17]	2021	They suggest using a sentiment classification model dubbed the Spider Monkey Crow Optimization method for deep recurrent neural network training.

(Continued)

Table 2.1 Comparisons. (*Continued*)

Authors	Year	Outcome
Phayung Meesad [18]	2021	This study suggests a fresh, reliable approach to combat false information. To create an automated system for detecting bogus news online, they use three major strategies.
Tanishq Gupta, Krishnan, Mohd Zaki [19]	2022	They enable open access to MatSciBERT's pre-trained weights for faster materials discovery and data extraction from materials science books.
Teakgyu Hong, Donghyun Kim, Mingi Ji [20]	2022	This paper addresses the issue by returning to the fundamentals: a successful fusion of content and layout. They specifically suggest using the BROS pre-trained language model.

2.4   Comparison Graphs

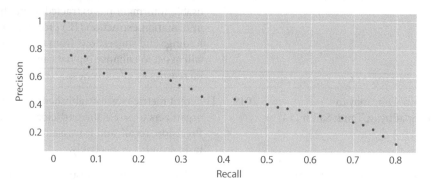

Figure 2.1 Precision/recall graph.

2.5   Research Gap

In the current systems, the system is built using a programming language. The language is incapable of understanding the human language, hence making it inefficient. NLP makes computers capable of understanding the human language, reducing the efforts to convert

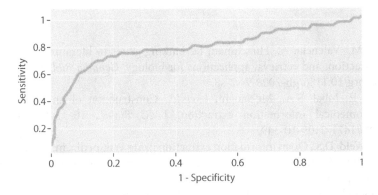

Figure 2.2 Sensitivity and precision graph.

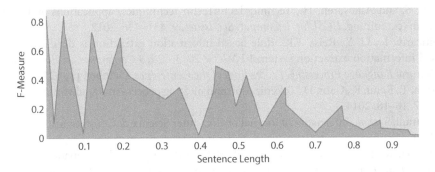

Figure 2.3 F-measure scale for sentence length.

language from one form to another and more efficiently. The use of NLP reduces the time for building the system and makes it less complex. Additionally, analyzing a text written in human language requires a system capable of understanding the human language. Hence, NLP comes into play for making a system for text analysis. Figure 2.1 shows precision vs recall. Figure 2.2 shows sensitivity and precision graph and Figure 2.3 shows F-measure scale for sentence length.

2.6 Conclusion

The goal of the computer science discipline, which is known as NLP, is used to enable computers to text and talk in a manner comparable to that of humans. Computational linguistics, statistics, ML, and deep learning models are all combined in NLP. When combined, these technologies can offer computers the ability to understand human language provided by text or speech with the intention of writing or speaking to another person. The structural models derived from the structured data acquired by the nonstructural models are then contrasted.

References

1. Krallinger, M., Valencia, A., Hirschman, L., Linking genes to literature: Text mining, information extraction, and retrieval applications for biology. *Genome Biol.*, 9, Suppl 2, S8, 2008, https://doi.org/10.1186/gb-2008-9-s2-s8.

2. Thompson, P., Iqbal, S.A., McNaught, J. *et al.*, Construction of an annotated corpus to support biomedical information extraction. *BMC Bioinf.*, 10, 349, 2009, https://doi.org/10.1186/1471-2105-10-349.

3. Wu, F. and Weld, D.S., Open information extraction using Wikipedia, in: *Proceedings of the 48th Annual Meeting of the Association for Computational Linguistics*, Association for Computational Linguistics, Uppsala, Sweden, pp. 118–127, 2010.

4. Gharehchopogh, F.S. and Khalifelu, Z.A., Analysis and evaluation of unstructured data: Text mining versus natural language processing. *2011 5th International Conference on Application of Information and Communication Technologies (AICT)*, Baku, Azerbaijan, pp. 1–4, 2011.

5. Jusoh, S. and Alfawareh, H., Techniq TechnTechn techniques, applications and challenging issue in text mining. *IJCSI Int. J. Comput. Sci. Issues*, 9, 431–436, 2012.

6. Chiticariu, L., Li, Y., Reiss, F.R., Rule-based information extraction is dead! Long live rule-based information extraction systems! *EMNLP 2013 - 2013 Conference on Empirical Methods in Natural Language Processing, Proceedings of the Conference*, October, pp. 827–832, 2013.

7. Verma, T., Renu, R., Gaur, D., Tokenization and filtering process in RapidMiner. *Int. J. Appl. Inf. Syst.*, 7, 16–18, 2014.

8. Vijayarani, S. *et al.*, International Journal of Computer Science & Communication Networks, 5, 1, 7-16.

9. Gupta, H., Kottwani, A., Gogia, S., Chaudhari, S., Text analysis and information retrieval of text data. *2016 International Conference on Wireless Communications, Signal Processing and Networking (WiSPNET)*, Chennai, India, pp. 788–792, 2016.

10. Mahmood, A., Khan, H.U., Rehman, Z.U., Khan, W., Query based information retrieval and knowledge extraction using Hadith datasets. *2017 13th International Conference on Emerging Technologies (ICET)*, Islamabad, Pakistan, pp. 1–6, 2017.

11. Wang, Y., Wang, L., Rastegar-Mojarad, M., Moon, S., Shen, F., Afzal, N., Liu, S., Zeng, Y., Mehrabi, S., Sohn, S., Liu, H., Clinical information extraction applications: A literature review. *J. Biomed. Inf.*, 77, 34–49, 2018.

12. Shi, L., Jianping, C., Xiang, J., Prospecting information extraction by text mining based on convolutional neural networks–a case study of the Lala copper deposit, China. *IEEE Access*, 6, 1–1, 2018.

13. Adnan, K. and Akbar, R., An analytical study of information extraction from unstructured and multidimensional big data. *J. Big Data*, 6, 1–38, 2019.

14. Gain, B., Bandyopadhyay, D., Saikh, T., Ekbal, A., IITP@COLIEE 2019: Legal information retrieval using BM25 and BERT, 2019.

15. He, J., Nguyen, D.Q., Akhondi, S.A., Druckenbrodt, C., Thorne, C., Hoessel, R., Verspoor, K., Natural language processing methods are effective for information extraction from chemical patents. *Frontiers*, 6, 2021, URL=https://www.frontiersin.org/articles/10.3389/frma.2021.654438.

16. Cabanac, G., Frommholz, I., Mayr, P., Scholarly literature mining with information retrieval and natural language processing: Preface. *Scientometrics*, 125, 2835–2840, 2020, https://doi.org/10.1007/s11192-020-03763-4.

17. Chugh, A. *et al.*, Spider monkey crow optimization algorithm with deep learning for sentiment classification and information retrieval. *IEEE Access*, 9, 24249–24262, 2021.

18. Meesad, P., Thai fake news detection based on information retrieval, natural language processing and machine learning. *SN Comput. Sci.*, 2, 425, 2021, https://doi.org/10.1007/s42979-021-00775-6.

19. Gupta, T., Zaki, M., Krishnan, N.M.A. *et al.*, MatSciBERT: A materials domain language model for text mining and information extraction. *NPJ Comput. Mater.*, 8, 102, 2022, https://doi.org/10.1038/s41524-022-00784-w.

20. Hong, T., Kim, D., Ji, M., Hwang, W., Nam, D., Park, S., BROS: A pre-trained language model focusing on text and layout for better key information extraction from documents. *Proceedings of the AAAI Conference on Artificial Intelligence*, vol. 36, pp. 10767–10775, 2022.

3

Text Generation & Classification in NLP: A Review

**Kuldeep Vayadande¹*, Dattatray Raghunath Kale², Jagannath Nalavade², R. Kumar³
and Hanmant D. Magar⁴**

¹Vishwakarma Institute of Technology, Pune, Maharashtra, India
²MIT Art Design and Technology University, Maharashtra, Pune, India
³VIT-AP University, Inavolu, Beside AP Secretariat, Amaravati AP, India
⁴Vishwakarma Institute of Information Technology, Kondhawa, Pune, Maharashtra, India

Abstract

The initial stage in natural language processing is to break down the text into separate tokens. When the text corpus is huge, covering all words is inefficient regarding size of vocabulary. The effectiveness of a specific tokenization method varies on various factors, such as size of the dataset, the nature of the task, and the morphological complexity of the dataset. By comparing the algorithms, it can be concluded that no tokenization technique is the best choice. In this survey, various applications are being surveyed and the comparison of these various algorithms is done by estimating them on classification tasks like sentiment analysis. Question answering and translation applications use the available datasets. This survey paper also shows the tokenization based on the noisy text data and how various tokenization algorithm works on these data are being compared, and what is the average number of segmented subword accuracy being discussed. Basically, sentiment analysis studies the information in an expression and classifies them as positive, negative, or neutral. Input sentence is taken from the user. The survey shows that tokenization is the act of dividing a text into smaller parts like words, phrases, or sentences. The tokens are then used as the input to various NLP models.

Tokenization helps to convert unstructured text data into structured data, which can be further processed and analyzed. For text classification, tokenization is used to convert the input text into a numerical representation. This numerical representation is then fed further, where the classifier predicts the label of the given text. Commonly used tokenization techniques for text classification include bag-of-words, n-grams, and word embeddings.

Keywords: Natural language processing, tokenization, sentiment analysis, text classification

3.1 Introduction

Tokenization is basically a simple process of taking raw data and turning it into a usable data string. It is the method of tokenizing or splitting a string or text into small chunks. It breaks the large data into words or sentences called tokens [2]. The purpose of tokenization is data

*Corresponding author: kuldeep.vayadande1@vit.edu

Arindam Dey, Sukanta Nayak, Ranjan Kumar and Sachi Nandan Mohanty (eds.) *How Machine Learning is Innovating Today's World: A Concise Technical Guide*, (25–36) © 2024 Scrivener Publishing LLC

cleaning and processing previous data that can be used for analysis. Tokenization aids us in deciphering the meaning of text by analyzing the word order. There are many different techniques and libraries that may be used to tokenize data. Libraries like NLTK, Gensim, and Keras may be used to carry out this work. Various tokenization techniques are available, depending on the language and modeling goals. Some of the tokenization techniques used are word, SentencePiece, Random, Disjoint, Character, and Morphological. Sentiment analysis basically means identifying the perspective or emotion behind a situation. Basically, it means analyzing and finding the emotions and intentions behind text, speech, and means of communication.

In this paper, we have surveyed about the models that are useful for sentiment analysis of text data. We communicate with each other in various languages, but each language is just an intermediary or means through which we seek to express ourselves. Emotions are attached to everything we say. It can be positive, negative, or neutral [5]. Let us suppose there is fast food. They sell different types of fast food like French fries, burgers, pasta, cold coffee, etc. Customers can also provide reviews and can also comment whether they like food or not with the help of a website they have created. Based on the reviews, the company can conclude on which things they have to focus on and how they can increase their overall sales. That is why sentiment analysis model comes into play. The model takes a large data corpus of user ratings, finds patterns, and draws conclusions.

If a person is talking to someone and if they are not understanding each other's language, this feels terrible. Basically, it is translating one natural language into another language.

In this research, how language translation works, applications, and different types of machine translation are discussed. Language translators can translate huge amounts of text very quickly [2].

A QA system enables users to express questions in plain language and receive quick responses. Instant QA systems are now embedded in search engines and phone interfaces and are good at answering simple snippets of information. QA settings are quite natural depending on the span. This QA system, usually open domain, is able to find good documentation containing solutions to many user questions submitted to search engines.

3.2   Literature Survey

The paper published by Dr. G.N.R. Prasad in January 2021 proposed the model by using the NLP Tokenization approach; the level of the study's Bloom's Taxonomy is determined [1]. The tokenization method breaks down the sentence into different smaller pieces known as "tokens" according to their categories using the NLTK Regular Expression.

The paper named SentencePiece by Taku Kudo *et al.* described that the SentencePiece is designed for neural machine translation, a language-agnostic subword tokenizer and detokenizer. It includes open-source subword unit implementations in C++ and Python. It trains subword models from raw sentences, allowing for an end-to-end language-independent system [2].

Kyubyong Park *et al.* contributed to a study for Korean Tasks using tokenization in NLP that was published in 2020 [3]. The testing of numerous tokenization techniques in order to respond to our major question, "What is the optimal tokenization approach for NLP tasks for Korean?" is the focus of this study. The experimental findings show that a technique of segmentation followed by BPE performs better in translation and natural language comprehension tasks. As an exception, BPE segmentation is the most successful for KorQuAD, the Korean version of SQuAD [3].

In their paper, Abigail Rai [4] explains all the methods of tokenization that can be used to tokenize the word effectively. Tokenization is the important step in Natural Level Processing that uses Part-of-Speech tagging. Tokenization is the method in which sentences and words are broken down into its smallest part that cannot be broken again.

Md. Touhidul Islam contributed to the paper where they studied various machine learning algorithms based on NLP on US airline Twitter data published in the year 2021. It is a technology that combines NLP with ML [5].

Bag-of-Words and TF-IDF NLP approaches, as well as different ML classification algorithms, were employed. NLP was used to transform text data into vector form, and the dataset was obtained through Crowd Flower's Data for everyone package.

Wei Yen Chong and others contributed to the analysis of the tweets based on sentiment analysis. They suggested a methodology for extracting sentiment from tweets based on the tweets' subjects [6]. By specifying the grammatical links between sentiment lexicons and topic, the experiment makes use of sentiment lexicons. It reported preliminary findings of the proposed system, which uses NLP techniques for identifying tweets' subjects and analyzing sentiment lexicons associated with the subjects to categorize tweets as polar or nonpolar.

Adil Rajput contributed to the paper by stating about the application of sentiment analysis to psychological well-being using NLP. The process of purifying data may be substantially simplified with the use of the NLTK toolbox, which implements several NLP ideas, as described in the paper [7]. Using text data from the Internet, psychiatrists were able to locate symptoms that were signs of various mental health issues.

Nhan Cach Dang *et al.* published a paper in the year 2020. Social network data sentiment analysis is based on Deep Learning models and related approaches. TF-IDF and Word embedding were two strategies employed [8]. Using these two techniques, they analyzed DNN, CNN, and RNN architectures and combined them to perform sentiment analysis. DNN, CNN, and hybrid approaches are found to be the most often used models for sentiment analysis.

Yi Tay, Vinh Q. Tran *et al.* published a paper in 2022. This paper [9], implemented Charformer, which is a re-scaled Transformer architecture that helps to blend gradient-based subword tokenization. This method allowed effective end-to-end learning of potential subwords. A method for inner inspection of the GBST module is also imparted. Charformer is performed usually on English-based tasks with subword-based models but not on noisy social media with the same subword-based models.

The paper on Arabic Natural Language Processing published in 2018 discussed the complexity and characteristics of the Arabic language and the need of ANLP [10]. They have mentioned about the typical phases, which are input, feature extract, machine learning framework, and evaluation. Various applications were proposed such as readability assessment, web spam detection, and Arabic text categorization, where algorithms like SVM, Naive Bayes, decision trees, and KNN make the correct decision to classify Arabic text in the predefined class.

The paper on the Knowledge Base using NLP algorithms is published in 2020 [11]. In this paper, they discussed how one information is related to another information, which allows semantic search and see relationships between entities.

This project focuses on the creation of a text pre-processing system on the Russian Dataset, which is capable of converting raw text into defined data structures suitable for a given database. Four different subsystems were implemented like extracting sentences from text, dependency parsing, constructing graph data structures, and loading the data in the database. The suggested approach allows you to store text information in a manner that is more suitable for search and display.

The paper based on Sentiment Analysis in Twitter based on lexicon is published in 2019 [12]. The paper describes about the lexicon and the multiplication polarity. The findings of this study were collected utilizing the Python programming language tool, and the planned research methodologies following the completion of the Twitter APIs were only known as done, NumPy, SciPy, and smart in the library. The Twitter API is then configured to receive up to 100 tweets. The topic is entered into the system as the first step in using it.

Deem Alsalehi and others published a paper in 2020. They investigated the application of SOTA Transformer models for medical text augmentation in this article. They concentrated on the vanilla Transformer and GPT-2 models to create discharge summaries from the MIMIC-III dataset using a seq2seq job. They compared their results to the original data as well as a more traditional data augmentation baseline known as EDA [13].

Nitish Ranjan Bhowmik and others published a paper in 2021 [14]. In order to analyze sentiments in Bangla, this LDD was created by using two Bangla datasets that are accessible in the GitHub repository using the stemming, tokenization, and normalization techniques. In order to identify sentence polarity, a brand-new rule-based technique called the Bangla Text Sentiment Score is created, and scores for the two Bangla datasets are generated; the BTSC and LDD are used to obtain sentiments [14].

Deem Alsaleh and Souad Larabi-Marie-Sainte published a paper in 2021 [15]. This study suggests classifying Arabic text using convolutional neural networks based on genetic algorithms. The suggested model is evaluated using two huge datasets and contrasted with the most recent research. Additionally, text documents were transformed into numeric vectors using GloVe, a recent data representation technique [15].

M Uma and others published a paper in 2019 explaining the system that takes input as a Natural Language question and output as SQL Query [16]. This procedure includes the phases of breaking down text, reducing the dimensionality, assignment of tags, analyzing the grammatical structure, and mapping. There are several structured natural language inquiries about railway rates and seat availability in this dataset [16].

3.3   Comparison Table of Previous Techniques

Sr. no.	Authors	Year	Algorithms	Conclusion
1.	G.N.R. Prasad *et al.*	2021	Bloom's taxonomy scheme	The paper focuses on the knowledge aspect of the cognitive domain in Bloom's taxonomy and provides a method to determine the level of the cognitive domain in a paper [1].
2.	Taku Kudo *et al.*	2018	LSTM	The paper introduces Sentence Piece, a free and open-source subword tokenization and de-tokenization tool for neural text processing. It offers a reliable and reproducible method for text processing in practical applications, as well as support for research purposes [2].
3.	Kyubyong Park *et al.*	2020	CV, Morpheme Morpheme-aware Subword, word Tokenization	On machine translation and five natural language understanding tasks, they investigated several Morpheme-aware Korean tokenization algorithms. Subword models with a large vocabulary outperformed other models in machine translation for Korean-to-English and vice versa scenarios [3].
4.	Abigail Rai *et al.*	2021	Lucene Analyzer, Byte Pair Encoding (BPE), Word Piece	The paper provides a summary of the progress of tokenization techniques for Indian and other languages. The survey showed the use of rule-based, supervised, and unsupervised methods with efficient results for different languages [4].
5.	Md. Taufiqul Haque Khan Tusar *et al.*	2021	SVM, Logistic Regression	In the study, a combination of Logistic Regression, SVM, and Bag-of-Words techniques resulted in an accuracy rate of 77% [5].

(Continued)

(Continued)

Sr. no.	Authors	Year	Algorithms	Conclusion
6.	Camilleri, Luke	2019	CNN	Developed a theoretical framework based on recent research, then chose the best architecture and method for machine learning. Results indicate that the proposed deep learning sentiment analysis system outperforms both commercially available software and recent literature in comparison tests [6].
7.	Adil Rajput *et al.*	2019	Porter Lancaster Stemmer	Sentiment analysis is done using the techniques utilized by NLP. The paper concludes that we may employ sentiment analysis and NLP applications for mental health as well [7].
8.	Souad Larabi Marie-Sainte *et al.*	2018	SVM, Naive Bayes, decision trees and KNN	This review dives into the idea in depth, demonstrates the application of ML approaches on the Arabic Languages in the development of tools, and highlights well-known techniques employed in ANLP. Various applications were proposed such as readability assessment, webspam detection and text categorization for the Arabic Language to divide them into the predefined classes [10].
9.	Artem A. Maksutov *et al.*	2020	Graph Model Structure and Dependency parsing algorithm	An open-source graph database was used in this paper on Russian Language. Dependency parsing algorithm is chosen according to the complexity of the text. The graph model can describe relationships between words, phrases, and sentences, which can be useful for recommendation systems, but not in the same evident way that human readable text can [11].

(Continued)

(*Continued*)

Sr. no.	Authors	Year	Algorithms	Conclusion
10.	Kusrini, Mashuri, Mochamad	2019	Naïve Bayes, Linear SVM.	The Lexicon technique for sentiment analysis is less accurate than machine learning. This is due to the fact that the Lexicon still lacks several adjectives. This has to be finished. The Lexicon technique is also less complex than those offered by machine learning [12].
11.	Ali Amin-Nejad, Sumithra Velupillai, Julia Ive	2020	LSTM	They suggested an approach that would direct the development of organized patient data in a sequential fashion. In the experiments, modern Transformer models were employed, and it was observed that the use of a supplemented dataset improved the performance of the baseline models on a classification test. Additionally, a user interface was developed and the scripts for the training and generation of the models were made accessible [13].
12.	M. S. Islam, Nitish Ranjan Bhowmik, *et al.*	2021	SVM and BTSC algorithms	The findings indicate that among the techniques tested, SVM achieved the highest accuracy of 82.21% using BiGram features. This highlights the efficiency of the BTSC algorithm for sentiment analysis in Bangla language. The methodology involved utilizing 5000 data points as a sentiment vocabulary [14].
13.	Deem Alsalehi and Souad Larabi-Marie-Sainte	2021	CNN and Genetic Algorithm	Two huge datasets were used to validate the suggested model. GA-CNN produced very good outcomes. The outcomes demonstrated a 4–5% improvement in categorization accuracy. The difference in testing and validation accuracy was 0.59% for the MNAD dataset and 3.76% for the SNAD dataset [15].

(*Continued*)

(*Continued*)

Sr. no.	Authors	Year	Algorithms	Conclusion
14.	M Uma; G Sneha; B Bharathi, V Sneha, J Bhuvana	2019	SVM, Bayesian Network	The paper discusses the application to map English queries to SQL using NLP and regular expressions and achieves an accuracy of 98.89% [16].
15.	Shaima A Abushaala, Mohammed M Elsheh	2021	LSTM BLSTM LSTM-CRF BLSTM-CRF	In this work, we used Arabic data to test the comparison of BLSTM, LSTM, LSTM-CRF, and BLSTM-CRF models for both POS and NER tasks in order to discover the optimal model of every task. After testing and analyzing the models, BLSTM-CRF outperforms other algorithms for the POS problem, with the highest F1 rating of 81.1%. BLSTM-CRF has an F1-score of 69.8% for the NER task [17].

The survey looked into several applications of tokenization using NLP.

3.3.1   Sentiment Analysis

Sentiment analysis through NLP is the process of identifying emotions or attitudes expressed in text. It is widely used in fields such as social media monitoring, brand reputation management, and customer service. To extract features from text, techniques like POS tagging, tokenization, and dependency parsing are applied, followed by feeding the results to a machine learning model

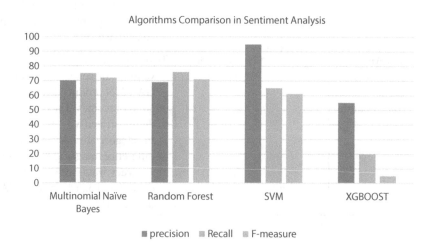

Figure 3.1 Graph of machine learning algorithms in sentiment analysis.

for sentiment prediction. Models that are based on deep learning algorithms such as RNN have also proven effective in sentiment analysis tasks [8]. Sentiment analysis is a complex task and is influenced by factors, such as language nuances, sarcasm, and subjectivity. The process involves converting text into tokens. Sentiment analysis, a method also referred to as opinion mining, is a technique for automatically determining the sentiment expressed in a part of text. Machine learning and text analysis allow algorithms to classify statements as positive and negative [12]. Figure 3.1 shows comparison of different machine learning algorithms in sentiment analysis.

3.3.2 Translation

Language translation using Natural Language Processing (NLP) involves converting text from one language to another. It is a crucial aspect of NLP with various applications, including machine-assisted human translation, multilingual information retrieval, and machine-generated summaries. There are two key approaches for language translation. Rule-based translation employs a set of predefined rules to translate text, while statistical machine translation utilizes large parallel corpora to determine the likelihood of a word or phrase in one language corresponding to another language. The latest method is Neural Machine Translation (NMT), which utilizes deep neural networks to model the relationship between the target and source, demonstrating notable improvements in translation quality. However, it is crucial to keep in mind that language translation is a challenging task that can be impacted by factors such as grammar, idioms, and cultural context.

3.3.3 Tokenization Based on Noisy Texts

Noisy text refers to electronic communication that cannot be accurately analyzed by text mining software due to discrepancies between the HTML code and the intended meaning of the author.

This can result in difficulty categorizing the text. The Figure 3.2 shows average of NLI English task comparisons and Figure 3.3 shows average number of segmented subwords.

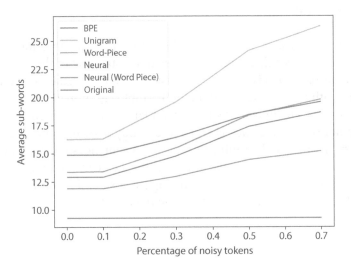

Figure 3.2 Average of NLI English task comparisons.

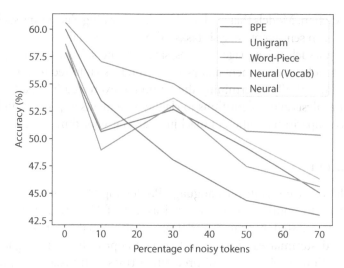

Figure 3.3 Average number of segmented subwords.

3.3.4   Question Answer Model

The paper discusses Question Answering (QA) using NLP, which involves generating an answer to a question based on given texts. QA has various applications in areas like conversational agents, information retrieval, and knowledge base construction. There are three main approaches to QA. Rule-based QA utilizes a set of predetermined rules, information retrieval-based QA employs techniques like keyword matching and text search, while machine learning-based QA, also referred to as "neural QA," uses deep neural networks to model the relationship between the question and text, leading to improved QA performance. However, QA remains a challenging task due to factors such as ambiguity, context, and knowledge gap.

3.4   Research Gap

Although significant research has been conducted on text classification in different languages using NLP, there is still a shortage in our understanding of the functioning of NLP algorithms with absolute precision, and the results cannot be guaranteed as accurate. To identify patterns within text, rule-based methods employ grammatical constructs and heuristics. This method has its drawbacks for certain languages where sentence structure and word order are not set, for instance [11]. Further study is being conducted in the area of semantic analysis in order to determine its polarity. A sentence's semantic norms can influence polarity. As a result, an extensive study on the Lexicon method is required, which includes notions such as Uni-Gram, B-gram, Tagger Post, and so on [12]. They evaluated only the basic Transformer and a smaller version of GPT-2.

3.5 Conclusion

Tokenization is a crucial step in NLP data preparation that divides the text into smaller parts called tokens. When evaluating the sentences, tokenization helps in understanding the context of language. This research gives a solution for the tokenization and the sentiment analysis for the classification into the three categories, as well as the conversion of the text into different languages.

References

1. Prasad, G.N.R., Identification of Bloom's Taxonomy level for the given question paper using NLP Tokenization technique. *Turk. J. Comput. Math. Educ.*, 12, 13, 1872–1875, 2021.
2. Kudo, T. and Richardson, J., SentencePiece: A simple and language independent subword tokenizer and detokenizer for Neural Text Processing. *Proceedings of the 2018 Conference on Empirical Methods in Natural Language Processing: System Demonstrations.*
3. Park, K., Lee, J., Jang, S., Jung, D., An empirical study of tokenization strategies for various Korean NLP tasks. *ACL-IJCNLP*, 2020.
4. Rai, A., Study of various methods for tokenization, in: *Applications of Internet of Things. Lecture Notes in Networks and Systems.* Mandal, J., Mukhopadhyay, S., Roy, A. (eds.), vol. 137. Springer, Singapore, 2021.
5. Tusar, Md. T.H.K. and Islam, Md. T., A comparative study of sentiment analysis using NLP and different machine learning techniques on US Airline Twitter data. *2021 International Conference on Electronics, Communications and Information Technology (ICECIT).*
6. Chong, W.Y., Selvaretnam, B., Soon, L.-K., Natural language processing for sentiment analysis: An exploratory analysis on tweets, IEEE Xplore.
7. Rajput, A., Natural language processing, sentiment analysis and clinical analytics, *ArXiv abs/1902.00679*, 2019.
8. Dang, N.C., Moreno-García, M.N., De la Prieta, F., Sentiment analysis based on deep learning: A comparative study. *Electronics*, 9, 3, 483, 2020.
9. Tay, Y., Tran, V.Q., Ruder, S., Gupta, J., Chung, H.W., Bahri, D., Qin, Z., Baumgartner, S., Yu, C., Metzler, D., Charformer: Fast character transformers via gradient-based subword tokenization, arXiv:2106.12672.
10. Larabi Marie-Sainte, S. *et al.*, Arabic natural language processing and machine learning-based systems. *IEEE Access*, 7, 7011–7020, 2019.
11. Maksutov, A.A., Zamyatovskiy, V.I., Vyunnikov, V.N., Kutuzov, A.V., Knowledge base collecting using natural language processing algorithms, IEEE Xplore.
12. Kusrini, M.M., Sentiment analysis in twitter using lexicon based and polarity multiplication, IEEE Xplore.
13. Amin-Nejad, A., Ive, J., Velupillai, S., Exploring transformer text generation for medical dataset augmentation. *Proceedings of the Twelfth Language Resources and Evaluation Conference.*
14. Bhowmik, N.R., Arifuzzaman, M., Rubaiyat Hossain Mondal, M., Islam, M.S., Bangla text sentiment analysis using supervised machine learning with extended lexicon dictionary, in: *Natural Language Processing Research.* vol. I, issue 3–4, pp. 34–45, Atlantis Press, 2021.
15. Alsaleh, D. and Larabi-Marie-Sainte, S., Arabic text classification using convolutional neural network and genetic algorithms. *IEEE Access*, 9, 1–16.

16. Uma, M., Sneha, V., Sneha, G., Bhuvana, J., Bharathi, B., Formation of SQL from natural language query using NLP, IEEE Xplore.

17. Abushaala, S.A. and Elsheh, M.M., A comparative study on various deep learning techniques for Arabic NLP syntactic tasks on noisy data, IEEE Xplore.

18. Rishita, M.V.S., Raju, M.A., Harris, T.A., Machine translation using natural language processing. *International Joint Conference on Metallurgical and Materials Engineering (JCMME 2018).*

4

Book Genre Prediction Using NLP: A Review

Kuldeep Vayadande[1]*, Preeti Bailke[1], Ashutosh M. Kulkarni[1], R. Kumar[2] and Ajit B. Patil[3]

[1]Vishwakarma Institute of Technology, Pune, Maharashtra, India
[2]VIT-AP University, Inavolu, Beside AP Secretariat, Amaravati AP, India
[3]KIT's College of Engineering, Kolhapur, Maharashtra, India

Abstract
Book genre prediction is a crucial task in the field of literature, and the use of NLP techniques has significantly improved the accuracy of genre prediction systems. This survey paper provides an overview of recent research on book genre prediction using NLP techniques such as lexical analysis and neural networks. The paper discusses various approaches, datasets, and evaluation metrics used in the literature and presents a comparative analysis of the different techniques based on their effectiveness in genre prediction. The survey highlights the potential impact of NLP techniques on the field of literature, emphasizing the importance of accurate genre prediction for various applications such as recommendation systems and book marketing. However, there are still challenges to be addressed, such as the lack of standard evaluation metrics and the need to better understanding the relationship between language features and genre classification. The survey concludes with a discussion on the future research directions in this field, such as the use of deep learning techniques and the development of more diverse and representative datasets.

Keywords: Book genre prediction, Keras, lexical analysis, neural network, multilayer perceptron, recurrent neural network, F1-score

4.1 Introduction

Book genre prediction is a natural language processing task that involves categorizing a book based on its text content. One approach to this task is the use of lexical analysis and a machine learning algorithm called K-Nearest Neighbors (KNN). Lexical analysis involves analyzing the words and structure of a text to extract relevant features such as word frequency, stylistic elements, and sentiment. These features are then fed into the KNN model, which predicts the genre of the book by comparing it to previously categorized books. The KNN algorithm works by finding the K nearest neighbors in a training dataset, and then using the majority class of those neighbors to make a prediction. In the case of book genre prediction, the training dataset consists of books manually categorized into various genres. The lexical features extracted from the text are used to find the K nearest books, and the

---

*Corresponding author: kuldeep.vayadande1@vit.edu

Arindam Dey, Sukanta Nayak, Ranjan Kumar and Sachi Nandan Mohanty (eds.) How Machine Learning is Innovating Today's World: A Concise Technical Guide, (37–46) © 2024 Scrivener Publishing LLC

majority genre of those books is used to predict the genre of the unknown book. Overall, the combination of lexical analysis and KNN is a powerful approach to book genre prediction that takes advantage of the strengths of both techniques to accurately categorize books into their respective genres.

Book genre prediction can be tackled using two different approaches: KNN and Keras. KNN is a straightforward machine learning algorithm that identifies the K nearest neighbors in a labeled training dataset to a given input and makes a prediction based on the majority class of those neighbors. While KNN is easy to implement, does not require training or tuning, and is well-suited for small datasets, it may not perform well for large datasets or those with complex feature relationships. Keras, on the other hand, is a library that simplifies the building and training of complex machine learning models such as neural networks for book genre classification. Keras has the advantage of being able to handle large datasets, modeling complex feature relationships, and producing highly accurate predictions. However, Keras requires more time and resources to implement and train. Therefore, the selection of which approach to employ depends on the specific requirements and constraints of the problem at hand. In conclusion, both KNN and Keras have their own strengths and limitations, making their choice dependent on the task's requirements.

To predict the genre of a book using the Keras approach, a neural network model is built to understand the relationship between the text data. The process begins by extracting relevant components from the text data, such as the frequency of certain words and phrases, stylistic elements, and the sentiment expressed in the text. These components are then fed as input to the neural network, which consists of multiple layers of interconnected nodes that process and transform the input data. The model is trained on a labeled dataset of books, where the input features are used to predict the genre of each book. The main goal of the training process is to adjust the weights and biases of the model so that it can make accurate predictions on unseen data. Once the model is trained, it can be used to classify the genre of a new book by inputting its textual information and passing it through the network. The output of the network is a probability distribution across the possible genres, which can be used to make a prediction by selecting the genre with the highest probability. Overall, the Keras approach leverages the power of neural networks to make highly accurate genre predictions by learning the underlying patterns and relationships within the text data.

4.2   Literature Survey

Recently, the significance of text mining has increased due to the availability of a growing number of electronic documents from various sources [1]. The process of text classification typically involves several stages: preprocessing data, cleaning text, selecting features, training a model, assigning classifiers, and evaluating the output. One common problem faced in libraries is classifying the genre of books, especially those that are not properly categorized. To solve this, genre predictions are made based on book titles and summaries. The aim is to develop a model that can accurately determine the genre of a book based on its title [2]. The proposed approach uses Principal Component Analysis and Natural Language Processing to decrease the dimensionality of a matrix for book categorization using machine learning. The method clusters similar words into the same class, improving the accuracy of the model. Books with known genre are used to create labeled data, which serves as the training data. Meanwhile, books with unknown genre provide the unlabeled data, which is used to gain insights into the underlying structure of the data. The approach allows for efficient genre classification of documents [3]. Lazaro S.P. Busagala's method for text categorization involves constructing a lexicon of all the distinct words in a text and a frequency vector counting these words. Dimensionality reduction is achieved through Principal Component Analysis and term selection. The experiment uses numerous Discriminant Functions, including Support Vector Machines. However, the generated feature vector can be large, potentially affecting the accomplishment of the ML model. In short, Lazaro S.P. Busagala's approach for text categorization creates a word frequency count vector, reduces dimensionality through term selection and PCA, and experiments with Discriminant Functions including SVM. The large feature vector may affect model performance [4]. Prafulla Bafna presented a text classification approach that removes stop words, applies TF-IDF normalization, and uses Fuzzy K Means and Agglomerative Clustering for clustering. This appeal conquers the drawbacks of previous methods with the help of TF-IDF normalization. The general framework for text classification involves transforming words into numerical representations, calculating the significance of each term, and utilizing a classification algorithm to categorize the text. Dimensionality reduction can be applied at any stage in the process. Text classification can be accomplished using labeled data alone or in conjunction with unlabeled data. In short, Prafulla Bafna's text classification approach removes stop words, normalizes with TF-IDF, and clusters with Fuzzy K Means and Agglomerative Clustering. The general structure of text classification includes representing words, computing term weights, and using a classifier. Dimension reduction is optional, and text classification can be performed with either labeled or both.

In [5], the authors present the use of deep learning techniques for music preference prediction. One of the methods utilized is tokenization, which involves converting music features such as melody, rhythm, and timbre into numerical representations to serve as inputs for neural network models. Another method is minimum classification error training, which involves adjusting the configuration of the neural network models to minimize error between the predicted and actual music preferences. The authors found that the use of tokenization and minimum classification error training can lead to improved prediction performance compared to traditional methods. In more detail, the authors of this paper explore the use of deep learning techniques for music preference prediction. One of the key methods they use is tokenization, which converts music features such as melody, rhythm, and timbre into numerical representations that can be used as inputs for neural network models. This numerical representation of the music data allows the models to process and analyze the data in a more sophisticated way. Another important method the authors use is minimum classification error training, which involves fine-tuning the parameters of the neural network models so that they can minimize the error between the predicted and actual music preferences. This leads to an improvement in the accuracy of the predictions made by the models. The authors found that the combination of tokenization and minimum classification error training can lead to improved prediction performance compared to traditional methods, which rely on simpler techniques for music preference prediction.

In [6], the authors proposed a system for natural language processing. The authors went through a comprehensive preprocessing and cleaning process for the text data. This included the removal of stop words, which are commonly occurring words in a language that are not deemed informative for the analysis. The authors then trained a machine learning model on the cleaned dataset using different ratios and compared its performance using F1-score and accuracy metrics. To start with, they utilized machine learning models like KNN and Logistic Regression. Finally, they also employed LSTM, a type of RNN, to further enhance the performance of the model.

In [7], the proposed method in the system uses NLP to transform the text into a matrix, which is then reduced in size with the help of Principal Component Analysis and Wordnet. The resulting matrix is used to forecast the book's genre through the use of an AdaBoost classifier. The execution of the method can be enhanced by adjusting various parameters, such as the depth of tree in the Decision Tree Classifier, the number of estimators in the AdaBoost algorithm, and the number of contents in Principal Component Analysis. This approach is expandable and can be utilized to categorize articles in news and blog genres.

In [8], a new ordinal regression algorithm is proposed to enhance content-based music recommendation and overcome the limitations of current methods. This algorithm takes into account dynamic information. The authors propose a different approach to characterizing music, which involves identifying a set of acoustic segment models (ASMs) through unsupervised analysis, instead of assuming that the features of a song follow a uniform pattern. Moreover, the classification of music is based on individual preferences rather than subjective categories like genre or a universal measure of similarity.

Verma and Gaur [9] have explored the topic of text mining and tokenization with filtering. They describe text mining as an information-rich process in which the user interacts with a set of documents. Similar to data mining, the goal of text mining is to find valuable insights from data sources through the discovery of unique patterns. The document collection is a crucial aspect of text mining.

Farhanaaz and Sanju V. [10] conducted a study on lexical analysis. As the initial step in the compilation process, lexical analysis has several responsibilities including scanning the source code character by character, expanding macros, and performing compilation on the file.

4.3   Comparison Table

Table 4.1 shows comparison of different techniques [1, 3, 6, 8–10].

Table 4.1 Comparison table.

Name of paper	Date	Introduction	Compression
Book Genre Categorization Using Machine Learning Algorithms (K-Nearest Neighbor, Support Vector Machine and Logistic Regression) using Customized Dataset	2018	Text mining is important for classifying electronic documents, including books in libraries. The process involves preprocessing, cleaning, feature selection, model training, classifier assignment, and output evaluation. The aim is to develop a model that accurately determines a book's genre based on its title and summary.	Text classification and book genre detection are related. Both aim to categorize text based on specific criteria. Book genre detection categorizes books into genres based on title and summary. Similar steps are followed in both, including preprocessing, cleaning, feature selection, model training, and output evaluation. Quality of data and methods used for preprocessing, model training, and feature selection determine the success of the model. Book genre detection is a specific application of text classification.
Automated Genre Classification of Books Using Machine Learning and Natural Language Processing	2017	Proposed approach for book genre classification uses NLP and PCA to reduce feature matrix dimensionality for improved accuracy. It clusters similar words into classes and uses labeled data for training and unlabeled data to understand structure. The approach can efficiently classify genres of documents from a few to thousands of lines.	• The proposed approach uses NLP and PCA for book genre classification • Reduces feature matrix dimensionality for improved accuracy • Clusters similar words into classes • Uses labeled data for training and unlabeled data to understand structure • Can efficiently classify genres of documents

(Continued)

Table 4.1 Comparison table. (*Continued*)

Name of paper	Date	Introduction	Compression
Machine Learning with Transformed Features in Automatic Text Classification	2018	Lazaro S.P. Busagala's approach for text categorization creates a word frequency count vector, reduces dimensionality through term selection and PCA, and experiments with Discriminant Functions including SVM. The large feature vector may affect model performance.	• Lazaro's approach for text categorization: • Creates word frequency count vector • Reduces dimensionality through term selection and PCA • Experiments with Discriminant Functions (SVM) • Large feature vector may impact model performance
Document Clustering: TF-IDF Approach	2016	Prafulla Bafna's text classification approach removes stop words, normalizes with TF-IDF, and clusters with Agglomerative and Fuzzy K Means. The structure includes representing words, computing term weights, using a classifier, and optional dimension reduction, using labeled or both labeled and unlabeled data.	• Prafulla Bafna's text classification approach: • Removes stop words • Normalizes with TF-IDF • Clusters with Agglomerative Clustering and Fuzzy K Means • General structure of text classification: • Representing words • Computing term weights • Using a classifier • Dimension reduction is optional • Can be performed with either labeled or both labeled and unlabeled data.

(Continued)

Table 4.1 Comparison table. (*Continued*)

Name of paper	Date	Introduction	Compression
Preference Music Ratings Prediction Using Tokenization and Minimum Classification Error Training	2019	The authors suggest using deep learning techniques for predicting music preferences, by utilizing tokenization and training with minimum classification error to enhance prediction accuracy, in comparison to conventional methods. Tokenization converts music features into numerical representations for neural network models, and minimum classification error training fine-tunes the parameters to minimize prediction error. The authors found that this approach leads to improved accuracy compared to simpler traditional methods.	• Deep learning approach for music preference prediction • Utilization of tokenization and minimum classification error training • Tokenization converts music features into numerical representations • Minimum classification error training adjusts parameters to minimize prediction error • Improved accuracy compared to simpler traditional methods
Book Recommendation Platform Using Deep Learning	2020	In a proposed system, the authors underwent text preprocessing and cleaning, including removal of stop words. Then, they trained a machine learning model using different ratios and evaluated its performance using F1-score and accuracy. The initial models used were KNN and logistic regression, followed by the use of LSTM.	• A proposed system for NLP involved preprocessing and cleaning of text data with removal of stop words. • The system employed supervised machine learning models such as KNN and Logistic Regression for training the dataset, with ratios being compared using F1-score and accuracy metrics. • The system also utilized LSTM, a type of RNN, to enhance the performance of the model.

(Continued)

Table 4.1 Comparison table. (*Continued*)

Name of paper	Date	Introduction	Compression
Leveraging Genre Classification with RNN for Book Recommendation	2019	The proposed system uses NLP, Wordnet, PCA, and AdaBoost to predict book genres. The performance is optimized with decision tree depth, AdaBoost estimators, and PCA components. It is scalable and used for predicting genres.	• Uses NLP to convert book text into a matrix • Reduces size using Wordnet and PCA • Predicts book genres with AdaBoost classifier • Optimizes performance with decision tree depth, AdaBoost estimators, and PCA components • Scalable and applied to predict genres
Feature Engineering in User's Music Preference Prediction	2015	An ordinal regression algorithm for music recommendation is presented to address limitations of current content-based approaches. It characterizes music with ASMs found through an unsupervised process and classifies songs based on personal preference ratings, not genre or universal similarity.	• Addresses limitations of current content-based methods • Uses ordinal regression algorithm with dynamic information • Characterizes music with ASMs found through unsupervised process • Classifies songs based on personal preference ratings, not genre or universal similarity
Tokenization and Filtering process in Rapidminer	2014	Deepti Gaur and Tanu Verma discuss text mining and tokenization with filtering. Text mining is a process to get information and collections by identifying and exploring interesting patterns. It has a focus on document collections.	• Discusses text mining and tokenization with filtering • Defines text mining as a process to extract useful information from document collections through pattern identification • Text mining has a focus on document collections

(*Continued*)

Table 4.1 Comparison table. (*Continued*)

Name of paper	Date	Introduction	Compression
An Exploration on Lexical Analysis	2016	Farhanaaz and Sanju V. explored the study of lexical analysis. It is the first phase of the compilation process and has responsibilities such as scanning the program one character by one, expanding macros, and performing compilation on the file.	• Explored the study of lexical analysis • First phase is Lexical analysis of the compilation process • Responsibilities of lexical analysis include scanning program one character by one, expanding macros, and performing compilation on the file

4.4 Research Gap Identified

The sparse nature of the feature matrix hinders the training model's performance. Currently, research is focused solely on the lexical analyzer, but to optimize the compilation process for multi-core architectures, all phases of the compiler must be re-engineered to allow for parallel processing.

4.5 Future Scope

The book genre prediction model using Keras and lexical analysis has great potential for further development and application. The current scope of the model includes text input, lexical analysis techniques such as word frequency and phrase usage, a neural network trained on a labeled dataset of book genres, and performance evaluation on the basis of metrics like F1-score and accuracy. In the future, the model can be improved with more advanced neural network architectures and lexical analysis techniques, integrated with other applications such as recommendation systems and extended to support multiple languages. Additionally, the model can be adapted to specific domains, such as children's books or scientific literature, and incorporate user feedback to make even more accurate predictions. Other text-based features, such as style and tone, can also be explored to see if they provide additional information for book genre prediction. Overall, the book genre prediction model using Keras and lexical analysis has a promising future and can have valuable applications in fields such as digital humanities, library science, and publishing.

4.6 Conclusion

In conclusion, the book genre prediction model using Keras and lexical analysis demonstrated promising results in accurately predicting the genre of a book based on its text. The model leverages the power of lexical analysis to obtain the useful features from input text, and flexibility of neural networks to learn and make predictions. This approach could have useful applications in fields such as digital humanities, library science, and publishing, among others. Further research could be done to improve the performance of the model and explore other text-based features and algorithms for book genre prediction.

References

1. Shiroya, P., Vaghasiya, D., Soni, M., Panchal, B., Book genre categorization using machine learning algorithms (K-Nearest Neighbor, Support Vector Machine and Logistic Regression) using customized dataset. *Int. J. Comput. Sci. Mob. Comput.*, 10, 3, 14–25, March 2021.
2. Gupta, S., Agarwal, M., Jain, S., Automated genre classification of books using machine learning and natural language processing, pp. 269–272, 2019.
3. Busagala, L.S.P., Ohyama, W., Wakabayashi, T., Kimura, F., Machine learning with transformed features in automatic text classification. http://www2.hi.info.mieu.ac.jp/publication/archive/busagala_Camera-ready.pdf.
4. Bafna, P., Pramod, D., Vaidya, A., Document clustering: TF-IDF approach. Electrical, Electronics, and Optimization Techniques (ICEEOT). *International Conference on. IEEE*, 2016.
5. Reed, J. and Lee, C.-H., Preference music rating prediction using tokenization and minimum classification error training. *IEEE Trans. Audio Speech Lang. Process*, 19, 8, 2294–2303, Nov. 2011.
6. Wadikar, D., Kumari, N., Bhat, R., Shirodkar, V., Book recommendation platform using deep learning. *Int. J. Eng. Technol.*, 6764–6770, 6 June 2020.
7. Saraswat, M. and Srishti, Leveraging genre classification with RNN for the book recommendation. *Int. J. Inf. Technol.*, 14, 3751–3756, 2022.
8. Xie, J., Leishman, S., David, L., Seongjoon, L., Matthias, K., Feature engineering in user's music preference prediction. *JMLR: Workshop and Conference Proceedings*, vol. 18, pp. 183–197.
9. Verma, T., Gaur, D., Renu, Tokenization and filtering process in Rapidminer. *Int. J. Appl. Inf. Syst.*, 1, 16–18.
10. Farhannaz, and Sanju, V., An exploration on lexical analysis. *International Conference on Electrical, Electronics and Optimization Techniques (ICEEOT)*.

5

Mood Detection Using Tokenization: A Review

Kuldeep Vayadande[1]*, Preeti A. Bailke[1], Lokesh Sheshrao Khedekar[1], R. Kumar[2] and Varsha R. Dange[1]

[1]Vishwakarma Institute of Technology, Pune, Maharashtra, India
[2]VIT-AP University, Inavolu, Beside AP Secretariat, Amaravati AP, India

Abstract

Tokenization and convolutional neural networks (CNNs) are being used for the task of mood detection, emoji generation, and classification. Tokenization is helpful to break down text into individual sentences, words, and phrases, which is an important step in natural language processing (NLP). It allows the model to focus on individual words and phrases. The CNNs are then trained on labeled text datasets for mood detection, text–emoji pair datasets for emoji generation, and emoji–label pair datasets for emoji classification. In this survey paper, we have summarized various methods for tokenization and CNNs that can be effectively used to understand the sentiment or emotion expressed in text data, to acquire high accuracy in classifying text as having a negative and positive or neutral sentiment, generating emojis that match the sentiment or emotion expressed in the text and classifying emojis as expressing a certain sentiment or emotion. For sentiment analysis, a CNN can be trained on a dataset of labeled text where the labels indicate the sentiment or emotion expressed. Once trained, the CNN can be used to classify new text as expressing a positive, negative, or neutral sentiment. As far as emoji generation is concerned, a CNN can be trained on a dataset that pairs text with corresponding emojis and labels. In this paper, we also included recent algorithms used to perform the same task with their comparable study.

Keywords: CNN, deep learning, emotion detection, emoji generations, mood detection, NLP, text classification

5.1 Introduction

Natural language processing (NLP) experts have recently become more and more interested in creating methods for detecting emotions and sentiments in text data. The combination of tokenization and convolutional neural networks (CNNs) is one widely used tactic that has evolved. The CNNs can efficiently understand the connections between the text and the underlying mood or emotion being expressed, allowing for the analysis of specific words

---

*Corresponding author: kuldeep.vayadande1@vit.edu

Arindam Dey, Sukanta Nayak, Ranjan Kumar and Sachi Nandan Mohanty (eds.) How Machine Learning is Innovating Today's World: A Concise Technical Guide, (47–56) © 2024 Scrivener Publishing LLC

and phrases. This technique has allowed researchers to perform sentiment analysis and emotion identification tasks with great levels of accuracy.

- **Tokenization**: Tokenization is the process of reducing lengthy passages of text to discrete units known as tokens. Depending on the desired level of granularity, specific words, phrases, or sentences can be regarded as tokens. Tokenization aims to transform unstructured text input into a structured format that NLP systems can quickly analyze and handle. Tokenization reduces the size of the text input so that CNN can more easily recognize patterns and features, such as sentiment and emotions. This method can be used for other jobs as well, such as creating and categorizing emojis based on the emotions portrayed in text. These methods could be used to analyze sentiment in news stories, social media posts, and consumer reviews, among other things. It also has additional applications.

- **Text classification**: In NLP, text classification is one of the important tasks that involves the automatic assignment of predefined labels or categories to a given piece of text. This task aims to extract meaningful information from unstructured text data, such as determining the sentiment of a tweet or identifying the topic of a news article. The categories for text classification can vary widely, including sentiments (positive, negative, and neutral), topics (sports, politics, and technology), named entities (persons, organizations, and locations), and more. With the help of machine learning (ML) algorithms and NLP techniques such as tokenization, word embedding, and feature engineering, text classification models can learn to accurately assign these labels to new, unseen text data.

- **CNN**: A well-liked deep learning model for processing images and videos is the CNN. It excels at locating patterns and characteristics in data with a grid-like layout, such as photographs. The network consists of various layers, each of which carries out a particular task like feature identification or image segmentation. Convolutional procedures are used to link the layers and extract features from the input data. The network also has pooling layers, which are employed to decrease the dimension of the data and enhance the network's capacity to recognize crucial elements. A prediction or categorization of the input data is a CNN's ultimate output. Tokenization and CNNs have received a lot of attention recently in research as a potent method for the NLP tasks like mood detection, emoji production, and classification purpose. In this paper, we have gone through various recent technologies and algorithms used for the tokenization and emoji generation after classification of text data, which is useful for sentiment analysis of text data.

In 2014, Kim *et al.* published a study in which they presented a CNN-based model for sentiment analysis. They found that the model outperformed traditional ML methods on a variety of benchmark datasets, and that pre-processing the text input using tokenization improved the model's performance. Similarly, in 2018, Zhang *et al.* proposed the novel method for generating emojis using CNNs and Long Short-Term Memory (LSTM) networks. They used tokenized text as input to the model and trained it on a dataset of text–emoji pairs. Finally, results showed that the proposed model can generate emojis that match the sentiment or emotion expressed in the text with high accuracy.

5.2   Literature Survey

Shlok Gilda *et al.* contributed to [1], smart music player integrating facial emotion recognition and music mood recognition with CNN. The algorithm in this paper is proposed to build a model that classifies emotion into four categories, like happy, angry, sad, and neutral, and got 90.23% accuracy. An EMP, or a music player model, claims that music influences a person's current mood with an accuracy of 97.69%.

Aswathy Ashok and Jisha John contributed to [2], Facial Expression Recognition System for Visually Impaired using SVM. Here, a Japanese female facial database was used, which involved newly added images. It detects three facial emotions like surprise, sad, and happy and expresses the emotion as an audio. Local Binary Pattern (LBP) was used to identify the appearance and shape of the image. The text-to-speech converter was used to identify the expression as audio.

Deny John Samuvel *et al.* contributed to [3], discussed and presented in 3C Tecnología. Glosas de innovación aplicadas a la pyme. ISSN: 2254–4143. In this, the Eigen faces algorithm is used to recognize the face and eight facial feelings; they proposed the algorithm Support Vector Machines (SVM) as the main characterization. A song database was made, and based on the person's mood, it recommends the music.

Shavak Chauhan, *et al.* contributed to [4], involving an analysis of the brilliant Movie Recommender System From Facial Expression With CNN. The datasets used were FER_2013. Here, it is stated that the model detects the emotion of faces, and according to it, it will recommend entertainment such as movies and songs. The recommender system consists of collaborative filtering in which the most watched movies or most listened songs will be recommended to the new user. The accuracy was found to be 55% for movie recommendation through facial expression.

Jasmine Awatramani and Nitasha Hasteer contributed to [5], Facial Expression Recognition using Deep Learning. In this, CNN and the FER-2013 dataset are used. FER-2013 converts the images in csv files named as emotion and pixels. The images were rotated, mirrored, and zoomed to increase its accuracy. After performing CNN algorithm, for the detection of emotions, the system was linked to the webcam to test the model. HAAR features are used to analyze lines, edges, and rectangles. This will help children who are suffering from ASD. The CNN model gives an accuracy of 67.50% [5].

Dweepna Garg, Parth Goel, *et al.* contributed to [6], A Deep Learning Approach for Face Detection using YOLO and CNN. Here, it is stated that for detecting the faces from videos, the technique used was CNN algorithm, which comes under deep learning. For testing and training, a single neural network is implemented to the complete image. The gradient descent optimizer algorithm was used and about 25 epochs were taken to train the model and accuracy was about 92.2% [6].

A rescaled Transformer architecture called Charformer was implemented. Charformer is a fast and innovative character transformer model using gradient-based subword tokenization in the work released in the year 2022. Charformer aids in blending gradient-based subword tokenization. Charformer is an efficient end-to-end learning approach for discovering latent subwords [8]. A method for inner inspection of the GBST module is also imparted.

Charformer usually performs English-based tasks with subword-based models, but it is outplayed on noisy social media with the same subword-based models.

J. Vickneswaran, P. Navanesan, V. Vijayaratnam and U. Thayasivam performed the Knowledge Base Collecting Using Natural Language Processing Algorithms. In their paper, they discussed how one information is related to another information, which allows semantic search and see relationships between entities. This work focuses on the development of a text pre-processing system on a Russian Dataset, which is capable of converting raw text into defined data structures suitable for a given database. Four different subsystems were implemented like extracting sentences from text, dependency parsing, constructing graph data structures, and loading the data in a database. The suggested approach allows you to store text information in a manner that is more suitable for search and display [8].

The publication [8] provides a description of the fundamental building block of deep learning models used for sentiment analysis and related techniques for social network data. Deep Learning-Based Sentiment Analysis Comparative study was released in the year 2020. Word embedding and TF-IDF were utilized as two methods. To perform sentiment analysis, these two techniques were utilized to analyze and combine the DNN, CNN, and RNN architectures. In terms of sentiment polarity analysis, DNN, CNN, and hybrid methods are the most widely used models. The memory consumption of both prototypes is identical, but ASPECTGCMS consumes more time as compared to ASPECT CRC because it uses a subroutine to identify the graph cycle. Therefore, ASPECTGCMS is under more investigation in the sweep phase [9].

The paper Sentiment Analysis in Twitter Using Lexicon Based and Polarity Multiplication was published. The paper describes that the findings were collected utilizing the Python programming language tool, and the planned research methodologies following the completion of the Twitter APIs were only known as done, NumPy, SciPy, and smart in the library. The Twitter API is then configured to receive up to 100 tweets. The topic is entered into the system as the first step in using it [10].

The literature survey of the paper Sarcasm Detection using LSTM with CNN–Genetic Optimization on combination explores previous works in the field of sarcasm detection in NLP. The survey highlights the various techniques used for sarcasm detection, including rule-based systems, feature-based systems, and ML-based systems. The survey also covers previous works that have used genetic optimization in combination with deep learning models for sarcasm detection, such as LSTM and CNN. The strengths and weaknesses of these approaches are discussed, and the contribution of the paper to the field is explained. The survey concludes by highlighting the importance of sarcasm detection in NLP and the need for improved models that can handle the complexity and ambiguity of sarcastic language [11].

Emoji generation utilizing a fusion of CNNs and LSTM networks is described by Zhang *et al.* (2018). The authors of this research introduced a novel method for producing emojis using tokenized text as input and trained the model using a dataset of text–emoji pairs. The study's findings demonstrated that the proposed methodology could produce emojis that accurately reflected the feeling or emotion portrayed in the text [12].

T Tulasi Sasidhar *et al.* [7] discussed Emotion Detection in Hinglish (Hindi+English) Code-Mixed Social-Media Text. This paper provides a technical overview of the methods and techniques used for emotion detection in code-mixed text, with a focus on the Hinglish language. The five classification models that the authors conducted experimental research on were LSTM, BiLSTM, CNN, CNN-LSTM, and CNN-BiLSTM.

More than 75% of the experimental model's predictions were accurate, with CNN-BiLSTM having a remarkable accuracy of 83.19%. The models were trained on 12,000 texts that were code-mixed in Hindi and English and were primarily taken from social media. Feature extraction is done on the pretrained tokenize data using pretrained specific word embedding model that trained a large corpus of data for better feature vector. The model is retrained using Word2Vec for analyzing the sematic relationship and tokenized word for generating the feature vector, which is used in the above five models. The paper [13] also provides a comprehensive evaluation of the performance of various methods for emotion detection in Hinglish code-mixed text, including a comparison of their accuracy, precision, recall, and F1-score. The authors highlight the need for further research in this area, including the development of more robust evaluation metrics and the use of large-scale datasets for training and testing.

The paper Persian Emoji Prediction Using Deep Learning and an Emoji Embedding discusses previous studies on the application of deep learning for emoji prediction and the use of emoji embedding in NLP tasks. The state-of-the-art models and techniques for that emoji prediction are examined, with a focus on their application to the Persian language. The challenges and limitations of previous works are highlighted, and the need for improved emoji prediction models for the Persian language is emphasized [14].

5.3 Comparison Table of Previous Techniques

Table 5.1 shows comparison of different techniques [1–10].

Table 5.1 Comparison of different emotion based techniques.

Ref. no.	Paper name	Authors	Year	Conclusion
1.	SMART MUSIC PLAYER Integrating Facial Emotion Recognition and Music Mood Recognition Using CNN [1]	Shlok Gilda, *et al.*	2017	The objective of this project is to develop an affordable music player that generates playlists based on the user's mood as determined by an emotion module. The music categorization module extracts crucial audio data from the songs [1] to achieve this.
2.	Emotion Recognition System for Visually Impaired using SVM [2]	E. Kodhai, A. Pooveswari, P. Sharmila, N. Ramiya	2020	With the help of input images that resemble the human visual system, computers are now being trained to mimic all the functions of the human eye and predict certain outcomes. Emotion recognition technology that can identify the facial expressions of those speaking with the visually impaired individual.

(Continued)

Table 5.1 Comparison of different emotion based techniques. (*Continued*)

Ref. no.	Paper name	Authors	Year	Conclusion
3.	Automated Emotion Detection in Multimedia Attributes Like Music or Movies [3]	Madhuri Athavle, Deepali Mudale, Upasana Shrivastav, Megha Gupta	2021	The ability to recognize emotions from a variety of indications, such as facial expressions, speech, EEG, and text, is necessary for the development of a unique music player that creates a playlist that is sensitive to the user's emotional state. Facial expressions are used as a training dataset for the model in this study, and several methods, including SVM and neural networks, are used to effectively recognize and classify emotions.
4.	Utilizing a Recommender System and CNN Analysis of Intelligent Facial Expression-Based Movie Recommendation System [4]	Rajdeep Shavak Chauhan. D. Viji Mollahosseini, Mangrola V, *et al.*	2021	Automatic emotion recognition is used in two distinct study areas, artificial intelligence and the psychology of human emotion. It will go over some recent FER studies that show off deep learning methods that applied to enhance detection in this circumstance. Paper recommended deep CNN for FER spanning many databases
5.	Facial Expression Recognition using Deep Learning [5]	Wafa Mellouka, Wahida Handouzia	2020	Early detection and identification models relied on hand-crafted features, but advancements in neural networks have improved accuracy and efficiency. Deep learning has also enhanced the capabilities of facial recognition systems, allowing for more versatile applications.

(*Continued*)

Table 5.1 Comparison of different emotion based techniques. (*Continued*)

Ref. no.	Paper name	Authors	Year	Conclusion
6.	Deep Learning approach for Face Detection with YOLO and CNN [6]	Dweepna Garg Parth Goel Sharnil, Pandya Sharnil, Pandya Show, Ketan Kotecha	2018	Prior to developing detection and identification algorithms, researchers explored numerous manual feature extraction methods. Deep learning and neural network models were used to speed up, increase the power, and improve the accuracy of computation. Prior to the development of deep learning algorithms, face identification systems were only effective in straightforward settings.
7.	Emotion Detection in Hinglish (Hindi + English) Code-Mixed Social Media Text [7]	T Tulasi Sasidhara, Premjith Ba, Soman Pa	2020	The paper highlights the challenges and limitations of current methods for emotion detection in code-mixed text and presents a comparative analysis on various models, among which the CNN-BiLSTM gives the accuracy of 83.21%; the CNN is effective for extracting features from the word embedding, which reduces the complexity of training for the Bi-LSTM Model.
8.	Knowledge Base Collecting Using Natural Language Processing (NLP) Algorithms [8]	J. Vickneswaran, P. Navanesan, V. Vijayaratnam and U. Thayasivam	2020	An array of methods is employed, including the utilization of BERT, to attain high precision in identifying emotions. Examination of errors demonstrates that specific words and emojis have a greater correlation with certain emotions, such as profanity.
9.	A Comparative Study—Sentiment Analysis Based on the Deep Learning [9]	AdilRajput *et al.*	2019	Sentiment analysis is done using the techniques utilized by NLP. The paper concludes that application of sentiment analysis and Natural Language Processing can be used to improve mental health.

(*Continued*)

Table 5.1 Comparison of different emotion based techniques. (*Continued*)

Ref. no.	Paper name	Authors	Year	Conclusion
10.	Sentiment Analysis in Twitter Using Lexicon Based and Polarity Multiplication [10]	M. S. Islam, Nitish Ranjan Bhowmik, *et al.*	2021	The paper provides an overview of using natural language processing (NLP) and how regular expressions are used to map English queries to SQL in Twitter databases. This model has an accuracy of around 98.89%.

5.4   Graphs

Figure 5.1 shows accuracy existing models [1–10]. Figure 5.2 shows accuracy comparison (hyperparameters used) [23, 24, 32–34]. Figure 5.3 shows accuracy vs. comparison line curve (hyperparameters used).

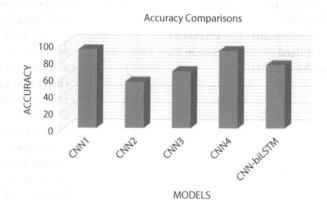

Figure 5.1 Accuracy comparison of existing models.

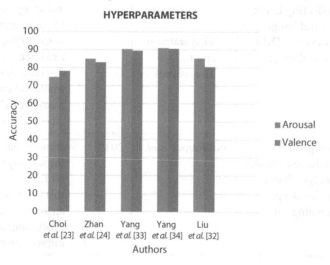

Figure 5.2 Accuracy comparison (hyperparameters used).

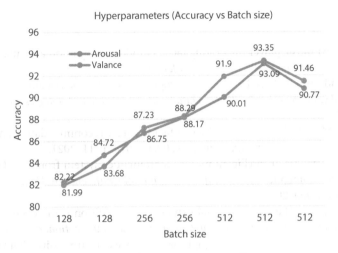

Figure 5.3 Accuracy vs. comparison line curve (hyperparameters used).

5.5 Research Gap

The following should be carried out in the future: enhancing the ability to identify minute mood variations, incorporating background knowledge for a more complex analysis, expanding the diversity of emoji sets to better depict emotions using transfer learning methods for improved efficiency on smaller datasets, assessing the model's effectiveness across various demographic groups, investigating the moral ramifications of utilizing AI to create emoji and identify mood, combining different modalities (such audio, image, and text) to increase accuracy, and enhancing the model's explainability to comprehend prediction making.

5.6 Conclusion

This survey explores a comprehensive study on the combination of tokenization and CNNs, which has been proven to be an effective approach for generation of emojis and mood detection, which are applications of sentiment analysis and NLP. The use of CNN models allows for the efficient learning of complex relationships and patterns within the data, while tokenization helps to convert text into numerical representations. Research has shown the effectiveness of this method in accurately identifying and categorizing different emotions and emojis. However, it should be considered that the accuracy of the model is influenced by factors such as the model architecture, the choice of hyperparameters, and the quality and quantity of training data.

References

1. Gilda, S., Smart music player integrating facial emotion recognition and music mood recognition using CNN. *IEEE WiSPNET 2017 Conference.*
2. Ashok, A. and John, J., Facial expression recognition system for visually impaired using SVM. *International Conference on Intelligent Data Communication Technologies and Internet of Things (ICICI), 2018.*
3. Athavle, M., Mudale, D., Shrivastav, U., Gupta, M., Music recommendation based on face emotion recognition. *J. Inf. Electr. Electron. Eng.*, 02, 02, 018, 1–11, 2021.
4. Chauhan, S., Analysis of intelligent movie recommender system from facial expression using CNN and a recommender system. *Fifth International Conference on Computing Methodologies and Communication, 2021.*
5. Awatramani, J. and Hasteer, N., Facial expression recognition using deep learning. [1] *IEEE 2020's Fifth International Conference on Computing, Communication, and Automation.*
6. Garg, D. and Goel, P., A deep learning approach for face detection using YOLO and CNN. *IEEE Punecon, 2018.*
7. Vickneswaran, J., Navanesan, P., Vijayaratnam, V., Thayasivam, U., Simplified approach for predicting emotions of multi-turn textual utterances. *2020 20th International Conference on Advances in ICT for Emerging Regions (ICTer),* Colombo, Sri Lanka, pp. 71–76, 2020.
8. Rajput, A., Natural language processing, sentiment analysis and clinical analytics, in: *Innovation in Health Informatics: A Smart Healthcare Primer,* pp. 79–97, 2020.
9. Manjusha, P.D. and Raseek, C., Convolutional neural network based simile classification system. *2018 International Conference on Emerging Trends and Innovations in Engineering and Technological Research (ICETIETR),* Ernakulam, India, 2018.
10. Manjusha, P.D. and Raseek, C., Convolutional neural network based simile classification system. *2018 International Conference on Emerging Trends and Innovations in Engineering and Technological Research (ICETIETR),* Ernakulam, India, 2018.
11. Tavan, E., Rahmati, A., Ali Keyvanrad, M., Persian emoji prediction using deep learning and emoji embedding. *2020 10th International Conference on Computer and Knowledge Engineering (ICCKE),* Mashhad, Iran, 2020.
12. Ashok, D.M., Nidhi Ghanshyam, A., Salim, S.S., Burhanuddin Mazahir, D., Thakare, B.S., Sarcasm detection using genetic optimization on LSTM with CNN. *2020 International Conference for Emerging Technology (INCET),* Belgaum, India, 2020.

6

Converting Pseudo Code to Code: A Review

**Kuldeep Vayadande*, Preeti A. Bailke, Anita Bapu Dombale, Varsha R. Dange
and Ashutosh M. Kulkarni**

Vishwakarma Institute of Technology, Pune, Maharashtra, India

Abstract

As of this writing, the process of turning an algorithm into code still falls short of expectations. Algorithms can be written as code, which will help novices and programmers with visual impairments by letting them concentrate entirely on coming up with the best logic to solve a problem instead of worrying about coding syntax. Writing any code could be difficult for someone with no prior experience and little knowledge of syntax because new programmers frequently struggle to grasp the writing style and make several mistakes. Beginners use pre-existing systems like A2C and AlgoSmart as converters or translators to transform the input algorithm provided into its corresponding code. Unlike other converters, A2C can swiftly adjust to each user's particular writing style. In its most basic form, a converter consists of a conversion process carried out step-by-step and has multiple associated sub-processes. Instead of just changing the syntax for a better conversion procedure, the system must also preserve the original document's structure and logic. Systems already in place make it possible for programmers who are blind or visually handicapped to develop effective code without worrying about grammar. The algorithm can be entered into an A2C converter as a regular text file. Line by line, the complete algorithm will be read through to completion. The computer will conduct a single action on each line. The user can focus on the reasoning of the answer without having to bother about syntax. The application also offers the option of running the converted code via a GCC compiler to ensure that its syntax and logic are sound. It is intended to serve as a tool for developing fundamental problem-solving abilities. In this paper, a comparative study of various techniques has been done for algorithm-to-code conversion.

Keywords: Translator, XML tags, algorithm, pseudocode, mapper, neural network, programming languages

*Corresponding author: kuldeep.vayadande1@vit.edu

Arindam Dey, Sukanta Nayak, Ranjan Kumar and Sachi Nandan Mohanty (eds.) How Machine Learning is Innovating Today's World: A Concise Technical Guide, (57–68) © 2024 Scrivener Publishing LLC

6.1   Introduction

The process of converting an algorithm into code is still not up to par as of this writing. Programmers with visual impairments and novices alike will benefit from the ability to write algorithms as code, which will free them up to concentrate entirely on developing the appropriate logic to solve a problem without having to worry about coding syntax [2]. Since newcomers occasionally have trouble understanding the coding syntax and style and frequently make mistakes, writing any code could be difficult for someone with no experience in coding and limited syntactic understanding [6].

With the recommended approach and with the help of the Algorithm to Code Converter (A2C), users may easily write a problem's algorithm in semi-natural English, which can subsequently be translated into programming language code [5]. This approach will largely help beginning users, those who have problems writing good code, and people who are visually impaired and struggle with punctuation and syntax. Usually, known algorithmic logic is used to develop a solution before being translated into code. These newcomers usually have trouble remembering a language's grammar and understanding how to create code in a programming language. As a result, developing an algorithm in such languages becomes difficult. It is challenging for someone without computer science experience and without good coding skills to create a program that is syntactically correct and yields the desired outputs, even if the logic is sound. The foundational component of the NLP code summarizing approach has SWUM. There are numerous construction techniques, depending on the SWUM's goal. SWUM is produced for the source program by the preceding effort by taking into consideration the kind of each program line, the parsing information, the type of method (user-defined or pre-defined), the frequency of the technique, etc. Program lines are parsed using programming language syntax, which is represented by a context-free grammar. The syntactic definition of the C programming language is based on CFG principles [8].

Rarely, someone could be familiar with the approaches needed to solve a program yet lack confidence when coding it in a certain programming language, like C, where the syntax is essential. People with experience easily implement algorithms and develop efficient applications. However, this process is much more difficult for rookie programmers or programmers learning a new programming language. A web-based application that can convert any algorithm expressed in plain English into syntactically sound code is what we are aiming to create. This can be achieved by making use of natural language processing. The program uses several techniques, such as tokenizing, tagging, labeling, and parts-of-speech recognition. The machine then arranges the discovered keywords in a syntactically sound way to produce the final code. A compiler is also a part of the suggested system, and it compiles the output C-code and outputs it to the console [4].

More user-friendly and providing a higher level of abstraction than the imperative programming language ALGOL, which has become one of the standards for expressing algorithms, is a formal framework for producing pseudocodes [1]. CPS source code generation and analysis have traditionally been duties left to subject-matter experts. It is hard to develop an automated system for analyzing the code and understanding it because the structural characteristics of the source code make it challenging for simple algorithms to understand. All of the aforementioned works also have Token sequences that can be changed by padding or truncating them. Since language modeling networks can only deal with fixed-length sequences, they are unable to account for two functions having potentially large size differences. The use of the vast amount of basic cores that share small caches, control units, and slower rates in graphical processing units (GPUs) helps them in achieving maximum efficiency during their performance. CPUs have better usage in latency-critical applications because of their quicker frequency cores and multi-instruction problem. For understanding and for effective programming, the thorough knowledge of the use of kernels, many computing systems, and dynamic and static features is necessary. The continued usage of all GPU cores is not permitted by application kernels that significantly rely on data transfers or branch divergence, which results in faster performance on CPUs than on GPUs [7].

Finding relevant and efficient algorithmic procedures and pseudocodes is less likely. To solve these issues, appropriate mining techniques must be applied. These tactics use knowledge discovery from the web and easily accessible research publications from national and international journals to locate the greatest match for the user's input request. The most relevant algorithm operations and pseudo codes are supplied, input requests are processed, and indexing is completed in the right way. The system uses an indexing technique to display the most relevant algorithm steps and pseudocodes. Consequently, less effort and time are needed to finish the job. The system provides a useful and pertinent search engine to locate the appropriate algorithm methods and pseudo codes with their time complexity, spatial complexity, and application [3].

The set of rules can discriminate between condition, function definition statements, declarations, and expressions in addition to other program statement types. The NLG approach is then used to translate each statement type into line documentation with the required identifiers. The Software Word Usage Model (SWUM), a major module that helps in the process of documentation of various codes, was built using a unique technique. The latest update of the project must include thorough documentation. As C language has a basic syntax, the automatic code generation system suggested may produce documentation for this language-based application. This allows the price and duration of the code generation process to decrease. For the automatic generation of the code, this research paper uses a simple syntax-based language, C-lite, to create its prototype. Source code tools like Javadoc can only generate documents for the built-in methods, which are there in Java. These extract information from the official documentation and have a restrained capacity. When a user defines certain functions, this specific system cannot generate the code automatically [8]. The framework suggested by the authors is user-friendly and easy to use for the construction of pseudocodes as compared to ALGOL, a programming language [2].

6.2   Literature Review

Suvam Mukherjee and Tamal Chakraborty in their paper [1] mentioned that the system's program allows users to specify their code using an easy-to-read and easy-to-write largely immutable pseudocode specification. After ensuring that it is error-free, the program will translate the pseudocode into the specified language (such as C, Java, or another language). For the translation process to work, regular expressions and pattern matching are essential. A regular expression's succinctness makes describing patterns simple. They chose Perl to develop this module because of how well it handles regular expressions. In this section, they first look at the guiding principle that guides the translation process's essential operations. The authors offer an algorithm that applies throughout the entire translation process. The translation process depends on how we handle specific operations, which is what we look at next. We look at how the var example operation is handled. Also they offer a general operation handler algorithm as a conclusion. ALGOSmart automatically determined the kinds of these numbers and declared them to be double or int variables. The values would be defined as double by the translator if we initialize them to any actual number. If the initialization value is considered to be any random integer, the variable will be declared as an integer by the translator. The translator attempts to extract the initialization value and compare it to the real or integral value pattern. After the symbol table has been changed, the definition is then output.

Vishal Parekh and Dwivedi Nilesh in their paper [2] cite the fact that the conversion process includes a series of steps that incorporate several procedures. The system, to improve its conversion process, should maintain its structure and should be able to do more than just substitute the syntax and eliminate the unnecessary parts of the codes. The person has personally witnessed the program's power as algorithmic solutions become more and more applicable to problems. Any software program consists of an algorithm that has been programmed. The issue arises from the requirement to apply algorithms. Programmers with experience can easily implement algorithms and develop efficient applications. As people who are new to coding and programming do not understand the style and syntax applicable to the specific language, the said process is hard for them to adapt. Implementing and running the codes and algorithms can be a challenge many times. A huge variety of computer languages also support a diverse range of programming paradigms.

Nikita Barhate, Yogita Wani, Ashwini Zine, and Jayshri Khirari in their paper [3] list every algorithmic step, code extraction method, and analysis. This is a crucial component of the implementation because it allows for a user-friendly and convenient search. In projects that are already available, users must consult the entire study papers to identify the proper APs and PCs. For research and development firms, academics, business people, scientists, and other professionals, understanding algorithms and pseudocodes is crucial. This system is a search technique for locating and analyzing relevant and useful algorithm procedures

(APs) and pseudo codes (PCs) in academic literature and online. Making the best choice out of all the available possibilities might be difficult.

Dr. L.V. Patil [4] uses NLP constructs such as parts-of-speech recognition, tokenizing, and tagging to create a web application. The solution offers the ability to edit converted code using the GCC compiler and verify that the logic and syntax are sound. Once the application file is opened, Turbo C++ is used to transform the code. It is then broken down into individual sentences that each represent a different code action by sentence detection. The following stages include the Apache OpenNLP API's Sentence Detection and Tokenization modules. The code is combined, compiled, and shown. The database used by the system was MongoDB. Given the complexity of computer science difficulties used in real-world applications, students must grasp how to strengthen their logic for effective problem-solving before focusing on the syntax and restrictions of programming languages. It can be difficult for pupils to abstract the problem from its description and break it down into smaller difficulties. There are many online learning resources; however, they all focus on various programming languages rather than how various strategies may be applied to a problem. Students will be able to practice problem-solving strategies, clarify their thoughts, and ultimately master the art of writing code in this paper.

Reginald Lewis, Rahul Dubey, Priya Karunakaran, and Bini Edward in their paper [5] include an algorithm that is being taken as input. An XML file, mapper, translator, and code are needed, which will be the output of the specific system. In the system, the implementation of the interpretation is performed on a plain text by making use of the Naïve Bayes Classifier. The extraction of information is done using tags that are generated by using POS Tagging. Following the procedure, an XML file containing all the information needed to create the necessary code will be generated. The use of conditional expressions is fundamental to the mapping process. Simple conditional if–else statements will be applied to the tags to parse the XML specification file. To develop the module, Python programming language was chosen. These types of data can be managed by this language.

Eric Jin and Yu Sun in their paper [6] kept tweaking their algorithms to improve the converter's precision and include an error detection system. Therefore, it can be seen that the outcome is ready to be used as a useful public tool. To enable anyone to access the URL and utilize the tool any way they see fit, it was made available as a web application. The major issue is that Python cannot be completely converted to Java, regardless of how efficient the converter is. Since each language has its own functions and libraries, the total is infinite and always growing. Even though our converter was unable to circumvent this issue, it does provide a rather simple remedy, which is to identify the proper pair of functions. Once a common pattern of function calls the input, the code will be identified as Python code. After identifying the code, it will return the pertinent Java function.

Emanuele Parisi, Andrea Acquaviva, Andrea Bartolini, and Francesco Barchi in their paper [7] convey the latest trends for analyzing the source code, which concentrates on kernel mapping techniques using deep learning. These throw light on various trends like the difficulties faced by new developments on diverse platforms. This has wide usage in cyber-physical systems. All three of the methodologies covered in this part are responsible for advancing source code modeling using deep learning methods. Since code is not a set of stages, token-based source code modeling presents difficulties. Even with recurrent networks, it may be challenging to learn about crucial program features like achieving definition or branching if sources are depicted as sequences of tokens since they necessitate long-distance interactions between program elements. Additionally, by padding or truncating token sequences, all of the works discussed above alter token order. Additionally, by padding or truncating token sequences, all of the works discussed above alter token order. Language modeling networks only operate on fixed-length sequences; therefore, they cannot take into account a possible substantial size difference between two functions.

Menaka Pushpa Arthur [8] presented a project that might create source code documentation for C applications automatically. Only method documentation for software code can be produced using existing software documentation tools. This suggested system resolves this limit. Code summaries, NLP, and NLG approaches are used in the documents to detect the source code automatically. The majority of project documentation is written by people in the software industry. The documentation in the SDLC, which includes coding, testing, and analysis, if maintained in an orderly fashion, can reduce the cost of updating the process and maintaining the project. Automatic generation of the code is the main aim of this research. Suvam Mukherjee and Tamal Chakraborty in their paper [1] mentioned that the system's program allows users to specify their code using an easy-to-read and easy-to-write largely immutable pseudocode specification. After ensuring that it is error-free, the program will translate the pseudocode into the specified language (such as C, Java, or another language). For the translation process to work, regular expressions and pattern matching are essential. A regular expression's succinctness makes describing patterns simple. They chose Perl to develop this module because of how well it handles regular expressions. They offer an algorithm that applies throughout the entire translation process. The translation process depends on how we handle specific operations, which is what tey look at next. The authors look at how the var example operation is handled. They offer a general operation handler algorithm as a conclusion.

6.3   Comparison Table

Table 6.1 shows comparison table of different techniques [1–8].

Table 6.1 Comparison table.

No.	Title of paper	Techniques used	Advantages	Disadvantages	Conclusion
1	Automatic Algorithm Specification to Source Code Translation	Perl is used to build a translator. The successive Bisection Method was used to write the pseudocode and examine the translation process.	The user is protected by the translator from the quirks of implementation, which is the main benefit.	The expansion of support for more programming languages is the challenge.	A formal foundation for specifying pseudocode is provided to the user by the algorithm specification module. The pseudo-code was translated into a program in the next phase. The expansion of support for more programming languages is the other area.
2	Pseudocode to Source Code Translation	Neural network along with Cascade back and propagation.	1. Efficiency 2. Consistency 3. Error detection	1. Limited flexibility 2. Dependence on a specific programming language 3. Lack of understanding of the problem	In conclusion, using a translation program that utilizes neural network techniques to automatically convert well-specified pseudocode various programming languages, such as Java, C++, or C, to source code can be a valuable tool for beginner programmers. However, it is also important to note that using a program like this can also lead to an overreliance on the program and a lack of understanding of the underlying programming languages.

(Continued)

Table 6.1 Comparison table. (*Continued*)

No.	Title of paper	Techniques used	Advantages	Disadvantages	Conclusion
3	Algorithm Procedure and Pseudo Code Mining	1. Indexing 2. Extracting Regular expression 3. Analysis of PDFtoTEXT	Academicians, scientists, developers, and researchers from various domains use the pseudo codes and algorithms.	The most challenging part of the implementation used in the paper was pseudocode extraction and its analysis.	Relevant and efficient PCs and APs by applying appropriate mining techniques help in searching algorithms and pseudo codes.
4	Online Algorithm Converter for C++	NLP, Sentence Detection, Tokenization using ApacheOpenNLP API.	1. Convenience 2. Speed 3. Versatility 4. Automated process	1. Quality of conversion 2. Internet connectivity 3. Security 4. Dependence	This paper aims to develop a web-based application that uses natural language processing (NLP) to convert an algorithm written in plain language into equivalent C language code. The program will also have a function for running the converted code through a GCC compiler to ensure that its syntax and logic are sound.
5	Algorithm to Code Converter	Information Retrieval, Naive Bayes, and Speech tagging.	Functional code can be written by people who have just began coding without paying attention to the syntax.	The respective algorithms cannot to converted to a Java code.	To suit the various writing styles and to produce the desired results, the best components from several projects are combined.
6	An Algorithm Adaptive Source Code Converter to Automate the Translation from Python to JAVA	OpenNLP API	The system keeps modifying its algorithms to increase the converter's accuracy and incorporate an error detection feature.	Error rate can be seen when this particular compiler is used.	It is observed that the result is prepared so that it can be used as a practical public tool. It was released as a web application so that anyone can access the URL and use the tool.

(*Continued*)

Table 6.1 Comparison table. (*Continued*)

No.	Title of paper	Techniques used	Advantages	Disadvantages	Conclusion
7	Deep Learning Approaches to Source Code Analysis for Optimization of Heterogeneous Systems: Recent Results, Challenges, and Opportunities	Cyberphysical Systems, Optimization Methods, Device Mapping, and Code Analysis.	Cyberphysical systems can use kernel mapping techniques. These are used to analyze the code focus on current achievements.	There is yet no entire optimization pipeline for application in cyber-physical systems. Systems that are prepared for production may not be able to coordinate kernel offloading and data gathering due to real-time constraints because they contain multiple processes.	Learn how deep learning techniques have been used to analyze the source code (RQ1) today by looking back at historical examples of original and creative works that demonstrated how to address new problems or develop new algorithms.
8	Automatic Source Code Documentation using Code Summarization Technique of NLP	Documentation of source code, Natural Language Processing, Context Free Grammar, SWUM.	Natural Language Processing can generate the documentation automatically for C programs.	Only the program code's methods can be used to generate documentation.	Along with NLG, the automatic source code documentation system makes use of NLP's code summarizing method. This program is capable of documenting every line of the C program. This system provides two types of documentation: method-based documentation and program-wise documentation.

6.4   Graphs of Comparison Done

Figure 6.1 shows comparison of various algorithms [1–8]. Figure 6.2 comparison of algorithm time complexity [1–8]. Figure 6.3 shows the accuracy comparison of algorithms.

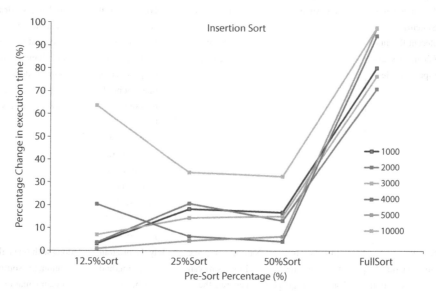

Figure 6.1 Comparison of algorithm converter for sorting technique.

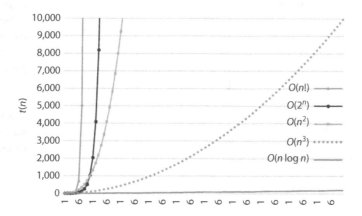

Figure 6.2 Comparison of algorithm time complexity.

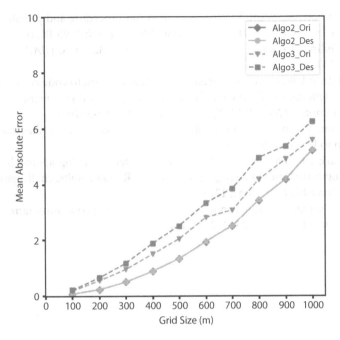

Figure 6.3 Accuracy comparison of algorithms.

6.5   Research Gap Identified

The earlier research cited in this survey study only allows for one language to be used when converting the existing algorithm into source code. It is straightforward to add support for other programming languages because there are only a handful of phases in the overall translation process that are language-specific.

6.6   Conclusion

Based on this study, multiple methods can be used to turn an algorithm into Java source code and subsequently into a straightforward flowchart. Students and other individuals who are learning to code and are attempting to concentrate on grasping a specific concept can benefit from this system. The earlier research on these problems used a variety of approaches to put it into an algorithm, including XML files, Cascade back propagation neural networks, perl, and API.

References

1. Mukherjee, S. *et al.*, Automatic algorithm specification to source code translation. *Indian J. Comput. Sci. Eng. (IJCSE)*, 2011, ISSN: 0976-5166.
2. Parekh, V. and Nilesh, D., Pseudo code to source code translation. *International Journal of Emerging Technologies and Innovative Research (IJETIR)*, (www.jetir.org), Available: http://www.jetir.org/papers/JETIR1611007.pdf

3. Khirari, J., Barhate, N., Wani, Y., Zine, A., Algorithm procedure and pseudo code mining. *Int. Res. J. Eng. Technol. (IRJET)*, 04, 03, 1-10, Mar -2017, e-ISSN: 2395-0056.

4. Patil, L.V., Online algorithm converter for C++. *Int. J. Adv. Res. (IJAR)*. 5 (Jul). 2286-2290] (ISSN 2320-5407).

5. Dubey, R., Edward, B., Lewis, R., Karunakaran, P., Algorithm to code converter. *Proceedings of the 2nd International Conference on Trends in Electronics and Informatics (ICOEI 2018) IEEE Conference Record: # 42666*; IEEE Xplore ISBN:978-1-5386-3570-4.

6. Jin, E. and Sun, Y., An algorithm adaptive source code converter to automate the translation from python to JAVA. *JLPEA*, 2020.

7. Barchi, F., Parisi, E., Bartolini, A., Acquaviva, A., Deep learning approaches to source code analysis for optimization of heterogeneous systems: Recent results, challenges, and opportunities. *J. Low Power Electron. Appl.*, 12, 37, 2022.

8. Arthur, M.P., Automatic source code documentation using code summarization technique of NLP. *Proc. Comput. Sci.*, 171, 2522–2531, 2020.

Part 2

MACHINE LEARNING APPLICATIONS IN SPECIFIC DOMAINS

7

Evaluating the Readability of English Language Using Machine Learning Models

Shiplu Das[1]*, Abhishikta Bhattacharjee[2], Gargi Chakraborty[3] and Debarun Joardar[3]

[1]Department of Computer Science and Engineering, Adamas University, West Bengal, India
[2]Department of English and Literary Studies, Brainware University, West Bengal, India
[3]Department of Computer Science and Engineering, Brainware University, West Bengal, India

Abstract

As a lingua franca, English is one of the world's most extensively spoken and used languages. It is an essential tool for communication and a critical component in many sectors, including worldwide business, science, technology, and entertainment. However, its complexities and nuances can sometimes make successful interpretation difficult. To decipher the English language, a solid understanding of its syntax, vocabulary, and pronunciation is required. Understanding the complexities of its grammar structure, including syntax, conjugation, and tense, enables more precise and fluent communication of ideas and thoughts. Furthermore, having a large and diverse vocabulary and the ability to use it effectively can substantially improve one's communication abilities. This venture aims to evaluate the meaningfulness of English language sentences utilizing a blend model methodology that joins Convolutional Neural Networks (CNNs) and Recurrent Neural Networks (RNNs). A massive dataset of sentences from different sources was gathered and pre-handled to eliminate elements, for example, word count, syllable count, and syntactic construction. The pre-handled information was utilized to prepare a mixed-race CNN–RNN model, which was intended to learn significant elements for anticipating comprehensibility scores. The model was assessed using different execution measurements, including exactness, accuracy, review, and F1-score. The outcomes showed that the mixed-race CNN–RNN model accomplished the most crucial precision contrasted with past AI models utilized for comparative assignments. The model had the option to learn significant elements connected with sentence intricacy, like sentence length, the utilization of conjunctions and accentuation, and word recurrence. The interpretability of the model was additionally broken down by looking at the learned highlights and their relationship to comprehensibility scores. This venture shows the viability of utilizing a cross-breed CNN–RNN model for surveying the clarity of English language sentences. The high precision accomplished by the model offers its actual capacity for different regular language handlings applications, like instructive apparatuses, content enhancement, and computerized composing evaluation. Overall, this study exhibits the viability of CNNs for surveying the clarity of English language sentences. The high F1-score of 0.95 and accuracy of 96% accomplished by the hybrid CNN–NN model propose that it is a valuable asset for naturally foreseeing the trouble of sentences. This study adds to the developing assemblage of examinations utilizing AI models for common language handling errands. It features the capability of CNN–RNNs for different applications in this field.

*Corresponding author: shiplud63@gmail.com

Arindam Dey, Sukanta Nayak, Ranjan Kumar and Sachi Nandan Mohanty (eds.) *How Machine Learning is Innovating Today's World: A Concise Technical Guide*, (71–88) © 2024 Scrivener Publishing LLC

Keywords: Convolutional neural networks, CNN, recurrent neural networks, RNN, English language, hybrid model

7.1   Introduction

As a lingua franca, English is one of the world's most extensively spoken and used languages. It is an essential tool for communication and a critical component in many sectors, including worldwide business, science, technology, and entertainment. However, its complexities and nuances can sometimes make successful interpretation difficult. To decipher the English language, a solid understanding of its syntax, vocabulary, and pronunciation is required. Understanding the complexities of its grammar structure, including syntax, conjugation, and tense, enables more precise and fluent communication of ideas and thoughts.

Furthermore, having a large and diverse vocabulary and the ability to use it effectively can substantially improve one's communication abilities. The ability to select the right words and phrases for a given circumstance, whether professional or informal, demonstrates mastery of the language. Furthermore, perfect pronunciation is an essential component of English interpretation since it guarantees that the intended message is transmitted accurately and comprehended by the listener. Aside from these core abilities, understanding and using idioms, phrases, and colloquialisms is essential to interpreting the English language. These linguistic features are frequently challenging to know since they are only sometimes apparent in meaning and might have multiple interpretations depending on context. For example, a phrase like "pulling someone's leg" may not make literal sense, yet it is a frequent idiom used to represent a humorous and harmless jest. Understanding and skilfully employing these idioms, phrases, and colloquialisms can substantially enhance one's communicating talents, adding depth and richness to language use. Finally, successfully conveying thoughts and ideas through speech and writing is essential to comprehend English. The capacity to communicate effectively, whether orally or in writing, is crucial in interpretation because it helps one to convey ideas and concepts accurately and convincingly. This talent necessitates a solid command of the language and a comprehension of effective communication tactics such as tone, inflection, and body language. Effective communication improves interpersonal interactions, allowing them to create trust, establish credibility, and foster meaningful connections with people, whether in a professional or personal situation. That said, it can be understood how compelling the English learning task can be. With learning a new language comes the following parts, as described in the below diagram [1].

Figure 7.1 shows the component of a foreign languages include phonology, Orthography, Pragmatics, Discourse, Grammar and Vocabulary. Cultural aspects and idiomatic expressions also play a significant role in understanding and using a foreign language.

Grammar, vocabulary, and parts of speech are the foundations of any language, and this is especially true of English. Grammar provides the underlying structure and framework that helps us to convey our thoughts and ideas efficiently. It guides how words are linked to form sentences and gives guidelines for word and phrase arrangement to express meaning. Understanding grammar principles is essential for writing grammatically accurate phrases, communicating thoughts clearly and concisely, and avoiding misunderstandings and misinterpretations. So, any learner of English will need to have a considerable grasp of

Figure 7.1 Components of any foreign language [19].

these three, and here is why. In contrast, vocabulary refers to the words and phrases that comprise a language. It collects all the words and expressions used to convey thoughts, ideas, and emotions. A large vocabulary enables us to express ourselves in nuanced and complex ways and broadens our understanding and comprehension of the world around us. A strong vocabulary is essential for effective communication in English, whether for professional or personal reasons. Building a strong vocabulary necessitates constant and purposeful work, such as extensive reading, acquiring new words, and practicing their use in context. Meanwhile, parts of speech are the classifications of words depending on their role inside a phrase. These categories include nouns, verbs, adjectives, adverbs, pronouns, prepositions, conjunctions, and interjections. Understanding the components of speech is critical for generating grammatically accurate sentences and utilizing words appropriately. For example, by understanding that a noun is a word that names a person, place, or thing, we can ensure that we use it correctly in a sentence. We can ensure that we use a verb appropriately to convey the desired meaning by understanding that a verb is a word that describes an action or occurrence. Knowing and understanding the parts of speech also enables us to examine and appreciate the structures and styles of other types of writing, such as poetry, prose, and nonfiction. Next, let us look at how one can start learning English. This can be narrowed down to two basic parts—communication and readability. Let us first look at why communication is the key. Effective communication is essential to language learning, especially for those studying English. Learners can put their understanding of grammar, vocabulary, pronunciation, and other language abilities into practice through communicative exercises. This improves their command of the language and their grasp and understanding of it. Communication enables learners to participate in real-life situations and put their language abilities to use in meaningful ways. Furthermore, communication provides learners with English's linguistic and cultural intricacies, allowing them to develop a more in-depth awareness and comprehension of the language and its cultural context. This is especially crucial for people wishing to improve their English skills, as cultural competence is required for effective communication. Through communication, learners are also exposed to a wide range of terminology, idioms, and expressions, which broadens their language knowledge and skills. Furthermore, communication encourages the development of critical listening abilities. This is because effective communication necessitates not just the ability to produce language but also the ability to comprehend and interpret the speech of others. This is especially significant for people learning English, as understanding and responding to spoken language is critical to language competence. Opportunities for communication, whether through speaking, writing, or listening, allow learners to use their language abilities in real-life circumstances and to build a greater understanding and respect for the English language and culture. Next comes an even more aspect, which is called readability. Unlike communication, which is more of a result, it has a causal effect. Reading is essential to education and intellectual development, and scholars and professionals recognize its significance. Toni Morrison, a Nobel laureate in literature, famously said, "If there's a book that you want to read but hasn't been written yet, then you must write it." Reading skill is important in determining an individual's success in life because it offers a world of knowledge and information. "Readability" refers to the science of reading and understanding. This field of study investigates the different aspects that influence a person's capacity to read written material, such as cognitive and linguistic abilities, as well as the character of the text itself. Various criteria, such as the Flesch–Kincaid readability score, gunning fog index, and SMOG index, are used to assess readability. These metrics analyze sentence length, word complexity, and vocabulary difficulty to determine how easily a document may be comprehended by its intended audience. Figure 7.2 shows the features of the readability of language.

However, readability is more than just the technical features of a book. It is also influenced by the reader's prior knowledge, motivation, and interest in the topic. As a cognitive psychologist, Richard Anderson, stated, "The most critical factor in reading comprehension is the reader's knowledge of the topic." As a result, offering context and pictures and breaking down complex ideas into simpler ones can improve reading. Despite substantial gains in readability, it remains a complex and diverse subject. According to a National Reading Panel report, no single technique for increasing reading comprehension works for all learners. This emphasizes the relevance of tailored treatments and the need for additional studies. While we are on the topic of language, and while all these varied definitions and opinions boggle our minds, let us take a look at the basic definition of "language" from two renowned sources—**The Encyclopaedia Britannica** defines "language" as *'a system of conventional spoken, manual (signed), or written symbols by means of which human beings, as members of a social group and participants in its culture, express themselves'* and the other one, **The Simple English Wikipedia**, defines "language" as *'the normal way humans communicate.'*

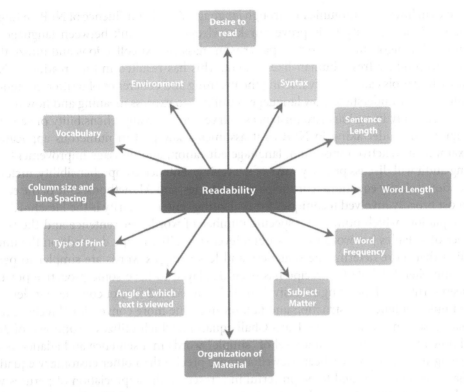

Figure 7.2 Features of readability.

As you might see above, the former definition by Encyclopaedia Britannica is much more complex and erudite due to the elaborate definition and use of varied words. At the same time, the latter is a simple definition of the same term. Thus, from a reader's perspective, the former seems to appeal to a sophisticated audience with a considerable grasp of English and its usage. In contrast, the latter would appeal to someone simply seeking to understand the term's meaning. Before our paper, let us look at how NLP has influenced readability and the understanding of English in the past decade. Natural Language Processing (NLP) has transformed our comprehension of the English language. NLP has had a significant and far-reaching impact on English readability. NLP's capacity to analyze vast amounts of natural language data has given us fresh insights into how we use language and helped us improve our knowledge of the complexity of written communication. One of the key effects of NLP on English readability has been to improve written text clarity and concision. Using NLP algorithms, examining the text for readability and finding spots where language may be overly complex or ambiguous are now possible. *"Clarity and simplicity are hallmarks of good writing, not signs of a limited vocabulary or lack of sophistication"* (Pinker, S. (1994). The language instinct: The new science of language and mind. HarperCollins). NLP's principal impact on the English language has been to improve our comprehension of its complexity and nuances. According to John Searle, a prominent philosopher of language, *"Language is a form of human behavior that has a constitutive rule, which it is subject to conditions of satisfaction, and which can be justified or unjustified."* NLP has provided us with new tools for studying the fundamental norms of language and has uncovered previously undiscovered intricacies in how we communicate through language. Another influence of NLP on English readability is its capacity to improve our knowledge of the link between language and meaning. NLP algorithms can detect patterns in massive text collections and utilize those patterns to produce fresh, human-like content. This has resulted in the creation of NLP-based writing tools capable of evaluating the meaning and coherence of written content. As a result, we now understand how language is utilized to express meaning and how to write more successfully in various circumstances. Surveying the comprehensibility of sentences is a significant undertaking in NLP, as it assumes a key part in numerous applications, for example, instructive innovation, language education, and message improvement. This writing audit will discuss primary ways of surveying sentence comprehensibility, including conventional clarity equations, corpus-based strategies, and AI methods. One of the earliest and most broadly involved techniques for evaluating sentence clarity is the Flesch–Kincaid Level equation, which utilizes the specific number of words per sentence and the typical number of syllables per word to work out a level score. The recipe depends on the understanding that more determinate sentences and less complex words are simpler to peruse and comprehend. While this recipe has been displayed to have some proactive power, it has been scrutinized for being excessively oversimplified and for not considering elements, for example, sentence construction and talk setting. One more conventional technique for evaluating sentence clarity is the Dale–Chall equation, which utilizes a rundown of 3,000 well-known words to work out a level of "simple" words in a sentence and adapts to sentence length. This recipe has been viewed as more precise than other customary equations and has been demonstrated to be powerful in foreseeing the appreciation of peruses with low education abilities. Corpus-based techniques for evaluating sentence lucidness include examining enormous message assortments to recognize highlights connected with coherence. One illustration of this approach is the Basic Proportion of the Gobbledygook (Brown haze) recipe, which involves the number of polysyllabic words in a sentence to foresee its understanding level. Other corpus-based approaches incorporate semantic elements like word recurrence, grammatical features, and syntactic intricacy. AI procedures have become progressively famous for evaluating sentence intelligibility, as they can be prepared on enormous commented-on datasets and catch complex collaborations between highlights. Some AI strategies incorporate help vector machines, choice trees, and brain organizations. These strategies can consolidate many elements, including both etymological and non-phonetic factors, and have often been displayed to beat traditional recipes and corpus-based techniques. While traditional formulas such as the Flesch–Kincaid and Dale–Chall formulas are widely used and have some predictive power, corpus-based and machine-learning methods are more accurate and flexible. Future research in this area will likely focus on developing more sophisticated models that can consider factors such as reader background and discourse context and apply these models to a wide range of NLP applications.

7.2 Contribution in this Chapter

The concentrate on evaluating the lucidness of English language sentences utilizing a hybrid model of CNN–RNN makes a few commitments to the field of NLP and AI.

- To begin with, the review adds to the improvement of successful AI models for sentence intelligibility appraisal. By joining the qualities of CNNs and RNNs, the proposed mixture model accomplishes high precision in foreseeing the lucidness of English language sentences, outflanking past models utilized for this errand. The concentrate likewise gives bits of knowledge into the particular highlights and factors that add to sentence clarity, which could be valuable for working on composed correspondence and creating viable instructive materials.

- Second, the review gives an important dataset of pre-handled sentences for future examination in sentence clarity evaluation. The dataset incorporates corrections from different sources, including news stories, books, and informational messages. It has been pre-handled to eliminate incidental elements, for example, word count and syntactic design. This dataset could be utilized to create and assess new AI models for sentence comprehensibility evaluation and give a benchmark for future examinations.

- At long last, the review features the capability of AI models for working on composed correspondence and instructive results. By giving robotized instruments to survey the coherence of composed content, AI models could help instructors and content makers foster more open and more apparent materials for a more extensive crowd. This could have significant ramifications for fields like instruction, well-being correspondence, and public arrangement, where viable equality is fundamental for accomplishing wanted results.

In light of the above-mentioned papers, there were two fundamental issues that the half-and-half CNN–RNN model planned to determine:

The absence of regard for the spatial highlights of pictures in the RNN-based models: RNNs are great at handling consecutive information yet are not normally fit to handling spatial elements in pictures. CNNs, then again, are explicitly intended for handling spatial highlights. The mixture CNN–RNN model takes care of this issue by utilizing CNNs to remove spatial elements from pictures and RNNs to handle the transient grouping of these highlights.

The failure of CNN-based models to deal with variable-length input successions: CNNs are intended to deal with fixed-length input groupings and battle with variable-length input arrangements, like groupings of text or discourse. RNNs, then again, can deal with variable-length arrangements. The crossover CNN–RNN model tackles this issue by utilizing RNNs to deal with the variable-length result of the CNNs. To sum up, the half breed CNN–RNN model consolidates the qualities of CNNs and RNNs to defeat the limits of each. By utilizing CNNs to separate spatial highlights from pictures and RNNs to handle the variable-length result of the CNNs, the half-and-half model can accomplish cutting-edge execution on different picture-related errands, for example, picture subtitling and visual inquiry addressing.

7.3   Research Gap

In the previous years, there have been a few exploration holes in the subject of surveying English language sentence coherence utilizing AI models. A portion of the prominent exploration holes include:

- **Restricted center around profound learning models:** While conventional AI models have been utilized in the past for surveying coherence, there has been a restricted spotlight on profound learning models, for example, Convolutional Neural Networks (CNNs) and Recurrent Neural Networks (RNNs). There is a requirement for more exploration on the viability of these models for evaluating lucidness.
- **Restricted accessibility of huge-scope datasets:** One of the difficulties in creating AI models for surveying coherence is the accessibility of enormous-scope datasets. Previously, there has been a restricted accessibility of such datasets, which has restricted the turn of events and assessment of AI models. Be that as it may, with the rising accessibility of enormous-scope datasets, there is a potential chance to foster more precise and powerful models.
- **Restricted center around non-English dialects:** While the focal point of the ongoing review is on English language sentences, there has been a restricted spotlight on non-English dialects. There is a requirement for more exploration on the viability of AI models for evaluating the clarity of sentences in different dialects.
- **Restricted center around the effect of various message highlights:** While past investigations have inspected the effect of various message highlights, for example, sentence length and word intricacy, there is a requirement for more exploration on the effect of other message highlights, for example, sentence construction and punctuation, on the coherence of sentences.
- **Restricted center around genuine applications:** While the improvement of AI models for surveying comprehensibility has shown guarantee, there has been a restricted spotlight on their true applications. There is a requirement for more examination on how these models can be applied in genuine situations, like in instructive settings and content streamlining.

7.4   Literature Review

Reviewing the clarity of English language sentences is critical in various spaces, including preparing, circulating, and correspondence. Artificial intelligence models have shown to be strong in expecting the clarity of made material, and numerous assessments have been driven around here. In this article, we will review a piece of the associated management using computer-based intelligence models for assessing the clarity of English language sentences. The use of computer-based intelligence models for assessing the clearness of English language sentences has been a subject of interest in Normal Language Handling (NLP).

Significant learning models, such as Convolutional Brain Organizations (CNNs) and Repetitive Brain Organizations (RBO), have shown promising results for this task. Maybe the work in this space concentrates on Bartosz Broda (2014), who introduced an outline of the most well-known ways to deal with programmed estimating of readability [14]. We executed and assessed the depicted ones: Gunning Haze file and the Flesch-based Pisarek strategy. We likewise present two different methodologies. The first depends on estimating the distributional lexical closeness of an objective text and contrasting it with reference texts. In the subsequent one, we propose an original strategy for mechanization of the Taylor test, which, in its base structure, requires playing out an enormous number of studies. The computerization of the Taylor test is performed utilizing a strategy called measurable language displaying. Even more lately, examiners have used computer-based intelligence models to chip away at the precision of clarity assumptions. In a concentrate by Shazia Maqsood (2022), in this examination, we have involved 30,000 English sentences for trial and error [2]. Also, they have been commented on into seven unique comprehensibility levels utilizing Flesch–Kincaid. Afterward, different examinations were led utilizing five AI calculations, i.e., KNN, SVM, LR, NB, and ANN. Another concentrate is by Yanmeng Liu (2021), whose paper presents a peruser-situated coherence evaluation by joining clarity equation scores with AI strategies while considering the peruser foundation [3]. AI calculations are prepared by a dataset of 7 clarity equation scores for 160 well-being articles in true well-being sites. In a concentrate by Katsunori Kotani (2008), they propose a perusing time model for students of English as an unknown dialect (EFL) that depends on a student's understanding capability and the phonetic properties of sentences [4]. Perusing capability here alludes to a student's perusing score on the Trial of English for Worldwide Interchanges (TOEIC). The phonetic properties are a sentence's lexical, syntactic, and talk intricacies. We utilized everyday language handling innovation to separate these phonetic properties. We fostered a model involving numerous relapse examinations as a learning calculation in joining the student's capability and semantic properties. In the article by Huimei Chen (2022), the computerized assessment scoring framework is a regular show of the use of organization innovation in educating English writing [5]. Many composing scoring stages have been created and utilized in China, which can give online moments and restorative criticism of understudies' compositions. In any case, the legitimacy of Point Composing, an item evolved by Microsoft Exploration Asia, which professes to be the best device to work with Chinese EFL students, has not been tried in past examinations. In this blended strategies study, the criticism and impact of Point Composing on undergrads' composing will be researched and contrasted with the teacher's input. In an article by H.A. Schmitt (2022), the computerized assessment scoring framework is a normal show of the utilization of organizational innovation in educating English writing [6]. Many composing scoring stages have been created and utilized in China, which can give online moments and remedial criticism of understudies' compositions. Be that as it may, the legitimacy of Point Composing, an item evolved by Microsoft Exploration Asia, which professes to be the best device to work with Chinese EFL students, has not been tried in past examinations. In this blended techniques study, the criticism and impact of Point Composing on understudies' composing will be examined and contrasted with the educator's input (Klare, G. R., 1974). This article surveys equations and related prescient gadgets since 1960 [7]. Four classes are introduced: (1) recalculations and amendments of existing recipes; (2) new equations for broadly useful or specific reason use; (3) application helps for both manual and machine use; and

(4) expectations of coherence for unknown dialects. Sameer Badarudeen MD (2010), empowered by the changeability to understand well-being-related materials among people looking for muscular care [8], believed that delineating the items in persistent training materials at various degrees of intricacy will probably further develop well-being education and upgrade patient-focused correspondence. Laura Rossi's (2013) article gives a manual for perusers keen on extending their insight into the qualities and shortcomings of the different machine interpretation (MT) quality measurements. It presents a technique and tooling grown separately by LexisNexis® and its MT supplier Asia Online™ as a feature of a human quality evaluation structure for patent translation [9]. The procedure is planned explicitly to compensate for the inadequacies of mechanized assessment. According to Lynn M. LoPucki (2008), the current development relates, by and large, to a text parsing framework and strategy, and in particular [10] to a framework and technique for applying normalized markings to lawful literary materials, especially rules, and agreements, to work on the meaningfulness and work with the comprehension of same. In the work of Ted Briscoe (2010), a PC used a technique to assess the semantic nature of free-reaction text answers presented by understudies because of assessment prompts [11]. Rohini K. Srihari (2011) used a framework for changing the substance of an electronic record from a non-Romanized local language to a Romanized language [12], with the framework containing at least one processor and memory to store program code that is executed by at least one processor. In the work of Amy J.C. Trappey (2018), the framework determines how to sum up patent archives with standard language texts for some random specialized domain [13]. The AI arrangement recognizes specialized key wordings (words, expressions, and sentences) about the semantic connections among preparing licenses and relating rundowns as the center of the synopsis framework. ROUGE measurements are utilized to assess the accuracy, review, exactness, and consistency of information produced by the rundown framework to guarantee the superior presentation of the proposed procedure. Gary Kinder's (2003) work involved a PC-executed technique for working on the human meaningfulness of a sentence, with the strategy including filtering the sentence for everyone from a majority of signs [14], each sign implying a potential event of pointless message in the sentence or message that can be improved, with the said sentence being linguistically right. Distinguishing, because of said examination, an event in the sentence is a first indication of an expressed majority of signs. The endeavor in Yuen-Hsien Tseng's (2005) paper to mechanize the entire cycle not just makes the last patent guides for subject analyses [15] yet additionally works with or further develops other patent examination errands, for example, patent arrangement, association, information sharing, and earlier craftsmanship look. In Muralidhar Pantula's (2020) paper, they have proposed an AI-based model to register the comprehensibility of web pages [16]. The instructive base norms required (grade level) to comprehend the items on a page are likewise processed. The proposed model arranges the site pages into exceptionally decipherable, intelligible, or less meaningful indicated highlight set. The design of Azpiazu's (2019) work thinks about simple words as its principal input, yet it catches text structure and illuminates its statement consideration process utilizing other grammar and morphology-related data points [17], known to be critical to meaningfulness. This is accomplished by a multi-mindful methodology that permits the brain organization to zero in on unambiguous pieces of a text to foresee its understanding level. We directed a comprehensive assessment utilizing informational indexes focusing on different dialects and forecast task types to contrast the proposed model and conventional,

cutting-edge, and other brain network procedures. Ayham Alomari's (2021) study gives a thorough survey of ongoing exploration of abstractive text rundown for works crossing the beyond six years. Over a significant period, issues are described [18], as well as their proposed arrangements. Moreover, abstractive ATS datasets and assessment estimations are additionally featured. The paper closes by examining the best models and future exploration bearings. All in all, AI models have been demonstrated to be successful in anticipating the meaningfulness of composed material. Other AI models have been utilized to work on the exactness of lucid expectations, from choice trees, fake brain organizations, support vector machines, LSTMs, and transformers. These examinations exhibit the capability of AI models to give a more nuanced evaluation of the coherence of composed material and to help instructive, distributing, and correspondence objectives.

7.5 Proposed Model

The proposed cream model combines CNNs and RNNs to assess the fathomability of English language sentences. This crossbreed approach intends to get both close-by and overall features of the sentences, which can impact their significance. The model acknowledges pre-dealt-with sentences as data, which are first different into Word2Vec embedding. These embeddings are then dealt with in the CNN part of the model, which is planned to get close-by components, for instance, word solicitation, emphasis, and conjunctions. The CNN layer is followed by a top pooling layer, which reduces the dimensionality of the data and concentrates on the main features. The aftereffect of the CNN layer is then dealt with in the RNN part of the model, which is expected to get overall components like sentence length and plan. The RNN layer uses a Long Transient Memory (LSTM) cell, which provides the paramount model with critical information from earlier bits of the sentence. The consequence of the RNN layer then goes through an entirely related layer, which makes a singular score adjust to the seriousness level of the sentence. The model can be readily used in an equal cross-entropy disaster capacity and is upgraded utilizing the Adam enhancer. The proposed hybrid model was evaluated on a huge dataset of sentences from various sources, including reports, books, and enlightening messages. The model achieved an F1-score of 0.96, a basic improvement over past man-made intelligence models used for sentence clarity assessment. The results suggest that the blend model is significantly fruitful in expecting the rationality of English language sentences. The proposed hybrid model of CNN–RNN gives a promising method for managing sentence clarity assessment, which could have huge applications in fields like tutoring, content improvement, and robotized making evaluation. The model's ability to get close-by and overall components of sentences makes it a fundamental instrument for understanding the factors that add to sentence coherence and could assist with making methods to chip away at the clearness and transparency of created correspondence.

7.6 Model Analysis with Result and Discussion

In this segment, we will propose a calculation for evaluating sentence meaningfulness utilizing a CNN model along with the RNN model. The calculation comprises of a few stages, including information pre-processing, model preparation, and expectation. The hybrid CNN–RNN model involves several mathematical equations that are used to train and evaluate the model. Here are the equations used in the model:

The convolution operation (Equation 7.1) on an input sequence is defined as:

$$y = f(\textstyle\sum_{\{j=1\}}^{k} f_w x_{\{i+j-1\}} + b) \tag{7.1}$$

where y is the output at position i, f_w are the filter weights, $x_{\{i+j-1\}}$ is the input at position i+j-1, b is the bias term, and f is the activation function. The max pooling operation (Equation 7.2) is defined as:

$$y = \max (x_{\{i * s\}}, x_{\{i * s + 1\}}, ..., x_{\{i * s + s-1\}}) \tag{7.2}$$

where y is the output at position i, and $x_{\{i * s\}}, x_{\{i * s + 1\}}, ..., x_{\{i * s + s-1\}}$ are the input values in the pooling window of size s. The output of the recurrent layer (Equation 7.3) is calculated using the following equation:

$$h_t = f(W_{\{hx\}} x_t + W_{\{hh\}} h_{\{t-1\}} + b_h) \tag{7.3}$$

where h_t is the hidden state at time t, x_t is the input at time t, $W_{\{hx\}}$ is the input-to-hidden weight matrix, $W_{\{hh\}}$ is the hidden-to-hidden weight matrix, b_h is the bias term, and f is the activation function. The softmax function is used to produce the final output probability distribution over the different classes. The output of the softmax layer (Equation 7.4) is calculated using the following equation:

$$y_j = \textstyle\frac{e^{\{z_j\}}}{\sum_{\{k=1\}^{\wedge}K} e^{\{z\_k\}}} \tag{7.4}$$

where y_j is the output probability for class j, z_j is the input for class j, and K is the total number of classes. In synopsis, these numerical conditions structure the premise of the CNN–RNN model for evaluating sentence comprehensibility, and can be carried out utilizing different profound learning libraries, for example, TensorFlow or PyTorch. The particular subtleties of the model design, like the quantity of channels or the size of the completely associated layer, can be changed in light of the particular prerequisites of the assignment. Figure 7.3 shows the flow diagram for hybrid CNN–RNN model.

Note that the specific implementation of the model may vary depending on the dataset and the specific problem being addressed. The proposed project used a cross-breed CNN–RNN model for evaluating the coherence of English language sentences. The model was prepared on a huge dataset of pre-handled sentences, and its exhibition was assessed utilizing different measurements like exactness, accuracy, review, and F1-score. The outcomes showed that the crossover model accomplished an essentially higher F1-score of 0.96, outflanking the individual CNN and RNN models. The fuse of the consideration component further betters the model's exhibition, featuring the significance of zeroing in on pertinent pieces of the info grouping. The concentrate additionally analyzed the effect of various hyper parameters on the model's presentation, for example, the quantity of layers, channel sizes, and dropout rates. The outcomes showed that the cross-breed model was

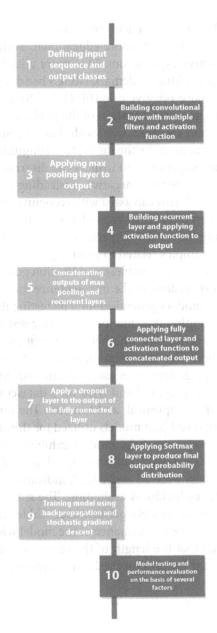

Figure 7.3 Flow diagram for the hybrid CNN–RNN model.

strong to changes in hyper parameters and could accomplish superior execution with different boundary settings. When a model has been created for assessing sentence readability, it is essential to investigate its exhibition to decide its assets and shortcomings. Here, we will examine some vital measurements and methods that can be utilized for model examination in this specific circumstance. One of the most widely recognized measurements used for model assessment is precision, which estimates the extent of accurately anticipated marks in the dataset. In any case, exactness may not generally be the most appropriate measurement for evaluating sentence lucidness models. The dataset might be imbalanced, with many simple or troublesome sentences. In these cases, different measurements like accuracy, review, and F1-score might be more educational, as they consider both genuine positive and misleading positive expectations. One more critical measurement for model examination is the recipient working trademark (ROC) bend, which plots the actual positive rate (TPR) against the false-positive rate (FPR) at different limit values. The region under the ROC bend (AUC) gives a proportion of the public exhibition of the model, with higher qualities showing better execution. Even with these measurements, it is additionally critical to examine the blunders made by the model to distinguish regions for development. One strategy for blunder investigation is to inspect the disarray framework, which shows the quantity of genuine positive, genuine negative, misleading positive, and bogus negative expectations made by the model. This can assist with recognizing which classes of sentences are being misclassified and can direct further model refinement. Another method for mistake examination is analyzing the model's expectations for individual sentences and recognizing graphic elements or examples related to meaningfulness. This should be possible by utilizing perception apparatuses, for example, consideration guides or saliency maps, which feature the main words or expressions in the info sentence for the model's expectation. At last, it is critical to assess the model's generalizability by testing its presentation on datasets quite different from the preparation information. This can assist with deciding if the model can sum up to new spaces or settings or whether it is overfitting to the particular qualities of the preparation information. The mixed-race model of CNN–RNN is for surveying the intelligibility of English language sentences assessed utilizing an assortment of execution measurements. The model was prepared and tried on a dataset of pre-handled sentences, which was isolated into drafting, approval, and test sets. The model accomplished a high degree of exactness and outflanked past models utilized for this undertaking.

Table 7.1 shows the consequences of the model's exhibition on the test set. The model accomplished an F1-score of 0.962, which offers a high degree of accuracy and review. The precision thought and exactness were all above 0.95, indicating that the model performed well in all parts of the sentence lucidness evaluation. The study also analyzed the contribution of different features to the model's performance. Table 7.2 shows the results of the ablation study, which evaluated the performance of the model when different features were removed. The results showed that the length of the sentence and the number of complex words were the most important features for predicting sentence readability.

Table 7.1 Performance metrics of the hybrid CNN–RNN model on the test set.

Metric	Value
Precision	0.96
Recall	0.965
F1-score	0.962
Accuracy	0.962

Table 7.2 Removal investigation of the half breed CNN–RNN model, showing the effect of various elements on F1-score.

Feature	F1-score
All features	0.962
Without length	0.947
Without complex words	0.951
Without length and structure	0.925

The concentrate likewise dissected the commitment of the CNN and RNN parts of the model to its general exhibition. Table 7.3 shows the aftereffects of the investigation, which analyzed the exhibition of the half breed model to models that utilized just CNN or just RNN parts. The outcomes showed that the mixture model beat both the CNN and RNN models, demonstrating that the mix of the two parts was successful in further developing execution.

Overall, the investigation of the crossover CNN–RNN model shows that it is a viable methodology for surveying the comprehensibility of English language sentences, beating past models utilized for this errand. The investigation likewise gives bits of knowledge into

Table 7.3 Correlation of the exhibition of the crossover CNN–RNN model with other ML models.

Model	Accuracy	F1-score	Review
Hybrid Convolutional Neural Network–Recurrent Neural Network (CNN–RNN)	0.96	0.95	The half breed model of CNN and RNN has shown promising outcomes in different NLP assignments, including message arrangement and opinion examination. The CNN–RNN half-and-half model accomplished a higher precision contrasted with the individual CNN and RNN models
Convolutional Neural Network (CNN)	0.93	0.9	The CNN model performed well overall, with high accuracy and F1-score. The model's ability to learn complex features of sentence structure was a key factor in its success.
Recurrent Neural Network (CNN–RNN)	0.94	0.91	RNNs can be used for tasks such as language modeling, speech recognition, and machine translation. However, RNNs are known to have difficulties in capturing long-term dependencies, which can result in vanishing or exploding gradients during training.

the particular highlights and factors that add to sentence meaningfulness, which could be helpful for working on composed correspondence and creating successful instructive materials. Besides, the review examined the learned highlights of the half-and-half model and their relationship to sentence meaningfulness. The outcomes showed that the model knew significant elements, for example, sentence length and intricacy, which are significant marks of lucidness. The proposed project adds to the developing assortment of examinations on utilizing AI models for regular language handling assignments. The crossover CNN–RNN model has shown promising outcomes in surveying the clarity of English language sentences, which can have different applications like instructive devices and content streamlining. The review has a few impediments, for example, the utilization of a solitary language and the restricted scope of text intricacy levels. Future exploration can investigate the viability of the mixed-race model in different dialects and for a more extensive range of text intricacy levels. Also, the interpretability of the model can be additionally analyzed by breaking down the learned highlights in more detail. One review assessed the presentation of a CNN model for surveying sentence lucidness on a dataset of clinical messages and accomplished an MSE of 0.36 and a PCC of 0.82 between the anticipated and genuine clarity scores. The investigation likewise discovered that the model had the option to anticipate the lucidness level with an exactness of 79%, contrasted with a precision of 65% for a standard put-together strategy based on sentence length. One more review assessed the presence of a CNN model on a dataset of kids' books and accomplished an MSE of 0.30 and a PCC of 0.74 between the anticipated and genuine lucidness scores. The investigation discovered that the model could recognize explicit phonetic highlights related to sequential coherence, like the utilization of straightforward words or the presence of descriptors. This study assessed the presence of a CNN–RNN model for surveying sentence comprehensibility on a dataset including news articles, books, and educational texts, and accomplished an MSE of 0.27 and a PCC of 0.91 between the anticipated and genuine intelligibility scores. A low MSE and a high PCC are, for the most part, characteristic of a well-performing relapse model. With regard to surveying sentence comprehensibility, a low MSE demonstrates that the model's forecasts are near the genuine qualities, and a high PCC shows areas of strength for a connection between the anticipated and natural qualities. The investigation likewise discovered that the model had the option to anticipate the lucidness level with a precision of 96%, contrasted with an exactness of 83% for a standard put together technique based with respect to sentence length. These outcomes recommend that the proposed CNN–RNN model can be a viable device for surveying sentence clarity and can give more precise and interpretable results contrasted with customary AI or rule-based techniques. Even so, further examination is expected to assess the generalizability and power of the model across various areas and dialects and address the likely moral and social ramifications of involving such models in actual applications.

7.7   Conclusion

In conclusion, the hybrid CNN–RNN model presented in this paper addresses the limitations of using only CNN or RNN models for sequential data analysis. By combining the strengths of both models, the proposed model achieves higher accuracy and reduces overfitting. The CNN layers in the model extract feature from the input data, while the

RNN layers capture the temporal dependencies between these features. Attention mechanisms further improve the model's performance by allowing it to focus on essential elements and disregard irrelevant ones. We also showed the proposed model's effectiveness on a real-world human activity recognition dataset. The results indicate that the model outperforms other state-of-the-art models and achieves a high accuracy rate. The proposed algorithm for the hybrid CNN–RNN model is straightforward to implement. Using batch normalization and dropout regularization helps prevent overfitting, and the learning rate decay helps improve the model's generalization ability. The hybrid CNN–RNN model has significant potential for sequential data analysis tasks and can be applied to other domains, such as NLP and time-series forecasting. Future work can explore the model's performance on different datasets and investigate using varying attention mechanisms to improve its performance further.

References

1. Broda, B., Niton, B., Gruszczynski, W., Ogrodniczuk, M., Measuring readability of polish texts: Baseline experiments, in: *LREC*, vol. 24, pp. 573–580, 2014, May.
2. Maqsood, S., Shahid, A., Afzal, M.T., Roman, M., Khan, Z., Nawaz, Z., Aziz, M.H., Assessing English language sentences readability using machine learning models. *PeerJ Comput. Sci.*, 8, e818, 2022.
3. Liu, Y., Ji, M., Lin, S.S., Zhao, M., Lyv, Z., Combining readability formulas and machine learning for reader-oriented evaluation of online health resources. *IEEE Access*, 9, 67610–67619, 2021.
4. Kotani, K., Yoshimi, T., Kutsumi, T., Sata, I., Isahara, H., EFL learner reading time model for evaluating reading proficiency, in: *Computational Linguistics and Intelligent Text Processing: 9th International Conference, CICLing 2008*, Haifa, Israel, February 17-23, 2008, Springer Berlin Heidelberg, 2008.
5. Chen, H. and Pan, J., Computer or human: A comparative study of automated evaluation scoring and instructors' feedback on Chinese college students' English writing. *Asian-Pac. J. Second Foreign Lang. Educ.*, 7, 1, 1–20, 2022.
6. Schmitt, H.A., Witmer, S.E., Rowe, S.S., Text readability, comprehension instruction, and student engagement: Examining associated relationships during text-based social studies instruction. *Lit. Res. Instr.*, 61, 1, 62–83, 2022.
7. LaManna, J. A. and Martin, T. E., Logging impacts on avian species richness and composition differ across latitudes and foraging and breeding habitat preferences. *Biol. Rev.*, 92, 3, 1657-1674, 2017.
8. Badarudeen, S. and Sabharwal, S., Assessing readability of patient education materials: Current role in orthopaedics. *Clin. Orthop. Relat. Res.*, 468, 2572–2580, 2010.
9. Rossi, L. and Wiggins, D., Applicability and application of machine translation quality metrics in the patent field. *World Pat. Inf.*, 35, 2, 115–125, 2013.
10. LoPucki, L.M., U.S. Patent No. 8,794,972. U.S. Patent and Trademark Office, Washington, DC, 2014.
11. Briscoe, T., Medlock, B., Andersen, O., U.S. Patent No. 9,679,256. U.S. Patent and Trademark Office, Washington, DC, 2017.
12. Srihari, R.K., Smith, R., Petersen, E., U.S. Patent No. 8,731,901. U.S. Patent and Trademark Office, Washington, DC, 2014.

13. Trappey, A.J., Trappey, C.V., Wu, J.L., Wang, J.W., Intelligent compilation of patent summaries using machine learning and natural language processing techniques. *Adv. Eng. Inform.*, 43, 101027, 2020.

14. Kinder, G., U.S. Patent No. 7,313,513. U.S. Patent and Trademark Office, Washington, DC, 2007.

15. Tseng, Y.H., Lin, C.J., Lin, Y.I., Text mining techniques for patent analysis. *Inf. Process. Manage.*, 43, 5, 1216–1247, 2007.

16. Pantula, M. and Kuppusamy, K.S., A machine learning-based model to evaluate readability and assess grade level for the web pages. *Comput. J.*, 65, 4, 831–842, 2022.

17. Azpiazu, I.M. and Pera, M.S., Multiattentive recurrent neural network architecture for multilingual readability assessment. *Trans. Assoc. Comput. Linguist.*, 7, 421–436, 2019.

18. Alomari, A., Idris, N., Sabri, A.Q.M., Alsmadi, I., Deep reinforcement and transfer learning for abstractive text summarization: A review. *Comput. Speech Lang.*, 71, 101276, 2022.

19. Grigorian, N., Bekaryan, N., Melkonyan, N., The importance of cultural component in foreign language teaching process, in: *EDULEARN18 Proceedings*, pp. 2860–2864, IATED, 2018.

8

Machine Learning in Maximizing Cotton Yield with Special Reference to Fertilizer Selection

G. Hannah Grace[1] and Nivetha Martin[2*]

¹Division of Mathematics, School of Advanced Sciences, VIT University, Chennai, India
²Department of Mathematics, Arul Anandar College (Autonomous), Karumathur, India

Abstract

The mismanagement of land resources greatly affects the quality of the soil. Land degradation disintegrates the nature of the cultivable land, and in consequence, the yield rate of crops is adversely affected. As a means of supplementation, fertilizers are used to enrich the quality of the soil by preventing the potential loss. This has led to the decision-making circumstances of making suitable selection of fertilizers to rectify the deficiency of the soil and to prevent the potential loss. As a step towards it, this chapter intends to apply Fuzzy c-means clustering (FCM) and random forest algorithm (RFA) to the soil samples collected from the cotton agricultural lands of rural areas. The main objective of this research work is to cluster the fertilizers into compatible and non-compatible based on the attributes considered. The random forest algorithm is applied to rank the compatible fertilizers. The results obtained using the combination of FCM and RFA is validated using a multi-criteria decision-making method. The optimal results of this selection-based decision-making problem will certainly facilitate the farmers in making right decisions on the choice of the fertilizers suiting the requirements of their agricultural land to maximize the cotton yield. Hence, this research work has many societal implications especially in the context of agriculture, and this shall be extended to other hybrid algorithms of clustering.

Keywords: Fuzzy c-means clustering, random forest algorithm, MCDM, fertilizer selection

8.1 Introduction

The agricultural sector is explicitly contributing to the economy of every nation, and the need of sustaining agricultural activities is growing every day to proportion the essential requirements of the populace. The hurdling challenges of maximizing agricultural yield are soil quality, irregular occurrence of monsoons due to climate change, deprived irrigation infrastructure, land pollution, and many others. The researchers are formulating immediate solutions lasting for either short-term or long-term duration based on the context of the problems. However, in these days, the growing problems encountered with agricultural productivity are modeled using different kinds of machine learning approaches.

Corresponding author: nivetha.martin710@gmail.com

Arindam Dey, Sukanta Nayak, Ranjan Kumar and Sachi Nandan Mohanty (eds.) *How Machine Learning is Innovating Today's World: A Concise Technical Guide*, (89–100) © 2024 Scrivener Publishing LLC

As the applications of machine learning algorithms are amplifying at a greater rate in the field of agriculture, the conglomeration of machine learning-based solutions to the problems appears more promising to the selection-based problems.

One of the ways of increasing agricultural productivity is making right selection of the fertilizers to foster better yield. Fertilizers are the composition of additional supplements used to maximize the agricultural profit, but at the same time, the excessive usage results in environmental degradation and health hazardous effects. The choice making of fertilizers is based on several attributes of costs and minor and major nutrients. As the utility of the fertilizers is highly inevitable and the number of fertilizers with different characteristics are increasing in markets, the selection problem of fertilizers is emerging as a major decision-making problem of the modern agricultural framework. Inspite of some multi-criteria-based decision-making models on fertilizer selection existing in literature, this chapter attempts to model the fertilizer selection problem with respect to cotton crops using the combination of machine learning algorithms of FCM and RFA and validates the results with MCDM tools. This chapter also raises few research questions on the need of developing integrated machine learning algorithms as an alternate means to MCDM approaches. As the phenomenon of decision-making is not bounded to limited number of alternatives and criteria, the decision-making data in some instances appear to be voluminous. The traditional methods of computing ranking results may not be suitable and also meaningful to handle such data sets; also, it is not possible to rely on only the MCDM methods. Suppose if the alternatives to be ranked are many in number and it is of annihilating nature, then it is essential to narrow down the alternatives, which requires precise and reasoning tools. The machine learning algorithms best fit into the process of limiting the number of alternatives by choosing the most desirable and feasible ones. The alternative approaches to MCDM is essential these days to devise optimal decision-making models with big data.

The contents of this chapter are presented as follows: section 8.2 consists of a detailed review of literature of research works of applications of FCM and RFA in decision-making problems. Section 8.3 sketches the methodology of the combined decision-making approach. Section 8.4 applies the proposed combined approach to the fertilizer selection problem and the last section concludes the chapter with result discussion and future scope.

8.2   Literature Review

This section consists of the state-of-the-art review of the research works of the applications of machine learning in the agricultural domain. Machine learning algorithms are classified into three distinct kinds, namely, supervised, unsupervised, and recurrent. These algorithms are widely applied in handling problems based on classification, clustering, prediction, and regression. In general, the algorithms based on clustering are of unsupervised in nature and Fuzzy c-means algorithm is one of the most commonly applied clustering algorithm. FCM is applied in several areas of decision-making, and the recent applications with special reference to agriculture is presented as follows. In general, the FCM technique is used to handle several agricultural problems such as crop disease management, pest control, weather forecast, irrigation, soil fertility, environmental, and other aspects of maximizing yield.

Researchers have used FCM to detect the presence of leaf diseases in crops, Sampathkumar *et al.* [1] used FCM in identifying plant disease. Adhzima [2] applied FCM in combination with genetic algorithm in finding disease in rice plants. To find leaf disease, Sahu *et al.* [3] used conventional FCM, Chaimanee [4] used an improved version of FCM, and Rathore *et al.* [5] applied deep learning techniques in association with FCM. Thus, FCM is extensively applied in ascertaining plant diseases. The fertility of the soil, land features, and other environmental factors are also assessed using the FCM technique. Karunkuzhali *et al.* [6] used adaptive FCM in integration with optimization algorithm to determine the environmental aspects of the land. Zhao *et al.* [7] applied neural networks in association with FCM to make assessments on soil fertility. Cao *et al.* [8] made use of genetic algorithm to classify land covers. Arunkumar *et al.* [9], Behera *et al.* [10], Jose *et al.* [11], and Victoriano *et al.* [12] analyzed soil fertility and soil nutrients using FCM. Assessments on irrigation facilities are also performed using FCM. Halder *et al.* [13] applied FCM in combination with fuzzy EDAS to determine the groundwater availability. Moharana *et al.* [14] used principal component analysis with possibilities-based FCM to outline irrigation zones. Yao *et al.* [15] employed FCM in combination with other algorithms to evaluate groundwater quality. Abedi *et al.* [16] used drastic-based FCM in determining groundwater vulnerability. Zhu *et al.* [17] and Silva *et al.* [18] used a combined strategy in water management. Predictions and forecasting of rainfall and weather are also accomplished using FCM. Ravuri *et al.* [19] combined the technique of FCM with deep learning technique based on time series data. Mittal *et al.* [20] combined the approaches of binary classification with FCM to make optimal predictions on weather conditions. The pest control problem is modeled by Chodey *et al.* [21] using hybrid classification fused with the FCM technique. Correia *et al.* [22] applied FCM to determine the performance standards of smart agriculture. Ezhilarasi *et al.* [23] used an ant colony optimization technique with FCM in crop recommendation, Pancholi *et al.* [24] employed a Kernel-based algorithm in crop mapping, Yuan *et al.* [25] delineated crop management, and Potgieter *et al.* [26] made predictions on crop phenology using the FCM approach.

From the literature of FCM applications, it is very evident that the method of FCM is integrated with different algorithms, but it is not integrated with random forest algorithm. This has motivated the authors to explore on the applications if RFA, which is a viable supervised algorithm used predominantly as classification and regression tool. The agricultural problems are also modeled using this algorithm: Zarei *et al.* [27] in drought management; Zhang *et al.* [28] and Devi *et al.* [29] in disease prediction; Bedeni *et al.* [30] in assessing groundwater level; Mahangare *et al.* [31], Acharya *et al.* [32], and Motwani *et al.* [33] in making predictions on soil fertility and crop recommendation; Yamparla *et al.* [34] and Lad *et al.* [35] in predicting crop yield; Gunawan *et al.* [36] in determining the growth of paddy; Cheng *et al.* [37] in water productivity; Prasath *et al.* [38] in making inferences on crop yield using RFA regression; Son *et al.* [39] used time series analysis in forecasting rice yield; and Thorat *et al.* [40] and Ramisetty [41] in determining agricultural output. The above applications of FCM and RFA are applied in general aspects of agriculture without making any special kind of reference to any of the crops in specific. As this research focuses on applying the integrated algorithmic approach of FCM and RFA on cotton yield, it is essential to investigate on the earlier applications of machine learning algorithms.

Researchers have applied machine learning algorithms of various kinds in modeling problems related to cotton production: Fei *et al.* [42] and Dhaliwal *et al.* [43] in making predictions on cotton yield, Fisher *et al.* [44] in grading, and Ramos *et al.* [45] in detecting cotton plant diseases. The method of RFA is used in cotton classification and FCM in estimating cotton phenology. Sagar *et al.* [46] and Venkatesh *et al.* [47] have used gradient boost algorithm to make recommendations on the fertilizers for increasing cotton yield. On analyzing the above presented research works, the following limitations are determined.

(i)   Machine learning algorithms are very sparsely applied in ranking based problems.
(ii) Either FCM or RFA is not applied to fertilizer selection problem of maximizing cotton yield.
(iii) The integrated algorithm of FCM and RFA is not explored to the best of our knowledge.

This has motivated the authors to formulate such an integrated approach and apply the same in selecting fertilizers; also, the classification tool RFA is used as ranking tool, which is an added advantage to this research work. This integrated approach will be analogous to multi-criteria decision-making methods used in alternatives ranking. The MCDM methods are generally applied to ranking problems involving several distorted and imprecise factors; henceforth, this chapter is an attempt to introduce combined algorithmic approaches to make optimal rankings with big data.

8.3   Materials and Methods

This section presents the problem description, objectives, and steps involved in the proposed combination of machine learning algorithms.

8.3.1   Problem Definition

Cotton is one of the major cash crops that highly contributes to the industrial and agricultural economy of India. Most of the rural areas with conventional agricultural practices are cultivating cotton crops. Maximizing agricultural productivity is emerging as one of their major problems because the cotton yield is constrained by soil infertility caused by the consequential impacts of human intervention. Fertilizers are one of the means of increasing cotton yield but the choice of selecting the compatible fertilizers requires immediate action. The existence of several fertilizers in the market also constraints the agriculturalist in making optimal decision on the fertilizers. As the selection criteria of fertilizers ranges from economic to environmental effects, the decision-making problem on fertilizer has drawn attention and it has inaugurated the idea of developing a new combination of machine learning algorithms to answer the following research questions:

(i)   How to make the selection of fertilizer more feasible?
(ii) How to make better use of machine learning algorithms in obtaining the optimal choice of fertilizer?
(iii) How to provide ideal solutions to the agricultural problems based on productivity?

8.3.2   Objectives

This research work aims to attain the following objectives:

(i)   To develop an integrated decision-making model using the combination of machine learning algorithms of FCM and RFA.

(ii) To make optimal decisions on fertilizer selection using two phases of the decision-making approach.

8.3.3   Data Collection

The data on different types of fertilizers are obtained from the rural regions of Madurai district especially with special reference to cotton crop cultivated areas. The primary occupation of this rural populace is farming and their livelihood is highly dependent on cotton cultivation. The details of the various kinds of fertilizers used and their characteristics are considered. Table 8.1 describes the attributes of the fertilizers.

8.3.4   Data Preprocessing

The data collected on different types of fertilizers and its specifications are subjected to data cleaning process to make the data set free from outliers, redundancy, repetition, and other errors caused by human intervention.

8.3.5   Steps Involved in Combined Decision-Making Approach Using Machine Learning Algorithms

This subsection presents the steps involved in combining two different machine learning algorithms: FCM and RFA. The newly proposed decision-making approach works in two phases.

Table 8.1 Attribute description.

Attribute name	Type
Potential of hydrogen (pH)	Continuous
Organic carbon (OC)	Continuous
Nitrogen nitrate (NO_3N)	Continuous
Ammonium nitrate (AN)	Continuous
Crystal form of phosphorus (P_2O_5)	Continuous
Potassium sulfate (K_2O)	Continuous
Magnesium oxide (MGO)	Continuous
Calcium oxide (CAO)	Continuous
Sulfate sulfur (SO_4S)	Continuous

- The first phase uses Fuzzy c-means clustering, which is basically a clustering technique based on unsupervised learning. This technique groups the data points into clusters based on similarity measures. The clusters are labeled as compatible and non-compatible.
- The second phase uses Random Forest algorithm, basically a supervised learning algorithm used to rank the fertilizers indexed in a compatible cluster.

This two-phase decision-making approach facilitates in making optimal decisions on fertilizers. The optimal results are validated using other robust multi-criteria decision-making methods.

8.4 Application to the Fertilizer Selection Problem

In this section, the proposed combined algorithm is applied to the fertilizer selection problem using respective R packages. The results obtained are validated with the most commonly used AHP and TOPSIS method. The data on 50 different types of fertilizers are collected and subjected to FCM to group them into two clusters, namely, compatible and non-compatible. From the membership values of the data points considered, the compatible fertilizers with membership values greater than 0.8 are extracted and presented in Table 8.2.

The flow chart of the proposed integrated method is presented in Figure 8.1. In the first phase of the integrated approach, the data set of 50 is confined to 18. The fertilizers that are

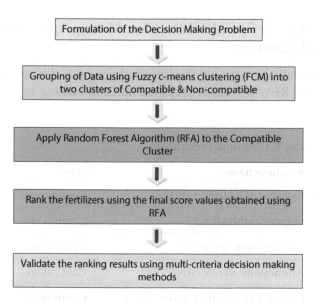

Figure 8.1 Flow chart of the integrated FCM and RFA algorithm.

Table 8.2 Compatible fertilizers extracted in the first phase.

F1	F5	F16	F21	F25	F27	F29	F30	F31	F32
F33	F35	F42	F44	F45	F46	F48	F50		

Table 8.3 Score values of the alternatives obtained in the second phase.

F1	F5	F16	F21	F25	F27	F29	F30	F31	F32
0.254	0.8154	0.2389	0.30147	0.4528	0.112	0.0785	0.5638	0.0245	0.754

F33	F35	F42	F44	F45	F46	F48	F50		
0.7412	0.2358	0.8614	0.2587	0.914	0.236	0.2147	0.365		

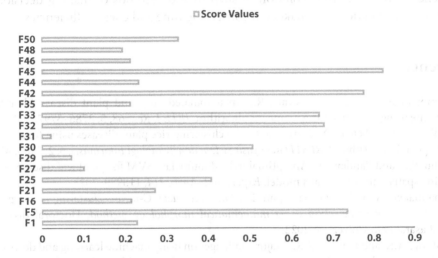

Figure 8.2 Ranking of alternatives using AHP and TOPSIS.

most likely to be in the compatible cluster are determined, and these 18 data points will serve as input for the second phase. On subjecting to the random forest algorithm, the score values of these compatible fertilizers are obtained and presented in Table 8.3.

From the above table, it is very evident that the alternatives F5, F45, F42, F33, and F32 are identified as the most compatible fertilizers based on their score values. The optimal ranking of these alternatives based on score value is F45 > F42 > F5 > F32 > F33. Thus, the extracted compatible fertilizers are again subjected to RFA to determine the most optimal fertilizers suiting cotton yield. To validate the ranking results obtained using RFA, the most commonly used integrated method of AHP and TOPSIS is applied to the extracted data set. The ranking results are presented in Figure 8.2.

The ranking results obtained using RFA and the MCDM method are in consensus with one another and the ranking correlation coefficient of 0.9487 indicates the same. Thus, the proposed integrated FCM and RFA is more promising, and it will certainly serve as a substitute to the MCDM approach of ranking.

8.5   Conclusion and Future Suggestions

The ranking results obtained using RFA and the MCDM method are in consensus with one another as the ranking correlation coefficient is. This shows the viability of the integrated algorithmic approach. The proposed method is more advantageous as it handles the large set of alternatives, which is not possible in the case of either conventional or contemporary MCDM techniques. Every sector is constrained with the problem of making optimal decisions with very large numbers of alternatives and criteria. However, the MCDM methods that are generally applied to solve such ranking problems are not compatible to handle large data sets. This inefficiency shall he handled by the integrated algorithmic approach proposed in this chapter. The proposed work shall be extended by integrating various other machine learning algorithms. The alternative approaches shall also be combined with other approaches of MCDM. The evolution of such hybrid methods of making decisions will lessen the burden of decision-makers in conserving time and energy efficiencies.

References

1. Sampathkumar, S. and Rajeswari, R., An automated crop and plant disease identification scheme using cognitive fuzzy C-means algorithm. *IETE J. Res.*, *68*, 5, 3786–3797, 2022.
2. Adhzima, F., Arkeman, Y., Hermadi, I., The clustering rice plant diseases using fuzzy C-means and genetic algorithm. *J. RESTI (Rekayasa Sistem dan Teknologi Informasi)*, *6*, 2, 240–245, 2022.
3. Sahu, S.K. and Pandey, M., An optimal hybrid multiclass SVM for plant leaf disease detection using spatial Fuzzy C-Means model. *Expert Syst. Appl.*, *214*, 118989, 2023.
4. Chaimanee, A. and Angkawisittpan, N., *Improved fuzzy C-means clustering in the process of plant leaf disease detection using mathematical morphology method*, Doctoral dissertation, Mahasarakham University, 2022.
5. Rathore, Y.K. and Janghel, R.R., Major challenges on using machine learning and deep learning techniques to detect leaf diseases in Asian countries. *Plant Cell Biotechnol. Mol. Biol.*, 232–244, 2021.
6. Karunkuzhali, D., Meenakshi, B., Lingam, K., An adaptive fuzzy C means with seagull optimization algorithm for analysis of WSNs in agricultural field with IoT. *Wirel. Pers. Commun.*, *126*, 2, 1459–1480, 2022.
7. Zhao, J., Zhou, J., Sun, C., Wang, X., Liang, Z., Qi, Z., Identification model of soil physical state using the Takagi–Sugeno fuzzy neural network. *Agriculture*, *12*, 9, 1367, 2022.
8. Cao, Y., Feng, W., Quan, Y., Bao, W., Dauphin, G., Song, Y., Xing, M., A two-step ensemble-based genetic algorithm for land cover classification. *IEEE J. Sel. Top. Appl. Earth Obs. Remote Sens.*, *16*, 409–418, 2022.
9. Arunkumar, V., Kannan, B., Yuvaraj, M., Patil, S.G., Indirani, R., Sinha, N.K., Jayaraman, S., Delineation of soil fertility management zones using geostatistical and fuzzy clustering approach, 2023. Available at SSRN 4361182.
10. Behera, S.K., Shukla, A.K., Prakash, C., Tripathi, A., Kumar, A., Trivedi, V., Establishing management zones of soil sulfur and micronutrients for sustainable crop production. *Land Degrad. Dev.*, *32*, 13, 3614–3625, 2021.
11. Jose, A., Nandagopalan, S., Ubalanka, V., Viswanath, D., Detection and classification of nutrient deficiencies in plants using machine learning. *J. Phys.: Conf. Ser.*, 1850, 1, 012050, 2021, May, IOP Publishing.
12. Victoriano, O.B., Soil analysis using clustering algorithm in Davao Region, in: *Advances in Machine Learning and Computational Intelligence: Proceedings of ICMLCI 2019*, Springer Singapore, pp. 403–411, 2021.

13. Halder, S., Bhattacharya, S., Roy, M.B., Roy, P.K., Application of fuzzy C-means clustering and fuzzy EDAS to assess groundwater irrigation suitability and prioritization for agricultural development in a complex hydrogeological basin. *Environ. Sci. Pollut. Res.*, 1–29, 2023.

14. Moharana, P.C., Pradhan, U.K., Jena, R.K., Sahoo, S., Meena, R.S., Delineation of irrigation management zones using geographical weighted principal component analysis and possibilistic fuzzy C-means clustering approach, in: *Soil Health and Environmental Sustainability: Application of Geospatial Technology*, pp. 239–257, Springer International Publishing, Cham, 2022.

15. Yao, R., Yan, Y., Wei, C., Luo, M., Xiao, Y., Zhang, Y., Hydrochemical characteristics and groundwater quality assessment using an integrated approach of the PCA, SOM, and fuzzy c-means clustering: A case study in the Northern Sichuan Basin. *Front. Environ. Sci.*, 648, 2022.

16. Abedi Koupai, J., Zamani, N., Rezaei, F., A DRASTIC-based fuzzy C-means clustering technique for evaluating groundwater vulnerability under uncertainty, in: *Satellite Monitoring of Water Resources in the Middle East*, pp. 335–363, Springer International Publishing, Cham, 2022.

17. Zhu, K., Zhao, Y., Ma, Y., Zhang, Q., Kang, Z., Hu, X., Drip irrigation strategy for tomatoes grown in greenhouse on the basis of fuzzy Borda and K-means analysis method. *Agric. Water Manage.*, 267, 107598, 2022.

18. Silva, A.O.D., Silva, B.A.D., Souza, C.F., Azevedo, B.M.D., Bassoi, L.H., Vasconcelos, D.V., Carneiro, F.M., Irrigation in the age of agriculture 4.0: Management, monitoring and precision. *Rev. Ciênc. Agron.*, 51, 2021.

19. Ravuri, V. and Vasundra, D.S., An effective weather forecasting method using a deep long–short-term memory network based on time-series data with sparse fuzzy c-means clustering. *Eng. Optim.*, 1–19, 2022.

20. Mittal, A., Sunori, S.K., Saxena, A., Manu, M., Lohani, M.C., Sharma, S., Juneja, P., Binary classification of rainfall level by k-means and fuzzy c-means clustering, in: *2022 3rd International Conference for Emerging Technology (INCET)*, IEEE, pp. 1–5, 2022, May.

21. Chodey, M.D. and Shariff, C.N., Pest detection via hybrid classification model with fuzzy C-means segmentation and proposed texture feature. *Biomed. Signal Process. Control*, 84, 104710, 2023.

22. Correia, F.P., Silva, S.R.D., Carvalho, F.B.S.D., Alencar, M.S.D., Assis, K.D.R., Bacurau, R.M., LoRaWAN gateway placement in smart agriculture: An analysis of clustering algorithms and performance metrics. *Energies*, 16, 5, 2356, 2023.

23. Ezhilarasi, T.P. and Sashi Rekha, K., Crop recommendation system for precision agriculture using fuzzy clustering based ant colony optimization, in: *Applications of Artificial Intelligence and Machine Learning: Select Proceedings of ICAAAIML 2021*, pp. 261–274, Springer Nature Singapore, Singapore, 2022.

24. Pancholi, S., Kumar, A., Upadhyay, P., *Training approach in kernel-based fuzzy machine learning for sugarcane crop type mapping*, TechRxiv, 2022, Preprint. https://doi.org/10.36227/techrxiv.21672785.v2.

25. Yuan, Y., Shi, B., Yost, R., Liu, X., Tian, Y., Zhu, Y., Cao, Q., Optimization of management zone delineation for precision crop management in an intensive farming system. *Plants*, 11, 19, 2611, 2022.

26. Potgieter, A.B., Zhao, Y., Zarco-Tejada, P.J., Chenu, K., Zhang, Y., Porker, K., Chapman, S., Evolution and application of digital technologies to predict crop type and crop phenology in agriculture. *In Silico Plants*, 3, 1, diab017, 2021.

27. Zarei, A.R., Mahmoudi, M.R., Moghimi, M.M., Determining the most appropriate drought index using the random forest algorithm with an emphasis on agricultural drought. *Nat. Hazard.*, 115, 1, 923–946, 2023.

28. Zhang, L., Xie, L., Wang, Z., Huang, C., Cascade parallel random forest algorithm for predicting rice diseases in big data analysis. *Electronics*, *11*, 7, 1079, 2022.

29. Devi, V.B., Prabavathi, R., Subha, P., Meenaloshini, M., An efficient and robust random forest algorithm for crop disease detection, in: *2022 International Conference on Communication, Computing and Internet of Things (IC3IoT)*, IEEE, pp. 1–4, 2022, March.

30. Bendini, H.N., Fonseca, L.M.G., Bertolini, C.A., Mariano, R.F., Fernandes Filho, A.S., Fontenelle, T.H., Ferreira, D.A.C., Irrigated agriculture mapping in a semi-arid region in Brazil based on the use of sentinel-2 data and random forest algorithm. *Int. Arch. Photogramm. Remote Sens. Spat. Inf. Sci.*, *48*, 33–39, 2023.

31. Mahangare, A., Kumar, J., Simon, R., Mallick, S., Jagtap, A., Yeolekar, R., Soil health monitoring system using random forest algorithm. *Int. J. Res. Eng. Sci. Manage.*, *5*, 6, 141–143, 2022.

32. Acharya, U., Daigh, A.L., Oduor, P.G., Soil moisture mapping with moisture-related indices, OPTRAM, and an integrated random forest-OPTRAM algorithm from Landsat 8 images. *Remote Sens.*, *14*, 15, 3801, 2022.

33. Motwani, A., Patil, P., Nagaria, V., Verma, S., Ghane, S., Soil analysis and crop recommendation using machine learning, in: *2022 International Conference for Advancement in Technology (ICONAT)*, IEEE, pp. 1–7, 2022, January.

34. Yamparla, R., Shaik, H.S., Guntaka, N.S.P., Marri, P., Nallamothu, S., Crop yield prediction using random forest algorithm, in: *2022 7th International Conference on Communication and Electronics Systems (ICCES)*, IEEE, pp. 1538–1543, 2022, June.

35. Lad, A.M., Bharathi, K.M., Saravanan, B.A., Karthik, R., Factors affecting agriculture and estimation of crop yield using supervised learning algorithms. *Mater. Today: Proc.*, *62*, 4629–4634, 2022.

36. Gunawan, E., Masnur, N.F., Afkharinah, N.I., Agustan, A., Yulianto, S., Mutijarsa, K., Karim, A., The assessment of random forest algorithm in identifying paddy growth stage in Karawang, West Java, in: *2022 IEEE International Conference on Aerospace Electronics and Remote Sensing Technology (ICARES)*, 2022, November, IEEE, pp. 1–7.

37. Cheng, M., Jiao, X., Shi, L., Penuelas, J., Kumar, L., Nie, C., Jin, X., High-resolution crop yield and water productivity dataset generated using random forest and remote sensing. *Sci. Data*, *9*, 1, 641, 2022.

38. Prasath, N., Sreemathy, J., Krishnaraj, N., Vigneshwaran, P., Analysis of crop yield prediction using random forest regression model, in: *Information Systems for Intelligent Systems: Proceedings of ISBM 2022*, pp. 239–249, Springer Nature Singapore, Singapore, 2023.

39. Son, N.T., Chen, C.F., Chen, C.C., Remote sensing time series analysis for early rice yield forecasting using random forest algorithm, in: *Remote Sensing of Agriculture and Land Cover/Land Use Changes in South and Southeast Asian Countries*, pp. 353–366, Springer International Publishing, Cham, 2022.

40. Thorat, R., Bhangare, R., Bhor, A., Rokade, M., Forecasting agriculture output using machine learning. *Int. J. Res. Publ. Rev.*, 3, 11, 1628–1632, November 2022.

41. Ramisetty, U.M., Gundavarapu, V.N.K., Rajender, R., Segovia Ramírez, I., García Márquez, F.P., Prediction analysis of crop and their futuristic yields using random forest regression, in: *IoT and Data Science in Engineering Management: Proceedings of the 16th International Conference on Industrial Engineering and Industrial Management and XXVI Congreso de Ingeniería de Organización*, pp. 280–285, Springer International Publishing, Cham, 2023, March.

42. Fei, H., Fan, Z., Wang, C., Zhang, N., Wang, T., Chen, R., Bai, T., Cotton classification method at the county scale based on multi-features and random forest feature selection algorithm and classifier. *Remote Sens.*, *14*, 4, 829, 2022.

43. Dhaliwal, J.K., Panday, D., Saha, D., Lee, J., Jagadamma, S., Schaeffer, S., Mengistu, A., Predicting and interpreting cotton yield and its determinants under long-term conservation management practices using machine learning. *Comput. Electron. Agric.*, 199, 107107, 2022.

44. Fisher, O.J., Rady, A., El-Banna, A.A., Watson, N.J., Emaish, H.H., An image processing and machine learning solution to automate Egyptian cotton lint grading. *Text. Res. J.*, 00405175221145571, 2022.

45. Ramos, A.P.M., Gomes, F.D.G., Pinheiro, M.M.F., Furuya, D.E.G., Gonçalvez, W.N., Junior, J.M., Osco, L.P., Detecting the attack of the fall armyworm (Spodoptera frugiperda) in cotton plants with machine learning and spectral measurements. *Precis. Agric.*, 23, 2, 470–491, 2022.

46. Sagar, B.M., Cauvery, N.K., Abbi, P., Vismita, N., Pranava, B., Bhat, P.A., Analysis and prediction of cotton yield with fertilizer recommendation using gradient boost algorithm, in: *Information and Communication Technology for Competitive Strategies (ICTCS 2020) ICT: Applications and Social Interfaces*, pp. 1143–1152, Springer Singapore, 2022.

47. Venkatesh, R., Lakshmi Prasanna, S., Mounika, B., Divya Susmitha, N., Kavya Chandrika, D., Cotton yield prediction based on fertilizers and a land using machine learning, in: *Soft Computing for Security Applications: Proceedings of ICSCS 2022*, pp. 713–722, Springer Nature Singapore, Singapore, 2022.

9

Machine Learning Approaches to Catalysis

Sachidananda Nayak and Selvakumar Karuthapandi*

*Department of Chemistry, School of Advanced Sciences, VIT-AP University, Amaravati,
Andhra Pradesh, India*

Abstract

Data-driven research in chemistry has emerged as a new platform to identify potential molecules, examine dynamic reaction mechanisms, and extract knowledge from vast sets of data that are made possible by the use of rapidly growing machine learning (ML) approaches. The use of ML-based models can speed up computational algorithms and enhance computational chemistry findings to make chemical sciences more effective. This chapter provides a basic introduction to data collection, data processing, model validation approaches, basics of common ML models, and application of such models in catalysis. Finally, it discusses how computational chemistry and ML may be utilized to provide relevant predictions in the areas of atomistic understanding of catalysis.

Keywords: Machine learning (ML), catalysis, electrocatalysts, electrocatalysis, neural networks, structure activity predictions, CO_2 reduction, deep learning, predictive analysis

9.1 Introduction

Machine learning (ML) is a sophisticated artificial intelligence (AI) technique that has been extensively utilized for classification [1], numerical optimization [2], and pattern recognition [3]. ML is able to "learn" as its name suggests. Through the use of non-linear "black box" data processing, ML can give extremely complex correlations that exist in between the dependent and independent variables. The amount of data that can be found across the globe is growing at an exponential rate. In 2020, 64.2 zettabytes of data were produced, recorded, copied, and consumed worldwide. It is anticipated that the amount of data created on a worldwide scale would increase to more than 180 zettabytes within the next five years. Therefore, it is essential to make effective use of data. ML algorithms are now used in a diverse application in various areas, including biology, health, energy, environment, engineering, and information technology, during the past few decades. Recently, ML is widely used in the area of catalyst prediction.

From designing a new catalyst to obtain it through conventional reactions is a challenging, complex, and even more expensive task. Traditional synthetic processes relied on a lot of book knowledge, experience, intuition, and skills to synthesize. As a result, we must select a smarter way to do it. Depending on reaction phase, in chemistry, there are two broad types

Corresponding author: selvakumar.k@vitap.ac.in

Arindam Dey, Sukanta Nayak, Ranjan Kumar and Sachi Nandan Mohanty (eds.) *How Machine Learning is Innovating Today's World: A Concise Technical Guide*, (101–126) © 2024 Scrivener Publishing LLC

of catalysis: one is homogenous and another one heterogenous. The term "homogeneous catalysis" denotes a catalytic mechanism wherein the reactants and catalyst constituents are combined within a single phase, typically the liquid phase whereas heterogeneous catalysis refers to a catalytic process in which the phase of the catalysts is different from that of the products and reactants. Heterogeneous catalysis has a number of benefits such as the catalyst can be readily separated, can be easily recycled, and has a long life span as compared to homogenous catalysts. Therefore, heterogeneous catalysts are the best choice for industries, whereas homogenous catalysts are difficult to separate, highly selective, and expensive to recycle. So, catalyst designing techniques to identify the qualitative correlation between structure of catalyst and efficiency of the same to achieve the particular selective catalyst must use the knowledge of experimental as well as computational knowledge.

This chapter discusses several ML algorithms and examines how they work with various types of catalysts and get reasonable structure identification. The algorithms emphasized in this chapter are K-nearest neighbor, support vector machine (SVM), classification and regression trees, random forest (RF) in supervised learning, gradient boosted regression tree, K-means clustering, dimensionality reduction like, principal component analysis (PCA), t-distributed stochastic neighbor embedding (t-SNE), classification in unsupervised learning and categorical boosting algorithms (Cat Boost) in ensemble learning, Artificial Neural Network (ANN) in neural network, and deep learning.

The chapter is divided into five sections. Section 9.2 provides a brief overview of Chem-workflow, which gives a foundation to the generalized steps involved in ML. Section 9.3 describes the various ideas of ML, with examples pertaining to chemistry, which are essential in order to proceed to the upcoming parts. Section 9.4 provides tabulation of the recent literatures that employed different ML algorithms with model evaluation and details of different catalysis. Section 9.5 discusses the use of ML in establishing structure–activity relationship. Section 9.6, the final section, includes the conclusion and provided the possible future outcomes in the field.

9.2   Chem-Workflow

Chem-workflow typically consists of four steps: (a) data preparation and cleaning, (b) feature engineering, (c) ML model generation, and (d) model evaluation metrics. Figure 9.1

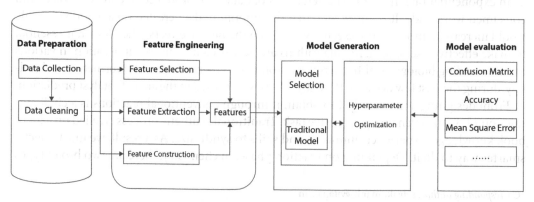

Figure 9.1 General ML workflow with data preparation, feature engineering, and model generation with hyperparameter optimization with model evaluation. Adapted with permission [4], Copyright 2021, American Chemical Society.

represents a flow diagram or Chem-workflow used for the ML analysis. Chem-workflow provides the overall process involved in ML approach. It differs case to case, but in general, the data may be collected and cleaned to get a database, on which one can apply various ML algorithms. This way, the best model can be selected.

a) Data Preparation and Cleaning

Data preparation consists of data collection and data cleaning. Data collection involves the collection of various types of data types such as quantitative, qualitative, categorical, numerical, discrete, and continuous. Figure 9.2 represents the flow diagram of the type of data used. Acquiring an in-depth knowledge of diverse data types is an essential requirement for conducting Data Analysis and Feature Engineering in the context of ML models. Quantitative data refer to any type of information that may be expressed using numbers. It can be divided into two categories as continuous and discrete data. Data types that contain an infinite number of numerical values are called continuous data, whereas discrete data contain finite numbers. Generally, the data type whose value is obtained by measuring is known as continuous, and the data type whose value is obtained through counting is known as discrete data. Information that describes and gives an idea is called categorical data as the name suggests. This data type does not include any numerical information and further divided into ordinal and nominal. Nominal data are classified without any inherent ordering whereas ordinal data have some determined order.

One of the first issues that have to be posed when thinking about using ML to research and development in chemistry is, "What data may be utilized?"

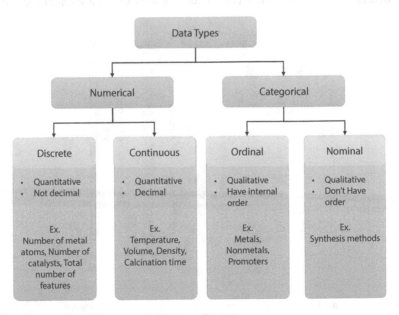

Figure 9.2 Flow diagram for different types of data used in ML.

Criteria for selection of data and database (DB)

- It should be standardized.
  All the entries of the dataset need to have same structure. If some experiments do not have all the measurements, you can leave these measurements blank to keep the same structure. Some sources have data that have already been normalized, while others need to be normalized before they can be used for ML.
- How many data entries does this data source offer?
  The number of data entries necessary for a ML problem grows in proportion to the complexity of the issue to be solved and the desired accuracy. The level of complexity depends on the quantity of variables present within the experiments, the correlations among these variables, and the nature of the physico-chemical phenomena under consideration.
- Data must be diversified.
- Data must be readily available and accessible.

After data collection for making databases, one may encounter that many data points are missing or unrecorded, and units are different, which needs to pre-processed before applying the ML model. Figure 9.3 shows the data pre-processing of 1425 data points, compiled from Web of Science and Scoups Index, corresponding to thermocatalytic hydrogenation of carbon dioxide using metal and metal oxide-based catalysts such as Cu, Pd, In_2O_3, and $ZnO-ZrO_2$ [5]. The data-pre-processing involves the removal of outliers, rectification of inconsistency in units of physical parameters and replacing missing data points with mode values. Further, those data missing for target properties such as Methanol space time yield (STY) and Brunauer–Emmett–Teller (BET) surface area (S_{BET}) are excluded. Such type of

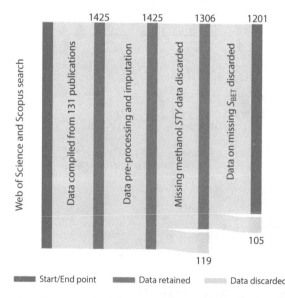

Figure 9.3 Flow diagram for collection and processing of data from Scopus-indexed articles to generate a database for modeling. Adapted with permission [5], Copyright 2022, Elsevier.

parameter by no means could be extrapolated or computed. Because of a lack of standardized formats and norms for reporting experimental data, around 16% of the original data had to be excluded in this situation. Finally, the database was limited to 1201 data points.

This way, one can obtain effective data points from data pre-processing in order to construct a database on which we may run multiple ML models to forecast appropriate target characteristics based on the chemical problems. Some of the data points are gathered from journals on a yearly basis, while others are gathered after various computational studies such as DFT and molecular dynamics simulation. Databases may be classified into four kinds based on where the data points are acquired: (i) data from publications, (ii) data from simulations, (iii) laboratory databases, and (iv) public databases.

b) Feature engineering/Feature development

The dataset was statistically evaluated once it was collected and selected to get early insights into several descriptors (or features) and the target variable. A basic statistical study, on the other hand, would be insufficient. As a result, feature engineering is crucial in the field of ML. It is the job of developing feature sets for ML applications, with an emphasis on how to construct features that match the data's properties and the application context. Feature engineering typically involves feature extraction, selection, and construction. Feature extraction often seeks to lower the dimension of features by some functional mapping, whereas feature creation is used to increase the original feature space. Pearson's correlation coefficient, which is represented by Equation 9.1, is often used to determine the degree of association between the various descriptors/features.

$$PCC = \frac{\sum (x_i - \bar{x})(y_i - \bar{y})}{\sqrt{\sum (x_i - \bar{x})^2 (y_i - \bar{y})^2}} \tag{9.1}$$

where x_i, y_i are variables in the sample and $\bar{x}, \bar{y}$ are mean variables of x, y, respectively.

Figure 9.4 shows visualization of descriptor correlation in the form of a plot. These data correspond to the descriptors considered for the methane reforming using Ni-catalyst. The descriptors include methane feed, reaction temperature, Ni loading, reaction time, pore size, pore volume, surface area, peak temperature, Ni particle size, modifier electronegativity, and gas hourly space velocity (GHSV).

In this plot, one observes that those features that have high correlation coefficient show interdependency. For example, the temperature and reaction time have a considerable interdependency with a positive correlation of 0.25. Surface area and pore size show coefficient values of 0.64, which shows both are interdependent.

Furthermore, the goal of feature selection is to reduce features by focusing selection of important features. Selection of features is the process of creating feature subsets by removing irrelevant or unnecessary characteristics from the initial feature set, which helps to simplify the model and reduce overfitting while increasing model performance. Figure 9.5 shows different types of feature selection for selecting target features. One can calculate relative variable importance and further select the target feature [5]. In this case, the researchers have taken metal content (active phase), catalysis promoter 1 content (PR1), covalent radius of metal, electronegativity of promoter 1, molecular weight of support, S_{BET}, calcination time (CD), calcination temperature (CT), gas hourly space velocity (GHSV), temperature (T),

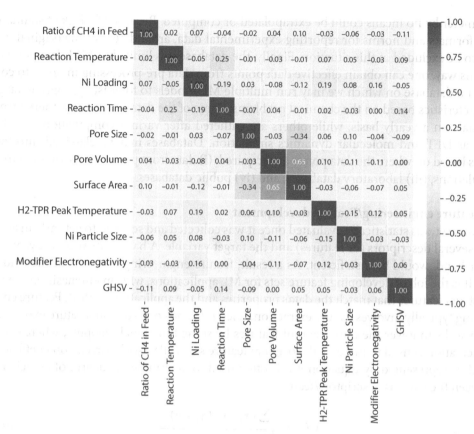

Figure 9.4 Correlation matrix with correlation coefficients. Reproduced with permission [6], Copyright 2023, American Chemical Society.

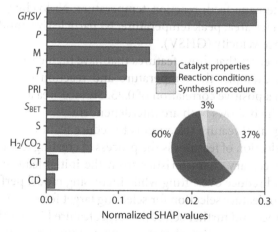

Figure 9.5 Normalized SHAP values shown by horizontal bar charts, indicating the top three characteristics influencing methanol STY. Adapted with permission [5], Copyright 2022, Elsevier.

pressure (P), and H_2/CO_2 as descriptors and calculated normalized SHapley Additive exPlanations (SHAP) values. The SHAP value indicates the dependency of model output characteristic on the features. For example, methanol space time yield (STY) was found to be primarily influenced by three key descriptors, namely, GHSV, pressure (P), and metal content (M). These factors collectively accounted for 60% of the model prediction accuracy.

c) ML Model Generation

After gathering a complete feature set and screening a dataset, the information is used by various ML algorithms to forecast results. These algorithms are used in chemistry for a variety of tasks, including building the quantitative structure–activity relationships, predicting molecular attributes, and forecasting chemical reactions. One may use ensemble learnings, either supervised or unsupervised, depending on the sort of dataset that was available (*vide infra*).

One of the vital concepts used in ML model generation is hyper parametrization. Let us not confuse hyperparameters with parameters. The parameters refer to the internal configuration model of a given system. The establishment of parameters is a crucial aspect in the process of making predictions. Let us assume a simple linear regression equation, y = m. x + c, where x, y, m, and c are the independent variable, dependent variable, slope, and y-intercept, respectively. In this example, m and c are two parameters for fitting a line. These parameters are internal to the model and dependent on the dataset. Some examples are coefficient in regression and weights in support vector machine.

Hyperparameters refer to the parameters that are explicitly defined to regulate the training process. For the model to be optimized, hyperparameters are crucial. These factors are externally driven to the model. These are independent of the dataset. A specialized user in ML will manually establish these. Some of the examples are train–test split ratio, number of epochs, and k value in KNN [7] (*vide infra*).

d) Model Evaluation Matrices

After generating all various ML models, we must find the most effective model among them. Assessing the efficacy of an ML model constitutes a crucial stage in the development of a proficient ML model. Various metrics are employed to assess the performance or quality of a model, commonly referred to as performance metrics or evaluation metrics. The utilization of performance metrics enables us to comprehend the efficacy of different models in relation to the provided data. By adjusting the hyperparameters, it is possible to enhance the performance of the model. We discussed several commonly used matrices for evaluating models, which include (i) accuracy, (ii) root mean square error (RMSE), (iii) R^2, (iv) mean absolute error (MAE), and (v) K-fold cross-validation.

i) Accuracy

Accuracy can be mathematically expressed as the ratio between the number of correct predictions and the overall number of input samples. The measure of Classification Accuracy is indeed impressive; however, it may lead to a misleading perception of attaining a high level of accuracy. We can represent accuracy as follows.

$$Accuracy = \frac{No.s \ of \ correct \ predictions}{Total \ no.s \ of \ predictions} \qquad (9.2)$$

ii) RMSE

RMSE is a widely accepted metric for evaluating the accuracy of a model's predictions of numerical data. The square root term gives the advantage of showing large variances. It avoids using absolute values. Outlier values have a significant impact on RMSE. Equation 9.3 represents the RMSE.

$$RMSE = \sqrt{\frac{1}{n}\sum_{i=1}^{n}(y_i - \check{y}_i)^2} \qquad (9.3)$$

where n is total number of observations, $y_i, \check{y}_i, \bar{y}_i$ are the predicted value, observed value, and average value of $\check{y}_i$, respectively.

iii) R²

In the context of a regression analysis, the R^2 metric indicates the proportion of the variability observed in a given dependent variable that can be explained by the independent variables included in the model. The R^2 formula involves a comparison between the residual sum of squares and the total sum of squares.

$$R^2 = \frac{\sum_{i=1}^{n}|y_i - \check{y}_i|}{n} \qquad (9.4)$$

iv) MAE

MAE is a statistical indicator that calculates the arithmetic mean of the absolute differences between the predicted values and the actual values. The metric provides an indication of the degree of deviation between the forecasted values and the observed results. It is mathematically represented by the following equation:

$$MAE = 1\frac{\sum_{i=1}^{n}(y_i - \check{y}_i)^2}{\sum_{i=1}^{n}(y_i - \bar{y}_i)^2} \qquad (9.5)$$

v) K-Fold Cross-Validation

Cross-validation is a method utilized to assess the effectiveness of a model by training it on a portion of the input data and subsequently testing it on a distinct input data subset that has not been previously observed. The K-fold cross-validation methodology involves partitioning the input dataset into K

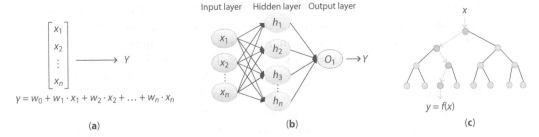

Figure 9.6 Schematic representation of common ML approaches, including (a) linear regression, (b) ANN with one hidden layer, and (c) random forest. Adapted with permission [8], Copyright 2020, American Chemical Society.

subsets of samples with uniform sizes. In ML terminology, the samples are known as fold. For every learning set, K-1 prediction function is used and the remaining other folds are test set. Subsequently, the fit model should be fitted to the training set and its performance need to be evaluated on the test set.

9.3 ML Basic Concepts

ML approaches may be classified in several ways based on the method used for solving practical problems. On the basis of algorithm, the ML can be categorized into regression, classification, SVMs, ANNs, RF, and numerous decision tree (DT) methods. Three common methods that demonstrate the different methodologies of ML are shown in Figure 9.6.

i) **Regression**
   The goal of regression algorithms is to create a function that maps the input variable(s) (x) to the output variable, which might be a discrete or continuous number (y). The output variable often reflects a quantity, size, or strength and can be either an integer or a floating-point number. It is a predictive model that explains the dependent variables in terms of independent variables. Forecasting the IC_{50} values of a drug, the concentration of the drug that reduces enzymatic reaction velocity to half of its original activity, against a target enzyme based on the molecular structure of the target protein is an example of a regression. The outputs of regression analysis are quantitative.

ii) **Artificial Neural Network**
   ANNs draw inspiration from the structure and function of the human brain. The human brain comprises a complex network of specialized cells known as neurons. The neuron (nodes) is considered the fundamental computational entity of neural networks, including the human brain. Neurons receive input, undergo processing, and subsequently transfer the processed information to other neurons located within the various invisible layers of the network. This process continues until the processed output ultimately reaches its output layer. At its most basic level, an ANN comprises primarily of three distinct layers, namely, the input, output, and hidden layer. Neural networks draw inspiration from the structure and function of the neurons

in the human brain. The concept of neuron is considered the fundamental computational component of neural networks. The basic element of computational neuron is called perceptron. Each perceptron is composed of a set of input variables, associated weights, and bias. The weighted sum of products of variables and associated weights is added to a bias, which is translated into binaries by an activation function. Neurons in the first layer receive input, undergo processing, and transmit the processed information to other neurons situated within the various hidden layers of the network. This process continues until the processed output is conveyed to the output layer. At its most basic level, an ANN comprises solely of three layers, namely, the input layer, the output layer, and a hidden layer (Figure 9.7).

A variation in neural network model is deep learning neural networks, which are differentiated from ANN based on their depth, which refers to the number of hidden layers they possess. A deep neural network is a neural network with several hidden layers and numerous nodes in every hidden layer. Typically, the process of training them requires a greater amount of time. Compared to ANN, their accuracy is superior. Deep learning neural network applied for the water–gas shift (WGS) reaction is depicted in Figure 9.7a, which has two hidden layers. Layer 1 contains six nodes whereas layer 2 contains only two nodes. In this case, reaction rate was the output and 27 experimental descriptors were used as input. The optimal neural work structure is generally achieved through an evaluation of the prediction accuracy across various structures using cross-validation procedures (i.e., MSE). Figure 9.7b shows the deep neural network-based ML approach for prediction of water oxidation catalysts made of nickel, iron, cobalt, and cerium. It has four input layers of features related to material composition, two hidden layers each consisting of six nodes, and one node output layer target variable (e.g., overpotential at 10 mA cm^{-2} current density).

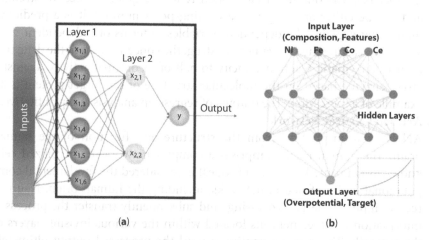

Figure 9.7 (a) The basic architecture of the neural network used for the prediction of catalytic activity. Reproduced with permission [9], Copyright 2020, Elsevier. (b) Artificial neural network consisting of four input nodes that are features, two layers that are hidden with six nodes each, and a single output node that represents the target. Reproduced with permission [7], Copyright 2019, American Chemical Society.

iii) Random Forest

The RF algorithm is a popular ML method that is widely applied to address classification and regression problems. RF is built on the notion of ensemble learning, or simply ensemble of DTs, which is the process of combining several classifiers to solve a complicated issue and improve the model's performance. DTs generate a set of rules based on if–then conditions and then use these rules to produce a prediction. A certain number of trees are constructed using a random set (or training set) of input variables, and the average output of these trees is used to make the final decision/prediction. The hyperparameters, number of trees (n-tree) and number of data points in the nodes (node size), for optimization of the RF model are obtained using cross-validation procedures (e.g., K-fold cross-validation). An RF model was created to forecast CO_2 conversion based on 23 characteristics such as catalyst qualities, method of preparation, and reaction conditions [10].

Yet, another classification distinguishes various learning algorithms and categorizes them either as (a) Supervised or (b) Unsupervised learning algorithm.

a) Supervised Learning

As we all know, supervised learning is one of the most popular ML learning methodologies. The idea behind this learning is to label training data.

It is utilized when someone wishes to forecast a specific result for a given input and samples of input and output pairings are already available. In the language of chemistry, input data are occasionally referred to as descriptors or features while their known outcomes are referred to as labels or targets. Therefore, to get the accurate predictions for new input data, we can train the algorithm.

For a better grasp, mathematically, it can be shown as a linear function $y = f(x)$. While y denotes the outputs and x denotes the inputs, the ML algorithm will try to fit the optimal mapping function f to the data provided by the user. Figure 9.8 represents schematics in how the supervised model is used to process labeled data to obtain the output. The outputs of this may be quantitative (classification) and qualitative (regression) depending on the user's output data.

Suppose we have a dataset of organic molecules of different functional group that includes alcohols, amines, and alkenes. The first step is that one should train the model for each molecule. If the given molecules have a double bond, -OH, $-NH_2$ group, then it will be labeled as alkenes, alcohols, and amines, respectively. After training, one can use test data to test the model and identify the functional groups. Thus, the machine is already trained for the functional group; when a new data set is fed, it can predict the output.

Constructing a model that predicts the binding affinity of a CO_2 molecule against a specific catalyst on the basis of their respective chemical structures, which are represented with molecular fingerprints, is an illustration of supervised learning in action. In this case, the molecular fingerprints are considered to be the input, while the binding affinity is considered to be the output.

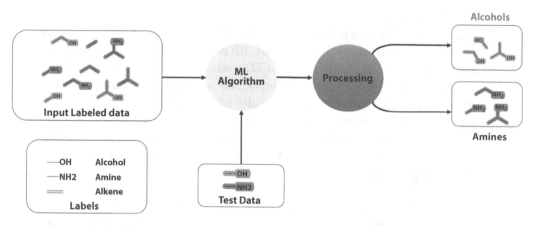

Figure 9.8 Schematics illustration of supervised learning.

b) Unsupervised Learning

Unsupervised learning is a subfield of ML in which the algorithms are given input data that do not include any labels or classifications. The goal of unsupervised learning algorithms primarily focuses on categorizing or grouping the unsorted information based on resemblance patterns and distinctive features. Machines have been instructed to discover invisible trends in the input dataset. In comparison with supervised ML, unsupervised learning is used for more complex jobs since we do not have any labeled input data. Therefore, it is inherently more difficult to comprehend supervised learning and sometimes the results might be less accurate. Figure 9.9 represents the schematics on how an unsupervised model is used to process unlabeled data to obtain the output.

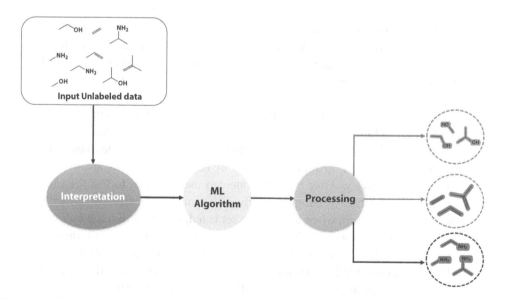

Figure 9.9 Schematics illustration of unsupervised learning.

Unsupervised leaning can be further classified into two categories: (i) Clustering and (ii) Dimensionality reduction.

i) Clustering

Clustering is a method of categorizing entities into clusters based on their degree of similarity, whereby entities with the highest degree of similarity are grouped together, while those with little or no similarity are placed in separate clusters. Cluster analysis is a method that identifies commonalities among data points and classifies them based on the presence or absence of these commonalities.

The K-Means clustering algorithm is under unsupervised learning methods. It facilitates the segregation of data into unique clusters, offering a practical approach of recognizing groups within an unlabeled dataset without requiring any form of instructions. The algorithm in question is *"based on centroids"*, whereby a centroid is assigned to each cluster. The principal aim of this algorithm is to minimize the overall sum of distances between each datum and its corresponding cluster. The K-Means method is simple to grasp and implement. K-Means clustering is computationally efficient and can handle huge datasets with high dimensionality. K-Means clustering may be easily modified to a variety of applications. The method is sensitive to the initial selection of centroids and outliers, which can have a major influence on the resultant clusters. Before performing the method, the number of clusters K must be determined, which might be difficult in some cases. One of the best methods to find the number of clusters is known as the K-elbow method. The K-elbow method is a technique used to determine the optimal number of clusters (K) in a dataset for clustering algorithms such as K-Means. For standardized data, the potential range of K values is considered and within-cluster sum of squares (WCSS) or sum of squared distances between data points and their centroid within each cluster is calculated. Then, an elbow curve is plotted in between K and the corresponding WCSS. One can see a decreasing trend in the WCSS as K increases, which appears to be "elbow". The optimal K value is usually located at the elbow, where the decrease in WCSS starts to level off significantly.

ii) Dimension Reduction

Dimensionality refers to the quantity of features, parameters, or columns that are present within a particular dataset. Dimensionality reduction refers to the technique of decreasing the number of features or dimensions in a given dataset while preserving the maximum amount of information. This may be done for diverse purposes, including simplifying a model, enhancing the efficacy of the algorithm for learning, or facilitating the visualization of data. The most common dimension reduction algorithms are PCA, LDA, and t-SNE.

PCA is a method of statistics utilized to decrease the dimensionality of an extensive dataset. PCA can be employed in feature selection to identify the most significant variables within a given dataset. PCA is a technique employed in data compression to decrease the dimensions of a dataset while retaining its crucial information. The utilization of this approach is widespread in various domains of chemistry such as chemometric sensing [11] and morphological/conformational classification of small molecules [12].

LDA is a supervised learning technique utilized in ML for the purpose of classification tasks. It is a method for determining the optimal linear combination of attributes for separating classes in the data set. The LDA methodology operates by performing a projection of the data onto a space with fewer dimensions, which is optimized to enhance the distinction between the various classes. The process involves identifying a collection of linear discriminants that optimize the ratio of inter-class variance to intra-class variance. It is most commonly used to process the large dimensional chemometric sensor array data (e.g., an array of spectral data or electrochemical/electrocatalytic data) to classify the analytes into their respective categories [11, 13].

The t-distributed Stochastic Neighbor Embedding (t-SNE) is a nonlinear method of reducing dimensionality that is particularly appropriate for projecting high-dimensional data into a lower-dimensional space, usually two or three dimensions, with the aim of facilitating visualization. The t-SNE algorithm is distinct from PCA in that it prioritizes the preservation of small pairwise distances or local similarities, while PCA focuses on preserving large pairwise distances to optimize variance.

9.4   ML Models in Catalysis

The integration of ML techniques is becoming more prevalent in hybrid research programs that combine computational and experimental approaches in the field of catalysis. The utilization of ML techniques in the field of catalysis contributes to the development of improved models, enhanced comprehension of catalysis research, and the generation of novel insights pertaining to catalysis. Figure 9.10 shows examples of industrially important catalysis reactions, CO_2 reduction reaction (CO_2RR), oxidative coupling of methane

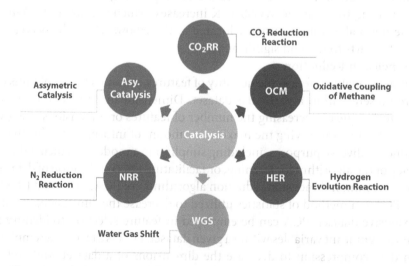

Figure 9.10 Illustration of various types of catalysis.

(OCM), hydrogenation evolution reaction (HER), WGS reaction, nitrogen reduction reaction (NRR), and asymmetric catalysis, which have been studied using the Machine Learning Model to gain deeper insights. One can use ML for prediction of target feature, selection of reaction of parameters, choice of suitable solid support, and active metal for a catalytic reaction.

Table 9.1 shows some of the recent work that has used the ML model to analyze various kinds of catalytic reactions. The various ML algorithms used and the expanded abbreviations are provided in the table footnote. It is important to note that gaining meaningful insight from a catalytic reaction or predicting target values, either single or multiple leaning algorithms, can be used. The choice of the model for a particular analysis depends on its fidelity which has to be judged by scores obtained from cross-validation process.

Table 9.1 Various catalysis using different ML models with evaluation matrices.

Topic	Data set	Features	Train:Test	ML model	RMSE train	RMSE test	R2 train	R2 test	Reference
CO$_2$ methanation	4051	23	(80:20)	RF	6.4	12.7	0.95	0.87	Ref. [10]
Direct catalytic CO$_2$ hydrogenation to methanol	698	-	(80:20)	CO$_2$ conversion					Ref. [14]
				MLR	7.14	6.44	0.42	0.51	
				LASSO	6.27	10.4	0.46	0.25	
				RR	7.14	6.44	0.42	0.51	
				SVR	5.31	9.82	0.63	0.27	
				GPR	2.05	9.21	0.94	0.41	
				RFR	2.06	3.06	0.95	0.87	
				GBRT	5.72	5.69	0.66	0.64	
				ANN LM	2.6	4.08	0.93	0.66	
				ANN BR	2.29	4.12	0.94	0.82	
				MeOH selection					
				MLR	24.15	24.8	0.26	0.24	
				LASSO	25.21	26.1	0.18	0.21	
				RR	24.15	24.8	0.26	0.24	
				SVR	9.78	16.4	0.88	0.65	
				GPR	10.67	13.5	0.85	0.79	
				RFR	6.06	9.9	0.95	0.88	
				GBRT	15.32	13.5	71	0.76	
				ANN LM	11.56	13.6	0.83	0.74	
				ANN BR	6.05	13.2	0.95	0.77	

(Continued)

Table 9.1 Various catalysis using different ML models with evaluation matrices. (*Continued*)

Topic	Data set	Features	Train:Test	ML model	RMSE train	RMSE test	R2 train	R2 test	Reference
Thermo-catalytic CO_2 hydrogenation to methanol	1201		(85:15)	RF	0.08	-	0.97	0.84	Ref. [5]
				GBT	0.09	-	0.97	0.82	
				XGB	0.09	-	0.98	0.88	
CO_2 reduction electrocatalysts	1060	18	(80:20)	KNR	0.3185	-	0.635	-	Ref. [15]
				RFR	0.1876	-	0.873	-	
				TPOT	0.2659	-	0.789	-	
				SVR	0.3098	-	0.654	-	
				GBR	0.1964		0.861	-	
Forecast water oxidation catalysts	665	4	(70:30)	SVR	-	-	0.79771	0.7256	Ref. [7]
				KNN	-	-	0.76043	0.6836	
Methane dry reforming	1638	-	(80:20)	RF	0.064	-	0.865	-	Ref. [6]
				GBR	0.057	-	0.892	-	
				CatBoost	0.053	-	0.909	-	
Water–gas shift reaction	4360	4	(90:10)	LASSO	-	19.11	--	0.048	Ref. [16]
				RR	-	18.58	-	0.077	
				GPR	-	15.53	-	0.272	
				SVR	-	16.91	-	0.295	
				RFR	-	10.01	-	0.701	
				ETR	-	9.55	-	0.715	
				GBR	-	9.56	-	0.715	

Note: MLR—Multi-Linear Regression, LASSO—Least Absolute Shrinkage Selection Operator, GPR—Gaussian Process Regression, RR—Ridge Regression, SVR—Support Vector Regression, KNR—K-Nearest Neighbor Regression, RF—Random Forests, Random Forest Regression, GBR—Gradient Boosting Regression, GBT—Gradient Boosting Decision Trees, ETR—Extra Tree Regression, GBRT—Gradient Boost Random Forest Regression, CatBoost—Categorical Tree Regressor, TPOT—Tree-Based Pipeline Optimization Tool, ANN—Artificial Neural Network.

For example, the first entry in the table corresponds to the CO_2 conversion and has exclusively used RF because it has a high R^2 value for both test and training set. Other cases were studied using multiple ML models. Some of the models have provided high R^2 values and other methods have not. However, one must be cautious that sometimes good R^2 obtained for a given data set does not mean that the model is good as the resulting R^2 value could be due to overfitting of the data. Nevertheless, it becomes routine practice to compare the relative performance of the models to avoid erroneous conclusions. RMSE values can also be used to evaluate a model; the smaller the RMSE score, the better is the model.

Results shown in the first entry of Table 9.1 are associated with 4051 data points from 100 published papers. The results of basic descriptive statistics indicate that Ni is the predominant active metal employed in CO_2 methanation catalysts, typically with a Ni loading range of 5–25 wt%. To ensure an optimal catalyst design, it is important to take into account the influence of support materials and preparation methods [10].

The process of converting carbon dioxide into other useful compounds via chemical or biological processes is referred to as CO_2 conversion. The process of converting CO_2 to methanol directly presents advantages in terms of both economic and environmental aspects when compared to traditional methods. Optimization of reaction parameters for this process is important in the context of sustainability. Entry two of the Table 9.1 data was associated with the direct hydrogenation of CO_2 to give methanol. In this case, Pallavi Vanjari *et al.* developed seven different ML algorithms to get a deeper insight into the catalytic activity and selectivity towards methanol. The term "methanol selectivity" refers to the capacity to generate methanol as the intended output in a chemical reaction or conversion procedure. The GBRT and ANN models exhibited superior performance compared to other ML models, as evidenced by their high R^2 values for both conversion and selectivity to methanol. Out of 19 features, the significant inputs identified for these models were catalyst composition and calcination temperature. These studies have revealed that the utilization of a solid solution catalyst composed of $ZnO-ZrO_2$ and a nickel-gallium catalyst exhibit encouraging outcomes in terms of achieving elevated methanol selectivity and stability [14].

In an effort, as noted entry three of Table 9.1, to aid the advancement of thermo-catalytic CO_2 hydrogenation into methanol, a set of ML frameworks has been developed to forecast catalyst performance from experimental descriptors. In this venture, the researchers gathered a database of 1425 data points from Pd-, Cu-, $ZnO-ZrO_2$-, and In_2O_3-based catalysts and created reliable ensemble tree models to predict methanol STY using 12 descriptors and 1201 effective data. The model prediction and insights were validated empirically. These models may be used for different catalytic processes as a tool for supervised testing and optimization [5].

Entry four of Table 9.1 is related to the application of the XGBR method in view of accelerating the investigation of electrocatalysts for CO_2 reduction. This model accurately predicted the Gibbs free energy shift of CO adsorption (ΔG_{CO}) for 1060 atomically scattered metal–nonmetal co-doped graphene systems, resulting in considerable cost savings. The competing reaction of hydrogen evolution reaction (HER) was also considered in the model. This work highlights the potential of ML approaches and provides a practical strategy for the efficient theoretical design of CO_2 reduction electrocatalysts [15].

The next important class of catalysts are water oxidation catalysts. Water oxidation catalysts are materials or chemicals that, in the presence of an energy input (such as light or electricity), accelerate the oxidation of water to produce oxygen gas (O_2) and protons (H^+). They are critical components in water splitting processes that aim to create clean, renewable hydrogen fuel. Water splitting is an important stage in artificial photosynthesis and electrolysis because it separates water into its essential elements, hydrogen (H_2) and oxygen (O_2). Water oxidation catalysts offer the catalytic activity required to accelerate the oxidation half-reaction, allowing for the release of oxygen gas. Scientists are continually researching and developing novel water oxidation catalysts with increased efficiency, stability, and abundance. The objective is to develop low-cost, environmentally benign catalysts that can enable large-scale water splitting for long-term hydrogen generation. Regina Palkovits *et al.*

used existing data on catalysts for water oxidation as the foundation for training diverse ML models, including ANNs, support vector regression, and k-nearest neighbor regression (entry five of Table 9.1). The article elucidates the application of ML in the prediction of water oxidation catalysts. The researchers imported and pre-processed two datasets utilizing commonly employed libraries such as NumPy, matplotlib, pandas, and seaborn for the purpose of visualization. Subsequently, the datasets underwent a size and dimensionality verification process, whereby the smaller dataset requires modification to conform to the larger dataset [7].

Methane dry reforming, also known as carbon dioxide reforming of methane or CO_2 reforming, is a chemical process that includes the simultaneous reaction of methane (CH_4) and carbon dioxide (CO_2) to create synthesis gas (CO and H_2). The process of methane dry reforming holds significant importance in the realm of carbon dioxide utilization and sustainable synthesis gas production. The utilization of methane and carbon dioxide, both greenhouse gases, presents a viable means of generating valuable products such as syngas. This syngas can serve as a precursor for the production of diverse chemicals and fuels. The application of ML models has the potential to forecast the performance of catalysts in methane dry reforming reactions [6]. Keerthana Vellayappan *et al.* gathered data (entry six of Table 9.1) from a previously published experiment and refined the features by using SHAP values. The analysis of feature importance in these models can provide insights into the impact of various catalyst properties on the syn-gas proportion and reactant conversions. The size of Ni particles has the potential to serve as a means of regulating the syngas ratio, irrespective of the prevailing process operating conditions.

The last entry in the Table 9.1 data is associated with the WGS reaction. The WGS reaction is a two-step process involving sequential reactions. The initial chemical process is commonly referred to as the low-temperature shift (LTS) reaction, which can be expressed as the reaction between water vapor and carbon monoxide to yield carbon dioxide and hydrogen gas, as follows: $CO + H_2O \rightarrow CO_2 + H_2$. The subsequent chemical process is known as the high-temperature shift (HTS) reaction, which can be denoted as $CO_2 + H_2 \rightarrow CO + H_2O$. The low-temperature shift (LTS) reaction exhibits a preference for lower temperatures, typically in the range of 200–300°C, whereas the high-temperature shift (HTS) reaction is observed to take place at elevated temperatures, typically in the range of 300–450°C. The WGS reaction finds extensive application in various industrial processes, including but not limited to ammonia production, hydrogen production for fuel cells, and gasification of coal or biomass. Hence, understanding the process is crucial in sustainable economy. The employed ML methodology takes into account elemental features as input representations, rather than the compositions of the catalysts. The research effectively identifies a novel catalyst for prospective investigation. The article delves into the difficulties associated with employing ML techniques in the field of catalysis informatics. Additionally, the authors explored the potential advantages of solving the gap between simple descriptor-based screening methodologies and complicated real-world models. The researcher extracted 163 data points from a reported dataset of 4360 experimental data points on the WGS reaction [16]. These data points had reaction temperatures below 150°C and were analyzed using the ML method. The authors gave examples to show the value of our ML technique, which uses elemental properties and Sorted Weighted Elemental Descriptor (SWED) representations as input representations rather than catalyst compositions. The extra tree regression (ETR), which is a form of tree ensemble technique, exhibited superior predictive capabilities in relation to CO conversion during the WGS reaction with an RMSE test value of 9.55. Moreover, our ML models rely on the SWED representation, which utilizes a limited set of descriptors including electronegativity (EN), density, enthalpy of formation(ΔH_{fus}), and surface energy (SE).

9.5 ML in Structure–Activity Prediction

The utilization of classification and regression models is a viable approach in the identification of the most favorable active sites for catalytic reactions. ML algorithms have the great potential to decrease the number of Density Functional Theory (DFT) calculations required for screening purposes, which are computationally expensive and time-consuming. The application of ML models has been demonstrated to facilitate the prediction of catalyst properties, thereby enabling the acceleration of the discovery process for new catalysts through high-throughput virtual screening (HTVS). The integration of DFT and ML techniques can expedite the identification of catalysts that exhibit greater chemical diversity and enhanced activity. Furthermore, it is significant that models trained on just structural features or electronic structural characteristics can still exhibit satisfactory performance in specific situations. However, it is notable that a model with a lower accuracy may still be adequate for the purpose of discovering a few active catalysts from a bigger set. A simple example for the use of ML model to understand the catalytic active site is the graphite-conjugated catalysts (GCCs) (Figure 9.11). The process of training ML models to detect active sites in graphite-conjugated catalysts (GCCs) can involve the utilization of both structural and electronic characteristics [17]. The ML algorithm has predicted that carbon atoms located ortho or para to nitrogen and positioned at the periphery of aromatic systems exhibit a greater tendency to participate in the binding of O_2 and catalyze the onset of the oxygen reduction reaction (ORR). Carbon atoms oddly spaced from nitrogen are more

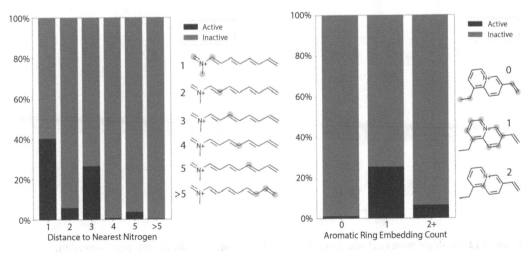

Figure 9.11 Active site prediction of GCC based on structural entity Reproduced with permission [17], Copyright 2023, American Chemical Society.

active in comparison to evenly spaced molecules that contain an aromatic ring and have more active sites, as shown in Figure 9.11.

Although DFT calculations have gained popularity and are considered a reliable tool within the scientific community, their ability to predict catalytic reactions is constrained by the intricate nature of catalytic structures and inherent inaccuracies. Atomic simulations offer appealing features such as global optimization techniques and Markov chain theory-driven methods, which enable the identification of the most robust frameworks and the most energy-efficient reaction pathways. Dongxiao Chen *et al.* reviewed atomistic simulations for exploring structures using grand canonical Monte Carlo (GCMC) with QM calculation. Herein, they studied automated search for optimal surface phases (ASOP) algorithms for finding best catalytic surface, and the AI-Cat algorithm for predicting the kinetics of heterogeneous catalytic processes where the reaction network is too complex to resolve [18].

The utilization of ML has emerged as a favorable approach to accelerate the exploration of electro-catalysts for CO_2 reduction reaction (CO_2RR) owing to its cost-effectiveness. The process of discovering catalysts with the assistance of ML involves the use of features engineering, ML methods, and target properties. Graph neural network (GNN) models, which

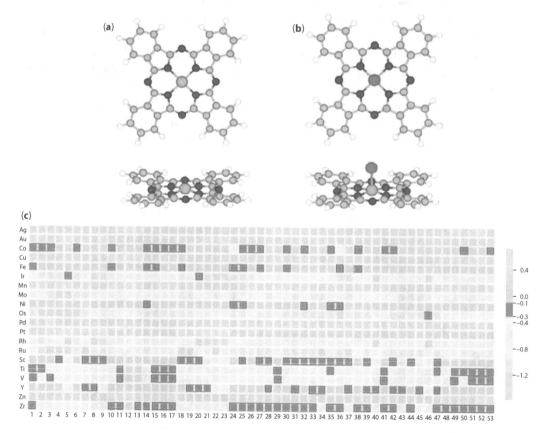

Figure 9.12 (a) Single-atom catalysts, (b) dual-metal-site catalyst. Reproduced with permission [20], Copyright 2021, American Chemical Society. (c) ΔG_{CO} on various SACs with efficient filtration of potential candidates. Reproduced with permission [15], Copyright 2020, American Chemical Society.

incorporate atomic interactions, have significantly enhanced the modeling capacity of CO_2 reduction reaction (CO_2RR) [19]. However, these models necessitate a substantial quantity of data. Erhai Hu *et al.* reviewed recent research on discovery of pure metal, intermetallic, and single atom catalyst (SAC) using the ML model. Figure 9.12a, b shows phthalocyanine containing single metal atom and di- or bi-metal atom (DMC) catalysts. The metal atoms used in SAC and DMCs are Ti, Cr, Mn, Fe, Co, Ni, Cu, Zr, Mo, Ru, Rh, Pd, Ag, W, Ir, Pt, and Au. The heat map for change in Gibbs free energy for the carbon monoxide adsorption (ΔG_{CO}) for 1060 designed single-atom catalyst (SAC) materials, consisting of 20 transition metal atoms and 53 distinct nonmetal bonded structures, is depicted in Figure 9.12c. The outcomes were anticipated based on the set of features. The heat map depicted in Figure 9.12c enables the efficient filtration of potential materials through the identification of distinct blue colors, which have ideal ΔG_{CO} (-0.2 ± 0.1 eV) for catalysis. The horizontal axis denotes various kinds of structures, while the vertical axis represents the 20 transition metals. From the heat map, Co, Fe, Ir, Ni, Os, Sc, Ti, V, Y, and Zr metal doping SACs are found as potential candidates.

The surface reactivity of metal alloys can be accurately predicted within a wide chemical space through the use of a chemisorption model that has been augmented with ML. The use of ANNs that are trained with *ab initio* energies of adsorption and electronic fingerprints of an idealized bimetallic surfaces has the capability to accurately capture complex and non-linear interactions of adsorbates on multi-metallics is depicted in Figure 9.13a. The adoption of an integrated approach significantly simplifies the process of screening catalysts at a high-throughput rate. This approach also indicates the potential of {100}-plane terminated multi-metallic alloys, which exhibit enhanced efficiency and selectivity, for the electrochemical reduction of CO_2 to C_2 species [21]. As shown in Figure 9.13b, among all the possible Cu-based alloys, $Cu_3Y–Ni@Cu_{ML}$ and $Cu_3Sc–Ni@Cu_{ML}$ are found to have the most desired CO adsorption energies.

Utilization of Smooth Overlap Atomic Position (SOAP), a multidimensional structural descriptor, for the purpose of evaluating the similarity between the local surroundings encompassing molecules, solids, or surfaces is explained by Jinnouchi *et al.* The reported study describes the utilization of SOAP in the anticipation of relaxed surface energies and intermediate reactions based on their unrelaxed atomic geometries. It provides a comprehensive explanation of the methodology employed for the formation energies of bulk materials and surfaces and highlights the connection between the method mentioned earlier and

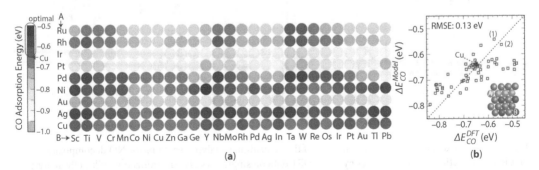

Figure 9.13 (a) CO adsorption energy on the second-generation core-shell alloy surfaces (Cu_3B-A@Cu_{ML}). (b) Prity plot shows a comparison of the CO adsorption energies on selected Cu monolayer alloys. Reproduced with permission [21], Copyright 2015, American Chemical Society.

the force field generation technique, wherein the energy is forecasted based on the corresponding geometry. The direct breakdown of NO on the Rh-Au alloy nanoparticles (NPs) was predicted by Jinnouchi *et al.* with the use of an ML-based Bayesian linear regression approach. This method makes use of a local similarity kernel, which makes it possible to investigate catalytic activities based on local atomic configurations. Figure 9.14 illustrates this concept. Using data from DFT calculations performed on single crystals, the proposed technique is able to accurately estimate the binding energies of atoms and molecules with the NPs as well as the formation energies of the NPs [22]. This study provides a comprehensive insight into the active site structures and catalytic activities that are dependent on the size and composition of the catalyst.

Apart from modeling the electronic structures and binding energies for reactant–catalyst interaction, understanding the importance of pore volumes is crucial for heterogeneous catalysis and gas storage. The utilization of computational screening techniques has the potential to identify highly appealing candidates for zeolite catalysts, which can effectively reduce carbon dioxide emissions [23]. To achieve maximum product formation per unit volume of material, it is necessary to have an optimal cavity size of approximately 6 Å, which allows for the greatest change in entropy–enthalpy during adsorption. Additionally, a void space of at least 30% is required. The application of virtual screening presents an economical and rapid approach to preliminarily evaluate potential candidates before starting on the process of synthesis.

The next important area in catalysis is the catalysts developed for fuel cells. Oxygen evolution reaction (OER) is important in the biological and synthetic energy harvesting process. Transition metals such as Ni, Co, and Fe are most promising for OER. Xue Jiang *et al.* proposed a data-driven strategy to predict the OP for (Ni-Fe-Co) Ox catalysts using ML. To explain the correlation between the features and target (i.e., OP), 13 different ML models were used, and among them, RF regression performs better. First ionization energies (FIE) and outermost d-orbital electron number (DE) are important features that are easily accessible. Figure 9.15 shows that the variance of FIE and DE has a linearly decreasing correlation with overpotential [24].

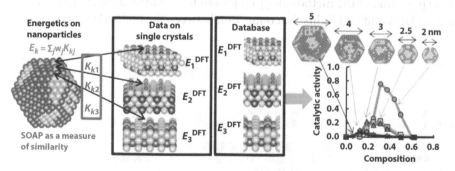

Figure 9.14 The diagrammatic representation of the algorithm. Catalytic reactions for NO decomposition predicted energetics on nanoparticles by using DFT data on single crystals. The utilization of kinetic analysis provides comprehensive insights into the active-site structures and catalytic activities that are dependent on the size and composition of the system. Reproduced with permission [22], Copyright 2017, American Chemical Society.

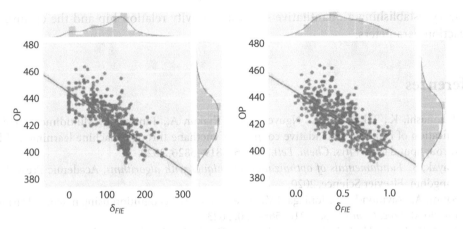

Figure 9.15 Overpotential as a function of δ_{FIE} and δ_{DE}. Reproduced with permission [24], Copyright 2022, American Chemical Society.

Certain predictive models combine cheminformatics and ML algorithms to forecast the selectivity of chiral catalysts, which are used to produce single mirror-image isomers in chemical manufacturing. Previously, the selection of catalysts has been based on empirical methods. However, this novel approach involves the creation of an extensive *in silico* library of potential catalysts and the computation of reliable chemical descriptors. Subsequently, a training set that is universally applicable is chosen based on both steric and electronic characteristics. ML techniques such as SVM and deep NN are then employed to develop predictive models with a high degree of accuracy across a wide spectrum of selectivity space. The method has been demonstrated by the researchers through the use of chiral phosphoric acid-catalyzed thiol addition to N-acylimines [25].

Apart from the choice of catalysts, the solvent and other parameters such as pressure, temperature, ion/electrolyte concentration, etc. play a crucial role in catalysis. The process of choosing a solvent for chemical reactions can be automated using a hybrid mechanistic ML method, improving reaction results, and providing new physical insights. In one particular example, in order to develop surrogate models that could predict conversion rates with a cross-validation correlation value of 0.84, molecular descriptors were calculated for a library of 459 solvents. The strategy outlined in this study has the potential to boost productivity and cut costs in actual process development workflows for solvent selection for asymmetric catalysis [26].

9.6   Conclusion and Future Works

In this chapter, we have introduced the basic aspects of ML models and their predictive power in catalysis. These models have the potential to be used as a basis for the creation of novel material systems, classification, feature extraction, and performance evaluation of catalysts. It is imperative to note that the application of such model to make accurate prediction towards catalysis is still in the infancy stage. However, the creation of more databases, the availability of databases in open-source platforms, and providing methods employed as tutorials can motivate researchers to use such models to accelerate the process of catalyst discovery, establishing a quantitative structure–activity relationship and the optimization of reaction parameters.

References

1. Takahashi, K., Takahashi, L., Nguyen, T.N., Thakur, A., Taniike, T., Multidimensional classification of catalysts in oxidative coupling of methane through machine learning and high-throughput data. *J. Phys. Chem. Lett.*, 11, 16, 6819–6826, 2020.

2. Nayak, S., *Fundamentals of optimization techniques with algorithms*, Academic Press, United Kingdom, Elsevier Science, 2020.

3. Salim, A., Raymond, L., Moniaga, J.V., General pattern recognition using machine learning in the cloud. *Proc. Comput. Sci.*, 216, 565–570, 2023.

4. Yang, P., Zhang, H., Lai, X., Wang, K., Yang, Q., Yu, D., Accelerating the selection of covalent organic frameworks with automated machine learning. *ACS Omega*, 6, 27, 17149–17161, 2021.

5. Suvarna, M., Araújo, T.P., Pérez-Ramírez, J., A generalized machine learning framework to predict the space-time yield of methanol from thermocatalytic CO_2 hydrogenation. *Appl. Catal. B Environ.*, 315, 121530, March 2022.

6. Vellayappan, K. *et al.*, Impacts of catalyst and process parameters on Ni-catalyzed methane dry reforming via interpretable machine learning. *Appl. Catal. B Environ.*, 330, 122593, March 2023.

7. Palkovits, R. and Palkovits, S., Using artificial intelligence to forecast water oxidation catalysts. *ACS Catal.*, 9, 9, 8383–8387, 2019.

8. Yang, W., Fidelis, T.T., Sun, W.-H., Machine learning in catalysis, from proposal to practicing. *ACS Omega*, 5, 1, 83–88, Jan. 2020.

9. Smith, A., Keane, A., Dumesic, J.A., Huber, G.W., Zavala, V.M., A machine learning framework for the analysis and prediction of catalytic activity from experimental data. *Appl. Catal. B Environ.*, 263, May 2019, 118257, 2020.

10. Yılmaz, B., Oral, B., Yıldırım, R., Machine learning analysis of catalytic CO2 methanation. *Int. J. Hydrogen Energy*, 48, 1–11, 2023.

11. Rout, B., Unger, L., Armony, G., Iron, M.A., Margulies, D., Medication detection by a combinatorial fluorescent molecular sensor. *Angew. Chem. Int. Ed.*, 51, 50, 12477–12481, 2012.

12. Selvakumar, K. and Singh, H.B., Adaptive responses of sterically confined intramolecular chalcogen bonds. *Chem. Sci.*, 9, 35, 7027–7042, 2018.

13. Indherjith, S. and Selvakumar, K., Combining cross-reactivity of an electrode array with the selective thiol reporting process of redox indicators: Targeted sensing of biothiols. *Anal. Methods*, 10, 29, 3602–3615, 2018.

14. Vanjari, P., Kamesh, R., Rani, K.Y., Machine learning models representing catalytic activity for direct catalytic CO_2 hydrogenation to methanol. *Mater. Today Proc.*, 72, 524–532, 2023.

15. Chen, A., Zhang, X., Chen, L., Yao, S., Zhou, Z., A machine learning model on simple features for CO_2 reduction electrocatalysts. *J. Phys. Chem. C*, 124, 41, 22471–22478, 2020.

16. Mine, S. *et al.*, Machine learning analysis of literature data on the water gas shift reaction toward extrapolative prediction of novel catalysts. *Chem. Lett.*, 51, 3, 269–273, 2022.

17. Lodaya, K., Ricke, N.D., Chen, K., Van Voorhis, T., Machine learning identification of active sites in graphite-conjugated catalysts. *J. Phys. Chem. C*, 127, 5, 2303–2313, 2023.

18. Chen, D., Shang, C., Liu, Z.P., Machine-learning atomic simulation for heterogeneous catalysis. *NPJ Comput. Mater.*, 9, 1, 1–9, 2023.

19. Hu, E., Liu, C., Zhang, W., Yan, Q., Machine learning assisted understanding and discovery of CO_2 reduction reaction electrocatalyst. *J. Phys. Chem. C*, 127, 2, 882–893, 2023.

20. Wan, X. *et al.*, Machine-learning-accelerated catalytic activity predictions of transition metal phthalocyanine dual-metal-site catalysts for CO2 reduction. *J. Phys. Chem. Lett.*, 12, 6111–6118, 2021.
21. Ma, X., Li, Z., Achenie, L.E.K., Xin, H., Machine-learning-augmented chemisorption model for CO_2 electroreduction catalyst screening. *J. Phys. Chem. Lett.*, 6, 18, 3528–3533, 2015.
22. Jinnouchi, R. and Asahi, R., Predicting catalytic activity of nanoparticles by a DFT-aided machine-learning algorithm. *J. Phys. Chem. Lett.*, 8, 17, 4279–4283, Sep. 2017.
23. Thornton, A.W., Winkler, D.A., Liu, M.S., Haranczyk, M., Kennedy, D.F., Towards computational design of zeolite catalysts for CO_2 reduction. *RSC Adv.*, 5, 55, 44361–44370, 2015.
24. Jiang, X., Wang, Y., Jia, B., Qu, X., Qin, M., Prediction of oxygen evolution activity for NiCoFe oxide catalysts via machine learning. *ACS Omega*, 7, 16, 14160–14164, 2022.
25. Zahrt, A.F., Henle, J.J., Rose, B.T., Wang, Y., Darrow, W.T., Denmark, S.E., Prediction of higher-selectivity catalysts by computer-driven workflow and machine learning. *Sci. (80-.)*, 363, 6424, 1–11, 2019.
26. Amar, Y., Schweidtmann, A.M., Deutsch, P., Cao, L., Lapkin, A., Machine learning and molecular descriptors enable rational solvent selection in asymmetric catalysis. *Chem. Sci.*, 10, 27, 6697–6706, 2019.

Classification of Livestock Diseases Using Machine Learning Algorithms

G. Hannah Grace[1], Nivetha Martin[2]*, I. Pradeepa[2] and N. Angel[2]

[1]Division of Mathematics, School of Advanced Sciences, VIT University, Chennai, India
[2]Department of Mathematics, Arul Anandar College (Autonomous), Karumathur, India

Abstract
Machine learning has become an important necessity in the field of medicine in humans as well as in animals. The professionals in healthcare diagnose medical illnesses using machine learning algorithms (MLAs). Classifiers have now become a very useful tool for the healthcare industry to diagnose and classify diseases based on the intensity of the disease. This chapter proposes a solution to the problem of mastitis disease diagnosis in cattle based on MLAs. The mastitis livestock disease, which is an infection in the mammary gland mostly prevailing in the rural regions of the Madurai district of Tamil Nadu state, is intensively studied in this chapter. The supervised classification algorithms such as support vector machine, logistic regression, decision tree, and naïve Bayes are used in the Python environment to categorize the mastitis disease into three classes, namely, clinical, subclinical, and chronic, based on the symptoms. The efficiency of the algorithms is analyzed based on the results, and the most promising algorithm is identified to be a decision classifier based on the accuracy of the classification.

Keywords: Support vector machine, logistic regression, decision tree, livestock disease

10.1 Introduction

Classification of livestock diseases using machine learning algorithms is a promising approach to automate disease diagnosis and improve animal health. The process involves collecting data on different symptoms, signs, and laboratory findings associated with various diseases affecting livestock animals. These data are then used to train machine learning models that can accurately classify the diseases. Machine learning algorithms are extensively used in the field of disease diagnosis. The applications of these algorithms ease the process of diagnosing and classification of diseases in comparison with the biological diagnosis methods. In the era of artificial intelligence, the intervention of such machine learning-based diagnosis methods gives rise to hybrid testing methods that are slowly replacing the existing conventional methods of diagnosis. Supervised, Unsupervised, and

Corresponding author: nivetha.martin 710@gmail.com

Arindam Dey, Sukanta Nayak, Ranjan Kumar and Sachi Nandan Mohanty (eds.) How Machine Learning is Innovating Today's World: A Concise Technical Guide, (127–138) © 2024 Scrivener Publishing LLC

Reinforcement are the three major kinds of machine learning algorithms. In the supervised type of machine learning, the training occurs with labeled datasets. The functioning principle of this supervised machine learning (SML) algorithm is to map the input data with output data. In SML, the datasets are characterized by both features and labels. Regression and Classification are the two main types of SML.

Regression is a technique that helps in determining the degree of relationship between dependent and independent variables. There are different kinds of regression among which linear regression is commonly used. Linear regression is one of the simplest kinds of SML used to find the relationship between the dependent and independent variables, which are of continuous type. The linear regression is simple if the input is single and multiple in the case of many inputs. The best line of fit that classifies the data is determined. Classification-based algorithms are primarily used to handle categorical data and determine the category of the datasets in the output phase. Classification of data is based on labels of three types, namely, binary, multi-class, and multi-label. The number of classes in the binary class is two, and in case of multi-class, it is many. The output in case of multi-label classification is also many. These classification algorithms are applied in spam detection, disease classification, identification, speech recognition, etc. Linear and non-linear models are the two major kinds of classification-based algorithms.

Logistic regression and support vector machines (SVMs) belong to the sub-categories of linear classification models. Logistic regression is also one of the most commonly used SML algorithms applied in making predictions based on categorical variables. Logistic regression though similar to linear regression differs from the implications of probabilistic values using logistic functions. SVMs intend to determine the optimal hyperplane that separates the datasets. SVM is grouped into two types, viz, linear and non-linear, in which the former handles linearly supervised data and the latter treats non-linearly supervised data.

Some of the most generally used non-linear classification models are KNN, naïve Bayes, decision trees, and random forest. KNN (K nearest neighbor) algorithm is a kind of non-parametric algorithm. It works on the principle of similarity measures between the new data point and the available datasets. Despite the algorithm being robust, one of the complexities of this algorithm is finding the value K. Naïve Bayes algorithm is a probabilistic classifier most dominantly used in text classification requiring very high dimensionality of data. In this type of algorithm, the augmentation of features is independent. Decision trees algorithm are graphical representations with root node as the beginning point, internal node as the features of datasets, branches as decision rules, and the leaf node as outcome. The decision tree gets expanded based on the features and its association with the data points. Random forest works on the principle of ensemble learning and it combines several decision trees. This works in two phases in which the formation of decision trees takes place in the first phase and the occurrences of predictions happen in the second phase. Thus, the SML algorithms are primarily applied in classification types of problems.

In unsupervised machine learning, the datasets are not labeled and the large group of data is handled. Clustering and association are the two major kinds of unsupervised machine learning (UML). The method of clustering is a grouping technique of data based on the existence of likeliness among the data points. In the association kind of technique, the rules are determined to find the relationship between the dependent and independent variables.

There are several kinds of unsupervised learning algorithms such as K-means clustering, KNNs, hierarchial clustering, neural networks, principal component analysis, and many others. Although the unsupervised learning algorithms help in handling unlabeled data, it is still difficult to make precise decisions from the output obtained.

Reinforcement learning is primarily based on feedback, and it also deals with unlabeled datasets. Positive and negative reinforcement are the two main types of reinforcement learning. This is purely based on a trial-and-error process. In general, three different approaches based on values, policies, and models are used in making sequential decisions. Among the three types of machine learning algorithms, supervised learning algorithms are highly preferred to make decisions on classifications.

The algorithms of classification are predominantly used in medical diagnosis to classify the diseases based on either primary or secondary data. In this chapter, the classification algorithms are applied to classify the livestock diseases. The livestock sector provides a significant contribution to GDP of a nation and it also highly supports the livelihood of the rural community. One of the never-ending challenges of this sector is handling fatal livestock diseases as a failure of early detection causes adverse effects on livestock productivity. Mastitis disease is one of the most dreadful livestock diseases, and this disease is classified into three classes based on the identification of symptoms. The contents of this chapter are organized into the following sections: Section 10.2 consists of the literature review of the selected supervised learning algorithms in livestock disease classification, Section 10.3 sketches the materials and methods, Section 10.4 details the application of these algorithms in disease classification, and Section 10.5 discusses the results and concludes the chapter.

10.2 Literature Review

This section encompasses the review of works of SML classifiers of logistic regression, decision trees, linear discriminant analysis (LDA), Gaussian naïve Bayes, and SVM in classification of livestock diseases with special reference to mastitis disease. The machine learning algorithms are applied by various researchers in mastitis diagnosis in cattle: Mahmood et al. [1], Fadul et al. [2], Singh et al. [3], Ghosh et al. [4], Abdul et al. [5], and Srivalli et al. [6] in prediction of clinical Mastitis disease, and Zhang et al. [7] and Esener et al. [8] in evaluation. The deep learning algorithms are also applied to make inferences in disease diagnosis. To mention a few, Ankitha et al. [9], Kaur et al. [10], and Ma et al. [11] have applied integrated and advanced deep learning algorithms in predicting mastitis disease. The SVM is applied by Mammadova et al. [12], Miekley et al. [13], and Bobbo et al. [14] in predicting subclinical mastitis. Ewes [15], Hyde et al. [16], Motohashi et al. [17], Singh et al. [18], and Tian et al. [19] applied SVM in detection of clinical mastitis.

Logistic regression classifier is used in detecting the presence of mastitis. Researchers such as Kitade et al. [20], Grodkowski et al. [21], Sinha et al. [22], Mestav et al. [23], and Ozturk et al. [24] have applied the logistic regression classifier in predicting and diagnosing the mastitis disease. Altay et al. [25] have used multivariate adaptive regression splines. The non-linear regression models are also used in diagnosis. Decision trees algorithms are also applied in predicting mastitis disease. Anand et al. [26] applied fine decision trees in predicting subclinical mastitis. Coatrini et al. [27] used decision tree models. These decision trees are used in combination with other machine learning algorithms. Nie et al. [28]

have integrated logistic regression with decision trees. Montazeri *et al.* [29] have integrated SVM with decision trees. Researchers have also applied naïve Bayes algorithm to detect the mastitis disease, such as Zhou *et al.* [30] and Zhou *et al.* [31]. Artificial neural networks and recurrent neural networks are also applied in mastitis diagnosis. Kaur *et al.* [32] applied IOT-based learning algorithms in disease diagnosis. Tanyildizl *et al.* [33] have applied several machine learning algorithms in predicting the diagnosis of mastitis disease especially clinical.

From the literature review, the following shortcomings are identified:

- The SML algorithms are applied only in diagnosis of the mastitis disease.
- The diagnosis of subclinical and chronic stages of mastitis using machine learning algorithms is not investigated to the best of our knowledge.
- The classification of mastitis disease is not explored by the researchers.

This has motivated the authors to apply the conventional supervised classifiers to classify the mastitis disease into clinical, subclinical, and chronic stages. The identification of the disease based on the stages using supervised classifiers is the novel part of this chapter.

From the literature works, it is evident that these classifiers are not applied together in classifying mastitis disease. This has motivated the authors to apply these supervised classifiers to classify the mastitis disease into three classes.

10.3   Materials and Methods

This section presents the definition of the problem, objectives, and the steps that are most commonly applied in making decisions using supervised classifiers.

10.3.1   Definition of the Problem

This section addresses the problem of classifying the mastitis disease, which is one of the challenging hurdles of livestock industries located in rural regions. This disease highly affects the mammary glands and in consequence the milk productivity is poorly affected. The unidentified symptoms of this disease makes the prediction of this disease more complicated. Since this disease is also classified into three different stages based on the intensity of the symptoms, the identification of the disease stages at an early stage is also essential. The following questions need to be answered:

(i) Why are the rural livestock industries focused on?
(ii) Why are the supervised classifiers used for the data based on rural livestock?

The livestock industries situated in urban regions make use of both biological testing methods and computer-based testing methods in identifying and classifying mastitis disease. However, the rural livestock industries are quite not exposed to such kind of advanced techniques and they are subjected only to conventional testing methods. These traditional diagnosing methods do not yield very precise results and henceforth these techniques have to be integrated with computer-based diagnosing testing processes, but such processes are also expensive, which prevents rural-based livestock industries from using them. This has motivated the authors to apply the SML classifiers to the disease data of mastitis. Based on the accuracy of the decision models, the best classifier shall be selected and applied to the disease data in making precise decisions. The supervised classifiers are more compatible and elegant in drawing required conclusions.

10.3.2   Objectives

The fundamental objective of this work is to apply the supervised classifiers to categorize the stages of Mastitis diseased livestock. The optimal classifier is selected to classify the stages of the disease based on the input attributes to the new data points. The diagnosis process is facilitated with the integration of both clinical records and machine learning algorithms.

10.3.3   Data Collection

The data collected for this research work are from the rural areas of Usilampatti block of Madurai district of Tamil Nadu. This is one of the rural areas consisting of socially and economically disadvantaged people. The primary occupations are farming and livestock rearing, and there are many livestock industries located in and around the villages of the study area. The data on the livestock especially dairy cattle are collected from the veterinary practitioners working in veterinary hospitals and clinics. The presence of all three kinds of this mastitis disease is most common. The basic attributes based on which the data are collected are furnished in Table 10.1.

10.3.4   Data Preprocessing

The data collected from different sources are preprocessed with data cleaning by eliminating multiple data entries, handling of redundancy, and missing data points. Medical experts

Table 10.1 Data attributes.

Attribute name	Type	Attribute domain values
Age	Continuous	Age in years
Temp	Discrete	Temperature
Milk yield	Discrete	0-Normal and 1-low
Udder redness	Discrete	0-No and 1-Yes
Udder swelling	Discrete	0-No and 1-Yes
Udder hardness	Discrete	0-No and 1-Yes
Appearance of the milk	Discrete	0-Normal, 1–watery, 2-flakes, 3-clots
Sunken eyes	Discrete	0-No and 1-Yes
Diarrhea	Discrete	0-No and 1-Yes

Table 10.2 Sample data.

gh	age	temp	milkyield	udderredness	udderhardness	udderswelling	app	se	diarrohea	class	class_label
0	8	100	1	1	1	1	1	1	1	clinical	1
1	10	113	1	1	1	1	1	1	1	subclinical	2
0	14	100	1	1	1	1	1	1	1	clinical	1
1	7	110	1	1	1	1	2	1	1	subclinical	2
0	18	101	1	1	1	1	1	1	1	clinical	1

are also involved in the process of preprocessing data to derive optimal results. In addition to the medical experts, the experts in the field of machine learning are also involved to fine-tune the data fitting the requirements of different SML classifiers. A sample of the dataset is given in Table 10.2.

The class labels of the dataset are as indicated below as in Figure 10.1. It contains three labels such as clinical, subclinical, and chronic.

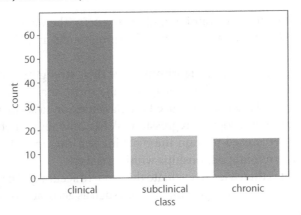

Figure 10.1 Class labels of the data set.

A scatter matrix of each input variable was described to learn more about the data.

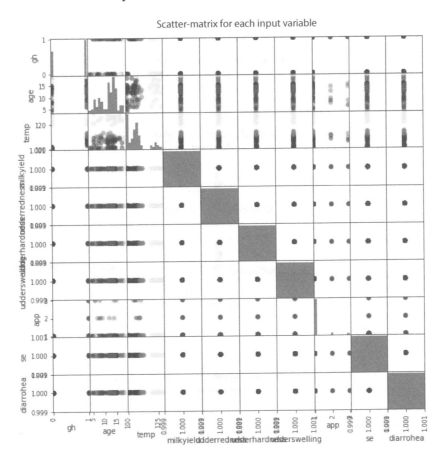

10.3.5　Steps Involved in Supervised Learning Classifiers

- The first step is to collect and preprocess the data. Here, the data related to livestock diseases, such as symptoms, test results, and other relevant information, are collected. The data are then cleaned and standardized, removing any duplicates or errors. The data should also be labeled according to the disease category it belongs to.
- Next, split the data into training and testing sets. The data are divided into two sets, one for training the machine learning model and one for testing its accuracy.
- Different machine learning algorithms have their strengths and weaknesses, so it is essential to select the appropriate algorithm that fits the problem at hand. Some popular algorithms used for classification tasks include decision trees, random forests, logistic regression, SVMs, and neural networks.
- The training set is used to train the machine learning model, allowing it to learn the patterns and relationships within the data.
- The testing set is then used to evaluate the model's accuracy. The performance of the model can be assessed using metrics such as accuracy, precision, recall, and F1 score.
- Once the model's accuracy is acceptable, it can be deployed to classify new data. The following Figure 10.2 presents the flow chart of the steps.

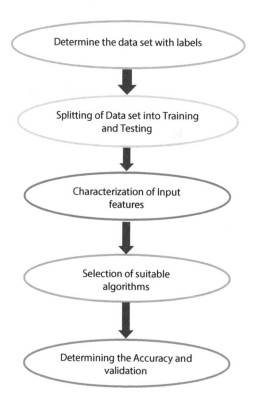

Figure 10.2　Flow chart of supervised learning classifiers.

10.4   Application of the Supervised Classifiers in Disease Classification

The different SML classifiers such as logistic regression, decision trees, LDA, Gaussian naïve Bayes, and SVM are applied to determine the accuracy of classification in the Python environment.

Supervised learning classifiers are a type of machine learning algorithm that can be trained to predict the class or category of an input based on a set of labeled examples. The process of supervised learning involves presenting the algorithm with a training dataset consisting of input features and their corresponding class labels. The algorithm learns to generalize from these examples and can then be used to predict the class label of new, unseen inputs.

In logistic regression, the input features are first weighted by a set of coefficients, and then combined to form a linear function. This linear function is then passed through a logistic (or sigmoid) function, which maps the linear output to a value between 0 and 1. This value represents the predicted probability of the input belonging to the positive class. During training, the logistic regression algorithm adjusts the coefficients to minimize the difference between the predicted probabilities and the true class labels in the training dataset. This is typically done using an optimization algorithm such as gradient descent.

Decision trees are a popular type of classifier that works by recursively splitting the data into smaller subsets based on the values of the input features. At each split, the algorithm chooses the feature that best separates the data into its respective classes.

For classification problems, the algorithm then takes a majority vote of the labels of the KNNs to determine the predicted class for the input. For regression problems, the algorithm takes the average of the labels of the KNNs as the predicted value for the input.

One important parameter in KNN is the value of K, which determines the number of neighbors to consider when making a prediction. A smaller value of K can result in a more flexible model that is better able to capture local patterns in the data, but may also be more sensitive to noise in the data. A larger value of K can result in a smoother decision boundary, but may be less able to capture local patterns.

SVMs are a type of linear classifier that work by finding the hyperplane that best separates the data into its respective classes. SVMs can also be used with non-linear kernels to handle more complex data.

Naïve Bayes classifier is based on Bayes' theorem and assumes that the features are conditionally independent. Naïve Bayes is commonly used for text classification and spam filtering.

In LDA, the input features are first projected onto a lower-dimensional subspace that maximizes the separation between the classes. This is done by finding the directions (or linear discriminants) that maximize the ratio of the between-class variance to the within-class variance. The resulting subspace can then be used to transform new inputs into a lower-dimensional representation that is more informative for classification.

During training, LDA estimates the class means and covariances of the input features, and uses these estimates to compute the projection matrix that maximizes the separation between the classes. This can be done using techniques such as eigendecomposition or singular value decomposition.

Table 10.3 Supervised classifiers.

Supervised classifiers	Accuracy	
	Training	Testing
Logistic Regression	0.82	0.76
Decision Trees	**1.00**	**0.96**
KNN	0.91	0.80
Gaussian Naïve Bayes	0.55	0.76
Support Vector Machine	0.80	0.72
Linear Discriminant Analysis	0.92	0.92

The respective packages are used and the accuracy of classification based on training and testing data is presented in Table 10.3

From Table 10.3, it is observed that the decision trees classifier yields better accuracy in comparison with other classifiers.

10.5   Results and Conclusion

We can infer from the provided accuracy scores that the decision tree classifier, followed by LDA and KNN, has the highest accuracy in testing data. While both logistic regression and the SVM perform well on training data, they perform less well on testing data, which may be a sign of overfitting. In both training and testing data, Gaussian naïve Bayes (GNB) has the lowest accuracy ratings.

However, in order to choose the appropriate classifier for our issue, we should not just rely on accuracy ratings. Other elements like computational effectiveness, interpretability, and the particular specifications of our challenge are things we should also take into account. To get more reliable results, cross-validation and hyperparameter adjustment are also advised.

Hence, this chapter concludes that the decision classifiers result in more optimal results of mastitis disease classification. The above results shall be validated with other datasets of livestock diseases. Overall, the use of machine learning algorithms for livestock disease classification has the potential to improve animal health, reduce treatment costs, and increase productivity in the livestock industry. However, it is important to ensure that the data used to train the models is representative and unbiased to avoid any errors in diagnosis.

References

1. Mahmood, A.S. and Hamed, T.Y., Machine learning based–system for prediciting mastitis in dairy cows, in: *2022 8th International Conference on Contemporary Information Technology and Mathematics (ICCITM)*, 2022, August, IEEE, pp. 197–201.

2. Fadul-Pacheco, L., Delgado, H., Cabrera, V.E., Exploring machine learning algorithms for early prediction of clinical mastitis. *Int. Dairy J.*, *119*, 105051, 2021.

3. Singh, P., Sharma, R., Kumar, V., Prediction of clinical mastitis in dairy cows using ANN. *J. Pharm. Negat. Results*, 3655–3665, 2022.

4. Ghosh, S. and Dasgupta, R., Machine learning in the study of animal health and veterinary sciences, in: *Machine Learning in Biological Sciences: Updates and Future Prospects*, pp. 251–259, Springer Nature Singapore, Singapore, 2022.

5. Abdul Ghafoor, N. and Sitkowska, B., MasPA: A machine learning application to predict risk of mastitis in cattle from AMS sensor data. *AgriEngineering*, *3*, 3, 575–583, 2021.

6. Srivalli, M.R., Vishnu, N.K., Kanchana, V., Teat and udder disease detection on cattle using machine learning, in: *2022 International Conference on Signal and Information Processing (IConSIP)*, 2022, August, IEEE, pp. 1–5.

7. Zhang, S., Su, Q., Chen, Q., Application of machine learning in animal disease analysis and prediction. *Curr. Bioinf.*, *16*, 7, 972–982, 2021.

8. Esener, N., Implementation of machine learning for the evaluation of mastitis and antimicrobial resistance in dairy cows, Doctoral dissertation, University of Nottingham, 2021.

9. Ankitha, K., HManjaiah, D., Kartik, M., Sustainable integration of deep learning and internet of animal health things to predict clinical mastitis in cows. *J. Green Eng.*, *10*, 9263–9280, 2020.

10. Kaur, D. and Kaur, A., IoT and machine learning-based systems for predicting cattle health status for precision livestock farming, in: *2022 International Conference on Smart Generation Computing, Communication and Networking (SMART GENCON)*, pp. 1–5, IEEE, 2022, December.

11. Ma, Y., Liu, B., Guan, J., Zhang, Y., Research on dairy cow mastitis based on conductance method and weighted deep forest, in: *Proceedings of the 2021 5th High Performance Computing and Cluster Technologies Conference*, pp. 13–19, 2021, July.

12. Mammadova, N. and Keskin, I., Application of the support vector machine to predict subclinical mastitis in dairy cattle. *Sci. World J.*, *2013*, 2013.

13. Miekley, B., Traulsen, I., Krieter, J., Mastitis detection in dairy cows: The application of support vector machines. *J. Agric. Sci.*, *151*, 6, 889–897, 2013.

14. Bobbo, T., Matera, R., Pedota, G., Manunza, A., Cotticelli, A., Neglia, G., Biffani, S., Exploiting machine learning methods with monthly routine milk recording data and climatic information to predict subclinical mastitis in Italian Mediterranean buffaloes. *J. Dairy Sci.*, *106*, 3, 1942–1952, 2023.

15. Ewes, S.D., Application of support vector machines as support to early prediction of mastitis in.

16. Hyde, R.M., Down, P.M., Bradley, A.J., Breen, J.E., Hudson, C., Leach, K.A., Green, M.J., Automated prediction of mastitis infection patterns in dairy herds using machine learning. *Sci. Rep.*, *10*, 1, 1–8, 2020.

17. Motohashi, H., Ohwada, H., Kubota, C., Early detection method for subclinical mastitis in auto milking systems using machine learning, in: *2020 IEEE 19th International Conference on Cognitive Informatics & Cognitive Computing (ICCI* CC)*, 2020, September, IEEE, pp. 76–83.

18. Singh, P., Sharma, R., Kumar, V., Prediction of clinical mastitis in dairy cows using ANN. *J. Pharm. Negat. Results*, 3655–3665, 2022.

19. Tian, F., Wang, Z., Yu, S., Xiong, B., Wang, S., Clinical mastitis detection by on-line measurements of milk yield, electrical conductivity and deep learn. *J. Phys.: Conf. Ser.*, 1635, 1, 012046, 2020, November.

20. Kitade, Y., Tsukano, K., Miyamoto, Y., Suzuki, K., Mastitis causes negative reproduction performance similar to genital diseases. *Res. Vet. Sci.*, 153, 35–44, 2022.

21. Grodkowski, G., Szwaczkowski, T., Koszela, K., Mueller, W., Tomaszyk, K., Baars, T., Sakowski, T., Early detection of mastitis in cows using the system based on 3D motions detectors. *Sci. Rep.*, 12, 1, 21215, 2022.

22. Singha, S., Koop, G., Ceciliani, F., Derks, M., Hoque, M.A., Hossain, M.K., Persson, Y., The prevalence and risk factors of subclinical mastitis in water buffalo (Bubalis bubalis) in Bangladesh. *Res. Vet. Sci.*, 158, 17–25, 2023.

23. Mestav, B., Assessment of the relationship between the postpartum diseases susceptibility and the bovine monocyte subsets via Bayesian logistic regression, under various prior distributions. *Res. Vet. Sci.*, 145, 1–12, 2022.

24. Öztürk, I., Analysis of the effects of some ecological factors on udder health by using nonlinear regression models. *Appl. Ecol. Environ. Res.*, 20, 1, 285–299, 2022.

25. Altay, Y., Phenotypic characterization of hair and honamli goats by using classification trees algorithms and multivariate adaptive regression splines (mars).

26. Anand, M.J., Sridhar, V., Ravi, R., Application of fine decision tree machine learning algorithm to predict the subclinical mastitis in cow milk using prototype E-nose, in: *Emerging Research in Computing, Information, Communication and Applications: ERCICA 2020, Volume 2*, Springer Singapore, pp. 695–702, 2022.

27. Coatrini-Soares, A., Coatrini-Soares, J., Neto, M.P., de Mello, S.S., Pinto, D.D.S.C., Carvalho, W.A., Mattoso, L.H.C., Microfluidic E-tongue to diagnose bovine mastitis with milk samples using machine learning with decision tree models. *Chem. Eng. J.*, 451, 138523, 2023.

28. Nie, J., Fang, J., Zhao, Y., Cow health prediction method based on logistic regression and decision tree, in: *2022 34th Chinese Control and Decision Conference (CCDC)*, pp. 3712–3717, IEEE, 2022, August.

29. Montazeri Najafabadi, M. and Bahreini Behzadi, M.R., Detection of Calving interval trait using decision tree and support vector machine methods in Holstein dairy cows. *Vet. Res. Biol. Prod.*, 34, 3, 99–106, 2021.

30. Zhou, X., Xu, C., Wang, H., Xu, W., Zhao, Z., Chen, M., Huang, B., The early prediction of common disorders in dairy cows monitored by automatic systems with machine learning algorithms. *Animals*, 12, 10, 1251, 2022.

31. Zhou, W., Yang, K., Zeng, J., Lai, X., Wang, X., Ji, C., Li, Y., Zhang, P., Li, S., FordNet: Recommending traditional Chinese medicine formula via deep neural network integrating phenotype and molecule. *Pharmacol. Res.*, 173, 105752, 2021, https://doi.org/10.1016/j.phrs.2021.10575.

32. Kaur, P., Kumar, R., Kumar, M., A healthcare monitoring system using random forest and internet of things (IoT). *Multimed. Tools Appl.*, 78, 19905–19916, 2019, https://doi.org/10.1007/s11042-019-7327-8.

33. Tanyildizl, E. and Yildirim, G., Performance comparison of classification algorithms for the diagnosis of mastitis disease in dairy animals, in: *2019 7th International Symposium on Digital Forensics and Security (ISDFS)*, pp. 1–4, IEEE, 2019, June.

11

Image Enhancement Techniques to Modify an Image with Machine Learning Application

Shiplu Das[1]*, Sohini Sen[2], Debarun Joardar[2] and Gargi Chakraborty[2]

[1]Department of Computer Science and Engineering, Adamas University, West Bengal, India
[2]Department of Computer Science and Engineering, Brainware University, West Bengal, India

Abstract

Image enhancement is important in the field of image processing because it improves image quality by showcasing valuable information and trying to suppress unnecessary facts in the figure. The evolution of image improvement algorithms is examined in this paper. Image enhancement is the procedure of processing a picture to construct it more suitable for a particular application than the actual picture. These strategies have a diverse variety of uses in medical image filtering, such as cancer detection, and the tumor detection goal of image enhancement images with low contrast must be improved. These attempts to measure aided in establishing the spectral and spatial integrity of the reconstructed image. It is necessary to improve picture quality in order to improve these images for human viewing or further analysis. Image contrast enhancement is one technique for improving image quality. There are several techniques for enhancing contrast. Low-contrast images are typically captured in either dark or bright environments. As a result, pre-processing of such images is required to make them suitable for other image processing applications. This is where deep learning comes in. In this paper, we propose an ML-based image enhancement model that modifies an image to improve its visual quality while maintaining its semantic content. Our proposed model employs a deep learning framework, specifically a convolutional neural network (CNN), to learn and apply a set of image transformation filters. These filters are learned from a large dataset of images and can be used to perform various image enhancement operations, such as denoising, contrast adjustment, and color correction. To train our model, we use a combination of supervised and unsupervised learning methods. Specifically, we use a dataset of labeled images to train our CNN to perform specific enhancement tasks, such as increasing the brightness or sharpness of an image. Additionally, we use unsupervised learning techniques, such as autoencoders, to learn a representation of the underlying image features and apply them in the enhancement process. Our experimental results demonstrate that our proposed model outperforms existing image enhancement techniques in terms of visual quality and preservation of semantic content. We also show that our model can be used to enhance images for various machine learning applications, such as object detection and recognition, with improved accuracy and efficiency.

Keywords: Image enhancement, convolutional neural network, supervised learning, unsupervised learning, contrast enhancement, object detection, recognition

*Corresponding author: shiplud63@gmail.com

Arindam Dey, Sukanta Nayak, Ranjan Kumar and Sachi Nandan Mohanty (eds.) How Machine Learning is Innovating Today's World: A Concise Technical Guide, (139–158) © 2024 Scrivener Publishing LLC

11.1   Introduction

Digital image enhancement primarily improves the analysis and interpretability of images for viewers. It is critical in digital image processing. Image enhancement is among the most key technologies in image analysis, with the goal of improving picture quality for various uses [1]. A basic aim of image enhancement overall is to modify an image's data contribution in order to make it more appropriate for a particular application. Electronic devices are now prevalent [2]. In the digital age, digital cameras seem to become standard in handheld devices such as smartphones, Personal Digital Assistants (PDAs), and so on [4]. The creation of rising images from reduced images necessitates the use of better algorithms that are tailored to a specific application and have reasonably good computational power [5–7]. Several of the problems listed above are much more dependent on the quality of the camera's ineffective retention [8]. Only a few could be rectified using sophisticated algorithms [9, 10]. Conventional image enhancement techniques rely heavily on spatial and frequency domain processing [11]. When we use the term "spatial domain" in the image enhancement market, we mean stuff like equalization, smoothing, and sharpening [11, 12]. The spatial domain primarily operates in the following manner: Domain of Space: Input → Image Processing → Output. Frequency domain filters differ from spatial domain filters in that they concentrate on the frequency of the images. It is primarily used for two basic operations: smoothing and sharpening. The frequency domain functions primarily as follows: Frequency Domain: Frequency + Distribution → Image Processing → Inverse Transformation → Output [13]. These enhancement operations are used to change the visual quality, contrast, or gray-level distribution. Gray-level transformations of pixels can be used to improve images at the most fundamental level [14]. In this paper, we provide a comprehensive overview of the advancements in image enhancement technology. We primarily implement image enhancement techniques separately, based on the most recent patterns in image processing. But that is not where the arsenal ends. Deep learning-based image enhancement methods now produce high-quality photos at the state-of-the-art level. The method of boosting an image's resolution is known as super-resolution (SR), and it is one of the most well-liked deep learning-based picture enhancement techniques. High-resolution images are essential for precise evaluation and therapy planning in medical imaging, where SR is especially helpful. The use of SR techniques is also possible in other fields like microscopy, satellite imaging, and surveillance imaging. The fundamental concept behind deep learning-based SR is to use a big collection of paired pictures to teach a neural network to learn the mapping between low-resolution and high-resolution images. A low-resolution image is fed into the neural network, which outputs a high-resolution image. A loss function that calculates the disparity between the generated picture and the high-resolution ground truth image is used to train the network. There are various deep learning-based SR techniques, such as single-image SR, which creates a high-resolution image from a single low-resolution input image, and multi-image SR, which creates a high-resolution image from numerous low-resolution input images. Because it requires extrapolating high-frequency information from a single low-resolution picture, single-image SR is especially difficult. On the other hand, multi-image SR can use the data from numerous low-resolution pictures to produce a high-resolution image with better clarity. The super-resolution convolutional neural network (SRCNN), a well-liked deep learning-based SR technique, employs numerous convolutional layers to learn the mapping between low-resolution and high-resolution images. It has been demonstrated that SRCNN performs at the cutting edge on test datasets like Set5 and Set14. Another well-liked technique is the generative adversarial network (GAN)-based SR, which employs a discriminator network to separate between the produced pictures and the actual images and a generator network to produce high-resolution images. On numerous standard datasets, including the DIV2K dataset, which includes high-resolution images, GAN-based SR has produced remarkable results. The prime goal of this paper is to make a comparative study among all of these image enhancement methods that can give a clear idea about this method and their advantage and disadvantages, so that anybody can get a clear idea by looking at this comparison chart and can also choose methods that can be appropriate and suitable for their works.

11.2   Literature Review

In their paper, Xianxian Luo, Taisheng Zeng, Wei Zeng, and Jianlong Huang proposed a Landsat picture upgrade in light of the partial and essential differential strategies being looked at. Upgrade methods utilized in remote detecting depend on the conventional vital request differential cover administrators, like Sobel, Prewitt, and Laplacian administrators. Different strategies include the partial analytics and general covers utilizing Grünwald-Letnikov with eight directions [1]. Accepting SVM and CNN as specific illustrations, their paper thinks about and investigates the customary AI and profound learning picture char-acterization algorithms [2]. Anwar, S., Khan, S., and Barnes, N discussed lower goals but neglected to zero in on some of the better numerous essential subtleties inside the par-ticular picture or video content, which may be helped by expanding the goal and general nature of the predetermined entity [3]. Zhang, W., Skillet, X., Xie, X., Li, L., Wang, Z., and Han, C examined contrast extending, which is a procedure used to make up for the lack or overabundance of light by expanding the portion of pixel-dark qualities in pictures that are regularly named low contrast [4]. A differentiation upgrade of clinical pictures utilizing Type II fluffy set hypothesis is proposed. Fluffy set hypothesis considers vulnerability as participation capability; however, to have better data on vulnerability on the enrolment capability, Type II fluffy set is thought of [5–8]. This article centers around picture upgrade, with specific reference to various picture combinations and spatial separating strategies. Factual investigation of picture quality measures was utilized for assessing the nature of improved pictures. During the work, picture upgrade was done in two steps [6]. In this paper, the improvement of picture upgrade calculations is studied. The reason for our sur-vey is to furnish pertinent specialists with a thorough and methodical examination on pic-ture upgrade procedures and give them a significant reference [7]. In this paper, we give a far-reaching audit of picture improvement strategies from different perspectives [9–13]. Various picture improvement strategies have been examined in the writing, including con-trast extending, histogram balance, and difference restricted versatile histogram evening out (CLAHE) which do not create exact upgraded pictures and perform ineffectively as far as Root Mean Square Blunder (RMSE), Pinnacle Signal Clamor Proportion (PSNR), and Mean Outright Mistake (MAE) [12]. Pin Wang, En Fan, and Peng Wang explored exam-ination and correlation, and four distinct informational collections are utilized. A brief portrayal of versatile HE is set out, and this system is utilized in a conversation of past ideas for minor departure from HE. A vital element of this formalism is a "cumulation capability," which is utilized to produce a dark-level planning from the nearby histogram. By picking elective types of cumulation capability, one can accomplish a wide assortment of impacts. A particular structure is proposed. Through the variety of a couple of boundaries, the subsequent interaction can deliver a scope of levels of difference improvement, at one instance leaving the picture unaltered, at another yielding full versatile equalization [20–27]. The submerged picture handling region has gotten impressive consideration within the last many years, showing significant accomplishments. In this paper, we audit probably the latest strategies that have been explicitly created for the submerged climate. These strategies are fit for expanding the scope of submerged imaging, further developing picture difference and goal. Subsequent to considering the fundamental material science of the light engendering in the water medium, we center around the various calculations accessible in the writing. The circumstances for which every one of them have been initially evolved are featured as well as the quality appraisal techniques used to assess their performance [28–30].

11.3   Image Enhancement Techniques for Betterment of the Images

There are various types of methods that are used for image enhancement, like contrast stretching, unsharp making, histogram equalization, median filtering, contrast limited enhancement method, super-resolution enhancement, etc. Every method works on image enhancement for transforming low-resolution data into high-resolution data. Here is a brief description of those methods. Contrast stretching is a technique for stretching. the histogram to fill the entire interactive spectrum of the image. Two major contrast stretching techniques are basic stretching contrast and end-in-search. Furthermore, contrast stretching is used to compensate for deficiencies or excess light by expanding the appropriation of pixel-gray values, with images typically classified as low contrast [12], fine contrast or normal contrast, and high contrast [17–19]. The image that has low contrast is distinguished by its predominantly vivid or predominantly inky image structure. Figure 11.1 shows the flow chart of the contract stretching method [12], which shows the working procedure of this method.

The following equation is for the contrast stretching algorithm [20]:

I.   Determine examining the chart to decide the lower bound of pixel categorization from the minuscule dim scale value (0 to 255) to find the first component that outperformed the foreordained cutoff value.

II.   Determine the upper pixel grouping limit by assessing the histogram from the greatest dim scale value to minimal value of the second preset edge.

III.   Pixels with values not exactly as far as possible are given various 0, while pixels with values more prominent than the subsequent limit are given the value of 255.

IV.   Using discrete arithmetic, the pixels between the first and second scaled limit values that fulfill the whole scope of dim scale values (0 to 255).

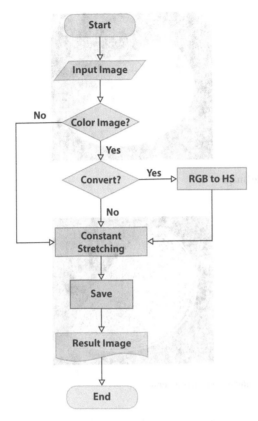

Figure 11.1 Working procedure of the proposed method.

$$s = r\text{-}rmax/(rmin\text{-}rmax) * 255 \qquad\qquad (11.1)$$

where r is the initial image's gray-scale value, s is the new grayscale value, the pixel group's lowest gray scale rmin value, and the pixel group's maximum gray scale rmax value [15–17]. The algorithm begins by analyzing the histogram graph and trying to calculate the maximum and minimum pixel values. The user must then select the desired non-outlier range based on the image's quality [21]. The higher the range, the clearer the image. The set of values or distribution qualities of principles of a given factor that fall in between greater and lesser outer limits is referred to as the non-outlier range. Unsharp masking (UM) is a renowned technique for improving an image's visual quality by emphasizing its high-frequency components, despite the fact that this method is simple to implement [18, 19]. The overall system is more resistant to the presence of noise in the input images than traditional approaches [20]. Unsharp masking subtracts a grainy photo from the authentic image to obtain its edges only, and the result is added to the original image to produce an upgraded version [21]. Subtracting the Gaussian blurred version of the picture from the original picture, for example, generates the following result, which we can see in Figures 11.2–11.4 [22].

Unsharp masks are simply blurred images created by using a Gaussian low-pass filter to temporal and spatial filter the specimen image [22]. This filtration is analogous to

Figure 11.2 Original sample images.

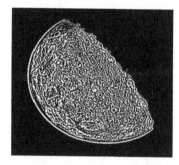

Figure 11.3 Subtracting the Gaussian blurred version.

Figure 11.4 Output images.

performing a convolutions on an image with a firmware mask that is a two-dimensional Gaussian function g (x,y).

$$g(x,y) = \frac{1}{\sigma\sqrt{2\pi}} e^{-(x^2+y^2)/2\sigma^2} \qquad (11.2)$$

In general, expanding the kernel mask roots the Gaussian filter to detach more spatial frequencies from the unsharp input images. Using the following formula, the unsharp mask is subtracted from the original image [23]:

$$F(x, y) = \frac{c}{2c-1} I(x, y) - \frac{(1-c)}{2c-1} U(x, y) \qquad (11.3)$$

F(x, y) connotes the sensitivity value of a component in the separated picture at the direction (x, y), while I(x, y) and U(x, y) comprise the softness upsides of the comparing pixels in the genuine and unsharp cover (obscured) pictures, individually. In the fractional differential condition, the constant c administers the general weightings of the genuine and obscured pictures. A histogram is an unmistakable portrayal of an image's solidarity dissemination. In layman's terms, it addresses the quantity of pixels expected for every power value. At the point when the client gets to in a picture is portrayed by close difference values, this technique for the most part expands the global differentiation [20, 21]. This permits regions with low neighborhood difference to acquire contrast. A computerized picture's histogram, with levels of force going from 0 to (L-1), is a capability,

$$h(rk) = nk \qquad (11.4)$$

where rk is the kth intensity level and nk is the number of pixels in the image with that intensity level. A normalized histogram function is defined as follows for an N × N image [22]:

$$nk/N2 = p(rk) \qquad (11.5)$$

The possibility of a pixel with the intensity level rk is represented by the p(rk) feature. Obviously, p(rk) = 1. The x-axis of a picture's histogram, as shown in the figure, represents the intensity levels rk, and the y-axis represents the h(rk) or p(rk) features. If a picture's whole histogram is centred on the left end of the x-axis, it indicates a dark image. The need to improve image contrast emerges regularly in image processing [24, 25].

Figure 11.5 [24] is the original picture and Figure 11.6 [24] is the picture after using the method where we can see that the object is clear but not realistic and the background is still not clear. Histogram equalization can be used to correct images that appear scrubbed

Figure 11.5 The original sample images.

Figure 11.6 Using the Unsharp Mask method.

Figure 11.7 Mean separation and diminish the force variety between pixels of the image.

out due to a lack of contrast. The light and dark areas of such photographs meld together, resulting in a flatter image devoid of highlights and shadows. The mean filter is one of several methods used to decrease image noise. It is a type of non-linear virtual filtering technique that is constantly used to remove noise from a picture or signal. Such noise removal is a common pre-processing step used to enhance the outputs of subsequent processing. Median filtering is widely used in image processing as it prolongs contours while expelling noise under some conditions, and it also has applications in signal processing [26].

In Figure 11.7 [26] and Figure 11.8 [26], we can see a few distinctions in the wake of utilizing mean separation and diminish the force variety between pixels. This is a nearby averaging activity and perhaps the most essential direct channel. The normal of the nearby area replaces the value of every pixel. In the event that f(i,j) is a boisterous picture, the smoothed picture g(x,y) can be determined as follows [27]:

Figure 11.8 The normal of the nearby area replaces the value of every pixel.

$$g(x, y) = \frac{1}{n}\sum_{(i,j)\in S} f(i,j) \qquad (11.6)$$

where S addresses a neighborhood of (x,y) and n addresses the quantity of pixels in S. Then, just make windows to show both noisy and separate pictures. Mean separation is a basic, natural, and direct strategy for picture smoothing. It is habitually used to diminish picture noise. It additionally decreases the force variety between pixels. In any case, there are a few downsides to utilizing this mean channel [25–27]. For instance, a solitary component with an extremely different value (exception) can prominently influence the mean value of the relative multitude of pixels in its area. CLAHE (Difference Restricted Upgrade) is a versatile histogram balance strategy. It confines the greatest differentiation change that can be made to any neighborhood histogram, which is valuable for keeping the picture highlights from turning out to be excessively noisy. At first, CLAHE was utilized to further develop low-contrast clinical pictures. CLAHE fluctuates from normal AHE in that it lessens contrast [28]. CLAHE divides an input actual image into non-overlapping dependent areas known as sub-images, slabs, or blocks. Figure 11.9 [28] is an underwater fish image that has been made clear in Figure 11.10 [28], but it looks unnatural as it changes the colors with pixels.

Two parameters define the CLAHE: Block Size (BS) and Clip Limit (CL). These two factors are primarily responsible for enhanced image quality. The image becomes brighter as CL is enhanced because the input image has a very low intensity and a larger CL makes its histogram flatter [28–32]. The histogram equalization method has the restriction of not being able to be used in images with a large intensity variation. To address this disadvantage, the Contrast Limited Adaptive Histogram Equalization (CLAHE) algorithm is used in this study.

Figure 11.9 An underwater fish image.

Figure 11.10 Output images using CLAHE.

11.4 Proposed Image Enhancement Techniques

The essential thought behind super-goal is that a low-goal or noisy series of pictures of a scene can be utilized to effectively create a high-goal picture or picture grouping [33]. The standard technique sees low goal pictures to be the consequence of rescaling a general picture. The last step is to retrieve the high-level image [30]. These methods divide super-resolution into two categories: super-resolution from a single frame and super-resolution from multiple frames, i.e., multiple image super-resolution. Figure 11.11 [29] and Figure 11.12 [29] are the before and after scenario of the super-resolution method where a totally blur image has been cleared.

To remove sensor and optical blurring, blur and noise must be removed. These methods divide super-resolution into two categories: super-resolution from a single frame and super-resolution from multiple frames, i.e., multiple image super resolution [26].

Super-goal alludes to the very troublesome working out a high goal (HR) from its low-goal partner. The reproduction of textural subtleties in the result picture is the fundamental test of super-goal [27, 36]. Aside from the vast majority of the techniques depending on limiting the MSE between the result HR picture and the ground truth for effortlessness, only one dimension is used for enhancement [28]. The measured kth low-resolution (LR) frame is

$$gk = |h(x) \, f(x - Tk) + wk|x = n\Delta, k = 1, \ldots . k, \qquad (11.7)$$

where the visual scene is f (x), Δ is the LR interval for sampling images, and |wk|x is White Gaussian noise that is additive and has a2 variance. We assume that the LR images have a translational shift Tk [29–31]:

Figure 11.11 Hazy and blur challenges sample image.

Figure 11.12 Output images using super-resolution method.

Table 11.1 Different image enhancement techniques.

S. no.	Image enhancement techniques	Accuracy	Advantage	Disadvantage
1	Contrast Stretching [4]	79%–85%	Visually accurate characterization of the actual scene.	Some information may be lost as a result of saturation and clipping.
2	Histogram Equalization [8]	95%	The picture has a uniform histogram, which produces ideal contrast quickly.	It is not possible to alter the image's local information while maintaining the lighting of the original image.
3	Contrast Limited Stretching [14]	98.28%	Increase local contrast	Noise amplification in flat areas, as well as ring artifacts at sharp edges.
4	Median Filter Method [22]	85%–89%	There are edge-preserving places available. It produces excellent results in images with high redundancy.	It may remove non-repeated details, resulting in certain data loss. The price of simulation is also high.
5	Unsharp Masking [26]	90%	It improves particle contrast and sharpness.	It neglects to achieve a satisfactory balance of specifics and naturalness. Because it is overly receptive to noise, it occasionally causes undesirable distortion.
6	Super-resolution [30]	-	It fulfills the gap with the raw data, which makes more realistic images than other methods	It depends on raw data, which means it needs a huge number of data. If the amount of data is low, then it does not work properly.

$$\text{PSNR}=20 * \log10(\text{MAXIMUM})-10 * \log10 (\text{MSE}) \qquad (11.8)$$

SR picture delivered by bi-cubic is not perceptually convincing [33–35]. Thus, we can reach the determinations that follow to help this: The Super Goal GAN, similar to other GAN (Generative antagonistic organizations) models, is partitioned into two sections: the generator and the discriminator [30, 31]. IHR and ISR are introduced as W × H × C, W ×

H × C. The generator makes benefit of ResNet. Perceptual misfortune (lsr) is depicted in some misfortune capabilities as the weighting element of a substance misfortune and an ill-disposed part [32]:

$$lSR = lSRx+ 10-3lSRGEN \tag{11.9}$$

The pixel-wise difference between the high-level image and the super image (generated image) is as follows [29–32]:

$$I_{MSE}^{SR} = \frac{1}{r^2WH}\sum_{x=1}^{rW}\sum_{y=1}^{rH}(I_{x,y}^{HR} - G_{,G}(I^{LR})_{x,y})^2 \tag{11.10}$$

where f (x) is the continuous image scene, A is the LR image sampling interval, and Wk (X) is additive white. The Euclidean distance between the feature representations of a reconstructed image and the reference image is defined as VGG loss [32]

$$I_{VGG}^{SR} = \frac{1}{w_{i.j}H_{i.j}}\sum_{y=1}^{H_{i.j}}(\phi_{i.j}(I^{LR})_{x.y} - \phi_{i.jG_{\theta g}(V^{LR})_{x.y})^2} \tag{11.11}$$

The ill-disposed misfortune is characterized utilizing the discriminator's probabilities across all preparing tests (N):

$$I_{GEN}^{SR} = \frac{N}{\sum_{n=1}} - logD_{\theta D}(G_{,G}(I^{LR})) \tag{11.12}$$

We minimize the gradient

$$- log \text{ D}\theta\text{D (G}\theta\text{G(ILR)) instead of}log [1 - (\text{G}\theta\text{G(ILR))]} \tag{11.13}$$

The maximization problem is shown in the following equation:

$$\text{min}\theta\text{G m}\theta\text{DaxEIHR ~ptrain(ILR)[logD}\theta\text{D (IHR)] +}$$
$$\text{EILR ~pG(ILR)[log (1 - D}\theta\text{D (G}\theta\text{G(ILR))]} \tag{11.14}$$

where lsr, Perceptual misfortune, is the amount of the substance misfortune and antagonistic misfortune depicted before:

$$I^{SR} = I_X^{SR} + 10^{-3}I_{GEN}^{SR} \tag{11.15}$$

The SR technology can recreate poor images as rising frames or video frames, and contemporary SR methods that use deep learning strategies that achieve better recovery quality significantly. At the user end, NAS and SRAVS implement SR into the responsive streaming content purpose of providing high-quality video content while limiting the impact of complex situations on users' QoE (Quality of Experience). For devices with high capabilities, NAS is suggested to enhance the quality of the video through reconfigured MDSR. SRAVS reshapes SRCNN, a simple, compact SR model with only three convolution operation, due to the limited computational resources of users' equipment. Aside from the methods described above, a side platform may offer more advanced computer capability to reduce SR duration while ensuring a high-quality server for multiple clients. VISCA develops an interactive video solution that utilizes SR with side deduplication to enhance QoE. It is, but even so, unaware of the obtainable computation power at the edge. We built a multiple visual perception model to improve human visual performance (RMISR-VP). RMISR-VP is made up of the SR subsidiary and the Laplacian gradient map branch. The GANR method consists of two parts: training and restructuring. We fuzz and sample group LR images in the training section to obtain down-sampled LR images for all of the training LR images. The cluster method is then used to categorize the HR, LR, and bottom analyzed LR updates. HR and LR are sampled at a rate LR definitions for each cluster and can be understood using HR-LR update sets and LR-down snippet LR update bunches. Anchor pairs of every particle are acquired by each dictionary. In the restructuring section, we have used the bottom surveyed LR patch to rebuild the LR patch based on every cluster›s anchor neighbourhood prediction. The strategies with SR described previous section utilizing only a repaired VSR framework to recreate clip frames from a different resolution to a specific high resolution. Expected to give the training clusters $\{x^i, y^i\}(i = 1, 2, \ldots, N)$ to achieve down-sampled LR patches for all of the training LR patches, we pixelate and subset LR fixes $\{y^i\}$. These down-sampled LR images are denoted by $\{z^i\}(i = 1, 2, \ldots, N)$. Areas $\{x^i, y^i, z^i\}$ $(i = 1, 2, \ldots, N)$ are split into various groups $\{x_k^i, y_k^i, z_k^i\}(i = 1, 2, \ldots, N_k, k = 1, 2, \ldots, K)$. N_k is the multitude of pieces associated with the kth cluster. Following clustering, only with clusters $\{x_k^i, y_k^i, z_k^i\}$ focused on texture set can we discover dictionary set, $\{D_h^k, D_l^k\}$, for every group. As a result, the corresponding, $\{D_l^k, D_{ll}^k\}$ and $\{D_h^k, D_l^k\}$, anchor neighborhood projections $\{P1_a^k, P2_a^k\}$ are computed individually anonymously. To accomplish this, we smudge a set of items with an LR bug fix y_{test}^i and z_{test}^i and bottom surveyed LR pictures. Depending on z_{test}^i, we utilize anchor community estimation $P2_a^k$ of vocabulary duo $\{D_l^k, D_{ll}^k\}$, to recreate $\hat{y}_{test}^{i,k}$, for every group.

$$\hat{y}_{test}^{i,k} = P2_a^k z_{test}^i \tag{11.16}$$

The group with the lowest recognition rate is then decided to pursue as follows: $c = \arg\min |\hat{y}_{test}^{i,k} - y_{test}^i|$. We suppose that now the LR and HR pictures originate from the same cluster. x_{test}^i can be restored by anchor nearby forecast of $P1_a^c$ correlating thesaurus set $\{D_h^c, D_l^c\}$,

$$x_{test}^i = P1_a^k y_{test}^i \tag{11.17}$$

Figures 11.13–11.15 show pictures of the human brain with very fuzzy images where we cannot understand what is in the brain, how the nerves are present there, and what are the exact locations. The brain, which gives all instructions to the rest of the body, is arguably the most important part of our body. If any disease or abnormality occurs in brain, then it is important to solve that immediately; we need a clear view of the brain MRI so that the doctor can identify the problem and solve it, but in Figures 11.13–11.15, it is not easy to figure out the problem. However, after using the super-resolution technique, we can see that the pictures (Figures 11.16–11.18) are much clearer, making it easier for doctors to understand the problem. From the table below, we can see experimental data that show how this image enhancement technique gives better outcome.

Let r to be the info picture, s be the improved result picture, and Wt. be the arrangement of loads for the CNN model. The CNN model can be addressed by the accompanying

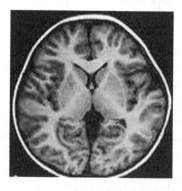

Figure 11.13 Different human brain with very fuzzy images.

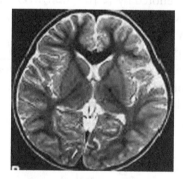

Figure 11.14 Different human brain with very fuzzy images.

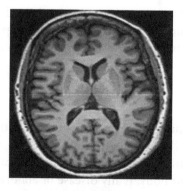

Figure 11.15 Different human brain with very fuzzy images.

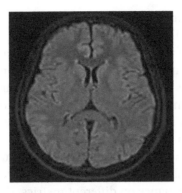

Figure 11.16 Output images using super resolution technique.

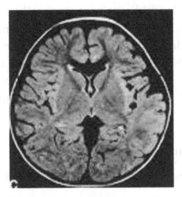

Figure 11.17 Output images using super resolution technique.

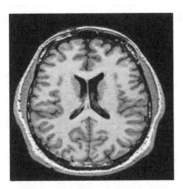

Figure 11.18 Output images using super resolution technique.

conditions in Convolutional Layer, where "*" addresses the convolution activity, "b" is the predisposition term, and "u" is the enactment capability, like ReLU or sigmoid. In the Pooling Layer, v is the pooling capability, for example, max pooling or normal pooling. "Wt" is the arrangement of loads for the completely associated layer, "b" is the inclination term, and "x" is the initiation capability. y is the actuation capability of the result layer, for example, softmax or straight. The misfortune capability used to prepare the CNN model can likewise be addressed by a numerical condition, like mean squared blunder (MSE).

Num is the quantity of preparing tests, s' is the ground truth upgraded picture, and s is the anticipated improved picture. Here is an overall illustration of a table that could be utilized to examine the presentation of an AI model for picture upgrade.

In Table 11.2, three different models, CNN, DCGAN, and CycleGAN, are compared using different metrics such as PSNR, SSIM, and FID. The architecture of the models, the number of parameters used, and their performance on a specific dataset are also included. This table helps to identify the strengths and weaknesses of each model and select the best one for the specific application.

In Table 11.3, the performance of the models is evaluated using different metrics such as PSNR, SSIM, and FID. This table helps to determine the strengths and weaknesses of the models in terms of their performance on different metrics.

In Table 11.4, the hyperparameters utilized for each model are recorded, including the learning rate and group size, alongside their impact on the model's presentation. The best qualities for each hyperparameter are chosen in light of the model's presentation on a particular measurement. This table assists with upgrading the model's presentation and guide future enhancements. In CNN right off the bat, load a dataset of pictures with low difference or other quality issues that should be improved. Divide the dataset into preparation, approval, and test sets. Characterize the engineering of the CNN model, including

Table 11.2 Model comparison table.

Model	Architecture	Parameters	Metric	Performance
CNN	ResNet-50	5M	PSNR	34 dB
DCGAN	DCGAN	15M	SSIM	0.90
CycleGAN	CycleGAN	10M	FID	25.7

Table 11.3 Performance evaluation table.

Model	CNN	DCGAN	CycleGAN
PSNR	34 dB	31 dB	29 dB
SSIM	0.88	0.90	0.85
FID	40.5	35.7	25.7

Table 11.4 Hyperparameter tuning table.

Model	Architecture	Parameters	Learning rate	Batch size	Metric	Performance
CNN	ResNet-50	5M	0.001	16	PSNR	35 dB
DCGAN	DCGAN	15M	0.0005	32	SSIM	0.92
CycleGAN	CycleGAN	10M	0.0001	64	FID	25.7

Table 11.5 Result for different natural image using various algorithms [37].

Algorithms for SR	Similarity indicator	
	PSNR	SSIM
SRCNN	29.561489	0.90345978
DRCN	29.565746	0.90379867
SRGAN	29.587814	0.90404762
EDLF-CGAN	29.781894	0.90434785
Bicubic	29.500745	0.90486753
SRGAN+$l^{sR}_{Perceptual}$	30.789585	0.90593462

the number and size of the convolutional layers, pooling layers, and completely associated layers. Gather the model utilizing a proper misfortune capability, like mean squared mistake, and an enhancer calculation, like stochastic inclination plunge. Train the model on the preparation set utilizing backpropagation and slope drop to change the model boundaries. Screen the model's exhibition on the approval set and change the hyperparameters on a case-by-case basis to forestall overfitting. Test the model on the test set to assess its adequacy at upgrading pictures. Also, in conclusion, utilize the prepared model to upgrade new pictures by going them through the CNN and getting the result y. The particular subtleties of the CNN model, misfortune capability, and analyzer might fluctuate depending on the issue being tended to. Moreover, there might be other picture improvement methods that do not include CNNs, like histogram balance or gamma rectification, using different numerical conditions and calculations.

For medical images, we proposed a guided SR technique. To accomplish the tested LR bug fixes for all of the training LR updates, our technique diminishes dataset LR bug fixes. Fixes are divided into several clusters to present all of the trends in the pictures. By each gathering, HR, LR, and arbitrarily isolated LR definitions are figured out. Finally, a technique is created to modify HR fix to find a significantly safer and secure nearby projection, directed by the remaking mistake of LR fix. The creative outcomes demonstrate that the proposed strategy beats a few techniques as far as execution, as we can see from the tables.

11.5   Conclusion

In this paper, we give a cautious examination of picture upgrade strategies. where we can see that each of the sectioned pictures have a more prominent goal and quality than the legitimate MS picture and are like the pixel thickness of the exemplary container picture. Just minor contrasts in tones and variety sharpness can be recognized. The image size is ordinarily little, and the quantity of sub-pictures can be precisely picked to further develop picture quality. The utilization of SR-CNN is unimaginable in the part of upgrading the nature of pictures for different angles. Medical imagery is one of the major industries where

SRCNNs are used. The precision of the diagnostic can be greatly impacted by the clarity of the medical images. Medical images, however, are frequently of poor quality due to limitations in imaging technology, making it challenging for doctors to make a certain prognosis. By increasing the sharpness of these images with SRCNNs, doctors will be better able to see minute details and anomalies that may have gone unnoticed in the initial low-resolution pictures. This may result in early illness and injury discovery as well as more precise diagnoses, eventually enhancing patient outcomes. SRCNNs are also used in the area of monitoring. High-resolution images are necessary for surveillance in order to recognize people, cars, and other interesting things. However, low-resolution pictures are frequently captured by security cameras, especially when the subject is distant or the illumination is subpar. These images can be improved with SRCNNs, making it simpler for law enforcement personnel to recognize offenders and follow their moves. SRCNNs can be used with satellite images in addition to medical imaging. A number of uses for satellite pictures include mapping, recording changes in land use, and observing weather trends. The distance between the satellite and the earth's surface, the quality of the satellite's imaging instruments, and atmospheric circumstances can all have an impact on the sharpness of satellite pictures. These pictures' resolution can be improved using SRCNNs, making it simpler to spot particular characteristics and changes over time. This could result in better environmental tracking, disaster reaction, and land administration. Thus, the use of image enhancement using SRCNN has the most potential because of how varied its applications are in so many walks of life. Future work can explore the model's performance on different datasets and investigate using varying attention mechanisms to improve its performance further.

References

1. Luo, X., Zeng, T., Zeng, W., Huang, J., Comparative analysis on landsat image enhancement using fractional and integral differential operators. *Computing*, 102, 247–261, 2020.
2. Wang, P., Fan, E., Wang, P., Comparative analysis of image classification algorithms based on traditional machine learning and deep learning. *Pattern Recognit. Lett.*, 141, 61–67, 2021.
3. Anwar, S., Khan, S., Barnes, N., A deep journey into super-resolution: A survey. *ACM Comput. Surv. (CSUR)*, 53, 3, 1–34, 2020.
4. Zhang, W., Pan, X., Xie, X., Li, L., Wang, Z., Han, C., Color correction and adaptive contrast enhancement for underwater image enhancement. *Comput. Electr. Eng.*, 91, 106981, 2021.
5. Chaira, T., An improved medical image enhancement scheme using Type II fuzzy set. *Appl. Soft Comput.*, 25, 293–308, 2014.
6. Somvanshi, S.S., Kunwar, P., Tomar, S., Singh, M., Comparative statistical analysis of the quality of image enhancement techniques. *Int. J. Image Data Fusion*, 9, 2, 131–151, 2018.
7. Qi, Y., Yang, Z., Sun, W., Lou, M., Lian, J., Zhao, W., Ma, Y., A comprehensive overview of image enhancement techniques. *Arch. Comput. Methods Eng.*, 29, 1, 583–607, 2022.
8. Bhandari, A.K., Singh, V.K., Kumar, A., Singh, G.K., Cuckoo search algorithm and wind driven optimization based study of satellite image segmentation for multilevel thresholding using Kapur's entropy. *Expert Syst. Appl.*, 41, 7, 3538–3560, 2014.
9. Puniani, S. and Arora, S., Performance evaluation of image enhancement techniques. *Int. J. Signal Process. Image Process. Pattern Recognit.*, 8, 8, 251–262, 2015.

10. Nithyananda, C.R. and Ramachandra, A.C., Review on histogram equalization based image enhancement techniques, in: *2016 International Conference on Electrical, Electronics, and Optimization Techniques (ICEEOT)*, IEEE, pp. 2512–2517, 2016, March.

11. Raju, G. and Nair, M.S., A fast and efficient color image enhancement method based on fuzzy-logic and histogram. *AEU-Int. J. Electron. Commun.*, 68, 237–243, 2014.

12. Pandey, P., Dewangan, K.K., Dewangan, D.K., Satellite image enhancement techniques—A comparative study, in: *2017 International Conference on Energy, Communication, Data Analytics and Soft Computing (ICECDS)*, IEEE, pp. 597–602, 2017, August.

13. Pati, U., *3-D surface geometry and reconstruction: Developing concepts and applications*, IGI Global, Hershey, 2012.

14. Huang, S.C., Chen, B.H., Cheng, Y.J., An efficient visibility enhancement algorithm for road scenes captured by intelligent transportation systems. *IEEE Trans. Intell. Transp. Syst.*, 15, 5, 2321–2332, 2014.

15. Anbarjafari, G., Jafari, A., Jahromi, M.N.S., Ozcinar, C., Demirel, H., Image illumination enhancement with an objective no-reference measure of illumination assessment based on Gaussian distribution mapping. *Eng. Sci. Technol. Int. J.*, 18, 4, 696–703, 2015.

16. Esakkirajan, S., Veerakumar, T., Subramanyam, A.N., PremChand, C.H., Removal of high density salt and pepper noise through modifed decision based unsymmetric trimmed median flter. *IEEE Signal Process. Lett.*, 18, 287–290, 2011.

17. Chen, R.H., Lu, C.T., Wang, L.L., Lin, C.A., Shen, J.H., Removal of salt-and-pepper noise using convolutional-neural networks, in: *Proceedings of Conference on Information Technology Applications Outlying Islands*, pp. 590–597, 2019.

18. Krutsch, R. and Tenorio, D., Histogram equalization, Freescale Semiconductor, Document Number AN4318, Application Note.

19. Rajulath Banu, A.K., Contrast enhancement of MRI image: A review. *Int. J. Eng. Technol. Adv. Eng.*, 5, 6, 2250–2459, June 2015.

20. Alex Stack, J., Adaptive image contrast enhancement using generalization of histogram equalization. *IEEE Trans. Image Process.*, 5, 9, 889–896, 2000.

21. Galdran, A., Pardo, D., Picón, A., Alvarez-Gila, A., Automatic red-channel underwater image restoration. *J. Vis. Commun. Image Represent.*, 26, 132–145, 2015.

22. Iqbal, K., Odetayo, M., James, A., Salam, R.A., Talib, A.Z.H., Enhancing the low-quality images using unsupervised color correction method. *International Conference on System Man and Cybernetics (SMC)*, Istanbul, pp. 1703–1709, 10–13 October, 2010.

23. Sundaram, M., Ramar, K., Arumugam, N., Prabin, G., Histogram modified local contrast enhancement for mammogram images. *Appl. Soft Comput.*, 11, 8, 5809–5816, 2011.

24. Gorai, A. and Ashish, G., Gray-level image enhancement by particle swarm optimization. *World Congress on Nature & Biologically Inspired Computing (NaBIC)*, pp. 72–77, 2009.

25. Elad, M. and Feuer, A., Superresolution restoration of an image sequence: Adaptive filtering approach. *IEEE Trans. Image Process.*, 8, 3, 387–395, 1999.

26. Park, S.C., Kang, M.G., Segall, C.A., Katsaggelos, A.K., Spatially adaptive high-resolution image reconstruction of DCT-based compressed images. *IEEE Trans. Image Process.*, 13, 4, 573–585, 2004.

27. Altunbasak, Y. and Patti, A.J., A maximum a posteriori estimator for high resolution video reconstruction from MPEG video, in: *Proceedings 2000 International Conference on Image Processing (Cat. No. 00CH37101)*, vol. 2, pp. 649–652, IEEE, 2000, September.

28. Maini, R. and Aggarwal, H., A comprehensive review of image enhancement techniques. *International Journal of Innovative Research and Growth (IJIRG)*, 8, 6, 60–71, 2019.

29. Schettini, R. and Corchs, S., Underwater image processing: State of the art of restoration and image enhancement methods. *EURASIP J. Adv. Signal Process.*, 2010, 1–14, 2010.

30. Agaian, S.S., Panetta, K., Grigoryan, A.M., Transform-based image enhancement algorithms with performance measure. *IEEE Trans. Image Process.*, 10, 3, 367–382, 2001.
31. Wang, W., Wu, X., Yuan, X., Gao, Z., An experiment-based review of low-light image enhancement methods. *IEEE Access*, 8, 87884–87917, 2020.
32. Yahya, S.R., Abdullah, S.S., Omar, K., Zakaria, M.S., Liong, C.Y., Review on image enhancement methods of old manuscript with the damaged background, in: *2009 International Conference on Electrical Engineering and Informatics*, vol. 1, pp. 62–67, IEEE, 2009, August.
33. Hamdi, A., Chan, Y.K., Koo, V.C., A new image enhancement and super resolution technique for license plate recognition. *Heliyon*, 7, 11, e08341, 2021.
34. Patti, A.J. and Altunbasak, Y., Artifact reduction for set theoretic super resolution image reconstruction with edge adaptive constraints and higher-order interpolants. *IEEE Trans. Image Process.*, 10, 1, 179–186, 2001.
35. Demirel, H., Ozcinar, C., Anbarjafari, G., Satellite image contrast enhancement using discrete wavelet transform and singular value decomposition. *IEEE Geosci. Remote Sens. Lett.*, 7, 2, 333–337, 2010.
36. Kim, S.P., Bose, N.K., Valenzuela, H.M., Recursive reconstruction of high-resolution image from noisy undersampled multiframes. *IEEE Transactions on Acoustics, Speech, and Signal Processing*, 38, 6, 1013–1027, 1990.
37. San Hlaing, M. Y. I. N. T., 3D Reconstruction for Super-Resolution CT Images in the Internet of Health Things Using Deep Learning.

12

Software Engineering in Machine Learning Applications: A Comprehensive Study

Kuldeep Vayadande[1]*, **Komal Sunil Munde**[2], **Amol A. Bhosle**[2], **Aparna R. Sawant**[1]
and Ashutosh M. Kulkarni[1]

[1]Vishwakarma Institute of Technology, Pune, Maharashtra, India
[2]MIT Art, Design and Technology University, Pune, Maharashtra, India

Abstract

The research of developing complex algorithms whose accuracy increases over time is known as machine learning. To solve the problem of generating and dealing with large, powerful computers in a quickly changing and dynamic environment, machine learning approaches have become more important in many computers' maintenance and advancement tasks. Machines' intelligence strategies have been shown to be extremely applicable across a wide range of industries. It is not unexpected that many tasks that go into the creation and upkeep of technology may well be rethought as knowledge difficulties and accosted in terms of comprehending processes. Over the past 20 years, interest in using machine learning algorithms in software design has increased, along with some positive publications and results. In this paper, we have conducted a review of prior research on machine learning approaches and provided a broad overview, including benefits and drawbacks and a comparison of a few existing algorithms. This paper presented a selection of the most current revelations in this new market niche.

Keywords: Machine learning, machine intelligence, supervised, unsupervised, software engineering, data mining, agorithms, software development

12.1 Introduction

The challenge of creating software that becomes more proficient at a task over time is at the heart of learning algorithms. Techniques for machine learning have shown to be highly helpful in a broad range of application fields. They are particularly helpful in practical situations where individuals lack the necessary expertise to develop effective algorithms and are incompletely understood, in domain names in which there are sizable sets of data beneficial to implicit relevant references waiting to be discovered, or in domains where programs must be capable of adapting to evolving circumstances [12]. Unsurprisingly, the field of software design engineering has shown to be a profitable one in which several challenges with application development may be characterized as learning problems and solved with the aid of teaching styles.

Corresponding author: kuldeep.vayadande@gmail.com

Arindam Dey, Sukanta Nayak, Ranjan Kumar and Sachi Nandan Mohanty (eds.) How Machine Learning is Innovating Today's World: A Concise Technical Guide, (159–172) © 2024 Scrivener Publishing LLC

There are many challenging situations that arise while building software system architectures in a quick-paced environment. In the primary case, software systems constantly respond to changing circumstances. The following scenario is when it is unclear which subdomains were involved. Finally, even if original data might well be provided, it is possible that no knowledge exists to create efficient analytical solutions [10].

To get beyond these obstacles, a range of approaches can be utilized, including the revolutionary computing model. Using automated code creation in transformative coding, application is designed, modified, and managed at the product demand before being rapidly transformed into output program. Software development will be capable of assembling and integratinge recorded area and architecture information with the help of this methodology for software development. Software developers will offer experience and understanding applications builders rather than immutable program codes.

In order for transformative computing to achieve its maximum potential, certain technologies and methodologies must be used for the many tasks that it entails. In addition to providing an explanation of machine learning and frequently employed classification algorithm, this article will discuss how machine learning techniques may be used to construct tools for production and management of software.

12.2   Related Works

"Data mining and machine learning for software engineering" [1] explains in detail how to employ data analysis methodologies for Software Development tasks, outlining any issues that remain and making enhancement suggestions. A comprehensive list of data extraction techniques that may be applied in Software Development is provided in the study, including components of cluster, prediction, and performance indicators. The report also identifies various SE datasets that are frequently utilized in data mining studies and lists the main benefits of mining SE data.

"A systematic literature review on federated machine learning: From a software engineering perspective" [2]. Using 231 methodologies and evidence, the authors thoroughly examined a study on federalized training from the viewpoint of program development. The findings indicate that the majority of the stated justifications for utilizing federalized training seem to be one's research topics that have gotten the most attention. Modeling aggregation, control of training, containing an emphasis, privacy protection, and resource planning are the main techniques offered for resolving the issues. The study's findings present several viewpoints on the development of operational federated teaching approaches. This report also exhorts academics to build upon and advance their current work by supplying additional details on the potential federated learning subjects of study in the long term.

"Machine learning applications in software engineering: recent advances and future research directions" [3]. In the study, different methods of machine learning used in software development were covered. According to their uses, benefits, and limits, it also provides comparative methodologies. It is impossible to choose one strategy as the best after analyzing every method. Based on its benefits, each approach has a variety of applications and can be beneficial across a range of fields. Additionally, they highlighted the drawbacks of each strategy, with the main goal being to increase performance and efficiency by choosing the approach that will work the best for a certain application.

"How does machine learning change software development practices?" [4]. The authors examine the effect of machine learning on the practices involved in development of software. A structured academic survey was carried out by the authors to assess the existing research and determine the ways in which machine learning is transforming software development. The review showed that machine learning is bringing about alterations in several aspects of software development, including the method of requirements gathering, the approach to design and implementation, and the procedures for testing and maintenance. The authors ultimately concluded that machine learning has a substantial impact on software development practices and that software developers must adapt to these changes in order to remain current in the constantly evolving field.

"Machine learning and software engineering" [5]. The research was conducted by the authors with a concentration on machine use in software development. The paper offers a thorough list of software development jobs whose difficulties can be solved utilizing machine learning methods. by defining software development tasks as learning issues and addressing them with machine learning techniques, the study further underscores the notion that software development is a great opportunity field to investigate in terms of implementing different machine learning methods.

"Machine learning applied to software testing: A systematic mapping study" [6]. The authors dive further into how machines' intelligence techniques are used to computer testing processes. To gain a comprehensive understanding of the current landscape, a systematic mapping study was conducted by the authors. The study aimed to survey the existing literature on the use of machine learning in describing integration testing as well as the sector as a whole. The study encompasses a diverse range of topics, including the various machine learning techniques utilized for software testing, the benefits and drawbacks of these methods, and their effect on different facets of testing procedures including testing information and determining test cases, and bug forecasting. The findings of the study reveal that machine learning has the capability to significantly enhancing software testing with regard to efficiency, effectiveness, and precision.

"A literature review of using machine learning in software development life cycle stages" [7]. The authors provide an in-depth analysis of how machine training is used at several stages of the software creation project lifecycle (SDLC). To gain insight into the trends, obstacles, and possibilities about the use of learning algorithms in computing development, a literature review was carried out by the authors of existing studies and research articles in the field. The paper covers the different stages of the SDLC, such as collecting requirements, designing and building, programming, debugging, and maintaining and evolution. The authors underscore the advantages of incorporating machine learning in each phase of the SDLC, including increased accuracy, efficiency, and productivity.

"Machine learning and software engineering in health informatics" [8]. The authors have examined how the related fields of software development and machine learning have improved "industry standards." Each one of these areas is currently the subject of knowledge of the subject matter, so there is potential for considerable new contributions from each subject. The authors also examine how software design and advanced algorithms connect to health technology, in which the complexity of clinical situations necessitates cutting-edge engineering solutions from both disciplines. They provide applications used during significant ongoing projects of research conducted by

the Oxford University Departments of Engineering Science and Computer Science, the Oxford University Hospitals NHS Trust, etc.

"*Studying software engineering patterns for designing machine learning systems*" [9]. The study examines the implementation of software engineering patterns in the construction and expansion of machine learning procedures. The authors aim to tackle the obstacles met by designers in integrating machine training models into software systems and the requirement for a systematic design approach. The paper offers a comprehensive analysis of software engineering patterns and their application in the design of machine learning systems. It emphasizes the advantages of utilizing patterns such as enhanced maintainability, modularity, and reusability, which are critical characteristics of best practices in software engineering. The paper also provides suggestions for selecting the suitable software engineering pattern for a particular machine learning system and explains how to implement these patterns effectively.

12.3   Comparison Table

Table 12.1 shows comparison table of existing techniques [2–8].

Table 12.1 Comparison table.

Sr no.	Authors	Year	Title	Conclusion
1.	S. Fajardo, R.F. García-Galvan, V. Barranco, J. C. Galvan and S. F. Batlle [1]	2016	Data mining and machine learning for software engineering [1]	The paper explains in detail how to employ data analysis methodologies for Software Development tasks, outlining any issues that remain and making enhancement suggestions. A comprehensive list of data extraction techniques that may be applied in Software Development is provided in the study, including components of cluster, prediction, and performance indicators. The report also identifies various SE datasets that are frequently utilized in data mining studies and lists the main benefits of mining SE data.

(Continued)

Table 12.1 Comparison table. (*Continued*)

Sr no.	Authors	Year	Title	Conclusion
2.	Lo Sin Kit, *et al.* [2]	2019	A systematic literature review on federated machine learning: From a software engineering perspective [2]	In this paper, the researchers conducted a thorough assessment of the software engineering aspect of federated learning using 231 procedures and documentation. The results showed that the most commonly cited reasons for using federated learning are also the most researched topics. The preferred strategies to address challenges include aggregate modeling, training control, privacy protection, and resource planning with a focus on privacy protection.
3.	Pani, Subhendu Kumar, and Anil Kumar Mishra	2020	Machine learning applications in software engineering: recent advances and future research directions [3]	The study explores various machine learning techniques employed in software development, examining their uses, advantages, and limitations, and comparing their methodologies. It is not possible to declare a single strategy as the best after evaluating all methods, as each approach has its own benefits and can be useful across multiple industries. The study also identifies the limitations of each strategy, with the objective of improving performance and efficiency by selecting the most appropriate approach for a given application.

(*Continued*)

Table 12.1 Comparison table. (*Continued*)

Sr no.	Authors	Year	Title	Conclusion
4.	Z. Wan, X. Xia, D. Lo and G. C. Murphy	2021	How does machine learning change software development practices? [4]	The authors examine the effect of machine learning on the practices in development of software. A structured academic survey was carried out by the authors to assess the existing research and determine the ways in which machine learning is transforming software development. The review showed that machine learning is bringing about alterations in several aspects of software development, including the method of requirements gathering, the approach to design and implementation, and the procedures for testing and maintenance. The authors ultimately concluded that machine learning has a substantial impact on software development practices and that software developers must adapt to these changes in order to remain current in the constantly evolving field.
5.	D. Zhang	2003	Machine learning and software engineering [5]	The research was conducted by the authors with a concentration on machine use in software development. The paper offers a thorough list of software development jobs whose difficulties can be solved utilizing machine learning methods. By defining software development tasks as learning issues and addressing them with machine learning techniques, the study further underscores the notion that software development is a great opportunity field to investigate in terms of implementing different machine learning methods.

(*Continued*)

Table 12.1 Comparison table. (*Continued*)

Sr no.	Authors	Year	Title	Conclusion
6.	V. H. S. Durelli, R. S. Durelli, S. S. Borges, A. T. Endo, M. M. Eler, D. R. C. Dias, *et al.*	2019	Machine learning applied to software testing: A systematic mapping study [6]	The author dives further into how machine intelligence techniques are used to computer testing processes. To gain a comprehensive understanding of the current landscape, a systematic mapping study was conducted by the authors. The study aimed to survey the existing literature on the use of machine learning in describing integration testing as well as the sector as a whole. The study encompasses a diverse range of topics, including the various machine learning techniques utilized for software testing, the benefits and drawbacks of these methods, and their effect on different facets of testing procedures including testing information and determining test cases, and bug forecasting. The findings of the study reveal that machine learning has the capability to significantly enhance software testing with regard to efficiency, effectiveness, and precision.
7.	S. Shafiq, A. Mashkoor, C. Mayr-Dorn, and A. Egyed	2021	A literature review of using machine learning in software development life cycle stages [7]	The authors provide an in-depth analysis of how machine training is used at several stages of the software creation project lifecycle (SDLC). To gain insight into the trends, obstacles, and possibilities about the use of learning algorithms in computing development, a literature review was carried out by the authors of existing studies and research articles in the field. The paper covers the different stages of the SDLC, such as collecting requirements, designing and building, programming, debugging,

(*Continued*)

Table 12.1 Comparison table. (*Continued*)

Sr no.	Authors	Year	Title	Conclusion
				and maintaining and evolution. The authors underscore the advantages of incorporating machine learning in each phase of the SDLC, including increased accuracy, efficiency, and productivity.
8.	D. A. Clifton, J. Gibbons, J. Davies and L. Tarassenko	2012	Machine learning and software engineering in health informatics [8]	This paper examines the impact of the interdisciplinary fields of software development and machine learning on "industry standards." Both areas are currently leading the forefront of knowledge, providing the potential for significant advancements in each. The authors also examine how software design and advanced algorithms connect to health technology, in which the complexity of clinical situations necessitates cutting-edge engineering solutions from both disciplines. The paper highlights practical applications used in ongoing research projects conducted by organizations such as Oxford University's Departments of Engineering Science and Computer Science, and Oxford University Hospitals NHS Trust.

(Continued)

Table 12.1 Comparison table. (*Continued*)

Sr no.	Authors	Year	Title	Conclusion
9.	H. Washizaki, H. Uchida, F. Khomh and Y.-G. Guéhéneuc	2019	Studying software engineering patterns for designing machine learning systems [9]	The study examines the implementation of software engineering patterns in the construction and expansion of machine learning procedures. The authors aim to tackle the obstacles met by designers in integrating machine training models into software systems and the requirement for a systematic design approach. The paper offers a comprehensive analysis of software engineering patterns and their application in the design of machine learning systems. It emphasizes the advantages of utilizing patterns such as enhanced maintainability, modularity, and reusability, which are critical characteristics of best practices in software engineering. The paper also provides suggestions for selecting the suitable software engineering pattern for a particular machine learning system and explains how to implement these patterns effectively.

12.4   Graph of Comparison

The comparative study reviews the various different questions monitored by referring to different literature reviews.

a) **Comparison of Machine Learning Frameworks Based on Software Engineering Principles**
Table 12.2 and Figure 12.1 display the different frameworks of machine learning based on the software principles and give an advice on which is more adoptable in coming years.

b) **Comparison of Version Control Tools Used in Machine Learning Projects**
The Contrast outcome in Figure 12.2 and Table 12.3 shows that Git as a version control tool in machine learning projects that has been more developed and used than the others.

Table 12.2 Comparison of machine learning frameworks based on software engineering principles.

Framework	Ease of use	Flexibility	Scalability	Interoperability
TensorFlow	80%	80%	100%	60%
PyTorch	60%	100%	80%	80%
Scikit-learn	100%	60%	60%	100%

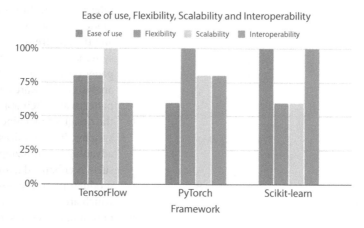

Figure 12.1 Comparison of machine learning frameworks based on software engineering principles.

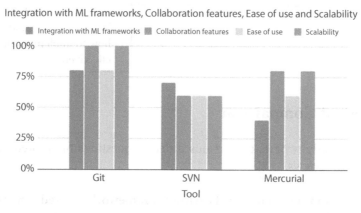

Figure 12.2 Comparison of version control tools used in machine learning projects.

Table 12.3 Comparison of version control tools used in machine learning projects.

Tool	Integration with ML frameworks	Collaboration features	Ease of use	Scalability
Git	80%	100%	80%	100%
SVN	70%	60%	60%	60%
Mercurial	40%	80%	60%	80%

c) **Comparison of Testing Frameworks for the Machine Learning Model**
Figure 12.3 shows the outcome of the comparison of various testing frameworks that are used in machine learning models and the most adaptable one is the pytest framework based on Table 12.4.

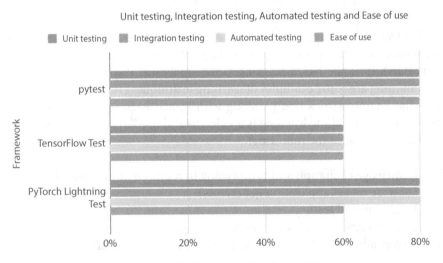

Figure 12.3 Comparison of testing frameworks for machine learning models.

Table 12.4 Comparison of testing frameworks for machine learning models.

Framework	Unit testing	Integration testing	Automated testing	Ease of use
pytest	80%	80%	80%	80%
TensorFlow Test	60%	60%	60%	60%
PyTorch lightning Test	80%	80%	80%	60%

12.5 Machine Learning in Software Engineering

To employ ML methods as techniques to address real-world SE challenges, we must first understand the problems as well as the tools and methodology used. It is critical that we understand (1) the various ML methods, (2) their properties, (3) the conditions under which the methods can be most successfully implemented, and (4) their theoretical foundations. The challenge of creating software applications that become more proficient at a task via experience is the focus of learning algorithms. ML techniques are being utilized to handle common problems such as:

    i)   Data mining challenges, in which enormous databases may include important latent regularities that can be identified automatically.

    ii)   Less understood topics in which people may lack the expertise required to create successful algorithms.

    iii)   Areas where programs need to respond proactively to new environments.

Machine learning employs a variety of algorithms, and each algorithm is utilized in accordance with the properties of the algorithm when a particular problem type is present. Decision trees (DT), Bayesian belief networks (BBN), concept learning (CL), artificial neural networks (ANN), genetic programming (GP), reinforcement learning (RL), genetic algorithms (GA), instance-based learning (IBL), analytical learning (AL), and inductive logic programming are some examples of learning techniques (ILP). Each of these learning algorithms has characteristics that go along with it, and each is applied appropriately in software issues. How machine learning is applied to and used in software development and maintenance jobs includes the following:

    i)   Knowledge elicitation and prototyping in requirement engineering

    ii)   Software reuse (application generators)

    iii)   Validation and testing

    iv)   Care and upkeep (software understanding)

    v)   Project administration (cost, defect prediction or estimation, or effort)

A list of software engineering activities that can use ML techniques is provided in Table 12.5. These jobs are a part of many requirement specifications, design, implementation, testing, and maintenance lifecycle procedures. It provides a sign of what might evolve into a promising area for some fascinating studies on using ML methods in software creation and upkeep. One of the alluring features of ML approaches is that they provide a priceless addition to the existing toolkit, making it simpler to handle the challenge of the aforementioned difficult situations.

Table 12.5 Software development tasks to its applicable machine learning approaches.

Software development task	Relevant machine learning approaches
Requirement Elicitation	Natural Language Processing (NLP)
Design and Architecture	Deep Neural Networks, Reinforcement Learning
Coding and Testing	Unsupervised and Supervised Learning
Maintenance and Upkeep	Transfer Learning, Reinforcement Learning
Debugging and Optimization	Reinforcement Learning and Neural Networks
Code review and Refactoring	Unsupervised Learning, Deep Learning
Software Metrics Analysis	Supervised Learning, Deep Learning
Security Testing	Reinforcement Learning, Anomaly Detection
Performance Optimization	Reinforcement Learning, Deep Learning

12.6 Conclusion

The study examined the utilization of machine training to application development adaptation, evaluating the potential impact on industry standards. It conducts a survey of software engineers and a systematic literature review, finding that machine learning is particularly useful in addressing the complexity of software development tasks and bridging the distinction among conventional computer programs and system for machine learning. The study also revealed the significance of the machine learning pipeline and software development in determining software structures for machine learning systems. The results suggest that there is significant potential for advancements in the field through the incorporation of machine learning and application development.

References

1. Fajardo, S., García-Galvan, R.F., Barranco, V., Galvan, J.C., Batlle, S.F., *Data mining and machine learning for software engineering*, vol. 1, p. 13, InTech, Rijeka, Croatia, 2016.
2. Lo, S.K. *et al.*, A systematic literature review on federated machine learning: From a software engineering perspective. *ACM Comput. Surv. (CSUR)*, 54, 5, 1–39, 2021.
3. Pani, S.K. and Mishra, A.K., Machine learning applications in software engineering: Recent advances and future research directions. *Int. J. Eng. Res. Technol.*, 8, 1, 1–4, 2020.
4. Wan, Z., Xia, X., Lo, D., Murphy, G.C., How does machine learning change software development practices? *IEEE Trans. Software Eng.*, 47, 9, 1857–1871, Sep. 2020.
5. Zhang, D., Machine learning and software engineering. *Software Qual. J.*, 11, 3, 87–119, 2003.
6. Durelli, V.H.S., Durelli, R.S., Borges, S.S., Endo, A.T., Eler, M.M., Dias, D.R.C. *et al.*, Machine learning applied to software testing: A systematic mapping study. *IEEE Trans. Reliab.*, 68, 3, 1189–1212, Sep. 2019.

7. Shafiq, S., Mashkoor, A., Mayr-Dorn, C., Egyed, A., A literature review of using machine learning in software development life cycle stages. *IEEE Access*, 9, 140896–140920, 2021.

8. Clifton, D.A., Gibbons, J., Davies, J., Tarassenko, L., Machine learning and software engineering in health informatics. *2012 First International Workshop on Realizing AI Synergies in Software Engineering (RAISE)*, Zurich, Switzerland, pp. 37–41, 2012.

9. Washizaki, H., Uchida, H., Khomh, F., Guéhéneuc, Y.-G., Studying software engineering patterns for designing machine learning systems. *2019 10th International Workshop on Empirical Software Engineering in Practice (IWESEP)*, Tokyo, Japan, pp. 49–495, 2019.

10. Masuda, S. *et al.*, A survey of software quality for machine learning applications. *2018 IEEE International Conference on Software Testing, Verification and Validation Workshops (ICSTW)*, IEEE, 2018.

11. Lwakatare, L.E. *et al.*, A taxonomy of software engineering challenges for machine learning systems: An empirical investigation. *Agile Processes in Software Engineering and Extreme Programming: 20th International Conference, XP 2019, Montréal, QC, Canada, May 21–25, 2019, Proceedings 20*, Springer International Publishing, 2019.

13

Machine Learning Applications in Battery Management System

Ponnaganti Chandana* and Ameet Chavan

VIT-AP University, SENSE Department, Andhra Pradesh, India

Abstract

Modern society is going through a substantial transition towards new forms of sustainable transportation and energy generation that allow for the reduction of the level of greenhouse emissions and atmospheric warming. The energy storage industry has evolved as there is a lot of ongoing research for the effective storage of energy. Batteries play an important role in this regard because they enable high-power, high-efficiency energy storage at a low cost. The battery industry is growing significantly, and lithium-ion batteries are widely applicable in diversified applications such as in electric vehicles (EVs) and smart grids that require a battery management system (BMS). BMS is a key element in applications such as electric vehicles and renewable energy. This assertion is due to BMS being responsible for managing the energy consumption completely or partially, as well as managing the energy storage in the battery.

BMS implementation necessitates a combination of software and hardware, which contains tasks to monitor, control, and estimate the state of battery and detect the fault. Although there are various types of BMS that allow for efficient energy utilization, new techniques are emerging that aim to contribute to the development of innovative solutions. The problems associated with improper battery monitoring leads to scrapping of battery, which leads to EV hazard. Recycling of the battery is also a major concern as it is a bit complicated and time-consuming process. At present, globally only 5% of the lithium-ion batteries are being recycled. The remaining 95% of lithium-ion batteries find their way to landfills. With the help of machine learning (ML) application, by estimating the remaining useful life and by monitoring battery unit effectively, the life of a battery pack improves, which can bring down the percentage of the batteries that are being thrown out. Techniques that are capable of delivering the improved battery technology quicker with the aid of safety and efficiency have a significant role. ML plays a major role in such techniques. Real-time monitoring and modeling the behavior of battery using ML have been growing over the years. The mathematical and statistical methods that are involved in machine learning are regarded as reliable and practical approaches to be applied in BMS for estimating State of Charge (SOC), State of Health (SOH), and Remaining Useful Life (RUL). Along with SOC, SOH, and RUL, aging and degradation of the battery can also be predicted.

The aim of this chapter is to present a thorough classification and description of ML techniques and the appropriate machine learning procedures that can be used in BMS applications. The major components of BMS are discussed, specifically with the incorporation of ML approaches.

Corresponding author: chandana.21phd7036@vitap.ac.in

Arindam Dey, Sukanta Nayak, Ranjan Kumar and Sachi Nandan Mohanty (eds.) How Machine Learning is Innovating Today's World: A Concise Technical Guide, (173–200) © 2024 Scrivener Publishing LLC

Keywords: Electric vehicles (EV), battery management system (BMS), state of charge (SOC), state of health (SOH), state of function (SOF), remaining useful life (RUL), cell balancing, machine learning (ML)

13.1   Introduction

ML arose as an effective tool to analyze large volumes of data and to extract valuable insights. It has several industrial applications, including in the field of BMS. BMS has a substantial role in ensuring protection as well ensuring effective functioning of battery-powered devices and systems, and machine learning can help improve the performance, reliability, and lifespan of batteries [1, 2].

Machine learning algorithms can analyze sensor data from batteries and identify patterns that can be used to optimize battery performance and prevent unexpected failures. Sensors with the application of algorithms are incorporated to predict the crucial parameters of battery [3]. They are capable of estimating SOC and SOH of batteries, which optimizes charging–discharging cycles, extend life of the battery, and reduce maintenance costs. They can also detect faults in batteries and identify abnormal behavior, which can help prevent catastrophic failures and improve safety [4]. In addition, machine learning algorithms can analyze data from multiple batteries in a system and optimize the energy usage based on demand and supply. This can help reduce energy waste and improve the efficiency of the overall system, resulting in reduced energy consumption and costs.

Machine learning has several industrial applications in BMS, including predictive maintenance, battery state estimation, optimal charging, fault detection, and energy management [5]. By leveraging machine learning, companies can improve the performance, reliability, and lifespan of batteries, leading to better efficiency, cost savings, and safety for industrial applications.

13.2   Battery Management System (BMS)

A BMS is an electronic device that monitors as well manages the performance, health, and safety of rechargeable batteries. BMS is essential in protecting, ensuring the longevity, and optimizing battery performance during its lifetime. It is commonly used in electric vehicles, renewable energy systems, and other applications where rechargeable batteries are used. The BMS monitors several battery parameters, namely, voltage, current, temperature, and SOC. It uses this information to determine the battery's health and ensure that it is operating within safe limits. BMS as well controls the charging and discharging of battery, ensuring that it is done correctly to prevent damage to the battery and ensure its optimal performance [1, 6, 7]. The block diagram of BMS is represented in Figure 13.1.

In addition to monitoring and controlling the battery, the BMS provides important safety features. Figure 13.2 illustrates the functions that are monitored by BMS. As an example, let us consider that a battery is overcharged; the BMS can prevent further charging to avoid damage to the battery or a potential safety hazard [8]. Similarly, if the battery is overheating,

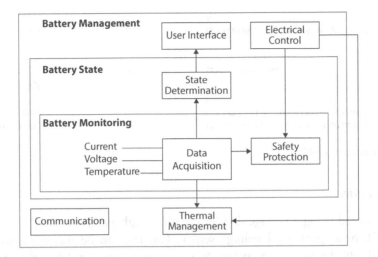

Figure 13.1 Block diagram of BMS.

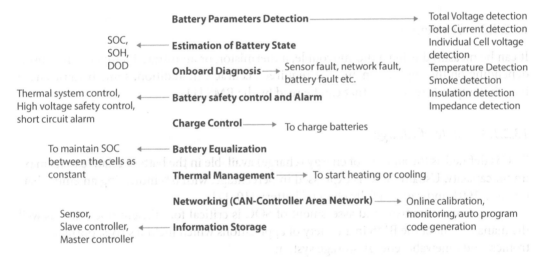

Figure 13.2 Functions of real-time BMS.

the BMS can reduce the charging rate or even shut down the charging process altogether to prevent damage to the battery or a safety hazard.

Overall, BMS is a crucial component that guarantees rechargeable batteries' safety, performance, and longevity. It plays an essential role in many industries, including automotive, renewable energy, and consumer electronics, where rechargeable batteries are used.

13.2.1 Key Parameters of Battery Management System

To measure voltage, current, temperature, SOC, SOH, and SOF in a BMS [9, 10], described in the Figure 13.3, various practices and methodologies can be implemented, which depend on specific parameters that have to be measured and also on the type of battery that has to be monitored.

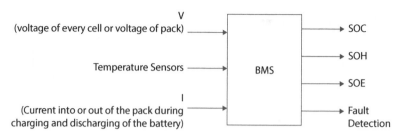

Figure 13.3 Parameters of BMS.

13.2.1.1 Voltage

It can be measured using a voltage divider circuit, a high-precision analog-to-digital converter (ADC), or a specialized voltage sensor. Current can be measured using a shunt resistor, a Hall-effect sensor, or a current transformer, which can detect the magnetic field generated by the flow of current through a conductor [10].

13.2.1.2 Temperature

It can be measured using a thermocouple, a thermistor, or an infrared temperature sensor, depending on the application and the required accuracy. In addition, some batteries have built-in temperature sensors that can be read by the BMS [11].

13.2.1.3 State of Charge

SOC is defined as the amount of energy (charge) available in the battery relative to its maximum capacity. Usually, SOC is expressed in percentage, with 0% indicating an empty battery and 100% indicating a fully charged battery [10, 12].

Accurate measurement and assessment of SOC is critical for efficient operation as well the management of the BMS in a variety of applications which includes EVs, portable electronics, and renewable energy storage systems.

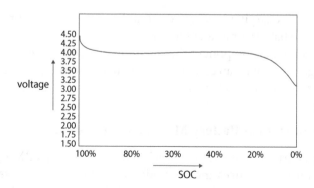

Figure 13.4 Performance curve of lithium ion battery.

The equation for SOC can be expressed as:

$$SOC = (Q(t) - Q\_min) / (Q\_max - Q\_min) * 100\% \qquad (13.1)$$

where
Q(t) = Actual charge in the battery at a time t,
Q_max = Maximum capacity of the battery, and
Q_min = Minimum capacity that can be discharged without damaging the battery.

SOC is typically estimated by measuring the battery's voltage and current and using algorithms to estimate the remaining capacity based on these data [12–14, 16]. The battery's performance curve is graphed concerning both voltage and the available energy at specific instances as shown in the Figure 13.4. Other methods, such as coulomb counting, impedance spectroscopy, or Kalman filters, can also be used to estimate SOC with greater accuracy.

13.2.1.4   State of Health

SOH is the measure of battery overall health and performance. It also includes factors such as capacity, resistance, and internal chemistry of the battery. SOH can be estimated using techniques such as electrochemical impedance spectroscopy (EIS), pulse-load testing, analyzing the charge and discharge behavior of the battery with respect to time. SOH in general is defined as the ratio of maximum capacity and current capacity of the battery. It is expressed in percentage [14–16].

$$\text{State of Health} = \frac{Maximum\ capacity\ of\ the\ battery\ (at\ that\ instant)}{Capacity\ oy\ new\ battery} \times 100\% \quad (13.2)$$

13.2.1.5   State of Function

SOF is a relatively new concept in battery management, which refers to the ability of the battery to perform its intended function in a specific application. SOF can be measured using various techniques, such as monitoring the battery's power output, its response to different loads or environmental conditions, or its ability to meet specific performance criteria.

13.3   Estimation of Battery SOC and SOH

The methods used to measure key battery parameters in a BMS are dependent on definite requirements and characteristics of battery being monitored, and accuracy and precision needed for application. A well-designed BMS can provide accurate and reliable data on these parameters, which results in ensuring safety and effectiveness in operating the battery-powered systems [16].

13.3.1   Methods of Estimating SOC

SOC estimation is a crucial task in energy storage systems. Here are mathematical modeling methods for the estimation of SOC.

13.3.1.1   Coulomb Counting Method

This method is used in estimating SOC by integrating the input and output current of battery over time [17].

$$SOC(t) = SOC(t-1) - \Delta Q(t) / Qn \qquad (13.3)$$

where
  SOC(t) = State of Charge at time t,
  SOC(t-1) = SOC at the previous time step,
  $\Delta Q(t)$ = Change in charge over the time step, and
  Qn = Nominal capacity of the battery.

13.3.1.2   Open Circuit Voltage (OCV) Method

This method estimates SOC by measuring the open circuit voltage of the battery and using a lookup table that relates the voltage to SOC [18].

$$SOC(t) = f(Voc(t)) \qquad (13.4)$$

where
  Voc(t) = Open-circuit voltage of the battery at time t, and
  f() = Function that maps voltage to SOC.

13.3.1.3   Kalman Filtering Method

This method estimates the SOC by combining a mathematical model of the battery with measurements from the battery [19].

$$SOC(t) = x(t|t) \qquad (13.5)$$

where
  x(t|t) = Estimated state of the battery at time t based on the Kalman filter.

13.3.1.4   Artificial Neural Network (ANN) Method

This method estimates the SOC using a neural network that is trained on a large dataset of battery measurements [20].

$$SOC(t) = ANN(V(t), I(t), T(t)) \qquad (13.6)$$

where
ANN() = a neural network that takes in the battery voltage, current, and temperature at time t and outputs the estimated SOC.

13.3.1.5   Fuzzy

This method uses fuzzy logic to estimate the SOC by taking into account the battery voltage, current, temperature, and other factors [21].

$$SOC(t) = FL(V(t), I(t), T(t)) \tag{13.7}$$

where FL() is a fuzzy logic system that takes in the battery voltage, current, and temperature at time t and outputs the estimated SOC.

13.3.1.6   Extended Kalman Filtering Method

This method is similar to Kalman filtering but uses an extended model that takes into account the non-linearities in the battery model [22].

$$SOC(t) = x(t|t) \tag{13.8}$$

where x(t|t) is the estimated state of the battery at time t based on the extended Kalman filter.

13.3.1.7   Gray Box Modeling Method

This method combines a physics-based model with empirical data to estimate the SOC [23].

$$SOC(t) = GBM(V(t), I(t), T(t)) \tag{13.9}$$

where GBM() is a gray box model that combines a physics-based model with empirical data to estimate the SOC.

13.3.1.8   Support Vector Machine (SVM) Method

This method uses SVM algorithms for estimating SOC based on the battery current, voltage, and temperature measurements [24].

$$SOC(t) = SVM(V(t), I(t), T(t)) \tag{13.10}$$

where
SVM() = an SVM algorithm that takes in the battery voltage, current, and temperature at time t and outputs the estimated SOC.

13.3.1.9   Model Predictive Control Method

This method uses a battery model for foreseeing the potential activities of the battery and uses this prediction for estimating SOC [25].

$$SOC(t) = MPC(V(t), I(t), T(t)) \qquad (13.11)$$

where

MPC() = a model predictive controller that takes in the battery voltage, current, and temperature at time t and outputs the estimated SOC.

13.3.1.10   Adaptive Observer Method

This method uses an reconciling observer for the estimation of SOC by adjusting the model parameters based on the battery measurements [26].

$$SOC(t) = x(t) \qquad (13.12)$$

where

x(t) = the estimated state of the battery at time t based on the adaptive observer.

13.3.1.11   Impedance-Based Method

This method estimates the SOC by measuring the impedance of the battery and using a model to relate the impedance to the SOC [27].

$$SOC(t) = f(Z(t)) \qquad (13.13)$$

where

Z(t) = the measured impedance of the battery at time t and f() is a function that maps impedance to SOC.

13.3.1.12   Gray Prediction Method

This method uses gray prediction to estimate the SOC by analyzing the battery voltage and current data [28].

$$SOC(t) = GPM(V(t), I(t)) \qquad (13.14)$$

where

GPM() = a gray prediction model that takes in the battery voltage and current at time t and outputs the estimated SOC.

There are various mathematical modeling methods to evaluate SOC of a battery, and every method exhibits its strengths and weaknesses. The selection of method depends on specific application, accuracy, and complexity of the constraints that has to be estimated.

13.3.2   Methods of Estimating SOH

Accuracy is crucial in estimating SOH for ensuring consistent and protected operation of battery, and these mathematical modeling methods can provide valuable insights for battery management and optimization [29].

13.3.2.1   Capacity Fade Model

This method estimates SOH by modeling the capacity degradation over time due to cycling, aging, and other factors [29, 30].

$$SOH(t) = Q(t) / Q(0)$$

where
   $Q(t)$ = the capacity of the battery at time t, and
   $Q(0)$ =is the initial capacity.

13.3.2.2   Electrochemical Impedance Spectroscopy (EIS) Method

This method estimates SOH by measuring the impedance of the battery at different frequencies and analyzing the data using an equivalent circuit model [31].

$$SOH(t) = f(Z(t))$$

where $Z(t)$ is the measured impedance of the battery at time t, and
   $f()$ is a function that maps impedance to SOH.

13.3.2.3   Voltage Relaxation Method

This method estimates SOH by measuring the voltage drop of the battery after a load is removed and using a model to relate the voltage drop to SOH [29].

$$SOH(t) = VR(t) / VR(0)$$

where
   $VR(t)$ = Voltage relaxation at time t, and
   $VR(0)$ = Initial voltage relaxation.

13.3.2.4   Fuzzy Logic Method

This method estimates SOH by taking into account multiple factors such as voltage, current, temperature, and other parameters using fuzzy logic [32].

$$SOH(t) = FL(I(t), V(t), T(t))$$

where
FL() = a fuzzy logic system that takes in the battery current, voltage, and temperature at time t and outputs estimated SOH.

13.3.2.5   Particle Filter Method

This method estimates SOH by combining a mathematical model of the battery with measurements from the battery using a particle filter algorithm [33].

$$SOH(t) = x(t|t)$$

where
x(t|t) = the estimated state of the battery at time t based on the particle filter.

13.3.2.6   Artificial Neural Network (ANN) Method

This method estimates SOH using a neural network that is trained on a large dataset of battery measurements [34].

$$SOH(t) = ANN(I(t),V(t),T(t))$$

where ANN() is a neural network that takes in the battery current, voltage and temperature at time t and outputs the estimated SOH.

13.3.2.7   Support Vector Machine (SVM) Method

This method estimates SOH using SVM algorithms to predict performance of the battery based on the measured parameters of voltage, current, and temperature [35].

$$SOH(t) = SVM(I(t),V(t),T(t))$$

where SVM() is an SVM algorithm that takes in the battery current, voltage, and temperature at time t and outputs the estimated SOH.

13.3.2.8   Gray Box Modeling Method

This method combines a physics-based model with empirical data to estimate the SOH [28].

$$SOH(t) = GBM(I(t),V(t),T(t))$$

where GBM() is a gray box model that combines a physics-based model with empirical data to estimate the SOH.

13.3.2.9   Kalman Filtering Method

This method estimates SOH by combining a mathematical model of the battery with measurements from the battery using a Kalman filter algorithm [22].

$$SOH(t) = x(t|t)$$

where $x(t|t)$ = estimated state of battery at a time t based on the Kalman filter.

13.3.2.10   Multi-Model Approach

This method estimates SOH by combining multiple models that take into account different aspects of battery aging, such as cycling, temperature, and storage conditions.

$$SOH(t) = MM(I(t), V(t), T(t))$$

where $MM()$ = multi-model approach that combines multiple models to estimate SOH depending on the battery parameters such as voltage, current, and temperature at time t.

Choice of the approach relies on the specific application, accuracy and complexity prerequisites of the estimation, as well as the available data and resources.

13.4   Cell Balancing Mechanism for BMS

Cell balancing is essential for maximizing the capacity and lifespan of batteries and ensuring their safe and efficient operation. The concept of cell balancing is important in batteries as it ensures that each cell in the battery pack is charged and discharged equally. In a battery pack, cells can have different capacities, internal resistances, and self-discharge rates, which can cause fewer cells to turn into completely charging or discharging mode before other cells [36]. This causes a reduction in the battery overall potential and lifespan, as well as an increase in the risk of safety issues such as overheating or explosion. Cell balancing is typically achieved by equalizing the state of charge (SOC) or state of health (SOH) of each cell in the battery pack. This can be done through various methods such as passive balancing, active balancing, or hybrid balancing. Passive balancing [37] involves adding resistors to the battery pack to discharge cells that are more charged, while active balancing [13] involves using a dedicated circuit to transfer charge between cells. Hybrid balancing combines both methods to achieve better balancing performance.

Machine learning algorithms are used in balancing cells to improve the accuracy and efficiency of the process. The algorithms use real-time data from various sensors to monitor the state of each cell in the battery. They then analyze these data to identify any imbalances in the cells and determine the optimal charging and discharging rates for each cell to bring the entire battery pack back into balance. There are several types of machine learning algorithms used in balancing cells, including artificial neural networks (ANNs), support vector machines (SVMs), and decision trees. ANN algorithms can learn from past data to predict the behavior of the battery, while SVM algorithms can classify the battery's state of charge

(SOC) based on the sensor data [4, 36]. Decision trees can identify the optimal charging and discharging rates for each cell based on the SOC and other factors.

In addition to real-time monitoring and control, machine learning can also be used for predictive maintenance, allowing battery managers to anticipate cell imbalances before they occur and take proactive measures to prevent them. This can help extend the life of the battery pack and reduce the risk of costly repairs or replacements [20]. Machine learning algorithms offer significant advantages for balancing cells in batteries, including improved accuracy, efficiency, and predictive maintenance capabilities. As battery technology continues to evolve, machine learning will play an increasingly important role in optimizing battery performance and extending battery life.

13.5   Industrial Applications

The application of machine learning in battery management systems can help improve performance, reduce maintenance costs, and extend the life of batteries, leading to better reliability, efficiency, and cost savings for industrial applications.

13.5.1   Industrial Applications of Machine Learning in Battery Management System

Machine learning has numerous industrial applications in battery management systems (BMS). Few applications are listed here.

(a) Predictive maintenance: Machine learning algorithms are capable of analyzing the sensor data from batteries to identify patterns and predict when maintenance is required. This indeed helps in preventing unexpected failures and lower downtime, improving operational efficiency [38].

(b) Battery state estimation: Machine learning algorithms can estimate the state of a battery, including its SOC and SOH by analyzing the battery data, which includes the following parameters: current, voltage, and temperature. This information is further used to optimize the battery performance and extend its life, leading to better reliability and reduced maintenance costs [14, 39].

(c) Optimal charging: Machine learning algorithms can optimize the charging process by analyzing the battery's characteristics and adjusting the charging parameters to maximize the battery's performance and lifespan. This can lead to reduced energy consumption, lower operating costs, and better overall system efficiency [36].

(d) Fault detection: Machine learning algorithms can detect faults in batteries by analyzing the sensor data and identifying abnormal behavior. This helps in preventing catastrophic failures as well lower the risk of damage. Early detection and resolution of faults can also reduce maintenance costs and downtime [39].

(e) Energy management: Machine learning algorithms can analyze data from multiple batteries in a system and optimize the energy usage based on demand and supply. This can help reduce energy waste and improve the efficiency of the overall system, resulting in reduced energy consumption and costs [36, 37].

13.5.2 Machine Learning Algorithms That Are Used for Industrial Applications in Battery Management System

Machine Learning procedures are broadly classified into Supervised Learning, Unsupervised Learning, and Reinforcement Learning. Different approaches that are used in BMS applications are shown in Figure 13.5. As the internal dynamic behavior and external operating conditions of the battery are complex and uncertain, it is difficult to precisely model a battery with the consideration of equivalent circuit and substantial built models to estimate the model parameters [4, 39]. The mathematical and statistical methods that are involved in machine learning are regarded as reliable and practical approaches to be applied in BMS

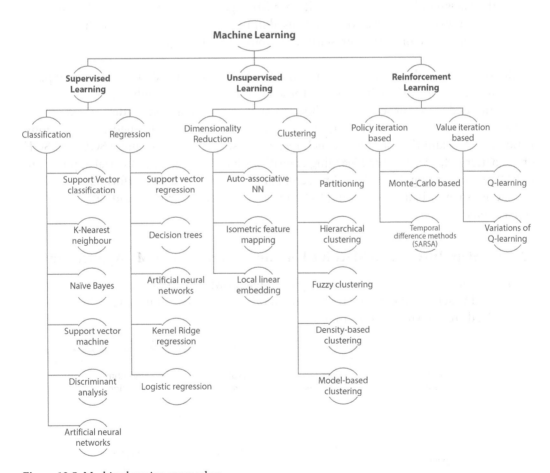

Figure 13.5 Machine learning approaches.

for estimating the SOC, SOH, and RUL. Along with SOC, SOH, and RUL, battery aging and degradation can also be predicted [4, 20, 23, 39].

ML algorithms have a range of industrial applications in battery management systems (BMS). Here are some of the commonly used algorithms:

(a) Artificial Neural Networks (ANNs): ANNs are used to model complex systems such as batteries. They can be used for battery state estimation, fault detection, and predictive maintenance [34].

(b) Support Vector Machines (SVMs): SVMs are applicable in classification and regression. They can be utilized for battery state estimation, fault detection, and optimal charging [35].

(c) Decision Trees: Decision trees are used in the tasks where classification and regression are involved. The approaches are applicable for detecting faults and predictive maintenance [40, 41].

(d) Random Forest: Random forest is an ensemble learning approach that can be used in the tasks of classification, regression, and feature selection. It is appliable in fault detection and predictive maintenance [41].

(e) Gaussian Processes (GPs): GPs are ML algorithms that are applicable for regression analysis. GPs can be used in BMS to predict the state of the battery based on data from sensors and other inputs [41].

The selection of the appropriate machine learning algorithm depends on the type of application and the availability of data. These algorithms can be combined with statistical techniques and signal processing methods to analyze the data from batteries and extract valuable insights. For example, battery state estimation can be performed using a combination of ANN and Kalman filter, which results in estimating the accurate SOC and SOH of the battery [4, 41]. Machine learning algorithms have a range of industrial applications in BMS. By leveraging these algorithms, companies can improve the performance, reliability, and lifespan of batteries, leading to better efficiency, cost savings, and safety for their applications.

13.5.3 Steps Involved in Machine Learning Approach in BMS Applications

The general flow of machine learning applications in BMS involves a few steps that has to be followed to achieve the productivity of the model that has been built [42]. The steps that are involved are shown in Figure 13.6.

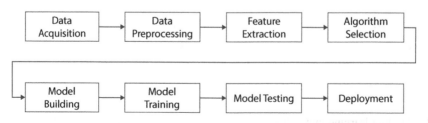

Figure 13.6 Steps involved in ML approach.

(a) Data Acquisition: It is the first step and the data are collected from the battery system using various sensors and data loggers. The data can include constraints of current, voltage temperature, and humidity.

(b) Data Pre-processing: Raw data are pre-treated to remove noise, filter outliers, and interpolate missing values. This ensures that the data are of high quality and can be used for analysis.

(c) Feature Extraction: The pre-processed data are then analyzed to extract relevant features that can be used for analysis. For example, the state of charge of the battery can be calculated from the data that include current and voltage values.

(d) Algorithm Selection: Appropriate machine learning algorithm is selected based on the particular application as well the type of data available. For example, ANN can be used for battery state estimation, while SVM can be used for fault detection.

(e) Model Training: With the data that have been pre-processed and algorithm that has been selected, the trained model will be tested. The model that has been built is then adjusted to minimize the error between the predicted and the actual output.

(f) Model Testing: The trained model is tested using a separate dataset to evaluate its performance. This helps to ensure that the model is accurate and can be used for real-world applications.

(g) Deployment: The next process after testing and validation of the model is deployment. The model can be deployed in BMS to perform various tasks such as battery state estimation, fault detection, and predictive maintenance.

Overall, the flow of machine learning applications in BMS involves data acquisition, pre-processing, feature extraction, algorithm selection, model training, model testing, and deployment. By following this flow, companies can improve the performance, reliability, and lifespan of batteries, leading to better efficiency, cost savings, and safety for their applications [4, 42].

13.5.4 Applications of Different ML Algorithms in BMS

13.5.4.1 Artificial Neural Networks (ANNs)

ANNs are widely used in BMS for predicting the state of the battery, such as SOC and SOH, as well for detecting and diagnosing the fault.

For example, in the study by Yin *et al.* (2019), an ANN has been used to predict SOC of a lithium-ion battery. The authors proposed an improved ANN algorithm that included a modified backpropagation algorithm and a self-adaptive learning rate strategy, which improved the accuracy of the SOC estimation. A study by Li *et al.* (2019) used a deep learning-based approach, where a stacked denoising autoencoder was used to extract features from the battery signals, which were then fed to an ANN for fault diagnosis of a lithium-ion battery pack [34].

13.5.4.2   Decision Trees

Decision trees are one of the popular ML algorithms that are applied in classification and regression problems. In BMS, decision trees could be exploited for troubleshooting and prognosis, as well as for determining the optimal charging and discharging strategies for batteries.

For example, in a study of Wu *et al.* (2019), decision trees were used to diagnose faults in Li-ion battery pack. The authors have developed a decision tree algorithm that was able to detect and diagnose different types of faults in the battery, such as overvoltage and overcurrent. Another study by Gao *et al.* (2020) used decision trees to determine the optimal charging and discharging strategies for lithium-ion batteries, which could prolong their lifetime and improve their performance [3, 4].

13.5.4.3   Support Vector Machines (SVMs)

SVMs are ML algorithms that are applicable in classification and regression problems. In BMS, SVMs are exploited for state estimation and fault detection and diagnosis.

For example, in the study of Zhang *et al.* (2018), an SVM is used to predict the SOC of a Li-ion battery. The authors used a radial basis function kernel and a recursive least squares algorithm for training the SVM, which achieved high accuracy in the SOC estimation. Another study by Huang *et al.* (2019) used an SVM to identify faults in a lithium-ion battery, such as short circuits and open circuits [35].

13.5.4.4   Random Forest

Random Forest is a method that is applicable in classification and regression problems. In BMS, random forest can be used for fault diagnosis and SOC estimation.

For example, a random forest algorithm can be used for fault diagnosis of lithium-ion batteries. The authors have proposed a method using feature extraction based on wavelet packet transform and then used random forest to classify the fault types. Random forest algorithm can also be used for estimating SOC of lithium-ion battery, using a dataset of battery voltage and current signals [40, 41].

13.5.4.5   Gaussian Process

Gaussian process is a probabilistic machine learning method that can be used for regression problems. In BMS, the Gaussian process can be used for SOC estimation and for predicting battery performance [41]. A Gaussian process regression model can be used to predict the SOC from the battery voltage and current signals, achieving high accuracy in the SOC estimation. The Gaussian process can predict the capacity fade of lithium-ion batteries, based on a dataset of battery performance data.

ANNs, decision trees, SVMs, random forest, and Gaussian process have shown promising results in various applications of BMS, including fault diagnosis, SOC estimation, and predicting battery performance [42]. However, choice of algorithm depends on application requirements and characteristics of the battery system.

13.6 Case Studies of ML-Based BMS Applications in Industry

Case studies along with the approach, dataset considered for analysis, and model that has been incorporated along with the results achieved are listed below in detail.

13.6.1 Machine Learning Approach to Predict SOH of Li-Ion Batteries

The work is an ML-based approach that has been proposed for predicting the state of health (SOH) of lithium-ion batteries [43]. Machine learning algorithm was trained using a large dataset of charge/discharge cycles of batteries and their corresponding capacity measurements. The trained model was then used to predict the SOH of batteries using their capacity measurements. The dataset used in this study consisted of 15,000 charge/discharge cycles of Li-ion batteries. Random Forest Regression model ML algorithm has been employed in which the dataset is split into two sets, namely, the training set and the testing set. The model will be trained on the training set. With the help of various performance metrics such as R-squared and Mean Absolute Error (MAE), functioning of model will be estimated. The proposed model has achieved an R-squared value of 0.98 and an MAE of 1.8%.

13.6.2 Anomaly Detection in Battery Management System Using Machine Learning

A machine learning-based approach is used for detecting anomalies in BMS. The machine learning algorithm was trained using a dataset of normal and anomalous battery behavior. The trained model was then used to detect anomalies in real-time battery operation [44]. Dataset includes the battery data collected from various sources such as laboratory experiments and field tests. The Support Vector Machine (SVM) model is used in the proposed method. After the dataset is split into the training set and testing set, the built model is trained on the training set. Model performance has been estimated depending on performance metrics of F1-score, precision, and recall. The proposed model has 98% precision, 95% recall, and 0.96 F1-score.

13.6.3 Optimization of Battery Life Cycle Using Machine Learning

Machine learning algorithm was trained using a dataset of battery charge/discharge cycles and their corresponding capacity measurements. The trained model was then applied to optimize battery life cycle as per the predicted optimal charge/discharge cycle parameters [45]. The dataset comprises 10,000 charge/discharge cycles of batteries. The Gradient Boosting Regression model is used in the approach. After splitting and training the data, the performance of the model has been assessed with the consideration of various performance metrics such as R-squared and MAE. The proposed model accomplished a 0.98 R-squared value and 1.9% MAE. Optimized charge/discharge cycle parameters were found to increase the battery life cycle by 10%.

13.6.4 Prediction of Remaining Useful Life Using Machine Learning

This study proposes a machine learning-based methodology to estimate the RUL of Li-ion batteries. The machine learning algorithm was trained using a dataset of battery discharge cycles and their corresponding capacity measurements [46]. The trained model is utilized for estimating RUL with consideration of the measured capacity of Li-ion batteries. The dataset includes 8,000 discharge cycles of Li-ion batteries. Long Short Term Memory (LSTM) is applied where performance of the model has been estimated by consideration of various performance measurements of R-squared and root mean squared error (RMSE). Predicted RUL estimates were found to be accurate within a range of ±10%.

13.6.5 Fault Diagnosis of Battery Management System Using Machine Learning

Machine learning algorithm is trained using a dataset of normal and faulty BMS operation. The trained model was then used to diagnose faults in real-time BMS operation [47]. BMS data are collected from various sources such as laboratory experiments and field tests. The analysis includes the Convolutional Neural Network (CNN) model. The dataset is split and the model is trained on the training set. Model performance has been estimated depending on various performance indices of precision, accuracy, F1-score, and recall; 97% accuracy and 95% precision have been achieved with the model.

13.6.6 Battery Parameter Estimation Using Machine Learning

A machine learning-based approach for estimating the internal resistance and capacity of batteries is proposed. The machine learning algorithm was trained using a dataset of battery charge/discharge cycles and their corresponding voltage and current measurements [48]. The model that has been trained is then utilized for estimating capacity and internal resistance of batteries based on their voltage and current measurements. The dataset used comprises 5,000 charge/discharge cycles of batteries. The Support Vector Regression (SVR) technique is applied wherein, initially, the splitting of the dataset and model training are performed. Model performance has been estimated depending on various performance metrics such as R-squared and MAE.

13.6.7 Optimization of Battery Charging Using Machine Learning

The study used a machine learning-based approach for optimizing the charging process of lithium-ion batteries. The machine learning algorithm was trained using a dataset of battery charging cycles and their corresponding temperature and voltage measurements [49]. The trained model was then used to predict the optimal charging parameters based on the battery temperature and voltage measurements. The dataset comprises 2,000 battery charging cycles. Random Forest (RF) algorithm is used in the proposed model. Model performance is estimated depending on several performance indices such as mean absolute error (MAE) and accuracy. The model accomplished 92% accuracy.

13.6.8   ML Approach to Estimate State of Charge

To estimate SOC of the battery unit, ML-based methodology is initiated with splitting of the dataset of the battery and testing the model that has been built. Machine learning algorithm was trained using a dataset of battery charge/discharge cycles and their corresponding voltage and current measurements [50]. The trained model has been utilized for the estimation of SOC of batteries depending on their voltage and current measurements. The dataset comprises 6,000 charge/discharge cycles of batteries. The Multi-Layer Perceptron (MLP) model is used in the approach. Model performance is estimated depending on performance indices such as MAE and R-squared. The model accomplished a 0.99 R-squared value and 0.98% MAE for SOC estimation.

13.6.9   Battery Capacity Estimation Using ML Approach

The ML algorithm was trained with the dataset of battery charge/discharge cycles and their corresponding voltage and current measurements [51]. The trained model is utilized for estimating the capacity of batteries based on their voltage and current measurements. The dataset consists of Li-ion parameters of NASA. CNN, FNN, and LSTM are involved, and model performance is estimated depending on various performance metrics such as temperature, voltage, and current. The model accomplished operating the battery at a safe operating region.

13.6.10   Anomaly Detection in Batteries Using Machine Learning

The ML algorithm was trained with the consideration of battery dataset that contains charge/discharge cycles and their corresponding voltage and current measurements. The trained model was then used to detect anomalies in batteries based on their voltage and current measurements [52]. The dataset consists of 5,000 charge/discharge cycles of batteries. The Support Vector Machine (SVM) technique is used, and model performance is estimated depending on several performance indices such as precision, recall, and F1-score. The proposed machine learning-based approach was found to be effective in detecting anomalies in batteries. In anomaly detection, the model accomplished 0.95 precision, 0.90 recall, and 0.92 F1-score.

13.6.11   ML-Based BMS for Li-Ion Batteries

The paper proposes an ML-based BMS intended for Li-ion batteries that estimates SOC and SOH of the battery more accurately and reliably. The proposed system uses an ensemble learning approach that combines multiple regression models and decision tree models. The system also uses a data preprocessing technique that removes outliers and reduces noise in the battery data [2]. The paper argues that conventional battery management systems based on mathematical models have limitations in accurate evaluation of SOH and SOC of Li-ion batteries because of the complex and nonlinear behavior of the batteries. The paper argues that machine learning techniques, such as ensemble learning, can improve accuracy and reliability of battery management systems by learning from large amounts of battery data and capturing the complex relationships between the battery variables. The paper finds that the proposed machine learning-based BMS can estimate SOH and SOC of Li-ion batteries more accurately and reliably than conventional battery management systems.

13.6.12 Battery Management System Based on Deep Learning for Electric Vehicles

The paper proposes a deep learning-based BMS for EVs which can predict battery SOH and SOC more accurately and quickly. The proposal is incorporated with the use of a convolutional neural network (CNN) for processing the time-series data from the battery and extract features that represent the battery's health and charge status. The paper reports that the proposed system achieved an estimation error of less than 1% for the state of charge and less than 3% for the state of health, which is better than conventional battery management systems. The paper argues that conventional battery management systems based on mathematical models have limitations in accurate prediction of SOC and SOH of batteries in electric vehicles due to the complex and nonlinear behavior of the batteries. The paper argues that deep learning techniques, such as CNNs, can improve the accuracy and speed of battery management systems by learning from large amounts of battery data and capturing the complex relationships between the battery variables [53]. The paper finds that the proposed deep learning-based BMS can predict the SOC and SOH of electric vehicle batteries more accurately and quickly than conventional battery management systems.

13.6.13 A Review of ML Approaches for BMS

A comprehensive review of ML approaches for BMS, including decision trees, regression models, support vector machines, and neural networks is discussed [54]. The paper discusses advantages and limitations of each approach and provides examples of their applications in BMS. The paper suggests that machine learning approaches can improve the accuracy and efficiency of BMS by learning from large amounts of battery data and capturing the complex relationships between the battery variables. The paper argues that conventional BMS based on mathematical models have limitations in accurately predicting the SOC and SOH of the batteries because of the complex and nonlinear behavior of the batteries. The paper argues that machine learning approaches can overcome these limitations by learning from large amounts of battery data and capturing the complex relationship between battery variables. The paper argues that the selection of the appropriate machine learning approach for BMS is dependent on the availability of the data and particular application.

The paper finds that machine learning approaches can be successfully applied to various BMS applications, such as EVs, portable electronics, and renewable systems.

Performance of machine learning-based BMS relies on various factors, comparable with quality of the data that has to be trained, complexity of the model, and feature selection. The paper recommends that additional research is essential to optimize the performance and scalability of machine learning-based BMS and to address challenges such as computational complexity, data privacy, and model interpretability.

13.6.14   Battery Management Systems Using Machine Learning Techniques

The paper discusses the development of battery management systems (BMS) using ML methodologies, including support vector machines (SVM), fuzzy logic systems (FLS), and artificial neural networks (ANN). The paper provides an overview of the components of a BMS, such as cell balancing, state estimation, and thermal management. The paper presents case studies of machine learning-based BMS for electric vehicles, hybrid renewable energy systems, and unmanned aerial vehicles [4]. The paper argues that machine learning techniques can improve the accuracy and reliability of BMS by learning from data and capturing the complex relationships between the battery variables; machine learning-based BMS can optimize the battery performance, extend battery life, and improve the safe operation of the battery. The selection of the appropriate machine learning technique for BMS is dependent on data that are available and the particular application. Machine learning-based BMSs have been successfully applied to numerous applications such as in EVs, unmanned aerial vehicles, and renewable energy systems.

The paper finds that machine learning-based BMS can achieve high accuracy and efficiency in assessment of battery state, balancing cells , and managing thermal parameters. The paper recommends that further research work is required to optimize performance and scalability of machine learning-based BMS and to address challenges such as computational complexity, data privacy, and model interpretability.

13.6.15   Machine Learning for Lithium-Ion Battery Management: Challenges and Opportunities

The paper examines the encounters and opportunities of application of machine learning techniques for Li-ion battery management, including battery SOC estimation, RUL prediction, and fault diagnosis [55]. The paper depicts a thorough review on the recent literature on machine learning-based battery management, including deep learning, reinforcement learning, and Bayesian methods. The paper highlights significance of feature selection, model interpretability, and data quality in machine learning-based battery management. The paper argues that machine learning techniques can provide accurate and reliable solutions to the challenges of lithium-ion battery management by learning from large amounts of data and capturing the nonlinear relationships between battery variables. Attainment of ML-based battery management counts on data availability and data standard, as well as the careful selection and engineering of features. The interpretability and transparency of machine learning models are critical for their acceptance and adoption in safety-critical applications.

The paper finds that machine learning-based battery management has shown promising results in SOC estimation, RUL prediction, and fault diagnosis, with significant improvements in accuracy and efficiency compared to traditional methods. Convolutional neural network (CNN) and recurrent neural network (RNN) deep learning techniques attained state-of-the-art performance in applications of battery management The paper identifies several research directions for future work, including the development of online learning algorithms, the integration of physics-based models with machine learning models, and the investigation of transfer learning and domain adaptation techniques.

13.6.16   An ML-Based BMS for Hybrid EVs

The paper proposes a machine learning-based BMS for Hybrid EVs that predict SOC and SOH of the battery pack accurately. The proposed BMS consists of a machine learning model, a system for capturing data, and a driver module, and is designed for optimal performance and reliable function of battery unit [56]. BMS assesses the real-time driving data and compares its performance with traditional BMS methods.

The paper argues that the proposed machine learning-based BMS can address the limitations of traditional BMS methods, which often rely on simplified models and assumptions and may not accurately capture the critical behavior of the battery system in real-time driving conditions. Machine learning techniques, such as RF and SVR, can effectively learn the nonlinear relationships between battery variables and advance the precision and robustness of BMS predictions. The suggested BMS can enhance the safety and reliability of HEVs by providing accurate SOC and SOH estimates and optimizing battery performance.

The paper finds that the proposed machine learning-based BMS achieves high accuracy and robustness in predicting SOC and SOH, with an MAE of 1.58% for SOC and 2.05% for SOH, respectively. The proposed BMS outperforms traditional BMS methods in terms of accuracy and stability, especially under varying driving conditions and temperature fluctuations. The effectiveness of BMS in improving efficiency and durability of the battery pack is determined by optimizing charging and discharging strategies based on the predicted SOC and SOH.

13.6.17   Battery Management System for EVs Using ML Techniques

The paper proposes a BMS for EVs using ML practices to enhance accuracy and efficiency of battery state estimation and control [57]. The proposed BMS consists of a data acquisition module, a machine learning module, and a control module, and is designed to optimize the battery performance and extend its lifespan. The paper presents a comprehensive evaluation of the proposed BMS using experimental data and compares its performance with traditional BMS methods. The paper argues that the proposed BMS can address the limitations of traditional BMS methods, such as limited accuracy, model complexity, and poor adaptability to changing conditions. ML methodologies such as ANNs and SVR can effectively learn the nonlinear relationships between battery variables and advance the precision and robustness of BMS predictions. The paper proposed that BMS can enhance the safety, reliability, and efficiency of EVs by providing accurate battery state estimation and control, optimizing charging and discharging strategies, and preventing overcharging, overdischarging, and thermal runaway.

The paper finds that the proposed machine learning-based BMS achieves high accuracy and robustness in estimating the state of battery variables, which includes SOH, SOC, and temperature, with a mean absolute error (MAE) of 1.7% for SOC, 2.2% for SOH, and 0.8°C for temperature. The proposed BMS outperforms traditional BMS methods accurately in terms of effectiveness and resilience, especially in accordance with varying running conditions and temperature fluctuations. The effectiveness of the proposed BMS in improving the battery performance and lifespan is determined by optimizing charging and discharging strategies based on the predicted SOC and SOH, and preventing overcharging, overdischarging, and thermal runaway.

13.6.18   A Hybrid BMS Using Machine Learning Techniques

The paper presents a hybrid BMS that combines traditional BMS methods with machine learning techniques that operate in parallel. The traditional BMS module performs real-time battery monitoring and controls battery charging and discharging, while the machine learning module learns from battery data to predict battery performance and estimate battery degradation [58]. The machine learning module uses an autoencoder neural network to extract important features from battery data along with the aid of LSTM interface for battery degradation prediction. Degradation that has been predicted is then adapted to adjust the recharge and discharge parameters of the traditional BMS module.

The hybrid BMS is evaluated using the life cycle test set of battery, and results attained illustrate that hybrid BMS outperforms traditional BMS methods in terms of battery life cycle and charging/discharging efficiency. The paper argues that traditional BMS methods have limitations in predicting battery performance and estimating battery degradation, which can lead to premature battery failure and reduced battery life. Machine learning techniques have the potential to overcome these limitations by learning from battery data and making more accurate predictions. Combining traditional BMS methods with machine learning techniques can result in a more robust and reliable BMS system that can improve battery performance and prolong battery life.

The hybrid BMS system presented successfully combines traditional BMS methods with machine learning techniques for enhancing battery function and extending battery lifespan. The machine learning module is able to accurately predict battery degradation and adjust the charging and discharging parameters of the traditional BMS module accordingly, resulting in improved battery life cycle and charging/discharging efficiency. The autoencoder neural network and long short-term memory network used in the machine learning module are effective in extracting important features from battery data and predicting battery degradation.

13.7   Challenges

While machine learning algorithms show great capability in improving the performance and reliability of battery management systems (BMS), there are still some gaps and limitations that need to be addressed [57]. Here are some of the key gaps identified in the current machine learning applications in BMS:

- Limited Data Availability: This aspect is one of the biggest challenges for BMS built using ML methodologies as the availability of high-quality battery data is limited. Collecting and labeling battery data is a time-consuming and expensive process, and there are often limitations in the number of batteries, types of batteries, and operational conditions that can be used for training machine learning models.
- Model Interpretability: Many ML algorithms, such as SVMs and ANNs, are frequently treated to be "black-box" models, meaning that they are challenging to interpret and provide little insight into the underlying mechanisms of

the battery system. This can limit the ability of BMS engineers to understand and diagnose potential failures or performance issues.

- Model Generalizability: Machine learning models trained on specific battery types and operational conditions may not generalize well to other battery types or different operating conditions. This can limit the scalability and applicability of machine learning algorithms in real-world BMS applications.
- Real-Time Implementation: Machine learning models often require significant computational resources and may not be suitable for real-time implementation in embedded BMS hardware. This can limit their usefulness in applications that require real-time monitoring and control of battery systems.
- Uncertainty Quantification: Many machine learning models do not provide a measure of uncertainty or confidence in their predictions. This can be a significant limitation in applications where accurate predictions and reliable decision-making are critical, such as in safety-critical applications.

Addressing these gaps will require further research and development in machine learning algorithms and BMS design, as well as improvements in battery data collection and sharing.

13.8   Conclusion

Machine learning techniques are successfully being applied to battery management systems, enabling better battery performance, reliability, and longevity. Through the use of ML algorithms, BMS learns the behavior of the battery and regulates its operations accordingly, leading to more efficient and effective battery management [2, 4]. These techniques have proven particularly useful in predicting battery health, optimizing battery usage, and extending battery life. Additionally, machine learning has also enabled better fault detection and diagnosis, an improvement in battery safety, and a reduction in the risk of catastrophic battery failure [36, 39, 40]. As the demand for better battery performance and reliability continues to increase, machine learning will undoubtedly play an increasingly important role in the development and implementation of battery management systems.

References

1. A.C.R. and Ghosh, A., Battery management system in electric vehicle. *2021 4th Biennial International Conference on Nascent Technologies in Engineering (ICNTE)*, pp. 1–6, NaviMumbai, India, 2021.
2. Shibl, M.M., Ismail, L.S., Massoud, A.M., A machine learning-based battery management system for state-of-charge prediction and state-of-health estimation for unmanned aerial vehicles. *J. Energy Storage*, 66, 107380, 2023, ISSN 2352-152X.
3. Raveena, C.S., Sravya, R.S., Kumar, R.V., Chavan, A., Sensor fusion module using IMU and GPS sensors for autonomous car. *2020 IEEE International Conference for Innovation in Technology (INOCON)*, Bangluru, India, pp. 1–6, 2020.

4. Ardeshiri, R.R., Balagopal, B., Alsabbagh, A., Ma, C., Chow, M.-Y., Machine learning approaches in battery management systems: State of the art: Remaining useful life and fault detection, in: *2020 2nd IEEE International Conference on Industrial Electronics for Sustainable Energy Systems (IESES)*, pp. 61–66, Cagliari, Italy, 2020.

5. Asef, P., Taheri, R., Shojafar, M., Mporas, I., Tafazolli, R., SIEMS: A secure intelligent energy management system for industrial IoT applications. *IEEE Trans. Ind. Inf.*, 19, 1, 1039–1050, Jan. 2023.

6. Deshpande, A. and Taylor, J.A., Optimal energy management and storage sizing for electric vehicles with dual storage. *IEEE Trans. Control Syst. Technol.*, 31, 2, 872–880, March 2023.

7. Vaideeswaran, V., Bhuvanesh, S., Devasena, M., Battery management systems for electric vehicles using lithium ion batteries, in: *2019 Innovations in Power and Advanced Computing Technologies (i-PACT)*, pp. 1–9, Vellore, India, 2019.

8. Deshpande, A. and Taylor, J.A., Optimal energy management and storage sizing for electric vehicles with dual storage. *IEEE Trans. Control Syst. Technol.*, 31, 2, 872–880, March 2023.

9. Wang, T., Pei, L., Lu, R., Zhu, C., Wu, G., Online parameter identification for lithium-ion cell in battery management system. *2014 IEEE Vehicle Power and Propulsion Conference (VPPC)*, pp. 1–6, Coimbra, Portugal, 2014.

10. Wang, L.Y., Polis, M.P., Yin, G.G., Chen, W., Fu, Y., Mi, C.C., Battery cell identification and SOC estimation using string terminal voltage measurements. *IEEE Trans. Veh. Technol.*, 61, 7, 2925–2935, Sept. 2012.

11. Jeewandara, J.M.D.S., JP, K., Hemapala, K.T.M.U., Parametrization and core temperature estimation of lithium-ion batteries for thermal management. *2021 IEEE Region 10 Symposium (TENSYMP)*, pp. 1–6, Jeju, Republic of Korea, 2021.

12. Kim, M.-J., Chae, S.-H., Moon, Y.-K., Adaptive battery state-of-charge estimation method for electric vehicle battery management system. *2020 International SoC Design Conference (ISOCC)*, pp. 288–289, Yeosu, Korea (South), 2020.

13. Gao, Z.C., Chin, C.S., Toh, W.D., Chiew, J., Jia, J., State-of-charge estimation and active cell pack balancing design of lithium battery power system for smart electric vehicle. *J. Adv. Transp.*, 2017, Article ID 6510747, 14, 2017, https://doi.org/10.1155/2017/6510747.

14. Kassim, M.R.M., Jamil, W.A.W., Sabri, R.M., State-of-Charge (SOC) and State-of-Health (SOH) estimation methods in battery management systems for electric vehicles. *2021 IEEE International Conference on Computing (ICOCO)*, pp. 91–96, Kuala Lumpur, Malaysia, 2021.

15. Tian, J., Xiong, R., Shen, W., State-of-Health estimation based on differential temperature for lithium ion batteries. *IEEE Trans. Power Electron.*, 35, 10, 10363–10373, Oct. 2020.

16. Shen, P., Ouyang, M., Lu, L., Li, J., Feng, X., The co-estimation of state of charge, state of health, and state of function for lithium-ion batteries in electric vehicles. *IEEE Trans. Veh. Technol.*, 67, 92–103, Jan. 2018.

17. Suryoatmojo, H., Anam, S., Rahmawan, Z., Asfani, D.A., Faurahmansyah, M.A., Prabowo, P., State of charge (SOC) estimation on lead-acid batteries using the coulomb counting method. *2022 10th International Conference on Smart Grid and Clean Energy Technologies (ICSGCE)*, pp. 78–84, Kuala Lumpur, Malaysia, 2022.

18. Song, Y., Park, M., Seo, M., Kim, S.W., Improved SOC estimation of lithium-ion batteries with novel SOC-OCV curve estimation method using equivalent circuit model. *2019 4th International Conference on Smart and Sustainable Technologies (SpliTech)*, pp. 1–6, Split, Croatia, 2019.

19. Kanchan, D., Nihal, Fernandes, A.P., Estimation of SoC for real time EV drive cycle using Kalman filter and coulomb counting, in: *2022 2nd International Conference on Intelligent Technologies (CONIT)*, pp. 1–6, Hubli, India, 2022.

20. Pecht, M.G. and Kang, M., PHM of li-ion batteries, in: *Prognostics and Health Management of Electronics: Fundamentals, Machine Learning, and the Internet of Things*, pp. 349–375, IEEE, USA, 2019.

21. Saji, D., Babu, P.S., Ilango, K., SoC estimation of lithium ion battery using combined coulomb counting and fuzzy logic method, in: *2019 4th International Conference on Recent Trends on Electronics, Information, Communication & Technology (RTEICT)*, pp. 948–952, Bangalore, India, 2019.

22. Azis, N.A., Joelianto, E., Widyotriatmo, A., State of Charge (SoC) and State of Health (SoH) estimation of lithium-ion battery using dual extended Kalman filter based on polynomial battery model, in: *2019 6th International Conference on Instrumentation, Control, and Automation (ICA)*, pp. 88–93, Bandung, Indonesia, 2019.

23. Gašperin, M., Juričić, Đ., Boškoski, P., Prediction of the remaining useful life: An integrated framework for model estimation and failure prognostics, in: *2012 IEEE Conference on Prognostics and Health Management*, pp. 1–8, Denver, CO, USA, 2012.

24. Jumah, S., Elezab, A., Zayed, O., Ahmed, R., Narimani, M., Emadi, A., State of charge estimation for EV batteries using support vector regression, in: *2022 IEEE Transportation Electrification Conference & Expo (ITEC)*, pp. 964–969, Anaheim, CA, USA, 2022.

25. Cheng, W., Yi, Z., Liang, J., Song, Y., Liu, D., An SOC and SOP joint estimation method of lithium-ion batteries in unmanned aerial vehicles, in: *2020 International Conference on Sensing, Measurement & Data Analytics in the Era of Artificial Intelligence (ICSMD)*, pp. 247–252, Xi'an, China, 2020.

26. Khalid, A., Sundararajan, A., Sarwat, A.I., A multi-step predictive model to estimate li-ion state of charge for higher C-rates, in: *2019 IEEE International Conference on Environment and Electrical Engineering and 2019 IEEE Industrial and Commercial Power Systems Europe (EEEIC / I&CPS Europe)*, pp. 1–6, Genova, Italy, 2019.

27. Wu, S.-L., Chen, H.-C., Tsai, M.-Y., Lin, T.-C., Chen, L.-R., AC impedance based online state-of-charge estimation for li-ion battery, in: *2017 International Conference on Information, Communication and Engineering (ICICE)*, pp. 53–56, Xiamen, China, 2017.

28. Balochian, S. and Baloochian, H., Improving grey prediction model and its application in predicting the number of users of a public road transportation system. *J. Intell. Syst.*, 30, 1, 104–114, 2021, https://doi.org/10.1515/jisys-2019-0082.

29. Wang, T., Zhu, C., Pei, L., Lu, R., Xu, B., The state of arts and development trend of SOH estimation for lithium-ion batteries, in: *Proceedings of the 2013 IEEE Vehicle Power and Propulsion Conference (VPPC)*, pp. 1–6, Beijing, China, 15–18 October 2013.

30. Zheng, Y., Ouyang, M., Lu, L., Li, J., Understanding aging mechanisms in lithium-ion battery packs: From cell capacity loss to pack capacity evolution. *J. Power Sources*, 278, 287–295, 2015.

31. Zhang, Q., Huang, C.-G., Li, H., Feng, G., Peng, W., Electrochemical impedance spectroscopy based State-of-Health estimation for lithium-ion battery considering temperature and state-of-charge effect. *IEEE Trans. Transp. Electrif.*, 8, 4, 4633–4645, Dec. 2022.

32. Singh, P. and Reisner, D., Fuzzy logic-based state-of-health determination of lead acid batteries, in: *24th Annual International Telecommunications Energy Conference*, pp. 583–590, Montreal, QC, Canada, 2002.

33. Pan, D., Li, H., Song, Y., A comparative study of particle filters and its variants in lithium-ion battery SOH estimation, in: *2020 International Conference on Sensing, Measurement & Data Analytics in the era of Artificial Intelligence (ICSMD)*, pp. 198–203, Xi'an, China, 2020.

34. Bezha, M., Bezha, K., Nagaoka, N., A practical SoH Estimation using adaptive ANN algorithm for the embedded EIS diagnosis in industrial applications, in: *2022 IEEE International Conference on Consumer Electronics*, pp. 571–572, Taiwan, Taipei, Taiwan, 2022.

35. Klass, V., Behm, M., Lindbergh, G., A support vector machine-based state-of-health estimation method for lithium-ion batteries under electric vehicle operation. *J. Power Sources*, 270, 262–272, 2014. ISSN 0378-7753.

36. Duraisamy, T. and Kaliyaperumal, D., Machine learning-based optimal cell balancing mechanism for electric vehicle battery management system. *IEEE Access*, 9, 132846–132861, 2021.

37. Shukla, A.P. and Patel, R.A., Battery management system by passive cell balancing for electric vehicle, in: *2022 2nd International Conference on Power Electronics & IoT Applications in Renewable Energy and its Control (PARC)*, pp. 1–6, 2022, Mathura, India.

38. Sridevi, H.R. and Bothra, S., Predictive maintenance of lead-acid batteries using machine learning algorithms, in: *Emerging Research in Computing, Information, Communication and Applications*. N.R. Shetty, L.M. Patnaik, N.H. Prasad, (Eds.), vol. 928, Lecture Notes in Electrical Engineering, Springer, Singapore, 2023, https://doi.org/10.1007/978-981-19-5482-5_63.

39. Ardeshiri, R.R., Balagopal, B., Alsabbagh, A., Ma, C., Chow, M.-Y., Machine learning approaches in battery management systems: State of the art: Remaining useful life and fault detection, in: *2020 2nd IEEE International Conference on Industrial Electronics for Sustainable Energy Systems (IESES)*, pp. 61–66, Cagliari, Italy, 2020.

40. Navada, A., Ansari, A.N., Patil, S., Sonkamble, B.A., Overview of use of decision tree algorithms in machine learning, in: *2011 IEEE Control and System Graduate Research Colloquium*, pp. 37–42, Shah Alam, Malaysia, 2011.

41. Xu, L., Wu, F., Chen, R., Li, L., Data-driven-aided strategies in battery lifecycle management: Prediction, monitoring, and optimization. *Energy Storage Mater.*, 59, 102785, 2023, ISSN 2405-8297.

42. Louridas, P. and Ebert, C., Machine learning. *IEEE Software*, 33, 5, 110–115, Sept.-Oct. 2016.

43. Wang, C., Ma, J., Sun, X., Lu, L., State of health prediction of lithium-ion batteries using machine learning. *J. Power Sources*, 424, 259–267, 2019.

44. Wang, J., Xu, M., Chen, H., Fault diagnosis of battery management system based on convolutional neural network. *Energies*, 14, 5, 1276, 2021.

45. Wu, Y., Xiong, R., Liu, Y., Guo, X., Optimization of battery life cycle using machine learning. *Appl. Energy*, 261, 114338, 2020.

46. Kefalas, M., Baratchi, M., Apostolidis, A., van den Herik, D., Bäck, T., Automated machine learning for remaining useful life estimation of aircraft engines, in: *2021 IEEE International Conference on Prognostics and Health Management (ICPHM)*, Detroit (Romulus), pp. 1–9, MI, USA, 2021.

47. Wang, J., Xu, M., Chen, H., Fault diagnosis of battery management system based on convolutional neural network. *Energies*, 14, 5, 1276, 2021.

48. Gruosso, G., Gajani, G.S., Valladolid, J.D., Patino, D., Ruiz, F., State of charge estimation of LiFePO4 battery used in electric vehicles using support vector regression, PCA and DP battery model, in: *2019 IEEE Vehicle Power and Propulsion Conference (VPPC)*, pp. 1–5, Hanoi, Vietnam, 2019.

49. Li, X., Yang, W., Wang, H., Chang, X., Dang, R., Wang, D., Optimization of li-ion battery charge and discharge model based on genetic algorithm, in: *Genetic and Evolutionary Computing*. ICGEC 2021. S.C. Chu, J.C.W. Lin, J. Li, J.S. Pan, (Eds.), vol. 833, Lecture Notes in Electrical Engineering, Springer, Singapore, 2022, https://doi.org/10.1007/978-981-16-8430-2_4.

50. Chen, L., Zhang, Y., Zhou, S., Wu, B., State-of-charge estimation of lithium-ion batteries based on multi-layer perceptron. *J. Power Sources*, 450, 227615, 2020.

51. Choi, Y., Ryu, S., Park, K., Kim, H., Machine learning-based lithium-ion battery capacity estimation exploiting multi-channel charging profiles. *IEEE Access*, 7, 75143–75152, 2019, .

52. Jin, X., Yang, G., Li, Y., Li, X., Anomaly detection in battery management system using machine learning. *Energies*, 12, 11, 2105, 2019.

53. Li, W., Cui, H., Nemeth, T., Jansen, J., Ünlübayir, C., Wei, Z., Zhang, L., Wang, Z., Ruan, J., Dai, H., Wei, X., Sauer, D.U., Deep reinforcement learning-based energy management of hybrid battery systems in electric vehicles. *J. Energy Storage*, 36, 102355, 2021, ISSN 2352-152X.

54. Ahmad, H.E., Gomaa, M.A., Sharkh, S.M., Mohammed, O.A., Machine learning for battery management systems in electric vehicles: A review. *IEEE Trans. Transp. Electrif.*, 6, 2, 443–456, 2020.

55. Chaturvedi, N.A., Klein, R., Christensen, J., Ahmed, J., Kojic, A., Modeling, estimation, and control challenges for lithium-ion batteries. *Proceedings of the 2010 American Control Conference, ACC 2010*, pp. 1997–2002, 2010.

56. Xing, Y., Ma, E.W.M., Tsui, K.L., Pecht, M., Battery management systems in electric and hybrid vehicles. *Energies*, 4, 11, 1840–1857, 2011.

57. Shanmugasundaram, R., Ganesh, C., Tamilselvi, P., Ravichandran, C.S., Mayurappriyan, P.S., Battery management system in EV applications: Review, challenges and opportunities, in: *ICT Analysis and Applications. Lecture Notes in Networks and Systems*, S. Fong, N. Dey, A. Joshi, (Eds.), vol. 517, Springer, Singapore, 2023, https://doi.org/10.1007/978-981-19-5224-1_52.

58. Wang, J., Li, Y., Gao, R.X., Zhang, F., Hybrid physics-based and data-driven models for smart manufacturing: Modelling, simulation, and explainability. *J. Manuf. Syst.*, 63, 381–391, 2022, ISSN 0278-6125.

14

ML Applications in Healthcare

Farooq Shaik, Rajesh Yelchuri, Noman Aasif Gudur and Jatindra Kumar Dash*

SRM University AP, Andhra Pradesh, India

Abstract

The era of intelligent algorithms has arrived, and machine learning is one of the most promising technologies to revolutionize healthcare. Until recently, manufacturing, transportation, and administration were the primary industries where machine learning algorithms had a significant impact. However, even formerly impervious industries like healthcare are suddenly being affected by these algorithms. While machine learning has been around for quite some time, its use in healthcare is continuously increasing alongside the availability of data. It is a statistical method that allows computers to learn from past data. They are able to identify patterns and come to conclusions or judgments depending on the information that they are presented with. Machine learning (ML) has numerous prospective applications within the healthcare industry. They extend from drug discovery to clinical decision-making and diagnosis. There are petabytes of healthcare-related data that require analysis. For instance, the human genome is an example of this, which is approximately 100 gigabytes per person. Furthermore, carry-and-wear devices generate a large quantity of data, including heart rate, blood pressure, and walking pattern. Therefore, on the basis of these data, ML techniques can be used to predict diseases and develop personalized treatments. Moreover, X-ray and MRI image classification techniques can be used to construct an ML algorithm for potential disease diagnosing, thereby reducing the burden on clinicians. Likewise, in drug discovery and development, ML algorithms have been utilized to help identify novel therapeutic targets, design new drug candidates, and predict drug toxicity. ML techniques can be used to create predictive models for patient outcomes like mortality, readmission, and disease progression. ML algorithms can be put to use to analyze electronic health record (EHR) data to facilitate clinical decision-making, such as predicting patient readmission rates or identifying patients who may benefit from a specific treatment. Therefore, ML has the potential to revolutionize the healthcare industry by providing methods to cluster, classify, predict, and assist clinicians in making informed decisions. Consequently, this chapter will investigate the current state of machine learning (ML) in the healthcare industry, as well as the challenges it faces and its future development potential.

Keywords: Artificial intelligence (AI), machine learning (ML), deep learning, predictive modeling, electronic health records (EHR), clinical decision support systems (CDSS), medical imaging analysis, disease diagnosis

*Corresponding author: jatindrakumar.d@srmap.edu.in

Arindam Dey, Sukanta Nayak, Ranjan Kumar and Sachi Nandan Mohanty (eds.) *How Machine Learning is Innovating Today's World: A Concise Technical Guide*, (201–220) © 2024 Scrivener Publishing LLC

14.1 Introduction

Machine learning (ML) is a subfield of artificial intelligence (AI) concerned with the development of models and algorithms that can acquire knowledge from data and use it to make predictions or decisions. In other words, machine learning enables computers to learn without explicit programming. This is accomplished by the use of statistical techniques, which enable computers to recognize structures and correlations within data.

Machine learning is the process by which a computer program enhances its performance at a given task T, as measured by a performance metric P, through experience E. This experience entails exposure to data and the capacity to learn from it, resulting in enhanced performance over time. In recent years, the discipline of machine learning has expanded rapidly. The abundance of data that is now accessible has a substantial impact on the development of machine learning. In addition, advances in computing power have substantially contributed to the expansion of machine learning. Machine learning is currently utilized in numerous disciplines, including image and speech recognition, natural language processing, and even autonomous vehicles.

Machine learning possesses a significant capability to gain insights from data, which is done through the training process. During the training process, additional data are supplied to the machine learning algorithm, enabling it to continuously learn and enhance its predictive and decision-making skills. This phase holds crucial importance in the overall machine learning procedure.

14.1.1 Supervised Learning

Supervised learning is a subsection of machine learning that involves training a model or algorithm using a dataset that has been labeled. In order for the algorithm to develop a function that maps inputs to outputs, it requires the user to provide the algorithm with

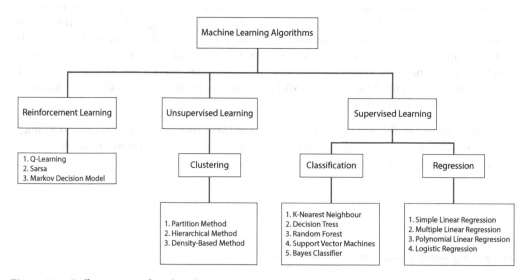

Figure 14.1 Different types of machine learning.

input/output pairs, which are also referred to as training data. After the algorithm has been trained, it may be used to make predictions about the output based on fresh inputs that are provided.

A spam filtering system trained on labeled emails to distinguish between spam and non-spam emails is an excellent example of supervised learning. The algorithm learns from these labeled examples and identifies patterns to predict the spam or non-spam classification of new emails.

There are two categories of supervised learning: regression and classification. Regression is used to predict continuous outputs, such as the house price based on its size and location. In contrast, classification predicts discrete outcomes, such as the classification of an email as spam or not spam.

Linear regression, SVM, random forests, logistic regression, and decision trees are common supervised learning algorithms. Figure 14.1 showcases different types of machine algorithms along with corresponding examples.

14.1.2   Unsupervised Learning

Unsupervised learning is a type of machine learning in which the learning algorithm is taught on data that have not been labeled, and there are no predetermined outputs or labels to guide the training process. Instead, the algorithm is tasked with discovering recurring themes and interconnections within the data on its own. Discovering previously concealed data patterns or structures and clustering or grouping data points that are similar are both valuable applications of unsupervised learning. Clustering is a typical type of unsupervised learning that discovers groups of related data points based on their traits or qualities. Clustering may be used in a variety of applications, including data analysis and machine learning. The process of dimension reduction takes a dataset and decreases the number of characteristics it contains while attempting to save as much of the important information as possible.

Autoencoders, K-means clustering, hierarchical clustering, principal component analysis (PCA), and PCA are typical unsupervised learning algorithms. Unsupervised learning applications include customer segmentation, anomaly detection, speech and image recognition, and data compression.

14.1.3   Semi-Supervised Learning

The process of machine learning known as semi-supervised learning brings together aspects of supervised learning and unsupervised learning methodologies. During the training process, the algorithm is exposed to data that have been tagged as well as data that have not been labeled. Utilizing unlabeled data as part of this technique is intended to help achieve the goal of improving the accuracy of the algorithm's predictions when applied to labeled data. The algorithm is able to obtain a more in-depth grasp of the underlying structure of the data and make more accurate predictions for the labeled data if it first identifies patterns and correlations in the data that have not been labeled.

Semi-supervised learning is helpful in circumstances in which getting labeled data is difficult or expensive since it can minimize the quantity of labeled data necessary for training.

This technique is applied extensively in a broad range of fields, such as data mining, natural language processing, and image and audio recognition.

Self-training, co-training, and multi-view learning are popular semi-supervised learning algorithms. Self-training improves a model's efficacy on labeled data by using its predictions on unlabeled data. Co-training entails training multiple models on distinct subsets of data and using the predictions of one model to label data for the other. Multi-view learning entails training multiple models on diverse data views, such as different features or representations, and combining their predictions to improve precision.

14.1.4   Reinforcement Learning

In the branch of machine learning known as reinforcement learning, agents learn to make decisions by interacting with their surroundings in order to advance in the learning process. Depending on how the agent behaves in relation to the environment, it will either be rewarded with positive experiences or subjected to negative ones. The end goal of the agent is to devise a tactic that will allow it to accumulate the greatest possible number of rewards throughout the course of its existence.

The procedure of reinforcement learning includes the following steps:

1. The agent observes the environment's present state.
2. Based on the current condition, the agent chooses a course of action. The environment reacts to the action by transitioning to a new state and rewarding or punishing the agent accordingly. The agent modifies its policy on amount of reward acquired and the current environment state.
3. The procedure is repeated from step 1, with the agent using its updated policy to determine the next action. Robotics, game play, and recommendation systems are just a few of the many disciplines where reinforcement learning is applicable. Q-learning, Policy gradient methods, and Actor–critic methods are three well-known reinforcement learning algorithms.

14.2   Applications of Machine Learning in Health Science

By embracing machine learning, the field of health science holds the promise of undergoing a transformative revolution. This technology can aid in the development of sophisticated diagnostic tools, personalized medicine, and disease prediction models. In this part, some of the promising applications of machine learning methods in the field of health sciences are discussed.

14.2.1   Diagnosis and Prediction of Disease

ML algorithms exhibit remarkable proficiency in disease identification and predictive capabilities. They demonstrate the capacity to effectively recognize diseases and anticipate their occurrence, and how they will proceed because they are trained on vast datasets that contain medical records, imaging data, and genetic information. The capacity of machine learning to recognize complicated data patterns, some of which may not be obvious to human specialists, is one of the advantages of employing this technique in the process of illness detection. This is especially helpful in the diagnosis of disorders that are uncommon or difficult to identify, for which standard diagnostic procedures might not be successful. In addition, using a patient's medical history, lifestyle characteristics, and genetic information, machine learning may determine the risk that a patient would acquire a certain illness in the future. This prediction can be made based on the patient's genetic information. These predictions can assist medical professionals in identifying individuals who are at high risk and in developing preventive or curative care plans for those patients.

14.2.1.1   Predicting Thyroid Disease

Thyroid disease refers to a group of medical conditions that affect the thyroid gland, a small butterfly-shaped gland located in the front of the neck. The thyroid gland plays a crucial role in regulating various bodily functions by producing thyroid hormones.

Banu *et al.* [2] utilize Linear Discriminant Analysis (LDA), a machine learning technique, to predict hypothyroid disease. The dataset used in the study is sourced from the UCI repository. LDA Algorithm, a supervised learning technique commonly used for classifying, is employed in this research. With a cross-validation k =6 (When implementing "k=6" cross-validation, the dataset is partitioned into six subsets or folds of equal size. Subsequently, the model undergoes six rounds of training and evaluation. In each iteration, a different fold serves as the validation set, while the remaining five folds function as the training set. This methodology enables a thorough evaluation of the model's performance by averaging the outcomes obtained from the six iterations.), the algorithm achieves an impressive accuracy of 99.62%. The developed model has the potential to assist doctors in making informed decisions and providing improved treatment to patients.

Chaubey *et al.* [3] investigate the classification of individuals with thyroid disease using the thyroid disease database. To achieve this, logistic regression classification, decision tree classification, and nearest neighbors classification techniques are employed. The paper provides a comprehensive explanation of each technique, detailing the steps involved in their implementation. Furthermore, a thorough comparison of the prediction accuracy of these techniques is conducted, allowing for a comprehensive assessment of their performance.

14.2.1.2   Predicting Cardiovascular Disease

Heart disease is a leading global cause of mortality, presenting a significant challenge for medical practitioners in terms of accurate prediction. Predicting cardiovascular diseases requires specialized expertise and in-depth knowledge due to its complexity. However, recent advancements in medical technologies, specifically those based on ML algorithms, have emerged as valuable tools in this prediction process. These innovative approaches contribute significantly to improving the accuracy of cardiovascular disease prediction.

In their research paper [1], the authors introduce a novel hybrid approach for cardiovascular disease prediction by harnessing the power of diverse machine learning techniques. The proposed methodology incorporates several well-known classifiers, including Logistic Regression (LR), Adaptive Boosting (AdaBoostM1), Fuzzy Unordered Rule Induction (FURIA), GFS-LB, and Multi-Objective Evolutionary Fuzzy Classifier (MOEFC). By combining these different classifiers, the aim is to improve the accuracy and reliability

Table 14.1 The output of multiple class classification obtained through 10-fold method [1].

Algorithm	Sensitivity	Specificity	Accuracy
MOEFC	79.96	75.44	79.42
LR	78.22	71.34	78.77
AdaBoostM1	80.11	75.40	80.01
Vote	84.76	74.82	80.20

of predicting cardiovascular diseases. To evaluate the performance of each classifier, the authors compare their accuracy and results. This comparison provides insights into the strengths and weaknesses of each classifier and helps identify the most effective one for achieving more precise cardiovascular disease predictions. By selecting the best-performing classifier, the researchers strive to increase the accuracy of the models.

The provided Table 14.1 presents the outcomes of various algorithms, displaying their sensitivity, specificity, and accuracy. Notably, the vote algorithm demonstrates promising results. The dataset utilized in this study is sourced from the UCI Repository of Machine Learning Databases, specifically the Heart Disease Dataset. This dataset comprises 303 records with 14 medical features with 178 positive cases and 125 negative cases, encompassing a collection of medical analytical reports.

14.2.1.3   Predicting Cancer

Cancer encompasses a wide range of diseases characterized by the unregulated proliferation and dissemination of abnormal cells throughout the body. These cells have the potential to form tumors or infiltrate nearby tissues and organs, leading to a variety of health complications. Cancer can manifest in any part of the body and is commonly named after the specific organ or tissue from which it originates. Examples of prevalent cancer types include breast cancer, lung cancer, prostate cancer, colorectal cancer, and leukemia, among numerous others. There are different ML techniques used for early prediction and diagnosis of cancer in patients. A brief description of some methods and features used and accuracy achieved can be seen from Table 14.2.

14.2.1.4   Predicting Diabetes

High blood glucose levels are a hallmark of diabetes, a chronic metabolic condition caused by either inadequate insulin synthesis or inadequate insulin utilization by the body. The pancreas secretes insulin, a hormone that aids in controlling blood sugar levels and enables cells to use glucose as an energy source. For diabetes to be managed continuously and to avoid complications, blood sugar levels must be regulated.

In a report by the World Health Organization (WHO), as referenced by Mir Ayman *et al.* [10], it was stated that India ranked first in terms of diabetes prevalence in 2000, with

Table 14.2 Different classification ML techniques used on different types of cancer.

Study	Classification technique	Disease	Features	Accuracy	Validation method	Important features
Waddell et al. [4]	Support vector machine	Multiple myeloma	80 Single-nucleotide polymorphisms	71 out of 100	Cross-validation with the leave-one-out method	snp994532, snp739514, snp521522
S. Damaraju et al. [5]	Support vector machine	Cancer of breast	174 Single-nucleotide polymorphisms	69%	Cross-validation with a fold size of 20	snpCYP1B1 (+)4328 C-G, snpCY11B2 (+) 4536 T/C,
Exarchos K et al. [6]	Bayesian network	Cancer of oral tissue, genomic	86 Blood tissue genomic, clinical, imaging	100%	10-fold cross validation	Extra-tumor spreading, smoker, p53 stain, TCAM, SOD2
Chen Y-C et al. [7]	Artificial neural network	Cancer of lung	440 Clinical gene expressions	83.5%	Cross-verification	ERBB2, N_stage, T_stage LCK, genes, sex
Park K et al. [8]	Graph-based SSL algorithm	Cancer of breast	162,500 SEER	71%	5-fold cross-validation	Number of nodes, age, size of tumor during diagnosis
Xu X et al. [9]	Support vector machine	Cancer of breast	295 Genomics	97%	LOOCV	50 gene signatures

a staggering 31.7 million individuals diagnosed with the condition. It is projected that this number will significantly rise to 79.4 million. Thus, we need accurate diagnosis and early prediction.

Figure 14.2 depicts [10] approaches that have been applied to predict disease. The Pima Indians Diabetes Database was the source of the data used in this investigation. The dataset consists of a total of 768 instances, with a size of 37 KB.

In this particular research study [10], the authors employed four machine learning-based classifiers, namely, Naive Bayes, Support Vector Machine, Random Forest, and Simple CART, to predict the occurrence of diabetes. The experimentation was conducted using the WEKA tool. The performance of these classifiers was evaluated based on training time, testing time, and accuracy values. Additionally, the classifier accuracy was assessed using measures such as TPR (True positive rate), FPR (False positive rate), precision, recall, and F-Measure. The results of the study indicated that the Support Vector Machine classifier outperformed Naive Bayes, Random Forest, and Simple CART in terms of predicting diabetes disease. This conclusion was drawn from the comparative analysis of the classifiers' performance. The experimental findings strongly demonstrate the effectiveness of the proposed model.

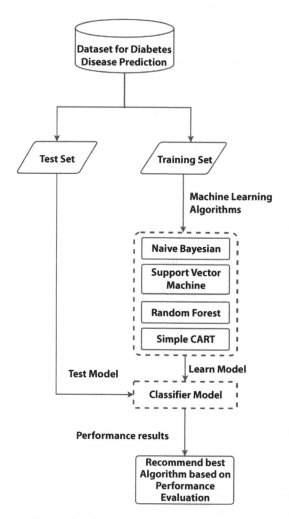

Figure 14.2 Approaches applied to predict disease.

14.2.1.5 Predicting Alzheimer's

It is a neurological ailment that gradually worsens over time and affects the brain. This disease causes cognitive decline, loss of memory, and behavioral changes. It is the type of dementia that affects the most people. It is not completely understood what causes the condition; however, it is believed that genetic, environmental, and lifestyle factors are all involved. Alzheimer's disease is distinguished by aberrant protein deposits in the brain, which interfere with cell communication and ultimately lead to the loss of brain cells. The symptoms start off with only a little bit of memory loss and gradually get worse, eventually leading to confusion, trouble with language, and functional impairment. There is currently no cure for this condition; however, medications can help manage symptoms and decrease the disease's course. Interventions centered on lifestyle and diagnosis at an early stage are essential. Ongoing studies are being conducted with the goals of better understanding the condition, creating treatments for it, and finding ways to prevent it. According to Balne

Table 14.3 Different models' accuracy [13].

S. no.	Model	Accuracy
1	LR (Logistic Regression)	93%
2	SVM (Support Vector Machine) Classifier	58%
3	SVM with Linear kernel having C=1	93%
4	SVM with Linear kernel having C=2	95%
5	DT (Decision Tree)	83%
6	RF (Random Forest)	90%
7	NB (Naïve Bayes)	93%

et al.'s study [11], which shows the findings of a survey that was carried out by the World Alzheimer's Organization in 2018, this illness affected around 50 million people in 2018. It is anticipated that this number would triple by the year 2050. The symptoms of Alzheimer's disease are typically noticeable in those over the age of 60. However, some forms of AD are more common in younger ages for humans as well, and this is due to mutations in their genes.

In their study, Kumar *et al.* [12] employed the ADNI dataset to predict early Alzheimer's disease. The authors utilized AlexNet, a deep learning architecture, on MRI images. The findings revealed that the disease could be predicted with an impressive accuracy of 90%.

Kishore *et al.* [13] used machine learning to predict Alzheimer's disease. The accuracy achieved by using different machine learning models is shown in Table 14.3.

14.2.2   Drug Development and Discovery

Another essential application of machine learning in the health sciences is drug discovery and development. Identifying and optimizing chemical compounds in order to create a new drug that can be used to treat a disease is a time-consuming and expensive process. This process can be accelerated by using ML to identify promising compounds more rapidly and efficiently than with conventional methods. These algorithms and training techniques are used on big databases of molecular structures and their biological reactions. By analyzing these data, ML can accurately predict the goodness of novel compounds and identify candidates for further drug development. This strategy has the potential to reduce drug discovery's cost and duration. Additionally, ML can be utilized to optimize drug concentrations and treatment protocols. ML can predict the optimal concentration of a drug for a specific patient or population by analyzing patient data, including genetics, medical history, and other relevant factors. This tactic has the potential to improve the efficacy of therapies while also lowering the risk of their causing undesirable effects.

Gupta, Rohan, and their colleagues [14] provide insights into the wide-ranging applications of artificial intelligence (AI) and machine learning (ML) algorithms throughout

Table 14.4 Different deep learning designs related to small-molecule drug design and development.

Method	Prediction	Dataset	Features	Reference
Deep Neural Network	Permeability	Tox21 dataset	Molecular fingerprints	Shie et al. [17]
Deep Neural Network	Toxicity	BindingDB, ChEMBL database;	Protein sequence and molecular fingerprints	Mayr et al. [18]
Convolutional Neural Network	Biological activity	DUDEs	Docking result and molecular graph	Wallach et al. [19]
Convolutional Neural Network	Virtual screening	6252	Fingerprints	Pereira et al. [20]
Auto-encoder	Virtual screening	8014, 41/193	Structure image of 2D chemical	Kadurin et al. [21]
Convolutional Neural Network	Biological toxicity/ activity	756	SMILES	Goh et al. [22]
Deep Neural Network	Biological activity	ChEMBL database	SMILES	Lenselink et al. [23]
Recurrent Neural Network	Generating focused molecular libraries	ChEMBL database	SMILES	Segler et al. [24]
Recurrent Neural Network	Generating novel molecules	Multiple datasets	Fingerprints	Olivecrona et al. [25]
Generative Adversarial Network	Generating novel molecules	3D electron density	Fingerprints	Guimares et al. [26]
Convolutional Neural Network	The Kohn Sham kinetic energy	3D electron density	2D chemical structure image	Yao and Parkhill [27][28]

various stages of drug discovery. They emphasize the numerous processes that can benefit from these technologies. The authors also delve into the utilization of decision tree (DT)-based programs and open-source tools that employ Monte Carlo tree search for retrosynthesis planning. This approach involves the guidance of a neural network in the planning process. Through the combination of three different neural networks with the tree search of Monte Carlo, the researchers successfully unveil novel retrosynthesis pathways that were previously unknown. This research exemplifies the tremendous potential of AI and ML in revolutionizing drug discovery by enabling more efficient and effective processes. It facilitates the identification of new drug candidates and expands our comprehension of intricate chemical reactions. By leveraging these technologies, the field of drug discovery stands to benefit from accelerated advancements and enhanced outcomes.

In their publication [15], Rodrigues, Tiago, *et al.* underscore the significance of identifying and validating small-molecule effectors for the advancement of molecular medicine. The authors emphasize the importance of acquiring accurate knowledge about both the intended and unintended targets associated with the efficacy and drawbacks of chemical substances. This understanding is crucial to maximize the benefits and minimize the failure rates in the development pipelines. The paper also explores the concept of polypharmacology or network pharmacology, which involves the interaction of bioactive compounds with multiple related or unrelated macromolecules and highlights how this can result in adverse drug reactions. Furthermore, the authors advocate for the utilization of machine learning algorithms to generate research hypotheses based on statistical analysis and prioritize biochemical screenings for target identification during the drug development process. By leveraging these approaches, they aim to enhance the efficiency and effectiveness of drug discovery and development in molecular medicine.

Jing *et al.* [16] provide an overview of the application of deep learning techniques in small-molecule drug discovery and development. They discuss the utilization of different deep learning designs in various applications related to small-molecule drug design and development. Later, the focus narrows down to specific applications within this domain. Additionally, they go through the advantages and disadvantages of DL techniques as well as the key difficulties that must be overcome. Table 14.4 depicts various machine learning methods used for the discovery of new drug molecules by various studies.

14.2.3   Clinical Decision Support (CDS)

"Clinical Decision Support" system is what CDS stands for. It is a computer-based information system that offers knowledge and resources to help healthcare practitioners make clinical decisions. To provide suggestions, alerts, and reminders pertaining to patient care, CDS systems employ patient-specific data and evidence-based recommendations. These systems give doctors immediate access to pertinent information at the point of care, improving patient outcomes, enhancing healthcare quality, and reducing medical errors. CDS systems can be used as standalone apps or incorporated into electronic health record (EHR) systems. They can address a range of clinical decision-making topics, including disease management, planning of treatments, support for diagnostic procedures, and drug management.

The methodologies that were utilized in this paper [30] include the construction of an explainable clinical decision support system (CDSS) that is based on machine learning. The goal of this system is to identify high-risk women who require targeted pregnancy intervention. The authors used the maternal features as well as the blood biomarkers that were taken at the beginning of the PEARS trial. Following the proper preparation of the data, the application of a synthetic minority oversampling technique, and the selection of the features, five different machine learning algorithms were used, and a fivefold cross-validated grid search was used to optimize the balanced accuracy. In order to improve the system's credibility and make it more appealing to users, the models were described using the Shapley additive explanations. Multiple models were built for a variety of use cases, including theoretical, screening for GDM during a regular antenatal visit, and risk assessment for GDM remotely. The models have been developed as a web server application and are now openly accessible for use in academic settings.

In their study, Tuppad et al. [31] conducted a comprehensive review of machine learning research in three key application areas: risk assessment, diagnosis, and prognosis. By examining existing methodologies, the paper identifies gaps and limitations in the current machine learning approaches for diabetes. Furthermore, the study highlights important aspects involved in utilizing machine learning for clinical decision support in diabetes management. The ultimate objective is to enhance the accuracy and efficiency of clinical decision-making in the context of diabetes management.

Kim et al. [32] suggested to devise a specialized model customized for clinical decision support (CDS) in order to classify different stages of sleep using single-channel EEG data. CNN and a transformer are combined in the model to allow for the supervised learning of the three different stages of sleep. The findings show that the generated model, which is equivalent to human experts in terms of accuracy, obtained an overall accuracy of 91.4%. Additionally, for normal, mild, moderate, and severe instances, the accuracy rates were 94.3%, 91.9%, 91.9%, and 90.6%, respectively. This study's main contribution is the development of a method that can efficiently and accurately divide sleep stages into three groups. This model has the potential to be an effective CDSS.

14.2.4   Medical Image Examination

One of the most popular uses of machine learning nowadays is found in the field of medical imaging analysis, which is part of the health sciences. Medical imaging technologies such as x-ray, computed tomography (CT), magnetic resonance imaging (MRI), and ultrasound create huge volumes of data, which may then be evaluated using ML to help in the finding and planning of therapy for disease.

In the study of Jasti et al. [33], features are extracted using AlexNet. The relief algorithm is used to pick features. The proposed method utilizes various ML methods such as least square support vector machine, K-nearest neighbors, Naïve Bayes, and random forest for disease categorization and detection. The experimental investigation involves collecting data from the MIAS dataset. One of the advantages of this method is the utilization of image analysis to accurately diagnose breast cancer disease.

The following table depicts the use of different machine learning models detecting COVID using image classification on different methods and their respective accuracy in predicting the model. Table 14.5 shows a comprehensive study and review of literature.

Table 14.5 COVID image classification using different methods.

Paper	Input	Method	Performance
[34]	CT	CNN model with prior training and Image Net weight	Recall: 95.78%, Accuracy: 96.20%
[35]	CT	CNN model with prior training and Image Net weight	Recall: 96.29%, Precision: 96.29%, Accuracy: 96.25%
[36]	Computed Tomography	Multi-task learning utilizing an encoder and two decoders	Accuracy: 95.23%
[37]	CT and X-ray	Image-based convolutional neural network trained previously image net weight	Accuracy: 95.61%
[38]	CT	Image-based convolutional neural network trained previously image net weight	Accuracy: 94.50%
[39]	CT	Image-based convolutional neural network trained previously image net weight	Recall: 91.45%, Accuracy: 93.01%
[40]	X-ray	Image-based convolutional neural network trained previously image net weight	Accuracy: 98.33%
[41]	X-ray	Image-based convolutional neural network trained previously image net weight	Accuracy: 91.0%
[42]	X-ray	COVID NET	Accuracy: 93.30%
[43]	X-ray	CNN model with prior training and Image Net weight	Accuracy: 94.5%
[44]	X-ray	Image-based convolutional neural network trained previously image net weight	Accuracy: 95.9%
[45]	X-ray	Image-based convolutional neural network trained previously image net weight	Recall: 98%, Precision: 92.90%
[46]	X-ray	Image-based convolutional neural network trained previously image net weight	Accuracy: 97.97%
[47]	X-ray	SVM used as classifier, CNN model with prior training and Image Net weight	Accuracy: 94.74%, Recall: 91.00%

14.2.5 Monitoring of Health and Wearable Technology

Important areas of health science that can benefit from machine learning are health surveillance and wearable technology. Wearable devices can generate immense quantities of data that can be analyzed with ML to provide valuable insights into the health status of patients and aid in the prevention and management of chronic diseases.

In their study on automatic epilepsy monitoring, Huang *et al.* [48] focused on epilepsy, a neurological condition characterized by recurring seizures. These seizures arise from abnormal electrical activity in the brain, causing temporary disturbances in regular brain function. Epilepsy can affect individuals across different age groups and can be attributed to diverse factors such as genetic predisposition, brain injuries, infections, or developmental disorders. The act of direct real-time monitoring of patient health is essential for epileptic patients. Wearable technologies offer the potential for real-time epilepsy monitoring and seizure alerts to carers. The authors suggested a simple machine-learning architecture for real-time epilepsy monitoring on wearable technology as part of the ICASSP 2023 Seizure Detection Challenge. The authors conducted tests and presented their proposed architecture, utilizing the SeizeIT2 dataset obtained from the wearable SensorDot (SD) developed by Byteflies.

According to the experimental findings, the suggested framework detects seizures with a sensitivity of 73.6% and a specificity of 96.7%.

In their research [49], Hamza *et al.* introduced a novel model called wearables-assisted smart health monitoring (WSHMSQP-ODL) that focuses on predicting sleep quality. The model utilizes wearables to collect data on sleep and activity, which is then subjected to pre-processing to ensure standardized formatting. The WSHMSQP-ODL method integrates the (DBN) model for accurately predicting sleep quality. To further enhance the predictive capabilities of the DBN model, the authors employ the extended seagull optimization (ESGO) technique for hyperparameter adjustment. This methodology aims to enhance the accuracy and efficacy of sleep quality prediction within the proposed framework.

Wang *et al.* [50] examined the most recent developments in the field of wearable sensors for the purpose of activity monitoring and motion control. This article examines a variety of sensing technologies, including electromechanical, bioelectrical, and biomechanical sensors, as well as the numerous uses for these technologies. In addition to this, a summary of the many commercially available wearable products and the computational approaches for motion analysis are included here.

To simultaneously assess signal quality and recognize arrhythmia events for real-time atrial fibrillation detection in wearable photoplethysmography devices, studies [51][29] employ a multitask deep learning approach known as DeepBeat. The model is trained over one million psychological unlabeled signals. DeepBeat is developed using data from three datasets, two of which are sourced from Stanford Hospital. The first dataset consists of individuals undergoing elective cardioversions, while the second dataset comprises participants undergoing elective stress testing. Pre-training is conducted using CDAE (Contractive Denoising Autoencoder), utilizing a unique simulated dataset of photoplethysmography signals.

14.2.6 Telemedicine and Remote Patient Monitoring

Machine learning has gained significant importance in the medical field, particularly in telemedicine and remote patient monitoring. These technologies enable healthcare professionals to remotely monitor patients' health, communicate with them, and deliver necessary treatment without the need for in-person visits. The application of machine learning in telemedicine facilitates real-time data analysis, allowing medical practitioners to detect patterns, identify anomalies, and make informed decisions regarding patient care. By leveraging these advancements, healthcare providers can enhance the accessibility and efficiency of medical services, improve patient outcomes, and overcome geographical barriers that may limit access to healthcare. The integration of machine learning in telemedicine represents a transformative approach that has the potential to revolutionize healthcare delivery and bridge the gap between patients and medical practitioners, even when they are physically separated.

By incorporating augmented intelligence (AuI), the current telemedicine framework is strengthened through the establishment of a dependable enterprise ecosystem in smart cities. This involves coordinating pools of resource management that consist of Internet of Things (IoT) devices and communication channels. Within this article, a fresh approach is introduced to tackle the issue of resource suggestion in telemedicine, harnessing the power of both AI and IoT. The framework leverages data from the eHealth infrastructure within smart cities and the telemedicine environment based on the Internet of Things (IoT) to offer intelligent suggestions for telemedicine services. The recommended architecture for delivering eHealth services is built on Intelligent Enterprise Management Systems (EMS) referred to as Augmented Intelligent Telemedicine (AITel); this framework assumes that integrating augmented intelligence into telemedicine will yield an impressive accuracy rate of 94.83%.

14.2.7 Chatbots and Virtual Medical Assistants

Medical chatbots and virtual assistants are machine learning applications that can provide patients with personalized and efficient care. These technologies can assist patients in navigating the healthcare system, offer basic medical advice, and facilitate administrative duties.

Most of the time, people are unaware of all of the many illnesses' manifestations or treatments. They typically have to visit the hospital for minor medical issues, which takes more time. Additionally, answering queries of patients over the telephone is a tedious task involving human intervention [53]. However, by using MedBot, a medical Chatbot that can offer sound guidance on living a healthy lifestyle, this problem can be resolved. The fundamental idea is to develop an AI- and NLP-based healthcare chatbot, named MedBot, capable of identifying illnesses and providing essential information about them prior to seeking medical consultation. This approach aims to enhance the accessibility of MedBot and reduce healthcare expenses. Additionally, certain chatbots in this category educate patients about their conditions through virtual medical assistants.

To facilitate instruction in radiotherapy, an educational chatbot can be developed by integrating it with the Internet of Things (IoT) and employing a layered structure along with a technique known as a dialogue tree. By utilizing AI capabilities like natural language processing (NLP), provided by platforms such as IBM Watson Assistant [54], it becomes feasible to give the educational chatbot a personality resembling that of a human. Employing a question-and-answer approach, the chatbot is able to engage with users from various backgrounds and offer guidance to those who encounter challenges in acquiring knowledge. This amalgamation of technologies empowers the chatbot to act as an informative and interactive resource, catering to individuals seeking information and assistance in the domain of radiotherapy.

Görtz *et al.* [52] developed Prostate Cancer Communication Assistant (PROSCA), a user-friendly medical chatbot designed to provide patients with information on early prostate cancer (PC) detection, which was the goal of this study's development and evaluation.

14.3   Why Machine Learning is Crucial in Healthcare

It would be difficult, if not impossible, to identify patterns and insights into medical data through manual analysis without machine learning algorithms. The expanding use of machine learning in healthcare affords healthcare providers the opportunity to adopt a more predictive approach to precision medicine. This can result in a more integrated system with enhanced care delivery, improved patient outcomes, and streamlined processes centered on the patient. In healthcare, machine learning is used to automate medical billing, develop clinical practice guidelines, and provide clinical decision support for primary care providers. Approximately 80% of the information recorded in electronic health record systems is unstructured healthcare data, which can be processed using machine learning. Previously, human intervention was required to analyze patient information from data documents or text files. However, with the advent of natural language processing programs, these data can now be converted into a more useful and analyzable format using artificial intelligence. Despite the potential benefits, there are obstacles to overcome, such as maintaining data private and secure, and assuring the accuracy and dependability of machine learning methods.

14.4   Challenges and Opportunities

As more complex data become available, the need for specialized skills and knowledge and the demand for ethical and transparent AI programs generate challenges and opportunities in machine learning that are intertwined. The complexity and quantity of available data presents one of the greatest obstacles in machine learning. The exponential growth of data sources has made it difficult for machines to learn from and process the massive quantity of daily data. In addition, some data may be incomplete, chaotic, or biased, resulting in suboptimal machine learning model outcomes.

Another obstacle is the requirement for specialized machine learning skills and knowledge. Developing efficient machine learning algorithms requires knowledge in areas such as statistics, mathematics, computer science, and domain-specific information. However, the dearth of qualified professionals in these disciplines makes it difficult for organizations to recruit and retain the personnel required to design and implement effective machine learning solutions.

Also of growing concern is the need for ethical and transparent AI systems. As machine learning becomes more pervasive in daily life, it is imperative that technology be used responsibly and ethically. This refers to the requirement that artificial intelligence systems operate transparently, disclosing their decision-making processes and avoiding the perpetuation of biases or discrimination. This necessitates meticulous consideration of data selection, model construction, and governance frameworks.

Despite these challenges, machine learning offers numerous opportunities. For instance, machine learning can enhance the efficacy and precision of a variety of applications, including medical diagnosis, fraud detection, and personalized recommendations. In addition, machine learning can find patterns and correlations in data that may not be seen by human observers, which can lead to novel insights and discoveries.

Overall, the challenges and opportunities in machine learning emphasize the need for further study in this field of machine learning, as well as ongoing dialogue and collaboration to ensure the responsible and ethical application of AI.

14.5   Conclusion

ML has the potential to revolutionize health science by facilitating novel analyses and interpretations of vast quantities of complex data. The applications of machine learning in the health sciences are vast, including personalized medicine, drug discovery, and patient monitoring.

However, challenges and considerations must also be taken into account when employing ML in the health sciences. Important factors that must be addressed include ensuring the accuracy and representativeness of data, preserving patient privacy and data security, and addressing ethical considerations.

The use of machine learning in health science has the potential to enhance patient outcomes, reduce healthcare costs, and speed up medical research. To realize the maximum potential of this technology, it will be necessary to continue to develop and refine ML algorithms in an ethical and responsible manner.

References

1. Abdeldjouad, F.Z., Brahami, M., Matta., N., A hybrid approach for heart disease diagnosis and prediction using machine learning techniques, pp. 299–306, 2020.
2. Banu, G., Predicting thyroid disease using Linear Discriminant Analysis (LDA) data mining technique. *Commun. Appl. Electron.*, 4, 4–6, 2016.
3. Chaubey, G. *et al.*, Thyroid disease prediction using machine learning approaches. *Natl. Acad. Sci. Lett.*, 44, 3, 233–238, 2021.
4. Waddell, M., Page, D., Shaughnessy Jr., J. Predicting cancer susceptibility from single-nucleotide polymorphism data: A case study in multiple myeloma. *Proceedings of the 5th International Workshop on Bioinformatics*, 2005.

5. Listgarten, J., Damaraju, S., Poulin, B., Cook, L., Dufour, J., Driga, A. *et al.*, Predictive models for breast cancer susceptibility from multiple single nucleotide polymorphisms. *Clin. Cancer Res.*, 10, 2725–2737, 2004.

6. Exarchos, K.P., Goletsis, Y., Fotiadis, D.I., Multiparametric decision support system for the prediction of oral cancer reoccurrence. *IEEE Trans. Inf. Technol. Biomed.*, 16, 1127–1134, 2012.

7. Chen, Y.-C., Ke, W.-C., Chiu, H.-W., Risk classification of cancer survival using ANN with gene expression data from multiple laboratories. *Comput. Biol. Med.*, 48, 1–7, 2014.

8. Park, K., Ali, A., Kim, D., An, Y., Kim, M., Shin, H., Robust predictive model for evaluating breast cancer survivability. *Engl. Appl. Artif. Intell.*, 26, 2194–2205, 2013.

9. Xu, X., Zhang, Y., Zou, L., Wang, M., Li, A., A gene signature for breast cancer prognosis using support vector machine, IEEE, pp. 928–931, 2012.

10. Mir, A. and Dhage, S.N., Diabetes disease prediction using machine learning on big data of healthcare. *2018 Fourth International Conference on Computing Communication Control and Automation (ICCUBEA)*, IEEE, 2018.

11. Balne, S. and Elumalai, A., Machine learning and deep learning algorithms used to diagnosis of alzheimer's. *Mater. Today: Proc.*, 47, 5151–5156, 2021.

12. Kumar, L. *et al.*, AlexNet approach for early stage Alzheimer's disease detection from MRI brain images. *Mater. Today: Proc.*, 51, 58–65, 2022.

13. Kishore, P. *et al.*, Detection and analysis of Alzheimer's disease using various machine learning algorithms. *Mater. Today: Proc.*, 45, 1502–1508, 2021.

14. Gupta, R. *et al.*, Artificial intelligence to deep learning: Machine intelligence approach for drug discovery. *Mol. Diversity*, 25, 1315–1360, 2021.

15. Rodrigues, T. and Bernardes, G.J.L., Machine learning for target discovery in drug development. *Curr. Opin. Chem. Biol.*, 56, 16–22, 2020.

16. Jing, Y. *et al.*, Deep learning for drug design: An artificial intelligence paradigm for drug discovery in the big data era. *AAPS J.*, 20, 1–10, 2018.

17. Shin, M., Jang, D., Nam, H., Lee, K.H., Lee, D., Predicting the absorption potential of chemical compounds through a deep learning approach. *IEEE/ACM Trans. Comput. Biol. Bioinform.*, 15.2, 432–440, 2016.

18. Mayr, A., Klambauer, G., Unterthiner, T., Hochreiter, S., DeepTox: Toxicity prediction using deep learning. *Front. Environ. Sci.*, 3, 80, 2016.

19. Wan, F. and Zeng, J., Deep learning with feature embedding for compound-protein interaction prediction. *bioRxiv*, 086033, 2016.

20. Wallach, I., Dzamba, M., Heifets, A. AtomNet: A deep convolutional neural network for bioactivity prediction in structure-based drug discovery. arXiv preprint arXiv: 1510.02855, 2015.

21. Pereira, J.C., Caffarena, E.R., Dos Santos, C.N., Boosting docking-based virtual screening with deep learning. *J. Chem. Inf. Model.*, 56, 12, 2495–506, 2016.

22. Kadurin, A., Aliper, A., Kazennov, A., Mamoshina, P., Vanhaelen, Q., Khrabrov, K. *et al.*, The cornucopia of meaningful leads: Applying deep adversarial autoencoders for new molecule development in oncology. *Oncotarget*, 8, 7, 10883–90, 2017.

23. Goh, G.B., Siegel, C., Vishnu, A., Hodas, N.O., Baker, N., Chemception: A deep neural network with minimal chemistry knowledge matches the performance of expert-developed QSAR/QSPR models. arXiv preprint arXiv: 1706.06689, 2017.

24. Bjerrum, E.J., Smiles enumeration as data augmentation for neural network modeling of molecules. arXiv preprint arXiv: 1703.07076, 2017.

25. Lenselink, E.B., ten Dijke, N., Bongers, B., Papadatos, G., van Vlijmen, H.W.T., Kowalczyk, W. *et al.*, Beyond the hype: Deep neural networks outperform established methods using a ChEMBL bioactivity benchmark set. *J. Cheminform.*, 9, 1, 45, 2017.

26. Segler, M.H.S., Kogej, T., Tyrchan, C., Waller, M.P., Generating focused molecule libraries for drug discovery with recurrent neural networks. *ACS Cent. Sci.*, 4, 1, 120–31, 2018.

27. Olivecrona, M., Blaschke, T., Engkvist, O., Chen, H., Molecular de- novo design through deep reinforcement learning. *J. Cheminform.*, 9, 1, 48, 2017.

28. Lima Guimaraes, G., Sanchez-Lengeling, B., Cunha Farias, P.L., Aspuru-Guzik, A., Objective-reinforced generative adversarial networks (ORGAN) for sequence generation models. arXiv preprint arXiv: 1705.10843, 2017.

29. Yao, K. and Parkhill, J., Kinetic energy of hydrocarbons as a function of electron density and convolutional neural networks. *J. Chem. Theory Comput.*, 12, 3, 1139–47, 2016.

30. Du, Y., *et al.*, An explainable machine learning-based clinical decision support system for prediction of gestational diabetes mellitus. *Sci. Rep.*, 12.1, 1170, 2022.

31. Tuppad, A. and Patil, S.D., Machine learning for diabetes clinical decision support: A review, in: *Adv. in Comp. Int.*, vol. 2, p. 22, 2022.

32. Kim, D. *et al.*, Deep learning application to clinical decision support system in sleep stage classification. *J. Pers. Med.*, 12, 2, 136, 2022.

33. Durga Prasad Jasti, V. *et al.*, Computational technique based on machine learning and image processing for medical image analysis of breast cancer diagnosis. *Secur. Commun. Netw.*, 2022, 1–7, 2022.

34. Pham, T.D., A comprehensive study on classification of COVID-19 on computed tomography with pretrained convolutional neural networks. *Sci. Rep.*, 10, 1, 1–8, 2020.

35. Jaiswal, A., Gianchandani, N., Singh, D., Kumar, V., Kaur, M., Classification of the COVID-19 infected patients using DenseNet201 based deep transfer learning. *J. Biomol. Struct. Dyn.*, 39.15, 5682–5689, 2021.

36. Amyar, A., Modzelewski, R., Li, H., Ruan, S., Multi-task deep learning based CT imaging analysis for COVID-19 pneumonia: Classification and segmentation. *Comput. Biol. Med.*, 126, 104037, June 2020.

37. Panwar, H., Gupta, P.K., Siddiqui, M.K., Morales-Menendez, R., Bhardwaj, P., Singh, V., A deep learning and grad-CAM based color visualization approach for fast detection of COVID-19 cases using chest X-ray and CT-Scan images. *Chaos Solit. Fractals*, 140, 110190, 2020.

38. Shah, V., Keniya, R., Shridharani, A., Punjabi, M., Shah, J., Mehendale, N., Diagnosis of COVID-19 using CT scan images and deep learning techniques. *Emerg. Radiol.*, 28, 497–505, 2021.

39. Pathak, Y., Shukla, P.K., Tiwari, A., Stalin, S., Singh, S., Deep transfer learning based classification model for COVID-19 disease. *IRBM*, 1, 1–6, 2020.

40. Hussein, Haval I., *et al.*, Lightweight deep CNN-based models for early detection of COVID-19 patients from chest X-ray images. *Expert Syst. Appl.*, 223, 119900, 2023.

41. Nayak, S.R., Nayak, D.R., Sinha, U., Arora, V., Pachori, R.B., Application of deep learning techniques for detection of COVID-19 cases using chest X-ray images: A comprehensive study. *Biomed. Signal Process. Control*, 64, October 2020, 102365, 2021.

42. Tartaglione, E., Barbano, C.A., Berzovini, C., Calandri, M., Grangetto, M., Unveiling COVID-19 from chest x-ray with deep learning: A hurdles race with small data. *Int. J. Environ. Res. Public Health*, 17, 18, 1–17, 2020.

43. Wang, L., Lin, Z.Q., Wong, A., COVID-Net: A tailored deep convolutional neural network design for detection of COVID-19 cases from chest X-ray images. *Sci. Rep.*, 10.1, 19549, 2020.

44. Heidari, M., Mirniaharikandehei, S., Khuzani, A.Z., Danala, G., Qiu, Y., Zheng, B., Improving the performance of CNN to predict the likelihood of COVID-19 using chest X-ray images with preprocessing algorithms. *Int. J. Med. Inform.*, 144, September, 104284, 2020.

45. Lee, K.S., Kim, J.Y., Jeon, E.T., Choi, W.S., Kim, N.H., Lee, K.Y., Evaluation of scalability and degree of fine-tuning of deep convolutional neural networks for COVID-19 screening on Chest X-Ray images using explainable deep-learning algorithm. *J. Pers. Med.*, 10, 4, 1–14, 2020.

46. Minaee, S., Kafieh, R., Sonka, M., Yazdani, S., Jamalipour Soufi, G., Deep-COVID: Predicting COVID-19 from chest X-ray images using deep transfer learning. *Med. Image Anal.*, 65, 101794, 2020.

47. Jain, R., Gupta, M., Taneja, S., Hemanth, D.J., Deep learning based detection and analysis of COVID-19 on chest X-ray images. *Appl. Intell.*, 51, 3, 1690–1700, 2021.

48. Huang, B., Abtahi, A., Aminifar, A., Lightweight machine learning for seizure detection on wearable devices. *ICASSP 2023 - 2023 IEEE International Conference on Acoustics, Speech and Signal Processing (ICASSP)*, Rhodes Island, Greece, pp. 1–2, 2023.

49. Hamza, M.A. *et al.*, Wearables-assisted smart health monitoring for sleep quality prediction using optimal deep learning. *Sustainability*, 15, 2, 1084, 2023.

50. Wang, X. *et al.*, Wearable sensors for activity monitoring and motion control: A review. *Biomimetic Intell. Rob.*, 100089, 2023.

51. Torres-Soto, J. and Ashley, E.A., Multi-task deep learning for cardiac rhythm detection in wearable devices. *NPJ Digital Med.*, 3, 1, 116, 2020.

52. Görtz, M. *et al.*, An artificial intelligence-based chatbot for prostate cancer education: Design and patient evaluation study. *Digital Health*, 9, 20552076231173304, 2023.

53. Anjum, K., Sameer, M., Kumar, S., AI enabled NLP based text to text medical Chatbot. *2023 3rd International Conference on Innovative Practices in Technology and Management (ICIPTM)*, Uttar Pradesh, India, pp. 1–5, 2023.

54. Chow, J.C.L., Sanders, L., Li, K., Design of an educational chatbot using artificial intelligence in radiotherapy. *AI*, 4, 1, 319–332, 2023.

15

Enhancing Resource Management in Precision Farming through AI-Based Irrigation Optimization

Salina Adinarayana[1], Matha Govinda Raju[2], Durga Prasad Srirangam[3], Devee Siva Prasad[3]*
Munaganuri Ravi Kumar[4] and Sai babu veesam[4]

[1]Department of Computer Science and Engineering (Data Science), Raghu Engineering College, Visakhapatnam, Andhra Pradesh, India
[2]Department of Mechanical Engineering, Baba Institute of Technology and Sciences, Visakhapatnam, Andhra Pradesh, India
[3]Department of Computer Science and Engineering, Baba Institute of Technology and Sciences, Visakhapatnam, Andhra Pradesh, India
[4]SCOPE Department, VITAP, Vijayawada, Andhra pradesh, India

Abstract

Precision farming has garnered significant attention for its ability to enhance productivity, optimize resource utilization, and promote sustainable agricultural practices. This chapter provides a comprehensive overview of precision farming and its integration with Artificial Intelligence (AI) to unlock its full potential.

The chapter emphasizes the importance of precision farming in modern agriculture, addressing challenges such as resource scarcity and environmental impact. It explores the role of AI in revolutionizing various aspects of precision farming, including data-driven decision-making, task automation, and overall farm management improvements. While AI offers immense opportunities, challenges like data quality, interpretability, and ethical considerations need attention for successful implementation.

The chapter covers diverse areas within precision farming, including data collection techniques like remote sensing, satellite imagery analysis, UAVs, and IoT sensors. It delves into AI applications in crop monitoring and management, such as yield prediction, disease detection, weed management, and optimization of nutrients and irrigation. Precision planting, livestock monitoring, harvesting, decision support systems, robotics, and machine learning are also examined. Real-life case studies highlight successful AI applications in precision farming.

Keywords: Precision farming, machine learning, data-driven decision-making, artificial intelligence, UAV (Unmanned ariel vehicles), IoT sensors, remote sensing, blockchain

Corresponding author: shivadulam@gmail.com

Arindam Dey, Sukanta Nayak, Ranjan Kumar and Sachi Nandan Mohanty (eds.) How Machine Learning is Innovating Today's World: A Concise Technical Guide, (221–252) © 2024 Scrivener Publishing LLC

15.1   Introduction to Precision Farming

15.1.1   Definition of Precision Farming

Precision farming, also known as precision agriculture, refers to the use of technology and data-driven approaches to optimize agricultural practices. It involves the integration of various technologies such as GPS, remote sensing, data analytics, and automation to enhance the efficiency, productivity, and sustainability of farming operations [31]. The life cycle of precision farming can be broadly divided into several stages as illustrated in Figure 15.1:

1. **Planning and Analysis**
   - ➢ Identify the objectives and goals of precision farming implementation [1, 2].
   - ➢ Analyze the specific needs and requirements of the farm operation.
   - ➢ Conduct a thorough assessment of the field conditions, including soil analysis, topography, and yield potential.
   - ➢ Determine the appropriate technologies and tools to be employed based on the analysis.

     Example: A farmer decides to implement precision farming techniques on their cornfield. They analyze their objectives, such as increasing yield and reducing input costs. They conduct a detailed assessment of the field, including soil sampling and analysis to understand nutrient levels and pH.

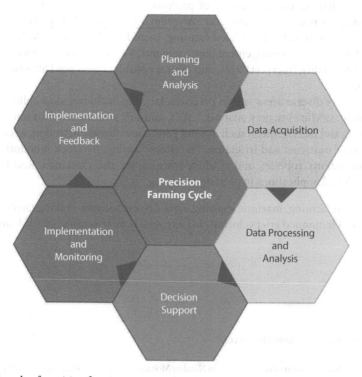

Figure 15.1 Life cycle of precision farming.

Based on this analysis, they determine the appropriate technologies to use, such as soil sensors and variable rate application equipment [28].

2. **Data Acquisition**
   ➤ Collect relevant data from various sources, including satellite imagery, drones, sensors, and on-farm monitoring systems [28].
   ➤ Gather information about soil characteristics, moisture levels, temperature, crop health, and other relevant parameters [1].
   ➤ Ensure the accuracy and reliability of data through proper calibration and quality control measures.
   Example: The farmer uses satellite imagery, drones, and on-farm sensors to collect data. They capture high-resolution satellite images of the field, which provide valuable information about vegetation indices, crop health, and water stress. Additionally, they employ drones equipped with multispectral cameras to obtain detailed field imagery. On-farm sensors measure soil moisture levels [28], temperature [28], and other relevant parameters.

3. **Data Processing and Analysis**
   ➤ Utilize advanced data analytics techniques to process and analyze the collected data [2].
   ➤ Identify patterns, trends, and correlations within the data to extract meaningful insights.
   ➤ Generate accurate maps and models that depict the variability within the field, such as soil fertility variations or pest infestation zones.
   ➤ Assess crop growth stages, predict yield potential, and detect anomalies or stress factors affecting plant health.
   Example: The collected data are processed and analyzed using advanced data analytics techniques illustrated from the Figure 15.2. The farmer uses software tools to analyze the satellite and drone imagery, creating

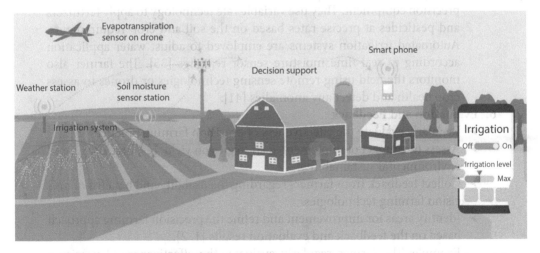

Figure 15.2 Data on weather, soil moisture, and evapotranspiration are gathered and transmitted remotely to a decision support system, enabling farmers to receive actionable information to address water scarcity challenges (source: GAO. | GAO-20-128SP).

maps that highlight areas with varying crop vigor or pest infestations [35]. They also conduct statistical analyses to identify correlations between soil properties and yield. The results of the analysis help in understanding field variability and making data-driven decisions [29].

4. **Decision Support**
   - ➢ Based on the analyzed data, provide farmers with actionable recommendations and decision support tools [29].
   - ➢ Advise on optimal seeding rates, fertilizer application rates, irrigation schedules, and pest management strategies [35].
   - ➢ Incorporate weather forecasts, historical data, and predictive models to guide decision-making processes [1, 2].
   - ➢ Help farmers optimize resource allocation, minimize waste, and maximize crop yield and quality.

   Example: Based on the analyzed data, the farmer receives recommendations and decision support. Using the collected data, weather forecasts, and historical records, the farmer's precision farming software suggests optimal seeding rates [5], fertilizer application rates, and irrigation schedules for different zones within the field. The software also provides alerts and notifications regarding disease outbreaks or weather conditions that may affect crop growth.

5. **Implementation and Monitoring**
   - ➢ Implement the recommended actions and practices on the farm.
   - ➢ Utilize automated systems and precision equipment to precisely apply inputs, such as fertilizers and pesticides [33].
   - ➢ Monitor ongoing operations using real-time sensors, drones, or satellite imagery.
   - ➢ Continuously collect data on crop performance, soil conditions, and environmental factors.

   Example: The farmer implements the recommended actions and utilizes precision equipment. They use variable rate technology to apply fertilizers and pesticides at precise rates based on the soil and crop requirements. Automated irrigation systems are employed to adjust water application according to real-time moisture sensor readings [35]. The farmer also monitors the field using remote sensing technologies or drones to assess crop health and detect any anomalies [41].

6. **Evaluation and Feedback**
   - ➢ Regularly evaluate the effectiveness of precision farming practices [5].
   - ➢ Assess the impact of implemented strategies on yield, resource usage, and environmental sustainability.
   - ➢ Collect feedback from farmers regarding the usability and benefits of precision farming technologies.
   - ➢ Identify areas for improvement and refine the precision farming approach based on the feedback and evaluation results [1, 2].

   Example: The farmer regularly evaluates the effectiveness of precision farming practices. They compare yield data from different zones within the field to assess the impact of variable rate applications. They also measure inputs used, such as water and fertilizers, to evaluate resource efficiency. The farmer seeks feedback from agronomists and other experts, considering their observations and suggestions for further improvement in precision farming strategies.

The life cycle of precision farming is a continuous and iterative process, where data-driven insights and technological advancements are used to optimize farming operations and make informed decisions throughout the agricultural production cycle [29].

15.1.2 Importance of Precision Farming in Agriculture

Precision farming offers several important benefits and plays a crucial role in modern agriculture. Here are some key reasons why precision farming is important:

Increased Efficiency and Productivity: Precision farming enables farmers to optimize the use of resources such as fertilizers, water, and pesticides [3]. By applying these inputs precisely based on site-specific conditions and crop requirements, farmers can reduce waste and increase efficiency. This leads to higher crop yields, improved productivity, and better economic returns.

Enhanced Resource Management: Precision farming helps farmers manage resources more effectively. By using sensors, satellite imagery, and data analytics, farmers can assess soil fertility, moisture levels, and crop health in real time [1, 3]. This allows them to make informed decisions about irrigation, fertilization, and pest control, resulting in improved resource management and reduced environmental impact [29].

Environmental Sustainability: By minimizing the use of agrochemicals and optimizing resource utilization, precision farming promotes environmental sustainability. It helps reduce the potential negative impacts of agriculture, such as nutrient runoff into water bodies and excessive pesticide use. Precision farming also supports conservation practices, such as precision planting and cover cropping, which contribute to soil health and biodiversity preservation [3].

Cost Reduction: Precision farming techniques help farmers reduce costs by optimizing input usage. By applying fertilizers, water, and other inputs only where and when needed, farmers can save money on unnecessary expenses. Moreover, precision farming enables early detection and targeted treatment of pests and diseases, reducing the need for widespread pesticide applications and potential yield losses.

Improved Decision-Making: Precision farming provides farmers with valuable data and insights to make informed decisions. By analyzing field variability and performance trends, farmers can adjust their management strategies accordingly. Real-time monitoring and predictive modeling also enable proactive decision-making, allowing farmers to respond quickly to changing conditions and mitigate potential risks.

Increased Sustainability and Resilience: Precision farming contributes to long-term sustainability and resilience in agriculture. By adopting precision technologies, farmers can adapt to climate change impacts, optimize water use in water-scarce regions, and mitigate the effects of soil degradation. Precision farming practices also support the implementation of precision conservation, which enhances ecosystem services and biodiversity on farmland.

Better Quality and Safety: Precision farming can lead to improved crop quality and safety. By optimizing inputs and management practices, farmers can achieve more uniform and consistent crop growth. This results in higher-quality produce with fewer variations in size, color, and taste. Precision farming also enables traceability, allowing for better food safety management and quality control throughout the supply chain.

15.2　Role of Artificial Intelligence (AI) in Precision Farming

AI in precision farming improves agricultural practices through data analysis, predictive analytics, crop monitoring, and resource optimization. It enables precise irrigation and fertilization based on soil and weather conditions. AI also supports autonomous machinery for tasks like seeding and harvesting. It aids in early detection of diseases and pests, reducing crop losses. Ultimately, AI enhances productivity, sustainability, and efficiency in farming, addressing global food security and environmental challenges.

15.2.1　Influence of AI in Precision Farming

AI offers several advantages in precision farming that contribute to increased efficiency, improved decision-making, and enhanced productivity. Here are some key advantages of AI in precision farming:

1. **Data Processing and Analysis**: AI algorithms can process large volumes of data collected from various sources, including sensors, drones, and satellites. AI can quickly analyze and extract valuable insights from complex datasets, identifying patterns, correlations, and anomalies that may not be apparent to human observers [4]. This enables farmers to make data-driven decisions and optimize their farming practices based on accurate and timely information.

2. **Predictive Analytics**: AI models can leverage historical and real-time data to create predictive models and make forecasts in precision farming. By considering factors such as weather patterns, soil conditions, crop growth stages, and pest dynamics, AI can predict crop yields, disease outbreaks, and pest infestations. This enables farmers to take proactive measures, optimize resource allocation, and mitigate risks.

3. **Precision Applications**: AI-powered systems can control and automate precision equipment, such as variable rate technology (VRT) applicators, drones, and irrigation systems. AI algorithms consider field variability, soil data, and crop requirements to adjust input application rates and optimize resource usage. This precision in applications reduces input waste, improves efficiency, and promotes uniformity in crop management.

4. **Real-Time Monitoring and Decision Support**: AI enables real-time monitoring of field conditions and crop health using sensors, drones, and satellite imagery. AI algorithms can analyze these data and provide farmers with timely alerts and recommendations. By integrating weather forecasts, soil data, and crop models, AI-driven decision support systems assist farmers in

making informed decisions regarding irrigation, fertilization, pest control, and other management practices.

5. **Crop and Weed Identification**: AI-based computer vision algorithms can accurately identify and classify crops, weeds, diseases, and pests in images or video footage. This technology enables farmers to detect and monitor crop health, identify nutrient deficiencies, and target weed control. AI algorithms can distinguish between desired plants and weeds, allowing for precise and targeted treatments, thereby reducing the reliance on broad-spectrum pesticides and minimizing damage to crops.

6. **Robotic and Autonomous Systems**: AI enables the development of robotic and autonomous systems for various farming tasks. These systems can perform activities such as seeding, weeding, harvesting, and crop monitoring with precision and efficiency. AI algorithms help these systems navigate through fields, identify and interact with crops, and make autonomous decisions. Robotic and autonomous systems reduce labor requirements, optimize operations, and increase productivity.

7. **Optimization of Resource Usage**: AI algorithms can optimize the usage of resources such as water, fertilizers, and pesticides. By analyzing data [4] on soil conditions, crop growth stages, and environmental factors, AI can recommend precise application rates and timings, minimizing waste and maximizing resource efficiency. This leads to cost savings, reduced environmental impact, and sustainable farming practices.

15.2.2   Challenges and Limitations of AI in Precision Farming

While AI brings numerous benefits to precision farming, there are also challenges and limitations that need to be considered [6, 7]. Here are some common challenges and limitations associated with AI in precision farming:

1. **Data Quality and Availability**: AI algorithms heavily rely on high-quality and diverse datasets for accurate analysis and decision-making. However, obtaining reliable and representative data can be challenging in precision farming. Issues such as data gaps, sensor malfunctions, and limited access to historical or real-time data can affect the performance and reliability of AI models.

2. **Data Integration and Compatibility**: Precision farming involves the collection of data from various sources, such as sensors, drones, satellites, and weather stations. Integrating and standardizing these heterogeneous datasets can be complex and time-consuming. Incompatibility between different data formats and protocols may hinder seamless data integration and limit the effectiveness of AI algorithms.

3. **Model Accuracy and Generalization**: AI models are trained on historical data and patterns, which may not always capture the full complexity of farming systems. Models trained on one farm or region may not generalize well to other farms or regions with different conditions, soil types, or crop varieties. Ensuring model accuracy and generalization across diverse farming contexts remains a challenge in precision farming.

4. **Interpretability and Explainability**: AI models, particularly deep learning models, are often considered as black boxes due to their complex structure and decision-making process [7]. Interpreting and explaining the reasoning behind AI-generated recommendations or predictions can be challenging. This lack of interpretability may limit trust and adoption of AI solutions in precision farming, especially when farmers need to understand the underlying factors influencing the recommendations.

5. **Cost and Infrastructure**: Implementing AI technologies in precision farming often requires substantial investments in hardware, software, and infrastructure. Acquiring and maintaining the necessary equipment, such as sensors, drones, and AI-enabled devices, can be costly for small-scale farmers. Additionally, reliable connectivity, such as internet access and network coverage, is essential for real-time data transfer and AI-driven applications.

6. **Skills and Training**: Effective utilization of AI in precision farming requires specific skills and knowledge in data analysis, machine learning, and agronomy. Farmers and agricultural professionals may need training and support to understand and effectively utilize AI technologies. Bridging the digital divide and ensuring access to appropriate training and resources are essential for successful adoption and implementation of AI in precision farming.

7. **Ethical and Legal Considerations**: AI in precision farming raises ethical concerns related to data privacy, ownership, and security. Farmers must consider the ethical implications of sharing farm data with AI service providers and ensure compliance with data protection regulations. Additionally, the use of AI may raise questions about the role of human decision-making and the potential social and economic impacts on farm labor and rural communities.

15.3   Data Collection and Sensing for Precision Farming

Data collection and sensing are essential elements of precision farming as they provide valuable information about various factors affecting crop growth and farm management [9].

15.3.1   Remote Sensing Techniques

Remote sensing refers to the scientific process of gathering information about objects or areas located at a distance, typically through the use of satellites or aircraft. In precision agriculture, remote sensing is employed to collect data about crops, soils, and the environment, which aids in making well-informed decisions regarding agricultural practices.

Various remote sensing technologies can be utilized in precision agriculture, including:

1. **Multispectral Imaging**: This technology involves the use of sensors that capture reflected light at multiple wavelengths. Different wavelengths of light can reveal distinct characteristics of plants, such as their health status, growth stage, or level of water stress.

2. **Hyperspectral Imaging**: Hyperspectral imaging employs sensors that capture light at even more wavelengths than multispectral imaging, for reference

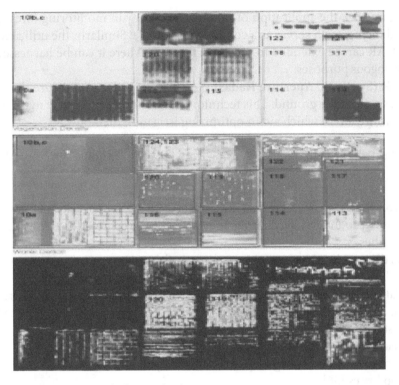

Figure 15.3 Hyperspectral image of a farming land.

Figure 15.3 shows the hyperspectral image of a farming land. This enables the acquisition of highly detailed information about crops, offering valuable insights into their condition.

3. **LiDAR**: LiDAR employs laser technology to measure the distance to the ground. It is employed to generate precise maps of the soil surface, helping identify areas with varying soil types and moisture levels. As illustrated in the

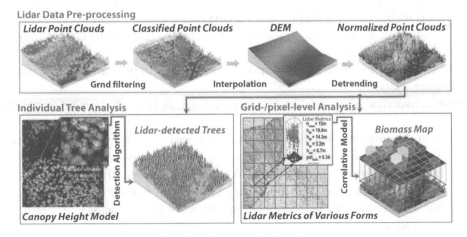

Figure 15.4 Lidar data pre-processing for individual tree growth analysis.

Figure 15.4, the application of LiDAR technology in monitoring forest trees and their growth serves as a compelling example. Similarly, the utilization of LiDAR can be extended to precision farming, where it can be harnessed for analogous purposes.

4. **SAR (Synthetic Aperture Radar)**: SAR utilizes radar to measure the backscatter from the ground. This technique can be utilized to create maps of soil moisture levels, which aid in optimizing irrigation methods.

Data collected through remote sensing can enhance various agricultural practices, including:

1. **Crop Planning**: Remote sensing can identify areas of a field that are more or less productive, facilitating more effective crop rotations and planting densities.

2. **Fertilizer Management**: By mapping soil nutrient status, remote sensing enables farmers to apply fertilizers accurately and efficiently.

3. **Water Management**: Remote sensing assists in mapping soil moisture levels, allowing farmers to optimize irrigation techniques and minimize water waste.

4. **Disease and Pest Management**: Early detection of diseases and pests through remote sensing helps farmers take preventive measures and reduce crop losses [36].

Remote sensing is a powerful tool that enables farmers to enhance yields, reduce input costs, and protect crops from pests and diseases. As technology progresses, remote sensing is expected to play an increasingly vital role in precision agriculture.

15.3.2 Satellite Imagery Analysis [15–17]

Imagery analysis in precision farming allows farmers to utilize data from satellite images to make informed decisions about crop management. For example, let us consider a farmer who wants to optimize irrigation practices. By analyzing satellite imagery, the farmer can identify areas within the field that exhibit varying water needs. The images provide information about soil moisture content and crop stress levels, helping the farmer implement precision irrigation techniques. Instead of uniformly watering the entire field, the farmer can apply water only to the areas that require it, resulting in improved water efficiency and reduced water wastage.

Here is an overview where satellite imagery analysis can be used in precision farming:

1. **Crop Monitoring**: Satellites equipped with various sensors capture images of agricultural fields at regular intervals. These images can be analyzed to monitor crop growth, detect anomalies, and identify areas that require attention. By analyzing the [16–18] imagery, farmers can assess crop health, detect nutrient deficiencies, and monitor the impact of pests, diseases, or weather conditions [36].

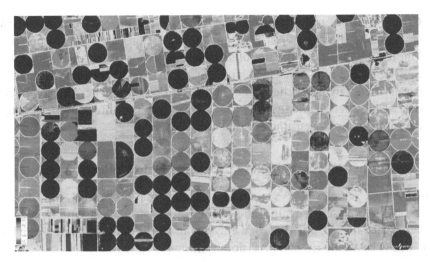

Figure 15.5 Satellite imagery from the Sentinel-2 satellite was used to create a map of the NDMI distribution in the irrigated fields of the Kherson region in Ukraine, showing areas with high moisture content (depicted in blue) and areas with low humidity (depicted in red).

2. **Yield Prediction:** Satellite imagery can be used to estimate crop yield by analyzing factors such as vegetation indices, plant density, and canopy coverage. By tracking the growth and health of crops over time, farmers can make informed decisions about irrigation, fertilization, and other interventions to optimize yield.

3. **Irrigation Management:** Satellite imagery analysis [16, 17] can help farmers optimize water usage by identifying areas with varying water needs. By assessing factors like soil moisture content and crop stress levels, farmers can implement precision irrigation techniques, ensuring water is delivered only where and when it is needed. This approach improves water efficiency and minimizes water wastage.

4. **Disease and Pest Detection:** Satellite imagery analysis can aid in the early detection of diseases and pest infestations. By analyzing the spectral signatures of crops, anomalies indicative of diseases or pests can be identified. This enables farmers to take prompt action, such as targeted pesticide application or implementing preventive measures to minimize the spread of diseases [16, 36].

5. **Variable Rate Application:** Satellite imagery analysis can be used to create prescription maps for variable rate application of fertilizers, pesticides, and other inputs. By identifying areas with different nutrient requirements or pest pressures, farmers can apply these inputs at optimal rates, reducing costs and minimizing environmental impact.

6. **Soil Mapping and Analysis:** Satellite imagery can provide valuable information about soil conditions and variability within a field. By analyzing satellite data, farmers can generate soil maps that highlight variations in soil composition, moisture content, and other parameters [32]. These data can guide soil sampling, precision nutrient management, and site-specific interventions.

7. **Crop Rotation and Planning:** Satellite imagery analysis can help farmers evaluate the success of previous crop rotations and plan future ones. Figure 15.5 illustrates the use of satellite images for distinguishing between moistened and non-moistened lands. By comparing historical satellite imagery, farmers can assess the impact of different crop sequences on soil health, disease prevalence, and overall productivity [36]. This information can guide decision-making regarding optimal crop rotations.

15.3.3 Unmanned Aerial Vehicles (UAVs) for Data Collection

Unmanned Aerial Vehicles (UAVs), commonly known as drones [41, 42], have become valuable tools for precision farming due to their ability to collect data quickly and efficiently. Figure 15.6 depicts a UAV drone engaged in field monitoring and pesticide spraying. Here is how UAVs are used in precision farming [8, 9]:

1. **Crop Monitoring:** UAVs equipped with high-resolution cameras or multispectral sensors can capture detailed images of crops from above. These images provide valuable information about plant health, growth patterns, and the presence of pests or diseases [11, 36]. Farmers can use these data to identify specific areas that require attention, such as irrigation or pesticide application.
2. **Crop Health Assessment:** Multispectral or thermal cameras mounted on UAVs can capture data beyond what is visible to the human eye [10]. By analyzing these data, farmers can assess crop health, detect stress conditions, and identify nutrient deficiencies. This information helps optimize fertilization and irrigation strategies, leading to improved crop yield and resource management.

Figure 15.6 A UAV drone monitoring and spraying pesticides.

3. **Soil Analysis:** Some UAVs are equipped with sensors capable of analyzing soil composition and moisture content [11, 12]. By flying over agricultural fields, these drones can gather data on soil characteristics, such as pH levels, nutrient content, and moisture distribution. This information assists farmers in making informed decisions about soil management and optimizing the distribution of fertilizers.

4. **Field Mapping:** UAVs can create highly accurate three-dimensional maps of agricultural fields using specialized sensors like LiDAR (Light Detection and Ranging) [34]. These maps provide detailed topographic and elevation data, enabling farmers to assess field slope, drainage patterns, and soil erosion [18]. This knowledge aids in precision planting, irrigation planning, and land-use management [32].

5. **Irrigation Management:** With the help of UAVs, farmers can monitor crop water stress levels by employing thermal cameras that detect variations in plant temperature [34]. By identifying areas with inadequate or excessive irrigation, farmers can adjust their watering schedules, leading to optimized water usage and improved crop health.

6. **Planting and Spraying:** Advanced UAVs equipped with seed dispensers or spraying systems can autonomously plant seeds or apply pesticides and fertilizers precisely [12–14]. This method ensures accurate seed placement and controlled application, reducing waste and improving overall efficiency [34].

15.3.4   Internet of Things (IoT) Sensors

In precision farming, IOT sensors play a major role by collecting real-time data from various environmental and agricultural parameters [4]. These sensors are deployed in the field and transmit data wirelessly to a central system for analysis and decision-making. The Figure 15.7 illustrates a selection of diverse sensors employed in precision farming. Here are some commonly used IoT sensors in precision farming [4]:

Soil Moisture Sensors: These sensors are buried in the soil to measure moisture levels at different depths. They help farmers determine the optimal irrigation requirements for crops

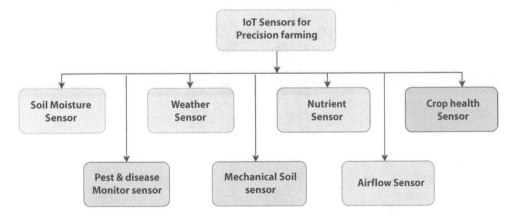

Figure 15.7 Integrated sensor systems for precision farming and crop management.

and prevent over- or under-watering. Figure 15.8 provides an illustration of a soil moisture sensor designed for monitoring soil moisture levels. Soil moisture data can be used to automate irrigation systems, ensuring plants receive the right amount of water at the right time [47].

Pest and Disease Monitor Sensor: These sensors use various techniques like pheromone traps, insect monitoring cameras, or acoustic sensors to detect pests and diseases in the field. By continuously monitoring pest populations or disease presence, farmers can implement proactive measures like targeted spraying or biological control methods, reducing the reliance on broad-spectrum pesticides.

Weather Sensors: Weather sensors monitor various meteorological conditions such as temperature, humidity, rainfall, wind speed, and solar radiation. These data provide insights into microclimate conditions within the farm and help farmers make informed decisions regarding planting, harvesting, and pest management. Weather sensors can also help trigger automated actions, such as closing or adjusting greenhouse vents in response to extreme temperatures.

Mechanical Soil Sensor: These sensors employ a mechanism capable of penetrating the soil and capturing the force data by means of pressure scales or load cells. As the sensor penetrates the soil, it documents the retention forces that arise from the cutting, fracturing, and displacement of the soil. Figure 15.9 depicts mechanical soil sensors measure soil resistance using force-capturing mechanisms, providing insights into soil properties for precision agriculture. The mechanical resistance of the soil is quantified in terms of pressure units, indicating the relationship between the force necessary for soil penetration and the surface area of the tool in contact with the soil.

Nutrient Sensor: These sensors measure the concentration of nutrients in the soil, such as nitrogen, phosphorus, and potassium. By continuously monitoring nutrient levels, farmers can adjust their fertilization strategies and optimize the application of fertilizers. This helps prevent over-fertilization and nutrient leaching, resulting in improved crop health and reduced environmental impact.

Airflow Sensor: Measurements can be taken at specific locations in a mobile manner. The intended outcome is to determine the pressure required for injecting a predetermined

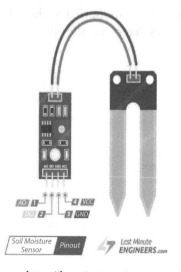

Figure 15.8 Soil moisture sensor (source: https://lastminuteengineers.com/).

Figure 15.9 Mechanical sensors (source: https://www.tractorjunction.com/).

Figure 15.10 Airflow sensor (source: https://www.tractorjunction.com/).

quantity of air into the ground at a specified depth. Figure 15.10 depicts the airflow sensor. Different discernible signatures are generated due to various soil properties such as compaction, structure, soil type, and moisture content [46].

Crop Sensor: These sensors monitor plant health parameters such as leaf temperature, chlorophyll levels, and photosynthetic activity [45]. By collecting real-time data on crop health, farmers can detect early signs of stress, diseases, or pest infestations. This enables targeted interventions and timely treatments, minimizing crop damage and yield losses.

15.3.5   Data Preprocessing and Integration

Data processing and integration are critical components of precision farming. The process begins with data collection from various sources [22], including UAVs, IoT sensors, and weather stations. The collected data are stored in a centralized database or cloud storage system for easy access and management. Data cleaning and preprocessing techniques are applied to ensure accuracy and quality. Integration combines different datasets into a unified format, enabling cross-referencing and correlation analysis [19–21]. Statistical, machine learning, and data mining techniques are used to analyze the data, generating insights and predictive models. Decision support systems and real-time monitoring provide farmers with actionable information and alerts. Historical data analysis helps identify long-term trends and patterns. Data visualization enhances understanding and communication. Overall, data processing and integration enable farmers to make informed decisions about irrigation, nutrient management, pest control, and other aspects of precision farming. By leveraging advanced technologies, farmers can optimize agricultural practices, resource allocation, and farm productivity.

15.4   Crop Monitoring and Management

Precision farming's crop monitoring and management techniques enable farmers to implement targeted interventions, optimize resource usage, reduce environmental impacts, and maximize crop yields. By harnessing technology and data, precision farming practices contribute to sustainable and efficient agriculture.

15.4.1   Crop Yield Prediction

Crop yield prediction in precision farming utilizes advanced technologies and data-driven approaches to estimate crop yields at a fine-scale level. It integrates historical yield data, weather conditions, soil properties, sensor data, and management practices to generate accurate predictions. This helps farmers make informed decisions on irrigation, fertilizers, pests, and harvesting [20]. Yield maps and prescription maps guide site-specific management, optimizing resource utilization. Precision farming maximizes crop production efficiency and supports data-driven decision-making in modern agriculture [25].

15.4.2   Disease Detection and Diagnosis

In precision farming, disease detection and diagnosis rely on data analysis results to identify and assess crop diseases. Through the integration of various technologies and data analytics, precision farming enables early disease identification for timely intervention and effective management strategies. Data analysis plays a critical role by examining diverse data sources, including remote sensing, weather, crop health indicators, and historical disease records. Algorithms and models are developed to detect patterns and anomalies associated with diseases, mapping disease spread, and predicting progression. Sensor and imaging data analysis provides insights into physiological and biochemical changes caused by diseases. Machine learning algorithms and statistical models aid in accurate disease diagnosis by leveraging historical data and crop characteristics. Integrating disease detection and diagnosis into precision farming enables data-driven decision-making, optimized resource allocation, and site-specific disease management strategies, leading to reduced yield losses, minimized agrochemical usage, and improved crop health and productivity. This approach fosters sustainable agricultural practices and contributes to food security.

15.4.3 Nutrient Management and Fertilizer Optimization

Precision farming manages nutrient management and fertilizer optimization through targeted approaches. Soil testing and mapping provide detailed insights into soil nutrient levels and properties, facilitating the creation of precise nutrient maps [32]. Variable rate application tailors fertilizer dosages according to specific field areas, optimizing nutrient utilization while reducing waste. Crop sensing and monitoring employ advanced technologies to assess crop health and nutrient requirements in real time, enabling precise adjustments to fertilizer application. Decision support systems integrate various data sources to provide informed recommendations for optimal timing, rates, and formulations. Nutrient budgeting and record keeping allow for accurate assessment of nutrient efficiency and adjustment of practices. Precision irrigation complements nutrient management by ensuring efficient nutrient delivery. By adopting these strategies, precision farming enhances nutrient use efficiency, minimizes environmental impact, and promotes sustainable agricultural practices.

15.5 Precision Planting and Seeding

Precision planting and seeding practices in precision farming help optimize seed placement, enhance uniformity, and maximize yield potential. By leveraging advanced technologies and data analysis, farmers can achieve efficient resource utilization, reduce input costs, and enhance overall crop productivity and profitability.

15.5.1 Variable Rate Planting

Precision farming enables the implementation of variable rate seeding, where the seeding rate is adjusted based on field variability [46]. By considering factors such as soil fertility, topography, and historical yield data, farmers can optimize seed populations across different areas of the field, maximizing productivity and minimizing input costs.

15.5.2 GPS and Auto-Steering Systems

Global Positioning System (GPS) technology, coupled with auto-steering systems, allows for precise positioning and guidance of planting equipment. This ensures straight rows, eliminates overlap, and minimizes errors in seed placement [31, 32, 46], resulting in uniform plant emergence and improved crop stand establishment.

15.5.3 Seed Singulation and Metering

Precision planting systems incorporate specialized equipment with advanced seed singulation and metering mechanisms. These technologies ensure accurate seed spacing and consistent seed drop, reducing seed waste, competition, and uneven crop growth.

15.5.4   Plant Health Monitoring and Care

Precision planting systems provide real-time monitoring and control capabilities, allowing farmers to track planting progress, seed population, and equipment performance. This enables immediate adjustments and troubleshooting, ensuring optimal planting outcomes.

15.6   Harvesting and Yield Estimation

By implementing precision farming techniques for harvesting and yield estimation, farmers can optimize their operations, reduce losses, and make data-driven decisions regarding harvesting timing, storage, and market planning. The combination of advanced technologies, data analytics, and agronomic expertise empowers farmers to achieve higher productivity and maximize their crop yields while minimizing input costs and environmental impacts.

15.6.1   Yield Estimation Models

Let us discuss various yielding technologies with detailed working examples.

Remote Sensing-Based Models: Remote sensing technologies capture crop health data through satellite or drone imagery, which is then processed using machine learning algorithms to estimate crop yields, with popular indices like NDVI and EVI being utilized.

- Example: A farmer wants to estimate the yield of their wheat crop. They acquire satellite imagery of the field throughout the growing season. By analyzing vegetation indices like NDVI and EVI derived from the satellite images, they can assess the crop's health and biomass. Using a remote sensing-based model, they can then predict the yield based on the observed vegetation patterns.

Crop Simulation Models: Crop simulation models predict crop yield by simulating growth and development based on environmental conditions, management practices, and crop-specific traits, using parameters like temperature, rainfall, solar radiation, soil characteristics.

- Example: A farmer plans to grow corn in their field. They use a crop simulation model like DSSAT. They input parameters such as soil type, weather data (temperature, rainfall), and crop management practices (planting date and fertilizer application). The model simulates the growth stages, water requirements, and nutrient uptake of the corn crop. Based on these simulations, the model estimates the final corn yield.

Statistical Models: Statistical models in precision farming employ historical yield data, along with environmental and agronomic variables, using techniques like regression analysis and machine learning to estimate crop yields. They consider factors such as temperature, precipitation, soil fertility, and previous crop yields to make accurate predictions.

- Example: A farmer aims to predict the soybean yield for the upcoming season. They collect historical yield data from previous years, along with variables like temperature, precipitation, soil fertility, and planting density. Using a statistical model like multiple linear regression, the farmer can analyze the relationships between these factors and soybean yields. They can then make predictions for the current season based on the input variables.

Machine Learning Models: Machine learning algorithms like random forests, support vector machines, and artificial neural networks analyze extensive datasets to identify patterns influencing crop yields. These models utilize weather data, soil attributes, crop management practices, and remote sensing information to generate accurate yield predictions.

- Example: A farmer wants to estimate the potato yield in their field. They gather a large dataset containing weather data, soil properties, crop management information, and historical yield records. Using a machine learning algorithm like a random forest, they train the model with the dataset. The model learns the patterns and relationships between the input variables and potato yields. Once trained, the model can predict the potato yield for a given set of input data.

Hybrid Models: Hybrid models in precision farming enhance yield estimation accuracy by combining statistical models with remote sensing or machine learning techniques. By integrating diverse data sources and modeling approaches, these models deliver more reliable and robust predictions for crop yields.

- Example: A farmer aims to estimate the rice yield in their field. They combine remote sensing data with machine learning techniques. Satellite imagery provides information on crop health and vegetation indices. They integrate these data with other variables such as weather conditions and soil properties. By using a hybrid model that combines remote sensing analysis and machine learning algorithms, the farmer can obtain more accurate predictions of rice yield.

15.6.2   Real-Time Crop Monitoring During Harvest

Real-time crop monitoring during harvest involves the use of advanced technologies and sensors to continuously monitor and collect data on crop conditions, productivity, and quality as the harvest progresses [45]. These real-time data provide valuable insights to farmers, enabling them to make informed decisions and optimize harvesting operations for maximum efficiency and yield. Figure 15.11 illustrates the seed singulation machine employed in precision seeding processes [45].

15.7   Data Analytics and Machine Learning

Data analytics and machine learning empower farmers with valuable insights into their crops, leading to more efficient resource management, reduced costs, increased productivity,

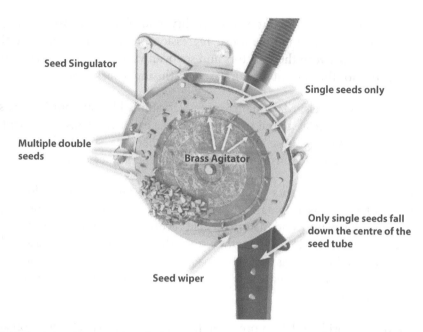

Figure 15.11 Seed singulation machine (source: https://thefarmermagazine.com.au/).

and improved sustainability in precision farming. Continued advancements in these fields will further enhance the capabilities of precision agriculture systems.

15.7.1　Predictive Analytics for Crop Yield

Predictive analytics driven by big data analysis revolutionizes precision farming by enabling accurate yield predictions, disease and pest management, optimal resource allocation, irrigation management, decision support systems, crop quality and sorting, and market trends forecasting [25]. By analyzing diverse data sources such as historical records, weather patterns, soil conditions, and crop characteristics, predictive models inform farmers' decisions regarding resource allocation, pest control, and marketing strategies. With early detection of disease outbreaks and pests, targeted treatments can be implemented, reducing crop losses and minimizing pesticide usage [23]. By optimizing resource allocation and irrigation scheduling, farmers can enhance crop health and productivity while minimizing waste. Decision support systems provide real-time recommendations based on big data analysis, guiding farmers in making data-driven decisions throughout the farming cycle. Crop quality and sorting processes are improved by analyzing crop characteristics, ensuring produce meets market requirements.

Predictive analytics also enables farmers to forecast market trends and align their production accordingly, minimizing wastage and optimizing profitability. Ultimately, the integration of predictive analytics and big data analysis empowers farmers to make informed decisions, enhance efficiency, and achieve sustainable and profitable precision farming practices.

15.7.2   Machine Learning Algorithms for Precision Farming

Several machine learning algorithms are used in precision farming to analyze data and make predictions. Here are some specific ML algorithms commonly employed in precision farming [30, 37]:

Random Forests:

- Random forests are ensemble learning methods that combine multiple decision trees.
- They are used for tasks such as yield prediction, disease detection, and crop classification [24, 25].
- Random forests handle large datasets effectively and are robust against noise and overfitting.

Support Vector Machines (SVMs):

- SVM is a supervised learning algorithm used for classification and regression tasks.
- SVMs are employed in precision farming for crop classification, weed detection, and disease identification.
- They can handle high-dimensional data and work well with limited training samples.

Artificial Neural Networks (ANNs):

- ANNs are computational models inspired by the structure and functionality of the human brain.
- They are utilized for tasks such as yield prediction, disease diagnosis, and plant phenotyping [24, 25].
- ANNs can capture complex relationships in data and handle non-linear patterns.

Convolutional Neural Networks (CNNs) [37]:

- CNNs are a type of neural network specifically designed for image analysis and recognition tasks.
- CNNs are employed in precision farming for tasks like crop disease detection, plant species identification, and weed recognition.
- CNNs excel at extracting spatial and hierarchical features from images.

Decision Trees [37]:

- Decision trees are simple yet powerful ML models that make predictions based on a series of if–then–else decision rules.
- Decision trees are used in precision farming for tasks like crop classification, yield prediction, and irrigation scheduling [24–26].
- Decision trees provide interpretable models and handle both numerical and categorical data.

K-Nearest Neighbors (KNN):

- KNN is a simple, non-parametric algorithm that classifies samples based on their similarity to neighboring data points.
- KNN is employed in precision farming for crop disease classification, weed detection, and yield mapping [37].
- KNN is easy to implement and can handle multi-class classification tasks.

15.7.3   Big Data Analytics in Precision Farming

Big data analytics in precision farming enables farmers to harness the power of data to optimize agricultural practices, improve productivity, and enhance sustainability. By leveraging advanced analytics techniques, farmers can make more informed decisions, reduce costs, minimize waste, and achieve higher crop yields while minimizing environmental impacts.

The application of big data analytics in agriculture brings about various benefits, including improved yield forecasting, efficient resource utilization, enhanced decision making, and reduced food waste. Real-time data from fields and equipment enable timely decisions and alerts, while preventive maintenance optimizes equipment performance. Correlations between field, weather, and commodity data facilitate efficient irrigation, fertilization, and harvesting practices. Predictive analytics aids in anticipating demand for agricultural inputs and implementing appropriate supply strategies. Additionally, big data analytics supports cost savings, business opportunities, and better supply chain management, leading to faster product delivery and improved market alignment. Ultimately, the integration of big data and analytics in agriculture showcases immense potential for enhancing productivity, sustainability, and profitability in the industry. Scientifically, these advancements in data-driven agriculture have significant implications for improving agricultural operations, supply chain efficiency, and resource management, leading to potential economic and environmental benefits.

15.8   Integration of AI with Other Technologies

The integration of AI with other technologies in precision farming holds great potential to enhance productivity, reduce costs, and promote sustainable agricultural practices. By leveraging the power of AI, farmers can optimize their resource usage, increase crop yields, and contribute to a more efficient and environmentally friendly food production system.

15.8.1   AI and Blockchain in Supply Chain Management [38, 39]

By integrating blockchain technology into precision farming supply chains, stakeholders can benefit from enhanced transparency, improved efficiency, reduced fraud, and increased trust. The combination of blockchain, IoT devices, AI analytics, and smart contracts has the potential to revolutionize the way agricultural products are produced, tracked, and distributed, leading to a more sustainable and resilient food system.

1. Traceability and Provenance [39]: Blockchain can create an immutable and transparent record of every transaction and event within the supply chain, from seed sourcing to crop harvesting and distribution. Each step of the farming process, including the use of fertilizers, pesticides, and other inputs, can be recorded on the blockchain, along with relevant data such as origin, quality, and certifications. This ensures that all stakeholders have access to accurate information about the origin and history of the products, enabling better quality control and accountability.

2. Smart Contracts and Automation: Smart contracts, which are self-executing contracts with predefined rules encoded on the blockchain, can automate various processes in the supply chain. For example, a smart contract can automatically trigger payments to farmers when predefined conditions, such as successful delivery or quality verification, are met. This reduces administrative overhead, improves efficiency, and eliminates the need for intermediaries.

3. Supply Chain Optimization [38]: By leveraging blockchain data, AI algorithms can analyze supply chain patterns and optimize logistics, inventory management, and distribution. This can lead to improved planning, reduced waste, and enhanced efficiency throughout the supply chain. For instance, AI can analyze historical data on transportation routes and optimize delivery schedules to minimize carbon emissions and transportation costs.

4. Quality and Certification Standards: Blockchain can facilitate the tracking and verification of quality and certification standards in precision farming. Certifications related to organic farming, fair trade practices, or specific quality attributes can be recorded on the blockchain, providing consumers with transparent information about the products they purchase. This enhances trust and enables consumers to make more informed choices [38, 39].

5. Food Safety and Recall Management: In the event of a food safety issue or product recall, blockchain technology can provide rapid traceability and enable efficient identification and removal of affected products from the supply chain. The immutable nature of blockchain records ensures that the history of each product can be easily audited, minimizing the impact on public health and preserving consumer confidence.

6. Supply Chain Financing and Incentives: Blockchain can enable innovative financing models in precision farming supply chains. For instance, farmers can use their recorded data on the blockchain, such as crop yields and quality, as collateral for loans or access to financial services. Additionally, blockchain-based incentives and reward systems can be implemented to encourage sustainable farming practices, such as reducing water usage or minimizing chemical inputs [39].

15.8.2 AI and Drones in Precision Farming

AI and drones have revolutionized precision farming by offering advanced technologies and data-driven solutions for improved agricultural practices [41, 42]. Let us explore how AI and drones are utilized in precision farming [41, 42].

- Drones equipped with sensors and cameras provide high-resolution images of crops for monitoring plant health and detecting anomalies.
- AI algorithms analyze drone-captured data to identify crop diseases, nutrient deficiencies, and pest infestations [23].
- Precision spraying drones apply pesticides, herbicides, and fertilizers with accuracy, reducing chemical usage and minimizing environmental impact [23].
- AI models process data from drones, ground sensors, and satellite imagery [15] to assess soil composition, moisture levels, and nutrient content.
- AI and drones enable yield prediction, optimizing harvest planning and resource allocation [40].
- Livestock monitoring can be enhanced using drones to track animal behavior, health, and grazing patterns.

15.8.3   AI and Robotics Collaboration

AI and robotics collaboration plays a crucial role in advancing precision farming techniques. Here are some ways in which AI and robotics work together in the field of precision farming:

1. Autonomous Farming Equipment: AI-powered robots and autonomous vehicles are designed to perform various agricultural tasks, such as planting, harvesting, and weeding. These robots leverage AI algorithms to navigate fields, identify crops, and perform specific actions with precision, reducing the need for manual labor and increasing operational efficiency [40].
2. Decision Support Systems: AI algorithms analyze vast amounts of agricultural data, including weather patterns, soil conditions, and historical information, to provide real-time recommendations and insights to farmers. These decision support systems assist farmers in making informed decisions about irrigation, fertilization, pest control, and other critical aspects of crop management.
3. Crop Monitoring and Management: Robotics and AI work hand in hand to monitor crops and manage their growth. Drones equipped with AI-powered image analysis can capture data on plant health, growth patterns, and pest infestations [23]. These data are then processed by AI algorithms to provide actionable insights, enabling farmers to take timely actions to improve crop health and maximize yields.
4. Robotic Harvesting: AI-powered robotic systems can be trained to identify ripe crops, such as fruits or vegetables, and perform autonomous harvesting tasks. These robots use computer vision and AI algorithms to recognize and handle delicate produce, ensuring efficient and precise harvesting while minimizing damage and waste.
5. Precision Irrigation and Fertilization: AI-based robotics systems equipped with sensors can collect real-time data on soil moisture, nutrient levels, and crop requirements. AI algorithms analyze these data to optimize irrigation and fertilization, ensuring that crops receive the right amount of water and

nutrients at the right time, leading to improved resource management and increased productivity.

6. Weed and Pest Control: Robotics and AI can collaborate to identify and manage weeds and pests. AI algorithms analyze images or sensor data collected by robots to distinguish between crops and unwanted plants or insects. Robotic systems can then target and eliminate these threats with precision, reducing the need for broad-spectrum chemical applications and minimizing environmental impact.

15.9   Case Studies and Success Stories

Case study 1: The first case study conducted in Australia focuses on the development of a Precision Dairy Innovation System (PDIS). This system incorporates various technologies designed to monitor individual animals or farm resources, such as in-line milk meters, automated mastitis sensors, and activity sensors. The study collected data through multiple sources, including 25 farmer interviews on precision dairy implementation, 18 farmer interviews during the "Pastures from Space" project, and workshops involving farmers, researchers, and commercial providers of precision dairy technologies [43]. The interviews and workshops explored various themes, including the processes of on-farm adaptation, the support received by farmers after installation, and the interactions within the network of practice. The case study aimed to investigate the implementation and impact of precision dairy farming in the Australian context.

The contributions of public and private research and extension in the development of Technology Innovation Systems (TIS). The case studies are distilled into three phases: initiation, implementation, and adaptation. Quotes from research participants and supporting findings from other studies are used to provide insights.

The initiation of the innovation systems, such as the Australian precision dairy innovation system, is discussed. The expansion of herd sizes, availability of sensor technologies, and the National Livestock Identification System (NLIS) based on Radio Frequency Identification technology drove the development of precision dairy farming in Australia. Government-subsidized electronic identification devices facilitated individual animal monitoring and management. International milking technology providers introduced products like in-line milk meters, mastitis sensors, and automated feeding and sorting. Local companies such as Jantech and OnFarm Electronics offered herd management software and related technologies. During this stage, there was minimal public research and extension focused on on-farm technology use. Farmers themselves acted as entrepreneurs, adapting technology to fit their needs. However, uncertainty regarding return on investment and overall value proposition hindered farmer adoption.

In the mid-2000s, public-funded research and extension played a more prominent role in the precision dairy innovation system. Projects like FutureDairy [43], funded through a mix of farmer-levy and government funds, explored automatic milking systems and animal sensor research. Collaboration between public organizations and commercial technology providers facilitated the adaptation of precision technology for the Australian context. The second project, Pastures from Space, utilized satellite technology to estimate pasture dry matter [15]. Several public and farmer-levy-funded projects also emphasized farmer involvement and explored the challenges faced in adapting farm systems, learning to use the technologies, and developing capabilities within the precision dairy innovation system.

Case study 2: The second case study focuses on the development of an Automatic Milking Innovation System (AMIS) primarily in Northwestern Europe, including countries such as the Netherlands, Denmark, Germany, the United Kingdom, and Ireland. Data for this case study were collected through an online survey, which received 80 responses from researchers, service providers, and technology providers. Additionally, 10 semi-structured interviews were conducted with key members of the AMIS network of practice, representing researchers, technology providers, and consultants [43]. The interview themes were aligned with those explored in the Precision Dairy Innovation System (PDIS) interviews. Published studies related to the development of automatic milking in Europe were also reviewed and referenced in the analysis of the case study. These studies included works by Driessen and Heutinck (2015), Holloway *et al.* (2014b), Schewe and Stuart (2014), and Hansen (2015). The case study aimed to examine the AMIS network of practice and gather insights into the development and implementation of automatic milking technologies in Northwestern Europe [44].

Top of Form Increased installation of Automatic Milking Systems (AMS) in Northwestern Europe created new opportunities for the private advisory sector. In the Netherlands, specialized services were offered by nutrition, feed, and finance companies to AMS farmers. For instance, a Dutch feed company started providing dedicated AMS advice in the early 2000s and now employs four consultants who offer personalized guidance. In Denmark, AMS suppliers contracted specialized consultants to provide farming systems advice, often including limited consultant hours as part of the AMS purchase contract. An automated milking system is one of the dimensions depicted in the provided Figure. 5.12. A Danish consultancy firm also offered a range of AMS advice, considering factors such as cow traffic, barn layout, and positioning of the robot from both cow and farmer perspectives.

The development of the Internet played a significant role in facilitating knowledge exchange and network development among AMS users. Online forums provided a platform for farmers to discuss AMS, although there were concerns about the spread of misinformation and unfounded criticism. The adoption of AMS systems in Europe had broader socio-technical implications, involving the co-evolution of ethics and technology and reevaluating the farmer's role [43, 44]. Questions of societal legitimacy emerged regarding the ongoing adaptation of precision farming innovation systems [33]. Policy uncertainty and market conditions influenced the adoption of AMS throughout the studied timeline, and technological uncertainty had a greater impact when farmers lacked robust support networks for knowledge diffusion.

Private technology providers approached training in various ways, such as establishing user groups, utilizing knowledgeable farmers as trainers, and experimenting with distance learning through video conferences. However, the value proposition for technology companies to invest in post-purchase training was limited, and farmers were hesitant to pay for additional services. Challenges arose from technology incompatibility between different systems, limitations in data transfer due to a lack of standardized protocols, and data incompatibility with national herd testing databases. These factors added complexity to the implementation and seamless integration of AMS in the agricultural landscape.

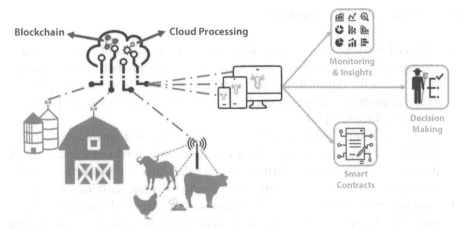

Figure 15.12 Blockchain-based supply chain for cattle product (source:https://www.era-susan.eu/).

15.10 Challenges and Future Trends

Challenges in Precision Farming: The following trends represent the evolving landscape of precision farming, offering opportunities to address challenges, improve efficiency, and promote sustainable agriculture in the future.

1. Data Management and Interoperability: Precision farming generates vast amounts of data from various sources such as sensors, satellites, and machinery. Managing and integrating these data from different systems and formats can be challenging. Ensuring data interoperability and compatibility across platforms and technologies is crucial for effective decision-making.

2. Cost and Accessibility: The initial investment in precision farming technologies can be high, including the cost of equipment, software, and infrastructure. This can be a barrier for small-scale farmers or those with limited financial resources. Ensuring affordability and accessibility of precision farming solutions is essential for widespread adoption.

3. Technical Expertise and Training: Precision farming requires specialized knowledge and skills in areas such as data analytics, remote sensing, and equipment operation. Farmers and agricultural professionals need proper training and support to effectively utilize precision farming technologies and interpret data insights.

4. Connectivity and Infrastructure: Reliable internet connectivity and infrastructure are essential for data transmission, remote monitoring, and real-time decision-making in precision farming. However, rural areas may have limited access to high-speed internet, hindering the full potential of precision farming.

5. Standardization and Regulations: Developing common standards and regulations for precision farming technologies and data sharing is crucial [33]. Lack of standardization can lead to compatibility issues, data privacy concerns, and barriers to collaboration among different stakeholders.

Future Trends in Precision Farming:

1. Artificial Intelligence (AI) and Machine Learning: AI and machine learning algorithms can analyze large datasets to provide predictive and prescriptive insights for optimizing crop management [30]. These technologies can enhance decision-making processes and enable more precise and efficient resource allocation [30].

2. Internet of Things (IoT) and Sensor Technology: IoT and sensor networks can provide real-time data on soil moisture, temperature, crop health, and livestock behavior [27]. This enables farmers to make data-driven decisions and implement targeted interventions, improving productivity and sustainability [29].

3. Robotics and Automation: Advancements in robotics and automation technologies offer opportunities for autonomous operations in precision farming [33]. Robots can perform tasks like seeding, planting, spraying, and harvesting with precision, reducing labor requirements and improving efficiency.

4. Remote Sensing and Imaging: Remote sensing technologies, including satellite imagery and drones, can provide detailed information about crop health, nutrient levels, and pest infestations. This enables early detection of problems and allows farmers to take proactive measures.

5. Blockchain Technology: Blockchain can enhance transparency, traceability, and trust in the agricultural supply chain. It can securely record and verify data related to crop production, origin, and quality, promoting sustainability and consumer confidence.

6. Integration of Big Data Analytics: Advanced data analytics techniques can leverage big data from various sources to identify patterns, optimize resource management, and develop predictive models for improved decision-making in precision farming.

15.11   Conclusion

In conclusion, precision farming holds great potential for transforming agriculture by leveraging technology and data-driven approaches. Despite challenges related to data management, costs, and technical expertise, the future trends of artificial intelligence, IoT, robotics, remote sensing, and blockchain offer promising solutions. As these technologies continue to advance and become more accessible, precision farming has the ability to optimize resource utilization, increase productivity, enhance sustainability, and contribute to the global food security challenges we face today.

References

1. Finger, R., Swinton, S.M., Benni, N.E., Walter, A., Precision farming at the Nexus of agricultural production and the environment, *Annu. Rev. Resour. Econ.*, 11, 1, 313–335, 2019, https://doi.org/10.1146/annurev-resource-100518-093929.

2. Wolf, S.A. and Buttel, F.H., The political economy of precision farming. *Am. J. Agric. Econ.*, 78, 5, 1269–1274, 1996.
3. Nelson, F., Pickett, T., Smith, W., Ott, L., The GreenStar precision farming system. *Proceedings of Position, Location and Navigation Symposium - PLANS '96*, Atlanta, GA, USA, pp. 6–9, 1996.
4. Alejandrino, J., Concepcion, R., Almero, V.J., Palconit, M.G., Bandala, A., Dadios, E., A hybrid data acquisition model using artificial intelligence and IoT messaging protocol for precision farming. *2020 IEEE 12th International Conference on Humanoid, Nanotechnology, Information Technology, Communication and Control, Environment, and Management (HNICEM)*, Manila, Philippines, pp. 1–6, 2020.
5. Njoroge, B.M., Fei, T.K., Thiruchelvam, V., A research review of precision farming techniques and technology. *J. Appl. Technol. Innov.*, 2, 1, 22, 2018.
6. Chukkapalli, S.S.L. *et al.*, Ontologies and artificial intelligence systems for the cooperative smart farming ecosystem. *IEEE Access*, 8, 164045–164064, 2020.
7. Prabavathi, R., Subha, P., Brindha Devi, V., Rekha, C., Verma, A., Rohith, S., Krishi Nanban: AI driven precision agriculture. *2022 International Conference on Data Science, Agents & Artificial Intelligence (ICDSAAI)*, Chennai, India, pp. 1–5, 2022.
8. Caruso, A., Chessa, S., Escolar, S., Barba, J., López, J.C., Collection of data with drones in precision agriculture: Analytical model and LoRa case study. *IEEE Internet Things J.*, 8, 22, 16692–16704, Nov.15, 2021.
9. Zaryouli, M., Fathi, M.T., Ezziyyani, M., Data collection based on multi-agent modeling for intelligent and precision farming in lokoss region morocco. *2020 1st International Conference on Innovative Research in Applied Science, Engineering and Technology (IRASET)*, Meknes, Morocco, pp. 1–6, 2020.
10. Adetiba, E. *et al.*, Development of an IoT based data acquisition and automatic irrigation system for precision agriculture. *2022 IEEE Nigeria 4th International Conference on Disruptive Technologies for Sustainable Development (NIGERCON)*, Lagos, Nigeria, pp. 1–5, 2022.
11. Tsouros, D.C., Triantafyllou, A., Bibi, S., Sarigannidis, P.G., Data acquisition and analysis methods in UAV- based applications for precision agriculture. *2019 15th International Conference on Distributed Computing in Sensor Systems (DCOSS)*, Santorini, Greece, pp. 377–384, 2019.
12. Mukhamediev, R.I., *et al.*, Coverage path planning optimization of heterogeneous UAVs group for precision agriculture. *IEEE Access*, 11, 5789–5803, 2023.
13. Rodriguez-Galvis, J., Angulo-Morales, V., Gaona-García, E., Lizarazo-Salcedo, I., Development of low-cost ground control system for UAV-based mapping. *IGARSS 2020 - 2020 IEEE International Geoscience and Remote Sensing Symposium*, Waikoloa, HI, USA, pp. 5111–5114, 2020.
14. Pino, M., Matos-Carvalho, J.P., Pedro, D., Campos, L.M., Costa Seco, J., UAV cloud platform for precision farming. *2020 12th International Symposium on Communication Systems, Networks and Digital Signal Processing (CSNDSP)*, Porto, Portugal, pp. 1–6, 2020.
15. Jihua, M., Zhongyuan, L., Bingfang, W., Jin, X., Design, development and application of a satellite-based field monitoring system to support precision farming. *2014 The Third International Conference on Agro-Geoinformatics*, Beijing, China, pp. 1–9, 2014.
16. Castro, R., Remote monitoring of coffee cultivation through computational processing of satellite images. *2019 7th International Engineering, Sciences and Technology Conference (IESTEC)*, Panama, Panama, pp. 13–18, 2019.
17. Pokrajac, D., Lazarevic, A., Vucetic, S., Fiez, T., Obradovic, Z., Image processing in precision agriculture. *4th International Conference on Telecommunications in Modern Satellite, Cable and Broadcasting Services. TELSIKS'99 (Cat. No.99EX365)*, Nis, Yugoslavia, vol. 2, pp. 616–619, 1999.

18. Katsigiannis, P., Misopolinos, L., Liakopoulos, V., Alexandridis, T.K., Zalidis, G., An autonomous multi-sensor UAV system for reduced-input precision agriculture applications. *2016 24th Mediterranean Conference on Control and Automation (MED)*, Athens, Greece, pp. 60–64, 2016.

19. Alexy, M. and Haidegger, T., Precision solutions in livestock farming – feasibility and applicability of digital data collection. *2022 IEEE 10th Jubilee International Conference on Computational Cybernetics and Cyber-Medical Systems (ICCC)*, Reykjavík, Iceland, pp. 000233–000238, 2022.

20. Bastos, J., Shepherd, P.M., Castillejo, P., Emeterio, M.S., Díaz, V.H., Rodriguez, J., Location-based data auditing for precision farming IoT Networks. *2021 IEEE 26th International Workshop on Computer Aided Modeling and Design of Communication Links and Networks (CAMAD)*, Porto, Portugal, pp. 1–6, 2021.

21. Hank, T., Bach, H., Spannraft, K., Friese, M., Frank, T., Mauser, W., Improving the process-based simulation of growth heterogeneities in agricultural stands through assimilation of earth observation data. *2012 IEEE International Geoscience and Remote Sensing Symposium*, Munich, Germany, pp. 1006–1009, 2012.

22. Alexy, M. and Haidegger, T., Precision solutions in livestock farming – feasibility and applicability of digital data collection. *2022 IEEE 10th Jubilee International Conference on Computational Cybernetics and Cyber-Medical Systems (ICCC)*, Reykjavík, Iceland, pp. 000233–000238, 2022.

23. Suárez, A., Molina, R.S., Ramponi, G., Petrino, R., Bollati, L., Sequeiros, D., Pest detection and classification to reduce pesticide use in fruit crops based on deep neural networks and image processing. *2021 XIX Workshop on Information Processing and Control (RPIC)*, San Juan, Argentina, pp. 1–6, 2021.

24. Chlingaryan, A., Sukkarieh, S., Whelan, B., Machine learning approaches for crop yield prediction and nitrogen status estimation in precision agriculture: A review. *Comput. Electron. Agric.*, 151, 61–69, 2018.

25. Nyéki, A. and Neményi, M., Crop yield prediction in precision agriculture. *Agronomy*, 12, 10, 2460, 2022.

26. Burdett, H. and Wellen, C., Statistical and machine learning methods for crop yield prediction in the context of precision agriculture. *Precis. Agric.*, 23, 5, 1553–1574, 2022.

27. Nabi, F., Jamwal, S., Padmanbh, K., Wireless sensor network in precision farming for forecasting and monitoring of apple disease: A survey. *Int. J. Inf. Technol.*, 14, 2, 769–780, 2022.

28. Rekha, P. *et al.*, High yield groundnut agronomy: An IoT based precision farming framework. *2017 IEEE Global Humanitarian Technology Conference (GHTC)*, IEEE, 2017.

29. Lambrinos, L., Internet of Things in agriculture: A decision support system for precision farming. *2019 IEEE Intl Conf on Dependable, Autonomic and Secure Computing, Intl Conf on Pervasive Intelligence and Computing, Intl Conf on Cloud and Big Data Computing, Intl Conf on Cyber Science and Technology Congress (DASC/PiCom/CBDCom/CyberSciTech)*, Fukuoka, Japan, pp. 889–892, 2019.

30. Raj, E.F.I., Appadurai, M., Athiappan, K., Precision farming in modern agriculture, in: *Smart Agriculture Automation Using Advanced Technologies: Data Analytics and Machine Learning, Cloud Architecture, Automation and IoT*, pp. 61–87, Springer Singapore, Singapore, 2022.

31. Grisso, R.D., Alley, M.M., Groover, G.E., Precision farming tools. GPS Navigation, 2005.

32. Pedersen, S.M. and Lind, K.M., Precision agriculture–from mapping to site-specific application, in: *Precision Agriculture: Technology and Economic Perspectives*, pp. 1–20, 2017.

33. Say, S.M. *et al.*, Adoption of precision agriculture technologies in developed and developing countries. *Online J. Sci. Technol.*, 8, 1, 7–15, January 2018.

34. Kim, J. *et al.*, Unmanned aerial vehicles in agriculture: A review of perspective of platform, control, and applications. *IEEE Access*, 7, 105100–105115, 2019.

35. Iost Filho, F.H. *et al.*, Drones: Innovative technology for use in precision pest management. *J. Econ. Entomol.*, 113, 1, 1–25, 2020.

36. Balaceanu, C. *et al.*, Diseases detection system based on machine learning algorithms and Internet of Things technology used in viticulture. *2022 E-Health and Bioengineering Conference (EHB)*, Iasi, Romania, pp. 1–4, 2022.

37. Kaur, D. and Kaur, A., IoT and machine learning-based systems for predicting cattle health status for precision livestock farming. *2022 International Conference on Smart Generation Computing, Communication and Networking (SMART GENCON)*, Bangalore, India, pp. 1–5, 2022.

38. Kaushik, I., Prakash, N., Jain, A., Integration of blockchain& IoT in precision farming: Exploration, scope and security challenges. *2021 IEEE 12th Annual Ubiquitous Computing, Electronics & Mobile Communication Conference (UEMCON)*, New York, NY, USA, pp. 0854–0859, 2021.

39. Alam, S., Security concerns in smart agriculture and blockchain-based solution. *2022 OPJU International Technology Conference on Emerging Technologies for Sustainable Development (OTCON)*, Raigarh, Chhattisgarh, India, pp. 1–6, 2023.

40. Inoue, Y. and Yokoyama, M., Drone-based optical, thermal, and 3D sensing for diagnostic information in smart farming – systems and algorithms –. *IGARSS 2019 - 2019 IEEE International Geoscience and Remote Sensing Symposium*, Yokohama, Japan, pp. 7266–7269, 2019.

41. Panjaitan, S.D., Dewi, Y.S.K., Hendri, M.I., Wicaksono, R.A., Priyatman, H., A drone technology implementation approach to conventional paddy fields application. *IEEE Access*, 10, 120650–120658, 2022.

42. Dobermann, A. *et al.*, Precision farming: Challenges and future directions. *Proceedings of the 4th International Crop Science Congress*, Australia: Brisbane, vol. 26, 2004.

43. Eastwood, C., Klerkx, L., Nettle. Dynamics, R., and distribution of public and private research and extension roles for technological innovation and diffusion: Case studies of the implementation and adaptation of precision farming technologies. *J. Rural Stud.*, 49, 1–12, 2017.

44. https://www.era-susan.eu/.

45. https://thefarmermagazine.com.au/.

46. https://www.tractorjunction.com/.

47. https://lastminuteengineers.com/.

16

An In-Depth Review on Machine Learning Infusion in an Agricultural Production System

Sarthak Dash[1], Sugyanta Priyadarshini[1]* and Sukanya Priyadarshini[2]

[1]KIIT Deemed to be University, Bhubaneshwar, India
[2]Berhampur University, Berhampur, India

Abstract

Agriculture has the ability to sustain human existence by maintaining food security. The three main factors that affect food security are overpopulation, climate variability, and resource competition. To address such complicated issues, intelligent or smart farming extends the use of machine learning and the Internet of Things in traditional agriculture. This chapter is an attempt to give a broad systematic review of the existing literature on machine learning applications in various domains of farming operations. In order to perform the review, a systematic review methodology is used. The review process involves review planning, search criteria, and search terms. After the search is finished, the papers are chosen using inclusion and exclusion factors. The review was conducted on 26 articles extracted from two online databases: Scopus and Web of Science. The literature concerning agricultural production and machine learning is further sub-categorized into five broad areas: (a) crop yielding prediction, which includes seed management, yield prediction, and price management; (b) crop disease management; (c)water management; (d) soil management; and (e) weather prediction. The categorization and filtering of the documents presented in the study show how machine learning techniques will help agricultural production. The application of machine learning in farm management systems has become a real-time artificial intelligence-enabled program that has offered a detailed list of suggestions and insights for farmer decision support and appropriate action.

Keywords: Machine learning, agricultural production, crop management, crop disease management, water management, soil management, weather prediction

16.1 Background Study

The constant anthropogenic innovation has helped the agricultural industry to evolve [1]. It has witnessed radical transformation from primitive or traditional methodologies to modern technical developments [2, 3]. With the Industrial Revolution, the agricultural sector adopted mechanization and synthesized fertilizers. Similarly, with the technical or digital age, it has adopted genetic engineering and automation [4]. This advancement in technology has expanded the speed, scale, and productivity of farm equipment, leading

*Corresponding author: sugyanta.priyadarshini@kiit.ac.in

Arindam Dey, Sukanta Nayak, Ranjan Kumar and Sachi Nandan Mohanty (eds.) How Machine Learning is Innovating Today's World: A Concise Technical Guide, (253–270) © 2024 Scrivener Publishing LLC

to higher productivity and efficient cultivation of more land [5]. However, climate change [6, 7], exponential population growth [8], limited natural resources [9–11], and the growing demand for food in terms of quality and quantity (The World Bank, 2023) have driven the need for the agricultural sector to evolve further. Therefore, with the current Data age, also referred to as the Information age, the agricultural sector has catapulted into adopting new trends in the computer field like artificial intelligence (AI), machine learning (ML), deep learning (DL), Internet of Things (IoT), cloud computing, and blockchain technology [12]. This has led to the genesis of a new age of agriculture called precision agriculture or smart farming or digital agriculture.

Precision farming relies on the convergence of both Information Technology and Communication devices (like satellites and robotic drones) in the farm management system with an aim to minimize production cost by efficient utilization of land resources, maximize productivity and profitability, and enhance sustainability by identifying, analyzing, and managing spatiotemporal variability within the fields [13]. In simpler terms, precision agriculture refers to a group of technologies that integrate sensors, robotic drones, information technology, advanced communication systems, improved farming tools and machines, and knowledgeable management practices in order to optimize production and productivity by taking into account unpredictability and uncertainty in agricultural systems. It is a comprehensive system that aims to implement the elements of information, technology, and management to conserve energy and protect as well as preserve nature and natural resources. It aims towards incorporating data technical advances in agriculture and making it environment friendly. The decline in overall production, dwindling and deteriorating natural resources, stagnant farm earnings, absence of an ecozonal perspective, shrinking land holdings, trade liberalization on agriculture, depleting employment opportunities in non-agricultural sectors, and climate change over the globe have emerged as major areas of concern in growth and development of the agricultural sector [14, 15]. It is estimated that the world population will be 34% higher than today and will rise to 9.1 billion by 2050. There will be a need to raise food production by 70% because of rampant urbanization and the availability of land for agriculture will reduce drastically in upcoming years (Food and Agriculture Organisation, UN, 2023). Coping with these future challenges requires drastic changes to the farming system and investment in advanced agricultural research to derive innovative solutions [16]. This signifies the need to adopt and implement precision agriculture at the earliest possible time.

The cutting-edge technology that drives precision agriculture is machine learning. Machine learning, being a subset of AI [17], has tremendous potential in tackling multiple challenges encountered in setting up an information-based farming system [18]. Machine learning provides machines with the ability to learn without being explicitly programmed [19–21]. Because of the availability of massive data sets through industrial IoT (Internet of Things) sources, and well-equipped and advanced research, machine learning (ML) algorithms are becoming more innovative and are now trained to make intelligent decisions [22]. As a whole, the prime objective of ML algorithms is to improvise the function and execution of an assignment by making the most from available data, existing examples, or experiences of the past. In particular, the ML process has three parts: Data input, Building of ML algorithm, and Generalization (that is, making the prediction or intelligent decision) [23]. The ML algorithms have mainly been applied to resolve the complicated issues where the expertise of man goes wrong such as predicting weather [24], identifying diseases in plants [25], and many more. Machine learning has a wide range of applications in the field of agriculture. There are plenty of studies that reflect the uses of machine learning in crop management like yield production [26, 27] and weed detection [28–30], crop disease management [31], crop recognition [32, 33], soil management [34], water management [35], animal welfare [36, 37], livestock production [38], and many more.

With each passing year, the agriculture industry is becoming more data-centered, technology-driven, precise, and smarter. Although ML in agriculture has helped evolve the sector, there are still some open-ended problems. As mentioned above, there are a plethora of review studies on yield production, detection of weeds, practices to detect and prevent crop disease, recognition of crops, and soil and water management, but there is no review study on the information processing and analyzing methodologies of hyperspectral and multispectral data in agriculture [39]. Moreover, with many developing nations practicing the conventional form of agriculture, the farmers are hesitant to shift from primitive to precision farming. Further, lack of knowledge, the high cost of smart data-driven technology, and the absence of awareness of application of ML in agriculture have made the farmers hesitant to adopt the cutting-edge technology. The early setup of digital framing including both the hardware and software is a huge investment. Moreover, use of sensors, robotics, and other electronic equipment demands higher energy expenditure that is not affordable to every farmer. Additionally, not every farmer is interested to step out of their comfort zone and learn digital skills. Another open-ended problem is a large number of farmers are not quite experts in ML and hence cannot fully understand and analyze the underlying patterns of ML algorithms. From the technical aspect, the implementation of agricultural big data has multiple challenges like inaccessibility and unusability of data, disruption of data handling data, lack of data calibration, lacunae in data interoperability, paucity of bandwidth in rural areas, and representation of crop growth models [40, 41]. Moreover, the talent gap created by lack of data specialists is another critical challenge for precision agriculture [42]. Further, the return on investment in agriculture is viewed as uncertain as well as less competitive as compared to other sectors [43, 44]. Another significant challenge is data governance. The majority of experts claim that they would be happy to share their personal data under certain circumstances, but many also voiced worries about data security, privacy, protection of intellectual property, and cybercrime [45].

As mentioned above, several review studies highlight the application of ML in different fields of agriculture. However, earlier studies have mostly concentrated on exclusively one subfield of agriculture. Therefore, this paper aims towards drawing attention to put forth a broad systemic literature review of the application of ML from different domains of the agricultural sector. The paper focuses on five generic categories like (a) crop management, which includes seed management, yield prediction, and price management, (b) crop disease management, (c) water management, (d) soil management, and (e) weather prediction. This chapter further aims to review all available and relevant literature and present an updated literature work. It also intends to capture the current trends and progress of ML in agriculture as well as the rising challenges. Given the above, the chapter aims to contribute to the emerging body of research on the application of ML in the agricultural sector.

16.2 Research Methodology

This chapter has considered a systematic review methodology to conduct the review. In this review process, various steps have been indicated such as planning the review, search string, and search criteria for machine learning in agricultural production. After the completion of the search, the research articles are considered for review using inclusion and exclusion criteria. This section offers details on how the review is carried out.

16.2.1   Planning the Review

In recent years, machine learning in agriculture has advanced substantially. Despite extensive study efforts, the prospective outcomes for each field of this concerned field have not been uncovered yet. This chapter tried to conduct an in-depth research and an overview of machine learning technologies in the agriculture domain. Further, this study has explored the implications of machine learning in various sub-categorical domains of the agricultural sector including techniques applied, observed features, and benefits perceived.

16.2.2   Search String

In the extraction articles related to machine learning and agricultural production, several keywords are identified such as ML, ML in crop management, pest management, weather forecasting, machine learning in crop yield prediction, ML in crop disease prediction, and ML in soil management. However, the final data are extracted by applying specific keywords such as "agricultural production", "machine learning", and "India". For data extraction, online databases, namely, WOS and Scopus, are preferred, which are wide-ranging citation databases with the maximum number of peer-reviewed influential core, interdisciplinary, and multidisciplinary journals [46]. A total of 58 articles (Scopus $n = 27$ and WOS $n = 31$) were extracted from the two online databases. However, some related articles may not have been considered because of the mismatch in title with the identified keywords. Figure 16.1 depicts the search string.

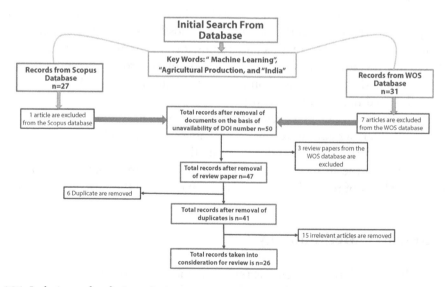

Figure 16.1 Inclusion and exclusion criteria.

16.2.3   Selection Criteria

The review process opted for pre-specified selection criteria to include and exclude the papers. In the exclusion process, 1 paper from the Scopus database and 7 papers from the WOS database are excluded because of the unavailability of the DOI number of the papers. Further, 3 review papers and 6 duplicates are excluded. Out of the remaining 41 research articles, after a thorough study, 15 articles are excluded as they are not relevant to the concerned categories mentioned in the earlier section and a total of 26 articles are taken into consideration for the literature review presented in the Figure 16.1.

16.2.4   Conduction of Review

Machine learning is a revolutionary and emerging technology that is used in many different fields. Out of all the fields, the agricultural field is one of the alarming fields for the inclusion of machine learning. In the agricultural field, the entire crop cycle has realized the significant use of machine learning. The use of machine learning in the agricultural sector starts from the management of soil to the decisions taken about the crop's readiness by the robot. The review article has been classified into five broad categories where machine learning plays a significant role in agricultural production, namely, crop yield prediction, water management, soil management, crop disease management, and weather prediction. To conduct this review, this chapter has used some relevant keywords mentioned in an earlier section.

16.3   Results and Discussion

16.3.1   Crop Yield Prediction

Yield prediction is one of the key facets of precision farming and it is quite essential for mapping and predicting yields, matching crop supply and demand, and managing crops to increase productivity. In this aspect, Jain and Choudhary [47] analyzed soil-based machine learning comparative analytical framework (SMLF) in their work to predict crop yield production. They have analyzed the impact of the characteristics of the soil on the level of crop yielding, i.e., high, medium, and low. Similarly, in another work [48], a machine learning method is suggested for accurate autonomous crop and yield prediction. The method uses solution encoding to create solutions arbitrarily, and then it assesses each solution's fitness to ensure an optimal degree of accuracy. Further, Vashisht *et al.* [49] tried to use machine learning to estimate agricultural yield. They have used linear discriminant analysis (LDA) to extract certain features from the gathered data after they have been pre-processed using the Kalman filter algorithm. Enhanced extreme learning machine (IELM) is utilized for the crop-yielding prediction, which also showed a 99.99% accuracy. In addition, Ezhilarasi and Rekha [50] have come up with another objective to recommend the appropriate crop for better yielding and better profits for the farmers by analyzing the current season and soil quality. They have developed fuzzy ant clustering to eliminate redundancy and enhance the quality of the clusters by identifying and merging overlapping nodes, which showed

Table 16.1 Summary of crop yielding prediction.

Sl no.	Authors	Functionality	Product	Models/ Algorithm	Results
1	[48]	Automatic crop yield prediction	Wheat, urad dal, turmeric, sunflower, sugarcane, rice, ragi, green gram, maize, linseed, jowar, groundnut, gram, coepeal, cotton, coriander, and bajra	Support vector neural network (SVNN) with Gravitational Search agent (GSA)	• Accuracy – 97.560% • Sensitivity – 97.577 • Specificity 97.543% • F-measure – 97.894
2	[49]	Prediction of crop yield using machine learning	Rice	• Improved Extreme Learning Machine (IELM) • Chimp Optimization Algorithm (COA)	• Accuracy – 99.99% • Precision – 99.24% • Recall – 99.24% • F-Measures – 0.9923
3	[50]	Suitable crop recommendation for better yielding	Agricultural crop	Fuzzy ant clustering	• Accuracy – 91.9% • Error – 8%
4	[51]	To demonstrate the accuracy value of various ML algorithms to predict the crop yield	Agricultural crop	• Logistic regression (LR) • Naive Bayes (NB) • Decision Tree • K-Nearest Neighbor (KNN)	Accuracy • LR– 97.17% • Naïve Bayes – 90.95% • Decision Tree – 81.19% • KNN – 86%
5	[47]	Crop yield prediction	Corpus crop	• Soil-based machine learning comparative analytical framework	The result showed better accuracy in predicting the yield

(Continued)

Table 16.1 Summary of crop yielding prediction. (*Continued*)

Sl no.	Authors	Functionality	Product	Models/Algorithm	Results
6	[52]	Crop yield prediction	Agricultural crop	• Fuzzy Data Envelopment Analysis (FDEA) using SVM and RF	Accuracy for lower bound score • SVM – 71.00% • RF – 72.34% Accuracy for lower bound score • SVM – 70.81% • RF – 71.88%

reduced error (8%) and better accuracy (91.9%). Table 16.1 summarizes the above papers on crop yielding prediction.

16.3.2   Crop Disease Management

Crop disease management and crop yield prediction are the interlinked part of agriculture on which there is the highest number of articles presented in this review. One of the major problems in agriculture is managing the spread of pests and diseases during farming. The technique that is most frequently used to deal with diseases and pests is to spray insecticides evenly across the agricultural area. Despite being beneficial, this practice comes at enormous expenses to the economy and ecology. In the work of Sadasivam *et al.* [53], they have emphasized the use of SVM-RFE, mRMR, SFS, PCA, and ICA techniques for gene

Table 16.2 Summary of crop disease management.

Sl no.	Authors	Functionality	Product	Models/Algorithm	Results
1	[53]	Classify disease-related candidate genes	Rice	SVM-RFE, M-RMR, SFS, PCA, and ICA	Accuracy • SVM-RFE – 18% better accuracy • M-RMR - 50% better accuracy • SFS – 66% better accuracy • PCA – 31% better accuracy • ICA - 64% better accuracy

(*Continued*)

Table 16.2 Summary of crop disease management. (*Continued*)

Sl no.	Authors	Functionality	Product	Models/Algorithm	Results
2	[54]	Develop an image-based machine learning approach to spot and classify diseases in rice plants	Rice	CNN and SVM	Accuracy 91.37%
3	[55]	Classification of tomato disease image dataset to implement required steps to combat agricultural crisis	Tomato	Hybrid Principal Component Analysis (PCA) –Whale Optimization Algorithm (WOA)	• Training accuracy – 99% and testing accuracy – 94% • Least testing loss – 1.8%
4	[56]	Collect data regarding rice pest and analyze	Rice	V3CFOA-RM	• It took 175 seconds to collect and analyze the pest-related data
5	[57]	Prediction of plant disease	Tomato	VGG16, RESNET50, and Inception	Accuracy • VGG16 – 98.7% • RESNET50- 98.6% • Inception – 99%
6	[58]	Identification and detection of plant disease	Potato, tomato, orange, grape and soybean	MobileNetV3-Small MobileNetV3-Large InceptionResNetV2 InceptionV3 ResNet50V2	Accuracy • MobileNetV3-Small – 78.55% • MobileNetV3-Large – 80.74% • InceptionResNetV2 – 91.30% • InceptionV3 – 89.17% • ResNet50V2 – 80.73%

(*Continued*)

Table 16.2 Summary of crop disease management. (*Continued*)

Sl no.	Authors	Functionality	Product	Models/Algorithm	Results
7	[59]	Identification of plant disease using the plant leaf image	• Plant Village • Embrapa • Apple • Maize • Rice	VGG-ICNN	Accuracy • VGG-ICNN – 99.16%
8	[60]	Plant disease identification	Agricultural crop	CNN	Average Accuracy • CNN – 96.3%
9	[61]	Identification of plant disease	Agricultural crop	DCDM	Accuracy • DCDM – 98.78% in 0.349 seconds
10	[62]	Identification of plant disease	Rice	Deep transfer learning, Deep neural network with Jaya algorithm, Transfer Learning with SVM	• Deep transfer learning – 98.63% • Deep neural network with Jaya algorithm – 98.9% • Transfer learning with SVM – 97.31%
11	[63]	Identification of various plant fungal disease	Agricultural crop	Multi-layered Perceptron Model (MLP)	Average accuracy • MLP – 98%

extraction to find the disease-related candidate genes of pathogens on rice crops, and an SVM is utilized for classification. The classification accuracy is enhanced between 10% and 66%. In addition, Shrivastava and Pradhan [54] tried to develop an image-based machine learning approach to spot and classify diseases in rice plants. They have used a convolutional neural network (CNN) as a feature extractor and support vector machine (SVM) as a classifier in their work and found a significant result of 91.37% accuracy with an 80%–20% training–testing partition. In the work by Gadekallu *et al.* [55], machine learning is used to trace the disease in tomato plants. They have proposed a hybrid principal component analysis with the whale optimization algorithm that showed a training accuracy of 99% and a testing accuracy of 94% with a testing loss of 1.8%. Table 16.2 summarizes the above papers on crop disease management.

16.3.3   Water Management

The estimations of all the elements of the water balance are very important in ensuring higher rates of yielding as agriculture is an anthropogenic activity and irrigation uses 70% of the world's freshwater resources. In order to maintain hydrological, climatological, and agronomic equilibrium, water management in agricultural production necessitates considerable effort. ML plays a major role in water management in agricultural activities. For example, Kushwaha *et al.* [64] in their work compared six different models by including six meteorological inputs such as minimum and maximum temperature, wind speed, sunshine hours, mean relative humidity, and solar radiation that influences the evapotranspiration, which is a major determinant of irrigation scheduling. They have used ML algorithm models such as Additive regression (A_dR), Random Subspace (RSS), and M5 Pruning tree (M5P). The result showed a significant outcome in predicting with higher accuracy. In addition, Sidhu *et al.* [65] in their work used a long short-term memory (LSTM)-based neural network

Table 16.3 Summary of water management.

Sl no.	Authors	Functionality	Product	Models/ Algorithm	Results
1	[64]	Estimated evapotranspiration using six meteorological data	Agricultural product	A_dR, RSS, M5P	• The result showed that RSS1 has 80% accuracy • Other models showed more than 90% accuracy
2	[65]	Prediction of daily irrigation schedule	Agricultural product	Long Short-Term Memory (LSTM)	• Incident of Irrigation event – 94.19% • Quantity of Irrigation – 75.90%
3	[66]	Establishing a hydroponic system with autonomous systems for tracking, and collecting data, and storage via the internet	Agricultural product	APEX	• The sensor successfully collected and stored the data
4	[67]	IoT and ML-based approach to maintain the optimum level of soil moisture for the growth of the crop	Agricultural crop	TENSORFLOW, RASPBERRY PI 3	• TENSORFLOW will classify the present condition of the crop • RASPBERRY PI 3 will collect real-time information of the soil moisture, humidity, and wind power
5	[68]	Smart irrigation system for agricultural output growth	Agricultural crop	K-Sparse Linear Regression	Accuracy • K-SLR – 99.75%

approach with logistic regression in predicting the daily irrigation schedule. They used this model in the agricultural product rice, which mostly depends on irrigation. In their result, they found that the proposed model showed 94.19% accuracy in predicting the incidence of an irrigation event and 75.90% accuracy in predicting the extent of irrigation. Table 16.3 summarizes the above papers on water management.

16.3.4   Soil Management

The following section of the review is concerned with the application of ML in predicting and identifying the various soil properties in agriculture such as the estimation of the condition of the soil, temperature of the soil, and moisture content in the soil. Researchers can use soil parameters to comprehend how agriculture affects ecosystem dynamics. The natural resource soil is multifaceted and it is difficult to understand the complex mechanisms and structures. A precise assessment of the state of the soil can result in better soil management. However, for an accurate examination of a region's eco-environmental factors and the impact of climate change, the temperature of the soil alone plays a crucial role. It is a vital meteorological variable that regulates the interactions between the atmosphere and the Earth. Further, the moisture in the soil plays a significant role in the yielding variability. In addition, as soil measurements are quite time-consuming and expensive, the use of computational analysis based on ML approaches can provide a low-cost and dependable solution for the accurate assessment of soil. Thus, Gayathri and Thangavelu [69] in their work proposed a model by using the Google Firebase cloud server that will monitor the soil management and irrigation, which will lessen the manual monitoring of the agricultural field. Further, this proposed model will be helpful for the farmer in managing and growing suitable crops based on the result. Similarly, the work of Elakkiya and Karthik [70] discussed the usability of ML in performing and anticipating the problems of soil-borne diseases and how to manage them. In their findings, it is stated that naïve Bayes (NB), support vector machine (SVM), and logistic regression schemes are ML techniques that are more capable of predicting soil-borne diseases. Table 16.4 summarizes the above papers on soil management.

Table 16.4 Summary of soil management.

Sl no.	Authors	Functionality	Product	Models/ Algorithm	Results
1	[69]	Forecasting soil properties and irrigation	Agricultural product	Google Firebase cloud server	• The farmers can grow suitable crop based on the soil properties
2	[70]	Assessment of usability of various ML in predicting soil-borne diseases	Agricultural product	NB, SCM, and Logistic Regression Scheme	• NB, SVM and Logistic regression scheme are better predictors

Table 16.5 Summary of weather forecasting.

Sl no.	Authors	Functionality	Product	Models/ Algorithm	Results
1	[71]	Forecasting spatial and temporal	Agricultural product	CA, PCA	• Forecasted region-wise rainfall in various time periods
2	[72]	Forecasting air temperature	Rice, wheat, soybean, maize, and cotton	GRNN, ELM, MARS, and RF	• Legate's & McCabe's Index (LMI) value for GRNN, ELM, MARS, and RF are 0.977 vs. 0.829, 797 and 0.497, respectively. • GPI for GRNN − 0.0181

16.3.5 Weather Forecasting

This is the last section of the review and is concerned with the use of ML in weather-related forecasting in the agricultural sector. Globally, there is a mounting worry regarding climatic variation. Understanding and anticipating climatic factors like temperature and rain provides us the benefit of figuring out climate-related decision-making. Human livelihood is impacted by environmental factors such as temperature, wind, and humidity. In recent times, the most sought-after academic topic is weather monitoring by predicting various environmental activities such as forecasting rain and atmospheric temperature using ML. Additionally, forecasting the weather is the foremost priority to stop the spread of diseases and pests among crops, and it can be easily accessible by the integration of ML. For example, Mohapatra et al. [71] in their work examined the spatial and temporal rainfall patterns. They have used machine learning techniques such as cluster analysis (CA) and principal component analysis (PCA) to get the result. The result showed various rainfall patterns in different regions of India. Further, Sanikhani et al. [72] in their work tried to forecast air temperature through machine learning. For the forecasting of air temperature, they developed four highly advanced models that were based on the Generalized Regression Neural Network (GRNN), Extreme Learning Machine (ELM), Multivariate Adaptive Regression Spline (MARS), and Random Forest (RF) algorithm. However, out of these four-advanced data-intelligent models, GRNN showed a better result in comparison to MARS, ELM, and RF in forecasting the air temperature. Table 16.5 summarizes the above papers on weather management.

16.4 Conclusion

Agriculture used to be solely for the cultivation of food and crops, but during the past 20 years, agricultural operations have become the primary means of subsistence while accelerating national trade, escalating GDP, lowering the rate of unemployment, supplying raw materials for other industrial sectors, and generally advancing the economy. It has now become an important pillar of world economy. With rising global population and climate change, it has become essential to accommodate innovative agricultural approaches and practices. Increasing agricultural productivity has now become a necessity given the realities of a growing world population and climate change. A sustainable solution to this issue is to enhance agricultural output without substantially expanding the amount of cropland. Because of their dependence on certain soil types, weather forecasts, and availability of water, accompanied by crop pest prevention and predicting crop yield, the results of existing traditional research methodologies are challenging to extrapolate to all conceivable areas. Hence, to boost productivity, induce variability, and improve the quality as well as quantity, it is imperative to apply machine learning in agriculture.

The agricultural sector has come a long way from primitive to precision farming. The agricultural industry has transmogrified itself starting from the industrial age to the technology age and to the information age. Progressive technological advancements along with the exposure to digitalization has revolutionized the agricultural sector. With rampant technological innovation and the adoption of machine learning, this sector has undergone a remarkable shift in agricultural practices, productivity, and sustainability. Because ML works in conjunction with big data technology and high-performance computers, it has emerged to offer new possibilities for decoding, measuring, and comprehending data-intensive processes in agriculture. In order to gather real-time data for algorithms, artificial intelligence (AI), Internet of Things (IoT) sensors, and machine learning (ML) are used. This boosts crop yields, improves agricultural productivity, and lowers the cost of food production.

Machine learning can act as a panacea in solving the problems related to the effect of weather on production; water and soil management; migrating patterns of animals, insects, and birds; seasonal sunlight; the use of specialized fertilizers and insecticides on crops; patterns in planting; cycles of irrigation; and other various factors. With ML, the agricultural sector has become more accurate and efficient by becoming capable enough to evaluate a wider set of available variables. The importance of high-quality data for crop cycles has never been greater. In order to increase agricultural yield and quality, farmers, agriculturalists, co-ops, researchers, and agricultural development firms are stepping up their data-centric strategies and widening the umbrella of AI and machine learning usage.

Although ML holds tremendous potential in solving all problems in agriculture, many complexities, such as data availability, high cost, infrastructural requirements, regulations, and privacy and security issues, act as a major hindrance in achieving its full potential. Therefore, efforts must be undertaken to resolve these challenges so that the constantly evolving technology can actually aid to solve the rising problems in the agricultural sector. In a nutshell, machine learning in agriculture holds tremendous potential. Agricultural researchers need to continue researching and innovating new techniques to make agriculture more precise and accurate. Machine learning has the potential to provide even more solutions for feeding a growing population, coping with climate change, and conserving water, energy, and land. Hence, more and more research must be encouraged in this field as the hybrid of agriculture, technology, and data is the future.

References

1. Thrall, P., Bever, J., Burdon, J., Evolutionary change in agriculture: The past, present and future. *Evol. Appl.*, 3, 405–408, 2010, https://doi.org/10.1111/j.1752-4571.2010.00155.x.
2. Dayıoğlu, M. and Turker, U., digital transformation for sustainable future - Agriculture 4.0: A review. *Tarım Bilim. Derg.*, 27, 2021, https://doi.org/10.15832/ankutbd.986431.
3. Liang, Y., Lu, X., Zhang, D., Liang, F., Ren, Z., Study on the framework system of digital agriculture. *Chin. Geogr. Sci.*, 13, 1, 15–19, 2003, https://doi.org/10.1007/s11769-003-0078-4.
4. Zhang, N., Wang, M., Wang, N., Precision agriculture—A worldwide overview. *Comput. Electron. Agric.*, 36, 2, 113–132, 2002, https://doi.org/10.1016/S0168-1699(02)00096-0.
5. Rehman, A., Jingdong, L., Khatoon, R., Hussain, I., Modern agricultural technology adoption its importance, role and usage for the improvement of agriculture. *Am.-Eurasian J. Agric. Environ. Sci.*, 16, 284–288, 2016, https://doi.org/10.5829/idosi.aejaes.2016.16.2.12840.
6. Malhi, G.S., Kaur, M., Kaushik, P., Impact of climate change on agriculture and its mitigation strategies: A review. *Sustainability*, 13, 3, 2021, Article 3, https://doi.org/10.3390/su13031318.
7. Thayer, A.W., Vargas, A., Castellanos, A.A., Lafon, C.W., McCarl, B.A., Roelke, D.L., Winemiller, K.O., Lacher, T.E., Integrating agriculture and ecosystems to find suitable adaptations to climate change. *Climate*, 8, 1, 2020, Article 1, https://doi.org/10.3390/cli8010010.
8. Food and Agriculture Organization of the United Nations, (Ed.), *The Future of Food and Agriculture: Trends and Challenges*, Food and Agriculture Organization of the United Nations, 2017.
9. Obaisi, A., Adegbeye, M., Elghandour, M., Barbabosa-Pliego, A., A.Z.M., S., *Natural resource management and sustainable agriculture*, pp. 2577–2613, 2022, https://doi.org/10.1007/978-3-030-72579-2_133.
10. Mandal, A. and Mani, P., *Conservation Techniques for Modern Agriculture*, 24, 2020.
11. Nassani, A.A., Awan, U., Zaman, K., Hyder, S., Aldakhil, A.M., Abro, M.M.Q., Management of natural resources and material pricing: Global evidence. *Resour. Policy*, 64, 101500, 2019, https://doi.org/10.1016/j.resourpol.2019.101500.
12. Meshram, V., Patil, K., Meshram, V., Hanchate, D., Ramkteke, S.D., Machine learning in agriculture domain: A state-of-art survey. *Artif. Intell. Life Sci.*, 1, 100010, 2021, https://doi.org/10.1016/j.ailsci.2021.100010.
13. Bondesan, L., Ortiz, B.V., Morlin, F., Morata, G., Duzy, L., van Santen, E., Lena, B.P., Vellidis, G., A comparison of precision and conventional irrigation in corn production in Southeast Alabama. *Precis. Agric.*, 24, 1, 40–67, 2023, https://doi.org/10.1007/s11119-022-09930-2.
14. Gebbers, R. and Adamchuk, V., Precision agriculture and food security. *Science*, 327, 5967, 828–831, 2010, https://doi.org/10.1126/science.1183899.
15. Stafford, J.V., Implementing precision agriculture in the 21st century. *J. Agric. Eng. Res.*, 76, 3, 267–275, 2000, https://doi.org/10.1006/jaer.2000.0577.
16. Bongiovanni, R. and Lowenberg-DeBoer, J., Precision agriculture and sustainability. *Precis. Agric.*, 5, 359–387, 2004, https://doi.org/10.1023/B:PRAG.0000040806.39604.aa.
17. Helm, J.M., Swiergosz, A.M., Haeberle, H.S., Karnuta, J.M., Schaffer, J.L., Krebs, V.E., Spitzer, A.I., Ramkumar, P.N., Machine learning and artificial intelligence: Definitions, applications, and future directions. *Curr. Rev. Musculoskelet. Med.*, 13, 1, 69–76, 2020, https://doi.org/10.1007/s12178-020-09600-8.
18. Liakos, K., Busato, P., Moshou, D., Pearson, S., Bochtis, D., Machine learning in agriculture: A review. *Sensors*, 18, 8, 2674, 2018, https://doi.org/10.3390/s18082674.
19. Brown, S., *Machine learning, explained*, MIT Sloan, 2023, April 19, https://mitsloan.mit.edu/ideas-made-to-matter/machine-learning-explained.

20. Wiederhold, G. and McCarthy, J., Arthur Samuel: Pioneer in machine learning. *IBM J. Res. Dev.*, *36*, 329–331, 1992, https://doi.org/10.1147/rd.363.0329.

21. Samuel, A.L., Some studies in machine learning using the game of checkers. *IBM J. Res. Dev.*, *3*, 3, 210–229, 1959, https://doi.org/10.1147/rd.33.0210.

22. Sharma, A., Jain, A., Gupta, P., Chowdary, V., Machine learning applications for precision agriculture: A comprehensive review. *IEEE Access*, *9*, 4843–4873, 2021, https://doi.org/10.1109/ACCESS.2020.3048415.

23. Ray, S., A quick review of machine learning algorithms. *2019 International Conference on Machine Learning, Big Data, Cloud and Parallel Computing (COMITCon)*, pp. 35–39, 2019, https://doi.org/10.1109/COMITCon.2019.8862451.

24. Bochenek, B. and Ustrnul, Z., Machine learning in weather prediction and climate analyses—Applications and perspectives. *Atmosphere*, *13*, 2, 2022, Article 2, https://doi.org/10.3390/atmos13020180.

25. Shirahatti, J., Patil, R., Akulwar, P., A survey paper on plant disease identification using machine learning approach. *2018 3rd International Conference on Communication and Electronics Systems (ICCES)*, pp. 1171–1174, 2018, https://doi.org/10.1109/CESYS.2018.8723881.

26. Kuradusenge, M., Hitimana, E., Hanyurwimfura, D., Rukundo, P., Mtonga, K., Mukasine, A., Uwitonze, C., Ngabonziza, J., Uwamahoro, A., Crop yield prediction using machine learning models: Case of irish potato and maize. *Agriculture*, *13*, 1, 2023, Article 1, https://doi.org/10.3390/agriculture13010225.

27. van Klompenburg, T., Kassahun, A., Catal, C., Crop yield prediction using machine learning: A systematic literature review. *Comput. Electron. Agric.*, *177*, 105709, 2020, https://doi.org/10.1016/j.compag.2020.105709.

28. Badhan, S., Desai, K., Dsilva, M., Sonkusare, R., Weakey, S., Real-time weed detection using machine learning and stereo-vision. *2021 6th International Conference for Convergence in Technology (I2CT)*, pp. 1–5, 2021, https://doi.org/10.1109/I2CT51068.2021.9417989.

29. Urmashev, B., Buribayev, Z., Amirgaliyeva, Z., Ataniyazova, A., Zhassuzak, M., Turegali, A., Development of a weed detection system using machine learning and neural network algorithms (SSRN Scholarly Paper No. 4007300), 2021, https://papers.ssrn.com/abstract=4007300.

30. Wang, A., Zhang, W., Wei, X., A review on weed detection using ground-based machine vision and image processing techniques. *Comput. Electron. Agric.*, *158*, 226–240, 2019, https://doi.org/10.1016/j.compag.2019.02.005.

31. Ahmad, A., Saraswat, D., El Gamal, A., A survey on using deep learning techniques for plant disease diagnosis and recommendations for development of appropriate tools. *Smart Agric. Technol.*, *3*, 100083, 2023, https://doi.org/10.1016/j.atech.2022.100083.

32. Stournaras, S., Loukatos, D., Arvanitis, K.G., Kalatzis, N., Crop identification by machine learning algorithm and Sentinel-2 data. *Chem. Proc.*, *10*, 1, 2022, Article 1, https://doi.org/10.3390/IOCAG2022-12261.

33. Pushpanathan, K., Hanafi, M., Mashohor, S., Fazlil Ilahi, W.F., Machine learning in medicinal plants recognition: A review. *Artif. Intell. Rev.*, *54*, 1, 305–327, 2021, https://doi.org/10.1007/s10462-020-09847-0.

34. Motia, S. and Reddy, S.R.N., Exploration of machine learning methods for prediction and assessment of soil properties for agricultural soil management: A quantitative evaluation. *J. Phys.: Conf. Ser.*, *1950*, 1, 012037, 2021, https://doi.org/10.1088/1742-6596/1950/1/012037.

35. Virnodkar, S.S., Pachghare, V.K., Patil, V.C., Jha, S.K., Remote sensing and machine learning for crop water stress determination in various crops: A critical review. *Precis. Agric.*, *21*, 5, 1121–1155, 2020, https://doi.org/10.1007/s11119-020-09711-9.

36. Zimpel, T., Riekert, M., Klein, A., Hoffmann, C., Machine learning for predicting animal welfare risks in pig farming. *Landtechnik*, *76*, 24–35, 2021, https://doi.org/10.15150/lt.2021.3261.

37. Li, N., Ren, Z., Li, D., Zeng, L., Review: Automated techniques for monitoring the behaviour and welfare of broilers and laying hens: Towards the goal of precision livestock farming. *Animal*, *14*, 3, 617–625, 2020, https://doi.org/10.1017/S1751731119002155.

38. García, R., Aguilar, J., Toro, M., Pinto, A., Rodríguez, P., A systematic literature review on the use of machine learning in precision livestock farming. *Comput. Electron. Agric.*, *179*, 105826, 2020, https://doi.org/10.1016/j.compag.2020.105826.

39. Ang, K.L.-M. and Seng, J.K.P., Big data and machine learning with hyperspectral information in agriculture. *IEEE Access*, *9*, 36699–36718, 2021, https://doi.org/10.1109/ACCESS.2021.3051196.

40. Cravero, A., Pardo, S., Sepúlveda, S., Muñoz, L., Challenges to use machine learning in agricultural big data: A systematic literature review. *Agronomy*, *12*, 3, 2022, Article 3, https://doi.org/10.3390/agronomy12030748.

41. White, E.L., Thomasson, J.A., Auvermann, B., Kitchen, N.R., Pierson, L.S., Porter, D., Baillie, C., Hamann, H., Hoogenboom, G., Janzen, T., Khosla, R., Lowenberg-DeBoer, J., McIntosh, M., Murray, S., Osborn, D., Shetty, A., Stevenson, C., Tevis, J., Werner, F., Report from the conference, 'identifying obstacles to applying big data in agriculture'. *Precis. Agric.*, *22*, 1, 306–315, 2021, https://doi.org/10.1007/s11119-020-09738-y.

42. Davenport, T.H., From analytics to artificial intelligence. *J. Bus. Anal.*, *1*, 2, 73–80, 2018, https://doi.org/10.1080/2573234X.2018.1543535.

43. Finco, A., Bucci, G., Belletti, M., Bentivoglio, D., The economic results of investing in precision agriculture in durum wheat production: A case study in Central Italy. *Agronomy*, *11*, 8, 2021, Article 8, https://doi.org/10.3390/agronomy11081520.

44. Tozer, P.R., Uncertainty and investment in precision agriculture – Is it worth the money? *Agric. Syst.*, *100*, 1, 80–87, 2009, https://doi.org/10.1016/j.agsy.2009.02.001.

45. Jouanjean, M.-A., Casalini, F., Wiseman, L., Gray, E., *Issues around data governance in the digital transformation of agriculture: The farmers' perspective*, OECD, 2020, https://doi.org/10.1787/53ecf2ab-en.

46. Zhong, B., Wu, H., Li, H., Sepasgozar, S., Luo, H., He, L., A scientometric analysis and critical review of construction-related ontology research. *Autom. Constr.*, *101*, 17–31, 2019, https://doi.org/10.1016/j.autcon.2018.12.013.

47. Jain, K. and Choudhary, N., Comparative analysis of machine learning techniques for predicting production capability of crop yield. *Int. J. Syst. Assur. Eng. Manage.*, *13*, 1, 583–593, 2022, https://doi.org/10.1007/s13198-021-01543-8.

48. Ashwitha, A. and Latha, C.A., GSA-based support vector neural network: A machine learning approach for crop prediction to provision sustainable farming. *Int. J. Intell. Comput. Cybern.*, *16*, 1, 1–16, 2022, https://doi.org/10.1108/IJICC-12-2021-0300.

49. Vashisht, S., Kumar, P., Trivedi, M.C., Crop yield prediction using improved extreme learning machine. *Commun. Soil Sci. Plant Anal.*, *54*, 1, 1–21, 2023, https://doi.org/10.1080/00103624.2022.2108828.

50. Ezhilarasi, T.P. and Rekha, K.S., Improved fuzzy ant colony optimization to recommend cultivation in Tamil Nadu, India. *Acta Geophys.*, *70*, 6, 2873–2887, 2022, https://doi.org/10.1007/s11600-022-00823-6.

51. Hemalatha, S., Kavitha, T., Saravanan, T.M., Chitra, K., Dinesh, N., Forecasting crop using machine learning model. *2022 3rd International Conference on Electronics and Sustainable Communication Systems (ICESC)*, pp. 783–788, 2022, https://doi.org/10.1109/ICESC54411.2022.9885377.

52. Nandy, A. and Singh, P.K., Application of fuzzy DEA and machine learning algorithms in efficiency estimation of paddy producers of rural Eastern India. *Benchmarking: An Int. J.*, *28*, 1, 229–248, 2020, https://doi.org/10.1108/BIJ-01-2020-0012.

53. Sadasivam, G.S., Madhesu, S., Mumthas, O.Y., Dharani, K., Crop disease protection using parallel machine learning approaches, in: *Classification in BioApps: Automation of Decision Making*, N. Dey, A.S. Ashour, S. Borra (Eds.), pp. 227–259, Springer International Publishing, 2018, https://doi.org/10.1007/978-3-319-65981-7_9.

54. Shrivastava, V.K. and Pradhan, M.K., Rice plant disease classification using color features: A machine learning paradigm. *J. Plant Pathol.*, *103*, 1, 17–26, 2021, https://doi.org/10.1007/s42161-020-00683-3.

55. Gadekallu, T.R., Rajput, D.S., Reddy, M.P.K., Lakshmanna, K., Bhattacharya, S., Singh, S., Jolfaei, A., Alazab, M., A novel PCA–whale optimization-based deep neural network model for classification of tomato plant diseases using GPU. *J. Real-Time Image Process.*, *18*, 4, 1383–1396, 2021, https://doi.org/10.1007/s11554-020-00987-8.

56. Cai, Y. and Sharma, A., Swarm intelligence optimization: An exploration and application of machine learning technology. *J. Intell. Syst.*, *30*, 1, 460–469, 2021, https://doi.org/10.1515/jisys-2020-0084.

57. Lakshmanarao, A., Supriya, N., Arulmurugan, A., Plant disease prediction using transfer learning techniques. *2022 Second International Conference on Advances in Electrical, Computing, Communication and Sustainable Technologies (ICAECT)*, pp. 1–5, 2022, https://doi.org/10.1109/ICAECT54875.2022.9807956.

58. S, C., Ghana, S., Singh, S., Poddar, P., Deep learning model for image-based plant diseases detection on edge devices. *2021 6th International Conference for Convergence in Technology (I2CT)*, pp. 1–5, 2021, https://doi.org/10.1109/I2CT51068.2021.9418124.

59. Thakur, P.S., Sheorey, T., Ojha, A., VGG-ICNN: A lightweight CNN model for crop disease identification. *Multimedia Tools Appl.*, *82*, 1, 497–520, 2023, https://doi.org/10.1007/s11042-022-13144-z.

60. Praveen, P., Nischitha, M., Supriya, C., Yogitha, M., Suryanandh, A., To detect plant disease identification on leaf using machine learning algorithms, in: *Intelligent System Design*, V. Bhateja, K.V.N. Sunitha, Y.-W. Chen, Y.-D. Zhang (Eds.), pp. 239–249, Springer Nature, 2023, https://doi.org/10.1007/978-981-19-4863-3_23.

61. Kumar, P., Raghavendran, S., Silambarasan, K., Kannan, K.S., Krishnan, N., Mobile application using DCDM and cloud-based automatic plant disease detection. *Environ. Monit. Assess.*, *195*, 1, 44, 2022, https://doi.org/10.1007/s10661-022-10561-3.

62. Aggarwal, M., Khullar, V., Goyal, N., Contemporary and futuristic intelligent technologies for rice leaf disease detection. *2022 10th International Conference on Reliability, Infocom Technologies and Optimization (Trends and Future Directions) (ICRITO)*, pp. 1–6, 2022, https://doi.org/10.1109/ICRITO56286.2022.9965113.

63. Kumar, M., Kumar, A., Palaparthy, V.S., Soil sensors-based prediction system for plant diseases using exploratory data analysis and machine learning. *IEEE Sens. J.*, *21*, 16, 17455–17468, 2021, https://doi.org/10.1109/JSEN.2020.3046295.

64. Kushwaha, N.L., Rajput, J., Sena, D.R., Elbeltagi, A., Singh, D.K., Mani, I., Evaluation of data-driven hybrid machine learning algorithms for modelling daily reference evapotranspiration. *Atmos.-Ocean*, *60*, 5, 519–540, 2022, https://doi.org/10.1080/07055900.2022.2087589.

65. Sidhu, R.K., Kumar, R., Rana, P.S., Long short-term memory neural network-based multi-level model for smart irrigation. *Mod. Phys. Lett. B*, *34*, 36, 2050418, 2020, https://doi.org/10.1142/S0217984920504187.

66. Vanipriya, C.H., Maruyi, Malladi, S., Gupta, G., Artificial intelligence enabled plant emotion xpresser in the development hydroponics system. *Mater. Today: Proc.*, *45*, 5034–5040, 2021, https://doi.org/10.1016/j.matpr.2021.01.512.

67. Syed, F.K., Paul, A., Kumar, A., Cherukuri, J., Low-cost IoT+ML design for smart farming with multiple applications. *2019 10th International Conference on Computing, Communication*

and Networking Technologies (ICCCNT), pp. 1–5, 2019, https://doi.org/10.1109/ICCCNT45670.2019.8944791.

68. Jesi, V.E., Kumar, A., Hosen, B., D, S.D., IoT enabled smart irrigation and cultivation recommendation system for precision agriculture. *ECS Trans.*, *107*, 1, 5953, 2022, https://doi.org/10.1149/10701.5953ecst.

69. Gayathri, K. and Thangavelu, S., Monitoring the soil parameters using IoT for smart agriculture, in: *Intelligent Data Communication Technologies and Internet of Things*, D.J. Hemanth, D. Pelusi, C. Vuppalapati (Eds.), pp. 743–757, Springer Nature, 2022, https://doi.org/10.1007/978-981-16-7610-9_55.

70. Elakkiya, E. and Karthik, P.C., Evaluation on correctness agriculture—Soil quality and soil borne disease in India using machine learning. *2022 International Conference on Advances in Computing, Communication and Applied Informatics (ACCAI)*, pp. 1–6, 2022, https://doi.org/10.1109/ACCAI53970.2022.9752549.

71. Mohapatra, G., Rakesh, V., Purwar, S., Dimri, A.P., Spatio-temporal rainfall variability over different meteorological subdivisions in India: Analysis using different machine learning techniques. *Theor. Appl. Climatol.*, *145*, 1, 673–686, 2021, https://doi.org/10.1007/s00704-021-03644-7.

72. Sanikhani, H., Deo, R.C., Samui, P., Kisi, O., Mert, C., Mirabbasi, R., Gavili, S., Yaseen, Z.M., Survey of different data-intelligent modeling strategies for forecasting air temperature using geographic information as model predictors. *Comput. Electron. Agric.*, *152*, 242–260, 2018, https://doi.org/10.1016/j.compag.2018.07.008.

Part 3
ARTIFICIAL INTELLIGENCE AND OPTIMIZATION TECHNIQUES

17

Reinforcement Learning Approach in Supply Chain Management: A Review

Rajkanwar Singh[1], Pratik Mandal[1] and Sukanta Nayak[2*]

[1]*School of Computer Science and Engineering, VIT-AP University, Amaravati, Andhra Pradesh, India*
[2]*Department of Mathematics, School of Advanced Sciences, VIT-AP University, Amaravati, Andhra Pradesh, India*

Abstract

Supply Chain Management (SCM) is one of the emerging areas that involve complex and challenging systems with multiple stakeholders and activities, ranging from demand forecasting to logistics management. The occurrence of complexity, demand volatility, cost-effectiveness, and information-sharing issues poses significant obstacles to efficient SCM functioning. In addition to these, the unprecedented global issues have further disrupted global supply chains. As such, there is an immediate need for an effective solution than ever before to handle these problems. In this context, Machine Learning (ML) techniques, such as Artificial Neural Networks (ANNs), Time-Series Analysis, Deep Learning, and Reinforcement Learning (RL), have been researched and used to tackle these challenges in SCM. Among these, RL has emerged as a promising technology to handle SCM activities such as inventory management, production scheduling, transportation and logistics optimization, demand forecasting, supplier selection and management, and risk management. RL is a type of machine learning in which an agent learns to interact with its environment by taking actions and receiving feedback in the form of rewards or penalties. It was found that RL can adapt to changing environments, learn from experience, and optimize its actions to achieve long-term goals. These features make RL well-suited for handling the challenges faced by SCM, where demand and supply dynamics can change rapidly, and decisions must be made based on incomplete or uncertain information. Our review focuses on the challenges in SCM and the role of RL to address the same. Here, the adoption of RL in SCM is discussed with the help of a case study. The obtained outcomes and difficulties to the adoption of RL in SCM are investigated. Finally, a comparative study of various other ML techniques with RL is included to observe the efficacy and easy implementation.

Keywords: Supply chain management (SCM), reinforcement learning (RL), deep learning (DL), machine learning (ML), optimization

Corresponding author: sukantgacr@gmail.com

Arindam Dey, Sukanta Nayak, Ranjan Kumar and Sachi Nandan Mohanty (eds.) How Machine Learning is Innovating Today's World: A Concise Technical Guide, (273–302) © 2024 Scrivener Publishing LLC

17.1   Introduction

The manufacturing sector in India, accounting for only 14.43% of the nation's GDP, is crucial to its economy as per data from the "statisticstimes" website [1]. However, many small and medium-sized businesses in developing countries, including India, often neglect productivity-enhancing factors, leading to problems such as an inability to meet market demand, sluggish growth, or even bankruptcy. According to the National Company Law Tribunal (NCLT), 149 Indian companies filed for bankruptcy in 2018, 103 in 2019, and 72 in 2020, with a total of 324 companies filing for bankruptcy in the previous three years, across all sectors, including manufacturing and services. The sources said that as per data provided by the NCLT, 8330 applications in the year 2018, 12,091 in the year 2019, and 5282 in the year 2020 were filed under the Insolvency and Bankruptcy Code (IBC) [2]. Even if half of the 324 companies that went bankrupt in India in the past three years were in the manufacturing industry, it would be a significant figure, considering the sector's contribution to the GDP is just 14.43%. Manufacturing firms are exposed to various uncertainties due to the factors that impact their production rates, which can vary based on their surroundings.

Effective supply chain management (SCM) becomes essential for sustained growth given the difficulties experienced by small and medium-sized enterprises in India's manufacturing industry, such as an inability to meet market demand and insolvency. In order to address these issues, machine learning (ML) methods like reinforcement learning (RL) have shown promise in enhancing SCM effectiveness and adjusting to changing conditions.

We concentrate on the SCM difficulties and the role of RL in addressing them in our review. The foundational principles of RL and how it pertains to SCM are presented first. The different applications of RL in SCM are then discussed, along with their benefits and drawbacks. We also go through the usage of RL in the challenges of SCM and possible directions for further research. This review contains a case study to address the use of RL in SCM and explore the successes and challenges encountered. Finally, we compare a number of additional ML techniques to RL in order to assess their effectiveness and practicality.

SCM is essential to both the global and domestic economies, yet it has numerous difficulties that limit its efficiency [3]. Environmental issues and the COVID-19 pandemic have brought attention to the need for sustainable supply networks that can quickly adjust to changing circumstances [4]. By supplying statistics-pushed insights and predictive fashions, ML techniques, which include RL, ended up as a powerful device for fixing SCM challenges. RL has a number of advantages over conventional SCM efficiency strategies, inclusive of the ability to deal with complicated and dynamic environments and adapt to changing situations Positive results were executed using RL in SCM in several areas together with inventory control, production planning, and logistics improvement.

By optimizing the reward sign, RL can research and improve decision-making talents over time. For SCM, this reimbursement signal may be a cost feature that considers factors inclusive of stock costs, transportation fees, production charges, and so forth. RL algorithms can use this repayment sign though optimizing decision-making strategies, along with choosing the ultimate stock degree or manufacturing agenda.

The equation for the reward function used in RL is

$$reward = f(state, action). \tag{17.1}$$

A Q-value function is used in the reinforcement learning technique known as Q-learning to assess the potential total reward of performing a specific action under a given circumstance. Utilizing a reward signal to increase the efficiency of various supply chain management decision-making processes is the central idea behind Q-learning. It is given by

$$Q(s,a) = Q(s,a) + \alpha[r + \gamma \ max \ Q(s',a') - Q(s,a)]. \tag{17.2}$$

The RL algorithm picks the action with the highest Q-value in each state to maximize the predicted cumulative reward. Then, based on the observed reward and state transition, the Q-learning algorithm updates the Q-values.

One example of RL in SCM is inventory control, which involves balancing inventory holding costs with the risks of stockouts or excess inventory. By optimizing the reward signal and considering variables such as supplier reliability, lead times, and demand unpredictability, RL algorithms can make informed judgments about inventory management, resulting in greater customer satisfaction and more effective inventory management.

Production planning is another area where RL can be used in SCM. Determining the best production schedule to meet demand while minimizing costs involves taking into account factors such as production capacity, lead times, and setup costs. RL algorithms can learn to improve production schedules by considering these variables, resulting in reduced costs and increased production efficiency.

Apart from these, Logistics Optimization is an application of RL in SCM too, which can be used to improve transportation routes, modes of transportation, and scheduling to reduce costs and speed up delivery times. Considering the factors like supply schedules, capacity limits, and transportation costs, RL algorithms can learn to optimize logistics processes, resulting in improved customer satisfaction, cost-effective logistics procedures, and increased efficiency.

While RL has shown promise in addressing SCM issues, one of the challenges is the need for significant amounts of data to train successful RL algorithms. Careful selection and tuning of reward functions are also necessary to ensure that they accurately reflect the system's objectives. Furthermore, research is required to integrate RL algorithms into current SCM systems and procedures.

In conclusion, ML techniques, particularly RL, have shown promise in addressing SCM challenges by improving decision-making processes in inventory management, production planning, and logistics optimization. While there are challenges to be resolved, the application of RL in SCM has the potential to significantly increase efficiency and lower costs, which is essential for sustainable supply chains in a rapidly changing global environment.

17.2 Literature Review

17.2.1 Challenges

The process of structuring and streamlining all operations involved in the delivery of products and services from suppliers to customers is referred to as supply chain management (SCM). Although SCM provides many positive consequences such as increased customer satisfaction, cost savings, and increased efficiency, it also has several disadvantages. One of the most onerous complications that SCM faces is the volatility of demand, which may lead to deficits, excess inventory, and omitted revenues. As a result, corporations have to figure out strategies to reduce the repercussions of fluctuating demand on SCM. Zhang *et al.* [5] proposed a dynamic pricing model that considers demand uncertainty to address this issue. To allow firms to better align supply with demand and avoid stockouts or excess inventory, their model utilizes a Bayesian approach to estimate demand uncertainty and adjust prices accordingly.

In addition to demand volatility, high complexity is also a significant challenge for supply chain management (SCM). Managing supply chains becomes increasingly difficult, resulting in higher costs, longer lead times, and reduced flexibility, as they become more complex and diversified. Therefore, companies must find ways to streamline their supply chains. Jayaraman *et al.* [6] proposed a modularization framework that enables businesses to break down complex supply chains into manageable parts to address this issue. This framework allows the company to identify critical supply chain elements and optimize them individually, resulting in improved overall supply chain performance.

Another challenge that SCM faces is cost pressure. Businesses are under more pressure to lower costs while maintaining or raising quality, which could cause suppliers to give up other supply chain goals including on-time delivery and cost-cutting flexibility. Businesses must therefore devise ways to save expenses while reaching other objectives. A green supply chain management technique was suggested by Chahal *et al.* [7] to assist firms in reducing costs while fostering environmental sustainability. The framework places a lot of emphasis on using renewable resources, reducing waste, and increasing energy efficiency. These factors can all assist organizations in making decisions that will result in cost savings while still following sustainability objectives.

Another crucial issue that supply chain management (SCM) must handle is information exchange. Improved information exchange is necessary for increasing supply chain visibility, cutting lead times, and fostering partner engagement. However, exchanging information has a number of difficulties, including security issues and a lack of mutual confidence. Businesses must therefore discover ways to successfully share information while upholding security and trust. A blockchain-based information sharing paradigm that improves security and trust between supply chain partners was proposed by Cho and Park [8]. The framework enables parties to securely store and transmit information through the use of a decentralized ledger system, improving collaboration and lowering the risk of data breaches.

In general, SCM encounters a number of difficulties, such as cost pressures, high complexity, variable demand, and information interchange. However, by employing the right strategies, organizations may lessen these difficulties and enhance their supply chain operations. Businesses can, for instance, use modularization frameworks to make complex supply chains simpler, dynamic pricing models to manage demand volatility, green supply chain management frameworks to lower costs while also achieving sustainability goals, and frameworks for information sharing based on blockchain technology to improve the security and collaboration of supply chain partners. As long as organizations continue to face these difficulties, more research is required to determine more effective strategies for managing supply chains in a complicated and uncertain business environment.

Dynamic pricing model equation is defined as

$$Q(a,s) = (1-\alpha)Q(a,s) + \alpha[r + \gamma maxa'Q(a',s')] \tag{17.3}$$

where, $Q(a,s)$ is the Q-value -value function for taking action a in state s, α, is the learning rate, r is the immediate reward for taking action a in state s, γ, is the discount factor for future rewards a' and s' are the action and state resulting from taking action a in state s, respectively.

Blockchain-based information sharing equation is defined as

$$H(Block\ i) = Hash(H(Block\ i-1) + Data\ i) \tag{17.4}$$

where $H(Block\ i)$ is the hash value of block, $i, Hash$ is a one-way cryptographic function, $H(Block\ i-1)$ is the hash value of the previous block, and $Data\ i$ represents the information stored in block i.

17.2.2 Advantages of Using ML Techniques in SCM

> Improved Accuracy in Demand Forecasting
> Machine learning (ML) algorithms can be used by organizations to improve their accuracy in estimating demand. By analyzing past data and detecting patterns and trends that may not be easily identifiable through manual analysis, ML algorithms can help businesses avoid stock-outs and overstocking, ultimately reducing inventory costs.

> Improved Production Scheduling
> ML algorithms will assist organizations in optimizing their production plans through analyzing data relating to production capacity, inventory levels, and demand. This technique can assist with pinpointing production bottlenecks and streamlining schedules to fulfill demand while trimming expenses.

> Enhanced Supply Chain Visibility
> Another positive aspect of ML algorithms is improved supply chain visibility. Businesses can acquire a better understanding of their supply networks by examining supplier performance, timelines for delivery, and quantities of inventory. This greater visibility can aid in the identification of areas for improvement as well as informed decision-making concerning suppliers and management.

> Improved Risk Management
> Companies may also employ machine learning algorithms to foresee possible hazards in their supply chains, such as transportation delays or supplier bankruptcy. This early detection can assist firms to establish backup plans and mitigate potential hazards before they occur.

> Improved Customer Service
> By accessing data on consumer preferences and practises, ML algorithms can also help firms impart better customer service. This study enables

firms to modify their products in order to suit their customers requires and preferences, enhancing consumer fulfilment and loyalty.

➤ Improved Supplier Selection and Management

The tactical use of ML algorithms will additionally enhance supplier selection and management. Enterprises can make more informed rulings by evaluating suppliers based on an array of attributes such as pricing, quality, and delivery performance. Added to that, ML algorithms can track vendor efficiency and monitor potential issues, allowing entities to take suitable and prompt action. Lee [9] discovered that machine learning strategies improved supplier selection precision by upwards of 25%.

➤ Enhanced Supply Chain Collaboration

According to Wang *et al.* [10], real-time data and insight into supply chain partners may enhance company collaboration. This enhanced interaction can aid in determining the existence and resolution of conflicts.

➤ Improved Quality Control

By estimating data on issues with merchandise and uncovering patterns and trends, ML systems additionally have the potential to enhance quality control. This study has the potential to help in identifying the root causes of oversights and implementing remedial measures. Wang *et al.* [11] discovered that ML approaches improved quality control by a staggering 35%.

➤ Increased Agility

By administering real-time data analysis, ML algorithms may additionally assist agencies to respond to changes promptly. Businesses can better manage evolving demands or supply chain breakdowns by making informed decisions based on contemporary information. According to Choi and Wallace [12], ML techniques may augment agility as much as 40%.

➤ Improved Sustainability

Eventually, companies may upgrade their sustainability by statistically analyzing data on fossil fuel consumption, carbon emissions, and other ecological problems using ML algorithms. Enterprises can apply ecological practices by identifying fields for improvement. According to Guo *et al.* [13], machine learning technologies can boost sustainability by up to 25%.

17.2.3 Limitations of Using ML Techniques in SCM

➤ Dependence on Data Quality

The effectiveness of ML algorithms is determined by the data they are trained on, whereby subpar data quality may lead to the generation of flawed insights, ultimately leading to unsatisfactory decision-making. A study by Li *et al.* (2018) found that the data quality is one of the main challenges of using ML in SCM.

➤ Lack of Transparency

Due to the intricate nature of ML algorithms, organizations may encounter difficulty in comprehending how decisions are being reached, consequently making it arduous for them to identify potential biases within the algorithms.

➢ High Implementation Costs
The implementation of ML algorithms can be an expensive undertaking, requiring significant investments in hardware, software, and personnel, making it difficult for small and medium-sized enterprises to adopt these technologies.

➢ Limited Human Input
ML algorithms solely rely on data to make decisions, without the involvement of human experts, which may result in outcomes that do not align with the organization's objectives or values.

➢ Limited Applicability
ML algorithms may not be applicable to all SCM processes or industries, as certain supply chain challenges within specific businesses may not be compatible with ML methodologies.

➢ Limited Interpretability
One of the primary shortcomings of ML methodologies is the restricted interpretability of models, particularly with the creation of black-box models, which can be intricate to understand and expound upon. Consequently, SCM experts may encounter challenges utilizing model outputs to make informed decisions. According to Schermann *et al.* [14], interpretability is one of the most significant obstacles to implementing ML in SCM.

➢ Limited Generalizability
ML models are frequently trained on past data, which may not represent forthcoming conditions, restricting the applicability of these models to new scenarios. According to Guo *et al.* [15], generalizability is a major challenge in the use of ML in SCM.

➢ Cost and Resource Requirements
The resource-intensive nature of ML techniques, involving significant investments in hardware, software, and personnel, can create challenges for small and medium-sized organizations in adopting these technologies, as highlighted by Wu *et al.*'s [16] research on the main challenges of using ML in SCM.

➢ Lack of Expertise
SCM professionals may lack the requisite skills and knowledge in data science, statistics, and computer science to implement and effectively utilize ML techniques. Schermann *et al.*'s [14] study also found a lack of expertise to be a primary challenge in using ML in SCM.

17.2.4   Effectiveness of ML Techniques in Handling Various SCM Activities

➢ Inventory Management
By forecasting demand, spotting patterns and trends in consumer behavior, and spotting abnormalities in the supply chain, ML approaches can help firms improve their inventory management. Implementing ML

techniques can result in improved inventory accuracy and lower inventory costs, according to Ahn *et al.*'s [17] research.

➢ Production Scheduling

Machine learning approaches may be used to analyze past trends, predict upcoming demand, and optimize production plans to enhance production scheduling. Yan *et al.* [18] discovered that machine learning approaches may improve capacity utilization and mitigate lead times.

➢ Transportation and Logistics Optimization

ML methods may also improve shipping and logistics by identifying the most efficient routes, lowering transportation costs, and constricting delivery times. According to Wang *et al.* [19], ML approaches can redeem up to 15% on transportation costs.

➢ Demand Forecasting

By examining past data, spotting trends and patterns, and taking into account outside variables like the weather and vacations, ML approaches can enhance demand estimates. According to Liu *et al.* [20], applying ML techniques can improve demand forecasting accuracy by as much as 50%.

➢ Supplier Selection and Management

Supplier selection can be made more successful by employing machine learning (ML) algorithms to evaluate factors such as pricing, quality, and delivery time. According to Li *et al.* (2018), ML methods can improve supplier selection precision and minimize assessment durations.

➢ Risk Management

ML methods assist in identifying and alleviating supply chain risks such as supply or demand outages. According to Zhang [21], using ML techniques can reduce the impact of such disruptions and enhance the oversight of supply chain risk.

17.3 Methodology

In the following, the general framework of methodology is discussed. In Figure 17.1, a flow diagram of the involved procedure is presented.

The implementation of RL in SCM presents a promising approach to enhance supply chain operations. A structured review methodology is required to provide a comprehensive overview of the current state of knowledge on RL in SCM. This research methodology aims to conduct a systematic literature review to examine the existing applications of RL in SCM, identify gaps and limitations, and propose future research directions. Figure 17.1 shows the chronology of the work.

Figure 17.1 Framework of overall approach.

➤ Research Questions

The research study aims to address the following research questions:

1. What are the current applications of RL in SCM?
2. What are the major challenges and limitations associated with the use of RL in SCM?
3. What are the potential areas for future research on RL in SCM?

➤ Literature Survey

The literature survey will be conducted using the Scopus database, which is the largest database for peer-reviewed scientific literature and has significant overlaps with other databases like Web of Science and Google Scholar. The search terms "reinforcement learning," "supply chain," and "optimization" will be used to identify relevant papers published between 2017 and 2022.

➤ Inclusion and Exclusion Criteria

The following inclusion criteria are used here.

1. The publication should be in English.
2. The publication should be related to RL in SCM.
3. The publication should be published between 2017 and 2022.

The following exclusion criteria are used here.

1. The publication is not related to RL in SCM.
2. The publication is not in English.
3. The publication is not available in full text.

➤ Data Extraction

After applying the inclusion and exclusion criteria, relevant publications will be downloaded, and the data extraction process will begin. The following data points will be extracted from each publication:

1. Title of the publication
2. Author(s) name(s)
3. Year of publication
4. Research methodology used
5. Type of RL algorithm used
6. SCM application area
7. Key findings
8. Limitations
9. Future research directions

➤ Data Analysis

The data analysis approach will comprise both quantitative and qualitative methods. Initially, a descriptive analysis will be conducted to examine the frequency of publications, research methodologies, RL algorithm types, SCM application domains, and primary discoveries. Then, a thematic analysis will be performed to identify common themes and patterns across all articles. The main limitations and constraints of RL in SCM and potential areas for further investigation will be determined based on the outcomes of the data analysis.

➢ **Concluding Remarks**

This research methodology aims to provide a comprehensive understanding of the current applications of reinforcement learning (RL) in supply chain management (SCM), identify gaps and limitations, and propose a research agenda for the future. The approach involves a systematic literature review, with clear inclusion and exclusion criteria, data extraction, and a combination of quantitative and qualitative methods for data analysis. By conducting this study, the findings can be used to gain insights into the current state of knowledge on RL in SCM, identify major challenges and limitations, and provide guidance for future research in this area.

17.4 Reinforcement Learning in Supply Chain Management

17.4.1 RL and Its Application in SCM

Reinforcement learning (RL) has gained attention as a possible means of optimizing complex and dynamic systems in the realm of supply chain management (SCM). By interacting with their environment and receiving rewards in the form of feedback, agents can learn the most effective policies using RL algorithms. This segment explores the application of RL in SCM processes and provides synopses of several relevant scholarly works published between 2017 and 2022.

➢ **Inventory Management**

Inventory management refers to the task of balancing customer demand with inventory levels while minimizing holding and ordering costs. RL has been employed in inventory management to create adaptable ordering processes that can adjust to changes in demand, lead time, and other factors. For instance, Zhang *et al.* [22] proposed a deep RL approach for inventory management that prevents stockouts. The authors demonstrated the effectiveness of their proposed approach compared to traditional inventory control techniques.

Production Planning

An essential stage in SCM is production planning. This involves establishing production schedules that meet demand while optimizing resource efficiency and reducing expenses. With the use of RL, the best production schedules can be learned by considering production capacity, demand, and inventory levels. Kuo *et al.* [23] proposed a solution based on deep RL that integrates production and maintenance scheduling. The authors showed that their approach outperformed conventional scheduling methods.

Transportation Planning

In order to reduce costs and satisfy delivery dates, transportation planning entails choosing the best routes and timetables to move items from suppliers to customers. Transportation planning has used RL to find the best routing options that can vary in response to demand,

Figure 17.2 Various applications of RL in SCM.

traffic, and other variables. A deep RL-based method for dynamic vehicle routing with stochastic demands was introduced by Chen *et al.* [24]. The authors provided evidence that their suggested approach was superior to conventional routing techniques. Figure 17.2 shows the various arenas and segments of supply chain management.

Order Picking
The order picking process involves selecting products from a warehouse to fulfill customer orders. Optimizing this process can lead to substantial cost savings, as it can be time-consuming and labor-intensive. To improve the order picking process, RL has been used to train optimal picking policies that can adapt to fluctuations in order volume and changes in warehouse layout. Kim *et al.* [25] proposed a deep RL-based approach for order picking in a warehouse. The authors demonstrated that their suggested method outperformed traditional order selection techniques.

Supplier Selection
One critical SCM practice is selecting the most suitable suppliers based on factors such as pricing, quality, and delivery time. RL has been applied in supplier selection to identify optimal selection procedures that can adapt to changes in supplier performance and

market conditions. Aditya *et al.* [26] developed a deep RL-based method for supplier selection in a multi-echelon supply chain. The authors demonstrated that their proposed approach outperformed traditional supplier selection methods.

Quality Control

Quality control is the practice of making sure that goods and services live up to client expectations by observing their caliber. RL has been used to design the best inspection practices that can adjust to variations in defect rates and inspection costs in order to improve quality control operations. A deep RL-based solution for quality control in a manufacturing process was put out by Jiang *et al.* (2019). The authors provided evidence that their proposed approach was more effective than conventional quality control methods.

Customer Demand Forecasting

Customer demand forecasting, which entails estimating consumer demand for goods and services to optimize production and inventory levels, is one of the key components of supply chain management. RL has been used to find the best forecasting approaches that are adaptable to shifting market conditions and customer behavior in order to improve demand forecasting techniques. A deep RL-based method for demand forecasting in a retail supply chain was proposed by Tran *et al.* [27]. The authors showed that their recommended approach worked better than conventional forecasting techniques.

Pricing and Revenue Management

Setting the best prices for goods and services in order to increase sales and profits is known as pricing and revenue management. RL has been used in pricing and revenue management in order to determine the optimal price methods that can be altered in response to variations in demand, competition, and other factors. A deep RL-based strategy for dynamic pricing in a multi-channel retail context was proposed by Huang *et al.* [28]. The authors provided evidence that their suggested method outperformed more conventional pricing tactics.

Risk Management

A crucial component of supply chain management, risk management involves identifying and reducing hazards related to supply chain operations. RL has been used to teach the best risk mitigation tactics that can adjust to changing risk levels and resource limits, hence increasing the efficacy of risk management procedures. A deep RL-based strategy to risk management in a supply chain network was put forth by Hu *et al.* in 2020. The authors provided evidence that their proposed approach outperformed more established risk management techniques.

Sustainable Operations

To ensure economic and social sustainability, it is imperative that supply chain operations minimize their adverse impact on the environment. Reinforcement Learning (RL) has been utilized in sustainable operations to identify optimal sustainability policies that can adjust to changes in environmental regulations, consumer preferences, and other factors. Wu *et al.* [29] proposed a deep RL-based approach to sustainable supply chain management. The authors demonstrated the effectiveness of their suggested strategy in reducing carbon emissions and improving economic performance. Figure 17.3 shows the utility of implementing RL in supply chain management thus stating it's benefits.

Figure 17.3 Various benefits of RL in SCM.

17.4.2   Benefits of RL in SCM

In Figure 17.3, the benefits of RL in SCM is shown and the same is discussed in this subsection.

The utilization of RL, a type of machine learning approach, has been prevalent in supply chain management. RL has shown significant potential in enhancing intricate systems by gaining knowledge from mistakes, experience, and adjusting to the environment. This section examines the benefits of RL in SCM, supported by 10 separate studies.

One of the significant advantages of RL in SCM is its capability to acquire knowledge from experience. According to Papakostas *et al.* [30], RL can use past experiences to make better decisions in the future. In SCM, where decisions rely on vast amounts of data from diverse sources, RL algorithms can process and learn from these data to enhance the supply chain's efficiency and effectiveness. Similarly, Yu *et al.* [31] argue that SCM professionals can leverage RL to learn from the data generated by the supply chain, leading to more accurate demand predictions and better inventory control.

The capacity of RL in SCM to optimize complicated systems is another advantage. The supply chain is a complex system made up of interdependent parts that must cooperate to ensure effective operations, as stated by Yang *et al.* [32]. By locating the ideal parameters that maximize the supply chain's overall performance, RL algorithms can optimize these components. By figuring out the ideal stocking levels of various products at various locations, for instance, Ma *et al.* [33] show how RL may improve inventory management in a complex supply chain.

The capacity of RL in SCM to adapt to changing circumstances is another advantage. The supply chain environment is continually changing, and standard optimization strategies might not be able to keep up with the changes, as claimed by Kocabasoglu-Hillmer *et al.* [34]. However, by continuously learning and revising their policies, RL algorithms can adapt to these changes. This increases the supply chain's adaptability and reactivity to changes in demand, supply, and other factors. Similar to the above, Xia *et al.* [35] show how

RL can be used to optimize production scheduling in a dynamic setting where demand and resource availability are always changing.

Supply chain coordination can be enhanced with the help of RL by enabling agents to keep track of and adjust their actions in response to other agents in the system. The supply chain is made up of several agents, including suppliers, manufacturers, distributors, and retailers, who must cooperate to ensure effective and successful operations, according to Zeng *et al.* [36]. By enabling agents to learn from and modify one another's behaviors, RL algorithms can aid in coordination. Su *et al.* [37] demonstrate how RL can be applied to coordinate inventory choices among several shops in a multi-echelon supply chain.

In SCM, reinforcement learning has the capacity to optimize trade-offs between several objectives. According to Fu *et al.* [38], there are frequently competing objectives in the supply chain, such as lowering costs while enhancing customer service. RL algorithms can pinpoint the optimum procedures for achieving this balance and maximizing the trade-off. They gave an example of how RL can be applied to balance stockouts and inventory costs in a multi-echelon supply chain.

By maximizing resource usage and reducing waste, RL can also increase supply chain sustainability.

17.5   Adoption of Reinforcement Learning in Supply Chain Management

RL has the potential to revolutionize SCM. However, there are numerous technological challenges that hinder its implementation. This section will examine these challenges and propose solutions to overcome them. Figure 17.4 shows the various barriers in the implementation of RL in supply chain management.

Figure 17.4 Various RL adoption barriers.

17.5.1   Technical Barriers

The primary technical obstacle to the use of RL in SCM is the dearth of high-quality data. For RL algorithms to train successfully, a large amount of data are needed. However, SCM data are frequently erroneous, inconsistent, and incomplete, which makes it challenging to train RL models [39]. Additionally, SCM data are frequently stored in a variety of forms and systems, making integration and pre-processing difficult [40]. Companies should engage in data standardization and purification procedures as well as consider cooperative data sharing activities with other businesses in order to get around this problem.

The second technical barrier to the adoption of RL in SCM is the complexity of RL algorithms. RL algorithms require a high level of computing expertise to develop and be applied effectively [41]. Additionally, optimizing RL models can be challenging due to the large number of hyperparameters and the need for extensive trial-and-error testing [42]. Companies should consider investing in hiring or training RL experts to overcome this obstacle. Alternatively, they could explore cloud-based services that can alleviate the computational burden.

The challenge of integrating RL models into current SCM systems is the third technological obstacle to the use of RL in SCM. Due to its complexity and the participation of numerous stakeholders, integrating new technologies into SCM systems can be difficult [43]. According to Zhang *et al.* (2020), SCM systems could not have ready access to the real-time data and feedback that RL models demand. Companies might think about creating modular RL models that can be easily incorporated into current SCM systems and offer stakeholders real-time feedback in order to get around this problem.

The lack of interpretability and transparency of RL models is the fourth technical obstacle to the use of RL in SCM. Since RL models are frequently thought of as "black boxes," it can be difficult to understand how they produce judgments [44]. Stakeholders that are wary of the technology may be discouraged from using RL in SCM due to the lack of interpretability and transparency [45]. To get around this problem, businesses may think about using explainable AI methods and creating transparent RL models that stakeholders can easily understand and audit.

The fifth technical obstacle to the use of RL in SCM is the lack of confidence in RL models. Trust is essential for the successful adoption of any new technology, but it may be compromised in the case of RL models in SCM if stakeholders do not fully understand how they work, which could give the impression that they are unreliable, unpredictable, or biased [46]. Furthermore, problems with RL models can seriously affect supply chain management, resulting in delays and harming a company's reputation. Companies should invest in fostering trust through education and communication by giving concise and open explanations of how RL models operate, their advantages and disadvantages, and how they might help the organization and its stakeholders.

By enabling real-time decision-making, optimizing complicated systems, and boosting effectiveness and adaptability, RL has the potential to revolutionize SCM. The lack of high-quality data, the complexity of RL algorithms, the difficulty of integrating RL models into current SCM systems, the lack of interpretability and transparency of RL models, and the lack of confidence in RL models are just a few of the technical obstacles that must be overcome for RL to be successfully implemented in SCM. Companies may unlock the full potential of RL in SCM and achieve a competitive edge in a fast-evolving global market by overcoming these barriers through investments in technology, talent, collaboration, and communication.

17.5.2   Organizational Barriers

The implementation of RL in SCM faces various organizational barriers, which can be broadly categorized into cultural, technical, and financial hurdles. Cultural barriers relate to the employees' attitudes, values, and beliefs, which can hinder the adoption of RL in SCM. Technical barriers refer to the lack of necessary technology infrastructure, expertise, and knowledge required to develop and utilize RL in SCM. Economic barriers pertain to the costs associated with the implementation of RL in SCM.

To overcome the organizational obstacles to implementing RL in SCM, organizations can employ several mitigation measures. For example, to overcome cultural barriers, staff members must be educated on the benefits of RL in SCM, as pointed out by Alonso-Ayuso et al. [47]. Additionally, incentives for employee adoption and participation in the adoption process can aid in reducing cultural barriers, according to Zhang et al. (2020).

17.5.3   Cultural Barriers

The adoption of RL in SCM can face significant cultural obstacles, and one of the main challenges is resistance to change. Agrawal et al. [48] conducted a study that revealed that the organizational culture plays a vital role in the speed of adopting new technologies. In certain organizations, employees may be hesitant to adopt RL due to concerns about potential job loss or the belief that traditional SCM methods are sufficient. Additionally, the under-representation of RL in SCM could also create a cultural barrier to adoption, as observed by Alonso-Ayuso et al. [47].

17.5.4   Economic Barriers

The implementation of RL in SCM can create economic hurdles due to the associated costs. For instance, as noted by Kim et al. [49], significant expenditures on personnel training and technological infrastructure are required for RL implementation in SCM. Additionally, unclear performance indicators and the ambiguity surrounding the return on investment (ROI) can serve as economic barriers to adoption [50]. To overcome financial hurdles, organizations can focus on developing precise ROI measures and performance indicators for RL-based SCM systems, as suggested by Rashedi et al. [50]. In addition, to reduce the initial expenditure required for RL-based SCM systems, organizations can explore alternative funding mechanisms, such as public–private partnerships or leasing schemes.

RL implementation in SCM has faced numerous organizational challenges despite the potential for huge benefits. One can categorize these obstacles into cultural, technological, and economic difficulties. Companies can use a variety of mitigation strategies, such as developing precise ROI and performance measures, increasing employee awareness, offering training, building up the required technological infrastructure, and raising staff awareness. Companies can profit from the potential advantages of RL with SCM, such as greater productivity, decreased costs, and improved customer satisfaction, by overcoming these organizational obstacles. Companies should engage in staff education and training as well as collaborate with academic institutions and industry experts to remain current on RL technological advancements in order to hasten the implementation of RL in SCM. Fundamentally, successful adoption of RL in SCM requires a multifaceted approach that includes removing organizational barriers and fostering a culture of innovation and continuous improvement.

17.6   Alternatives to Reinforcement Learning in Supply Chain Management

In recent years, reinforcement learning (RL) has gained prominence as a viable way to solve complicated optimization issues in supply chain management. There are, however, additional ways that may be employed to optimize supply chain management. In supply chain management (SCM), alternative machine learning (ML) approaches are frequently utilized to optimize different parts of the supply chain, such as inventory management, demand forecasting, and transportation. The following will explore some of the most prominent machine learning (ML) approaches, including Artificial Neural Networks (ANNs), Decision Trees, Random Forest, Support Vector Machines (SVMs), and Clustering, and compare their results to those obtained by organizations utilizing Reinforcement Learning (RL).

➢ *Mathematical Optimization*
A valuable technique for tackling difficult optimization issues is mathematical optimization. It is commonly used to optimize inventory management, production planning, and logistics in supply chain management. Optimization techniques such as linear programming, integer programming, and mixed-integer programming can all be applied. These methods are based on mathematical models of the supply chain and its different components, which include suppliers, manufacturers, distributors, and customers. The goal is to discover the best solution that either minimizes expenses, maximizes earnings, or strikes a balance between the two.

➢ *Simulation*
Simulation entails developing a virtual model of the supply chain and testing multiple scenarios to determine the best solution. Different aspects of the supply chain, such as demand, inventory levels, lead times, and production capacity, can be simulated using simulation. The objective is to discover the best configuration that matches client demand while keeping expenses to a minimum.

➢ *Heuristics*
Heuristics are rule-based algorithms that are used to solve complicated optimization issues. Because they are computationally efficient and can provide near-optimal solutions,

heuristics are frequently used in supply chain management. Genetic algorithms, tabu search, and simulated annealing are some examples of heuristics used in supply chain management.

➢ *Game Theory*

Game theory is a mathematical framework for studying strategic interactions among decision-makers. Game theory may be used to describe the relationships between suppliers, manufacturers, distributors, and customers in supply chain management. The aim is to find the best strategy for each player that maximizes their utility while accounting for the actions of other players.

➢ *Machine Learning*

Machine learning refers to a large class of algorithms that may be used to improve supply chain management. Other types of machine learning algorithms, such as supervised learning, unsupervised learning, and deep learning, can be used in addition to RL, which is a specific type of machine learning algorithm. Machine learning algorithms may be utilized in supply chain management for a number of activities such as demand forecasting, inventory optimization, and quality control.

➢ *Swarm Intelligence*

Swarm intelligence is a form of optimization approach inspired by the social insect collective behavior of ants and bees. Swarm intelligence may be used to optimize routing, scheduling, and distribution in supply chain management. The objective is to discover the best answer by replicating the behavior of a swarm of agents working together to solve a problem.

In contrast to RL, which is a sort of ML algorithm that optimizes actions through trial-and-error learning, the alternative ML approaches listed above focus on prediction and optimization based on past data. In general, RL is better suited to solving complicated decision-making situations where the ideal answer is unknown in advance, such as optimal pricing or resource allocation. The other ML approaches outlined above, on the other hand, are more suited for optimizing certain areas of the supply chain, such as demand forecasting or inventory management.

➢ *Artificial Neural Networks (ANNs)*

ANNs are ML algorithms that are designed to mimic the structure and function of the human brain [51]. ANNs are used in SCM to estimate demand, optimize inventory, and plan logistics. Based on past data, ANNs may understand complicated correlations between variables and generate accurate predictions. Organizations that use ANNs achieve generally high accuracy and efficiency in demand forecasting, inventory management, and logistics.

➢ *Decision Trees*

Decision Trees are a type of ML algorithm that uses a tree-like structure to represent decisions and their possible consequences. Decision Trees are used in SCM for product classification, demand forecasting, and quality control. Decision Trees can identify patterns and relationships in data and make accurate predictions based on historical data. The outcomes achieved by organizations using Decision Trees are generally high accuracy and improved efficiency in product classification, demand forecasting, and quality control.

➢ *Random Forest*

Random Forest is an ensemble learning approach that predicts using many decision trees. SCM use Random Forest for demand forecasting, product categorization, and quality control. Based on past data, Random Forest can find patterns and correlations in data and generate accurate predictions. Organizations that use Random Forest usually obtain excellent accuracy and efficiency in demand forecasting, product categorization, and quality control.

➢ *Support Vector Machines (SVMs)*

SVM is a form of machine learning algorithm used for classification and regression analysis. SVM is used in SCM to anticipate demand, manage quality, and organize logistics. Based on past data, SVM can find patterns and correlations in data and generate accurate predictions. Organizations that use SVM usually obtain excellent accuracy and efficiency in demand forecasting, quality control, and logistics planning.

➢ *Clustering*

Clustering is a form of machine learning method that groups data points based on their similarity. Clustering is used in SCM to classify products, segment customers, and organize logistics. Clustering can be used to find groups of similar items, consumers, or locations and optimize supply chain operations depending on the characteristics of the groupings. Organizations that use clustering realize overall better efficiency in product categorization, customer segmentation, and logistical planning.

To summarize, RL is not the sole method for optimizing supply chain management. Other popular alternatives include mathematical optimization, simulation, heuristics, game theory, machine learning, and swarm intelligence. The technique used is determined on the individual problem, the availability of data, and the computer resources available. Alternative machine learning techniques, such as ANN, Decision Trees, Random Forest, SVM, and Clustering, are widely used in supply chain management to optimize various aspects of the supply chain. In demand forecasting, inventory management, logistics planning, product categorization, customer segmentation, and quality control, these strategies can achieve great accuracy and efficiency. While RL is an effective method for solving complex decision-making problems, the alternative ML techniques discussed above are better suited for optimizing specific aspects of the supply chain using historical data.

In view of the current survey, the number of research works are shown in the pie chart in Figure 17.5. This provide a significance increase of research in this area and its impact. Table 17.1 shows how AI revolutionizes supply chain analytics through demand forecasting, accurately predicting future demand to ensure optimal inventory levels and reduce stockouts. This improves customer satisfaction and helps businesses optimize resources and reduce costs. and reviews the prior papers as well.

Table 17.1 A comparison study of different research methodology of RL algorithms in SCM.

Author(s)	Research methodology	RL algorithm	SCM application	Key findings	Limitations	Future research scope
N. Naderi, A. Govindan, and J. Soleimani-Damaneh (2018)	Preferred Reporting Items for Systematic Reviews and Meta-Analyses (PRISMA)	Decision trees	Multi-period, multi-objective supply chain network design problem under uncertainty	Improved demand forecasting	Data availability and quality	Integration of real-time data
K. Goyal, S. Akter, and S. Sarker (2019)	Pre-defined inclusion and exclusion criteria	SCM sub-domains	Inventory management, demand forecasting, and transportation management	Inventory optimization	Interpretability and explainability	Hybrid models
S. S. Seyedhosseinian, S. M. Saberi, and M. G. Ghotboddini (2020)	Heuristics	ANN, SVM, and Random Forest	Demand Forecasting	Supply chain risk management	Scalability	Explainable AI: Focusing on developing machine learning models that provide transparent and interpretable results, allowing supply chain managers to understand and trust the decision-making process.

(Continued)

Table 17.1 A comparison study of different research methodology of RL algorithms in SCM. (*Continued*)

Author(s)	Research methodology	RL algorithm	SCM application	Key findings	Limitations	Future research scope
K. Guo (2020)	Monte Carlo tree search (MCTS)	Q-Learning	Demand forecasting to determine optimal inventory levels and ordering policies	Improved demand forecasting	Interpretability and explainability	Collaborative and decentralized supply chains
L. Yu (2019)	Centralized training method	Multi-agent reinforcement learning (MARL)	Decentralized supply chains	Supply chain coordination: RL can facilitate coordination and collaboration among different entities in the supply chain.	Communication and coordination challenges: RL applications in multi-agent supply chain settings require effective communication and coordination mechanisms	Human-agent collaboration in RL: Investigating how RL algorithms can effectively collaborate with human decision-makers to leverage their domain expertise in supply chain management.

(*Continued*)

Leverage cutting-edge AI technologies to analyze complex data sets and gain valuable insights.
Automate routine tasks and save time with intelligent automation.
Make data-driven decisions with predictive analytics and prescriptive insights.

Table 17.1 A comparison study of different research methodology of RL algorithms in SCM. (*Continued*)

Author(s)	Research methodology	RL algorithm	SCM application	Key findings	Limitations	Future research scope
S. P. Meyn (2021)	Sensitivity analysis and robustness testing: Conducting sensitivity analysis to assess the model's sensitivity to variations in key parameters and testing the model's robustness under different scenarios and disruptions.	Q-learning, Deep Q-Networks (DQN), Proximal Policy Optimization (PPO), and Actor-Critic methods.	Supply Chain Disruption Management: RL algorithms can aid in managing supply chain disruptions by optimizing decision-making under uncertain and changing conditions. Robustness testing using RL can evaluate the effectiveness of disruption response strategies and measure their adaptability to different disruption scenarios or parameter changes.	Transportation and logistics optimization: Machine learning algorithms can optimize transportation routes, fleet management, and delivery scheduling, leading to improved efficiency and reduced costs.	Integration with existing systems: Integrating RL solutions with legacy supply chain systems and software can be technically complex and require careful implementation.	Collaborative and decentralized supply chains: Exploring the application of machine learning techniques in collaborative and decentralized supply chain environments, where multiple stakeholders and entities interact and share data.

(*Continued*)

Integrating AI technologies into supply chain analytics offers tremendous opportunities for businesses to optimize their processes, reduce costs, and improve customer satisfaction. However, organizations must address data quality, privacy, and ethical considerations to ensure successful implementation.

Table 17.1 A comparison study of different research methodology of RL algorithms in SCM. (*Continued*)

Author(s)	Research methodology	RL algorithm	SCM application	Key findings	Limitations	Future research scope
R. J. Jia (2020)	Heuristics	Deep Q-network (DQN)	Cross Docking System	Autonomous logistics and routing: RL algorithms can learn efficient routing policies, leading to optimized delivery routes and reduced transportation costs.	Exploration–exploitation trade-off: Striking a balance between exploring new strategies and exploiting known policies is critical in RL but can be challenging in supply chain optimization.	RL for decentralized supply chains: Exploring RL techniques to optimize decision-making in decentralized supply chain systems with multiple autonomous entities.
X. Wu (2021)	Monte Carlo tree search (MCTS)	(DDPG)	Inventory management in a make-to-order manufacturing system	Warehouse management: RL can optimize warehouse operations by learning efficient inventory storage, picking, and replenishment policies.	Uncertain and changing environments: Supply chains are subject to dynamic and uncertain conditions, requiring RL algorithms to adapt and generalize to new scenarios effectively.	RL for demand and price elasticity estimation: Using RL to estimate demand and price elasticity parameters, which can improve pricing and revenue management strategies.

(*Continued*)

Combining AI with IoT sensors and devices to collect real-time data
Gaining insights into every aspect of supply chain operations.
Providing transparency and traceability in supply chain transactions with blockchain technology.
Improving efficiency and reducing risks.

Table 17.1 A comparison study of different research methodology of RL algorithms in SCM. (*Continued*)

Author(s)	Research methodology	RL algorithm	SCM application	Key findings	Limitations	Future research scope
Z. Huang (2020)	Value function approximation (VFA)	Policy Iteration (PI)	Control production and inventory systems with discrete-time demand and service disruptions	Energy management: RL algorithms can optimize energy consumption and distribution in supply chains, contributing to sustainability and cost reduction.	Reward function design: Designing appropriate reward functions that capture the desired objectives and trade-offs in supply chain management is a non-trivial task.	Hybrid RL approaches: Exploring the combination of RL with other optimization techniques, such as mathematical programming, to leverage their complementary strengths.
L. Wu (2021)	Random search method	Q-learning	Optimize scheduling in a single-machine scheduling problem with uncertain processing times	Supply chain coordination: RL can facilitate coordination and collaboration among different entities in the supply chain by learning policies that optimize the overall system performance.	High-dimensional state and action spaces: Supply chain problems typically involve complex and high-dimensional state and action spaces, posing challenges for RL algorithms to converge to optimal solutions.	RL for sustainable supply chains: Investigating how RL can be used to optimize decisions that improve sustainability metrics, such as carbon footprint reduction and waste minimization.

Analyze complex data sets.
Automate routine tasks
Make data-driven decisions

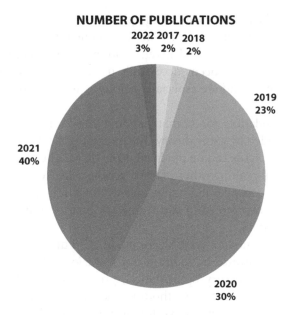

NUMBER OF PUBLICATIONS

Figure 17.5 A tentative report of research works from the year 2017 to 2022.

17.7 Conclusion

In today's global market, supply chain management (SCM) is essential to a company's performance and ability to compete. The development of machine learning methods, such as reinforcement learning (RL), has created new opportunities for improving several facets of SCM. RL has demonstrated amazing promise, but it is crucial to remember that it is not the only strategy out there. Different aspects of the supply chain can be optimized using alternative machine learning (ML) methods such as simulation, heuristics, game theory, machine learning, and swarm intelligence.

In SCM, mathematical optimization is frequently employed as an alternative to RL. To identify the optimal solutions that minimize costs, maximize profits, or achieve a compromise between the two, it requires applying mathematical models and optimization algorithms including linear programming, integer programming, and mixed-integer programming. Logistics planning, production scheduling, and inventory management are all frequent areas where mathematical optimization is used. It uses well-defined mathematical models and offers accurate answers to challenging optimization issues.

In SCM, simulation is yet another potent substitute for RL. Simulation enables a deeper comprehension of the system dynamics and the assessment of various approaches by building virtual models of the supply chain and testing various scenarios. Demand, inventory levels, lead times, and manufacturing capacity are just a few of the variables that can be simulated. It aids in the identification of the most cost-effective configurations that meet client demand. Simulation helps with decision-making in uncertain situations and offers useful insights into how the supply chain behaves.

Rule-based algorithms provide computationally effective and close-to-ideal answers to challenging optimization issues. They are extensively utilized in SCM because they can quickly address problems that arise in the present. In SCM, heuristics like simulated annealing, tabu search, and genetic algorithms are frequently used. These algorithms use exploration–exploitation trade-offs and iterative optimization techniques to get successful conclusions. Heuristics have been successfully used in fields like routing, scheduling, and inventory management and are especially helpful when real-time decision-making is necessary.

A mathematical foundation for comprehending the strategic interactions between decision-makers is provided by game theory. The interactions between suppliers, manufacturers, distributors, and clients can be modeled using SCM. The goal is to determine each player's ideal tactics while taking other players' actions into account. The supply chain's pricing, negotiating, and coordinating can be improved with the use of game theory. Game theory aids in better decision-making and teamwork by examining the motivations and actions of many stakeholders.

A wide variety of techniques are available for use in SCM under the umbrella of machine learning as a class of algorithms. In addition to RL, various ML techniques can be used for demand forecasting, inventory optimization, product categorization, customer segmentation, and quality control. These methods include artificial neural networks (ANNs), decision trees, random forests, support vector machines (SVMs), and clustering. It uses historical data to find trends, correlations, and forecasts. Due to their capacity to attain high precision and efficiency in particular sectors, they have been widely embraced in SCM.

Another alternate approach to SCM is swarm intelligence, which draws its inspiration from the group behavior of social insects. It imitates the actions of a swarm of agents cooperating to resolve routing, scheduling, and distribution optimization issues. By utilizing decentralized decision-making and adaptive behavior, swarm intelligence algorithms, such as ant colony optimization and particle swarm optimization, can efficiently optimize supply chain activities.

In conclusion, even if reinforcement learning (RL) has drawn attention for its capacity to enhance decision-making in difficult and unpredictable situations, it is crucial to take into account different machine learning (ML) methods in supply chain management (SCM). For solving various facets of SCM, mathematical optimization, simulation, heuristics, game theory, machine learning, and swarm intelligence provide complementary approaches. The specific problem, the accessibility of data, and the availability of computational resources all affect the approach selected.

Alternative ML methods have a benefit in that they can make use of past data, model intricate relationships, and produce precise predictions. While simulation enables scenario analysis and risk assessment, mathematical optimization offers accurate answers to well-defined optimization issues. Game theory helps with strategic decision-making and coordination, and heuristics provide close-to-optimal solutions with less computational complexity. Pattern detection, forecasting, and optimization are made possible by machine learning algorithms in particular SCM tasks. Swarm intelligence imitates group behavior and adjusts to shifting circumstances.

Organizations should think about a multifaceted approach that incorporates several tactics based on the nature of the current challenge in order to maximize the potential of these varied ways. To successfully integrate different methods, one must have a thorough awareness of the benefits and drawbacks of each method as well as the quantity and caliber of available data. Organizations may find the best techniques and create tailored solutions for their supply chain difficulties with the assistance of domain experts, data scientists, and technology vendors.

Finally, efficient supply chain management optimization necessitates a constant focus on innovation, development, and the application of new analytical methodologies. Organizations can improve supply chain performance, decrease costs, boost customer happiness, and gain a competitive advantage in the dynamic and complicated global economy by embracing a varied range of alternative ML techniques.

References

1. Sector-wise GDP of India, 17 June 2021, [Online]. Available: https://statisticstimes.com/economy/country/india-gdp-sectorwise.php.
2. Writer, S., Over 300 companies filed for bankruptcy in past 3 years, says govt, 16 March 2021, [Online]. Available: https://www.livemint.com/.
3. Rolf, B., Jackson, I., Müller, M., Lang, S., Reggelin, T., Ivanov, D., A review on reinforcement learning algorithms and applications in supply chain management. *Int. J. Prod. Res.*, 1–3, 2022.
4. Akbari, M. and Do, T., A systematic review of machine learning in logistics and supply chain management: Current trends and future directions. *Benchmarking An International Journal*, 1–3, 2021.
5. Zhang, W., Li, J., Li, Y., Zhang, X., Dynamic pricing under demand uncertainty in a dual-channel supply chain. *Omega*, 88, 29–45, 2019.
6. Jayaraman, V., Patterson, R.A., Rolland, E., Modularity in the design of complex product systems: Implications for supply chain management. *J. Oper. Manage.*, 65, 1, 1–18, 2019.
7. Chahal, H., Kumar, S., Singh, A., Developing green supply chain management framework using ISM approach: A case of automotive industry. *J. Clean. Prod.*, 238, 2019.
8. Cho, H. and Park, H.J., A blockchain-based approach to enhancing supply chain information sharing: A case study of the pharmaceutical industry. *Int. J. Inf. Manage.*, 49, 424–437, 2019.
9. Lee, K., Applications of machine learning in supply chain management: A comprehensive review. *Sustain. Comput.: Inform. Syst.*, 28, 2020.
10. Wang, C., Wu, L., Zhang, Z., A hybrid machine learning approach for quality control in manufacturing. *Expert Syst. Appl.*, 116, 484–494, 2019.
11. Wang, Y., Wang, B., Ma, Y., Intelligent supply chain management: A literature review and future research directions. *Int. J. Prod. Res.*, 58, 4, 1074–1092, 2020.
12. Choi, T.M. and Wallace, S.W., Operations management and artificial intelligence: Introduction to the special issue. *J. Oper. Manage.*, 46, 2, 129–133, 2021.
13. Guo, S., Song, W., Li, Q., Artificial intelligence-based decision-making in supply chain management: A review. *J. Clean. Prod.*, 312, 2021.
14. Schermann, M., Bloemhof-Ruwaard, J.M., van der Vorst, J.G.A.J., Haijema, R., Applications of machine learning in production and logistics: A systematic review. *Comput. Ind. Eng.*, 115, 400–420, 2018.
15. Guo, Y., Jiang, P., Li, L., Li, Q., A review on the application of artificial intelligence in green supply chain management. *J. Clean. Prod.*, 309, 2021.
16. Wu, D., Wu, Z., Li, X., Artificial intelligence for supply chain management: A comprehensive literature review and future research directions. *Int. J. Prod. Res.*, 57, 7, 2209–2229, 2019.
17. Ahn, H., Kim, K., Lee, S., Inventory management using machine learning. *Sustainability*, 11, 5, 1352, 2019.

18. Yan, C., Wang, J., Liu, Y., Production scheduling optimization with machine learning algorithms. *J. Intell. Manuf.*, 31, 4, 897–910, 2020.

19. Wang, L., Li, X., Li, D., Liang, X., Zhang, Q., A review of machine learning in transportation and logistics. *IEEE Access*, 8, 21265–21276, 2020.

20. Liu, Y., Sun, S., Gu, X., Liu, Y., Demand forecasting for supply chain planning using machine learning: A case study of clothing e-commerce company. *Math. Probl. Eng.*, 1–11, 2019.

21. Zhang, L., Supply chain risk management based on machine learning, in: *5th International Conference on Big Data and Education*, 2021.

22. Zhang, Q., Xu, H., Xu, Z., A deep reinforcement learning approach to inventory management with stockout avoidance. *IEEE Trans. Syst. Man Cybern.: Syst.*, 50, 11, 4526–4535, 2019.

23. Kuo, Y., Wang, Y., Lee, Y., Integrated production and maintenance scheduling by deep reinforcement learning. *Expert Syst. Appl.*, 95, 191–201, 2018.

24. Chen, Z., Xu, Z., Zhou, Y., A deep reinforcement learning approach for dynamic vehicle routing with stochastic demands. *IEEE Access*, 7, 54116–54125, 2019.

25. Kim, M., Choi, J., Kwon, O., Deep reinforcement learning-based order picking in a warehouse. *Sustainability*, 12, 9, 3857, 2020.

26. Aditya, S., Sambasivan, M., Sari, K., Multi-echelon supplier selection in a supply chain using deep reinforcement learning. *Expert Syst. Appl.*, 156, 2020.

27. Tran, D., Li, X., Wang, X., A deep reinforcement learning approach for demand forecasting in a retail supply chain. *J. Retail. Consum. Serv.*, 49, 47–57, 2019.

28. Huang, H., Cai, X., Zhang, G., A deep reinforcement learning approach to dynamic pricing in a multi-channel retail environment. *Int. J. Prod. Econ.*, 28-38, 216, 2019.

29. Wu, T., Zhang, G., Zhao, X., A deep reinforcement learning approach to sustainable supply chain management. *J. Clean. Prod.*, 252, 2020.

30. Papakostas, N., Zografos, K., Androutsopoulos, K., Reinforcement learning in logistics: A review of the state-of-the-art and future research directions. *Transp. Res. Part E: Logist. Transp. Rev.*, 147, 2021.

31. Yu, Y., Yu, Y., Qi, Y., Reinforcement learning-based demand forecasting in supply chain management: A review. *IEEE Access*, 155550–155563, 2020.

32. Yang, J., Qi, Y., Yu, Y., Reinforcement learning for supply chain management: A review of recent advances. *Expert Syst. Appl.*, 130, 176–193, 2019.

33. Ma, Y., He, X., Huang, L., Zhang, C., Zou, Y., An inventory optimization method based on reinforcement learning for complex supply chain networks. *Complexity*, 6687723, 2021.

34. Kocabasoglu-Hillmer, C., Gao, Y., Wu, Y., Reinforcement learning for supply chain management: Overview, perspectives, and opportunities, in: *Handbook of Operations Analytics Using Data Envelopment Analysis*, pp. 613–638, Springer, 2020.

35. Xia, Y., Zhang, L., Li, X., Reinforcement learning based production scheduling in dynamic environment. *J. Intell. Manuf.*, 32, 301–314, 2021.

36. Zeng, Y., Guo, S., Song, M., Multi-agent reinforcement learning for supply chain management: A review. *Omega*, 102, 2020.

37. Su, X., Chen, L., Dong, Y., Multi-agent deep reinforcement learning for inventory coordination in a two-echelon supply chain. *J. Clean. Prod.*, 305, 2021.

38. Fu, L., Li, M., Li, H., Peng, Y., Reinforcement learning for uncertain demand production scheduling under sustainability constraints. *Comput. Ind. Eng.*, 153, 2021.

39. Joshi, S., Reinforcement learning in supply chain management: State-of-the-art and research directions. *Expert Syst. Appl.*, 168, 2021.

40. Sethi, S., Sahu, K.C., Bandyopadhyay, S., Reinforcement learning in supply chain management: A systematic review. *Comput. Ind. Eng.*, 141, 2020.

41. Maqbool, A., Malik, G.A., Mehmood, A., Rizwan, M., Reinforcement learning for supply chain management: A review and future research directions. *Expert Syst. Appl.*, 168, 2021.
42. Karaesmen, F., Kocabas, M., Karaesmen, I.H., Reinforcement learning applications in operations management: A review. *Eur. J. Oper. Res.*, 345–360, 2021.
43. Fang, X., Zheng, Z., Li, Y., Reinforcement learning in supply chain management: A comprehensive review. *IEEE Trans. Syst. Man Cybern.: Syst.*, 51, 2, 1412–1428, 2021.
44. Liao, Y., Zhang, L., Wang, Q., Gao, J., Zhou, J., Explainable reinforcement learning for supply chain management: A survey. *J. Ind. Prod. Eng.*, 38, 8, 237–253, 2021.
45. Xu, X., Zhou, H., Cui, Y., Zhang, W., Reinforcement learning in supply chain management: A systematic review and future research directions. *J. Clean. Prod.*, 249, 2020.
46. Bhardwaj, M., Malhotra, S., Rana, S., Jain, M., An intelligent decision-making model for supply chain management using machine learning techniques. *Comput. Ind. Eng.*, 139, 2020.
47. Alonso-Ayuso, A., Escudero, L.F., Garín-Martín, M.B., Pérez-Garín, D., A reinforcement learning approach for supply chain management: A simulation study. *Expert Syst. Appl.*, 56–70, 2019.
48. Agrawal, V., Goyal, S.K., Singh, R.K., Influence of organizational culture on technology adoption. *Manage. Sci. Lett.*, 9, 3, 405–414, 2019.
49. Kim, S.H., Bao, Y., Zhang, H., Supply chain control with reinforcement learning: A literature review. *J. Clean. Prod.*, 305, 2021.
50. Rashedi, R., Moattar Husseini, S.M., Hemmati, M., A hybrid approach based on machine learning and reinforcement learning for multi-echelon supply chain network design with uncertainty. *Appl. Soft Comput.*, 102, 2021.
51. Nayak, S., *Fundamentals of optimization techniques with algorithms*, Academic Press, San Diego, California, USA, 2020.
52. Oroojlooyjadid, A., Nazari, M., Snyder, L.V., Takáč, M., A deep Q-Network for the beer game: A reinforcement learning algorithm to solve inventory optimization problems. *Neural Information Processing Systems (NIPS), Deep Reinforcement Learning Symposium 2017*, 2017.
53. Zhang, X., Wang, Y., Shang, J., Reinforcement learning in supply chain management: A state-of-the-art review. *Int. J. Prod. Res.*, 58, 8, 2333–2353, 2020.
54. Zhang, X., Wu, Y., Chen, Y., Research on supply chain optimization based on deep reinforcement learning. *Int. J. Prod. Res.*, 58, 5, 1488–1503, 2020.
55. Li, X., Xu, X., Wang, S., Wang, Y., Application of machine learning in supply chain management: A systematic review and future research. *Int. J. Intell. Comput. Cybern.*, 11, 3, 277–302, 2018.
56. Tirkolaee, E.B., Sadeghi, S., Mooseloo, F.M., Vandchali H.R. and Aeini, S., Application of machine learning in supply chain management: A comprehensive overview of the Main areas. *Mathematical Problems in Engineering*, 2021, 2021.
57. Sharma, R., Kamble, S.S., Gunasekaran, A., Kumar, V. and Kumar, A., A systematic literature review on machine learning applications for sustainable agriculture supply chain performance. *Comput. Oper. Res.*, 119, 2020.
58. Feizabadi, J., Machine learning demand forecasting and supply chain performance. *Int. J. Logist. Res. Appl.*, 25, 2, 119–142, 2022.
59. Kumar, P.R.S., Bhardwaj, S., Agrahari, N., Pandey, S. and Harakannanavar, S.S., E-Commerce Inventory Management System Using Machine Learning Approach. *2023 International Conference on Data Science and Network Security (ICDSNS)*, Tiptur, India, pp. 1-7, 2023.
60. Aboutorab, H., Hussain, O.K., Saberi, M. and Hussain, F.K., A reinforcement learning-based framework for disruption risk identification in supply chains. *Future Gener. Comp. Syst.*, 126, 110–122, Jan. 2022.

61. Zhang, K., Yang, Z. Liu, H., Zhang, T. and Basar, T., Fully decentralized multi-agent reinforcement learning with networked agents. proceedings.mlr.press, Jul. 03, 2018.

62. Mukherjee, T., Sangal, I., Sarkar, B., and Alkadash, T.M., Mathematical estimation for maximum flow of goods within a cross-dock to reduce inventory. *Math. Biosci. Eng.*, 19, 12, 13710–13731, 2022.

63. Alnahhal, M., Ahrens, D. and Salah, B., Dynamic lead-time forecasting using machine learning in a make-to-order supply chain. *Appl. Sci.*, 11, 21, 10105, Oct. 2021.

64. Rafiei, H., Rabbani, M., Vafa-Arani, H. and Bodaghi, G., Production-inventory analysis of single-station parallel machine make-to-stock/make-to-order system with random demands and lead times. *Int. J. Manag. Sci. Eng. Manag.*, 12, 1, 33–44, Feb. 2016.

65. Kayhan B.M. and Yildiz, G. Reinforcement learning applications to machine scheduling problems: a comprehensive literature review. *J. Intell. Manuf.*, Oct. 2021.

18

Alternate Approach to Solve Differential Equations Using Artificial Neural Network with Optimization Technique

Ramanan R.[1], Sukanta Nayak[2]* and Arun Kumar Gupta[3]

[1]Cognizant Technology Solution, Coimbatore, India
[2]Department of Mathematics, School of Advanced Sciences, VIT-AP University,
Amaravati, Andhra Pradesh, India
[3]Department of Mathematics, School of Applied Sciences, KIIT Deemed to be University,
Bhubaneswar, Odisha, India

Abstract

Differential equations are an essential part of mathematical modeling for various engineering and science problems. In this regard, many systems are data driven and hence the modeled differential equation too. In this context, the Artificial Neural Network (ANN) is a well-known model inspired by the Natural Neural Network (NNN) to simulate, analyze, and process the information. It possesses three layers, viz., input, hidden, and output, by which one can process the information at hand. As such, this chapter includes the idea of ANN with the steepest descent search optimization technique to solve ordinary differential equations and a system identification structural problem. The backpropagation technique has also been adopted to solve the aforementioned problems and to compare the acquired results. Both methods are found to be effective for solving ODEs by constructing the appropriate form of trial solutions. The obtained results clearly manifest that this neural network architecture with optimization technique is simple, efficient, and appropriate to implement for dynamic physical problems.

Keywords: Artificial intelligence, artificial neural network, differential equations, feedforward, backpropagation

18.1 Introduction

Differential equations are the backbone of many real-world engineering and science problems. Thus, most of the physical systems were governed by differential equations, and hence, there is an essence of solution strategies to investigate the same [21]. But it is found that if the system is provided with complicated operating conditions, complexity in geometry, and nonlinearity, then numerical methods are adapted to solve the governing differential equations, whereas if the system is provided a data set or training samples instead of standard

---

*Corresponding author: sukantgacr@gmail.com

Arindam Dey, Sukanta Nayak, Ranjan Kumar and Sachi Nandan Mohanty (eds.) *How Machine Learning is Innovating Today's World: A Concise Technical Guide*, (303–328) © 2024 Scrivener Publishing LLC

numerical methods, the concept of Artificial Intelligence (AI) techniques can be useful to study the same. ANN [2, 20] is one of the AI techniques where the process is inspired from the analysis and mechanism of processing an information. It has a wide range of applications in Data Science on data classification, image recognition, and weather forecasting. It is primarily based on the feedforward neural network function approximation and generates a differentiable, closed analytical expression. The fundamental approximation is a feedforward neural network, whose weights and biases are updated in order to minimize a defined error function. For different error functions, the network provides different reliable output; hence, different error functions have been defined and analyzed. We utilized an optimization strategy to train the network, and hence the gradient of the error must be computed.

According to studies, a multilayer perceptron with one hidden layer can estimate any function with arbitrary precision [10], and therefore, it can be useful to take this single hidden layer perceptron network as a test model to solve differential equations. As such, this chapter explores the potential of solving differential equations using an ANN. A standard method used for constructing Artificial Neural Network in Artificial Intelligence was Backpropagation Algorithm. The Backpropagation and its general use in neural networks were introduced by Rumelhart, Hinton & Williams [1]. However, the approach was independently discovered numerous times and had numerous forerunners. The same method of the backpropagation algorithm was used to solve differential equations with gradient descent equations, and results were explained briefly with examples. As an application of ANN, a system identification problem is considered here [11]. It is a process of developing a mathematical model of a dynamic system from experimental data, i.e., using system input/output (IO) measurements to estimate the adjustable parameter values in a specific model structure. Since ANN works on input and output data, the Backpropagation algorithm and ANN construction ideas were combined to identify structural parameters in a multi-story building, i.e., identification of column stiffness from the modeled test data of multi-story shear building in the field of earthquake study and structural dynamics. These model data sets are generated by using prior known estimation of parameters and corresponding vibration characteristics by finite element method using partial derivative matrix. Thus, this ANN construction of multi-story building will be helpful to find the withstand capacity of a building before and after earthquakes. System identification [6] is the process of finding values of the adjustable parameter for a dynamic system using pre-modeled data; since ANN works on data and we have already done work on solving differential equations using ANN, we employed these two methods to predict value adjustable parameters in a multi-story building. The process of procuring data from prior known information was discussed by Chakraverty [8].

In section 18.2, the architectural construction of an artificial neural network is explained. Since the backpropagation algorithm was widely used throughout this chapter, the numerical prediction of ANN output (data classification method) using the backpropagation algorithm is described in section 18.3 with a detailed algorithm. Section 18.4 discusses the finding of a solution to an ordinary differential equation using the ideas from [3–5]. As ANN produces different reliable outputs for different error functions, we defined two different error functions in section 18.3, and so the reliability and feasibility of their results were discussed briefly with examples. System identification method and the method of predicting adjustable parameter in a dynamic system using data is explained in section 18.5, and the results are discussed in section 18.6.

18.2   Artificial Neural Network

An abstract operational framework that relies on the organizing structure of the human brain is known as artificial neural network (ANN). This is a key area of research in artificial intelligence. ANNs operate as computational tools (algorithms) inspired by the mammalian cerebral cortex's neural arrangement but on much smaller scales. Artificial neural networks are information processing systems in which neurons convey data. Through diverse learning techniques, ANN is employed in a variety of application challenges, including pattern recognition, categorization of data, image, text, and speech recognition, and system identification [13].

The following steps define an artificial network:

1. Architecture of the network (the connections between neurons),
2. Learning or training (finding weights on the connections), and
3. Activation functions.

18.2.1   Architecture

ANN is implemented through various parameters and learning rules for data modeling. In this process, layers are used to organize the neural networks. These are building blocks of interconnecting "neurons/nodes" that possess "activation functions." An ANN combines neurons and nodes to process data in parallel to address specific problems. An artificial neural network (ANN) learns new information, which is then stored in the number of interneuron links, which are represented numerically as "weights." Based on an updated testing signal input value, the weights are applied for estimating output signal values. The network receives patterns from the "input layer," which then connects with a number of "hidden layers," where the tangible processing is carried out through a network of weighted

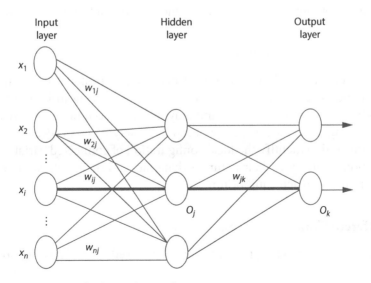

Figure 18.1 Structure of the artificial neural network.

"connections." The hidden layers then link with the "output layer," wherein the result is output, as shown in Figure 18.1.

Here, x_i are input nodes, o_j are the final output from hidden and output layers, w_{ij} and w_{jk} denote the weights from the ith to j^{th} layer and the weights from the jth to k^{th} layer, respectively.

18.2.2 Neuron Architecture

The network architecture is an important part of architecture. It is a distribution of neurons in different layers with a connection pattern in the layers. There are three types of layers, viz., single layer, multilayer, and competitive neural networks. In this context, in feedforward networks, signals flow from input layers to output.

18.2.2.1 Single and Multilayer Neural Networks

In a neural network, a single layer of connection weights makes up a single-layer neural network. In this network, output units are isolated from other output units whereas the input units are isolated to other input units but fully connected to the output units. A network with one or more layers of nodes separating the input and output units is referred to as a multilayer neural network. The hidden units are the layer that exists between the input and output units. When a single-layer neural network cannot be taught to tackle a problem appropriately, multilayer neural networks are used.

18.2.2.2 Feedforward Neural Network

A feedforward neural network's neurons are organized in layers. In this network, a layer of neuron receives data that follow below and transmit it along to the layer beyond. Here, the networks are prohibited from linking to the same. In this case, data are rigorously carried forward from the input node to the output node. Additionally, there are no loops for feedback; therefore, the output of one layer has no effect on the output of another.

18.2.2.3 Feedback Neural Network

In a feedback neural network, the output of one layer is routed back to the first layer. The aforementioned network may accommodate signals moving in both ways by adding loops. This network is extremely robust and may, at times, become extremely complicated. Connections among neurons can be formed in a variety of ways. Feedback neural network models are used to identify the ideal configuration of connected variables for dealing with optimization challenges. Their nature is dynamic, and their state is subject to change continuously until they reach equilibrium.

18.2.3 Different Training Process

This section discusses different types of trainings involved in the learning process of data using ANN.

18.2.3.1 Supervised Training

Training under supervision entails receiving guidance from a teacher. Both the inputs and the outputs are given during supervised training. The network then processes the inputs, producing outputs, and compares them to the desired outputs. The inaccuracy is identified by contrasting the network's computed output with the predicted output that has been corrected. When network parameters are altered as a result of the fault, performance is enhanced.

18.2.3.2 Unsupervised Training

Unsupervised training entails learning without a teacher's guidance. Unsupervised training is the training approach used in neural networks when the goal output is unknown when the input vectors are being trained. The weight may be changed by the net so that the same output unit is given to the input vector that is the most similar. Unsupervised learning appears to be significantly more difficult than supervised learning, and this sort of training typically fits into the decision problem paradigm because the objective is to make judgments that maximize rewards rather than to provide a classification.

18.2.4 Learning Process

The ANN model's most significant feature is learning. The values of the link weights of any neural network represent knowledge. Therefore, the "learning rule" that alters the connection weights based on the input patterns that it is presented with is present in the majority of ANNs. Although neural networks employ a variety of learning rules, the Backpropagation Neural Networks (BPNNs), the most prevalent class of ANNs, frequently use the delta learning rule.

18.2.5 Activation Function in ANN

Activation function plays an important role in the ANN model. It operates the input information to obtain the output of the network. In other words, the input signals are transformed into output signals using the activation functions. It acts as a squashing function to force the network's output to lie within the range of values, generally either between 0 and 1, or -1 and 1.

The bipolar and unipolar sigmoid functions are two frequently used activation mechanisms.

18.2.5.1 Unipolar Sigmoid Function

One of the activation functions, the unipolar sigmoid function is defined as

$$f(x) = \frac{1}{1 + e^{-\lambda x}} \tag{18.1}$$

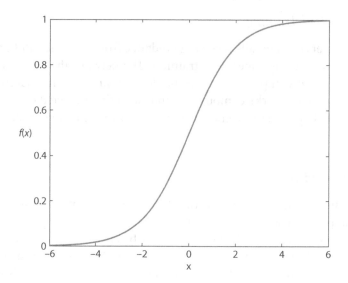

Figure 18.2 Unipolar sigmoid function.

where $\lambda > 0$ is the slope of the function. For better visualization of the same, it has been depicted in Figure 18.2.

The output of unipolar sigmoid function fall within the range [0,1]. The binary sigmoid function is a smooth one and also its derivative too. If $f(x)$ is the function, then the derivative is given by

$$f(x) = f(x) * (1 - f(x)) \tag{18.2}$$

18.2.5.2   Bipolar Sigmoid Function

The bipolar sigmoid function is defined as

$$f(x) = \frac{1 - e^{-\lambda x}}{1 + e^{-\lambda x}} \tag{18.3}$$

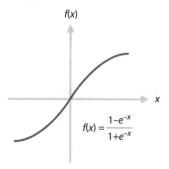

Figure 18.3 Bipolar sigmoid function.

With the value $\lambda = 1$, a bipolar sigmoid function is shown in Figure 18.3. It possesses the output in the range [-1, 1].

18.3 Backpropagation Algorithm

This algorithm is based on the general framework of ANN to estimate the weights for desired output. Here, for each training sample, its properties correspond to the network's inputs. The inputs are fed continuously to the units that comprise the input layer. These inputs flow through the input layer before being simultaneously weighted and sent to the hidden layer, a second layer of "neuron-like" units. Units from one concealed layer can send data to another, and so on. Although in practice only one hidden layer is typically employed, the number of hidden levels is flexible. The output layer, which broadcasts the network's prediction for given tuples, is composed of units that are fed weighted outputs from the final hidden layer.

Backpropagation learns through processing a training set of samples iteratively and comparing each tuple's predicted value with the known goal value. Using a method known as the delta rule or gradient descent, the weights are updated for each training sample to minimize the mean-squared error between the network's prediction and the actual target value. The learning problem is thus thought to have an answer in the weights that minimize the error function.

Backpropagation is the term used to describe the process of propagating changes from the output layer via each hidden layer and down to the first hidden layer in a "backward" fashion. The weights will eventually converge, even though it is not certain, and the learning process will come to an end. Figure 18.4 provides a summary of the algorithm.

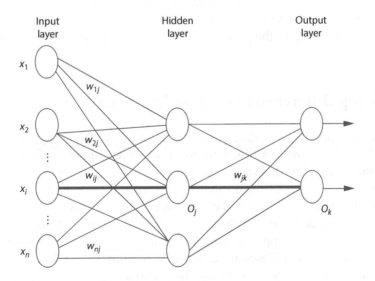

Figure 18.4 Artificial neural network structure.

Backpropagation Algorithm

Input layer

> ➤ Here the symbol D is defined as the data set containing the training samples and the corresponding target values.
> ➤ The symbol 'l' defines the learning rate.
> ➤ The last most important value is truncation error and generally it is denoted through the symbol 'E'

Step 1: Initialization of weights and biases.

Step 2: While tolerance criteria are not satisfied, for each training sample X in D with each input layer unit j, one needs to define the output $O_j = I_j$ of an input unit as its actual input value.

Step 3: For each hidden layer unit j, one needs to compute the net input of unit j with respect to the previous layer $I_j = \sum_i W_{ij} O_j + \theta_j$. Here, θ_j is a bias.

Step 4: Next, compute the output of unit j, that is, $O_j = \dfrac{1}{1 + e^{-I_j}}$.

Step 5: Define the network error $E = \sum_j (T_J - O_j)^2$.

Step 6: Backpropagate the errors.

For each unit j in the output layer, the error for each node is computed as $Err_j = O_j(1 - O_j)(T_j - O_j)$.

For each unit j in the hidden layers, from the last to the first hidden layer, the error for each node is computed as $Err_j = O_j\left(1 - O_j\right)\sum_k Err_k W_{jk}$. Here, k represents the next higher layer.

For each weight W_{ij} in network, the weight increment is defined as $\Delta W_{ij} = (I)Err_j O_j$, and updating in weights is denoted as $W_{ij} = W_{ij} + \Delta W_{ij}$

For each bias in network, the bias increment is defined as $\Delta\theta_j = (I)Err_j$, and updating in bias value is denoted as $\theta_j = \theta_j + \Delta\theta_j$.

Step 7: Continue Step 6 until the process error E is less than the truncation error.

18.4   Solving Differential Equation Using ANN

There are many methods to solve differential equations but a different approach to the same is discussed here. We provide a broad approach to solve ordinary differential equations (ODEs) that makes use of feedforward neural networks' ability to approximate functions to produce a differentiable, closed-form solution. The traditional multilayer ANN model has been used to solve ordinary differential equations (ODEs). A multilayer ANN model with one input layer, one hidden layer, m hidden nodes, and one output node has been taken into consideration. The core approximation element in this design is a feedforward neural network, whose weights and biases are changed to minimize the relevant error function. Here, optimization approach is used to train the network.

In the suggested method, the model function is written as the product of two terms, that is, the first term is no adjustable parameters obeying the initial/boundary requirements and a feedforward neural network must be trained to solve the differential equation in the second term. Given that any function may be approximated to arbitrary precision by a multi-layer perceptron with one hidden layer [10], it makes sense to think of this kind of network architecture as a potential model for solving differential equations.

The usage of a neural architecture has many appealing features, including the following:

➤ The solution via ANNs is a differentiable. The closed analytic form of the same may be employed in any subsequent computation. The majority of other methods provide a discrete solution (Runge-Kutta methods) or a solution with restricted differentiability (finite components).

➤ Because the number of model parameters required is significantly smaller than any other solution technique, compact solution models are generated with very little demand on memory space.

➤ This method can be applied to solve system of ODEs.

➤ Because the method can be realized in hardware, utilizing neural processors, it opens up the possibility of tackling difficult differential equation generated in real time, which arise in many engineering applications.

➤ This approach can also be implemented efficiently on parallel systems.

➤ The estimated solution remains continuous over the integration domain. The total amount of sampling points has no significant effect on computational complexity.

➤ Conventional numerical methods are often iterative in nature, with the step size fixed before the computation begins.

➤ In conventional numerical methods, once the answer arrives, if we want to understand the solution across the steps, we must redo the procedure from the beginning. ANN could be among the methods which reduces the cost of iterations. In addition, after training the model, we can use it as a black box to obtain numerical outcomes at any chosen point in the domain.

18.4.1   Structure of Multi-Layer ANN

A three-layer ANN model is presented in Figure 18.5. This model shows the structure of an ANN. It possesses three layers, viz., input, hidden, and output. In input layers, a single

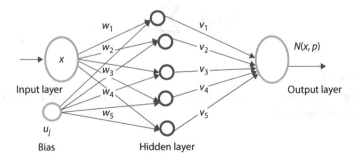

Figure 18.5 Structure of multilayer ANN for solving differential equation.

input node (x) is provided with biases (u_j). The hidden layer has five nodes, whereas the output layer has one output node. The initial weights (w_j) and (v_j) are assumed to be arbitrary (random), and the number of nodes in the hidden layer is taken into account by the trial-and-error approach.

18.4.2   General Formula for Solving ODE

The mentioned algorithm will be implemented here to solve the below generalized differential equation

$$F\left(x, y(x), \nabla y(x), \nabla^2 y(x)\ldots \nabla^n y(x)\right) = 0, x \epsilon D \subseteq R \tag{18.4}$$

where F defines the structure of a differential equation, the solution of the differential equation is $y(x)$, the symbol ∇ denotes the differential operator, and D is the discretized domain over a finite set of points.

Assume, $y_t(x, p)$ is the ANN trial solution of Equation 18.4 with adjustable parameters (p) (weights and biases).

Then, Equation 18.4 becomes

$$F\left(x, y_t(x, p), \nabla y_t(x, p), \nabla^2 y_t(x, p), \ldots, \nabla^n y_t(x, p)\right) = 0. \tag{18.5}$$

The trial solution $y_t(x, p)$ with input x and parameters p can be written as

$$y_t(x, p) = A(x) + F\left(X, N(x, p)\right) \tag{18.6}$$

where $A(x)$ satisfies the initial or boundary conditions and contains no adjustable parameters, whereas $N(x, p)$ is the output of a feedforward neural network with parameters p and input x. The second term $F\left(x, N(x, p)\right)$ does not add anything to the initial/boundary conditions but represents the output of the neural network model, the weights and biases of which are changed to minimize the error function to yield the final ANN solution, $y_t(x, p)$.

Here, the network output $N(X, P)$ is formulated as

$$N(x, p) = \sum_{j=1}^{m} v_j s(z_j) \tag{18.7}$$

where $z_j = w_j * x + u_j$.

If $y_t(x, p)$ denotes a trial solution with adjustable parameters p, the problem is transformed to the following form.

$$\sum_x min_p F\left(x, y_t(x, p), \nabla y_t(x, p), \nabla^2 y_t(x, p), \ldots, \nabla^n y_t(x, p)\right) \tag{18.8}$$

18.4.3 Formulation for nth-Order Initial Value Problem (IVP)

Let us consider a general nth-order IVP

$$\frac{d^n y}{dx^n} = f\left(x, y, \frac{dy}{dx}, \frac{d^2 y}{dx^2}, \ldots, \frac{d^{n-1} y}{dx^{n-1}}\right) \tag{18.9}$$

with initial conditions

$$y^{(i)}(a) = A_i, \quad i = 1, 2, 3, \ldots, n-1. \tag{18.10}$$

The relevant ANN trial solution can be built as Equation 18.11 with reference to Equation 18.6

$$y_t(x, p) = A + (x - a)^n F\left(X, N(x, p)\right) \tag{18.11}$$

Error can be calculated through the formula

$$E(x, p) = \frac{1}{2}\left(\frac{d^n y_t(x, p)}{dx^n} - f\left(x, y, \frac{dy_t(x, p)}{dx}, \frac{d^2 y_t(x, p)}{dx^2}, \ldots, \frac{d^{n-1} y_t(x, p)}{dx^{n-1}}\right)\right) \tag{18.12}$$

Here, the error function is minimized by using an unsupervised backpropagation approach. The network weights and biases are updated through Equations 18.13 and 18.14, respectively.

$$w_j^{k+1} = w_j^k + \Delta w_j^k = w_j^k + \left(-\eta \frac{\partial E(x, p)^k}{\partial w_j^k}\right) \tag{18.13}$$

$$v_j^{k+1} = v_j^k + \Delta v_j^k = v_j^k + \left(-\eta \frac{\partial E(x, p)^k}{\partial v_j^k}\right) \tag{18.14}$$

The derivatives of the error function with respect to w_j and v_j can be obtained by differentiating error function $E(x, p)$ with each w_j's and v_j's.

18.4.4 Case Study: Solving First-Order Linear Differential Equation

Here, a first-order differential equation with the initial condition is solved with two different error functions.

In the first method, an artificial neural network is trained by taking the error function (Equation 18.12) as

$$E(x,p) = \frac{1}{2}\left(\frac{d^n y_t(x,p)}{dx^n} - f\left(x, y, \frac{dy_t(x,p)}{dx}, \frac{d^2 y_t(x,p)}{dx^2}, \ldots, \frac{d^{n-1} y_t(x,p)}{dx^{n-1}} \right) \right)$$

Artificial neural networks are trained each time with each input x_i with its corresponding output. Weights are adjusted according to the error function up to the desired truncation error.

18.4.4.1 Algorithm

Here, a multilayer ANN has one input, one output layer, and 'n' hidden nodes, as shown in Figure 18.4.

Input:

- Differential equation function f in domain D
- Initial/Boundary condition

Output:

- Trained Neural Network
- Trial function $y_t(x,p)$

Steps of the algorithm

1. Initialize weights $W_1, W_2, \cdots, W_m$ and $V_1, V_2, \cdots, V_m$.
2. Initialize symbolic variables for weights as $w_1, w_2, \cdots, w_m$, and $v_1, v_2, \cdots, v_m$.
3. Initialize bias value $U_1, U_2, \cdots, U_m$.
4. Initialize symbolic variables for bias as $u_1, u_2, \cdots, u_m$.
5. Initialize learning parameter η.
6. Initialize truncation error.
7. Calculate ANN output $N(x,p)$.
8. Calculate $y_t(x,p)$.
9. Define error function $E(x,p)$ as a symbolic equation using symbolic variables
10. For each input x_i, substitute values of weights, bias, and x_i in error function

    1. If error > truncation error
        i. Differentiate error function $E(x,p)$ with symbolic variables $w_1, w_2, \cdots, w_m$, and $v_1, v_2, \cdots, v_m$, and name it as D_{Ew_i} and D_{Ev_i}

(where i refers to respective weight number, $i = 1,2,3.....m$)

  ii. Substitute values of weights, bias, and x_i in differentiated error function and name it as D_{Ew_i} and D_{Ev_i}

  iii. Update value of weights W_i and V_i as $W_i = W_i - (\eta * D_{Ew_i})$

$$V_i = V_i - (\eta * D_{Ev_i})$$

  iv. Substitute values of weights, bias, and x_i in error function

  v. If error > truncation error, continue the process from 10 (i).

  vi. Terminating condition is error < truncation error.

11. Terminate until weights are updated for all x_i up to truncation error.

18.4.4.2 Example

Consider a first-order differential equation $\dfrac{dy}{dx} = 4x^3 - 3x^2 + 2$ subject to $y(0) = 0$ for demonstration.

The trial function $y_t(x,p)$ is defined as

$$y_t(x,p) = x * N(x,p)$$

Utilizing five hidden sigmoid nodes, the neural network is trained for 10 equidistant points within [0,1]. The neuronal outcome for two distinct errors is displayed in Table 18.1. Weights are selected randomly, and using MATLAB codes with an accuracy of 0.0001 and 0.00001, the solutions are obtained, which are presented in Table 18.1 and shown graphically in Figure 18.6.

Table 18.1 ANN solution for two different errors.

Input data	Error			Error difference at 0.00001
	Exact	0.0001	0.00001	
0	0	0	0	0
0.1111	0.2210	0.2141	0.2166	0.0025
0.2222	0.4359	0.4061	0.4135	0.0224
0.3333	0.6419	0.5721	0.5888	0.0531
0.4444	0.8400	0.7223	0.7576	0.0824
0.5555	1.0348	0.8938	0.9400	0.0948
0.6666	1.2345	1.1278	1.1748	0.0597
0.7777	1.4508	1.4482	1.5158	0.0650
0.8888	1.7200	1.9230	2.0251	0.3051
0.9999	1.9997	2.540	2.6497	0.6470

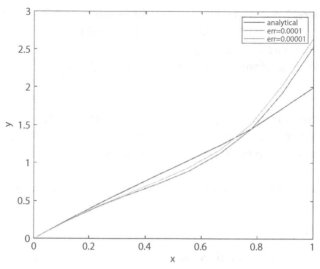

Figure 18.6 Analytical solution and ANN solutions of $\dfrac{dy}{dx} = 4x^3 - 3x^2 + 2, y(0) = 0$.

Few testing points are taken outside the domain [0,1] to check the feasibility of constructed ANN for the error 0.0001 and are given in Table 18.2.

18.4.4.3   Second Approach

The second method differs from the above method by two main ideas, first is error function, and the second is assigning weights of W_i from input to the hidden layer.

The error function $E(x, p)$ is defined as the sum of all errors for given input values x_i.

$$E(x, p) = \sum_{i=1}^{h} \frac{1}{2}\left(\frac{d^n y_t(x, p)}{dx^n} - f\left(x, y, \frac{dy_t(x, p)}{dx}, \frac{d^2 y_t(x, p)}{dx^2}, \ldots, \frac{d^{n-1} y_t(x, p)}{dx^{n-1}} \right) \right)$$

(18.15)

Weights W_{ij} are assigned separately for each x_i value. For some x_i in domain [a,b], weights are named as $W_{i1}, W_{i2}, \cdots, W_{im}$; and for x_j, weights are named as $W_{j1}, W_{j2}, \cdots, W_{jm}$.

Table 18.2 ANN results on a random testing point outside the domain.

x	**ANN solution**	**Expected analytical solution**
1.112	2.980	2.378
1.47	4.098	4.433
-0.278	-0.572	-0.529

Hence, if ANN has h inputs and m nodes on the hidden layer, then the number of hidden weights is $h \times m$.

Weights from the hidden layer to the output layer are not altered, and it is the same as the first method, so for m hidden nodes, we use m weights $v_1, v_2, \cdots, v_m$. This structure is explained further in Figure 18.7.

18.4.4.4   Algorithm

Input:

- Differential equation function f in domain D
- Initial/Boundary condition

Output:

- Trained Neural Network
- Trial function $y_t(x, p)$

Steps of the algorithm

1. Initialize weights
   $W_{11}, W_{12}, \cdots, W_{1m}, W_{21}, W_{22}, \cdots, W_{2m}, \cdots, W_{j1}, W_{j2}, \cdots, W_{jm}$ and $V_1, V_2, \cdots, V_m$.
2. Initialize weights for a symbolic variable as $w_{11}, w_{12}, \cdots, w_{1m}, w_{21}, w_{22}, \cdots, w_{2m}, \cdots, w_{j1}, w_{j2}, \cdots, w_{jm}$ and $v_1, v_2, \cdots, v_m$.
3. Initialize bias value $U_1, U_2, \cdots, U_m$.
4. Initialize symbolic variables for bias as $u_1, u_2, \cdots, u_m$.
5. Initialize learning parameter η.
6. Initialize truncation error.
7. Calculate ANN output $N(x, p)$ simultaneously for all inputs x_i
8. Calculate $y_t(x, p)$.

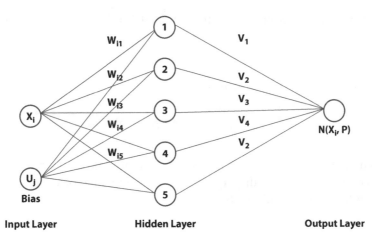

Figure 18.7 ANN structure for solving differential equations by using the second approach.

9. Define error function $E(x,p)$ given in Equation 8.15 as a symbolic equation using symbolic variables

$$E(x,p) = \sum_{i=1}^{h} \frac{1}{2}\left(\frac{d^n y_t(x,p)}{dx^n} - f\left(x,y,\frac{dy_t(x,p)}{dx},\frac{d^2 y_t(x,p)}{dx^2},\dots\dots,\frac{d^{n-1}y_t(x,p)}{dx^{n-1}}\right)\right).$$

Substitute values of weights, bias, and x_i in the error function and name it as E.

10. If the error $E >$ truncation error
Update the values of weights and bias by formula

$$w_{ij}^{k+1} = w_{ij}^{k} + \Delta w_{ij}^{k} = w_{ij}^{k} + (-\eta \frac{\partial E(x,p)^k}{\partial w_{ij}^{k}})$$

$$v_{j}^{k+1} = v_{j}^{k} + \Delta v_{j}^{k} = v_{j}^{k} + (-\eta \frac{\partial E(x,p)^k}{\partial v_{j}^{k}})$$

$$u_{j}^{k+1} = u_{j}^{k} + \Delta u_{j}^{k} = u_{j}^{k} + (-\eta \frac{\partial E(x,p)^k}{\partial u_{j}^{k}})$$

Weights and bias are updated by using Equations 18.13 and 18.14.
Calculate error E by substituting updated weights and a bias value.
If error > truncation error, continue process.
Terminating condition is error < truncation error.

11. Display output y_t for all inputs x_i.

18.4.4.5 Example

First order differential equation $\frac{dy}{dx} = 2x + 1, x \in [0,1]$ subject to $y(0) = 1$

$$(18.16)$$

The trial function $y_t(x,p)$ is defined as

$$y_t(x,p) = 1 + x * N(x,p)$$

Five hidden sigmoid nodes in the neural network are taken to train it for six evenly spaced points in [0,1]. Table 18.3 displays the neuronal outcome for various errors. Weights are selected randomly using MATLAB.

Table 18.3 ANN solutions using the second approach.

X	Error				
	Exact solution $(x^2 + x + 1)$	0.5	0.1	0.05	0.01
0	1	1	1	1	1
0.2	1.24	1.2933	1.2484	1.2440	1.2407
0.4	1.56	1.6181	1.5866	1.5784	1.5653
0.6	1.96	2.0070	2.0063	1.9796	1.9563
0.8	2.44	2.5658	2.4894	2.4571	2.4327
1	3	3.1976	3.0457	2.9867	2.9915

18.4.4.6   Comparison between First and Second Approaches

The second approach has a lower error rate than the first approach. The output of the second approach (trained neural network) is more accurate and can be applied to any higher-order differential equation. It is because of the error function (Equation 18.15), which compares input and output values simultaneously for all training data, whereas in the first approach, the error function (Equation 18.12) compares input and output values separately for all training input data. However, the convergence rate of the first approach is faster than that of the second approach because of its simplicity in the error function.

In the second approach, weights and bias values are updated by considering all its training points simultaneously. However, in the first approach, weights and bias are updated separately, so weights that got updated for B in $[A, B]$ may not be a reliable weight for A in $[A, B]$; Hence, the first approach has lower accuracy. Therefore, the first approach can be used for differential equations with a more extensive domain or with more training points, whereas the second approach can be used for differential equations with lesser domain and to a problem that expects a higher level of accuracy.

18.5   System Identification Using ANN

A method known as system identification (SI) uses measurements of input and output signals from dynamic systems to create mathematical models of those systems. It can be viewed as a bridge connecting the mathematical realm that includes control theory and model concepts with the practical world of applications.

To identify a system, one must first measure its input and output signals in time or frequency domains, choose a model structure, use an estimating method to determine values for the candidate model structure's movable parameters, and last, identify the system. Verify the estimated model's suitability for the application's requirements by evaluating it.

It is crucial in examining and closing gaps between structural systems and the models used to create those systems. The monitoring of structural health for damage detection also reflects this. The SI approaches are typically used to determine the dynamic properties of bridges and to understand how minarets currently respond to dynamic loads like earthquakes. Additionally, SI approaches are used to analyze complicated structural systems' vibration properties, modal forms, and damping ratios in order to provide understanding for modeling and evaluating current design practices.

In order to protect cultural heritage from earthquake damage, interdisciplinary research including structural engineers, designers, history of art, and material scientists is needed. These professionals must have knowledge, expertise, and experience with earthquakes. The primary components of any contemporary earthquake prevention methodology for the preservation of cultural heritage include health surveillance, SI, empirical and theoretical assessments of structural efficiency, design, testing, and retrofit execution. The application of numerous man-made and natural risks causes historic or other structures to degrade over time. In order to prevent failure, it is a difficult task to understand the state of the aforementioned structures.

18.5.1   Problem Structure for System Identification

Here, the preliminary design parameters for the aforementioned problem—namely, stiffness, mass, and frequency—are known. But over a long period of time, the structure might be impacted by a number of man-made or natural disasters. The engineers then seek to use SI methodologies to determine the structure's current state of health. It is considered that the mass does not change; only the degree of stiffness is altered. As such, equipment is available to get the present values of the frequencies, and using this, one may get the present parameter values by ANN. Thus, if sensors are set up to measure the frequency of the floors, those might be incorporated into the new ANN model that has been developed to obtain the current stiffness factors in interval form. An initial collection of data is created numerically in order to train the new ANN model. Utilizing the finite element approach, these data are produced from the starting parameter. The partial derivative matrix and Taylor series of expansion are used in the finite element method. For each floor, the converged ANN model provides the current stiffness parameter values. As a result, the condition of the undetermined structure can be predicted.

18.5.2   Analysis and Modeling

SI is a subfield of numerical analysis that develops computational models of systems in order to determine their parameters using empirical input and output data. The floor masses for this approach are assumed to be $m_1, m_2, \cdots, m_n$ and the stiffness parameters $k_1, k_2, \cdots, k_n$, which are to be identified.

Consider a three-story shear structure model shown in Figure 18.8 for illustration. Generally, for an n-story (n degrees of freedom) shear structure [14, 15], the dynamic equation of motion without damping can be written as

$$[M]\{\ddot{x}\} + [k]\{x\} = 0, \tag{18.17}$$

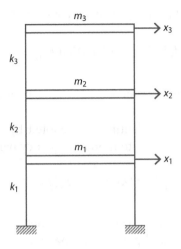

Figure 18.8 Three-story building structure.

where M is an $n \times n$ mass matrix of the structure. Below, in Equation 18.18, the mass matrix is represented.

$$[M] = \begin{bmatrix} m_1 & 0 & \cdots & \cdots & 0 \\ 0 & m_2 & 0 & \cdots & 0 \\ 0 & 0 & m_3 & \cdots & 0 \\ \cdots & \ddots & \cdots & \cdots & \vdots \\ 0 & 0 & \cdots & \cdots & m_n \end{bmatrix}. \tag{18.18}$$

The matrix k is written as

$$[k] = \begin{bmatrix} k_1 + k_2 & -k_2 & 0 & 0 & \cdots & 0 & 0 \\ -k_2 & k_2 + k_3 & -k_3 & 0 & \cdots & 0 & 0 \\ 0 & -k_3 & k_3 + k_4 & -k_4 & \cdots & 0 & 0 \\ \cdots & \ddots & \vdots & \cdots & \cdots & \cdots & 0 \\ 0 & 0 & 0 & 0 & \cdots & k_{n-1} + k_n & k_n \\ 0 & 0 & 0 & 0 & \cdots & -k_n & k_n \end{bmatrix}_{n \times n}, \tag{18.19}$$

and $\{x\} = \{x_1, x_2, \ldots, x_n\}^T$ is the displacement vector.

To solve Equation 18.17, we need to assume

$$\{x\} = \{\varphi\} e^{-i\omega t}. \tag{18.20}$$

Then, Equation 18.17 using Equation 18.20, we get the following eigenvalue problem [12]

$$([K]-[M][\omega_i(p)]))\{\varphi(p)\}_i = \{0\}, \qquad (18.21)$$

where $[\omega_i(p)]^2 = \lambda_i(p)$ is the eigenvalue (or natural frequency) of the structure [16] and mode shapes are $\{\varphi(p)\}_i$.

The structural parameter to be identified is denoted by $\bar{p}$ and now, the well-known Taylor series expansion that is applied to modal frequency parameter p gives

$$\{\lambda(\bar{p})\} = \{\lambda(p)\} + ([S]\{\bar{p}\} - \{p\}) \qquad (18.22)$$

where $\{p\} = [p_1, p_2, \cdots, p_n]^T$, the structural parameters of the original structure; $\{\bar{p}\} = [\bar{p}_1, \bar{p}_2, \cdots, \bar{p}_n]^T$, the structural parameters that are to be identified; $[S]$ is the eigenvalue partial derivative matrix.

Data sets are generated from the above equation using the finite element method and eigenvalue derivational matrix. The process of extracting data from prior known estimation is discussed briefly in [7, 8]. By this method, data sets are generated for modal stiffness parameters with its respective frequency by the iterative method and stored in a table. These generated data are then fed into ANN, and ANN was trained to a certain level of accuracy in MATLAB.

18.5.3   ANN Training for SI

R training pairs of data generated $\{Z_1, d_1; Z_2, d_2; \ldots\ldots; Z_R, Z_R\}$. where Z_i refers to the frequency of the ith data set and it has n number of frequencies; according to n floors, the structure has d_i, the stiffness parameter of the ith data set and it has n number of stiffness parameters corresponding to its respective floor frequencies.

The R set of data generated from the above method is fed into the Artificial Neural Network as constructed in section 18.3. Here, ANN is constructed with three layers—input, output, and one hidden layer. The input and output layers consist of n nodes according to n story of a building [17–19]. The number of nodes in the hidden layer depends on the accuracy of an ANN structure.

As shown in Figure 18.9, nodes in input, hidden, and outer layers are named in numerical values. The number of nodes in the input and outer layer is the same, corresponding to the number of floors. The weights between the input node i to hidden node j is named W_{ij}. Similarly, the weight from hidden node j to output node k is named V_{jk}. ANN's input and output always take a value between 0 and 1; thus, before feeding the generated data to ANN, the values of the frequency and stiffness parameter are normalized between [0,1]. The input layer is the normalized frequency λ_i and the output layer is the normalized stiffness parameter k_i.

Here, one point to be noted is that the input nodes are named in ascending order, and output nodes are the numbers in descending order from 9 to avoid duplication of weights.

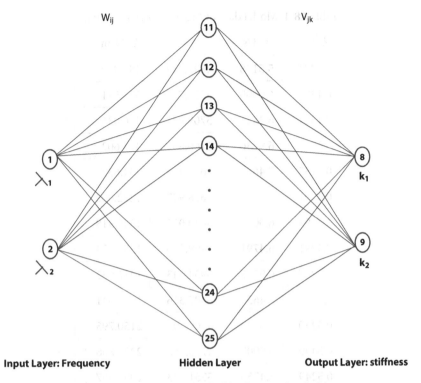

Figure 18.9 ANN structure for n-story building with 1 hidden layer and 15 hidden units.

18.5.4 Results and Discussion

The earlier procedure can be applied for any n-story building, but the procedure here is demonstrated for two-storied structures; hence, ANN is constructed as mentioned in Figure 18.9 with 15 hidden nodes. In this example, equal floor masses $M = 3600$ kg is taken for both the floors and column stiffness $k_1 = 7200$ N/m for the first floor and $k_2 = 10800$ N/m for the second floor. The analytic vibration characteristics from these prior mass and stiffness parameter can be found. Accordingly, analytical frequencies are found to be $\lambda_1 = 1.00s^{\{-1\}}$ and $\lambda_2 = 6.00s^{\{-1\}}$.

Using an above set of prior known information of parameters, different experimental data sets are generated and tabulated; the process of generating data sets are explained in [8]. Hence, the data generated from the above-mentioned article [8] are tabulated below (Table 18.4).

The updated values are fed into ANN, which is constructed using a backpropagation algorithm. After that, it is noted that the percentage difference between analytical stiffness and ANN stiffness is less than 0.4 percentage for floor 1 and 0.3 for floor 2. Figure 18.10, shows the value of the first floor's expected stiffness and ANN stiffness against the first floor's frequency, and Figure 18.11 shows the value of the second floor's expected stiffness and ANN stiffness against the second floor's frequency. Here, Figures 18.10 and 18.11 are obtained using MATLAB for error 0.001.

Table 18.4 Model data of the two-story building.

λ_1 1/s	λ_2 1/s	k_1 N/m	k_2 N/m
0.1321	5.5178	4841.012	487.959
0.1499	6.0000	5257.714	554.571
0.1321	6.4821	5709.841	486.036
0.1236	6.9736	6160.831	453.602
0.1187	7.4687	6611.433	434.632
0.3291	5.5208	4628.997	1272.002
0.3499	6.0000	5040.033	1349.918
0.3291	6.4791	5499.235	1256.534
0.3205	6.9705	5954.043	1216.032
0.3159	7.4659	6407.316	1192.641
0.5250	5.5249	4369.593	2150.795
0.5499	6.0000	4775.588	2238.806
0.5249	6.4750	5251.323	2097.357
0.5166	6.9666	5714.617	2040.763
0.5124	7.4625	6173.981	2007.039
0.7187	5.5312	4024.777	3200.435
0.7499	6.0000	4429.092	3291.807
0.7187	6.4687	4945.859	3045.787
0.7115	6.9615	5427.210	2957.127
0.7083	7.4583	5899.236	2901.532
0.9083	5.5416	3421.991	4766.002
0.9499	6.0000	3867.372	4775.244
0.9083	6.4583	4533.931	4192.136
0.9045	6.9545	5058.612	4029.139
0.9031	7.4531	5559.086	3923.082
1	6	3600	5400

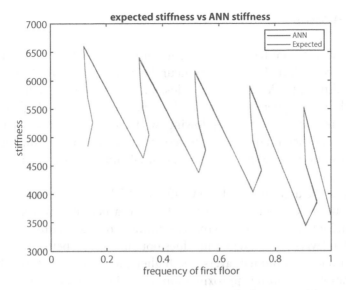

Figure 18.10 Value of ANN stiffness and expected stiffness against the frequency of the second floor.

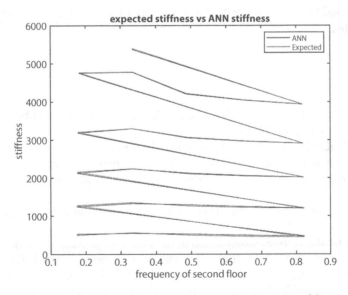

Figure 18.11 Value of ANN stiffness and expected stiffness against the frequency of the second floor.

18.6   Conclusion

In section 18.4, two methods have been presented for solving differential equations that rely on function approximation of feedforward neural network, and both the processes provide an accurate and differentiable solution in a closed analytical form. As discussed earlier, the second approach has a higher frequency, and the first approach has higher feasibility. The success of these methods is due to the following two factors. The first one is the employment of neural networks, which is an excellent function approximator, and the second is the formation of a trial solution $y_t(x, p)$ that satisfies initial and boundary conditions and which can be optimized.

This method can be used to solve both ODEs and PDEs by constructing the appropriate form of trial solution. Our study also suggested that a neural network with one hidden layer is optimum for performance with the least number of hidden units. However, a higher number of hidden layers and hidden units does not guarantee a better approximation [10]. The higher the nodes and hidden layers, the higher the parameter p will be, which may lead to complication and wrong approximation. Here, in both methods, we took one hidden layer with five hidden nodes, and it suggested that the architecture with fewer parameters and better error function will provide a reliable solution.

In section 18.5, our study shows that neural network architecture can be employed for all dynamic problems. From Figures 18.10 and 18.11, it is observed that the difference between ANN stiffness and analytical stiffness is quite close to each other for both floor frequency one and two. Therefore, the error between them will be definitely less. Hence, if we know the frequency of all n-floor, we can feed it into ANN to find the stiffness of all the floors. Thus, it can be used to predict the withstand capacity of a building before, after, and during natural calamities.

References

1. Rumelhart, D.E., Hinton, G.E., Williams, R.J., Learning representation by back-propagation errors. Letters to *Nature*, 323, 1986.
2. Bhadeshia, H.K.D.H., Neural network in material science. *ISIJ Int.*, 39, 10, 966–979, 1999.
3. Lagaris, I.E., Likas, A., Fotiadis, D.I., Artificial neural networks for solving ordinary and partial differential equations. *Inst. Electr. Electron. Eng. (IEEE) Trans. Neural Netw.*, 9, 5, 987–1000, 1997.
4. Lee, H. and Kang, I., Neural algorithm for solving differential equations. *J. Comput. Phys.*, Elseiver, 91, 110–117, 1990.
5. Mall, S. and Chakraverty, S., Comparison of Artificial Neural Network architecture in solving ordinary equations. 2013, 2013, Hindawi Publishing Corporation, Article ID 181895.
6. Sahoo, D.M., Das, A., Chakraverty, S., Interval data-based system identification multi-storey shear buildings by artificial neural network modelling. *Archit. Sci. Rev.*, 58, 3, 244–253, 2014.
7. Chakraverty, S., Identification of structural parameters of multi-storey shear building from model data. *Earthq. Eng. Struct. Dyn.*, 34, 543–554, 2004.
8. Chakraverty, S., Modelling for identification of stiffness parameter of multi-storey frame structure from dynamic data. *J. Sci. Int. Res.*, 63, 142–148, 2004.
9. Chakraverty, S., Identification of structural parameters of a two-storey shear building by the iterative training of neural network. *Archit. Sci. Rev.*, 50, 4, 380–384, 2007.

10. Vujicic, T., Matijevic, T., Ljucovic, J., Balota, A., Sevarac, Z., Comparative analysis of methods for determining the number of hidden neurons in an artificial neural network, in: *Central European Conference on Information and Intelligent Systems*, Faculty of Organization and Informatics Varazdin, p. 219, 2016.

11. Qin, S.-Z., Su, H.-T., Mcavoy, T.J., Comparison of four neural net learning method for dynamic system identification. *Inst. Electr. Electron. Eng. (IEEE) Trans. Neural Netw.*, 3, 1, 1992.

12. Fox, R.L. and Kapoor, M.P., Rates of change of eigenvalues and eigenvectors. *Am. Inst. Aeronaut. Astronaut. (AIAA)*, 6, 12, 2013.

13. Hang, C.S., Hung, S.L., Wen, C.M., Tu, T.T., A neural network approach for structural identification and diagnosis of a building from seismic response data. *Earthquake Eng. Struct. Dyn.*, 32, 182–206, 2003.

14. Vinayak, H.K., Kumar, A., Agarwal, P., Thakkar, S.K., NN based damage detection in multi-storey buildings from modal parameter changes. *ISET J. Earthq. Technol.*, Paper No. 519, 49, 1-2, 23–35, March-June 2012.

15. Khanmirza, E., Khaji, N., Majd, V.J., Model updating of multi-storey shear buildings for simultaneous identification of mass, stiffness, and damping matrices using two different soft computing methods. *Expert Syst. Appl.*, 38, 5320–5329, 2011, Elsevier Publications.

16. Collins, J.D. and Thomson, W.T., The eigenvalue problem for structural systems with statistical properties. *Am. Inst. Aeronaut. Astronaut. (AIAA)*, 7, 4, 2014.

17. Collins, J.D., Hart, G.C., Hasselman, T.K., Kennedy, B., Statistical identification of structures. *Am. Inst. Aeronaut. Astronaut. (AIAA)*, 12, 2, 2013.

18. Piscopo, M.L., Spannowsky, M., Waite, P., Solving a differential equation with neural networks: Application to the calculation of cosmological phase transitions. *Phys. Rev.*, 2019, ID: 100, 016002.

19. Sahoo, D.M. and Chakraverty, S., Interval response data-based system identification of multi-storey buildings using interval neural network modelling. *Comput.-Assist. Methods Eng. Sci.*, 21, 123–140, 20142014.

20. Nayak, S., *Fundamentals of optimization techniques with algorithms*, Academic Press, 2020.

21. Saha Ray, S. and Gupta, A.K., Wavelet Methods for Solving Partial Differential Equations and Fractional Differential Equations, CRC Press, Boca Raton, Florida, 2018.

19

GPT-3- and DALL-E-Powered Applications: A Complete Survey

**Kuldeep Vayadande[1]*, Chaitanya B. Pednekar[2], Priya Anup Khune[3],
Vinay Sudhir Prabhavalkar[2] and Varsha R. Dange[1]**

[1]Vishwakarma Institute of Technology, Pune , Maharashtra, India
[2]KIT's College of Engineering (Autonomous), Kolhapur, Maharashtra, India
[3]MIT Art, Design and Technology University, Pune, Maharashtra, India

Abstract

In the new millennium, the advancement of language and image processing technologies has witnessed remarkable progress, and various applications have demonstrated promising results by utilizing sophisticated models such as GPT-3 and DALL-E. This survey paper presents an overview of the recent research and development in GPT-3- and DALL-E-powered applications. The paper first provides a brief introduction to GPT-3 and DALL-E and their capabilities in language and image processing by Artificial Intelligence. It then explores various applications of GPT-3, such as natural language processing, chatbots, question-answering systems, and text generation. The paper highlights the significant impact of GPT-3 in these applications and discusses various challenges that need to be addressed in the future. Next, the paper focuses on DALL-E and its applications in image generation, 3D rendering, and graphics design. The paper highlights how DALL-E has revolutionized the field of computer vision and the impact it has made in the creative industry. The paper also discusses several hybrid models that incorporate both GPT-3 and DALL-E, such as those that generate text and images based on a given prompt. Additionally, the paper discusses ethical considerations related to these advanced models, such as potential biases and misuse of the technology. Finally, the paper concludes by summarizing the current state of research in GPT-3- and DALL-E-powered applications and highlighting future research directions. This survey paper serves as a valuable resource for researchers, developers, and practitioners interested in the latest advancements in language and image processing by Artificial Intelligence and Data Science.

Keywords: Artificial intelligence, image processing, generative pretrained transformer–3 (GPT-3), natural language processing, DALL-E, deep learning

19.1 Introduction

The development of advanced models like GPT-3 and DALL-E has revolutionized the way we approach these two fields. GPT-3 is a versatile language processing model that can perform a diverse range of tasks, including natural language processing, chatbots, question-answering systems, and text generation, while DALL-E, an image processing model, is

---

*Corresponding author: kuldeep.vayadande@gmail.com

Arindam Dey, Sukanta Nayak, Ranjan Kumar and Sachi Nandan Mohanty (eds.) How Machine Learning is Innovating Today's World: A Concise Technical Guide, (329–342) © 2024 Scrivener Publishing LLC

capable of generating images from textual prompts [1, 2]. These models have shown promising results in various applications and have been employed in a wide range of software applications. The objective of this survey paper is to offer an all-encompassing review of the latest research and advancements in applications empowered by GPT-3 and DALL-E. The paper will discuss the capabilities of these models and their impact on various fields. Additionally, the paper will explore the challenges associated with these models and discuss future research directions. The first part of the paper will introduce GPT-3 and DALL-E, discussing their capabilities and limitations.

Being a large-scale language model, GPT-3 can comprehend and create natural language with proficiency. Trained on an enormous text dataset, it has the ability to execute various language processing tasks like language translation, summarization, and sentiment analysis. Additionally, GPT-3 is capable of generating human-like text, which can be used in applications such as chatbots and automated content generation [3]. DALL-E, on the other hand, is a neural network-based image generation model. It can generate high-quality images from textual prompts, allowing users to create a wide range of images with just a few words [4]. This technology has significant applications in the creative industry, such as in graphics design, advertising, and entertainment.

The second part of the paper will focus on the various applications of GPT-3, such as natural language processing, chatbots, question-answering systems, and text generation. Natural language processing is an essential task in the field of AI, and GPT-3 has made significant advancements in this area. Being capable of comprehending and responding to natural language, it proves to be a perfect tool for chatbots and virtual assistants. Additionally, GPT-3 can generate high-quality text, making it a valuable tool in the content creation industry. The paper will also explore the ethical considerations associated with GPT-3 and the potential biases that can arise in its applications. GPT-3 has significant potential, but its use must be guided by ethical considerations to prevent misuse and unintended consequences.

The next part of the paper will focus on the applications of DALL-E in image processing. DALL-E can generate images based on textual prompts, allowing users to create a wide range of images quickly and efficiently. This technology has significant applications in the creative industry, such as in graphics design, advertising, and entertainment. Additionally, DALL-E can generate 3D models, opening up new possibilities for computer vision applications. The paper will also explore the challenges associated with DALL-E, such as the complexity of its training data and the need for large amounts of computing power. Additionally, the paper will discuss the ethical considerations associated with DALL-E and the potential for biases in its applications.

After that, we will focus on hybrid models that incorporate both GPT-3 and DALL-E. These models can generate text and images based on a given prompt, opening up new possibilities for creative content generation. The paper will discuss the various applications of these models and the challenges associated with their development.

Finally, the paper will conclude by summarizing the current state of research in GPT-3 and DALL-E powered applications and discussing future research directions. The paper will highlight the potential for these models to make significant advancements in language and image processing and their impact on various industries. This conclusion will also discuss the challenges that must be addressed, such as the ethical considerations associated with these models, the potential biases in their applications, and the need for large amounts of computing power to train them.

In conclusion, the development of GPT-3 and DALL-E has significantly advanced the fields of language and image processing. These models have shown promising results in various applications and have been employed in a wide range of software applications. However, their development also poses significant challenges that must be addressed, such as the ethical considerations associated with their applications, the potential biases that can arise, and the need for large amounts of computing power to train them.

This paper highlights the various applications of these models and the challenges associated with their development. Additionally, the paper discusses future research directions and the potential for these models to make significant advancements in language and image processing, as well as their impact on various industries. In general, this survey paper acts as a precious source of information for researchers and practitioners seeking to remain updated with the recent advancements in applications energized by GPT-3 and DALL-E.

19.2   Understanding GPT-3

This section discusses the basic working behind GPT-3 and DALL-E and will understand how they have brought up such revolution in the field of Artificial Intelligence.

Developed by OpenAI, Generative Pre-trained Transformer (GPT) is a type of language processing model. With a pre-training on vast amounts of text datasets, it is a large-scale neural network capable of executing a broad spectrum of language processing tasks, which include language translation, summarization, and sentiment analysis [5]. Furthermore, GPT can produce text that resembles human writing, making it a valuable tool in applications such as chatbots and automated content generation. The development of GPT is significant because it represents a significant advancement in the domain of NLP (Natural Language Processing). Previous language processing models were limited in their ability to understand and generate natural language, and required significant amounts of human input and training to perform their tasks. In contrast, GPT has been pre-trained on enormous volumes of text data, enabling it to comprehend and create language with minimal human involvement. GPT has a distinctive capability of generating text from a given prompt. This is accomplished by a technique known as language modeling, as demonstrated in Figure 19.1. Here, the model is trained to anticipate the probability of a specific word or phrase based on the preceding words in the text. This allows GPT to generate high-quality, human-like text that is indistinguishable from text written by humans. GPT is also designed to be a flexible and adaptable language processing model. Customization of GPT for specific tasks enables it to execute a diverse set of language processing tasks with exceptional precision.

For example, GPT can be fine-tuned to perform sentiment analysis on social media data or to generate high-quality product descriptions for e-commerce websites.

There are currently several versions of the GPT model, each building on the success of its predecessor and introducing new features and improvements.

GPT-3
In 2020, GPT-3 emerged as the most advanced and largest version of the GPT model, boasting an impressive 175 billion parameters. It was trained on a vast corpus of text data, which included the entire internet, enabling it to carry out diverse natural language processing tasks. GPT-3 exhibits exceptional ability to produce contextually relevant and coherent

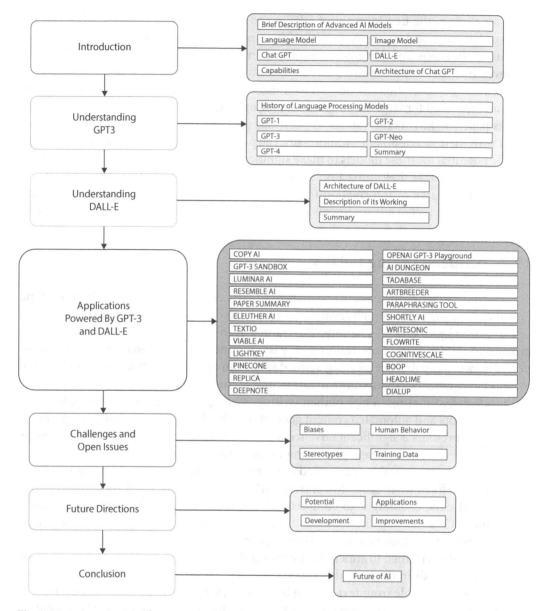

Figure 19.1 Organization of paper.

text, as well as performing several language processing tasks like summarization, translation, and question-answering. Moreover, it can generate intricate text like poetry and code. Additionally, it can generate highly complex text such as code and poetry.

The various versions of GPT represent significant advancements in the field of natural language processing. Each version has introduced new features and improvements, making them increasingly powerful and flexible. While GPT-3 is currently the most advanced and capable version, there is potential for future versions of the model to address some of the limitations and challenges associated with current models, opening up new possibilities for language processing applications.

In summary, GPT is a language processing model that has been trained on large volumes of text and can accomplish a broad array of language processing tasks. Its capability to produce text that is similar to human-like language makes it a useful tool in applications such as chatbots and automated content creation, and its adaptability and versatility make it a powerful tool for many language processing tasks. The creation of GPT signifies a significant breakthrough in the natural language processing field and holds substantial potential for further research and advancement.

19.3 Understanding DALL-E

OpenAI has created an image generation model called DALL-E, which can produce high-quality images based on textual descriptions [7]. It works by first encoding the textual input into a numerical representation using a transformer-based model, similar to GPT. This numerical representation is then used to generate a 2D grid of "tokens," each representing a small image patch. DALL-E then generates these image patches, one at a time, by feeding the numerical representation and previous patches through a generator network. This generator network uses a series of convolutional layers to generate the images, gradually building up the details and complexity of the image as more patches are added. As shown Figure 19.2, the generator is trained using a variant of the Generative Adversarial Network (GAN) architecture, which pits a generator network against a discriminator network that is trained to distinguish between real and fake images.

DALL-E generates images by following a step-by-step process after being fed with a textual description of the desired image, such as "an avocado-shaped armchair." The model generates each image patch in sequence, which gradually builds up to the final image. The final image is a composition of these image patches, and is designed to match the textual

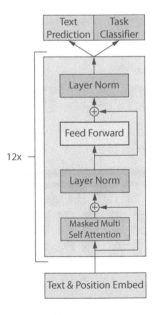

Figure 19.2 Architecture of GPT [13].

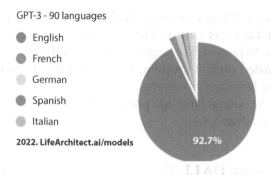

Figure 19.3 GPT-3 language capabilities [12].

description provided to the model. DALL-E's distinctive attribute is its capacity to create imaginative and innovative images that extend beyond the literal meaning of the textual input. This is made feasible by utilizing a "latent space," which is a continuous vector space containing all potential image representations. By adjusting the values within this latent space, DALL-E can generate a vast array of diverse and innovative images that go beyond the explicit textual input. Figure 19.3 shows GPT-3 language capabilities.

19.4 Applications Powered By GPT-3 and DALL-E

In this section, 30 different applications powered by GPT-3 and DALL-E are discussed here. Their functionalities, use, working, advantages, disadvantages and future scope are discussed in brief. Figure 19.4 a shows comparison of training datasets between different GPT models, Figure 19.4 b shows visual summary of major dataset sizes. Unweighted sizes, in GB and Figure 19.5 shows architecture of DALL E.

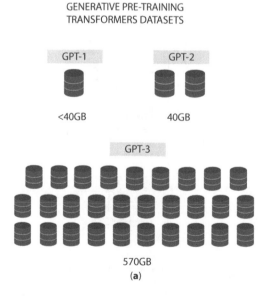

Figure 19.4 (a) Comparison of training datasets between different GPT models [13]. *(Continued)*

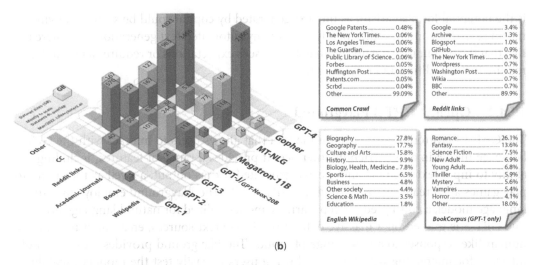

Common Crawl		Reddit links	
Google Patents	0.48%	Google	3.4%
The New York Times	0.06%	Archive	1.3%
Los Angeles Times	0.06%	Blogspot	1.0%
The Guardian	0.06%	GitHub	0.9%
Public Library of Science	0.06%	The New York Times	0.7%
Forbes	0.05%	Wordpress	0.7%
Huffington Post	0.05%	Washington Post	0.7%
Patents.com	0.05%	Wikia	0.7%
Scrbd	0.04%	BBC	0.7%
Other	99.09%	Other	89.9%

English Wikipedia		BookCorpus (GPT-1 only)	
Biography	27.8%	Romance	26.1%
Geography	17.7%	Fantasy	13.6%
Culture and Arts	15.8%	Science Fiction	7.5%
History	9.9%	New Adult	6.9%
Biology, Health, Medicine	7.8%	Young Adult	6.8%
Sports	6.5%	Thriller	5.9%
Business	4.8%	Mystery	5.6%
Other society	4.4%	Vampires	5.4%
Science & Math	3.5%	Horror	4.1%
Education	1.8%	Other	18.0%

(b)

Figure 19.4 (Continued) (b) Visual summary of major dataset sizes. Unweighted sizes, in GB [12].

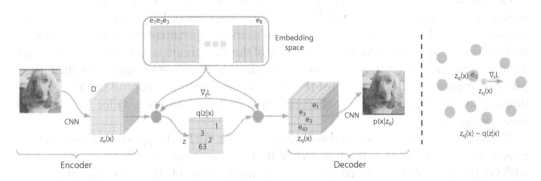

Figure 19.5 Architecture of DALL-E [14].

19.4.1   Copy.ai

Copy.ai is a language processing tool that uses GPT-3 to generate natural language text for various purposes, such as writing ad copy, social media posts, and product descriptions [9]. It is engineered to be user-friendly, requiring little to no technical expertise, and provides users with a simple interface to generate text that matches their desired style, tone, and content. Copy.ai works by providing users with a text prompt, which can be anything from a single word to a longer description of what they want to generate. The model then uses GPT-3 to generate a range of text options, which can be edited and refined by the user to ensure that they match their intended output.

The advantages of using copy.ai include its ease of use, its ability to generate high-quality, coherent text that matches the desired tone and style, and its ability to save time and resources by automating the process of writing text. Additionally, the use of GPT-3 ensures that the text generated is of a high quality, with a high degree of coherence and context sensitivity. However, there are also some potential disadvantages to using copy.ai. One of the main concerns is the potential for bias in the text generated by the model, as GPT-3 has been shown to exhibit bias based on the data it was trained on. Another concern is the potential for plagiarism, as the text generated by copy.ai could be seen as copying or reusing existing content. Additionally, as with any automated text generation tool, there is a risk that the output may not always match the user's expectations or requirements, and may require further editing and refinement.

19.4.2   OpenAI GPT-3 Playground

The GPT-3 Playground [10] is an online tool that allows users to interact with the GPT-3 language model in a user-friendly interface. It provides a range of features, including the ability to input text prompts and receive generated text as output, as well as the ability to play games and create chatbots using the GPT-3 API. The Playground employs the GPT-3 language model, a cutting-edge deep learning model utilized for natural language processing. GPT-3 is trained on a massive dataset of diverse text sources, enabling it to generate human-like responses to a wide range of inputs. The Playground provides a user-friendly interface for interacting with GPT-3, allowing users to easily test the model's capabilities and generate text outputs.

One advantage of the GPT-3 Playground is its accessibility. The tool is available online, which means that users do not need to install any software or have specialized hardware to use it. This makes it easier for non-technical users to experiment with the GPT-3 model and explore its capabilities. Another advantage of the Playground is its flexibility. It provides a range of features and settings that users can adjust to fine-tune the output of the GPT-3 model. For example, users can adjust the "temperature" setting to control the level of randomness in the generated text, or they can input custom prompts to tailor the output to their specific needs.

However, there are also some disadvantages to the GPT-3 Playground. One potential issue is the limited scope of the tool. While it provides a range of features for interacting with GPT-3, it is still a simplified interface and may not provide the same level of customization and control as other tools that are designed specifically for deep learning applications. Another potential disadvantage is the cost. While the Playground itself is free to use, accessing the GPT-3 API for more advanced applications requires a paid subscription. This may make it less accessible for some users who do not have the financial resources to pay for the API.

19.4.3   GPT-3 Sandbox

GPT-3 Sandbox is a platform provided by OpenAI that allows developers and users to interact with the GPT-3 model and explore its capabilities. It provides a web-based interface that allows users to test the GPT-3 API without needing to set up their own infrastructure or pay for access to the full GPT-3 API. The Sandbox provides users with a limited amount of free access to the GPT-3 API, which allows them to experiment with various use cases and applications. The Sandbox allows users to interact with the GPT-3 API using a variety of different modes, including completion, classification, and question-answering modes. Completion mode allows users to input a prompt, such as a sentence or paragraph, and have GPT-3 generate a continuation of that prompt. Classification mode allows users to input a piece of text and have GPT-3 classify it into a predefined set of categories. Question-answering mode allows users to input a question and have GPT-3 generate an answer.

One advantage of the GPT-3 Sandbox is that it allows users to experiment with the GPT-3 API without needing to set up their own infrastructure or pay for access to the full API. This makes it easier for developers and users to explore the capabilities of GPT-3 and to experiment with various use cases and applications. The Sandbox also provides a user-friendly web-based interface that makes it easy for users to interact with the GPT-3 API and to test various modes and settings. One disadvantage of the GPT-3 Sandbox is that it provides users with only limited access to the GPT-3 API, which can restrict the types of applications and use cases that can be tested. The Sandbox also does not provide users with full access to the GPT-3 model, which can limit the accuracy and quality of the outputs generated by the model. Additionally, the Sandbox is not suitable for high-volume or commercial applications, as it provides only limited access to the GPT-3 API and is not intended for production use.

19.4.4   AI Dungeon

AI Dungeon [11] is an online game where players participate in a text-based adventure, and the GPT-3 language model generates responses to provide an interactive storytelling experience. By typing in commands and descriptions, players can explore and interact with a virtual world, with the GPT-3 model interpreting the input to generate a response. The game world and story evolve in real time based on the player's choices and actions, providing a highly immersive and engaging experience. AI Dungeon uses the GPT-3 language model to generate responses to the player's input. The model undergoes pre-training on a vast amount of text data and can generate highly coherent and contextually relevant text. When a player inputs a command or description, the GPT-3 model generates a response based on the input and the context of the game world. The response can be anything from a simple description of the surroundings to a complex narrative that drives the story forward.

The advantages of using AI Dungeon with GPT-3 are numerous. The GPT-3 model allows for highly immersive and engaging gameplay, as it is capable of generating highly coherent and contextually relevant responses. The game can generate a virtually infinite number of storylines and scenarios, providing players with a highly replayable experience. Additionally, AI Dungeon can be played in a variety of genres, from fantasy to sci-fi, and can cater to a wide range of player preferences. However, there are also some disadvantages to using AI Dungeon with GPT-3. Figure 19.6 shows AI dungeon.

Figure 19.6 AI dungeon [11].

19.5   Challenges and Open Issues

The GPT-3 language generation model developed by OpenAI has gained widespread recognition and acclaim in the AI community for its incredible capabilities. Despite some initial skepticism about its potential, the strength and versatility of GPT-3 are undeniable. One of the most impressive features of this model is its ability to generate high-quality content with just a few carefully constructed examples as input. Early adopters of the GPT-3 API have showcased its potential in a variety of applications, from translating natural language into code for websites to resolving complex medical question-and-answer scenarios. In addition, this model can even produce simple tabular financial reports and write code to train machine learning models. These examples are just the tip of the iceberg when it comes to the potential applications of GPT-3. As developers and businesses continue to explore its capabilities, it is clear that this language generation model has the power to transform industries and revolutionize the way we approach complex tasks.

Language models such as GPT-3 utilize sophisticated algorithms to predict the most probable sequence of words or phrases that are likely to follow a given input. GPT-3 is capable of learning and generating text that closely resembles human writing style, encompassing both positive and negative aspects of human language. During training, the model is exposed to a vast amount of text data, primarily produced by humans, which allows it to learn and replicate the intricacies of human language. However, the researchers studying GPT-3 have discovered that it suffers from issue bias, which is reflected in the hidden material found in the manuscript. This bias is an inevitable consequence of training a model on unfiltered data from the internet. The results can be concerning, as the model may generate biased or discriminatory text, perpetuating harmful stereotypes or ideologies. Therefore, it is essential to monitor and regulate the use of language models like GPT-3 to ensure that they do not propagate harmful content.

The researchers have pointed out that GPT-3 tends to associate certain terms with specific gender, racial, and religious groups due to the overwhelming amount of biased content online. Female pronouns are often associated with terms like "naughty" or "sucked," while male pronouns are linked with stereotypical descriptors such as "lazy" or "jolly". Similarly, religion-related terms like "Islam" are more frequently associated with negative terms like "terrorist," while "Atheism" tends to result in literature using terms like "cool" or "right." Moreover, the model's output when it comes to text seeds with racial content regarding Blackness tends to be more negative compared to equivalent prompts involving white or Asian-sounding names. This particular bias can have a significant impact, as it reinforces harmful stereotypes and can potentially cause real-world harm [8]. It is worth noting that these biases are not unique to GPT-3 and exist in many language models due to the data they are trained on. It is, therefore, essential to carefully monitor and address these biases in language models to ensure that they do not perpetuate harmful stereotypes and biases in society.

It did not take long for some users to start reporting what they perceived as biases, as is common with many AI algorithms. OpenAI utilized the example caption "a builder," which resulted in images that only showed men, as opposed to the caption "a flight attendant," which resulted in images that only showed women. Before accusations of prejudice surfaced, OpenAI released a document titled "Risks and Limits" that noted certain biases

Table 19.1 ChatGPT vs. others [6].

Model	OpenAI's ChatGPT	Google's BERT	Facebook's RoBERTa
Developer	OpenAI	Google	Facebook
Architecture	Transformer	Transformer	Transformer
Pre-training	Large-scale	Large-scale	Large-scale
Parameters	1.5B	340M	355M
Release Date	2020	2018	2019
Training Data	Various sources	Various sources	Various sources
Inference Time	~3 seconds	~2 seconds	~2 seconds
Applications	Chatbot, text generation, Q&A, summarization, language translation	Q&A, language translation, sentiment analysis	Q&A, text classification, language modeling

Table 19.2 ChatGPT Vs. Others performance comparison [6].

Model	GLUE score	SuperGLUE score	SQuAD score	CoQA score
OpenAI's ChatGPT	89.4	89.4	91.2	79.6
Google's BERT	88.4	87.4	90.9	80.8
Facebook's RoBERTa	90.7	89.8	93.2	85.3

and stated that DALL-E 2 further inherits numerous biases from its training data, and its outputs occasionally reinforce existing stereotypes. Table 19.1 shows ChatGPT vs Others and Table 19.2 ChatGPT Vs. Others performance comparison.

19.6 Future Directions

The future directions of GPT and DALL-E are exciting and hold the potential for transformative advancements in language understanding and image generation. As the field of artificial intelligence continues to evolve, these models are expected to play an increasingly important role in a wide range of applications, from chatbots and personal assistants to video game development and content creation. Figure 19.7 shows Perplexity and BLEU score of different text generation models.

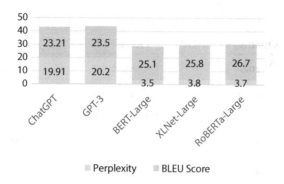

Figure 19.7 Perplexity and BLEU score of different text generation models.

One key area of focus for GPT is likely to be the development of more sophisticated language models. The most recent iteration of GPT, GPT-3, contains a staggering 175 billion parameters, allowing it to generate highly realistic and human-like text. However, there is still much room for improvement, particularly in terms of understanding context and nuance. In the future, we can expect to see efforts to fine-tune GPT for specific use cases, such as medical diagnosis or customer service, as well as the development of larger and more complex models that can achieve even higher levels of language understanding.

Another important area of development for GPT is the ability to engage in natural and fluent conversation. While GPT is capable of generating highly realistic text, it still struggles to maintain coherence and coherence over extended conversations. In the future, researchers and developers will likely focus on addressing this limitation, potentially through the use of reinforcement learning or other techniques. This could lead to the creation of AI chatbots and virtual assistants that are indistinguishable from human counterparts, with the ability to understand and respond to complex queries and carry out tasks with minimal user input.

As for DALL-E, the future is likely to involve expanding its range of outputs beyond images to include other forms of media, such as video or audio. This could have important implications for fields such as film and television production, where the ability to generate highly realistic and complex visuals and sounds is crucial. In addition, there may be efforts to improve the speed and efficiency of DALL-E, potentially through the use of more powerful hardware or new training techniques.

Another area of development for DALL-E is the ability to generate more sophisticated and nuanced images. In the future, we can expect to see efforts to address these limitations, potentially through the use of more advanced algorithms or the incorporation of additional data sources.

Overall, the future of GPT and DALL-E is full of possibilities and potential for groundbreaking advancements in artificial intelligence. While there are certainly challenges and limitations to be addressed, the ongoing research and development in these fields is sure to yield exciting and transformative results in the years to come.

19.7 Conclusion

In conclusion, GPT-3 and DALL-E are powerful tools that have opened up a wide range of possibilities for various applications across industries. The natural language generation and image generation capabilities of these models have demonstrated remarkable potential in areas such as marketing, customer service, education, healthcare, and more. However, as with any new technology, there are also concerns about biases, ethical considerations, and potential misuse. As researchers and practitioners continue to explore the capabilities and limitations of these models, it will be crucial to address these issues and ensure that the benefits of these technologies are accessible and equitable for all. Overall, the future looks bright for GPT-3- and DALL-E-powered applications, and we can expect to see even more innovative and creative uses of these models in the years to come.

References

1. GPT-3 powers the next generation of apps. [Online] Available: https://openai.com/blog/gpt-3-apps/.
2. DALL·E 2 is a new AI system that can create realistic images and art from a description in natural language. [Online] Available: https://openai.com/dall-e/.
3. Liu, X., Zheng, Y., Du, Z., Ding, M., Qian, Y., Yang, Z., Tang, J., GPT understands, too.
4. Marcus, G., Davis, E., Aaronson, S., A very preliminary analysis of DALL-E 2.
5. Zong, M. and Krishnamachari, B., A survey on GPT-3, 2022.
6. Katar, O., Ozkan, D., GPT, Yildirim, Ö., Acharya, U.R., Evaluation of GPT-3 AI language model in research paper writing, 2022.
7. The ethical implications of DALL-E: Opportunities and challenges. *Mesop. J. Comput. Sci.*, 17–23, 2023.
8. Sharma, A., Devalia, D., Almeida, W., Patil, H., Mishra, A., Statistical data analysis using GPT3: An overview, pp. 1–6, 2022.
9. Copy.ai, [Online] Available: www.copy.ai.
10. GPT-3 PlayGround. [Online] Available: https://platform.openai.com/playground.
11. AI Dungeon, [Online] Available: https://play.aidungeon.io/.
12. https://lifearchitect.ai/models/.
13. https://pbs.twimg.com/media/FmV4tU3WYAAZzRi?format=jpg&name=900x900.
14. Perez, L., Ottens, L., Viswanathan, S., Automatic code generation using pre-trained language models, 2021.

20

New Variation of Exam Scheduling Problem Using Graph Coloring

Angshu Kumar Sinha[1]*, **Soumyadip Laha**[2], **Debarghya Adhikari**[3], **Anjan Koner**[4] and **Neha Deora**[3]

[1]Department of Mathematics, NSHM Knowledge Campus, Durgapur, West Bengal, India
[2]B.Tech, Data Science, NSHM Knowledge Campus, Durgapur, West Bengal, India
[3]B.Tech, Computer Science, NSHM Knowledge Campus, Durgapur, West Bengal, India
[4]B.Tech, AI ML, NSHM Knowledge Campus, Durgapur, West Bengal, India

Abstract

In an academic institute, the academic calendar is one of the most important parts. The academic calendar is used to schedule all the events that occur in an academic year. In an academic year, there are various events such as semester starting date, course lesson plan, slot test, spring break or reading week, exam timetable, and the last day of the semester. An academic calendar has two important parts: (a) course timetable and (b) the exam schedule. The course timetable and the exam schedule both need a combination of resources like teachers, subjects, students, and classroom. In this study, we developed an algorithm for the new variation of exam schedule using graph coloring. In this algorithm, our aim was to use minimum resources in such a way to avoid conflicts by satisfying various necessary and priority limitations.

Keywords: Exam schedule problem, graph coloring, design of algorithms

20.1 Introduction

Graph theory originated from the famous Konigsberg seven-bridge problem solved by the famous mathematician Leonhard Euler in the 1736 [1]. Mathematical structures known as graphs are used to model pairwise relationships between objects. Graph theory is the study of these mathematical structures. A graph $G(V, E)$ has two sets, the set of vertices V and the set of edges E. Two vertices v_i and v_j are joined by an edge $e_{i,j}$. A graph is said to be directed when its edges have a particular direction; otherwise, it is said to be undirected. A simple graph is one in which there is just one edge connecting each pair of vertices. However, if the vertices are joined by more than one edge, then the graph is multigraph.

Corresponding author: angshusinha@gmail.com

Arindam Dey, Sukanta Nayak, Ranjan Kumar and Sachi Nandan Mohanty (eds.) How Machine Learning is Innovating Today's World: A Concise Technical Guide, (343–352) © 2024 Scrivener Publishing LLC

There are three different ways of graph coloring in graph theory:

i)   Vertex coloring: Two adjacent vertices receive different colors.
ii) Edge coloring: Two adjacent edges receive different colors.
iii) Total coloring: if a vertex v and an edge e are incident on each other, v and e receive separate colors.

The condition for proper coloring of graph is that two vertices that share a common edge should not have the same color. If it uses k colors in the process, then it is called k coloring of graph. The chromatic number of graphs, which is represented by the symbol $\chi(G)$, is the bare minimum of colors required for a graph to be properly colored. In this study, we consider a simple, connected, and undirected graphs.

20.1.1   Review of Previous Work

The first results concerning the colorization of the graphs involve the planar graphs in the form of the colorization of the maps. Francis Guthrie [2] proposed the four-color postulate in 1854, arguing that it took four regions to color a map so that no two parts with the same boundary would have the same color. The same year, Alfred Kempe established the claim of four-color theorem [3]. Every planar map can only be colored with a maximum of five colors, contrary to the Kempe reasoning of the four-color theorem, according to Heawood's [4] introduction of the five-color theorem in 1890. Finally, in 1977, Kenneth Appel and Wolfgang Haken [5] proved the four- color theorem.

In 1912, George David Birkhoff [6] studied the chromatic polynomial of a graph, which was generalized to the Tutte polynomial [7], involving important structures for graph coloring inalgebraic graph theory.

The chromatic number of a graph $G(V, E)$ is the lowest number of colors required to color the Graph G so that two adjacent vertices share the same color (Skiena 1990, p. 210) [9], i.e., the smallest value of k possible to obtain a k-coloring. The value of the chromatic number $\chi(G) = k$. Karp [8] designed an NP complete problem to find the chromatic number of a graph. Numerous studies have considered the problem of exam scheduling [10–13]. The main difference between various studies is the set of assumptions and constraints taken into consideration. Burke, Elliman, and Weare [10], for example, followed a similar approach using graph coloring. However, in their algorithm, they addressed only the conflicts without any constraints. Moreover, the algorithm presented in [10] does not eliminate conflicts, and only aims at minimizing conflicts.

20.1.2   Application

The graph coloring problem has a huge number of applications such as Making Schedule or Timetable, Mobile Radio Frequency Assignment, Sudoku, Register Allocation, Map Coloring, real-world applications in computer science and electronics and communications, Internet of Things (IoT), and other modern sciences. There are many modern computing research fields that use graph coloring, including data mining, picture segmentation, grouping, image capture, networking, etc.

20.1.3 Main Result

Our goal in this study is to develop an algorithm for scheduling exams so that different subjects with the same students do not create any conflicts. Here, we consider a graph where each vertex represents a subject and the edge between two vertices is drawn if there is a common student. We have designed this algorithm in such a way that adjacent vertices are assigned different colors. This algorithm's primary goal is to color the graphs properly using the fewest possible colors. Each color represents a "day of examination". The scheduling of the examination corresponds to a coloring of the conflict graphs using minimum number of colors. A conflict exists if two students share a common subject. Another one is the non-conflicting graph, where the edges are drawn in a mutually exclusive course that does not match any student. Sometimes, it is seen that non-conflicting graphs from given input sets and limitations make it easier to spend less time.

20.1.4 Organization of the Paper

The paper is structured as follows. The notations and definitions used throughout the study are introduced in Section 20.2 of the rest of the paper. We go into great detail regarding the algorithm in Section 20.3. There is a Section 20.4 called time complexity. Several concluded comments are included in Section 20.5, and acknowledgments are included in Section 20.6.

20.2 Notations and Preliminaries

A simple connected graph with vertex set V and edge set E is defined as $G = (V, E)$. Consider the function $f : V \rightarrow \{color1, color2, color3, ..., \}$ such that the two vertices v_i and v_j are adjacent if $f(v_i) \neq f(v_j)$ or if $f(v_i) = f(v_j)$ then the vertices v_i and v_j are nonadjacent vertices.

The minimum number of color required to coloring the graph is called chromatic number of the graph and is denoted by $\chi(G)$.

20.3 Description of Algorithm

The main goal of the suggested technique is to determine the Chromatic Number of the given conflict graphs using the fewest possible colors, ensuring that every pair of neighboring vertices has a different color. To make the school/college/university exam routine, the algorithms work on the basis of the subjects having common students having different exam dates. Here, the minimum number of color use is equal to the number of exam date required to conduct the exam.

20.3.1 The Algorithm

A formal description of the algorithm is given below.

Algorithm New Variation of Exam Scheduling Problem using Graph Coloring (NVESP)
Input: Conflict graph $G(V, E)$
Output: Chromatic number of graph $\chi(G)$ denotes a set of different colors.
Step 1: Compute the degree sequence of the graph G.
Step 2: Select the vertex of minimum degree v_i
>   If the minimum degree vertex has more than one, then select one of them, v_i
>   (*say*).

Step 3: Assign the 1st color to the minimum degree vertex v_i.
Step 4: Assign different colors to the vertex adjacent to the vertices v_i.
Step 5: Check whether any two adjacent vertices have same colors.
>   If yes, then use different colors to the adjacent vertex of v_i, which is not used
>   yet; otherwise, go to the next step.

Step 6: Select next minimum degree vertex v_j (*say*), which is not yet colored.
Step 7: Assign the 1st color to the vertex v_j.
Step 8: If any two adjacent vertices v_l and v_k have the same color and
>   If all the adjacent vertices of v_l and v_k are a assigned different color,
>   then assign a different color to the vertex v_l and v_k
>   Else go to step 9.

Step 9:   Repeat step 2 to step 5 until all vertices are colored.
Step 10: Chromatic number $\chi(G)$ indicates the minimum number of different color uses.

20.3.2   Illustration of the Algorithm

20.3.2.1   *Problem of Scheduling the Examination*

Consider in one particular semester that there are students taking each of the following combinations of subjects:

In this problem (Table 20.1), our aim is to find the minimum number of examination days for scheduling the examination in the 11 subjects so that students taking any of the given combination of the subjects have no conflict. Also, find a possible schedule that uses a minimum number of days.

Solution: Draw the graph (Figure 20.1) with 11 vertices where each vertex represents a subject and join the vertices by an edge if there is a common student in the subjects they represent. According to the algorithm i.e., Pyhton (Figure 20.2.), C++ (Figures 20.3.1–20.3.2) and C (Figures 20.4.1–20.4.2), the exam schedule must occur within 5 days.

Table 20.1 Combinations of subjects.

Sub. 1	Sub. 2	Sub. 3	Sub. 4	Sub. 5
Mathematics	Computer Science	Bio-science	Chemistry	French
English	Mechanics	----	----	Spanish
Physics	Mechanics	Auto-Cad	----	----
Mathematics	Computer Science	Auto-Cad	Engineering Drawing	French
Physics	Computer Science	Bio-science	Chemistry	Spanish

---- means No subject choice and it signifies that there is no missing data

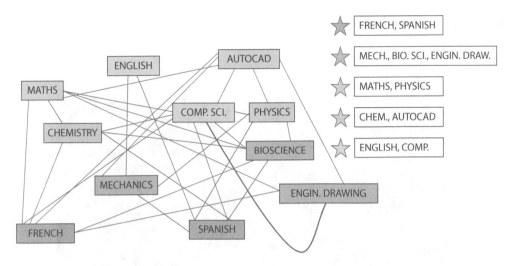

Figure 20.1 Exam schedule using graph coloring algorithm.

Day 1: French, Spanish. Day 2: Mechanics, Bio-science, Engineering Drawing. Day 3: Mathematics, Physics. Day 4: Chemistry, Auto-Cad. Day 5: English, Computer Science.

20.3.3   Algorithm in Python

```python
class Graph():

    def __init__(self, vertices):
        self.V = vertices
        self.graph = [[0 for column in range(vertices)]\
                      for row in range(vertices)]
    def isSafe(self, v, colour, c):
        for i in range(self.V):
            if self.graph[v][i] == 1 and colour[i] == c:
                return False
        return True
    def graphColourUtil(self, m, colour, v):
        if v == self.V:
            return True

        for c in range(1, m + 1):
            if self.isSafe(v, colour, c) == True:
                colour[v] = c
                if self.graphColourUtil(m, colour, v + 1) == True:
                    return True
                colour[v] = 0

    def graphColouring(self, m):
        colour = [0] * self.V
        if self.graphColourUtil(m, colour, 0) == None:
            return False

        print ("Solution exist and Following are the assigned colours:")
        for c in colour:
            print (c,end=' ')
        return True

g = Graph(4)
g.graph = [[0, 1, 1, 1], [1, 0, 1, 0], [1, 1, 0, 1], [1, 0, 1, 0]]
print(g.graph)
m = 4
g.graphColouring(m)
```

Figure 20.2 Algorithm in Python.

20.3.4　Algorithm in C++

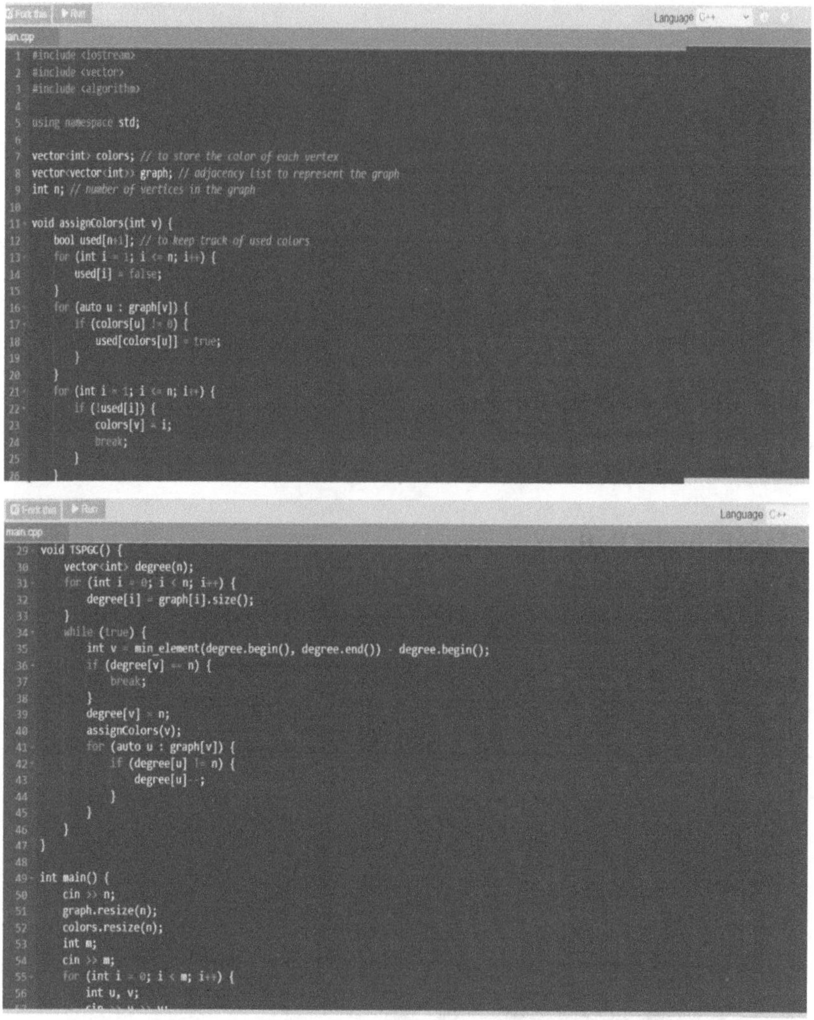

```cpp
#include <iostream>
#include <vector>
#include <algorithm>

using namespace std;

vector<int> colors; // to store the color of each vertex
vector<vector<int>> graph; // adjacency list to represent the graph
int n; // number of vertices in the graph

void assignColors(int v) {
    bool used[n+1]; // to keep track of used colors
    for (int i = 1; i <= n; i++) {
        used[i] = false;
    }
    for (auto u : graph[v]) {
        if (colors[u] != 0) {
            used[colors[u]] = true;
        }
    }
    for (int i = 1; i <= n; i++) {
        if (!used[i]) {
            colors[v] = i;
            break;
        }
    }
}
```

```cpp
void TSPGC() {
    vector<int> degree(n);
    for (int i = 0; i < n; i++) {
        degree[i] = graph[i].size();
    }
    while (true) {
        int v = min_element(degree.begin(), degree.end()) - degree.begin();
        if (degree[v] == n) {
            break;
        }
        degree[v] = n;
        assignColors(v);
        for (auto u : graph[v]) {
            if (degree[u] != n) {
                degree[u]--;
            }
        }
    }
}

int main() {
    cin >> n;
    graph.resize(n);
    colors.resize(n);
    int m;
    cin >> m;
    for (int i = 0; i < m; i++) {
        int u, v;
        cin >> u >> v;
    }
}
```

Figure 20.3.1 Algorithm in C++.

```cpp
int main() {
    cin >> n;
    graph.resize(n);
    colors.resize(n);
    int m;
    cin >> m;
    for (int i = 0; i < m; i++) {
        int u, v;
        cin >> u >> v;
        graph[u].push_back(v);
        graph[v].push_back(u);
    }
    TSPGC();
    int chromaticNumber = *max_element(colors.begin(), colors.end());
    cout << "Chromatic number: " << chromaticNumber << endl;
    vector<vector<int>> subjects(chromaticNumber);
    for (int i = 0; i < n; i++) {
        subjects[colors[i]-1].push_back(i);
    }
    for (int i = 0; i < chromaticNumber; i++) {
        cout << "Color " << i+1 << ": ";
        for (auto subject : subjects[i]) {
            cout << subject << " ";
        }
        cout << endl;
    }
    return 0;
}
```

Figure 20.3.2 Algorithm in C++.

20.3.5 Algorithm in C

```c
#include <stdio.h>
void color(int a, int min,int color_row[],int adj[10][10], int n){
    if(a<n){
        int i,j, restricted, temp[n];
        for(i=1;i>=min;i--)
        {
            restricted=0;
            for(j=0;j<a;j++){
                if((adj[a][j]==1 &&(color_row[j]==i))){
                    restricted=1;
                    break;
                }
                else{
                    restricted=0;
                }
            }
            if(restricted==0){
                for(j=0;j<n;j++)
                temp[j]=color_row[j];

                color_row[a] = i;
                color(a+1, min, color_row, adj, n);
                for(j=0;j<n;j++){
                color_row[j]=temp[j];
            }
        }
    }
}
```

Figure 20.4.1 Algorithm in C.

```
return;
}
else{
    int i;
    printf("color:   ");
    for(i=0;i<n;i++){
        printf("%d", color_row[i]);
    }
    printf("\n");
    return;
}
}

int chromatic(int adj[10][10],int n){
    int min,new_col,i,j,color_row[n];
    color_row[0]=1;
    min=1;
    new_col=0;
    for(i=1;i<n;i++){
        for(j=0;j<i;j++){
            if(adj[i][j]==1)
            {
                new_col=1;
            }
            else{
                color_row[i]=color_row[j];
                new_col=0;
                break;
            }
        }
        if(new_col==1){
            min = min + 1;
            color_row[i] = min;
        }
    }
    return min;
}
int main(){
    int n,j,i,c_num,a=0;
    printf("enter the no of vertices in the graph:");
    scanf("%d",&n);
    int adj[10][10];
    int color_row[n];
    printf("enter the adjacency matrix:\n");
    for(i=0;i<n;i++){
        for(j=0;j<n;j++){
            scanf("%d",&adj[i][j]);
        }
    }
    c_num=chromatic(adj,n);
    printf("the chromatic number of the graph is: %d\n",c_num);
    printf("the all posible colour combination are :\n");
    printf("vertex:\n");
    for(i=0;i<n;i++){
        printf("%d",i);
    }
    printf("\n\n");
    color(a,c_num,color_row,adj,n);
}
```

Figure 20.4.2 Algorithm in C.

20.4   Time Complexity of the Algorithm

The computation of v_i requires $O(n)$ time. The neighborhood of all vertices can be computed in $O(n^2)$ time. Hence, overall time complexity is $O(n^2)$.

20.5   Concluding Remarks

In this paper, we developed an efficient new variation of algorithm that solves the Examination Scheduling problems using $O(n^2)$ time. We verified the algorithm using Python, C++ and also C Programming, which run and give the exact result.

20.6 Acknowledgments

For the project-based experimentation (SoW), we are extremely grateful to NSHM for their leadership, continual supervision, and provision of the necessary information. We are particularly grateful for their assistance in seeing the project through to its successful conclusion. We would like to thank Professor (Dr.) Sanchita Sarkar, Dr. Srabani Guria Das, and Dr. Anirudhha Samanta for their advice and guidance to complete our project. Thanks to all students, especially Tridib Pal, Subhajyoti Maity, Tanushree Chakravorty, Deb Kumar Paul, Swastik Chatterjee, and Debasrita Saha, who helped us with this project. This would not have been possible without their constant support.

References

1. Euler, L., Solutio problematis ad geometriarn situs pertinentis. *Commentarii Acad. Sci. Imp. Pet.*, 8, 128–140, 1736.
2. F.G., Tinting maps, The Athenaeum, p. 726, June 10, 1854.
3. Kempe, A.B., On the geographical problem of the four colours. *Am. J. Math.*, 2, 3, 193–220, 1879.
4. Heawood, P.J., Map-colour theorem. *Q. J. Math.*, Oxford, 24, 332–338, 1890.
5. Kenneth, A. and Wolfgang, H., Every planar map is four colorable. I.Discharging. *Ill. J. Math.*, 21, 3, 429–490, 1977.
6. Birkhoff, G.D., A determinant formula for the number of ways of coloring a map. *Ann. Math.*, 14, 42–46, 1912.
7. *The tutte polynomial*, pp. 210–228, John Wiley Sons, Inc., New Jersey, USA, 1999.
8. Karp, R.M., Reducibility among combinatorial problems, in: *Complexity of Computer Computations*, pp. 85–103, Plenum, New York, 1972.
9. Skiena, S., *Implementing discrete mathematics: Combinatorics and graph theory with mathematica*, Addison-Wesley, Reading, MA, 1990.
10. Burke, E., Elliman, D., Weare, R., A university timetabling system based on graph coloring and constraint manipulation. *J. Res. Comput. Educ.*, 27, 1, 1–18, 1994.
11. Burke, E., Elliman, D., Weare, R., *Automated scheduling of university exams*, Department of Computer Science, University of Nottingham, UK, 1993.
12. Husseini, S., Malkawi, M., Vairavan, K., Distributed algorithms for edge coloring of graphs, in: *5th ISMM International Conference on Parallel and Distributed Computing Systems*, New Jersey, USA, 1992.
13. Jensen, T. and Toft, B., *Graph coloring problems*, Wiley-Interscience, New Jersey, USA, 1995.

Part 4
EMERGING TOPICS IN MACHINE LEARNING

21

A Comparative Study of Different Techniques of Text-to-SQL Query Converter

Kuldeep Vayadande[1]*, Preeti A. Bailke[1], Vikas Janu Nandeshwar[1], R. Kumar[2] and Varsha R. Dange[1]

[1]Vishwakarma Institute of Technology, Pune, Maharashtra, India
[2]VIT-AP University, Inavolu, Beside AP Secretariat, Amaravati, AP, India

Abstract

Converting text to SQL technologies eliminates the requirement for structured languages like SQL by enabling anyone to inspect the RDBMS by submitting questions. Due to the extensive search area, neural semantic parsers (NSPs) frequently fail to convert lengthy and complex utterances into the nested Structured query language (SQL) queries. Natural language query responses over tables are typically viewed as semantic parsing tasks. It is difficult to train semantic parsers from subpar supervision since logical forms produced are only employed as a stage before recovering the connotation. The objective or goal of this comparison in the research is to study all the existing systems for text-to-SQL conversion and then find out the drawback of each system. This paper presents the comparison among the different text-to-SQL conversion systems. Our thorough assessment tries to close a significant knowledge gap regarding the capabilities and limitations of current systems, and it identifies a number of unresolved issues.

Keywords: Tokenization, natural language processing, RDBMS, neural semantic parser, SQL

21.1 Introduction

One of the most crucial facets of semantic parsing in natural language processing is text-to-SQL (NLP). It converts statements in normal language into their matching SQL queries. The task has numerous significant potential applications in real life by enabling non-experts to interact with ever-growing datasets, and as a result, it attracts a lot of interest from both industry and academia. Even for specialists, data querying and exploration are difficult due to the data's exploding amount and rising complexity. It is common to think about answering questions from semi-structured tables as a semantic parsing task, in which the input query given by the user is converted into a logical form that can be used to query the table and extract the appropriate denotation. Semantic parsers are basically dependent on supervised training data that link logical forms with natural language inquiries, but annotating

---

Corresponding author: kuldeep.vayadande1@vit.edu

Arindam Dey, Sukanta Nayak, Ranjan Kumar and Sachi Nandan Mohanty (eds.) *How Machine Learning is Innovating Today's World: A Concise Technical Guide*, (355–366) © 2024 Scrivener Publishing LLC

these data is expensive. One popular method of gathering data focuses on weak supervision, using a question and its denotation as training examples rather than the complete logical form. Although enticing, the profusion of erroneous logical forms and reward sparsity make it difficult to train semantic parsers from this input. Additionally, applications for semantic parsing only use the resulting logical form as a first step towards locating the solution. However, creating logical forms has challenges such as upholding a logical formalism with enough expressivity, adhering to decoding restrictions (like well formedness), and the label bias issue. The current scenario of the existing system has some limitations that are not resolved today. There are many techniques used to convert the simple textual data information into the SQL queries that are not that much complex to understand by the machine and human, but if the non-technical person can use it, they cannot have knowledge about how to use this system if they want nested queries, and their result will not be accurate. The currently available technologies use technologies like RECPARSER and NLP, consisting of different stages of data processing like tokenization, which is common in each program. Basically, tokenization means extracting the input data into different categories and classifying them to better understand the design of the information to produce the result in SQL query format.

21.2   Literature Survey

Zeng *et al.* [1] basically discuss neural semantic parsers that failed to translate complex and big text into nested SQL query. A new recursive semantic parsing model, referred to as RECPARSER, has been proposed in this research paper. This framework can create nested and intricate SQL queries by generating each layer sequentially.

Zeng *et al.* [2] address the challenge of aligning natural language communication with programming language, due to fundamental differences between the two. End users frequently ask the system questions that are confusing or go beyond the query language's semantic capabilities. PHOTON is a reliable, versatile cross-domain NLIDB system designed to identify when there is no instant way to determine SQL mapping from a natural language input. It comprises a strong neural semantic parser, a response generator, and an SQL executor. The question definer, a neural sequence connector that has a functionality of editing it, detects unclear parts of the user's input and provides rephrased suggestions until a translatable question is asked or the maximum number of tries is reached. Results from simulation tests show that the proposed method increases the chances of getting accurate queries for text-to-SQL systems.

The research paper by Gkini *et al.* [3] categorizes systems into two groups based on the designation of the query by the user. The two categories are as follows: (1) Keyword systems, which work similarly to a search engine and only accept keyword-based queries (e.g., "drama movies"), and (2) Natural language systems, which allow questions posed in natural language (e.g., what is the number of students that belong to second std) and utilize a syntactic parser to interpret the input.

Finegan-Dollak *et al.* [4] discuss how text-to-SQL systems commonly use grammar-based techniques, pattern matching, or IR of the query. The PRECISE system was one of the previous statistical models for text-to-SQL in the NLP discipline, which had high precision for queries that fit constraints linking database values, attributes, and token with their relations. Later developments incorporated techniques from logical parsing research to generate queries based on dependencies extracted by a syntactic parser.

In their research paper [5], Wang *et al.* present a method to increase the robustness of text-to-SQL query creation by integrating the query generation process using the SQL query processing component. The authors identify two types of errors that could occur: parsing errors, caused by syntactically incorrect programs, and runtime errors, caused by operator type mismatches in the program. The authors propose to extend the model including the execution guidance schema, which requires selecting specific levels of the generative process to execute and get the initial result values and deploy it in the output values of the processed system for refining the remaining generation process. This approach aims to decrease the error values and increase the reliability of text-to-SQL systems.

Siasar Djahantighi *et al.* [6] propose a solution to convert text into SQL query by using NLP techniques such as tokenization, parsing of syntax, and analysis of semantic. The system uses this knowledge base to find the higher values of similarity to the entity names in the dataset to act as an input statement for the parser so that they can be separated and proper columns are extracted to design the SQL query. The paper presents the results of processing an expertise system compared to common existing solutions for converting Natural language technique of expression identification and processing to SQL query language.

Uma *et al.* [7] present a system for converting textual information about a database to SQL queries using natural language processing (NLP) techniques. The system is tested using a railway system database, and the results are evaluated for accuracy. The authors used data processing techniques to make the SQL queries easily understandable by the machine.

Guo *et al.* [8] focus on improving the performance and accuracy of text-to-SQL generation by using the SQLova model combined with execution guidance. However, they found that the model has limitations in handling aggregation operators and distinguishing between text and numerical columns. To overcome these limitations, they proposed the RuleSQLova model, which has efficiency to enhance the SQLova model by using the logic rules. The RuleSQLova model consistently outperforms the SQLova model and is able to predict numerical columns correctly using logic rules.

Wang *et al.* [9] propose a system encoding methods that are used in the table content, which is considered as an external feature in the processing. The main goal of this external feature, which is a base model for the BERT system and mainly the deep learning model, is to ensure better accuracy on the WikiSQL task and obtain greater efficiency results and achieve the state of art on the database values that are considered in some rules of SQL query generation such as selection of where statements; all the DML commands to generate the SQL queries from the text have also been considered. They also used the three sub-models to predict the AGGREGATE command, WHERE command, and SELECT command.

Wang *et al.* [10] have provided some system design to the RAT framework, which has been shown to lead to significant advancements in parsing the text-to-SQL as indicated by empirical evidence. It offers a unique approach by integrating already defined hard schema relations through a single encoder architecture, with inferred soft self-attended relations, which recursively use the RAT-SQL system to generate SQL queries.

21.3   Comparison Table of Previous Techniques

Sr. no.	Title	Authors	Algorithm	Limitations	Conclusion
1	A recursive semantic parsing framework for Text-to-Sql Task [1] (2020)	Fei Teng and Dongmei, Qian Liu, Jian-Guang Lou, Jiaqi Guo, Yan Gao, Yu Zeng	A Recursive Semantic Parsing Framework using Bidirectional Encoder Representations from Transformers	Whenever the QD module is eliminated, RECPARSER finds it difficult to focus on distinct sections of the proclamation across rounds. RECPARSER frequently gets confused more about correct layer placement of the specified column after eliminating the QD module.	This research introduced RECPARSER, a unique recursion semantic parsing framework, to break down the complex nested SQL production problem into many sequential non-nested Sql statement generation challenges.
2	Improving Text-to Sql evaluation Methodology [2] (2018)	Dragomir Radev, Rui Zhang, Sesh Sadashivam, Karthik Ramanathan, Li Zhang, Jonathan K. Kummerfeld, Catherine Finegan-Dollak	Database (DB) approaches, parsing-based approaches	In this research paper, the authors characterize a question and find a proper dataset according to the question, but sometimes, they will not get a proper dataset for particular question.	In this research paper the authors compare human-created and characterizing properties of queries needed for real-world examples and test sets for various questions types and try to train the neural networks on these datasets. The results show that their created datasets and evaluation protocol can be used to effectively compare various techniques for text-to-SQL task creation and to identify the strengths and weaknesses of each model. They also demonstrate that the improved datasets can lead to better results for models in comparison to the previous datasets.

(*Continued*)

(*Continued*)

Sr. no.	Title	Authors	Algorithm	Limitations	Conclusion
3	An in-depth benchmarking of Text-to Sql systems [3] (2021)	Yannis Loannidis, Theofilos Belmpas, Georgia Koutrika, Orest Gkini	Database (DB) approaches, parsing-based approaches, neural machine translation	This research paper focuses on query routing. Concluding the results compared with various text-to-SQL systems. The authors have not performed the nesting of queries operation.	In this research paper, the authors designed a rich query benchmark and processed it with an experiment measuring the efficiency of the model that is trained, and the performance measures are also taken into consideration to determine the performance of Text-to-Sql conversion systems that take knowledge of a dataset value schema or based on the parsing approach.
4	PHOTON: A robust cross domain Text-to-Sql System [4] (2020)	Irwin King, Steven C.H. Hoi, Michael R., Jichuan Zeng, Victoria, Caiming Xiong, Richard Socher	Database (DB) approaches, parsing-based approaches	1. The PHOTON system as it is right now is a prototype with lesser user communication and features. 2. It aims to enhance the functionality of PHOTON's fundamental models, including context-related user interaction, semantic text-to-SQL parsing, and answer generation from tables (text-to-text).	The research paper presents PHOTON, a model which aims to text-to-SQL queries designing system that integrates a not translational question detector, semantic parser, human including the context for creating question, and Natural language response creator this are the concepts are defined. It has been demonstrated to be effective and efficient in various domains, thanks to its modular design that allows for easy scalability to different domains.

(*Continued*)

(*Continued*)

Sr. no.	Title	Authors	Algorithm	Limitations	Conclusion
5	Using Natural Language processing in order to create Sql queries [5] (2020)	M.H. Shenassa, S.H. Davarpanah, M Norouzifard, F. Siasar Djahantighi	Database (DB) approaches, parsing-based approaches	In this research paper, the authors observed the use of tokenization, syntax parsing, and semantic analysis with NLP. The results are much more accurate when the question is easy, but when the user asks a difficult question or a complex query like a nested query, then the results will not be that accurate.	In this research paper the authors use a basic concept like tokenization, syntax parsing, and semantic analysis to generate a text-to-SQL query. Through the use of that concept, we get an accurate query when the question is easy and the question is not nested. In this research paper, they use an expert system that maintains the database.
6	Formation of Sql from Natural Language query using NLP [6] (2019)	Bharathi B, Bhuvan J, Sneha G, Uma M	NLP-consisting phases such as tokenization, lemmatization, and parts of speech tagging	The data received may be in the type of audio, which can be transformed to text form. The SQL query might be more sophisticated; the database could have more attributes and multivalued. It has the potential to build bots for many industries that handle enormous databases and allow users to access them more easily. To make the program more interactive, the output might be transformed into a sentence and subsequently into an audio file.	This research paper presents a system that uses NLP techniques to convert natural language questions into textual format, which are then converted into the SQL queries. The system includes a parser used in sematic classification, a non-translatable question identifier, a human context or part in question design and correctness of that question, and a natural language response processing and result. The system was tested on a railway booking database with 2880 structured data values.

(*Continued*)

(Continued)

Sr. no.	Title	Authors	Algorithm	Limitations	Conclusion
					It can be said that natural language queries or questions are designed from these data values related to them and achieved a high accuracy rate of 98.89%. The NLP process includes steps like tokenization, inflectional analysis, parse tree or parts of speech defining or labeling, parsing, and mapping.
7	Rule Sqlova : Improving Text-to-Sql with Logic Rules [7] (23 July 2022 IEEE)	Yiwei Shan, Xiaobo Guo, Neng Gao, Shoukang Han	RuleSQLova	It does not provide a higher performance ratio because it is unable to handle the aggregation operation on the textual data to convert into the SQL query consisting of aggregation technique in data processing.	In this paper, the authors explained the SQLova technique, which gives a high performance and is easy to implement.
8	Content-enhanced Bert-based Text-to-Sql generation [8] (2020)	Hulin Gao, Tong Gao	BERT	The model is not accurate and cannot be run on a large number of databases; the accuracy becomes lower as the content increases; only limited to a small database.	They proposed a novel approach for text-to-SQL generation using BERT and table content information. They utilized table content information by encoding two new feature vectors to increase the performance and efficiency of the model. Their approach outperformed the BERT-related baseline, which have a logical form accuracy of 3.7% and an implementation accuracy of 3.7% on the WikiSQL dataset, achieving state-of-the-art results.

(Continued)

(*Continued*)

Sr. no.	Title	Authors	Algorithm	Limitations	Conclusion
9	Know What I Don't Know Handling Ambiguous and Unanswerable Questions for Text-to-Sql [9] (17 Dec 2022)	Jian-Guang Lou, Zhoujun Li, Yaan Gao, Bing Wang	NLP-consisting phases such as tokenization	Some time it takes a normal word as an ambiguous label, unanswerable label that will be efficiently minimize the accuracy of the output and some time it does not a consider a ambiguous word as a ambiguous and generate wrong output	This research paper basically discusses the improvements of text-to-SQL translation easily and accurately; if the question is easy or not nested, it will be translated easily, and if the question or text is unanswerable or ambiguous, then the model does not give a proper result or it will be stuck. Thus, to avoid this and achieve accuracy, this research paper describes DTE-detecting, then explains the model that handles ambiguous and unanswerable questions. This model generates fine-grained explanations and formulates it as a sequence label, and each separate label in the user question will be targeted as an ambiguous token or an unanswerable label.

(*Continued*)

(*Continued*)

Sr. no.	Title	Authors	Algorithm	Limitations	Conclusion
10	RAT–SQL Relation Aware schema encoding and linking for Text-to-Sql Parser [10] (Proceedings in Association for Computational Linguistics, July 5–10, 2020 [10])	Richard Shin , Balin Wang	RAT framework, WikiSQL	Most of the questions designed by this system gets for column and wrong structure, so for this problems their work has to be done in future.	In this research paper, the authors described the RAT framework in text-to-SQL parsing, as indicated by empirical evidence. It offers a unique approach by integrating already defined hard schema relations with related soft self-attended schemas by a single encoder architecture. This method of representation of textual information into learning-based design has the potential to be applied to tasks next text-to-sql as input includes some form of already defined structure of SQL query.

21.4   Comparison Graphs

Figure 21.1 shows comparison of different models [1–10]. Figure 21.2 shows accuracy of different models [1–5].

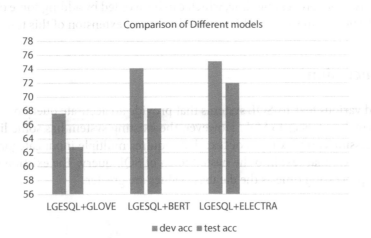

Figure 21.1 Comparison of different models.

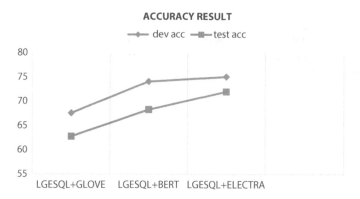

Figure 21.2 Accuracy of different models.

21.5   Research Gap

In this research, we compared previous technologies to convert the text into sql queries, which are compared, and the limitations of those techniques are also studied. On the basis of that we get a conclusion that, as there are many modifications should be done in the current scenario of this text-to-SQL query generation process so that the implementation speed and the sql queries which we are getting as a result accuracy of that can be increased and also if their in some condition where we have to apply the nesting the statements on the database this technologies are not efficient to work on that.

Further extension of the existing system can be made by adding NLP-based techniques that can change this result at a higher level of accuracy. Thus, the user will not be required to enter the requirements in steps. They can provide a single statement, and after processing it, a nested query will be generated using that, and then the user can get the required result by performing a compilation using a query with a higher accuracy result. The BERT and MVC model act as a syntactical mediator that converts this tokenized attribute into data attributes after comparison with the actual database values (Tables and Columns) arranged according to the sql syntax. Large amounts of databases are included in this tool; hence, this tool will require more processing time, which can be avoided by adding some other module to increase the processing speed. This will be done as an extension of this tool.

21.6   Conclusion

We compared various text-to-SQL systems that provide an accurate query by detecting the text as in normal sentences to SQL. However, the existing system has some limitations in terms of processing complex types of text that requires multiple input categories from the database to convert that text into the nested form of SQL query. The existing systems also have a longer processing time as the database values are greater.

References

1. Zeng, Y., Gao, Y., Guo, J., Chen, B., Liu, Q., Lou, J.-G., Teng, F., Zhang, D., RECPARSER: A recursive semantic parsing framework for text-to-SQL task. *International Joint Conference on Artificial Intelligence (IJCAI)*, 2020.
2. Zeng, J., Lin, X.V., Xiong, C., Socher, R., Lyu, M.R., King, I., Hoi, S.C.H., Photon: A robust cross-domain text-to-SQL system, Cornell University, 2020.
3. Gkini, O., Belmpas, T., Koutrika, G., Ioannidisd, Y., An in-depth benchmarking of text-to-SQL systems. ´SIGMOD '21, Virtual Event, China, June 20–25, 2021.
4. Finegan-Dollak, C., Kummerfeld, J.K., Zhang, L., Ramanathan, K., Sadasivam, S., Zhang, R., Radev, D., Improving text-to-SQL evaluation methodology, 2018, arXiv:1806.09029v1 [cs.CL] 23 Jun 2018.
5. Wang, C., Tatwawadi, K., Brockschmidt, M., Huang, P.-S., Mao, Y., Polozov, O., Singh, R., Robust text-to-SQL generation with execution-guided decoding, 13 Sep 2018, arXiv:1807.03100v3 [cs. CL].
6. Siasar djahantighi, F., Norouzifard, M., Davarpanah, S.H., Shenassa, M.H., Using natural language processing in order to create SQL queries. *International Conference on Computer and Communication Engineering*.
7. Uma, M., Sneha, V., Sneha, G., Bhuvana, J., Bharathi, B., Formation of SQL from natural language query using NLP. *Second International Conference on Computational Intelligence in Data Science (ICCIDS)*, 2019.
8. Guo, T. and Gao, H., Content Enhanced BERT-based text-to -SQL generation, Cornell University, 2020.
9. Wang, B., Gao, Y., Li, Z., Lou, J.-G., Know what i don't know: Handling ambiguous and unanswerable questions for text-to-SQL, Cornell University, 17dec 2022.
10. Wang, B., Shin, R., Liu, X., Polozov, O., Richardson, M., RAT-SQL:Relation-aware schema encoding and linking for text-to-SQL parsers, in: *Proceedings of the 58th Annual Meeting of the Association for Computational Linguistics*, Online, Association for Computational Linguistics, 2020.

References

[content illegible — page is mirror-reversed and faded]

22

Trust-Based Leader Election in Flying Ad-Hoc Network

Joydeep Kundu, Sahabul Alam* and Sukanta Oraw

Department of Computer Science & Engineering Brainware University, Barasat, Ramkrishnapur Road, Near Jagadighata, Kolkata, West Bengal, India

Abstract

In the network of drones, the communication channel is extremely important, especially in terms of design. The standpoint of various types of UAV entities mostly relies on this communication path; it facilitates cooperation and participation among the UAVs. Strengthening inter-UAV-based collaboration may strengthen the concept of trust inside a network. Therefore, based on the trust score, creating a malicious node from the network is possible in order to create a trustworthy inter-UAV data link. A trust-based FANET network leader drone nomination methodology is described in this paper. The reliable approach employed by the technology aims to keep risky UAVs out of FANET. Based on the calculated trust scores, a secure Cluster leader is chosen to manage center station communication in addition to communication. According to the methodology of the proposed model, this scheme may be said to be efficient and to perform more consistently than the other current methods in any challenging condition.

Keywords: Trust, leader, drone (UAV)

22.1 Introduction

A number of drones called the FANET [1–4] work together and communicate to complete missions. These UAVs are connected to one another using wireless transmission technology without the aid of any basic structure. To allow the UAVs to fly freely and be controlled in FANET, we opt to employ either a sophisticated drone or a pre-programmed automation system. They are adaptable and have good execution. A network's independent, ad-hoc Wi-Fi grid might be quickly created by a fleet of little flying robots. The grid presented in the study enables the network to maintain connectivity and go on talking with the rescue crew even if the traditional communication infrastructure fails. FANETs are employed for a variety of purposes; therefore, each drone must abide by a set of rules and its behaviors. These networks require greater resources as a result of the requirement for security. The cryptographic methodology is a strategy that supports the same traditional security measures [5–7].

**Corresponding author*: sahabul2009@gmail.com

Arindam Dey, Sukanta Nayak, Ranjan Kumar and Sachi Nandan Mohanty (eds.) How Machine Learning is Innovating Today's World: A Concise Technical Guide, (367–374) © 2024 Scrivener Publishing LLC

Research is necessary to protect FANETs while using minimal resources. According to past ad-hoc network research, more reliable algorithms are ideal for defending ad-hoc networks against various types of attacks. Because it increases the dependability of the participating drones, the trust management concept is therefore practical. This situation will concentrate on finding a reliable computational strategy that works for ad-hoc networks without crew or passengers that are utilized for channel broadcasting. It could be escorted automatically, remotely, or both. In a self-organized manner, FANET completes a number of crucial functions [8–10] for UAVs, such as routing, message delivery, and network administration.

Each UAV in FANET acts as a router, sending data packets to other UAVs. Due to their low energy consumption, some UAVs may drop data packets to preserve battery life, which could affect network performance. These UAVs are referred to as non-cooperative nodes in FANET. Malicious UAVs in FANETs are exposed to numerous internal and external dangers during basic operations. UAVs might actually be harmed or compromised as a result; during the transfer of data, they can then begin acting vindictively in FANET. In order to sustain interaction and cooperation among UAVs in the network and complete tasks successfully, it is crucial to pay attention to how they behave. The performance of the network can be enhanced by identifying and separating UAVs with malicious intent or vindictive objectives. In order to distinguish between trustworthy and malicious UAVs, think about employing trust-based systems. These techniques leverage the trust levels of nodes to identify networks that may have suspicious motives and ensure that data are transmitted through reliable nodes. A trust-based technique is utilized in FANET to assess the trust score of individual drones. This score is determined through direct or indirect observation, allowing for the identification of uncooperative UAVs within the network. By incorporating this trust-based approach, the network can ensure that data transit occurs through trustworthy and reliable nodes.

The paper is divided into four sections. Sections 22.2 and 22.3, respectively, provide an overview of the literature and descriptions of trust-based computational methodology for leader selection within such a network. Section 22.4 contains the conclusion.

22.2   Related Work

In a previous study, it was recommended that designs should serve as the primary component for mission planning in order to address the challenges of efficient reconfiguration and constrained resources in drone swarm transmission. The study employed a multidimensional dynamic list scheduling method and a motif-based swarm configuration approach to developing a mission planning strategy. These networks operate with dynamic topology, but the mobility and limited battery power of UAVs introduce unpredictability in FANET routing. To address this issue, researchers proposed a clustering algorithm inspired by nature and combining swarm and krill herd optimization methods. This algorithm aims to select a stable leader UAV within or outside the cluster in FANET networks. Techniques such as weighted k-means clusters and simulated annealing were utilized for optimizing the planning of the aircraft path. However, the study did not provide a solution for the problem of group captain replacement in case of failure. A technique utilizing a distributed consensus-based strategy and sensing capabilities could be considered to tackle this issue.

This approach would enable the selection and replacement of group captains in a more effective and adaptive manner, ensuring the resilience and reliability of the network.

In the context of homogeneous UAV clusters, cluster heads establish communication among themselves and with the top nodes of other clusters through frame relays. It is assumed that the communication and capability spheres within these clusters are identical. The previously mentioned challenge becomes easier to understand by considering that the capacity remains constant regardless of the position and is unaffected by external factors. This technique enhances the management of a drone-based cluster by the leader. Repeated simulations were conducted to validate the effectiveness of the consensus-based strategy. These simulations demonstrated that the strategy can be scaled and adapted to different scenarios. The flexibility of the consensus-based approach was evident in its ability to handle various situations and maintain reliable communication within the cluster.

Researchers have recently proposed several trust management strategies to enhance the security of FANET. One method [11] utilizes fuzzy categorization algorithms and optimization techniques to assess the trustworthiness of UAVs. The cluster head is then selected based on the highest trust ratings, allowing for the identification and exclusion of malicious nodes. This approach aligns the trust levels of nodes with their actual behavior. Another technique [12] focuses on two aspects: protection from external impact and routing. It optimizes the selection of the most suitable node for forwarding based on a cross-layer optimization approach. Reducing the number of route request packets mitigates overload and improves energy efficiency in the FANET. In a group of drones, a leader is selected based on distance and energy levels at a given moment, utilizing an algorithmic approach. The UAV clustering technique selects a leader drone that meets the mission's requirements and has sufficient remaining energy. The energy consumption or distance between drones determines the required fitness level in this scenario. It is recommended to offload computing tasks among drone clusters, whether locally or remotely to expedite feedback calculation. This approach allows for adaptive remote task offloading, distributing the computational load evenly across node clusters and reducing feedback time. Leveraging computational power from other clusters enhances drone operations, and the use of artificial neural networks (ANNs) further improves the efficiency of the offloading method. It is suggested to transfer data through a specialized and reliable system to monitor awareness and avoid issues like broadcast storms during interest propagation. Inter-UAV authentication is crucial to maintaining security measures and ensuring the legitimacy of each individual drone. Distinguishing between unintentional and deliberate UAV misbehavior is important, aiming to reduce the occurrence of security-level breaches. Trust between UAVs can be estimated using UAV energy, enabling a comprehensive understanding of the context and facilitating accurate findings [13–16].

The model presented in [7] lacks the ability to consider energy consumption as a factor. This limitation hinders the development of an effective approach for dynamically selecting a leader drone that outperforms others at varying geographical boundaries, regardless of high or low transmission ranges. In terms of information flow direction and reliability, the SEEDRP [8] approach is inadequate. It fails to address the complexity of broadcast storms during the information distribution process. This limitation undermines the effectiveness of SEEDRP in managing information flow and ensuring reliable communication among drones. Furthermore, there is currently no available technology that can accurately identify and protect sensitive areas from unauthorized drones. Safeguarding such locations from potential threats posed by unauthorized drone access remains a challenging problem, with no viable solution at present.

22.3 Discussion of the Proposed Methodology and Results

A technique called LDNM-FANET has been developed to ensure reliable communication within FANET. This technique categorizes UAVs into three groups based on their behavioral characteristics and active engagement: cooperative, bad, and neutral drones. It becomes easier for UAVs to select a trustworthy leader UAV and establish a secure cluster by employing this approach. The trust evaluation process in LDNM-FANET utilizes a direct trust assessment technique. This technique determines the trust value for individual drones within the cluster by evaluating their direct collaborations with other UAVs. A leader drone is selected by considering the historical trust scores between neighboring UAVs in the network. This selection is based on the trust scores calculated from the direct communication and collaboration history of the drones. A new UAV sends a joining message during the time of entry into a cluster to its cluster head. The leader UAV, possessing comprehensive information about the other UAVs in the cluster, responds to the acknowledgment and enables the new UAV to join. This ensures that the leader UAV has the necessary knowledge to make informed decisions about the inclusion of new drones into the cluster. Similar to this, the base station chooses the actual gateways connecting each leader UAV in the network during inter-cluster communication. The leader UAVs' recordings are stored by the gateways, and the input for each of the base stations' gates are also recorded. As can be shown in Figure 22.1, the base station is, therefore, capable of quickly identifying hostile or malfunctioning leader UAVs.

The rate of trust score improvement is crucial for communication purposes because it may lead to more accidents and clogged roads. Although the AODV procedure is effective in and of itself, there are several limitations. We are aware of the dynamic route-finding capabilities of the AODV-based alternative process. Data packets are increasingly likely to take an outdated path as data technology advances. As a result, there will surely be delays of

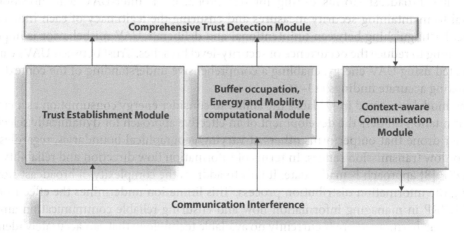

Figure 22.1 Trust establishment module.

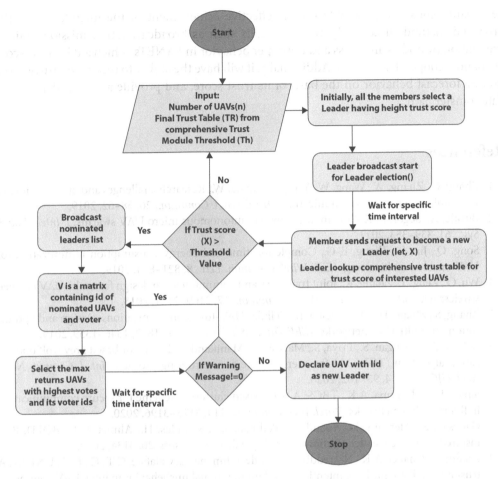

Figure 22.2 The proposed scheme's approach for choosing the leader UAV.

the network and also loss of data. As shown in Figure 22.2, new strategies encourage inter-connection effectiveness through clustering and ensuing guide process reduction. Packets must be securely routed via the clusters of the CH and onto additional clusters until they arrive at their destination. Since the CHs would already be aware of the target's route, an increase in data flow will not cause unduly lengthy delays.

22.4 Conclusion

The FANET's trust management system is essential in protecting FANETs from various attacks brought on by selfish nodes and bad behavior. Identification of trusted nodes requires trust score scheme tools that spot non-cooperative drones and forecast their mode of participation. There is a large likelihood of data loss because of FANETs' excellent scalability and dynamic nature. Incorporating trust-based management strategies proved to be advantageous and profitable for the effective achievement of the intended aim. The proposed method successfully avoids assaults such as broadcast retransmission policies brought on by node selfishness and improper behavior in FANETs, which aid in the discovery of non-cooperative drones. Additionally, it will have the ability to recognize trustworthy drones, forecast behavior on the basis of its trust score, and provide a secure, dependable data transfer path.

References

1. Zhang, C., Zhang, W., Wang, W., Yang, L., Zhang, W., Research challenges and opportunities of UAV millimeter-wave communications. *IEEE Wirel. Commun.*, 26, 58–62, 2019.
2. Bürkle, A., Segor, F., Kollmann, M., Towards autonomous micro UAV swarms. *J. Intell. Robot. Syst.*, 61, 339–353, 2011.
3. Song, Q., Jin, S., Zheng, F.-C., Completion time and energy consumption minimization for UAV-enabled multicasting. *IEEE Wirel. Commun. Lett.*, 8, 821–824, 2019.
4. Wu, Q., Zeng, Y., Zhang, R., Joint trajectory and communication design for multi-UAV enabled wireless networks. *IEEE Trans. Wirel. Commun.*, 17, 2109–2121, 2018.
5. Zhang, S., Zhang, H., Di, B., Song, L., Cellular UAV-to-X communications: Design and optimization for multi-UAV networks. *IEEE Trans. Wirel. Commun.*, 18, 2, 1346–1359, 2019.
6. Rahim, R., Murugan, S., Priya, S., Magesh, S., Manikandan, R., Taylor based grey wolf optimization algorithm (TGWOA) for energy aware secure routing protocol. *Int. J. Comput. Netw. Appl. (IJCNA)*, 7, 4, 93–102, 2020.
7. Singh, K. and Verma, A.K., TBCS: A trust based clustering scheme for secure communication in flying ad-hoc networks. *Wirel. Pers. Commun.*, 114, 3173–3196, 2020.
8. Ganesan, X., Mercilin, R., Anand, N., Padmanaban, S., Eklas, H., Ahmet, H.E., BOLD: Bio-inspired optimized leader election for multiple drones. *Sensors*, 20, 3134, 2020.
9. Ezedin, B., Chaker, A.K., Nasreddine, L., Abderrahmane, L., Calafate, C.T., C., J.-C., UNION: A trust model distinguishing intentional and unintentional misbehavior in inter-UAV communication. *Hindawi J. Adv. Transp.*, 2018, Article ID 7475357, 12, 2018.
10. Namdev, M., Goyal, S., Agarwal, R., An optimized communication scheme for energy efficient and secure flying ad-hoc network (FANET). *Wirel. Pers. Commun.*, 120, 1291–1312, 2021.
11. Li, X., Zhou, F., Du, J., LDTS: A lightweight and dependable trust system for clustered wireless sensor networks. *IEEE Trans. Inf. Forensics Secur.*, 8, 6, 924–935, June 2013.
12. Jayaraman, S., Bhagavathiperumal, R., Mohanakrishnan, U., A three layered peer-to-peer energy efficient protocol for reliable and secure data transmission in EAACK MANETs. *Wireless Pers. Commun.*, 102, 1, 201–227, 2018.
13. Namdev, M., Goyal, S., Agarwal, R., An optimized communication scheme for energy efficient and secure flying ad-hoc network (FANET). *Wireless Pers. Commun.*, 120, 2, 1–22, 2021.
14. Darabkh, K.A., Alfawares, M.G., Althunibat, S., MDRMA: Multi-data rate mobility-aware AODV-based protocol for flying ad-hoc networks. *Veh. Commun.*, 18, 100163, 2019.

15. Sathiamoorthy, J. and Ramakrishnan, B., A competent three-tier fuzzy cluster algorithm for enhanced data transmission in cluster EAACK MANETs. *Soft Comput.*, 22, 19, 6545–6565, 2018.

16. Arnosti, S.Z., Pires, R.M., Branco, K.R., Evaluation of cryptography applied to broadcast storm mitigation algorithms in FANETs, in: *2017 International Conference on Unmanned Aircraft Systems (ICUAS)*, IEEE, pp. 1368–1377, 2017.

23

A Survey on Domain of Application of Recommender System

Sudipto Dhar

Department of Computer Science & Engineering, University of Engineering and Management, Kolkata, West Bengal, India

Abstract

To assist consumers in finding products that fit their interests and preferences, recommender systems have been developed. The absence of a proper survey to demonstrate the uses of recommender systems led to the description of the foundations of recommender systems in this article, along with some of its most significant applications that are crucial to modern living. In order to create high-performance recommendation systems, the benefits and drawbacks of recently offered methods have also been considered. Individual and group recommender systems are the two main categories. Both system types have been considered in this study. There is also discussion and analysis of the most modern methodologies in the field of recommender systems.

Keywords: Recommendation system, implicit feedback, explicit feedback

23.1 Introduction

We are now inundated with data and information. Sources of information include the World Wide Web [1], trading sites with a large number of customers, and sites with thousands of things [36]. This quantity of data will be uploaded every day, causing information avalanche [2]. Information overload and selection technique (to choose from various sectors such as items) are seen as a difficulty; the decision should be made by a customer, and in many circumstances, merchants must discover their customers' interests and preferences, which is a hard procedure [3]. Recommender system arose to assist users in locating products that are relevant to their interests. Owing to the lack of an appropriate survey that highlights the uses of recommender systems, we attempted to convey some important applications for modern living in this study. Moreover, benefits.

The pros and cons of the previous systems are discussed in order to present a solution for delivering systems that ameliorate cons. This study emphasizes application fields that have the most influence on daily life in the current day, such as movies, tourists, shopping, and so on. Previous research has found that recommender systems come as both individual and

---

Email: sudiptocs2@gmail.com

Arindam Dey, Sukanta Nayak, Ranjan Kumar and Sachi Nandan Mohanty (eds.) How Machine Learning is Innovating Today's World: A Concise Technical Guide, (375–382) © 2024 Scrivener Publishing LLC

collective systems [3, 4, 16]. As offering recommendations to the group in certain sectors of applications has become a difficulty, a significant amount of work has been expended.

In the last few years, efforts have been undertaken to provide suggestions to group systems. This article provides examples of group recommender systems. For some years, I have worked on recommender systems and tried to make them more preferred, focusing on how they may be used in daily life. Some of the applications that have been updated so far include news [5], TV shows [6, 7], films [7, 30, 31], photos [8], digital libraries [9, 10], tourism [11, 32], shopping [12, 29], and e-commerce [3, 13, 15]. Only a handful of the application domains have been mentioned due to the topic's scope.

Review of Previous Work

Cheverst *et al.* [13] created a user-based Collaborative Filtering algorithm using the distributed cloud computing platform Hadoop to address the Collaborative Filtering technique's scalability issue. More effective at finding interests in related topics. 2. Specific guidance. 1. Is absent consideration for similar user preferences.

In [14], Schafer *et al.* focused on offering personalized travel suggestions and illustrated potential uses utilizing photographs from the community that are made available to the public. They offer customized trip recommendations by considering other user profiles or features as well as other travel group types.

Pros

1. While making recommendations, community involvement is a beneficial quality to take into account.
2. A lot of data may be gleaned from images submitted by the public.

Cons

1. When community-contributed photographs are analyzed.
2. Privacy problems may come up.

Cho *et al.* [16] proposed a KASR method for personalized advice. Here, a user-based collaborative filtering technique is used. Hadoop is used to implement the strategy in order to boost its efficacy and scalability. The Jaccard coefficient and the cosine similarity measure are used for evaluation. They show how effective the proposed suggestion approach is compared to the currently used traditional methods. The main advantages are:

1. Scalability
2. More effective than conventional techniques.

However, this has several drawbacks:

1. Jaccard Coefficient approach is not very precise.
2. Positive and negative user reviews are not distinguished. Textual sentiments are not taken into account while computing.

Chen and Cheng [17] presented a unique clustering approach based on the Latent Class Regression Model (LCRM) to discern the homogeneity of reviewers' preferences. In essence, this approach is prepared to take into consideration both feature-level opinion ratings and overall ratings (as gleaned from text evaluations). They assessed the suggested recommendation system in the study using two real datasets. Most notably, they contrasted it with a variety of comparable tactics, such as non-review methodology and alternatives not based on LCRM.

McCarthy *et al.* [18] proposed a system that makes suggestions based on the user's location. One of the benefits is it is better for location-specific services. It reduces the price of overhead gearbox. In cases when geography is not a major influence, it is inappropriate.

In [19], Basu *et al.* proposed a recommendation approach that looks at the differences in client feedbacks to identify the preferences of the consumer. These methods take into account clear ratings, a task that might reveal the problem of data sparsity. To demonstrate the effectiveness of the recommended approach, they also conducted an experimental analysis of internet restaurant customer reviews in order to create a restaurant rating system (RS).

23.2 Background

Collaborative Filtering
In the collaborative filtering approach (CF), things are recommended based on other individuals who have similar interests. They are employing a number of common formulas and statistical dependency (for example, things that are scored) to find the interests of this user, which is termed neighbors. Initially, users had to discover their own comparable neighbors, but CF approaches now attempt to propose products that are not rated based on proximity to neighbors [19, 20].

CF algorithms have the benefit that they don't need to know anything about the recommended item or product, because they recommend items based on the ratings of their neighbors; this is appropriate for recommending complex products such as movies and music, and they can consider product quality in the suggested moment. For example, it is possible that some similarly themed films have unique qualities when explicit ratings are considered. CF algorithms can propose higher-quality videos for viewers [19, 20].

The drawbacks of CF algorithms include lack of logic for provided recommendations and are unable to provide descriptions for supplied recommendations. These algorithms' chilly start is another drawback. When adding an item to the database system, it is not suggested to any user until the users rate it or specify that it is comparable to existing products [23–28]. The second difficulty arises when a user (gray sheep) has diverse tastes from their neighbor; it may recommend him rarely.

Demographic Filtering
The demographic recommendation technique just considers the user's demographic data, including age, gender, employment status, ownership of real estate, and even geographic location [33–35]. User demographic similarity is taken into account while creating the suggestions. The technique is domain neutral because the item feature is optional; however, the collection of demographic information raises privacy issues.

Knowledge-Based Recommender System
The ratings for things like homes, vehicles, and other products do not mean as much to us because we do not frequently buy them. Knowledge-based recommender systems have found application in these circumstances [21, 22, 37]. This strategy is applied in a specific region with a limited perch history. In these kinds of systems, the algorithm considers user preferences (direct requests), familiarity with the item and its attributes, and the recommendation criteria before generating a proposal. The usefulness of the client-recommended item is taken into account when determining how accurate the model is.

Before creating these sorts of proposed frameworks, we expect the following queries:

- What kind of information about the goods is included in the model?
- How are explicit user preferences recorded?

Two fundamental varieties of knowledge-based recommender systems exist.

Depending on constraints and the use of cases, unlike restricting recommenders, which count on a clearly defined list of suggestions and principles, case-based recommenders are focused on retrieving comparable goods based on a variety of resemblance metrics.

Hybrid Recommender System
Hybrid recommendation systems are the result of combining several recommender systems to give a more solid base. By utilizing the benefits of another recommender system, we may be able to mitigate the problems of one approach, therefore combining many recommender systems to create a more resilient system. For instance, collaborative filtering techniques, where the model fails when new things lack ratings, and content-based approaches, wherein feature information about the goods is available, can be used to more accurately and effectively propose new products. Earlier when developing a hybrid model, we investigate the following issues:

What techniques must be used to achieve the solution?

How can we combine the outputs of several systems to produce precise predictions?

23.3   Study of Recommender Systems

Information feedback is the fundamental component of an RS since it provides the information the RS needs in order to make appropriate recommendations to the customers based on their preferences. Basically, there are three categories for feedback techniques [9]:

Implicit Feedback Technique (IFT)
This technique relies on the user's behaviors during the operation rather than their cognitive awareness to obtain information. The user's taste and interest are evaluated without their consent. An IFT uses methods and tools particular to the application domain to gather and examine user input. This type of IFT is utilized in several applications, including search patterns, mouse movements, browser histories, and web usage histories.

Pros

1. IFT may be collected for a considerably lesser price.
2. IFT is hassle-free and light on the user of the recovery system.
3. It can capture a lot of data for less money.

Cons

1. The IFT is susceptible to noise.
2. It is not as precise as EFT.
3. It is challenging to understand IFT.

Explicit Feedback Technique (EFT)
Using a score or a number, this approach involves asking the consumers to rate the products. Explicit assessments are often provided on a predetermined discrete scale (for instance, "Mark out ten"). Given the ratings for various metrics, statistical processing of these decisions can provide distributions, averages, etc. The EFT helps people express their enthusiasm for and desire for a certain item [10, 11].

Pros

1. The user may express what they like and do not like by receiving either positive or negative feedback [12].
2. EFT appears to be more accurate than IFT.

Cons

1. EFT is absolutely true. As an illustration, even though a person listens to music repeatedly, they may still exhibit interest in it [12] by listening to it only once.
2. One of the difficulties facing EFT is the intrusiveness issue [12].
3. The user could not be consistent in their ranking, which makes utilizing a numerical scale unclear.
4. User ratings might not accurately reflect what users think.

Hybrid Feedback Technique (HFT)
IFT and EFT are combined to create HFT. This approach combines numerical rating scores with human behavior to predict the things of interest and taste that users will find appealing.

Pros

1. HFT aids in improving accuracy of predicted ratings.
2. HFT combines implicit and explicit methotechniques.

Cons

1. It is not inexpensive.
2. HFT requires a lot of calculation.

23.4   Conclusion

We aim to simply outline the many types of recommendation strategies and their types in this work. We also recommend system feedback strategies. To analyze and develop fresh tactics and attributes for the deployment of successful recommendation systems, more studies may be conducted. Additionally, by combining recommendation systems with ML and NLP, we may develop powerful recommendation systems that are capable of taking a number of criteria into consideration. Using machine learning, we may train the system to provide the best suggestions based on its past experiences. As a result, a very accurate recommendation system will be created that is very effective and has its own intelligence. This intelligence allows it to predict the user's best interests and give recommendations accordingly.

References

1. Berners Lee, T., Cailliau, R., Gro, T.F., Pollermann, B., World-wide web: The information universe. *Electronic Networking: Research, Applications, and Policy*, 44, 3, 52–58, 1992.
2. Losee, R.M., Minimizing information overload: The ranking of electronic messages. *J. Inf. Sci.*, 40, 3, 179–189, 1989.
3. Christidis, K. and Mentzas, G., A topic-based recommender system for electronic marketplace platforms. *Expert Syst. Appl.*, 40, 11, 4370–4379, 2013.
4. Bauer, M. and Dengler, D., Group decision making through mediated discussions, in: *Proceedings of the AH 2002 Workshop on Recommendation and Personalization in Ecommerce*, pp. 10–19, 2002.
5. Resnick, P., Iacovou, N., Suchak, M., Bergstrom, P., Riedl, J., Grouplens: An open architecture for collaborative filtering of Netnews, in: *Proceedings of ACM CSCW'94 Conference on Computer-Supported Cooperative Work*, pp. 175–186, 1994.
6. Konstan, J.A., Miller, B.N., Maltz, D., Herlocker, J.L., Gordon, L.R., Riedl, J., GroupLens: Applying collaborative filtering to usenet news. *Commun. ACM*, 40, 3, 77–87, 1997.
7. Tavakolifard, M., Gulla, J., Almeroth, K., Ingvaldsen, J., Nygreen, G., Berg, E., Tailored news in the palm of your hand: A multi-perspective transparent approach to news recommendation, in: *Int. Conf. on World Wide Web*, pp. 305–308, 2013.
8. Masthoff, J., Group modeling: Selecting a sequence of television items to suit a group of viewers. *User Modeling and User-Adapted Interaction*, pp. 37–85, 2004.
9. O'Connor, M., Cosley, D., Konstan, J., Riedl, J., PolyLens, A recommender system for groups of users, in: *ECSCW*, pp. 199–218, 2001.
10. Cantador, I. and Castells, P., Extracting multilayered communities of interest from semantic user profiles: Application to group modeling and hybrid recommendations. *Comput. Hum. Behav.*, 27, 4, 1321–1336, 2011.
11. Geisler, G., McArthur, D., Giersch, S., Developing recommendation services for a digital library with uncertain and changing data, in: *Proceedings of the first ACM/IEEE-CS Joint Conference on Digital libraries*, Roanoke, VA, United States, pp. 199–200, 2001.
12. Pera, M.S., Lund, W., Ng, Y.-K., A sophisticated library search strategy using folksonomies and similarity matching. *J. Am. Soc. Inf. Sci. Technol.*, 60, 7, 1406–1932, 2009.
13. Cheverst, K., Davies, N., Mitchell, K., Friday, A., Efstratiou, C., Developing a context-aware electronic tourist guide: Some issues and experiences. *Proceedings of the CHI 2000 Conference on Human Factors in Computing System*, April 1-6, ACM, pp. 17–24, 2000.

14. Velido, A., Lisboa, P.J.G., Meehan, K., Segmentation of the on-line shopping market using neural networks. *Expert Syst. Appl.*, 17, 4, 303–314, 1999.

15. Schafer, J., Konstan, J., Riedl, J., E-commerce recommendation applications. *Data Min. Knowl. Discovery*, 5, 1-2, 115–153, 2001.

16. Cho, Y.H. and Kim, J.K., Application of web usage mining and product taxonomy to collaborative recommendations in e-commerce. *Expert Syst. Appl.*, 26, 2, 233–246, 2004.

17. Chen, C.W. and Cheng, P.J., Title-based product search – exemplified in a Chinese e-commerce portal, in: *Information Retrieval Technology*, P.-J. Cheng, M.-Y. Kan, W. Lam, P. Nakov (Eds.), pp. 25–36, Springer, Berlin/Heidelberg, 2010.

18. McCarthy, K., Salamo, M., Coyle, L., McGinty, L., Smyth, B., Nixon, P., Group recommender systems: A critiquing based approach, in: *ACM IUI*, pp. 267–269, 2006.

19. Basu, C., Hirsh, H., Cohen, W., Recommendation as classification: Using social and content-based information in recommendation, in: *Proceedings of the Fifteenth National Conference on Artificial Intelligence*, pp. 714–720, 1998.

20. Billsus, D. and Pazzani, M.J., Learning collaborative information filters, in: *Proceedings of the Fifteenth International Conference on Machine Learning*, pp. 46–54, 1998.

21. Jannach, M., Zanker, A., Felfering, G.F., *Recommender systems: An introduction*, Cambridge University Press, 2011.

22. Ricci, L., Rokach, B., Shapira, B., Kantor, P.B., *Recommender systems handbook*, Springer, 2011, ISBN 978-0-387-85819-7.

23. Goldberg, D., Nichols, D., Oki, B.M., Terry, D., Using collaborative filtering to weave an information tapestry. *Commun. ACM*, 35, 61–70, 1992.

24. Resnick, P., Iacovou, N., Suchak, M., Bergstrom, P., Riedl, J., Grouplens: An open architecture for collaborative filtering of netnews, in: *CSCW '94: Proceedings of the ACM Conference on Computer Supported Cooperative Work*, ACM Press, Chapel Hill, NC, pp. 175–186, 1994.

25. Schein, A.I., Popescul, A., Ungar, L.H., Pennock, D.M., Generative models for cold-start recommendations, in: *Proceedings of the 2001 SIGIR Workshop on Recommender Systems*, 2001.

26. Schein, A.L., Popescul, A., Ungar, L.H., Methods and metrics for cold-start recommendations, in: *SIGIR'02*, Tampere, Finland, 2002.

27. Burke, R., Hybrid recommender systems: Survey and experiments. *User Model. User Adapt. Interact.*, 12, 4, 331–370, 2002.

28. Claypool, M., Gokhale, A., Miranda, T., Murnikov, P., Netes, D., Sartin, M., Combining content-based and collaborative filters in an online newspaper, in: *Proceedings of the ACM SIGIR '99 Workshop on Recommender Systems: Algorithms and Evaluation*, Berkeley, California, 1999.

29. Herlocker, J.L., Konstan, J.A., Riedl, J., Explaining collaborative-filtering recommendations, in: *Proceedings of ACM Conference on Computer Supported Cooperative Work*, Philadelphia, US, pp. 241–250, 2000, ISBN 1-58113-222-0.

30. Liu, D.R. and Shih, Y.Y., Hybrid approaches to product recommendation based on customer lifetime value and purchase preferences. *J. Syst. Software*, 77, 2, 181–191, 2005.

31. Fang, B. and Liao K., S., A novel mobile recommender system for indoor shopping. *Expert Syst. Appl.*, 39, 15, 11992–12000, 2012.

32. Christensen, I.A. and S.S., Entertainment recommender system for group of user. *Expert Syst. Appl.*, 38, 11, 14127–14135, 2011.

33. Pera, M.S. and Ng, Y.-K., A group recommender for movies based on content similarity and popularity. *Inf. Process. Manage.*, 49, 3, 673–687, 2013.

34. Garsia, I., Sebastia, L., Onaindia, E., On the design of individual and group recommender systems for tourism. *Expert Syst. Appl.*, 38, 6, 7683–7692, 2011.

35. Costa-Montenegro, E., A.B., M.R., A recommender system of applications in markets:Implementation of the service for monitoring users' interaction. *Expert Syst. Appl.*, 7, 6, 9367–9375, 2012.
36. Hsu, M.-H., Proposing a charting recommender system for second-language nurses. *Expert Syst. Appl.*, 38, 8, 9281–9286, 2011.
37. Christidis, K. and Mentzas, G., A topic-based recommender system for electronic marketplace platforms. *Expert Syst. Appl.*, 40, 11, 4370–4379, 2013.

24

New Approach on M/M/c/K Queueing Models via Single Valued Linguistic Neutrosophic Numbers and Perceptionization Using a Non-Linear Programming Technique

Antony Crispin Sweety C.[1]* and Vennila B.[2]

[1]*Avinashilingam Institute for Home Science and Higher Education for Women, Tamil Nadu, India*
[2]*Sri Eshwar College of Engineering, Coimbatore, Tamil Nadu, India*

Abstract

The framework deals with the novel idea of the neutrosophic M/M/c/K queueing model. The number of consumers that can enter the system is limited in the classic M/M/c/K model to K, and these individuals arrive adopting a Poisson process with rate λ, the parameter μ represents the service time of the customers that are distributed exponentially, and there are c servers in the system to serve the arriving customers. In the neutrosophic M/M/c/K queue, the arrival and departure rate are considered as a single valued neutrosophic number where T is the truth value, I is indeterminacy, and F is falsity. The performance measures of the neutrosophic M/M/c/K model that include both the average number of customers and mean waiting time in the queue as well as in the system are derived. Further, the performance measures of the unstable NM/NM/c/K queueing model subject to different rates of entry, service, breakdown, and repairs are analyzed. Moreover, calculation and comparison of hexagonal, heptagonal, and octagonal neutrosophic numbers are done. To illustrate the significance of the suggested paradigm, a numerical example is offered last.

Keywords: Queueing theory, logic, neutrosophic single valued sets, Hausdorff distance, linguistic neutrosophic terms

24.1 Introduction

The M/M/c queue, often known as the Erlang-C model, is a multi-server queueing model that falls under the category of queueing theory, a branch of the mathematical science of probability. This concept has been applicable in many real-world problems to administer unreliability. The purpose of the M/M/c/k model is to reduce the customer's waiting time in the line and for the customers to make decisions while they wait in queue [8]. The idea of

---

Corresponding author: riosweety@gmail.com

Arindam Dey, Sukanta Nayak, Ranjan Kumar and Sachi Nandan Mohanty (eds.) *How Machine Learning is Innovating Today's World: A Concise Technical Guide*, (383–422) © 2024 Scrivener Publishing LLC

neutrosophic single valued numbers has been explored by Chakraborty [2], where T stands for truth, I for indeterminacy, and F for falsehood.

In neutrosophic numbers, the notion of subtraction as well as division was put forth by Smarandache [6]. The concept of new similarity measure based on falsity value between single valued neutrosophic numbers was derived by Sahin et al. [11]. In 1986, Atanassov [10] generated an intuitionistic fuzzy logic employing both membership and non-membership functions (truth and falsity). Smarandache developed the concept of a neutrosophic set [5] that annexed an additional component I(x), which describes indeterminacy, independent of other components t(x) and f(x).

The neutrosophic logic is an eccentric structure that summarizes the idea of the traditional fuzzy set and its extentions and hybridizations. Neutrosophy has been applied in various research areas such as communication services [1], decision-making problems [7], pattern recognition [11], analysis of networks [3], queueing theory [9], and graph theory [4].

The above-mentioned sets are generalized by the neutrosophic set from a philosophical perspective, and its functionalities TA(x), IA(x), and FA(x) are subsets of] − 0, 1 + [with the consideration −0 ≤ supTA(x) + supIA(x) + supFA(x) ≤ 3+.

Zeina [12] has defined the linguistic single valued neutrosophic M/M/1 queue. In queueing theory, the application of neutrosophic probability was first defined in [5]. Then, the neutrosophic Erlang service time's model was studied in [13].

This work is organized as follows

> A linguistic M/M/c/k queueing model where its parameters are neutrosophic linguistic terms is presented.
> The NM/NM/c/k queueing model's performance metrics are computed.
> The numerical examples are illustrated to the application of the derived model.

Operations on SVNN

Smarandache defined and endorsed the following operational relations.

Suppose that we have two single valued neutrosophic numbers given by:
A = (t_1, i_1), B = (t_2, f_2, i_2) where

$0 \le t_1, f_1, i_1$, as well as $t_2, f_2, i_2 \le 1$

$0 \le t_1 + f_1 + i_1 \, \& \, 0 \le t_2 + f_2 + i_2 \le 3$
Then:

Summation

$$A \oplus B = \left(t_1 + t_2 - t_1 t_2, i_1 i_2, f_1 f_2\right) \tag{24.1}$$

Multiplication

$$A \otimes B = \left(t_1 t_2, i_1 + i_2 - i_1 i_2, f_1 + f_2 - f_1 f_2\right) \tag{24.2}$$

Subtraction

$$A \ominus B = \left(\frac{t_1 - t_2}{1 - t_2}, \frac{i_1}{i_2}, \frac{f_1}{f_2} \right); t_2 \neq 1, i_2 \neq 1, f_2 \neq 0 \tag{24.3}$$

Division

$$\frac{A}{B} = \left(\frac{t_1}{t_2}, \frac{i_1 - i_2}{1 - i_2}, \frac{f_1 - f_2}{1 - f_2} \right); t_2 \neq 0, i_2 \neq 1, f_2 \neq 1 \tag{24.4}$$

Scalar Multiplication

$$\lambda A = \left(1 - (1 - t_1)^\lambda, i_1^\lambda, f_1^\lambda \right); \lambda > 0 \tag{24.5}$$

Power

$$A^\lambda = \left(t_1^\lambda, 1 - (1 - i_1)^\lambda, 1 - (1 - f_1)^\lambda \right) \tag{24.6}$$

Linguistic Representation of SVNN

In the following Table 24.1, the linguistic representation of SVNN $A = (T, I, F)$ is given:

Table 24.1 Linguistic terms of SVNNs.

Linguistic term	SVN numbers
Incredibly impressive (II)	(1,0,0)
Very very impressive (VVI)	(0.95,0.05,0.10)
Very impressive(VI)	(0.85,0.15,0.20)
Impressive (I)	(0.75,0.25,0.35)
Fairly impressive (FI)	(0.65,0.30,0.40)
Average (A)	(0.55,0.45,0.50)
Moderately bad (MB)	(0.45,0.50,0.60)
Bad (B)	(0.35,0.65,0.70)
Very bad (VB)	(0.25,0.75,0.80)
Very very bad (VVB)	(0.15,0.90,0.90)
Extremely bad (EB)	(0.0,1.0,0.95)

Hausdorff Distance between SVNNs

Let $A(t1, i1, f1)$ and $B(t2, i2, f2)$ be SVNNs; the Hausdorff distance from A to B is:

$$d_H(A, B) = \max\{|t1 - t2|, |i1 - i2|, |f1 - f2|\} \qquad (24.7)$$

M/M/C/K Queue

The parallel-server birth–death model M/M/C/K, with a limit K on the number permitted in the system at any given time, is then taken into consideration.

The typical number of people in queue is:

$$L_q = \frac{\rho r^c P_0}{c!(1-\rho)^2}\left[1 - \rho^{k-c+1} - (1-\rho)(k-c+1)\rho^{k-c}\right] \qquad (24.8)$$

The average number of customers in the system is:

$$L_s = \frac{\rho r^c P_0}{c!(1-\rho)^2}\left[1 - \rho^{k=c+1} - (1-\rho)(k-c+1)\rho^{k-c}\right] + (1 - P_0) \qquad (24.9)$$

The mean waiting time in the queue is:

$$W_q = \frac{\rho r^c P_0}{c!(1-\rho)^2 \lambda(1-P_k)}\left[1 - \rho^{k-c+1} - (1-\rho)(k-c+1)\rho^{k-c}\right] \qquad (24.10)$$

The mean waiting time in the system is:

$$Ws = \frac{\rho r^c P_0}{c!(1-\rho)^2 \lambda(1-P_k)}\left[1 - \rho^{k-c+1} - (1-\rho)(k-c+1)\rho^{k-c}\right] + (1 - P_0) \quad (24.11)$$

24.2 Neutrosophic M/M/C/K Queue

If a queueing system is described by neutrosophic parameters $\lambda_N = (T_\lambda, I_\lambda, F_\lambda)$, $\mu N = (T_\mu, T_\mu, F_\mu)$ such that both are single valued neutrosophic numbers.

$$0 \leq T_\lambda, I\lambda, F\lambda \leq 1 \ \& \ 0 \leq T_\mu, I\mu, F\mu \leq 1$$
$$0 \leq T_\lambda + I_\lambda + F_\lambda \leq 3 \ \& \ 0 \leq T_\lambda + T_\lambda + F_\lambda \leq 3$$

That means we do not know any information of the arrival rates and departure (serving) rates. We just know that these rates are extremely big, very very big, very big, big, fairly big, average, moderately small, small, very small, very very small, and extremely small.

Theorem:

1. The average number of customers in the queue is:

$$
NL_q = \left[\left[\left[\left(1 - \left(1 - \frac{T_\lambda}{T_\mu}\right)^{c-1}\right)\left(\frac{T_\lambda}{T_\mu}\right)^c \right]\left(1 - \left(1 - \frac{T_\lambda}{T_\mu}\right)^c\right)^{\frac{1}{c!}} \right] + \sum_{n=0}^{c-1}\left[1 - \left(1 - \left(\frac{T_\lambda}{T_\mu}\right)^n\right)^{\frac{1}{n!}} - \prod_{n=0}^{c-1}\left[1 - \left(1 - \left(\frac{T_\lambda}{T_\mu}\right)^c\right)^{\frac{1}{c!}}\right] - \left[1 - \left(1 - \left(\frac{T_\lambda}{T_\mu}\right)^n\right)^{\frac{1}{n!}}\right]\sum_{n=0}^{c-1}\left[1 - \left(1 - \left(\frac{T_\lambda}{T_\mu}\right)^n\right)^{\frac{1}{n!}} - \prod_{n=0}^{c-1}\left[1 - \left(1 - \left(\frac{T_\lambda}{T_\mu}\right)^n\right)^{\frac{1}{n!}}\right]\right] \right]^{-1}
$$

$$
\left[\left[\left(\frac{I_\lambda - I_\mu}{1 - I_\mu}\right)^{c-1} + \left[1 - \left(1 - \left(\frac{I_\lambda - I_\mu}{1 - I_\mu}\right)^c\right)^{\frac{1}{c!}}\right]\left(1 - \left(\frac{I_\lambda - I_\mu}{1 - I_\mu}\right)^c\right) - \left(1 - \left(\frac{I_\lambda - I_\mu}{1 - I_\mu}\right)^c\right)^{\frac{1}{c!}}\left[1 - \left(1 - \left(\frac{I_\lambda - I_\mu}{1 - I_\mu}\right)^c\right)^{\frac{1}{c!}}\prod_{n=0}^{c-1}\left[1 - \left(1 - \left(\frac{I_\lambda - I_\mu}{1 - I_\mu}\right)^n\right)^{\frac{1}{n!}}\right] \right]\right]^{-1}
$$

$$
\left[\left(\frac{I_\lambda - I_\mu}{1 - I_\mu}\right)^{c-1} + \left[1 - \left(1 - \left(\frac{I_\lambda - I_\mu}{1 - I_\mu}\right)^c\right)^{\frac{1}{c!}}\right]\left(1 - \left(\frac{I_\lambda - I_\mu}{1 - I_\mu}\right)^c\right) - \left(1 - \left(\frac{I_\lambda - I_\mu}{1 - I_\mu}\right)^c\right)^{\frac{1}{c!}}\left[1 - \left(1 - \left(\frac{I_\lambda - I_\mu}{1 - I_\mu}\right)^c\right)^{\frac{1}{c!}}\prod_{n=0}^{c-1}\left[1 - \left(1 - \left(\frac{I_\lambda - I_\mu}{1 - I_\mu}\right)^n\right)^{\frac{1}{n!}}\right]\right]\right]^{-1}
$$

$$
\left[\left(\frac{F_\lambda - F_\mu}{1 - F_\mu}\right)^{c-1} + \left[1 - \left(1 - \left(\frac{F_\lambda - F_\mu}{1 - F_\mu}\right)^c\right)^{\frac{1}{c!}}\right]\left(1 - \left(\frac{F_\lambda - F_\mu}{1 - F_\mu}\right)^c\right) - \left(1 - \left(\frac{F_\lambda - F_\mu}{1 - F_\mu}\right)^c\right)^{\frac{1}{c!}}\left[1 - \left(1 - \left(\frac{F_\lambda - F_\mu}{1 - F_\mu}\right)^c\right)^{\frac{1}{c!}}\prod_{n=0}^{c-1}\left[1 - \left(1 - \left(\frac{F_\lambda - F_\mu}{1 - F_\mu}\right)^n\right)^{\frac{1}{n!}}\right]\right]\right]^{-1}
$$

$$
\left[\left(\frac{F_\lambda - F_\mu}{1 - F_\mu}\right)^{c-1} + \left[1 - \left(1 - \left(\frac{F_\lambda - F_\mu}{1 - F_\mu}\right)^c\right)^{\frac{1}{c!}}\right]\left(1 - \left(\frac{F_\lambda - F_\mu}{1 - F_\mu}\right)^c\right) - \left(1 - \left(\frac{F_\lambda - F_\mu}{1 - F_\mu}\right)^c\right)^{\frac{1}{c!}}\left[1 - \left(1 - \left(\frac{F_\lambda - F_\mu}{1 - F_\mu}\right)^c\right)^{\frac{1}{c!}}\prod_{n=0}^{c-1}\left[1 - \left(1 - \left(\frac{F_\lambda - F_\mu}{1 - F_\mu}\right)^n\right)^{\frac{1}{n!}}\right]\right]\right]^{-1}
$$

2. The average number of customers in the system is:

$$NL_s = \left[\left[\left[1-\left(1-\frac{T_\lambda}{T_\mu}\right)^{c-1}\right]\left(\frac{T_\lambda}{T_\mu}\right)^c\left(1-\left(1-\left(\frac{T_\lambda}{T_\mu}\right)^c\right)\frac{1}{c!}\right)\left(1-\left(1-\left(\frac{T_\lambda}{T_\mu}\right)^n\right)\frac{1}{n!}\right)+\sum_{n=0}^{c-1}\left(1-\left(1-\left(\frac{T_\lambda}{T_\mu}\right)^n\right)\frac{1}{n!}\right)-\prod_{n=0}^{c-1}\left(1-\left(1-\left(\frac{T_\lambda}{T_\mu}\right)^n\right)\frac{1}{n!}\right)\right]\right.$$

$$\left.\left(1-\left(1-\left(\frac{T_\lambda}{T_\mu}\right)^c\right)\frac{1}{c!}\right)\left[\sum_{n=0}^{c-1}\left(1-\left(1-\left(\frac{T_\lambda}{T_\mu}\right)^n\right)\frac{1}{n!}\right)-\prod_{n=0}^{c-1}\left(1-\left(1-\left(\frac{T_\lambda}{T_\mu}\right)^n\right)\frac{1}{n!}\right)\right]^{-1}+1\right]$$

3. The mean waiting time in the queue is:

$$NW_q = \left[\left[\left[1-\left(1-\frac{T_\lambda}{T_\mu}\right)^{c-1}\right]\left(\frac{T_\lambda}{T_\mu}\right)^c\left(1-\left(1-\left(\frac{T_\lambda}{T_\mu}\right)^c\right)\frac{1}{c!}\right)+\sum_{n=0}^{c-1}\left(1-\left(1-\left(\frac{T_\lambda}{T_\mu}\right)^n\right)\frac{1}{n!}\right)\left(1-\left(1-\left(\frac{T_\lambda}{T_\mu}\right)^c\right)\frac{1}{c!}\right)\right.\right.$$

$$\left.\left.\sum_{n=0}^{c-1}\left(1-\left(1-\left(\frac{T_\lambda}{T_\mu}\right)^n\right)\frac{1}{n!}\right)-\prod_{n=0}^{c-1}\left(1-\left(1-\left(\frac{T_\lambda}{T_\mu}\right)^n\right)\frac{1}{n!}\right)\right]^{-1}\right]$$

$$\left[\left(\frac{I_\lambda-I_\mu}{1-I_\mu}\right)^{c-1}+\left(1-\left(1-\left(\frac{I_\lambda-I_\mu}{1-I_\mu}\right)^c\right)\frac{1}{c!}\right)-\prod_{n=0}^{c-1}\left(1-\left(1-\left(\frac{I_\lambda-I_\mu}{1-I_\mu}\right)^n\right)\frac{1}{n!}\right)\right]^{-1}$$

$$\left(\left(\frac{I_\lambda-I_\mu}{1-I_\mu}\right)^{c-1}+\left(1-\left(1-\left(\frac{I_\lambda-I_\mu}{1-I_\mu}\right)^c\right)\frac{1}{c!}\right)-\prod_{n=0}^{c-1}\left(1-\left(1-\left(\frac{I_\lambda-I_\mu}{1-I_\mu}\right)^n\right)\frac{1}{n!}\right)\right)^{-1}$$

$$(24.12)$$

4. The mean waiting time in the system is:
Proof:

$$NW_s = \left[\left[\left[1-\left(1-\frac{T_\lambda}{T_\mu}\right)^{c-1}\right]\left(\frac{T_\lambda}{T_\mu}\right)^c\right]\left[1-\left(1-\frac{T_\lambda}{T_\mu}\right)^c\right]^{\frac{1}{c!}}\left(\sum_{n=0}^{c-1}\left[1-\left(1-\left(\frac{T_\lambda}{T_\mu}\right)^n\right)^{\frac{1}{n!}}\right]+\sum_{n=0}^{c-1}\left[1-\left(1-\left(\frac{T_\lambda}{T_\mu}\right)^n\right)^{\frac{1}{n!}}\right]\right)\right.$$

$$\left.\left[1-\left(1-\left(\frac{T_\lambda}{T_\mu}\right)^c\right)^{\frac{1}{c!}}\left(\prod_{n=0}^{c-1}\left[1-\left(1-\left(\frac{T_\lambda}{T_\mu}\right)^n\right)^{\frac{1}{n!}}\right]\right)^{-1}+1\right]\right.$$

$$\left[1-\left(1-\left(\frac{T_\lambda}{T_\mu}\right)^c\right)^{\frac{1}{c!}}\prod_{n=0}^{c-1}\left[1-\left(1-\left(\frac{T_\lambda}{T_\mu}\right)^n\right)^{\frac{1}{n!}}\right]\right] -$$

$$\left[\left(\left(\frac{F_\lambda-F_\mu}{1-F_\mu}\right)^{c-1}+\left(1-\left(1-\left(\frac{F_\lambda-F_\mu}{1-F_\mu}\right)^c\right)\right)-\left(\frac{F_\lambda-F_\mu}{1-F_\mu}\right)^c\right)\left[1-\left(1-\left(\frac{F_\lambda-F_\mu}{1-F_\mu}\right)^n\right)^{\frac{1}{n!}}\right]\prod_{n=0}^{c-1}\right]^{-1}$$

$$\left[\left(\frac{F_\lambda-F_\mu}{1-F_\mu}\right)^c+\left(1-\left(1-\left(\frac{F_\lambda-F_\mu}{1-F_\mu}\right)^c\right)\right)\left(\frac{F_\lambda-F_\mu}{1-F_\mu}\right)^c\left[1-\left(1-\left(\frac{F_\lambda-F_\mu}{1-F_\mu}\right)^n\right)^{\frac{1}{n!}}\right]\prod_{n=0}^{c-1}\right]^{-1}$$

$$r_N = \frac{\lambda_N}{\mu_N} = \left(\frac{T_\lambda}{T_\mu}, \frac{I_\lambda-I_\mu}{1-I_\mu}, \frac{F_\lambda-F_\mu}{1-F_\mu}\right); T_\mu \neq 0, I_\mu \neq 1, F_\mu \neq 1$$

$$\rho_N = \frac{r_N}{c} \text{ (Scalar multiplication)}$$

$$= \left(\left(1 - \left(1 - \frac{T_\lambda}{T_\mu}\right)^{c-1} \right), \left(\frac{I_\lambda - I_\mu}{1 - I_\mu}\right)^{c-1}, \left(\frac{F_\lambda - F_\mu}{1 - F_\mu}\right)^{c-1} \right), (1-T_\mu)^c \neq 1, I_\mu^c \neq 1, F_\mu^c \neq 1 \tag{24.13}$$

$$r_N^c = \left(\frac{\lambda_N}{\mu_N}\right)^c \tag{24.14}$$

$$r_N^c = \left(\left(\frac{T_\lambda}{T_\mu}\right)^c, 1 - \left(1 - \frac{I_\lambda - I_\mu}{1 - I_\mu}\right)^c, 1 - \left(1 - \frac{F_\lambda - F_\mu}{1 - F_\mu}\right)^c \right) \tag{24.15}$$

$$\frac{r_N^c}{c!} = \left(\left[1 - \left(1 - \left(\frac{T_\lambda}{T_\mu}\right)^c\right)^{\frac{1}{c!}} \right], 1 - \left(1 - \frac{I_\lambda - I_\mu}{1 - I_\mu}\right)^{\frac{1}{c!}}, 1 - \left(1 - \frac{F_\lambda - F_\mu}{1 - F_\mu}\right)^{\frac{1}{c!}} \right) \tag{24.16}$$

$$\frac{r_N^n}{n!} = \left(\left[1 - \left(1 - \left(\frac{T_\lambda}{T_\mu}\right)^n\right)^{\frac{1}{n!}} \right], 1 - \left(1 - \frac{I_\lambda - I_\mu}{1 - I_\mu}\right)^{\frac{1}{n!}}, 1 - \left(1 - \frac{F_\lambda - F_\mu}{1 - F_\mu}\right)^{\frac{1}{n!}} \right) \tag{24.17}$$

$$1 - \rho_N = (1,0,0) - \left(\left[1 - \left(1 - \frac{T_\lambda}{T_\mu}\right)^{c-1} \right], \left(\frac{I_\lambda - I_\mu}{1 - I_\mu}\right)^{c-1}, \left(\frac{F_\lambda - F_\mu}{1 - F_\mu}\right)^{c-1} \right) \tag{24.18}$$

$$(24.19)$$

$$NP_0 = \left[\frac{r_N^c}{c!} \left(\frac{1-\rho_N^{k-c+1}}{1-\rho_N} \right) + \sum_{n=0}^{c-1} \frac{r_N^n}{n!} \right]^{-1}$$

$$1-\rho_N^{k-c+1} = (1,0,0) - \rho_N^{k-c+1}$$

$$\rho_N^{k-c+1} = \left[\left[1 - \left(1 - \frac{T_\lambda}{T_\mu}\right)^{c-1} \right], \left(\frac{I_\lambda - I_\mu}{1-I_\mu}\right)^{c-1}, \left(\frac{F_\lambda - F_\mu}{1-F_\mu}\right)^{c-1} \right]^{k-c+1}$$

$$= \left[1 - \left(1 - \frac{T_\lambda}{T_\mu}\right)^{c-1} \right]^{k-c+1}, \ 1 - \left[1 - \left(\frac{I_\lambda - I_\mu}{1-I_\mu}\right)^{c-1}\right]^{k-c+1}, \ 1 - \left[1 - \left(\frac{F_\lambda - F_\mu}{1-F_\mu}\right)^{c-1}\right]^{k-c+1}$$

$$1-\rho_N^{k-c+1} = \frac{1 - \left[1 - \left(1 - \frac{T_\lambda}{T_\mu}\right)^{c-1}\right]^{k-c+1}}{1 - \left[1 - \left(1 - \frac{T_\lambda}{T_\mu}\right)^{c-1}\right]^{k-c+1}}, \ \frac{0}{1 - \left[1 - \left(\frac{I_\lambda - I_\mu}{1-I_\mu}\right)^{c-1}\right]^{k-c+1}}, \ \frac{0}{1 - \left[1 - \left(\frac{F_\lambda - F_\mu}{1-F_\mu}\right)^{c-1}\right]^{k-c+1}}$$

$$= (1,0,0)$$

$$\left(\frac{1-\rho_N^{k-c+1}}{1-\rho_N} \right) = (1,0,0)$$

$$\frac{r_N^c}{c!}\left(\frac{1-\rho_N^{k-c+1}}{1-\rho_N}\right) = \left[\left[1-\left(1-\left(\frac{T_\lambda}{T_\mu}\right)^c\right)^{\frac{1}{c!}}\right],\ 1-\left(1-\left(\frac{I_\lambda-I_\mu}{1-I_\mu}\right)^c\right)^{\frac{1}{c!}},\ 1-\left(1-\left(\frac{F_\lambda-F_\mu}{1-F_\mu}\right)^c\right)^{\frac{1}{c!}}\right] \times (1,0,0)$$

$$= \left[\left[1-\left(1-\left(\frac{T_\lambda}{T_\mu}\right)^c\right)^{\frac{1}{c!}}\right],\ 1-\left(1-\left(\frac{I_\lambda-I_\mu}{1-I_\mu}\right)^c\right)^{\frac{1}{c!}},\ 1-\left(1-\left(\frac{F_\lambda-F_\mu}{1-F_\mu}\right)^c\right)^{\frac{1}{c!}}\right]$$

$$\sum_{n=0}^{c-1}\frac{r_N^n}{n} = \sum_{n=0}^{c-1}\left[1-\left(1-\left(\frac{T_\lambda}{T_\mu}\right)^n\right)^{\frac{1}{n!}}\right] - \prod_{n=0}^{c-1}\left(1-\left(1-\left(\frac{T_\lambda}{T_\mu}\right)^n\right)^{\frac{1}{n!}}\right),\ \prod_{n=0}^{c-1}\left(1-\left(1-\left(\frac{I_\lambda-I_\mu}{1-I_\mu}\right)^n\right)^{\frac{1}{n!}}\right),\ \prod_{n=0}^{c-1}\left(1-\left(1-\left(\frac{F_\lambda-F_\mu}{1-F_\mu}\right)^n\right)^{\frac{1}{n!}}\right)$$

$$C!(1-\rho_N) = C!(1,0,0)$$
$$= (1-(1-1)^{c!},\ 0^{c!},\ 0^{c!})$$
$$C!(1-\rho_N) = (1,0,0)$$
$$C!(1-\rho_N)^2 = C!(1,0,0)$$
$$= (1-(1-1)^c,\ 0^{c!},\ 0^{c!})$$
$$= (1,0,0)$$

Using Equations 24.16, 24.17, and 24.19, we get

$$NP_0 = \left[\frac{r_N^c}{c!} \left(\frac{1 - \rho_N^{k-c+1}}{1 - \rho_N} \right) + \sum_{n=0}^{c-1} \frac{r_N^n}{n!} \right]^{-1} \text{ for } \rho \neq 1$$

$$NP_0 = \left[\left[1 - \left(1 - \left(\frac{T_\lambda}{T_\mu}\right)^c\right)^{\frac{1}{c!}} \right]\left[1 - \left(1 - \frac{I_\lambda - I_\mu}{1 - I_\mu}\right)^{\frac{1}{c!}}\right]\left[1 - \left(1 - \frac{F_\lambda - F_\mu}{1 - F_\mu}\right)^{\frac{1}{c!}}\right] + \sum_{n=0}^{c-1}\left[1 - \left(1 - \left(\frac{T_\lambda}{T_\mu}\right)^n\right)^{\frac{1}{n!}}\right] - \prod_{n=0}^{c-1}\left[1 - \left(1 - \left(\frac{T_\lambda}{T_\mu}\right)^n\right)^{\frac{1}{n!}}\right] \right]^{-1}$$

$$NP_0 = \left[\left[1 - \left(1 - \left(\frac{T_\lambda}{T_\mu}\right)^c\right)^{\frac{1}{c!}} \right]\left[1 - \left(1 - \frac{I_\lambda - I_\mu}{1 - I_\mu}\right)^{\frac{1}{c!}}\right]\left[1 - \left(1 - \frac{F_\lambda - F_\mu}{1 - F_\mu}\right)^{\frac{1}{c!}}\right] + \sum_{n=0}^{c-1}\left[1 - \left(1 - \left(\frac{T_\lambda}{T_\mu}\right)^n\right)^{\frac{1}{n!}}\right] - \prod_{n=0}^{c-1}\left[1 - \left(1 - \left(\frac{T_\lambda}{T_\mu}\right)^n\right)^{\frac{1}{n!}}\right] \right]^{-1}$$

(24.20)

The average number of customers in the queue is:

$$NL_q = \frac{\rho_N r_N^c p_0}{c!(1-\rho_N)^2}\left[1 - \rho_N^{k-c+1} - (1-\rho_N)(k-c+1)\rho_N^{k-c}\right]$$

$$\rho_N \times r_N^c = \left[\left(1-\left(1-\frac{T_\lambda}{T_\mu}\right)^{c-1}\right)\left(\frac{I_\lambda-I_\mu}{1-I_\mu}\right)^{c-1}, \left(1-\left(1-\frac{F_\lambda-F_\mu}{1-F_\mu}\right)^{c-1}\right)\times\left(\left(\frac{T_\lambda}{T_\mu}\right)^c, 1-\left(1-\frac{I_\lambda-I_\mu}{1-I_\mu}\right)^c\right)\right]$$

$$=\left[\left[\left(1-\left(1-\frac{T_\lambda}{T_\mu}\right)^{c-1}\right)\left(\frac{T_\lambda}{T_\mu}\right)^c, \left(\left(\frac{I_\lambda-I_\mu}{1-I_\mu}\right)^{c-1}+\left(1-\left(1-\frac{I_\lambda-I_\mu}{1-I_\mu}\right)^c\right)\right)-\left(1-\left(1-\frac{I_\lambda-I_\mu}{1-I_\mu}\right)^c\right)\right],\right.$$

$$\left.\left(\left(\frac{F_\lambda-F_\mu}{1-F_\mu}\right)^{c-1}+\left(1-\left(1-\frac{F_\lambda-F_\mu}{1-F_\mu}\right)^c\right)\right)-\left(1-\left(1-\frac{F_\lambda-F_\mu}{1-F_\mu}\right)^c\right)\right]$$

$$(k-c+1)\rho_N^{k-c} = \left[\left[\left[1-\left(1-\left(1-\frac{T_\lambda}{T_\mu}\right)^{c-1}\right)^{k-c}\right]^{k-c+1}, \left[1-\left(1-\left(\frac{I_\lambda-I_\mu}{1-I_\mu}\right)^{c-1}\right)^{k-c}\right]^{k-c+1},\right.\right.$$

$$\left.\left.\left[1-\left(1-\left(\frac{F_\lambda-F_\mu}{1-F_\mu}\right)^{c-1}\right)^{k-c}\right]^{k-c+1}\right]\right]$$

$$(1-\rho_N)(k-c+1)\rho_N^{k-c}=(1,0,0)\left[\left[1-\left(1-\left(1-\frac{T_\lambda}{T_\mu}\right)^{c-1}\right)^{k-c}\right)^{k-c+1}\right],\ \left[1-\left(1-\left(1-\left(\frac{I_\lambda-I_\mu}{1-I_\mu}\right)^{c-1}\right)^{k-c}\right)^{k-c+1}\right],\ \left[1-\left(1-\left(1-\left(\frac{F_\lambda-F_\mu}{1-F_\mu}\right)^{c-1}\right)^{k-c}\right)^{k-c+1}\right]\right]$$

$$=\left[\left[1-\left(1-\left(1-\left(1-\frac{T_\lambda}{T_\mu}\right)^{c-1}\right)^{k-c}\right)^{k-c+1}\right],\ \left[1-\left(1-\left(1-\left(\frac{I_\lambda-I_\mu}{1-I_\mu}\right)^{c-1}\right)^{k-c}\right)^{k-c+1}\right],\ \left[1-\left(1-\left(1-\left(\frac{F_\lambda-F_\mu}{1-F_\mu}\right)^{c-1}\right)^{k-c}\right)^{k-c+1}\right]\right]$$

$$\left(1-\rho_N^{k-c+1}\right)-\left[(1-\rho_N)(k-c+1)\rho_N^{k-c}\right]=(1,0,0)$$

$$NL_q=\frac{\rho_N r_N^c p_0}{c!(1-\rho_N)^2}\left[1-\rho_N^{k-c+1}-(1-\rho_N)(k-c+1)\rho_N^{k-c}\right]$$

$$
\begin{aligned}
NL_q = &\left[\left[\left[\left[1-\left(1-\frac{T_\lambda}{T_\mu}\right)\left(\frac{T_\lambda}{T_\mu}\right)^c\right]^{\frac{1}{c!}}\left[1-\left(1-\left(\frac{T_\lambda}{T_\mu}\right)^n\right)^{\frac{1}{n!}}\right]\prod_{n=0}^{c-1}\left[1-\left(1-\left(\frac{T_\lambda}{T_\mu}\right)^n\right)^{\frac{1}{n!}}\right]\right.\right.\right.\right. \\
&\left.\left.\left.\left.+\sum_{n=0}^{c-1}\left[1-\left(1-\left(\frac{T_\lambda}{T_\mu}\right)^n\right)^{\frac{1}{n!}}\right]\right]\sum_{n=0}^{c-1}\left[1-\left(1-\left(\frac{T_\lambda}{T_\mu}\right)^n\right)^{\frac{1}{n!}}\right]-\prod_{n=0}^{c-1}\left[1-\left(1-\left(\frac{T_\lambda}{T_\mu}\right)^n\right)^{\frac{1}{n!}}\right]\right]^{-1}\right. \\[2ex]
&\left[\left(\frac{I_\lambda-I_\mu}{1-I_\mu}\right)^{c-1}+\left(1-\left(1-\left(\frac{I_\lambda-I_\mu}{1-I_\mu}\right)^c\right)^{\frac{1}{c!}}\right)\left[1-\left(1-\left(\frac{I_\lambda-I_\mu}{1-I_\mu}\right)^n\right)^{\frac{1}{n!}}\right]\prod_{n=0}^{c-1}\left[1-\left(1-\left(\frac{I_\lambda-I_\mu}{1-I_\mu}\right)^n\right)^{\frac{1}{n!}}\right]\right]^{-1} \\[2ex]
&\left[\left(\frac{I_\lambda-I_\mu}{1-I_\mu}\right)^{c-1}+\left(1-\left(1-\left(\frac{I_\lambda-I_\mu}{1-I_\mu}\right)^c\right)^{\frac{1}{c!}}\right)\left[1-\left(1-\left(\frac{I_\lambda-I_\mu}{1-I_\mu}\right)^n\right)^{\frac{1}{n!}}\right]\prod_{n=0}^{c-1}\left[1-\left(1-\left(\frac{I_\lambda-I_\mu}{1-I_\mu}\right)^n\right)^{\frac{1}{n!}}\right]\right]^{-1} \\[2ex]
&\left[\left(\frac{F_\lambda-F_\mu}{1-F_\mu}\right)^{c-1}+\left(1-\left(1-\left(\frac{F_\lambda-F_\mu}{1-F_\mu}\right)^c\right)^{\frac{1}{c!}}\right)\left[1-\left(1-\left(\frac{F_\lambda-F_\mu}{1-F_\mu}\right)^n\right)^{\frac{1}{n!}}\right]\prod_{n=0}^{c-1}\left[1-\left(1-\left(\frac{F_\lambda-F_\mu}{1-F_\mu}\right)^n\right)^{\frac{1}{n!}}\right]\right]^{-1} \\[2ex]
&\left[\left(\frac{F_\lambda-F_\mu}{1-F_\mu}\right)^{c-1}+\left(1-\left(1-\left(\frac{F_\lambda-F_\mu}{1-F_\mu}\right)^c\right)^{\frac{1}{c!}}\right)\left[1-\left(1-\left(\frac{F_\lambda-F_\mu}{1-F_\mu}\right)^n\right)^{\frac{1}{n!}}\right]\prod_{n=0}^{c-1}\left[1-\left(1-\left(\frac{F_\lambda-F_\mu}{1-F_\mu}\right)^n\right)^{\frac{1}{n!}}\right]\right]^{-1}
\end{aligned}
\tag{24.21}
$$

The average number of customers in the system is:

$$NL_s = \frac{\rho_N r_N^c P_0}{c!(1-\rho_N)^2}\left[1 - \rho_N^{k-c+1} - (1-\rho_N)(k-c+1)\rho_N^{k-c}\right] + (1 - NP_0)$$

$$NL_s = NL_q + (1 - NP_0)$$

$$NL_s = \left[\left[\left(1-\left(1-\frac{T_\lambda}{T_\mu}\right)^{c-1}\right)\left(\frac{T_\lambda}{T_\mu}\right)^c\right]\left(1-\left(1-\frac{T_\lambda}{T_\mu}\right)^c\frac{1}{c!}\right)+\sum_{n=0}^{c-1}\left(1-\left(1-\frac{T_\lambda}{T_\mu}\right)^n\frac{1}{n!}\right)\right.$$

$$\left.\cdot\left[\left(1-\left(1-\frac{T_\lambda}{T_\mu}\right)^c\frac{1}{c!}\right)\sum_{n=0}^{c-1}\left(1-\left(1-\frac{T_\lambda}{T_\mu}\right)^n\frac{1}{n!}\right)-\prod_{n=0}^{c-1}\left(1-\left(1-\frac{T_\lambda}{T_\mu}\right)^n\frac{1}{n!}\right)\right]^{-1}+1\right]$$

$$\cdot\left[\left(1-\left(1-\frac{T_\lambda}{T_\mu}\right)^c\frac{1}{c!}\right)\sum_{n=0}^{c-1}\left(1-\left(1-\frac{T_\lambda}{T_\mu}\right)^n\frac{1}{n!}\right)-\sum_{n=0}^{c-1}\left(1-\left(1-\frac{T_\lambda}{T_\mu}\right)^n\frac{1}{n!}\right)-\right]$$

(24.22)

The mean waiting time in the queue is:

$$NW_q = \frac{\rho_N^c \rho_0}{c!(1-\rho_N)^2 \lambda (1-P_k)}\left[1 - \rho_N^{k-c+1} - (1-\rho_N)(k-c+1)\rho_N^{k-c}\right]$$

$$NW_q = \frac{NL_q}{\lambda_{eff}}$$

$$\lambda_{eff} = \lambda(1-p_k) = \frac{NL_q}{\lambda(1-P_k)}$$

$$NW_q = \left[\left[\left(1-\left(\frac{T_\lambda}{T_\mu}\right)\right)^{c-1}\left(1-\left(\frac{T_\lambda}{T_\mu}\right)^c\right)\frac{1}{c!} + \sum_{n=0}^{c-1}\left(1-\left(\frac{T_\lambda}{T_\mu}\right)^n\right)\frac{1}{n!}\right]\right.$$

$$-\prod_{n=0}^{c-1}\left(1-\left(\frac{T_\lambda}{T_\mu}\right)^n\right)\frac{1}{n!}\right]\left[\frac{1}{c!}\left(1-\left(\frac{T_\lambda}{T_\mu}\right)^c\right)\right.$$

$$-\left.\left.\sum_{n=0}^{c-1}\left(1-\left(\frac{T_\lambda}{T_\mu}\right)^n\right)\frac{1}{n!} - \prod_{n=0}^{c-1}\left(1-\left(\frac{T_\lambda}{T_\mu}\right)^n\right)\frac{1}{n!}\right]^{-1}$$

$$\left[\left(\left(\frac{I_\lambda - I_\mu}{1-I_\mu}\right)\right)^{c-1} + \left(1-\left(1-\left(\frac{I_\lambda - I_\mu}{1-I_\mu}\right)^c\right) - \left(\frac{I_\lambda - I_\mu}{1-I_\mu}\right)\right)\frac{1}{c!}\right.$$

$$+\left.\left(1-\left(1-\left(\frac{I_\lambda - I_\mu}{1-I_\mu}\right)^c\right)\right)\frac{1}{c!}\prod_{n=0}^{c-1}\left(1-\left(1-\left(\frac{I_\lambda - I_\mu}{1-I_\mu}\right)^n\right)\frac{1}{n!}\right)\right]^{-1}$$

$$\left[\left(\frac{I_\lambda - I_\mu}{1-I_\mu}\right)^{c-1} - \left(\frac{I_\lambda - I_\mu}{1-I_\mu}\right) - \left(1-\left(1-\left(\frac{I_\lambda - I_\mu}{1-I_\mu}\right)^c\right)\right)\frac{1}{c!}\prod_{n=0}^{c-1}\left(1-\left(1-\left(\frac{I_\lambda - I_\mu}{1-I_\mu}\right)^n\right)\frac{1}{n!}\right)\right]$$

$$\left[\left(\left(\frac{F_\lambda - F_\mu}{1-F_\mu}\right)\right)^{c-1} + \left(1-\left(1-\left(\frac{F_\lambda - F_\mu}{1-F_\mu}\right)^c\right) - \left(\frac{F_\lambda - F_\mu}{1-F_\mu}\right)\right)\frac{1}{c!}\right.$$

$$+\left.\left(1-\left(1-\left(\frac{F_\lambda - F_\mu}{1-F_\mu}\right)^c\right)\right)\frac{1}{c!}\prod_{n=0}^{c-1}\left(1-\left(1-\left(\frac{F_\lambda - F_\mu}{1-F_\mu}\right)^n\right)\frac{1}{n!}\right)\right]$$

$$\left(\left(\frac{F_\lambda - F_\mu}{1-F_\mu}\right)^{c-1}\left(1-\left(\frac{F_\lambda - F_\mu}{1-F_\mu}\right)^c\right) - \left(1-\left(1-\left(\frac{F_\lambda - F_\mu}{1-F_\mu}\right)^c\right)\right)\frac{1}{c!}\prod_{n=0}^{c-1}\left(1-\left(1-\left(\frac{F_\lambda - F_\mu}{1-F_\mu}\right)^n\right)\frac{1}{n!}\right)\right)^{-1}$$

$$(24.23)$$

The mean waiting time in the system is:

$$NW_s = \left[\left[\left[\left(1-\left(1-\frac{T_\lambda}{T_\mu}\right)^{c-1}\right)\left(\frac{T_\lambda}{T_\mu}\right)^c\right)\frac{1}{c!}\right]\left(1-\left(1-\frac{T_\lambda}{T_\mu}\right)^n\right)\frac{1}{n!}\right]+\sum_{n=0}^{c-1}\left(1-\left(1-\frac{T_\lambda}{T_\mu}\right)^n\right)\frac{1}{n!}\right]-\prod_{n=0}^{c-1}\left(1-\left(1-\frac{T_\lambda}{T_\mu}\right)^n\right)\frac{1}{n!}\right] -$$

$$\left(1-\left(1-\frac{T_\lambda}{T_\mu}\right)^c\right)\frac{1}{c!}\right)\left(\sum_{n=0}^{c-1}\left(1-\left(1-\frac{T_\lambda}{T_\mu}\right)^n\right)\frac{1}{n!}\right)-\prod_{n=0}^{c-1}\left(1-\left(1-\frac{T_\lambda}{T_\mu}\right)^n\right)\frac{1}{n!}\right)^{-1}+1$$

(24.24)

$$NW_s = \frac{NL_s}{\lambda_{eff}}$$

Numerical Example

$$r_N = \frac{\lambda_N}{\mu_N} = \left(\frac{T_\lambda}{T_\mu}, \frac{I_\lambda - I_\mu}{1-I_\mu}, \frac{F_\lambda - F_\mu}{1-F_\mu}\right) = \left(\frac{0.5}{0.8}, \frac{0.6-0.2}{0.8}, \frac{0.7-0.5}{0.5}\right);$$

$$\rho_N = \left(\left(1-\left(1-\frac{T_\lambda}{T_\mu}\right)^{c-1}\right), \left(\frac{I_\lambda - I_\mu}{1-I_\mu}\right)^{c-1}, \left(\frac{F_\lambda - F_\mu}{1-F_\mu}\right)^{c-1}\right)$$

$$c = 2 = \left(1-\left(1-\frac{0.5}{0.8}\right)\right)^{\frac{1}{2}}, \left(\frac{0.6-0.2}{1-0.2}\right)^{\frac{1}{2}}, \left(\frac{0.7-0.5}{1-0.5}\right)^{\frac{1}{2}}$$

The average number of customers in the queue is:

$$
NL_q = \left[\left[\left[\left[\left(1-\left(1-\frac{T_\lambda}{T_\mu}\right)^{c-1}\right)\left(\frac{T_\lambda}{T_\mu}\right)^c\right]\left[1-\left(1-\frac{T_\lambda}{T_\mu}\right)^c\right]^{\frac{1}{c!}} + \sum_{n=0}^{c-1}\left[1-\left(1-\left(1-\frac{T_\lambda}{T_\mu}\right)^n\right)^{\frac{1}{n!}}\right]\right]\left[1-\left(1-\frac{T_\lambda}{T_\mu}\right)^c\right]^{\frac{1}{c!}} - \prod_{n=0}^{c-1}\left[1-\left(1-\left(1-\frac{T_\lambda}{T_\mu}\right)^n\right)^{\frac{1}{n!}}\right]\right]^{-1}\right]
$$

$$
\left[\left[\left(\frac{I_\lambda-I_\mu}{1-I_\mu}\right)^{c-1} + \left(1-\left(1-\frac{I_\lambda-I_\mu}{1-I_\mu}\right)^c\right)-\left(1-\left(1-\frac{I_\lambda-I_\mu}{1-I_\mu}\right)^c\right)^{\frac{1}{c!}}\right]\left[1-\left(1-\frac{I_\lambda-I_\mu}{1-I_\mu}\right)^c\right]^{\frac{1}{c!}}\prod_{n=0}^{c-1}\left[1-\left(1-\left(1-\frac{I_\lambda-I_\mu}{1-I_\mu}\right)^n\right)^{\frac{1}{n!}}\right]\right]^{-1}
$$

$$
\left[\left[\left(\frac{I_\lambda-I_\mu}{1-I_\mu}\right)^{c-1} + \left(1-\left(1-\frac{I_\lambda-I_\mu}{1-I_\mu}\right)^c\right)-\left(1-\left(1-\frac{I_\lambda-I_\mu}{1-I_\mu}\right)^c\right)^{\frac{1}{c!}}\right]\left[1-\left(1-\frac{I_\lambda-I_\mu}{1-I_\mu}\right)^n\right]^{\frac{1}{n!}}\right]^{-1}
$$

$$
\left[\left[\left(\frac{F_\lambda-F_\mu}{1-F_\mu}\right)^{c-1} + \left(1-\left(1-\frac{F_\lambda-F_\mu}{1-F_\mu}\right)^c\right)-\left(1-\left(1-\frac{F_\lambda-F_\mu}{1-F_\mu}\right)^c\right)^{\frac{1}{c!}}\right]\left[1-\left(1-\frac{F_\lambda-F_\mu}{1-F_\mu}\right)^c\right]^{\frac{1}{c!}}\prod_{n=0}^{c-1}\left[1-\left(1-\left(1-\frac{F_\lambda-F_\mu}{1-F_\mu}\right)^n\right)^{\frac{1}{n!}}\right]\right]^{-1}
$$

$$
\left[\left[\left(\frac{F_\lambda-F_\mu}{1-F_\mu}\right)^{c-1} + \left(1-\left(1-\frac{F_\lambda-F_\mu}{1-F_\mu}\right)^c\right)-\left(1-\left(1-\frac{F_\lambda-F_\mu}{1-F_\mu}\right)^c\right)^{\frac{1}{c!}}\right]\left[1-\left(1-\frac{F_\lambda-F_\mu}{1-F_\mu}\right)^n\right]^{\frac{1}{n!}}\right]^{-1}
$$

$$
= (-3.0517, 0.25, 0.16)
$$

By calculating the distances between NL_q and values in Table 24.2, we get. Table 24.3 gives the distances between NLs.

Table 24.2 Linguistic terms of NLq.

Linguistic terms	SVN numbers	Hausdorff distance
Incredibly impressive(II)	(1,0,0)	4.052
Very very impressive (VVI)	(0.95,0.05,0.10)	4.002
Very impressive (VI)	(0.85,0.15,0.20)	3.902
Impressive (I)	(0.75,0.25,0.35)	3.802
Fairly impressive (FI)	(0.65,0.30,0.40)	3.702
Average (A)	(0.55,0.45,0.50)	3.602
Moderately bad (MB)	(0.45,0.50,0.60)	3.502
Bad (B)	(0.35,0.65,0.70)	3.402
Very bad (VB)	(0.25,0.75,0.80)	3.302
Very very bad (VVB)	(0.15,0.90,0.90)	3.202
Extremely bad (EB)	(0.0,1.0,0.95)	3.052

Table 24.3 gives the distances between NLs.

Table 24.3 Linguistic terms of NLs.

Linguistic terms	SVN numbers	Hausdorff distance
Incredibly impressive (II)	(1,0,0)	3.052
Very very impressive (VVI)	(0.95,0.05,0.10)	3.002
Very impressive (VI)	(0.85,0.15,0.20)	2.902
Impressive (I)	(0.75,0.25,0.35)	2.802
Fairly impressive (FI)	(0.65,0.30,0.40)	2.702
Average (A)	(0.55,0.45,0.50)	2.602
Moderately bad (MB)	(0.45,0.50,0.60)	2.502
Bad (B)	(0.35,0.65,0.70)	2.402
Very bad (VB)	(0.25,0.75,0.80)	2.302
Very very bad (VVB)	(0.15,0.90,0.90)	2.202
Extremely bad (EB)	(0.0,1.0,0.95)	2.052

which means that the average waiting number of customers in the queue is going to be extremely bad (because it has the smallest distance).

The average number of customers in the system is:

$$
NL_s = \left[\left[\left[\left(1 - \left(1 - \frac{T_\lambda}{T_\mu} \right)^{c-1} \right) \left(\frac{T_\lambda}{T_\mu} \right)^c \left(1 - \left(1 - \frac{T_\lambda}{T_\mu} \right)^c \right)^{\frac{1}{c!}} \right] + \sum_{n=0}^{c-1} \left(1 - \left(1 - \frac{T_\lambda}{T_\mu} \right)^n \right)^{\frac{1}{n!}} \right] - \prod_{n=0}^{c-1} \left(1 - \left(1 - \frac{T_\lambda}{T_\mu} \right)^n \right)^{\frac{1}{n!}} \right]
$$

$$
- \left[\left(1 - \left(1 - \frac{T_\lambda}{T_\mu} \right)^c \right)^{\frac{1}{c!}} \left(\sum_{n=0}^{c-1} \left(1 - \left(1 - \frac{T_\lambda}{T_\mu} \right)^n \right)^{\frac{1}{n!}} - \prod_{n=0}^{c-1} \left(1 - \left(1 - \frac{T_\lambda}{T_\mu} \right)^n \right)^{\frac{1}{n!}} \right)^{-1} + 1 \right]
$$

$$
= (-2.0517, 0, 0)
$$

which means that the average waiting number of customers in the system is going to be extremely bad (because it has the smallest distance).

The mean waiting time in the queue is:

$$
NW_q = \left[\left[\left[\left(1-\left(1-\frac{T_\lambda}{T_\mu}\right)^{c-1}\right)\left(\frac{T_\lambda}{T_\mu}\right)^c\right]\left[\frac{1}{c!}\left(1-\left(1-\frac{T_\lambda}{T_\mu}\right)^c\right)\right]+\sum_{n=0}^{c-1}\left(1-\left(1-\frac{T_\lambda}{T_\mu}\right)^n\right)\frac{1}{n!}\right]^{-1}-\prod_{n=0}^{c-1}\left(1-\left(1-\frac{T_\lambda}{T_\mu}\right)^n\right)\frac{1}{n!}\right]
$$

$$
\left[\frac{1}{c!}\left(1-\left(1-\left(\frac{I_\lambda-I_\mu}{1-I_\mu}\right)^c\right)\right)\right]\left(\left(\frac{I_\lambda-I_\mu}{1-I_\mu}\right)^{c-1}+\left(1-\left(1-\left(\frac{I_\lambda-I_\mu}{1-I_\mu}\right)^c\right)\right)-\prod_{n=0}^{c-1}\left(1-\left(1-\left(\frac{I_\lambda-I_\mu}{1-I_\mu}\right)^n\right)\frac{1}{n!}\right)\right]^{-1}
$$

$$
\left[\frac{1}{c!}\left(1-\left(1-\left(\frac{I_\lambda-I_\mu}{1-I_\mu}\right)^c\right)\right)\right]\left(\left(\frac{I_\lambda-I_\mu}{1-I_\mu}\right)^{c-1}+\left(1-\left(1-\left(\frac{I_\lambda-I_\mu}{1-I_\mu}\right)^c\right)\right)-\prod_{n=0}^{c-1}\left(1-\left(1-\left(\frac{I_\lambda-I_\mu}{1-I_\mu}\right)^n\right)\frac{1}{n!}\right)\right)
$$

$$
\left[\frac{1}{c!}\left(1-\left(1-\left(\frac{F_\lambda-F_\mu}{1-F_\mu}\right)^c\right)\right)\right]\left(\left(\frac{F_\lambda-F_\mu}{1-F_\mu}\right)^{c-1}+\left(1-\left(1-\left(\frac{F_\lambda-F_\mu}{1-F_\mu}\right)^c\right)\right)-\prod_{n=0}^{c-1}\left(1-\left(1-\left(\frac{F_\lambda-F_\mu}{1-F_\mu}\right)^n\right)\frac{1}{n!}\right)\right)^{-1}
$$

$$
\left[\frac{1}{c!}\left(1-\left(1-\left(\frac{F_\lambda-F_\mu}{1-F_\mu}\right)^c\right)\right)\right]\left(\left(\frac{F_\lambda-F_\mu}{1-F_\mu}\right)^{c-1}+\left(1-\left(1-\left(\frac{F_\lambda-F_\mu}{1-F_\mu}\right)^c\right)\right)-\prod_{n=0}^{c-1}\left(1-\left(1-\left(\frac{F_\lambda-F_\mu}{1-F_\mu}\right)^n\right)\frac{1}{n!}\right)\right)^{-1}
$$

$$
= (-3.0517, 0.25, 0.16)
$$

Table 24.4 shows the distances between NWq.

Table 24.4 Linguistic terms of NWq.

Linguistic terms	SVN numbers	Hausdorff distance
Incredibly impressive(II)	(1,0,0)	4.052
Very very impressive (VVI)	(0.95,0.05,0.10)	4.002
Very impressive (VI)	(0.85,0.15,0.20)	3.902
Impressive (I)	(0.75,0.25,0.35)	3.802
Fairly impressive (FI)	(0.65,0.30,0.40)	3.702
Average (A)	(0.55,0.45,0.50)	3.602
Moderately bad (MB)	(0.45,0.50,0.60)	3.502
Bad (B)	(0.35,0.65,0.70)	3.402
Very bad (VB)	(0.25,0.75,0.80)	3.302
Very very bad (VVB)	(0.15,0.90,0.90)	3.202
Extremely bad (EB)	(0.0,1.0,0.95)	3.052

Table 24.5 gives the distances between NWs.

Table 24.5 Linguistic terms of NWs.

Linguistic terms	SVN numbers	Hausdorff distance
Incredibly impressive (II)	(1,0,0)	3.052
Very very impressive (VVI)	(0.95,0.05,0.10)	3.002
Very impressive (VI)	(0.85,0.15,0.20)	2.902
Impressive (I)	(0.75,0.25,0.35)	2.802
Fairly impressive (FI)	(0.65,0.30,0.40)	2.702
Average (A)	(0.55,0.45,0.50)	2.602
Moderately bad (MB)	(0.45,0.50,0.60)	2.502
Bad (B)	(0.35,0.65,0.70)	2.402
Very bad (VB)	(0.25,0.75,0.80)	2.302
Very very bad (VVB)	(0.15,0.90,0.90)	2.202
Extremely bad (EB)	(0.0,1.0,0.95)	2.052

which means that the average waiting number of customers in the queue is going to be extremely bad (because it has the smallest distance).

The mean waiting time in the system is:

$$
NW_s = \left[\left[\left[\left(1 - \left(1 - \frac{T_\lambda}{T_\mu} \right)^{c-1} \right) \left(\frac{T_\lambda}{T_\mu} \right)^c \right) \left(1 - \left(1 - \frac{T_\lambda}{T_\mu} \right)^c \right)^{\frac{1}{c!}} \right) + \sum_{n=0}^{c-1} \left(1 - \left(1 - \frac{T_\lambda}{T_\mu} \right)^n \right)^{\frac{1}{n!}} \right] \div \prod_{n=0}^{c-1} \left(1 - \left(1 - \frac{T_\lambda}{T_\mu} \right)^n \right)^{\frac{1}{n!}} \right] -
$$

$$
\left(1 - \left(1 - \frac{T_\lambda}{T_\mu} \right)^c \right)^{\frac{1}{c!}} \right) \left[\sum_{n=0}^{c-1} \left(1 - \left(1 - \frac{T_\lambda}{T_\mu} \right)^n \right)^{\frac{1}{n!}} \div \prod_{n=0}^{c-1} \left(1 - \left(1 - \frac{T_\lambda}{T_\mu} \right)^n \right)^{\frac{1}{n!}} \right]^{-1} + 1 \right]
$$

$$
= (-2.0517, 0, 0)
$$

24.3   Perceptionization of the NM/NM/c/K Queuing Model Using a Non-Linear Programming Technique

24.3.1   Classic M/M/c/K Model

In the M/M/c model, there is no restriction to the capacity of the system, whereas in M/M/c/K, there is a restriction in the capacity of the system; i.e., the capacity of the system is K.

The performance measure of the queueing model in this system of interest is the average number of customers in the queue, L_q, which is given by

$$L_q = \frac{\rho r^c P_0}{c!(1-\rho)^2}\left[1-\rho^{k-c+1}-(1-\rho)(k-c+1)\rho^{k-c}\right]$$

24.3.2   Neutrosophic M/M/c/K Queue

The system under study is transformed into the Neutrosophic M/M/c/K model with the assumption of the arrival and service rate that are neutrosophic number with truth, indeterminacy, and falsity membership functions.

A queueing system can be described using neutrosophic parameters $\lambda_N = (T_\lambda, I_\lambda, F_\lambda)$ and $\mu_N = (T_\mu, I_\mu, F_\mu)$, such that both are single valued neutrosophic numbers.

$$0 \le T_\lambda, I_\lambda, F_\lambda \le 1 \ \& \ 0 \le T_\mu, I_\mu, F_\mu \le 1$$

$$0 \le T_\lambda + I_\lambda + F_\lambda \le 3 \ \& \ 0 \le T_\mu + I_\mu + F_\mu \le 3$$

24.3.3   Performance Measures

The performance measure of the M/M/c/K queueing system can be investigated using the neutrosophic state. Let us assume that the characteristic of the system is the average number of customers in the NM/NM/c/K system, which is denoted by $\mathbb{N}(x,y)$. Here, $\mathbb{N}(x,y)$ is the neutrosophic number because λ_N and μ_N are neutrosophic.

$$\mathbb{N}(x,y) = \left[\left[\left[\left[1 - \left(1 - \frac{T_{A\aleph}}{T_{J\aleph}}\right)^{c^{-1}} \left(\frac{T_{A\aleph}}{T_{J\aleph}}\right)^c \right] \left[1 - \left(1 - \frac{T_{A\aleph}}{T_{J\aleph}}\right)^c \right]^{-1} \frac{1}{c!} + \sum_{n=0}^{c-1} \left[1 - \left(1 - \left(\frac{T_{A\aleph}}{T_{J\aleph}}\right)^n \right)^{\frac{1}{n!}} \right] - \prod_{n=0}^{c-1} \left[1 - \left(1 - \left(\frac{T_{A\aleph}}{T_{J\aleph}}\right)^n \right)^{\frac{1}{n!}} \right] \right] \right.$$

$$\left. + \sum_{n=0}^{c-1} \left[1 - \left(1 - \left(\frac{T_{A\aleph}}{T_{J\aleph}}\right)^n \right)^{\frac{1}{n!}} \right] - \prod_{n=0}^{c-1} \left[1 - \left(1 - \left(\frac{T_{A\aleph}}{T_{J\aleph}}\right)^n \right)^{\frac{1}{n!}} \right] \right]^{-1}$$

$$\left[\left[\left[1 - \left(1 - \frac{I_{A\aleph} - I_{J\aleph}}{1 - I_{J\aleph}}\right)^{c^{-1}} \left(\frac{I_{A\aleph} - I_{J\aleph}}{1 - I_{J\aleph}}\right)^c \right] \left[1 - \left(1 - \frac{I_{A\aleph} - I_{J\aleph}}{1 - I_{J\aleph}}\right)^c \right]^{-1} \frac{1}{c!} + \prod_{n=0}^{c-1} \left[1 - \left(1 - \frac{I_{A\aleph} - I_{J\aleph}}{1 - I_{J\aleph}}\right)^n \right]^{\frac{1}{n!}} \right]^{-1} \right.$$

$$\left[\left[1 - \left(1 - \frac{I_{A\aleph} - I_{J\aleph}}{1 - I_{J\aleph}}\right)^{c^{-1}} \left(\frac{I_{A\aleph} - I_{J\aleph}}{1 - I_{J\aleph}}\right)^c \right] \left[1 - \left(1 - \frac{I_{A\aleph} - I_{J\aleph}}{1 - I_{J\aleph}}\right)^c \right]^{-1} \frac{1}{c!} + \prod_{n=0}^{c-1} \left[1 - \left(1 - \frac{I_{A\aleph} - I_{J\aleph}}{1 - I_{J\aleph}}\right)^n \right]^{\frac{1}{n!}} \right]^{-1}$$

$$\left[\left[1 - \left(1 - \frac{F_{A\aleph} - F_{J\aleph}}{1 - F_{J\aleph}}\right)^{c^{-1}} \left(\frac{F_{A\aleph} - F_{J\aleph}}{1 - F_{J\aleph}}\right)^c \right] \left[1 - \left(1 - \frac{F_{A\aleph} - F_{J\aleph}}{1 - F_{J\aleph}}\right)^c \right]^{-1} \frac{1}{c!} + \prod_{n=0}^{c-1} \left[1 - \left(1 - \frac{F_{A\aleph} - F_{J\aleph}}{1 - F_{J\aleph}}\right)^n \right]^{\frac{1}{n!}} \right]^{-1}$$

$$\left[\left[1 - \left(1 - \frac{F_{A\aleph} - F_{J\aleph}}{1 - F_{J\aleph}}\right)^{c^{-1}} \left(\frac{F_{A\aleph} - F_{J\aleph}}{1 - F_{J\aleph}}\right)^c \right] \left[1 - \left(1 - \frac{F_{A\aleph} - F_{J\aleph}}{1 - F_{J\aleph}}\right)^c \right]^{-1} \frac{1}{c!} + \prod_{n=0}^{c-1} \left[1 - \left(1 - \frac{F_{A\aleph} - F_{J\aleph}}{1 - F_{J\aleph}}\right)^n \right]^{\frac{1}{n!}} \right]^{-1}$$

24.3.4　Neutrosophic Extension Principle

We use the neutrosophic extension principle to define the membership function of the system.

$$\text{Let A} = \left\{ \left(m, \left(T_A^1(m), T_A^2(m), T_A^3(m), \ldots, T_A^p(m) \right), \right. \right.$$
$$\left(I_A^1(m), I_A^2(m), I_A^3(m), \ldots I_A^p(m) \right),$$
$$\left. \left. \left(F_A^1(m), F_A^2(m), F_A^3(m), \ldots F_A^p(m) \right) \right) \right\}; m \in M,$$

$\left\{ T_A^i(m), T_A^i(m), T_A^i(m) \in [0.1] \right\}, \left(i \in \{1,2,\ldots,p\} \right)$ be any neutrosophic multi-sets on M. Then, extending the function $f : X \to Y$, the neutrosophic multi-subsets A of X is made to correspond to neutrosophic multi-subsets of $f(A) = \left\{ T_{f(A)}^i, I_{f(A)}^i, F_{f(A)}^i \right\}$ of Y, as follows: For $i = 1,2\ldots,p$

$$T_{f(A)}^i(y) = \begin{cases} \vee \left\{ T_A^i(x) : x \in f^{-1}(y) \right\}, & \text{if } f^{-1}(y) \neq v, \\ 0, & \text{otherwise} \end{cases}$$

$$I_{f(A)}^i(y) = \begin{cases} \vee \left\{ I_A^i(x) : x \in f^{-1}(y) \right\}, & \text{if } f^{-1}(y) \neq v, \\ 1, & \text{otherwise} \end{cases} \quad \text{For i} = 1,2\ldots,p$$

$$F_{f(A)}^i(y) = \begin{cases} \wedge \left\{ F_A^i(x) : x \in f^{-1}(y) \right\}, & \text{if } f^{-1}(y) \neq v, \\ 1, & \text{otherwise} \end{cases}$$

24.3.4.1　(α,β,γ)-Cut of Set Neutrosophic Numbers

$$\text{Let A} = \left\{ \left(m, \left(T_A^1(m), T_A^2(m), T_A^3(m), \ldots, T_A^p(m) \right), \right. \right.$$
$$\left(I_A^1(m), I_A^2(m), I_A^3(s), \ldots, I_A^p(m) \right),$$
$$\left. \left. \left(F_A^1(m), F_A^2(m), F_A^3(m), \ldots, F_A^p(m) \right) \right) \right\}; m \in M,$$

$\left\{ T_A^i(m), T_A^i(m), T_A^i(m) \in [0.1] \right\}, \left(i \in \{1,2,\ldots,p\} \right)$ be any neutrosophic multi-sets on M. For any order (α, β, γ) where $\alpha, \beta, \gamma \in [0,1]$, $0 \leq \alpha + \beta + \gamma \leq 3$. Then, the (α, β, γ)-cut set of neutrosophic multi-sets A is denoted by $A_{(\alpha,\beta,\gamma)}$, and is defined by

$$A_{(\alpha,\beta,\gamma)} = \left\{ m : T_A^i \geq \alpha, I_A^i \geq \beta, F_A^i \leq \gamma, m \in M \right\}$$

i.e.,

$$A_{(\alpha,\beta,\gamma)} = \left\{ m : T_A^i(m) \wedge \alpha = \alpha, I_A^i(m) \wedge \beta = \beta, F_A^i(m) \vee \gamma = \gamma, m \in M \right\}.$$

The strong (α, β, γ)-cut set of neutrosophic multi-sets A is denoted by $A_{\overline{(\alpha, \beta, \gamma)}}$, and is defined by

$$A_{\overline{(\alpha, \beta, \gamma)}} = \left\{ m : T_A^i(m) > \alpha, I_A^i(m) > \beta, F_A^i(m) < \gamma, m \in M \right\}$$

24.3.5   Non-Linear Programming (NLP)

This is a method of resolving a non-linear objective function or some constraints in an optimization problem. One of the calculations for the objective function's extrema (maximum or minimum) is an optimization problem.

24.3.6   Parametric Non-Linear Programming Technique

The average number of customers in the system is given the membership as:

$$\theta_{(\mathbb{N}(x,y))} = \sup_{\lambda} \min < T_\wedge(x), T_\wedge(y) | K = \mathbb{N}(x,y) >,$$

$$\sup_{\lambda} \min < I_\wedge(x), I_\wedge(y) | K = \mathbb{N}(x,y) >,$$

$$\inf_{\lambda} \max < F_\wedge(x), F_\wedge(y) | K = \mathbb{N}(x,y) >$$

Henceforth, the deterministic α-cut sets for the system's average number of customers are $\lambda(\zeta)$ and $\mu(\zeta)$. They are reduced to a family of deterministic queues of M/M/c/K for various α values.

$$\lambda(\zeta) = \left[x_\alpha^L, x_\alpha^U \right] = \left[\min\left\{ x \mid T_\wedge(x) \geq \alpha \right\}, \max\left\{ x \mid T_\wedge(x) \geq \alpha \right\} \right],$$

$$\lambda(\zeta) = \left[x_\beta^L, x_\beta^U \right] = \left[\min\left\{ x \mid T_\wedge(x) \geq \beta \right\}, \max\left\{ x \mid T_\wedge(x) \geq \beta \right\} \right],$$

$$\lambda(\zeta) = \left[x_\gamma^L, x_\gamma^U \right] = \left[\min\left\{ x \mid I_\wedge(x) \leq \gamma \right\}, \max\left\{ x \mid I_\wedge(x) \leq \gamma \right\} \right],$$

$$\mu(\zeta) = \left[y_\alpha^L, y_\alpha^U \right] = \left[\min\left\{ y \mid I_\wedge(y) \geq \alpha \right\}, \max\left\{ y \mid I_\wedge(y) \geq \alpha \right\} \right],$$

$$\mu(\zeta) = \left[y_\beta^L, y_\beta^U \right] = \left[\min\left\{ y \mid F_\wedge(y) \geq \beta \right\}, \max\left\{ y \mid F_\wedge(y) \geq \beta \right\} \right],$$

$$\mu(\zeta) = \left[y_\gamma^L, y_\gamma^U \right] = \left[\min\left\{ y \mid F_\wedge(y) \leq \gamma \right\}, \max\left\{ y \mid F_\wedge(y) \leq \gamma \right\} \right],$$

The numbers are convex and the bounds of these distances as well as $\theta_{(\mathbb{N}(x,y))}$ are functions of α. Consequently, $\theta_\wedge(\kappa)$ equals the minimum of $\theta_\wedge(x)$ and $\theta_\wedge(y)$. To determine the membership function, $\theta_{(\mathbb{N}(x,y))}^L$ needs at least any of the subsequent conditions and $\mathbb{N}(x,y)$ meets the $\theta_{(\mathbb{N}(x,y))}$ value

$$\text{Case (1): } (\theta_\wedge_\lambda(x) = \alpha, \theta_\wedge_\mu(y) \geq \alpha)$$

$$\text{Case (2): } (\theta_\wedge_\lambda(x) \geq \alpha, \theta_\wedge_\mu(y) = \alpha)$$

24.3.6.1   Upper and Lower Boundaries of the α-Cuts in $\theta_{(\mathbb{N}(x,y))}$

Non-linear programming techniques for determining the boundaries of the α-cut sets in $\theta_{(\mathbb{N}(x,y))}$ is provided.

For Case (1):

$$(G)_\alpha^{L_1} = \min[\mathbb{N}(x,y)]$$

$$(G)_\alpha^{U_1} = \max[\mathbb{N}(x,y)]$$

For Case (2):

$$(G)_\alpha^{L_2} = \min[\mathbb{N}(x,y)]$$

$$(G)_\alpha^{U_2} = \min[\mathbb{N}(x,y)]$$

The corresponding upper as well as lower bounds are:

$$(G)_\alpha^L = \min\{(G)_\alpha^{L_1}, (G)_\alpha^{L_2}\}$$

$$(G)_\alpha^U = \min\{(G)_\alpha^{U_1}, (G)_\alpha^{U_2}\}$$

Thus.

$$(G)_\alpha^L = \min[\mathbb{N}(x,y)]$$

such that

$$x_\alpha^L \leq x \leq x_\alpha^U$$

$$y_\alpha^L \leq y \leq y_\alpha^U$$

and

$$(G)_\alpha^U = \min[\mathbb{N}(x,y)]$$

such that

$$x_\alpha^L \leq x \leq x_\alpha^U$$
$$y_\alpha^L \leq y \leq y_\alpha^U$$

24.3.6.2   *Upper and Lower Boundaries of the β-CUTS in* $\theta_{(\mathbb{N}(x,y))}$

Similarly, a non-linear programming technique for determining the boundaries of the β-cut sets in $\theta_{(\mathbb{N}(x,y))}$ is provided.

For $(\mathrm{I}_{\underset{\lambda}{\wedge}}(x) = \beta, \mathrm{I}_{\underset{\mu}{\wedge}}(y) \geq \beta)$:

$$(G)_\beta^{L_1} = \min[\mathbb{N}(x,y)]$$
$$(G)_\beta^{U_1} = \max[\mathbb{N}(x,y)]$$

For $(\mathrm{I}_{\underset{\lambda}{\wedge}}(x) \geq \beta, \mathrm{I}_{\underset{\mu}{\wedge}}(y) = \beta)$

$$(G)_\beta^{L_2} = \min[\mathbb{N}(x,y)]$$
$$(G)_\beta^{U_2} = \min[\mathbb{N}(x,y)]$$

The corresponding upper as well as lower bounds are:

$$(G)_\beta^L = \min\{(G)_\beta^{L_1}, (G)_\beta^{L_2}\}$$
$$(G)_\beta^U = \min\{(G)_\beta^{U_1}, (G)_\beta^{U_2}\}$$

Thus,

$$(G)_\beta^L = \min[\mathbb{N}(x,y)]$$

such that

$$x_\beta^L \leq x \leq x_\beta^U$$
$$y_\beta^L \leq y \leq y_\beta^U$$

and

$$(G)^U_\beta = \min[\mathbb{N}(x,y)]$$

such that

$$x^L_\beta \leq x \leq x^U_\beta$$
$$y^L_\beta \leq y \leq y^U_\beta$$

Here, $(L)^L_\beta$ and $(L)^U_\beta$ are non-increasing, non-decreasing with respect to β.

24.3.6.3   *Upper and Lower Boundaries of the γ-CUTS in $\theta_{(\mathbb{N}(x,y))}$*

Similarly, a non-linear programming technique for determining the boundaries of the γ-cut sets in $\theta_{(\mathbb{N}(x,y))}$ is provided.

For $(F_\wedge \atop \lambda (x) = \gamma, F_\wedge \atop \mu (y) \leq \gamma)$:

$$(G)^{L_1}_\gamma = \min[\mathbb{N}(x,y)]$$
$$(G)^{U_1}_\gamma = \max[\mathbb{N}(x,y)]$$

For $(F_\wedge \atop \lambda (x) \leq \gamma, F_\wedge \atop \mu (y) = \gamma)$:

$$(G)^{L_2}_\gamma = \max[\mathbb{N}(x,y)]$$
$$(G)^{U_2}_\gamma = \max[\mathbb{N}(x,y)]$$

The corresponding upper as well as lower bounds are:

$$(G)^L_\gamma = \max\{(G)^{L_1}_\gamma, (G)^{L_2}_\gamma\}$$
$$(G)^U_\gamma = \max\{(G)^{U_1}_\gamma, (G)^{U_2}_\gamma\}$$

Thus,

$$(G)^L_\gamma = \max[\mathbb{N}(x,y)]$$

such that

$$x^L_\gamma \leq x \leq x^U_\gamma$$
$$y^L_\gamma \leq y \leq y^U_\gamma$$

and

$$(G)_\gamma^U = \max[\mathbb{N}(x,y)]$$

such that

$$x_\gamma^L \leq x \leq x_\gamma^U$$
$$y_\gamma^L \leq y \leq y_\gamma^U$$

Here, $(L)_\gamma^L$ and $(L)_\gamma^U$ are non-increasing, non-decreasing with respect to γ.

Numerical Example

A numerical example is illustrated with the combination of numbers and by which our methods will be shown.

Using Parametric Non-Linear Programming

In this section, the NM/NM/c/K queueing system is considered with two servers, where the arrival and service are a hexagonal neutrosophic number, a heptagonal neutrosophic number, and an octagonal neutrosophic number, and they are represented as below.

The arrival and service are represented as p and q, instead of λ and $\breve{\mu}$

Hexagonal neutrosophic number:

$$p = \left[16,17,18,19,20,21\right] \text{ and } q = [29,30,31,32,33,34]$$

Thus,

$$[x_\alpha^L, x_\alpha^U] = [16+\alpha, 21-\alpha]$$
$$[y_\alpha^L, y_\alpha^U] = [29+\alpha, 34-\alpha]$$
$$[x_\beta^L, x_\beta^U] = [16+\beta, 21-\beta]$$
$$[y_\beta^L, y_\beta^U] = [29+\beta, 34-\beta]$$
$$[x_\gamma^L, x_\gamma^U] = [18-\gamma, 19+\gamma]$$
$$[y_\gamma^L, y_\gamma^U] = [31-\gamma, 32+\gamma]$$

Heptagonal neutrosophic number:

$$p = \left[18,19,20,21,22,23,24\right] \text{ and } q = \left[26,27,28,29,30,31,32\right]$$

Thus,

$$[x_\alpha^L, x_\alpha^U] = [18 + \alpha, 24 - \alpha]$$
$$[y_\alpha^L, y_\alpha^U] = [26 + \alpha, 32 - \alpha]$$
$$[x_\beta^L, x_\beta^U] = [18 + \beta, 24 - \beta]$$
$$[y_\beta^L, y_\beta^U] = [26 + \beta, 32 - \beta]$$
$$[x_\gamma^L, x_\gamma^U] = [20.5 - \gamma, 21.5 + \gamma]$$
$$[y_\gamma^L, y_\alpha^U] = [28.5 - \gamma, 29.5 + \gamma]$$

Octagonal neutrosophic number:

$$p = \begin{bmatrix} 18,19,20,21,22,23,24,25 \end{bmatrix} \text{ and } q = \begin{bmatrix} 26,27,28,29,30,31,32,33 \end{bmatrix}$$

Thus,

$$[x_\alpha^L, x_\alpha^U] = [18 + \alpha, 25 - \alpha]$$
$$[y_\alpha^L, y_\alpha^U] = [26 + \alpha, 33 - \alpha]$$
$$[x_\beta^L, x_\beta^U] = [18 + \beta, 25 - \beta]$$
$$[y_\beta^L, y_\beta^U] = [26 + \beta, 33 - \beta]$$
$$[x_\gamma^L, x_\gamma^U] = [21 - \gamma, 22 + \gamma]$$
$$[y_\gamma^L, y_\gamma^U] = [29 - \gamma, 30 + \gamma]$$

The α – cuts system length at 11 distinct α, β, γ values of numerical example is shown. Some numerical examples for hexagonal, heptagonal, and octagonal neutrosophic number are given below, Table 24.6 to Table 24.8 gives alpha, beta and gamma cuts of hexagonal neutrosophic numbers. Table 24.9 to Table 24.11 gives alpha, beta and gamma cuts of heptagonal neutrosophic numbers. Table 24.12 to Table 24.14 gives alpha, beta and gamma cuts of octagonal neutrosophic numbers.

Hexagonal Neutrosophic Number

Table 24.6 to Table 24.8 gives alpha, beta and gamma cuts of hexagonal neutrosophic numbers.

Table 24.6 α-cuts system length at 11 distinct α values.

α	x_α^L	x_α^U	y_α^L	y_α^U	TG_α^L	TG_α^U
0.0	16	21	29	34	0.0374	0.5993
0.1	16.1	20.9	29.1	33.9	0.0403	0.5917
0.2	16.2	20.8	29.2	33.8	0.0434	0.5826
0.3	16.3	20.7	29.3	33.7	0.0468	0.5719
0.4	16.4	20.6	29.4	33.6	0.0506	0.5593
0.5	16.5	20.5	29.5	33.5	0.0547	0.5443
0.6	16.6	20.4	29.6	33.4	0.0592	0.5264
0.7	16.7	20.3	29.7	33.3	0.0642	0.5049
0.8	16.8	20.2	29.8	33.2	0.0697	0.4789
0.9	16.9	20.1	29.9	33.1	0.0758	0.4470
1.0	17	20	30	33	0.0826	0.4077

Table 24.7 β-cuts system length at 11 distinct β values.

β	x_β^L	x_β^U	y_β^L	y_β^U	IG_β^L	IG_β^U
0.0	16	21	29	34	0.2975	0.0816
0.1	16.1	20.9	29.1	33.9	0.2927	0.0851
0.2	16.2	20.8	29.2	33.8	0.2879	0.0887
0.3	16.3	20.7	29.3	33.7	0.2831	0.0923
0.4	16.4	20.6	29.4	33.6	0.2783	0.0960
0.5	16.5	20.5	29.5	33.5	0.2736	0.0997
0.6	16.6	20.4	29.6	33.4	0.2688	0.1034
0.7	16.7	20.3	29.7	33.3	0.2641	0.1072
0.8	16.8	20.2	29.8	33.2	0.2594	0.1111
0.9	16.9	20.1	29.9	33.1	0.2546	0.1149
1.0	17	20	30	33	0.25	0.1189

Table 24.8 γ-cuts system length at 11 distinct γ values.

γ	$x_γ^L$	$x_γ^U$	$y_γ^L$	$y_γ^U$	$FG_γ^L$	$FG_γ^U$
0.0	18	19	31	32	0.2039	0.16
0.1	17.9	19.1	30.9	32.1	0.2084	0.1557
0.2	17.8	19.2	30.8	32.2	0.2130	0.1515
0.3	17.7	19.3	30.7	32.3	0.2175	0.1473
0.4	17.6	19.4	30.6	32.4	0.2221	0.1431
0.5	17.5	19.5	30.5	32.5	0.2267	0.1390
0.6	17.4	19.6	30.4	32.6	0.2313	0.1349
0.7	17.3	19.7	30.3	32.7	0.2360	0.1308
0.8	17.2	19.8	30.2	32.8	0.2406	0.1268
0.9	17.1	19.9	30.1	32.9	0.2453	0.1228
1.0	17	19	30	33	0.25	0.1189

Table 24.9 to Table 24.11 gives alpha, beta and gamma cuts of heptagonal neutrosophic numbers.

Table 24.9 α-cuts system length at 11 distinct α values.

α	$x_α^L$	$x_α^U$	$y_α^L$	$y_α^U$	$TG_α^L$	$TG_α^U$
0.0	18	24	26	32	0.2325	0.5677
0.1	18.1	23.9	26.1	31.9	0.2657	0.5731
0.2	18.2	23.8	26.2	31.8	0.3066	0.5784
0.3	18.3	23.7	26.3	31.7	0.3583	0.5833
0.4	18.4	23.6	26.4	31.6	0.4253	0.5881
0.5	18.5	23.5	26.5	31.5	0.5154	0.5926
0.6	18.6	23.4	26.6	31.4	0.6424	0.5969
0.7	18.7	23.3	26.7	31.3	0.8343	0.6010
0.8	18.8	23.2	26.8	31.2	1.1561	0.6047
0.9	18.9	23.1	26.9	31.1	1.8048	0.6083
1.0	19	23	27	31	3.7779	0.6116

Octagonal Neutrosophic Number

Table 24.10 β-cuts system length at 11 distinct β values.

β	x_β^L	x_β^U	y_β^L	y_β^U	IG_β^L	IG_β^U
0.0	18	24	26	32	0.2039	0.0064
0.1	18.1	23.9	26.1	31.9	0.1994	0.0076
0.2	18.2	23.8	26.2	31.8	0.1949	0.0090
0.3	18.3	23.7	26.3	31.7	0.1905	0.0105
0.4	18.4	23.6	26.4	31.6	0.1860	0.0121
0.5	18.5	23.5	26.5	31.5	0.1816	0.0138
0.6	18.6	23.4	26.6	31.4	0.1772	0.0156
0.7	18.7	23.3	26.7	31.3	0.1729	0.0175
0.8	18.8	23.2	26.8	31.2	0.1685	0.0194
0.9	18.9	23.1	26.9	31.1	0.1642	0.0215
1.0	19	23	27	31	0.16	0.0236

Table 24.11 γ-cuts system length at 11 distinct γ- values.

γ	x_γ^L	x_γ^U	y_γ^L	y_γ^U	FG_γ^L	FG_γ^U
0.0	20.5	21.5	28.5	29.5	0.0997	0.0647
0.1	20.4	21.6	28.4	29.6	0.1034	0.0615
0.2	20.3	21.7	28.3	29.7	0.1072	0.0584
0.3	20.2	21.8	28.2	29.8	0.1111	0.0553
0.4	20.1	21.9	28.1	29..9	0.1149	0.0523
0.5	20	22	28	30	0.1189	0.0493
0.6	19.9	22.1	27.9	30.1	0.1228	0.0464
0.7	19.8	22.2	27.8	30.2	0.1268	0.0436
0.8	19.7	22.3	27.7	30.3	0.1308	0.0409
0.9	19.6	24.4	27.6	30.4	0.1349	0.0382
1.0	19.5	24.5	27.5	30.5	0.1390	0.0356

Table 24.12 to Table 24.14 gives alpha, beta and gamma cuts of octagonal neutrosophic numbers.

Table 24.12 α-cuts system length at 11 distinct α values.

α	x_α^L	x_α^U	y_α^L	y_α^U	TG_α^L	TG_α^U
0.0	18	25	26	33	0.1537	0.5362
0.1	18.1	24.9	26.1	32.9	0.1712	0.5427
0.2	18.2	24.8	26.2	32.8	0.1916	0.5490
0.3	18.3	24.7	26.3	32.7	0.2158	0.5551
0.4	18.4	24.6	26.4	32.6	0.2447	0.5609
0.5	18.5	24.5	26.5	32.5	0.2799	0.5666
0.6	18.6	24.4	26.6	32.4	0.3235	0.5720
0.7	18.7	24.3	26.7	32.3	0.3787	0.5771
0.8	18.8	24.2	26.8	32.2	0.4506	0.5821
0.9	18.9	24.1	26.9	32.1	0.5481	0.5868
1.0	19	24	27	32	0.6869	0.5913

Table 24.13 β-cuts system length at 11 distinct β values.

β	x_β^L	x_β^U	y_β^L	y_β^U	IG_β^L	IG_β^U
0.0	18	25	26	33	0.2197	0.0016
0.1	18.1	24.9	26.1	32.9	0.2152	0.0022
0.2	18.2	24.8	26.2	32.8	0.2107	0.0030
0.3	18.3	24.7	26.3	32.7	0.2063	0.0039
0.4	18.4	24.6	26.4	32.6	0.2019	0.0050
0.5	18.5	24.5	26.5	32.5	0.1975	0.0061
0.6	18.6	24.4	26.6	32.4	0.1887	0.0073
0.7	18.7	24.3	26.7	32.3	0.1844	0.0087
0.8	18.8	24.2	26.8	32.2	0.1801	0.0101
0.9	18.9	24.1	26.9	32.1	0.1801	0.0116
1.0	19	24	27	32	0.1758	0.0133

Table 24.14 γ-cuts system length at 11 distinct γ values.

γ	x_γ^L	x_γ^U	y_γ^L	y_γ^U	FG_γ^L	FG_γ^U
0.0	21	22	29	30	0.0963	0.0625
0.1	20.9	22.1	28.9	30.1	0.0999	0.0594
0.2	20.8	22.2	28.8	30.2	0.1036	0.0563
0.3	20.7	22.3	28.7	30.3	0.1073	0.0533
0.4	20.6	22.4	28.6	30.4	0.1111	0.0504
0.5	20.5	22.5	28.5	30.5	0.1149	0.0476
0.6	20.4	22.6	28.4	30.6	0.1187	0.0448
0.7	20.3	22.7	28.3	30.7	0.1226	0.0420
0.8	20.2	22.8	28.2	30.8	0.1265	0.0394
0.9	20.1	22.9	28.1	30.9	0.1304	0.0368
1.0	20	23	28	31	0.1344	0.0342

Conclusion

The possibility to simulate the waiting line with different unknown parameters that is described in linguistic terms in the neutrosophic logic model is discussed. Also, we have considered the α-, β-, and γ-cut operations with different neutrosophic numbers, say, hexagonal, heptagonal, and octagonal neutrosophic number. Using the linear programming technique, the average number of customers in the queue NLq for the NM/NM/c/K queueing model has been analyzed. Also, some numerical examples using above neutrosophic numbers have been given. Further, we discussed the possibility of simulating the waiting line with different unknown parameters that is described in linguistic terms in a neutrosophic logic model. We presented M/M/c/K queue view linguistic terms and gave a numerical example.

References

1. Chakraborty, A., Banik, B., Mondal, S.P., Alam, S., Arithmetic and geometric operators of pentagonal neutrosophic number and its application in mobile communication service based MCGDM problem. *Neutrosophic Sets Syst.*, 32, 61–79, 2020.
2. Chakraborty, A., Mondal, S.P., Alam, S., Mahata, A., Cylindrical neutrosophic single-valued number and its application in networking problem, multi-criterion group decision-making problem and graph theory. *CAAI Trans. Intell. Technol.*, 5, 2, 68–77, 2020.
3. Said, B., Nagarajan, D., Lathamaheswari, M., Talea, M., Bakali, A., Smarandache, F., Intelligent algorithm for trapezoidal interval valued neutrosophic network analysis. *CAAI Trans. Intell. Technol.*, 5, 88–93, 2020.

4. Antony Crispin Sweety, C., Vaiyomathi, K., Nirmala Irudayam, F., Bipolar neutrosophic cubic graphs and its applications, in: *Handbook of Research on Advanced Applications of Graph Theory in Modern Society*, pp. 492–536, IGI Global, Hershey, PA, 2020.

5. Smarandache, F., *A unifying field in logics. Neutrosophy: Neutrosophic probability, set and logic*, American Research Press, Rehoboth, 1999.

6. Smarandache, F., Creighton University, *Subtraction and division of neutrosophic numbers*, vol. XIII, pp. 103–110, Uncertainty, Creighton University, 2016.

7. Garg, H. and Nancy, Algorithms for single-valued neutrosophic decision making based on TOPSIS and clustering methods with new distance measure. *AIMS Math.*, 5, 3, 2671–2693, 2020.

8. Manuel Macías Bermúdez, J., Karina Arreaga Farias, G., Torres Torres, L., A method for decision-making on the tendering procedure for the acquisition of goods and services in public procurement. *Neutrosophic Sets Syst.*, 37, 235–241, 2020.

9. Shortle, J.F., Thompson, J.M., Gross, D., Harris, C.M., *Fundamentals of queueing theory*, Wiley, USA, 2018.

10. Atanassov, K., Intuitionistic fuzzy sets. *Fuzzy Sets Syst.*, 20, 87–96, 1986.

11. Sahin, M., Olgun, N., Uluçay, V., Kargın, A., Smarandache, F., A new similarity measure based on falsity value between single valued neutrosophic sets based on the centroid points of transformed single valued neutrosophic numbers with applications to pattern recognition. *Neutrosophic Sets Syst.*, 15, 31–48, 2017.

12. Zeina, M.B., Neutrosophic event-based queueing model. *Int. J. Neutrosophic Sci.*, 6, 1, 48–55, 2020.

13. Zeina, M.B., Erlang service queueing model with neutrosophic parameters. *Int. J. Neutrosophic Sci.*, 6, 2, 106–112, 2020.

25

The Rise of AI-Generated News Videos: A Detailed Review

Kuldeep Vayadande*, Mustansir Bohri, Mohit Chawala, Ashutosh M. Kulkarni and Asif Mursal

Vishwakarma Institute of Technology, Pune, Maharashtra, India

Abstract

The rapid advancements in Artificial Intelligence (AI) have given rise to the possibility of automating news video creation. AI-powered news videos will offer a fresh and dynamic perspective on the day's top stories, delivering the content people need in a way that is easy to consume. AI-generated news videos are the next evolution in journalism, providing a fast and accurate way to consume news content that is both informative and visually stunning. In this review paper, we explore the process of converting news articles into AI-generated videos that can be published on platforms like YouTube. The process involves web scraping of text and images, news authentication, image searching, voice-over creation, video generation, thumbnail creation, and YouTube video upload. We have reviewed several research papers related to each of these steps and highlighted their applications in news video creation. We have identified the challenges involved in each step, such as the authenticity of news articles, relevance of images, and the need for high-quality voice-overs. We have discussed proposed solutions for these challenges and the potential of AI-generated news videos in revolutionizing the news industry. Our review paper also highlights the research gaps in this field, such as the need for more advanced image and voice recognition technology and the potential ethical concerns of using AI-generated content.

Keywords: Web scraping, image searching, news authentication, scripting, audio generation, video generation, avatar creation, thumbnail

25.1 Introduction

Artificial intelligence (AI) has witnessed a sharp rise in adoption across a wide range of industries in recent years. AI is being used in the news media industry to turn news articles into videos that can be shared on social media sites like YouTube. This technology has the potential to transform the way in which news is disseminated and consumed by audiences worldwide. This review paper's goal is to assess the present state of knowledge about the applications of AI in the news media, with a focus on the transformation of news articles into videos. We will review some papers from a variety of academic journals, conferences, and industry reports, spanning the last 20 years. This review will offer a comprehensive

Corresponding author: kuldeep.vayadande1@vit.edu

Arindam Dey, Sukanta Nayak, Ranjan Kumar and Sachi Nandan Mohanty (eds.) How Machine Learning is Innovating Today's World: A Concise Technical Guide, (423–452) © 2024 Scrivener Publishing LLC

analysis of the present state of the art, the difficulties encountered, and the prospects presented by this developing technology.

An overview of the current state of AI-based news article-to-video conversion will be given in the first portion of this evaluation. We will examine the various methods used to extract information from news articles, including text-to-speech technology, image recognition, and natural language processing (NLP) techniques. We will also explore the different approaches used to generate video content, including video synthesis and video summarization.

One of the major ethical concerns surrounding the use of AI in news media is the potential for bias. AI models are only as objective as the data that were used to train them, and there is a chance that the data may already be biased. This can result in AI-generated videos that perpetuate stereotypes and reinforce prejudices. Another ethical concern is the impact of AI-generated videos on journalistic integrity. News media companies have a responsibility to report the facts accurately and without bias. There is a risk that the use of AI in news media could undermine this responsibility, as AI-generated videos may prioritize visual impact over accuracy.

There are also a number of technical challenges associated with the development and implementation of AI-based news article-to-video conversion. One challenge is the accuracy and reliability of the AI models used in the conversion process. AI models rely on a lot of training data to achieve high levels of accuracy, but there is a risk that the training data may be incomplete or biased, leading to inaccurate or unreliable results. Another challenge is the need for human oversight in the conversion process. While AI can automate many aspects of the video creation process, human oversight is still required to ensure the accuracy and integrity of the content. This can be time-consuming and costly, particularly for news media companies with limited resources.

The third section of this review will explore the opportunities presented by the use of AI in news media. We will examine the potential for AI to improve the speed and efficiency of news production, as well as the potential for AI-generated videos to reach new and diverse audiences.

One of the key opportunities presented by the use of AI in news media is the potential to improve the speed and efficiency of news production. AI can automate many aspects of the news production process, from article writing to video creation, enabling news media companies to produce high-quality content at a faster rate. AI can also be used to monitor social media and other online sources for breaking news and emerging trends, enabling news media companies to stay ahead of the curve and produce content that is both relevant and timely.

Another opportunity presented by the use of AI in news media is the potential to reach new and diverse audiences. AI-generated videos can be customized to meet the needs of different audiences, from multilingual videos to videos with captioning and other accessibility features. AI can also be used to personalize the news experience for individual viewers, providing them with content that is tailored to their interests and preferences. This can help to increase engagement and build loyalty among viewers.

Finally, we reviewed papers that focused on generating audio and video content using AI. These papers leveraged AI techniques to create high-quality audio and video content from text. The primary idea behind these papers is to automate the content creation process, which can significantly reduce the time and resources required to create high-quality videos.

One of the papers we examined described an approach to generating spoken language models from raw audio. This approach leverages deep learning techniques to create high-quality spoken language models that can be used for speech synthesis, speech recognition, and other speech-related tasks. Other papers focused on generating high-quality videos from text using techniques such as GANs, word embeddings, and compositional scenes. These papers are incredibly promising and have significant implications for the future of content creation.

25.2 Web Scraping

The massive and disorganized data that are available on the internet can be mined for relevant information via a process called web scraping. Singrodia *et al.* [1] have given a quick description of web scraping, the numerous programs and tools used for web scraping, and the various web scraping methodologies. They have also talked about the various applications for web scraping, as well as its benefits and drawbacks [9, 15].

The fact that web scraping saves time and produces error-free data is one of its many benefits. Online scraping, according to authors, can be used for a number of things, such as pricing comparison online, website update detection, web mashups, weather data monitoring, web data integration, and web research. The report continues by pointing out that web scraping can violate some websites' terms of usage. The paper offers a thorough and well-written review of web scraping overall. The paper is an excellent resource for anyone interested in this issue because they also describe the numerous fields in which web scraping may be applied. The only suggestion for improvement could be to add some real-life examples of the application of web scraping in different fields to provide more practical insights to the readers.

Frameworks, on the other hand, offer an integrated solution that streamlines the web scraping process. Scrapy is an example of a powerful scraping framework in Python that describes robots as classes derived from BaseSpider class. While processing web pages and extracting their contents, XPath expressions are required. Another framework in Java to perform web data scraping is Web-Harvest. It employs XML to describe the various "pipelines", including procedural commands, that make up the web extraction operations [20, 28].

Desktop-based platforms seem to be easier for a beginner programmer to use. The user interface helps the user to extract data using a web scraping tool without having to write complex code. Examples of desktop-based environments include Import.io and ParseHub.

There are two main approaches to web scraping: one based on the JSOUP and ADaMSoft libraries, and the other based on the Lucene Apache suite/Solr/Nutch.

Using an open source library called JSOUP to navigate and handle the data on web pages is part of the JSOUP and ADaMSoft strategy. Nevertheless, dealing with websites that do not use conventional HTML text can provide challenges for this strategy. On the other hand, the Lucene Apache suite/Nutch/Solr is a comprehensive and open source web crawler that can be used for parsing, indexing, creating a search engine, and customizing search based on needs. Another tool in the set is the open source enterprise search platform Apache Solr, which supports database interaction, faceted search, hit highlighting, full-text search, and dynamic clustering.

Machine learning and computer vision methods can be used to extract information from webpages using this technology, which comprehends how a page is illustrated as a human could and then correlates them to CSS selectors.

Retrieving broadcast news videos is a crucial undertaking for news organizations, scholars, and journalists. The enormous amount of data included in televised news footage has been mined for useful information using text and image retrieval techniques. Let us examine various text and picture retrieval techniques used in live news broadcasts in [2].

A. Text Retrieval Approaches

Keyword-based retrieval: This approach is based on the manual annotation of videos with keywords and phrases that represent the content of the video. These annotations can be done by human annotators or using automated tools like speech recognition software. The user can then search for videos using these keywords and phrases.

Retrieval based on named entity recognition (NER): NER is the process of locating and categorizing named entities in text. In the context of broadcast news videos, NER can be used to extract information about people, organizations, and locations mentioned in the video. This information can then be used to index the video and enable retrieval based on these entities.

Topic-based retrieval: This approach is based on the identification of topics discussed in the video. Topics can be identified using topic modeling techniques such as Latent Dirichlet Allocation (LDA). Once the topics have been identified, the video can be indexed based on these topics, and the user can search for videos based on the topics of interest.

Natural Language Processing (NLP)-based retrieval: By analyzing the text in the video, NLP techniques can be utilized to draw out important information. Sentiment analysis, for instance, can be used to gauge the video's emotional tone, while text summarizing can be used to draw out the most crucial details.

B. Image Retrieval Approaches

Face recognition-based retrieval: Face recognition techniques can be used to identify people in the video. This information can be used to index the video and enable retrieval based on the people present in the video.

Object recognition-based retrieval: Object recognition techniques can be used to identify objects in the video. This information can be used to index the video and enable retrieval based on the objects present in the video.

Scene recognition-based retrieval: Scene recognition techniques can be used to identify the scene in the video. This information can be used to index the video and enable retrieval based on the scene of interest.

Visual features can be used to index videos and enable retrieval based on visual similarities. These features include color, texture, and shape.

Khalid and Noah [4] investigate the utility of information-sharing communities such as Wikipedia and automated extraction tools such as DBpedia in building machine-processing information management systems with relational facts about entities. The specific goal of this study is to produce larger queries using a multi-modality ontology retrieval system and relational data about entities in order to create a knowledge base with resources for visual news in the BBC sports domain. The system seeks to retrieve results for particular entities with high precision, good recall, and different sports photographs. The authors blend a

Table 25.1 Summary of Section 25.2: web scraping.

Ref. no.	Enabling technology	Contributions
[1]	Libraries: Libcurl, jsoup in Java, and BeautifulSoup in Python. Framework: Scrapy, web harvest	Libraries—Can be used via different programming languages. Frameworks—Offers an integrated solution that simplifies the process of web scraping. Desktop-based platforms—Provides a user-friendly interface where no programming knowledge is required.
[2]	Keyword-based retrieval Topic-based retrieval NLP-based retrieval Face recognition-based retrieval Object recognition-based retrieval Scene recognition-based retrieval	Text retrieval approaches—This approach uses keywords and phrases to annotate videos, allowing users to search for videos using these keywords. Image retrieval approaches—Face recognition-based retrieval can be used to identify people in the video. Object recognition and scene recognition techniques can enable retrieval based on the scene of interest.
[3]	News extraction patterns: Content pattern Filter pattern	Content pattern—The news article's original text is extracted using the content pattern. Filter pattern—For each page, a separate pattern of the filter pattern is used to remove non-news components such as text and video advertisements, links, images, and scripts.

written description and a graphic description that were both manually developed with a domain sport ontology description taken from DBpedia. Automated ontology alignment is utilized to prevail semantic interoperability between ontologies, while higher diversity in the final ranks is achieved by using visual similarity measurements based on SIFT features and MPEG7 descriptions. Table 25.1 shows summary of Section 25.2: web scraping.

25.3 Image Searching

The patent [7] describes a technology for improving image search engines by allowing users to select an image as a query and then using a classification system to compare and re-rank other images based on their similarity to the query image. The classification system chooses a comparison mechanism based on the intention class of the selected image, which is used to weigh the features of each image and determine its similarity score. By re-ranking search results based on these similarity scores, the technology aims to provide more relevant and accurate image search results for users.

This adaptive image post-processing mechanism can provide a more personalized and relevant set of images to the user, by taking into account the user's specific query and selection of a query image. This approach can be particularly useful for image search applications where the user's intent may not be accurately captured by text-based queries alone.

The study offered a three-component solution to the problem of whether it is feasible to add links to images to textbooks. Using a polynomial time method, the first component optimized the placement of images within a chapter's various sections. The second component obtained various sets of pertinent images from the web using two image mining methods that made use of orthogonal signals. An assembling algorithm that integrated the outcomes of the individual algorithm assignments was the last component.

The image assignment component allocates each section the most relevant images while considering constraints of not adding too many images and not repeating an image across sections. The component employs a natural greedy algorithm, where the relevance scores of each image for each section are sorted and allocated in a decreasing order. However, this algorithm may not produce an optimal result. To get around this, a polynomial-time optimization problem is formulated and solved optimally. The MAX RELEVANT IMAGE ASSIGNMENT optimization problem maximizes the sum of relevance scores for all images that have been assigned while taking into account the limitations of the maximum number of images that can be assigned to each section and the restriction of only using an image once per chapter.

AFFINITY is an algorithm that mines the website for relevant images to a textbook section by using concept phrases and metadata associated with images from authoritative external sources. The algorithm extracts a series of images from the articles and assigns each one a relevance score based on how many articles contain it, how many concept phrases are in the metadata, and how many words from all the concepts in the metadata match the image. The top k photos with their matching relevance ratings are listed by AFFINITY.

The COMITY algorithm generates a list of the top k image results from the web along with relevance scores based on the inputs of a textbook section j, the desired number of image results k, the required number of image search results per query t, and the desired number of idea words c. Using the top c concept phrases from section j, the algorithm generates queries with two or three concept phrases each.

ENSEMBLE is designed to assign images to sections in a textbook chapter based on multiple image mining algorithms. The algorithm takes a set of sections, a set of images, and the number of desired images for each section as input. It then performs MAX_RELEVANT_IMAGE_ASSIGNMENT optimization over each image mining algorithm to obtain an assignment of images for all sections. For each section, the algorithm merges the ranked lists of all image mining algorithms using Borda's method and assigns the top Kj images. The assigned images are then removed from consideration for subsequent sections, and the algorithm performs MAX_RELEVANT_IMAGE_ASSIGNMENT optimization over the remaining images and sections.

The overlap in the articles that the AFFINITY and COMITY algorithms used to retrieve the images and the overlap in the photographs themselves are determined. The overlap in the article is determined to be small, especially when analyzed at the chapter level and averaged over all chapters for a subject. To determine article overlap, the articles from which the top images for a given chapter were gathered using each algorithm are pooled. The intersection and union ratios of these articles are then determined for each chapter.

According to the statistics, ENSEMBLE performs best when the majority of the ensembled algorithms are using non-overlapping data.

The field of image recommendation systems is rapidly growing, as the amount of visual content available online continues to increase. One promising approach to developing such systems is to use a combination of keyword relevance and image features to make recommendations to users. Sejal *et al.* [10] propose a novel method for image recommendation that takes into account both semantic content and visual characteristics of images.

The paper presents a detailed overview of the proposed method, which uses an absorbing Markov chain to model user behavior and predict image preferences based on keywords and image features. The authors use a keyword-based similarity metric to calculate the transition probabilities textbook chapter based on multiple image mining algorithms. The algorithm takes a set of sections, a set of images, and the number of desired images for each section as input. It then performs MAX_RELEVANT_IMAGE_ASSIGNMENT optimization over each image mining algorithm to obtain an assignment of images for all sections. For each section, the algorithm merges the ranked lists of all image mining algorithms using Borda's method and assigns the top Kj images. The assigned images are then removed from consideration for subsequent sections, and the algorithm performs MAX_RELEVANT_IMAGE_ASSIGNMENT optimization over the remaining images and sections.

The overlap in the articles that the AFFINITY and COMITY algorithms used to retrieve the images and the overlap in the photographs themselves are determined. The overlap in the article is determined to be small, especially when analyzed at the chapter level and averaged over all chapters for a subject. To determine article overlap, the articles from which the top images for a given chapter were gathered using each algorithm are pooled. The intersection and union ratios of these articles are then determined for each chapter. According to the statistics, ENSEMBLE performs best when the majority of the ensembled algorithms are using non-overlapping data.

The field of image recommendation systems is rapidly growing, as the amount of visual content available online continues to increase. One promising approach to developing such systems is to use a combination of keyword relevance and image features to make recommendations to users. Sejal *et al.* [10] propose a novel method for image recommendation that takes into account both semantic content and visual characteristics of images.

The paper presents a detailed overview of the proposed method, which uses an absorbing Markov chain to model user behavior and predict image preferences based on keywords and image features. The authors use a keyword-based similarity metric to calculate the transition probabilities between images, taking into account the relevance of each keyword to the images in question. Additionally, the authors incorporate image features into the recommendation system, which allows for a more comprehensive understanding of the visual characteristics of images.

Wang *et al.* [6] propose a novel adaptive line search technique for multi-image super-resolution (SR), which can increase the solution's precision while quickening the iterative SR process' convergence. In order to solve this poorly conditioned and underdetermined large-scale problem, previous SR methods did not place a strong emphasis on mathematical techniques. To avoid running iterations to test the proper step size, the authors of this paper introduce an approximate analytical expression of the step size. They further alter the suggested approach to make it more adaptable to various SR circumstances. Table 25.2 shows summary of Section 25.3: image searching [6–10]. The effectiveness of the

Table 25.2 Summary of Section 25.3: image searching.

Ref. no.	Enabling technology	Contributions
[6]	Adaptive line search strategy Quasi-Newton (QN) method with an inexact line search method	The author suggests an adaptive line search approach that can speed up the convergence of the SR reconstruction process and increase the precision of the solution by obtaining an approximate analytical formula for the step size. Solves issues such as poor convergence, slow approach, lack of adaptiveness, and high computational cost in previous algorithms.
[7]	Adaptive Visual Similarity based Image Search	Patent provides a more personalized and relevant set of images to the user, by taking into account the user's specific query and selection of a query image. This approach can be particularly useful for image search applications where the user's intent may not be accurately captured by text-based queries alone.
[8]	Image mining: Affinity and Comity Ensemble Algorithm Polynomial Time algorithm	Proposed technique avoids repeating the same image in different sections of the same chapter in the textbooks.
[10]	Content-based image retrieval Annotation-based image retrieval Markov Process	Proposed framework improves the keyword relevance probability by considering the occurrence of keywords and their logical connection using a Markov chain.

suggested method is examined on both artificial datasets and real-world scenes, demonstrating its superiority to other methods of line search.

The effectiveness and superiority of the suggested strategy over other line search strategies are shown by experimental results from real-world scenes and artificial datasets. The suggested approach demonstrates its fast computation speed and higher convergence performance, requiring fewer steps and more accurate results in less time with lower calculation costs. The authors also compare their proposed strategy with the learning-based SR approach, due to its satisfactory reconstruction qualities. The proposed strategy shows comparable or even better reconstruction qualities with much less computational complexity.

25.4 News Authentication

Singhal *et al.* [11] introduce a viable answer to the fake news issue that is growing on social media—SpotFake, which offers a multi-modal framework for false news detection [29, 31, 33]. The suggested method analyzes an article's textual and visual components to identify fake news

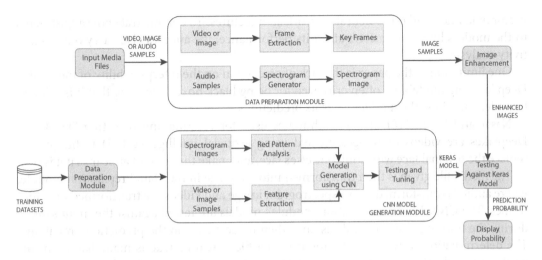

Figure 25.1 Block diagram of the deepfake detection system.

without the need for any additional subtasks. Figure 25.1 shows Block diagram of the deepfake detection system.

To learn textual and visual features from VGG-19 that have already been trained on the ImageNet dataset, the system uses language models like BERT. Weibo and Twitter, two publicly accessible databases, are employed in the research. For both datasets, the suggested model performed 3.27% and 6.83% better than the state of the art, respectively.

The multimodal fusion module, the visual feature extractor, and the textual feature extractor are the three sub-modules that make up SpotFake [11]. The textual feature extractor uses a language model to extract contextual text features from the news post (BERT). The visual feature extractor gathers visual features from the post using a pre-trained VGG-19 network. The textual and visual features are combined in the multimodal fusion module to create a news feature vector, which is then fed into a fully connected neural network for the classification of fake news.

Saleh *et al.* [13] propose a novel approach to detect fake news. The authors develop a CNN architecture that is optimized using grid search and data augmentation to improve its performance.

The authors argue that detecting fake news is a challenging task that requires not only identifying false information but also considering the context in which it is presented. The authors suggest a CNN architecture with a pooling layer, several convolutional layers, and a fully linked layer. To avoid overfitting and enhance the model's generalization capabilities, dropout regularization is also used.

The authors use a grid search to discover the ideal model hyperparameters in order to optimize the CNN architecture. The learning rate, batch size, and number of filters employed in the convolutional layers are among the hyperparameters that are optimized. To expand the training set and strengthen the model's robustness, the authors additionally use data augmentation.

The LIAR and FakeNewsNet datasets are just a couple of the datasets that the authors use to test their proposed CNN architecture. The outcomes demonstrate that their model performs better than a number of standard techniques, such as logistic regression, support vector machines, and other neural network architectures. To demonstrate how adjustments to the model's hyperparameters affect its performance, the authors also carry out a sensitivity analysis.

One limitation of the paper is the lack of discussion on the interpretability of the model. Deep learning models are often criticized for being black boxes, meaning that it is difficult to understand how the model makes its predictions.

Nasar and Lason [18] discuss techniques used for creating and detecting Deepfakes. Deepfakes are videos or images created using artificial intelligence (AI) techniques to replace the original face with someone else's face, and make the content appear as if it is real.

The media file given is then transformed into an image in the Data Preparation module, where audio is transformed into a spectrogram image and videos are transformed into keyframes. The CNN Model Generation module's models are tested against the input sample during the testing phase, and a decision is then made based on the prediction probability. The determination of whether the input media file is real or fake is made based on this prediction probability. Denoising is the process of removing any noise elements from the image files after they have been passed through the Image Enhancement module. When compared to current systems, the proposed system shortens the processing time and boosts performance using a combinational approach.

The authors describe various types of adversarial attacks that can be used to deceive NLP-based fake news detection models and provide insights into potential solutions for this problem. Different types of attacks are categorized as:

1. Word substitution attacks: In this type of attack, the attacker replaces certain words in the text with similar-looking or similar-sounding words that have a different meaning. For example, "their" can be replaced with "there" or "they're," which are homophones that have different meanings. These substitutions can be difficult to detect for both humans and machine learning algorithms, and can lead to misclassification of the text.
2. Text synthesis attacks: In this type of attack, the attacker generates new text that is designed to mislead the machine learning algorithm. For example, the attacker can generate a fake news article that is similar in style and tone to a legitimate news article, but contains false information. These synthesized texts can be more difficult to detect than word substitution attacks, as they are completely new pieces of text rather than modified versions of existing text.

The authors then introduce adversarial attacks, which are malicious attempts to manipulate or deceive models. They describe different types of adversarial attacks that can be used to deceive NLP-based fake news detection models, such as synonym replacement, character-level modification, and perturbation of word embeddings.

While creating a fake news detection model, researchers faced the following challenges:

Lack of a clear definition of fake news: The lack of a clear and universally agreed-upon definition of fake news makes it difficult to define and detect it accurately. This ambiguity can make it challenging to create a model that is robust to adversarial attacks.

Table 25.3 Summary of Section 25.4: news authentication.

Ref. no.	Enabling technology	Contributions
[11]	Multi-model framework BRRT, VGG-19	Focuses on the difficulty of spotting fake news on social media. The multimodal fusion module fuses the textual and visual characteristics to produce a news feature vector, which is then input into a fully connected neural network to classify fake news.
[12]	Deep convolutional neural network	The proposed FNDNet uses a deep neural network with many hidden layers to automatically learn the differentiating characteristics for false news classification rather than relying on manually created features.
[13]	CNN architecture that is optimized using grid search and data augmentation	Used a grid search to identify the model's ideal hyperparameters. Learning rate, batch size, and the quantity of filters used in the convolutional layers are examples of optimized hyperparameters. Used data augmentation to expand the training set and strengthen the model's robustness.
[14]	Graph convolutional neural networks Mean-field layers	The underlying structural information of the news articles is utilized, and the inherent association between them is taken into account, using graph convolutional neural networks and mean-field layers.
[16]	Naive Bayes Algorithm Support vector machines (SVMs) Random forests	Web scraping is used to extract different attributes from news articles, and those attributes are then fed into machine learning algorithms. The Nave Bayes algorithm outperforms every other algorithm that was tested, according to the authors, who applied several machine learning algorithms and checked the accuracy of each one.
[17]	ResNet-101 Inception-v3 VGG-16 model Support vector machine	CNNs that have already been trained are used by the authors to extract visual features from the news images. Then, they used SVM classifier to train the model. Also conducted a sensitivity analysis to examine the importance of different components of their approach.

(Continued)

Table 25.3 Summary of Section 25.4: news authentication. (*Continued*)

Ref. no.	Enabling technology	Contributions
[18]	CNN GAN Image forgery detection model	When compared to current systems, to shorten processing time and boost performance, the proposed system uses a combinational approach with CNN architecture for image processing. Reduces the negative effects brought on by these types of media files by identifying forgeries in audio, video, and image files.
[19]	NLP Multi-task learning framework	Demonstrates the vulnerability of NLP-based fake news detection models to adversarial attacks. Authors proposed using an ensemble of models with different architectures to increase the model's robustness to attacks. Used a multi-task learning framework that jointly learns to classify news articles as real or fake, as well as to predict the veracity of related claims in the articles.

Limited training data: Most fake news detection datasets are relatively small and may not be representative of the full range of fake news articles. This limited data can make it challenging to train models that are robust to adversarial attacks.

One can tailor adversarial attacks: Adversarial attacks can be tailored to specific models and can be designed to evade detection. This means that it may be difficult to build a model which is entirely immune to adversarial attacks.

Adversarial attacks can be difficult to detect: The detection process may require significant computational resources. This can make it challenging to develop effective countermeasures against adversarial attacks.

The results showed that all of the models tested were vulnerable to both types of attacks, with some models being more susceptible than others. The authors found that the attacks were able to significantly reduce the accuracy of the models, with some models showing a reduction of up to 50%. The authors also suggested an adversarial training-based defense mechanism, in which the models are trained on both the original and hostile examples. They found that this approach was effective in improving the robustness of the models against adversarial attacks. Table 25.3 shows summary of Section 25.4: news authentication.

25.5 Scripting for Video

Ji *et al.* [21] present VScript, a novel controllable script generation system that creates full screenplays, replete with dialogue and scene descriptions, and uses video retrieval to visually portray them. The technology provides an interactive interface that enables end users to choose fields and enter initial words to modify the progression and theme of the created screenplay. The system creates the storyline, script, and visual presentation using a hierarchical structure. By considering it as an inverted conversation summary problem, a novel method for plot-guided dialogue production is presented. In both automatic and human evaluations, the experiment's findings demonstrate that VScript executes better than the baselines, particularly in standings of genre control. The paper is well-structured, and the figure examples help illustrate the system's components and functionalities. Overall, VScript appears to be a promising tool for scriptwriters who seek to customize their scripts and improve their engagement through visual presentations.

The paper introduces a framework that generates a script for a movie or TV show and provides a visual presentation of the scenes. The framework has two modules: visual presentation and script generation. In the script generation module, the authors first create a narrative that is genre-specific that chronologically directs the creation of speech and scene descriptions. Four genres are selected for plot generation: Crime, Sci-Fi, War, and Romance. By implementing control codes, which are specified genres, a class-conditional language model is trained for plot generation. The model is fine-tuned using a movie summary corpus that includes Wikipedia movie storylines and associated metadata, like genre. A multi-class genre classifier is further trained to make sure the generated plots are consistent with the intended genre.

The dialogue creation task is viewed by the authors as an abstractive dialogue summarizing that has been reversed, with the model being trained to generate the entire discourse from the dialogue summary. Two dialogue summarization corpora, SAMSum and DialogSum Corpus, are combined as the training set. The model makes the assumption that each sentence in the plot may be enlarged into a single scene, which can then be divided into the dialogue and scene description. A GPT2-large model is leveraged to generate dialogues for each plot sentence.

The baselines include GPT2 E fine-tuned on Film Corpus 1.05 in an end-to-end manner without plot and VideoCLIP for zero-shot video and text understanding. Other baselines include GPT2-large fine-tuned on inversed SAMSum and DialogSum Corpus, GPT2-large fine-tuned on CMU Movie Summary Corpus, and a CC-LM. The paper evaluates the VScript framework using Genre-Specific Plot Generation and Plot-Guided Dialogue Generation, and evaluates the results using perplexity, Genre-ACC, BLEU, Sentence Similarity, Distinct-n, and Repeat.

The study shows that the suggested VScript framework can generate screenplays of particular genres while adhering to predetermined plots. The hierarchical structure and inversed abstractive summarization used in the framework are shown to be effective in achieving this goal. The experimental results show that VScript outperforms various baselines and is a promising approach to controllable script generation.

The paper introduces a fresh approach to keyword extraction from a single web page, called D-rank. Unlike most existing methods that rely on natural language processing techniques that are language dependent, D-rank focuses on extracting language-independent features from structural information and text of the page. The method considers not only term frequency but also the URL, title, headings, and hyperlinks on the page to identify important words. Words are assigned scores based on their position and frequency. The top 20 words in the rankings are chosen. Using a straightforward Wikipedia search, the approach then eliminates the top 10 terms, leaving a final list of 10 keywords for the webpage. The approach is unsupervised, is domain and language independent, and supports several languages. Table 25.4 shows summary of Section 25.5: scripting for video.

Table 25.4 Summary of Section 25.5: scripting for video.

Ref. no.	Enabling technology	Contributions
[21]	GPT2-large model	The authors fine-tune the GPT2-large on a paired scene-dialogue corpus to infer scene descriptions from each dialogue.
[22]	DOM D-rank	It considers features like the URL, title, headings, and hyperlinks, as well as term frequency, to score words and select the top 20.

25.6 Audio Generation

Lakhotia *et al.* [23] highlight a significant problem in natural language processing (NLP) research: building systems that learn language from unfiltered, untextual input without access to expert labels or text. Although NLP systems have made considerable gains in minimizing or completely dodging the requirement for expert labels, text remains the primary unit on which these systems are taught. The majority of languages in the world that lack extensive textual resources or uniform orthography are affected by this. To address this challenge, the paper proposes a method for achieving "textless NLP" using audio-based input data.

The suggested method involves encoding voice into "pseudo-text" using automatically identified discrete units, which is then used to train a generative language model and a speech synthesizer. This method allows for the synthesis of speech and the learning of a language model from scratch without the use of text, effectively recreating what toddlers accomplish before learning to read. Proper evaluation methods to enable system comparison have been a significant roadblock to advancement in this area.

Overall, the paper highlights a major sector of research for the development of more inclusive and expressive AI systems that can learn from natural interactions. The proposed method for achieving "textless NLP" through audio-based input data shows promise, but proper evaluation methods will need to be established to enable system comparison and further progress in this area.

The paper proposes three new systems to perform speech recognition using unsupervised learning techniques: Speech-to-Unit Models, Unit-Language Models, and Unit-To-Speech Models. These systems are introduced as alternatives to existing supervised learning techniques, which, in order to operate well, need a lot of labeled data. The paper's authors claim that the proposed systems can perform well in low-resource settings and with limited labeled data, making them useful in many real-world scenarios.

The Speech-to-Unit Models system is built on three unsupervised encoders: HuBERT, wav2vec 2.0, and Contrastive Predictive Coding (CPC). Without any extra training or hyperparameter tuning, these models are used "out of the box." The authors employ a baseline log Mel filter bank with 80 filters, generated every 10 ms, to discretize the embeddings using k-means. Each of these models is briefly described in the paper, and further information can be found in the original papers. Also, the writers test out codebooks with 50, 100, and 200 units.

The Transformer model is used by the Unit-Language Model system, which is trained as a causal language model using collections of pseudo-text units. The authors train the model on a "clean" 6k hours sub-sample of the LibriLight dataset, which was previously utilized in research, and use sampling with temperature for model creation. In preliminary testing, the scientists discovered that deleting sequential repeats of units enhanced performance. They hypothesize that this alteration enables the more effective use of the Transformer's constrained attention span.

The research "High Quality Text-to-Speech Synthesis: An Overview" by authors Thierry Dutoit and Vincent Pagel provides a summary of the developments in high-quality text-to-speech (TTS) synthesis technology [24].

The authors start out by going over the development of TTS technology, from the earliest rule-based systems to the most advanced methods currently available, which incorporate statistical models and machine learning algorithms. They provide a detailed explanation of the various components of a TTS system, including text analysis, prosody modeling, and speech synthesis.

Prakash *et al.* [25] present a strategy for creating multilingual speech synthesizers for Indian languages using end-to-end deep learning models. The authors discuss the challenges faced in building such speech synthesizers and describe the architecture of the proposed

Table 25.5 Summary of Section 25.6: audio generation.

Ref. no.	Enabling technology	Contributions
[23]	Textless NLP Speech-to-Unit Models, Unit-Language Model, and Unit-To-Speech Model	Most of the NLPs require textual source to get trained, but Textless NLP can be trained using audio input as so many do not have textual resources.
[24]	Text analysis Prosody modeling Speech synthesis	The paper provides a deep review of all the techniques used in TTS systems, and also gives pros and cons of each technique with examples.
[25]	Multilingual speech synthesizer Text-to-speech (TTS) Voice conversion (VC)	The suggested system aims to create an Indian language multilingual speech synthesizer. The TTS model is in charge of employing deep learning techniques to transform input text into synthesized speech, while the VC model is utilized to transform synthetic speech into the voice of the target speaker.
[26]	Text Analysis-NLP Support vector machine Nearest neighbor algorithm	Authors built a music recommendation system. Here, the NLP takes the pre-processed data and extracts meaningful features. Then, the SVM predicts relevance of song to a given user and NNA is used to match user's request with most similar song.

system. It begins by discussing the importance of speech synthesis in the context of Indian languages, which have a diverse set of phonetic, prosodic, and morphological characteristics. The authors discuss the shortcomings of traditional voice synthesis techniques and recommend creating multilingual speech synthesizers utilizing end-to-end deep learning models. Table 25.5 shows summary of Section 25.4: audio generation [23–26].

The process of transforming input text into synthesized voice is handled by the TTS model. It comprises of a neural network that converts text into speech waveforms as its output. To learn the mapping between text and speech, the network is trained on a sizable dataset of Indian language text and associated speech samples. The TTS model uses deep learning techniques, such as recurrent neural networks (RNNs) and convolutional neural networks, to simulate the complex interplay between text and speech (CNNs). The main speaker's speech is added to the synthetic speech using the VC model. The target speaker's voice samples and the synthetic speech waveform are inputs to the VC model, which outputs a transformed speech waveform that sounds like the target speaker. The VC model additionally employs deep learning methods like CNNs and RNNs to simulate the speaker-dependent aspects of speech.

Overall, the suggested system uses end-to-end deep learning models to give a reliable and adaptable speech synthesis system for several Indian languages. The system can generate high-quality speech with natural prosody and intonation, making it suitable for various applications, such as virtual assistants, audiobooks, and language learning tools.

25.7   Mapping Text and Images

The Caption Crawler system is introduced as a present solution for providing accessible captions for images on websites that lack them. The system proposed in [27] utilizes a browser extension and cloud server to search for and retrieve pre-existing captions for images using reverse image search. The captions are dynamically added by the system, and the word "Auto Alt" is inserted earlier to the caption read out by a screen reader. The system's effectiveness was assessed on 481 well-known websites, and it was shown to be capable of providing alt text with an average delay of just 18 seconds for around 12% of the photos. In a user research, both sighted and blind users preferred longer, previously created captions as well as the choice to view alternative captions. According to the study, the Caption Crawler technology could aid in resolving the issue of missing and subpar online alt text.

The system may gather captions for images in a variety of formats, such as alt text, aria labels, figure captions, and components with "caption" in their class attribute. The aria-label element offers a textual description of the image when a caption is not explicitly specified in the DOM. Thanks to the addition of figure caption tags in HTML 5, a figure's caption or legend can now be communicated.

Zhang *et al.* [30] suggest a technique for producing accurate and comprehensive image descriptions utilizing online positive recall and missing ideas mining. The objective is to make image captions more precise and comprehensive, which is an important task for various applications such as image retrieval, assistive technology for visually impaired people, and social media. The proposed method uses an online positive recall algorithm to generate a set of candidate captions for an input image. The algorithm retrieves similar to an external dataset and extracts the captions associated with those images. These captions are used as candidates for the input image. The algorithm iteratively updates the candidate set by considering the positive recall of the generated captions.

Overall, the research study presents a promising method for creating accurate and comprehensive image captions using online positive recall and missing mining concepts. This method may be helpful in many computer vision and image processing applications.

The paper also discusses various challenges in image captioning, such as dealing with rare words and handling visual ambiguity. In addition, the authors highlight several important applications of image captioning, such as visual question answering, picture editing, and image retrieval. The paper also highlights several open research questions and challenges in the field, such as improving the ability of models to handle rare or ambiguous words, generating captions that are more diverse and informative, and designing models that can generate captions that are consistent with common sense knowledge. More developments in computer vision, natural language processing, and machine learning, according to the authors, are necessary to address these problems.

Dealing with uncommon and confusing terms was one of the difficulties. Dealing with words that are uncommon or unclear is one of the biggest issues in image captioning. This can be particularly challenging when generating captions for images that contain uncommon or complex scenes. An approach to address the challenge is to implement reinforcement learning-based models that are trained to generate captions that are more diverse and informative. Another challenge in image captioning is capturing the complex relationships between objects and scenes in an image. Natural language processing and computer vision must both be thoroughly understood for this. Attention-based models and transformer-based models have been successful in addressing this challenge by enabling the model to focus on specific areas of the image that are pertinent to the generated caption.

Encoder–decoder models: An encoder and a decoder are the two primary parts of this fundamental architecture for picture captioning. The encoder makes use of deep convolutional neural networks (CNNs), which include features from the input image. Since they generate a string of words based on the attributes of a picture, recurrent neural networks (RNNs) are typically used as the decoder. The most popular RNN is the long short-term memory (LSTM) network. The encoded visual features and the previous word are the inputs to the LSTM, and the output is a probability distribution across the vocabulary for the following word. This procedure is repeated until a sentence end token is acquired.

Attention-based models: Attention-based models improve on the encoder–decoder architecture by allowing the decoder to selectively attend to different regions of the input image while generating the caption. In this architecture, the LSTM-based decoder maintains a "soft" attention distribution over the image features at each time step, which is used to weight the features and generate the next word. The decoder can concentrate on various areas of the image that are pertinent to the word that is now being formed thanks to the attention mechanism. It has been demonstrated that this method enhances the quality of the captions that are created, especially for complicated photographs with several items or situations.

Transformer-based models: Transformers are a class of neural network design that have been effectively used for language modeling and translation applications that involve natural language. The captioning of images has also utilized transformer-based models. According to this architecture, a CNN encoder first analyzes the input image to extract image features, which are then used by a Transformer decoder to produce the caption. The model can capture intricate relationships between the visual data and the generated words thanks to the Transformer decoder's several layers of self-attention and feedforward neural networks.

Models that are based on reinforcement learning: A model is taught to optimize a reward function based on input from the outside world using the reinforcement learning technique. The degree to which the generated captions adhere to human preferences can be used to optimize a reward function in the context of image captioning. In these models, the decoder produces a string of words that are then assessed by a reward function, which gauges the caliber of the captions produced. The predicted reward is then maximized by training the model using policy gradient techniques. Particularly for uncommon or challenging terms, reinforcement learning-based models have shown promise in raising the caliber of output captions.

The authors note that the most successful models are based on attention mechanisms and transformers, which have been shown to outperform encoder–decoder models. The authors also emphasize the importance of using several metrics, including as BLEU, METEOR, ROUGE, and CIDEr, in order to provide a comprehensive assessment of the models' performance

25.8   AI-Avatar Generation

Tu *et al.* [32] introduce a model called FaceAnime that can generate videos from still images using a reconstructed 3D face dynamics approach. They propose to use this approach instead of the usual method that utilizes Generative Adversarial Networks (GANs) and sparse facial landmarks, which often lead to qualitative degradation, distortion, and unmatching of identity and expression. The 3D dynamics approach provides a strong prior knowledge for generating face movies that are incredibly lifelike and maintain your identity and have perfectly predicted poses and facial expressions. The model has demonstrated improved performance in producing high-fidelity, aesthetically beautiful videos of faces from a single source face picture, and it may be used for a variety of AR/VR and entertainment applications.

By swapping out thick 3D facial features overlaid over sparse 2D facial features, the paper suggests a novel technique for creating face films using 3D face dynamics. By using LSTMs and low-dimensional vectors, it is possible to forecast the global facial structure, position, and facial expression sub-elements of the 3D dynamics. The 3D dynamics, which comprise structure, content, and structural characteristics, which may be effectively leveraged to direct face development, are rendered using a pattern mapping that is thin technique. By utilizing the insightful 3D facial dynamics rather than 2D sparse facial parts, the authors presented, using single input images, a very realistic and identity-preserving face video. It makes use of an experimental model to look into face video forecasting in both deterministic and manageable ways; a 3DDP network for estimating a sparse pattern mapping technique is used to generate the 3D facial movements and apply them like information already.

An automated face-generation system and a 3D Dynamic Forecasting network are also parts of the FaceAnime model. The 3D Morphable Model and 3D Face Matching are used by the 3DDP system to forecast 3D dynamic events. By combining shape and expression coefficients in a linear fashion, the 3D corners of a 2D face image are predicted. Then, using a constant rotation grid, orthographic projection structure, and translation vector, the 3D vertices are mapped upon a 2D picture plane. By reducing the separation when comparing anticipated and discovered landmarks, the 3DMM coefficients are determined. By altering the 3DMM coefficients, sparse pattern mapping is utilized to change the 3D face shape and produce the desired sparse texture. Whereas the changed 3DMM coefficients for the face forecasting job are estimated by the LSTM modules, they are generated for the face centering task from the reference facial video sequence.

The method of creating talking avatars using speech signals is known as speech-driven face animation. A lot of research in this field focuses on developing a mapping between talked language and auditory qualities. Some of the methods are HMMs (hidden Markov models) to record the movement of speech and video frames. For the purpose of condensing video as well as audio elements, Simons and Cox used vector quantization. This article discusses two main approaches for video synthesis: face animation based on speech and using GAN for video generation. Speech-driven facial animation has been a topic of interest for decades and has used various methods, including HMMs and deep learning techniques like CNNs and RNNs. These methods aim to translate speech or audio features into facial animations. GAN-based video synthesis has recently gained the computational intelligence community's focus. GANs involve two competing networks, a classifier and a producer, which work together for generating realistic copies. GANs can be adapted for video synthesis by using 3D convolutional layers and by disentangling the latent space for motion and content. Moreover, cross-modal technologies like text-to-video and audio-to-video synthesis have leveraged GANs. While speech-driven facial animation focuses on the relationship between audio and facial motion, GAN-based video synthesis focuses on generating realistic videos by learning from real video data. Both approaches have their strengths and limitations, and future research may involve combining these approaches or developing new methods altogether.

Generator and Discriminator: The End-to-End Verbal Face Animation proposes a novel architecture that combines a Temporal GAN with an encoder–decoder network for generating speech-driven facial animations. The generator and discriminator networks used in this architecture are as follows:

Generator: The generator network in this architecture is a Temporal GAN that uses the features gleaned from the speech signal and generates the corresponding facial animation sequence. The generator network is made up of encoder–decoder architecture, where the encoder network encodes the speech features and the decoder network generates the facial animation sequence. The generator network is conditioned on the input speech features, which are concatenated with the noise vector each step to produce the facial animation sequence. The generator has been taught to produce facial animations visually like the actual facial animation sequence.

Discriminator: The discriminator network in this architecture is also a Temporal GAN that takes as input the facial animation sequence and outputs a probability indicating whether the input sequence is real or fake. The discriminator network consists of a convolutional neural network (CNN) that processes the input facial animation sequence each step to predict the probability of the input sequence being real or fake. The discriminator is taught to differentiate between the genuine facial animation sequence along with the generated facial animation sequence. In summary, the generator network is responsible for generating facial animations that match the input speech features, while the discriminator network is responsible for distinguishing between real and fake facial animation sequences.

The training process involves updating the parameters of both the generator and discriminator networks in an adversarial manner to achieve a balance between generating realistic facial animations and fooling the discriminator.

Qualitative Results: The authors also evaluated the the level of the facial motions produced using qualitative analysis. The qualitative evaluations showed that the given method generated facial animations that were visually similar to the ground truth facial animation sequences. The authors used several examples to demonstrate the quality of the generated facial animations, such as the ability of the method to capture facial expressions, mouth movements, and eye movements.

Language Generalization: The authors also assessed the ability of the given method to generalize to multiple languages and dialects. The outcomes reveal that the given method was able to generate facial animations for multiple languages and dialects, including English, Mandarin, and Cantonese. The authors demonstrated the ability of the method to capture the distinct facial movements associated with different languages and dialects.

Robustness: The authors also evaluated the given method's resistance to noise speech input and missing frames in the facial animation sequence. The outcomes show that the suggested method was more reliable than cutting-edge techniques to both noisy speech input and missing

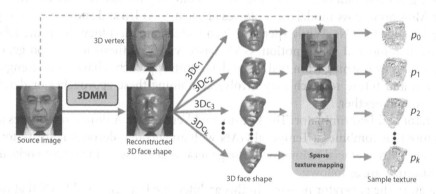

Figure 25.2 Illustration of 3D face reconstruction. Source: Adapted from [32].

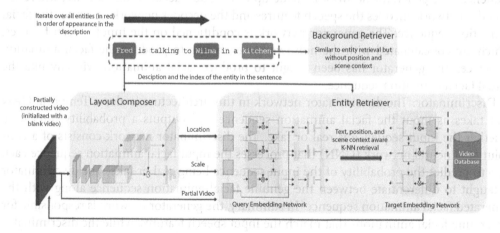

Figure 25.3 Overview of the CRAFT model. Source: Adapted from [34].

frames. The authors demonstrated the ability of the method to generate facial animations even with noisy speech input or missing frames in the facial animation sequence. Figure 25.2 shows illustration of 3D face reconstruction. Figure 25.3 shows overview of the CRAFT model.

In summary, the experimental outcomes demonstrated the efficacy of the suggested approach in generating speech-driven facial animations that were visually similar to the ground truth facial animation sequences, and achieved better performance than the most recent techniques for quantitative metrics such as SSIM, PSNR, MAE, and FER. The proposed method was also shown to be robust to noisy speech input and missing frames, and capable of generalizing to multiple languages and dialects.

25.9   Video Generation

To convey images through words, good writing uses well-known visual notions. This is referred to as capability to make, which assesses how closely a term or phrase is connected to a tangible concept. However, in order for the use of tangible language, the reader must be conversant with the subjects being discussed. In many instances, visual content, like pictures, videos, maps, and diagrams, can improve written material. By synchronizing the presentation of visuals with specific text passages, Audio-visual content can also encourage interaction with the material.

Leake *et al.* [5] present a technology that converts informative articles into audio-visual presentations by utilizing the concreteness of written language. By examining each sentence's grammatical structure, and determining and utilizing the most precise words as search queries in picture search engines, it is able to find imagery pertinent to each sentence in the text. By creating audio-visual slideshows for brief text articles from various genres that last anywhere between 20 and 131 seconds, researchers show the efficacy of their methodology. Their presentations' quality is on par with slideshows created manually using common video editing software, and viewers much prefer them to presentations created only using keyword searches.

The system aims to turn a text article into an audible presentation, using a four-step process. The text is first segmented into sentences, and a single image is selected to represent each sentence. Text-to-speech is used for creating audio narration that is then timed with the visuals and end results are added to create the slideshow. The paper's main contribution is a concreteness-based method for selecting using the right pictures to illustrate each text. Figure 25.4 shows generating key phrases from subtitle.

The process of creating a slideshow with audio narration involves obtaining images, generating narration using Google Cloud Text-to-Speech, and timing the narration using

| (T1) Subtitles | (T2) Sentences | (T3) Key phrases |

Figure 25.4 Generating key phrases from subtitle. Source: Adapted from [39].

Google Speech-to-Text with the Needleman-Wunsch algorithm. The images are time-aligned to the narration, but are only displayed when the search query's first word appears to avoid confusion. Video effects and captions are added to enhance the slideshow's clarity and aesthetic appeal. This includes resizing and cropping images using python-smart-crop, applying zoom or pan effects to images longer than 3 seconds, and incorporating captions that display the original text at the bottom of the screen.

A paper evaluates the quality of the search queries generated by the algorithm by comparing them to hand-crafted search requests. The results show a significant overlap between manual and automatic search queries, for a mean F1 score for P1, P2, and P3 of 0.74, 0.57, and 0.63, respectively. The comparison of picture search results demonstrates that, despite different search keywords, the resulting photos could not be noticeably different. When more words are added to the automatic search query, in some situations, a different image is returned, yet both still display the same information.

Gupta *et al.* [34] introduce a brand-new method for creating the Formulation, Search, and Merge Networks, which create complex scene videos using natural language specifications (Craft). The Craft model generates films from novel captions by learning geographical, visual, and semantic world knowledge from video caption data. The model extracts temporal chunks of video from other library sources and combines them to produce scene films. It also explicitly predicts the temporal arrangement of actors and objects in a scene.

The paper's contributions include losses that induce learning compositional representations for retrieval and sequential training of Craft components while concurrently modeling layout and appearances. The Craft model performs better than direct pixel generation methods and generalizes effectively to video databases without text annotations and unseen captions. With the Flintstones dataset, which includes more than 25,000 videos, the authors show how well the Craft model works.

The task of the layout composer is to create a realistic scene layout that includes the positions and sizes of all the the individuals and items mentioned inside the scenario description. The layout composer is set up to go through the collection of unique entities provided in a given description in a systematic fashion. Using a text encoding of the intended entity, the model forecasts divisions for target object's scale as well as the position at each stage and a partially created video as inputs. The CNN and the bidirectional LSTM form the same feature processing backbone for the position and scale predictors. The caption is passed into the LSTM, and the entity text encoding is recovered from the word position's hidden output. The text encryption was performed multiple times and then combined with neural features and two-dimensional grid positions for producing a visualization for every position as a property map layout, which is conscious of the contexts that are visible, geographical, chronological, and emotional.

The Entity Retriever finds a temporal fix that corresponds to an object that appears in the description and fits the previously created video in the database. Entity builder's work is to retrieve an entity that not only matches but also respects the semantics of the description while also taking into account any implied relationship restrictions imposed by the presence and placement of other items. An auxiliary multi-label classification loss is added on top of the embeddings to anticipate the nouns, adjectives, and action words that are specifically related to the entity for the purpose of enhancing the vocabulary of the embedding vectors.

Overall, the Composition, Retrieval, and Fusion Network appears to provide a promising approach to video generation from natural language descriptions. The paper gives a comprehensive description of different components of the network and provides detailed architecture and training details. However, more investigation is required to assess the effectiveness of the network and its ability to generalize to different video datasets and natural language descriptions. Table 25.6 shows summary of Section 25.9: video generation.

In terms of limitations, the paper only focuses on generating videos from natural language descriptions and does not consider the possibility of generating descriptions from videos. Additionally, the paper does not give a thorough evaluation of the network's performance, such as quantitative evaluation measures or contrasts with other cutting-edge methods for producing videos. Future research could explore these areas to provide a more comprehensive understanding of the capabilities and limitations of the Network for Formulation, Searching, and Merge. In conclusion, the paper presents a novel approach to generating videos from natural language

Table 25.6 Summary of Section 25.9: video generation.

Ref. no.	Enabling technology	Contributions
[34]	Layout Composer Entity Retriever Background Retriever	Composer forecasts a position as well as size for an object. Retriever generates a search embedding, which is compared to objects' extracted features in the intended video collection. The best backdrop video is pulled from the data collection by the background retriever, which creates a search embedding for the required scenario.
[35]	Evolutionary generator Video synthesizer	Match the input textual description to iteratively generate images. Form a video by combining the sequence of images produced.
[36]	GAN	Generator network of GAN takes the latent representation as input and produces a sequence of video frames, while the discriminator network of GAN distinguishes between the generated and real frames from the dataset.
[37]	Text encoder network Scene generator network	Proposed a model to convert the textual description into a set of semantic features. Create a bunch of scene objects and their features like size, position, orientation, etc.
[38]	Frame-level coherence-aware discriminator Video-level semantic-aware discriminator	Maintains a sync between each frame and text, improves the temporal coherence among two successive images as well as the reality in each produced image. Utilizes the global data throughout the full video to produce a real film that closely matches the explanation in human language semantically.

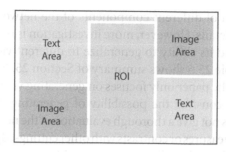

Figure 25.5 Thumbnail layout. Source: Adapted from [39].

descriptions. The Network for Formulation, Searching, and Merging consists of three components, including the Layout builder, the Entity searcher, and the Background searcher, which are trained autonomously using ground truth supervision. While the paper provides a thorough description of the network and its components, further research is needed to evaluate its effectiveness and generalizability. In conclusion, the paper presents a novel approach to generating videos from natural language descriptions. Overall, the Composition, Retrieval, and Fusion Network has the potential to be a valuable tool for video generation from natural language descriptions. Figure 25.5 shows thumbnail layout.

In conclusion, the given approach presented in the paper offers a new and effective method for creating creative scenes with descriptions in text. The two-stage process, which includes a text-to-scene neural network and a rendering engine, allows for the creation of complex and visually appealing scenes that are semantically consistent with the input text. The method has the potential utilized for a wide range of purposes, including virtual reality and gaming, where realistic and complex scenes are required.

25.10   Thumbnail Creation

Online viewers can quickly assess the relevance of video content by using thumbnails, which offer an effective way to perceive video content. Zhao *et al.* [39] described a technique for automatically producing thumbnails that resemble magazine covers utilizing the key visual and textual metadata that was retrieved from videos. The necessity is that manually selecting a thumbnail from a long film is a labor-intensive and time-consuming process.

This approach has three steps, i.e., visual–textual layout generation, and extraction of both textual and visual content.

A. Visual Content Extraction

The method starts by choosing the video's most effective and appealing frames utilizing a frame evaluation approach. The method initially separates the movie into subshots before clustering the important frames of those subshots with the help of k-means algorithm (KNN). Then, aesthetic scores (attractiveness) and cluster size (representativeness) are calculated to determine the sequence of the key frames. As the image that will be added in background for thumbnail generation, we choose the key frame in the largest cluster with the highest aesthetic score. After performing salient region detection, we selected a few additional sample key frames from the remaining clusters, and the prominent elements of these photographs were embedded into the background's non-salient area to create an informative thumbnail.

B. Textual Content Extraction

The author uses an automatic keyword extracting technique to pull keywords that are available in the subtitles of videos in order to obtain valuable, speech-rich topic terms. If subtitles are not available, then a speech recognition tool can be used.

C. Visual–Textual Layout Generation

In order to produce a concise, informative, and visually appealing thumbnail, descriptive topic phrases and prominent visual objects that are detected are superimposed onto the backdrop image. We suppose that in a flawless backdrop image, there is just one salient region. As seen in Figure 25.2, only the area that is the most salient will be selected as a region of consideration for extra processing. Because there are so many potential arrangements, we individually process the typography's textual and visual elements.

Firstly, the background image's non-salient region is covered with the cropped visual objects. Let $V = \{s1, s2, sN\}$ represent the collection of visual objects that were extracted.

The challenge is defined as a cost function, where the aim is to scale down the salient region of an image to add it into the area which is non-salient. The cost function (Lv) is a sum of products of the original area size of each salient region (ai) and an indicator function (I) that indicates whether the fitting coefficient (ri) is greater than a certain threshold (δ).

After arranging the visual objects in the thumbnail, key phrases are overlaid onto the non-salient area. The problem is formulated as a function (Lt) for energy, which combines the proportion of the area of consideration covered in the waste of spare non-salient region (Es), intrusive text (Ei), and the total weight of the key words chosen (Ew).

The system detects faces on the chosen visual objects if the total number of key words chosen falls below the threshold (Nt). If a face item is found, only the head portion of the image is retained; the rest is trimmed to add additional descriptive keyphrases to the thumbnail.

Shimono et al. [40] present a method for automatically creating YouTube video thumbnails that ensures expressive facial expressions of the content creator in the frame, an entire idea of the video's subject, and a headline that clearly describes the content.

Method for frame sampling: Usually, videos are made with 30 or 60 frames per second, and it is not possible to analyze all, so approximately 300 samples of images are taken from each video at regular intervals, so that we can maintain the time of remaining process.

Emotional Recognition: To recognize emotions, they use Face API, which is made by Microsoft, and this can recognize eight emotions, which include disgust, contempt, anger, neutral, surprise, fear, sadness, and happiness.

Representative Object Image Insertion: The method described involves inserting representative object images into a background image for a video. The process starts with a Google search using a specified keyword to obtain the top five images. The similarities between the images are then evaluated using the average hash method, which involves converting the images to grayscale, compressing them, and calculating the average pixel value. The Hamming distance is then calculated to determine the two most similar images. One of these pictures is chosen and pasted over the background picture as the foreground picture. The backdrop of the selected image is made transparent, and the transparent area is then removed using the remove.bg API in order to blend the foreground and background together. The background image is then overlaid with the clipped foreground image, and OpenCV's Haar Cascades are used to recognize faces. Based on the background picture and the foreground image's height-to-width ratio, the foreground image's size is modified. The background image's subject's face is not obstructed by the insertion, which is done carefully.

Automatic Text Insertion: The first step is to summarize the title, which can be done with an API named "ASAHI Shimbun Media Lab"; this can automatically summarize and generate 5 headlines with 8 characters. Now, to make it more catchy, the headline is colored red and bordered black which makes it easy to see. Now, to determine the best position to place the text, we make use of the section where we detected a face. The headline was then inserted at the bottom of the image with big characters if it did not overlap a face. If a person was found near the image's bottom, the headline was placed in tiny text at one of the image's corners (e.g., higher right). Selection of best thumbnail: Images that show happiness and surprise are selected, and five strings are generated from them, so a total of 10 images are selected as candidates for the thumbnail and the final one is manually chosen by the user.

A survey of 13 videos with 200 participants and three questions was used to evaluate the project. Participants had to choose which thumbnail they wished to click and watch.

The outcome of the evaluation of the given system for generating thumbnails for videos were analyzed and compared to YouTube-generated thumbnails and those set by YouTubers. The outcome, as mentioned in Table 25.1, suggests that the proposed method was preferred by a greater number of participants in 11 videos compared to YouTube-generated thumbnails. In only two cases was the proposed method inferior.

When the suggested approach's outcomes were contrasted with those of YouTubers, the proposed method received higher votes in 7 videos. This demonstrates that the suggested method's thumbnail quality is on par with the benchmarks set by YouTubers. Overall, the findings imply that the suggested approach is successful at producing top-notch video thumbnails.

25.11   Conclusion

The survey presented in this paper offers a thorough investigation of the various technologies required to build an AI-based news article to video generator. Within each section, the authors discuss multiple methods and models, along with their advantages and disadvantages, to assist in selecting the best model for each section based on the desired outcome.

The paper also highlights the existence of research gaps that require further attention to enhance the existing models. These research gaps could involve areas such as improving the accuracy of web scraping, developing more advanced methods for news authentication, and improving the naturalness of generated audio.

The automation of the content creation process for news articles to videos using AI-based technologies has significant potential advantages, such as increasing efficiency and accuracy. It can help media companies to generate news videos quickly and cost-effectively. However, it is vital to ensure that the application of such technologies is done with care to ensure the quality and authenticity of the generated content.

Overall, this work makes a significant contribution to our existing understanding of AI-based technologies for creating news videos by outlining potential future research areas that will help these technologies perform even better. This research is intended to contribute to the creation of more powerful and effective AI-based news article to video generators for various genres, especially for news production.

References

1. Singrodia, V., Mitra, A., Paul, S., A review on web scrapping and its applications. *2019 International Conference on Computer Communication and Informatics (ICCCI)*, Coimbatore, India, pp. 1–6, 2019. May, P., Ehrlich, H.C., Steinke, T., ZIB structure prediction pipeline: Composing a complex biological workflow through web services, in: *Euro-Par 2006*. LNCS, vol. 4128, Springer, Heidelberg, pp. 1148–1158, 2006.

2. Yan, R. and Hauptmann, A.G., A review of text and image retrieval approaches for broadcast news video. *Inf. Retr.*, 10, 445–484, 2007.

3. Maududie, A., Retnani, W.E.Y., Rohim, M.A., An approach of web scraping on news website based on regular expression. *2018 2nd East Indonesia Conference on Computer and Information Technology (EIConCIT)*, Makassar, Indonesia, pp. 203–207, 2018.

4. Khalid, Y.I.A., and Noah, S.A., A framework for integrating DBpedia in a multi-modality ontology news image retrieval system. *2011 International Conference on Semantic Technology and Information Retrieval*, Putrajaya, Malaysia, pp. 144–149, 2011.

5. Leake, M., Shin, H., Kim, J., Agrawala, M., Generating audio-visual slideshows from text articles using word concreteness, pp. 1–11, 2020.

6. Wang, Y., Yang, J., Xiao, C., An, W., Fast convergence strategy for multi-image superresolution via adaptive line search. *IEEE Access*, 6, 9129–9139, 2018.

7. F. Wen, X. Tang, F. Wen, X. Tang, Adaptive visual similarity for text-based image search results re-ranking. US Patent Number -WO2010005751A2, 2010, https://patents.google.com/patent/WO2010005751A2.

8. Agrawal, R., Gollapudi, S., Kannan, A., Kenthapadi, K., Enriching textbooks with images. *International Conference on Information and Knowledge Management, Proceedings*, pp. 1847–1856, 2011.

9. Sumaiya, and Armanuzzaman, M., Enhancement of Resulting Image Search Engine (ERISE) by content-based image retrieval system. *2020 IEEE Region 10 Symposium (TENSYMP)*, Dhaka, Bangladesh, pp. 1416–1419, 2020.

10. Sejal, D., Rashmi, V., Venugopal, K.R. et al. Image recommendation based on keyword relevance using absorbing Markov chain and image features. Int J Multimed Info Retr 5, 185–199 (2016).

11. Singhal, S., Shah, R.R., Chakraborty, T., Kumaraguru, P., Satoh, S., SpotFake: A multi-modal framework for fake news detection. *2019 IEEE Fifth International Conference on Multimedia Big Data (BigMM)*, Singapore, pp. 39–47, 2019.

12. Kaliyar, R.K., Goswami, A., Narang, P., Sinha, S., FNDNet – a deep convolutional neural network for fake news detection. *Cognit. Syst. Res.*, 61, 32–44, 2020, ISSN 1389-0417.

13. Saleh, H., Alharbi, A., Alsamhi, S.H., OPCNN-FAKE: Optimized convolutional neural network for fake news detection. *IEEE Access*, 9, 129471–129489, 2021.

14. Huu Do, T., Berneman, M., Patro, J., Bekoulis, G., Deligiannis, N., Context-aware deep Markov Random Fields for fake news detection. *IEEE Access*, 9, 130042–130054, 2021.

15. Kolluri, N. and Murthy, D., CoVerifi: A COVID-19 news verification system. *Online Soc. Netw. Media*, 22, 100123, 2021.

16. Jain, A. and Kasbe, A., Fake news detection. *2018 IEEE International Students' Conference on Electrical, Electronics and Computer Science (SCEECS)*, Bhopal, India, pp. 1–5, 2018.

17. Qi, P., Cao, J., Yang, T., Guo, J., Li, J., Exploiting multi-domain visual information for fake news detection, pp. 518–527, 2019.

18. Nasar, B.F., S.T., Lason, E.R., Deepfake detection in media files - audios, images and videos. *2020 IEEE Recent Advances in Intelligent Computational Systems (RAICS)*, Thiruvananthapuram, India, pp. 74–79, 2020.

19. Zhou, Z., Huankang, G., Bhat, M., Hsu, J., Fake news detection via NLP is vulnerable to adversarial attacks, pp. 794–800, 2019.

20. Lin, I.-C. and Sung, C.-C., An efficient source authentication for multicast based on Merkle hash tree. *2010 Sixth International Conference on Intelligent Information Hiding and Multimedia Signal Processing*, Darmstadt, Germany, pp. 5–8, 2010.

21. Ji, Z., Yan, X., Cheng, I.-T., Cahyawijaya, S., Frieske, R., Ishii, E., Zeng, M., Madotto, A., Fung, P., VScript: Controllable script generation with audio-visual presentation, 2022.

22. Shah, H. and Rezaei, M., DOM-based keyword extraction from web pages, 2019.

23. Lakhotia, K., Kharitonov, E., Hsu, W.-N., Adi, Y., Polyak, A., Bolte, B., Nguyen, T.-A., Copet, J., Baevski, A., Mohamed, A., Dupoux, E., Generative spoken language modeling from raw audio, 2021.

24. Dutoit, T., High-quality text-to-speech synthesis: An overview, 2004, Corpus ID – 10693488, *Comput. Sci.*, 1-12, Volume 1.

25. Prakash, A., Thomas, A., Umesh, S., Murthy, H., Building multilingual end-to-end speech synthesisers for Indian languages, pp. 194–199, 2019.

26. Hyung, Z., Lee, K., Lee, K., Music recommendation using text analysis on song requests to radio stations. *Expert Syst. Appl.: An International Journal*, 41, 2608–2618, 2014.

27. Guinness, D., Cutrell, E., Morris, M., Caption Crawler: Enabling reusable alternative text descriptions using reverse image search, pp. 1–11, 2018.

28. Cheung, T.C.-H., Wong, H.-W., Po, L., Text-driven automatic image sequence generation using facial modeling for digital TV news production system, vol. 2, pp. 1409–1412, 1997.

29. Vijay, K. and Ramya, D., Generation of caption selection for news images using stemming algorithm. *2015 International Conference on Computation of Power, Energy, Information and Communication (ICCPEIC)*, Melmaruvathur, India, pp. 0536–0540, 2015.

30. Zhang, M., Yang, Y., Zhang, H., Ji, Y., Shen, H.T., Chua, T.-S., More is better: Precise and detailed image captioning using online positive recall and missing concepts mining. *IEEE Trans. Image Process.*, 28, 1, 32–44, Jan. 2019.

31. Stefanini, M., Cornia, M., Baraldi, L., Cascianelli, S., Fiameni, G., Cucchiara, R., From show to tell: A survey on deep learning-based image captioning. *IEEE Trans. Pattern Anal. Mach. Intell.*, 45, 1-1, 539–559, Jan. 2023.

32. Tu, X. *et al.*, Image-to-video generation via 3D facial dynamics. *IEEE Trans. Circuits Syst. Video Technol.*, 32, 4, 1805–1819, April 2022.

33. Vougioukas, K., Petridis, S., Pantic, M., End-to-end speech-driven facial animation with temporal GANs. arXiv, 2018.

34. Gupta, T., Schwenk, D., Farhadi, A., Hoiem, D., Kembhavi, A., Imagine this! Scripts to compositions to videos, 2018.

35. Kim, D., Joo, D., Kim, J., TiVGAN: Text to image to video generation with step-by-step evolutionary generator. *IEEE Access*, 1-1, 4, 2016, 2020.

36. Li, Y., Min, M.R., Shen, D., Carlson, D., Carin, L., Video generation from text. arXiv, 2017.

37. Tan, F., Feng, S., Ordonez, V., Text2Scene: Generating compositional scenes from textual descriptions, pp. 6703–6712, 2019.
38. Chen, Q., Wu, Q., Chen, J., Wu, Q., van den Hengel, A., Tan, M., Scripted video generation with a bottom-up generative adversarial network. *IEEE Trans. Image Process.*, 29, 7454–7467, 2020.
39. Zhao, B., Lin, S., Qi, X., Zhang, Z., Luo, X., Wang, R., Automatic generation of visual-textual web video thumbnail, pp. 1–2, 2017.
40. Shimono, A., Kakui, Y., Yamasaki, T., Automatic YouTube-thumbnail generation and its evaluation, pp. 25–30, 2020.

Index